Winning Results with Google AdWords

Winning Results with Google AdWords

Andrew Goodman

McGraw-Hill/Osborne

New York   Chicago   San Francisco   Lisbon
London   Madrid   Mexico City   Milan   New Delhi
San Juan   Seoul   Singapore   Sydney   Toronto

The *McGraw·Hill* Companies

McGraw-Hill/Osborne
2100 Powell Street, 10th Floor
Emeryville, California 94608
U.S.A.

To arrange bulk purchase discounts for sales promotions, premiums, or fund-raisers, please contact **McGraw-Hill**/Osborne at the above address. For information on translations or book distributors outside the U.S.A., please see the International Contact Information page immediately following the index of this book.

Winning Results with Google AdWords

567890 CUS CUS 019876

ISBN 0-07-225702-4

Acquisitions Editor	Megg Morin
Project Editor	Janet Walden
Acquisitions Coordinator	Agatha Kim
Technical Editor	Brad Geddes
Copy Editor	Judith Brown
Proofreader	Pam Vevea
Indexer	Claire Splan
Composition	International Typesetting and Composition
Illustration	International Typesetting and Composition
Series Design	Michelle Galicia, Peter F. Hancik
Cover Design	Jeff Weeks

This book was composed with Adobe® InDesign®.

To the memory of Carol Shortreed,
my aunt, and
everyone's friend.

About the Author

Andrew Goodman is founder and principal of Page Zero Media, a Toronto-based search marketing firm that helps clients with paid search strategy, campaign management, and ROI tracking. As cofounder of Traffick.com, an acclaimed "Guide to Portals," Andrew enjoyed a quasi-journalistic front-row seat as search engines went from niche specialty, to dot-com roadkill, to big business, in the years 1999–2005.

Andrew's views on paid search are frequently cited in the press, including *The New York Times, The Washington Post, Fortune Small Business, The Globe and Mail, Bloomberg Markets,* and *New Media Age.* He is a regular speaker at industry conferences such as Jupitermedia's Search Engine Strategies and Nielsen Norman Group User Experience.

Thirty-eight-year-old Goodman lives in Toronto with his wife Carolyn. On non-smog days he rollerblades along the Toronto waterfront near his home.

Contents at a Glance

Contents

Acknowledgments

The size and might of one's Rolodex remains a power symbol in the business world, even though no one uses a Rolodex anymore. (I happen to use a Yahoo address book—sorry, Google.) I am grateful to nearly all of my address-book people for the small kindnesses they've offered directly or indirectly as I've worked on this book. It seems impossible to cover them all. But to give it the best possible shot, I'll organize my thanks by categories. Apologies in advance to information retrieval professionals if the categories seem as loosely slapped together as the Yahoo directory circa 1995.

This book would not have been possible without Google itself. Google employees who have guided and accommodated me include Mike Mayzel, Barry Schnitt, Peter Norvig, Sheryl Sandberg, Nate Tyler, Wendy Muller, Eric Morris, Daniel Cytrynbaum, Jill Randell, Sukhinder Singh, David Fischer, David Krane, and Salar Kamangar. As for Messrs. Page, Brin, and Schmidt: I do believe they're mentioned in the book.

Pioneers in fields such as search marketing and usability have shaped my thinking and also have provided with me with a platform to share those thoughts with others. In particular I thank Danny Sullivan and Jakob Nielsen. Also, Mike Grehan, Ralph Wilson, Jill Whalen, Larry Chase, and Anne Holland. Others who have been valued colleagues, correspondents, and fellow travelers for some time now include Chris Sherman, Detlev Johnson, Anne Kennedy, Elisabeth Osmeloski, Gary Price, Ed Kohler, Jim Sterne, Christine Churchill, Shari Thurow, Grant Crowell, Bryan Eisenberg, Eric Ward, Matt Van Wagner, Derrick Wheeler, Keith Boswell, Noel McMichael, Mikkel Svendsen, Nacho Hernandez, Matt Bailey, Catherine Seda, Misty Locke, Josh Stylman, Jessie Stricchiola, Adam Eisner, and Jennifer Laycock. Seth Godin, Andy Bourland, and Chris Locke provided encouragement at the most unexpected times. James Gifford offered special wisdom about the publishing business. Tara Calishain was instrumental in recommending me to the publisher.

Clients, who have become good friends, provide the feedback so vital to keeping up with developments. For starters, thanks to Ray Allen, Elliot Noss, Dirk Plantinga, and Jim Peterson.

My Page Zero colleagues apply their professionalism and single-minded passion to the paid search enterprise, eclipsing my own day-to-day efforts to put theory into practice. I salute Scott Perry, Mona Elesseily, and Mark Shawera. I thank Dean Towers for his support, client satisfaction record, and business acumen as we shared fantastic delusions about the growth of our industry. Traffick.com cofounder Cory Kleinschmidt has been a constant friend and seamless collaborator.

If I could, I'd give a shout-out to every person who matters in the blogosphere, and every search industry executive who has consented to be interviewed by me over the years—people like Jeremy Zawodny (Yahoo's most famous blogger), John Battelle (*Wired* founder who moderates Web 2.0 conferences and blogs about search), Eytan Elbaz (cofounder of Applied Semantics, acquired by Google), Paul Gardi (Teoma), Karen Yagnesak (formerly of FindWhat), Rich Skrenta (ODP, Topix.net), and Nick Denton (Moreover.com, Gawker Media). None of you march to the beat of the same ol' corporate drummer, yet economic productivity continues to rise. If our society is falling under the grip of a *Revenge of the* (good-looking) *Nerds*–type scenario, so be it, because your pursuit of the deviant's advantage has created some incredible mutations that offer the promise of a better life for a wide segment of the population.

At McGraw-Hill, heartfelt thanks to Megg Morin, in particular, for her wisdom in overseeing the editorial process. Also, to Katie Conley for her early enthusiasm, and to Janet Walden, Judith Brown, Brad Geddes, and Pam Vevea for eagle-eyed editorial support. And Mark Shawera provided valuable research assistance.

Last but never least, to my wife, Carolyn Bassett, who didn't seem much fazed by my moods and who by now groks most of the incessant search marketing industry banter. I remember how proud I was when I witnessed the successful completion of her magnum opus (a PhD dissertation on fiscal policy in South Africa). The prospect of enjoying the rest of 2005 together with no more talk of chapters should make up for time lost over the past 18 months. Now entrenched in our respective roles as professor and businessman, I feel we've doubled our chances of changing the world for the better.

Introduction

Even if you're a grizzled search engine marketing veteran, you'll probably still learn a few new tricks from this book. This is because I have been so obsessed with getting the answers to tough AdWords questions. But admittedly, if you're in the hyper-advanced crowd, you'll use this book mainly to confirm some of your convictions, convince clients of certain indisputable facts, and help your staff to better plan and execute campaigns. (In which case you should run out right now and buy three or four extra copies!)

For those who are new to paid search, you'll find that you're better suited to the task if you have some relevant marketing experience or formal education that intersects with some of the key skill sets required of online marketers. This book is meant to help you, the educated reader, find the answers to hard questions about AdWords campaign strategy and tactics that you won't necessarily discover by asking Google staff or by reading gossip on the message boards. It can be comfortably read straight through, front-to-back, or you can pull out useful tidbits using the index and table of contents.

Although sometimes I make assertions without referring to the source, most everything in this book is grounded in science. For nearly every point, I've sought either direct empirical evidence from my own campaigns or those run by colleagues, or have researched sources that have data about key facets of online marketing. I've also disputed those findings when I think they're misleading.

As enamored as I am with getting the facts straight, I'm also a big believer in context. How much energy you put into any task depends on situating that task both in terms of the economics of an industry generally, and in terms of the strategies your competitors might be using to reach customers. Chapter 1 erases all doubt about matters such as how big the search engine marketing industry is in relation to offline advertising, and the size of Google's market share. Chapter 2 examines how Google's advertising program got here and how the company's unique culture will affect your results.

If you're eager to get going though, skip right to Chapter 3, which orients you to the nature of paid search marketing and the nature of the user's search process. Chapter 4 presents the key secret to AdWords success, as well as the critical campaign setup parameters that you'll want to have right from the start. Chapter 5 gets you into setting up your campaign and explains the genius of ad groups. It also discusses tricky issues like editorial policy.

Starting in Chapter 6, you'll move into the intermediate-level work of generating appropriate keywords and figuring out what to bid on them. Discovering bargain keyword inventory isn't easy, but it is another key secret to success, and it takes time and savvy. This chapter isn't just a narrowly technical approach to keywords; it's really about targeting and understanding your market. I also cover the ins and outs of matching options, third-party keyword research and bid management tools, and advanced topics like dayparting.

Should you inject "flair" into your ad copy? How can you split-test ads head to head in AdWords to determine which one performs better? How long should you run a test? To find out, read Chapter 7. It contains six rules for writing AdWords advertising copy, and is full of examples to get your creative juices flowing. Chapter 8 contains tips on planning and budgeting, and on interoffice politics related to your role as a marketing manager (if that's what you do) who must report to higher-ups.

OK, so you're making a profit, and now you want more. How to pump up the volume? For tips, read Chapter 9.

Chapter 10 covers the vital topic of how to best measure and interpret campaign results (especially those related to return on your marketing investment), and how to choose a web analytics tool. I warn you: it's often difficult to interpret the numbers. I provide case studies to illustrate some of the subtleties that can trip you up. Chapter 11 goes one better than this, exploring state-of-the-art thinking about how to increase conversion rates once users arrive on your site. You'll see a mix of big-picture thinking about creating the right kind of image and environment for strong online sales, on one hand, and specific tactics and landing page examples, on the other. In Chapter 12, I speculate about the future of paid search and examine the competitive landscape facing Google. The future is bright, but the competition is fierce, both for Google and its advertisers. Not everyone will win, but developing a thorough understanding of the marketing fundamentals that I cover in this book will increase your odds significantly.

Part I

The Paid Search Opportunity

Chapter 1

How Big Is This Market?
The Rapid Rise of Paid Search

Advertising annoys people. Advertising works. Many in the advertising business have long assumed that both of these statements are true. But the more annoying advertising gets as a whole, the harder it becomes for any particular advertiser to break through the clutter. Tellingly, a grassroots backlash has arisen against the most bothersome ways of interrupting people, to the point where legislation is now being enforced against telemarketing, junk faxing, and email spam.

But what if you could come up with a way to advertise that doesn't annoy people and achieves measurable results at the same time—a form of advertising that targets potentially interested customers, yet doesn't bother people needlessly? This is the underlying premise of AdWords and why you should be considering it as part of your ad campaign.

In the Beginning: Advertising on the Internet

The idea of the Internet as a marketing medium was so energizing to so many not just because of its superior targeting and interactive potential, but because of the potential to annoy fewer people. Somewhere along the way (around 1998–2000, when they smelled money), online marketers forgot the promising principles of targeting. Suddenly our favorite websites, search engines, and portals were crammed with intrusive, blinking banner ads.

Those kinds of ads still "work" in the sense that they get noticed. But research now proves that the most intrusive forms of online advertising might also erode consumer loyalty and do serious damage to the brand image of advertisers and publishers alike.[1]

Until I began my career as an Internet entrepreneur in 1999, I'd never given such issues much thought. Then I discovered a writer who put a new spin on the history of the advertising business: Seth Godin. He changed the world of advertising forever when he wrote *Permission Marketing*. Godin's narrative relegated so-called interruption marketing to the dustbin of history (at least in his enlightened fantasies). Godin's premise was that email marketing would change the way companies developed relationships with prospects by offering a means to contact prospects who had "raised their hands for" (opted into) marketing messages that were "anticipated, personal, and relevant."[2] The skeptical reader might wonder, though, how that permission was going to be gained in the first place. Wouldn't some kind of unsolicited message be needed at some point to initiate the process?

I was already beginning to sense the unraveling of the promise of "permission" as I looked with dismay at the clutter building up in my own email inbox.[3] The game of permission marketing seemed to be over before it had truly gained traction, in part due to spam, in part because corporate marketers bent the rules and abused the concept of permission. Everyone wanted in your face, now that your face was stuck in your email box. With no theoretical limit on the number of emails that might pile up, we all wound up receiving too many. People began unsubscribing from opt-in publications, switching email addresses, ignoring and filtering their email. What started out looking like a magic bullet became more like a rapid-fire hailstorm of ammo opening gaping holes in our daily work routines. The recipients of the daily volley of "anticipated" messages ran for cover.

Nonetheless, Godin's theories stuck in my mind because he was evidently working on a broader analysis of the rapidly changing context for marketing and advertising. And he kept publishing these timely ideas. In *Purple Cow*, he explored more deeply how irrelevant big ad campaign methods had become, as they were more suitable for a time (in the 1950s and 1960s) when consumers needed to be trained to adopt leading brands in product categories that had never existed before. Now, with product proliferation, the old "virtuous circle" of the "TV-industrial complex" (advertise product, take massive profits, and reinvest in yet more advertising) wouldn't work, especially not to introduce new products in old categories.[4]

What does work in this new era? "Think small," argues Godin. "One vestige of the TV-industrial complex is the need to think mass. ... No longer. Think of the smallest conceivable market and describe a product that overwhelms it with its remarkability. Go from there."[5] Want an example? How about the Powerbar (now owned by Nestlé), which spread by word of mouth from humble beginnings among a few cycling enthusiasts.[6] Although the energy-bar category eventually became crowded, there was plenty of room for a few more independent growth stories in this same market; most recently, the highly successful Clif bar.

Quietly, and seemingly unrelated to all of this background learning about marketing and advertising, I was writing about emerging search engine technologies. In October 1999, shortly after launching my site Traffick.com (at the time, subtitled "The Guide to Portals"), I reviewed two new entries, Google and Ask Jeeves, that were facing off against powerful incumbents like AltaVista, AllTheWeb, and Inktomi. Google got a positive rating. I concluded the review: "Best of all, the Google site is devoid of advertising. Enjoy it while it lasts."[7]

At that time, the one-year-old startup, led by Stanford computer science doctoral candidates Larry Page and Sergey Brin, had few ideas about how the company would make money. Unlike portal companies such as Yahoo, they didn't scheme about how to "lock users in" or how to "make their site sticky." They didn't spend days in investing seminars spreading hype about how they would "monetize the eyeballs." They basically stuck to improving their web search technology. Based on initially favorable reviews from journalists, researchers, librarians, and enthusiasts like myself (in short, the technorati), word spread rapidly about the quality of search results on Google's site, the lack of clutter on the page, and the speed with which results were served. Google's index passed its challengers in terms of index size at 500 million documents in June 2000 and never looked back.[8]

Many observers assumed Google would make its money by licensing the technology as an enterprise search solution (Google now does this, but earns little from the effort), or by distributing its results through a major portal that required a search index. (Google got its biggest push forward by inking just such a deal with Yahoo, which ended the relationship when Google became a competitive threat.) Today, Google Search is a leading online destination in every country in the world. It may come as a surprise to some readers to learn that 98% of Google's nearly $4 billion in annual revenues are currently derived from advertising.[9]

Happily, the experience of using Google Search today is not so different from the way it was when there was no advertising. Google wisely realized that their biggest asset was a large population of search engine users, so they released their ad program cautiously, making sure that the ads were in a nonintrusive format.

Thanks in large part to Google's efforts, search engine advertising is now the leading engine of growth in online advertising. Few would argue that to this point, it's been a genuine success story in marrying the ideal of less-intrusive marketing methods with the ability to build a business by reaching out to interested prospects. In the remainder of this chapter, I'll present additional evidence to prove to you how big a deal search advertising has become. It's not going away anytime soon. And Google is the category leader, which means that most online advertisers need to consider Google AdWords as their top priority in any paid search campaign.

Search Marketing Facts and Figures

Although my specialty is paid search, and in particular, AdWords, I consider my own consulting shop to be a *search marketing* firm. Many of my colleagues are self-described search marketers. Only recently have we been able to gather reliable statistical information about this market. Understanding the size and dimensions of the search advertising market is important because it helps put things in perspective. You don't want to underestimate the power of your search marketing efforts, but you don't want to have unrealistic expectations of the medium, either. It will grow, but for now, it's dwarfed by the advertising industry as a whole.

Size of the Advertising Market

How much do companies spend on advertising in general? As you'll see, this is a huge sector. It's only a matter of time before some of this spending moves over to the relatively small search marketing arena. This will start happening as more advertisers recognize the effectiveness of search marketing.

What Large Companies Spend on Ad Campaigns

The size of the advertising market as a whole is enormous. Search marketing looks pretty small by comparison, as you'll see. The real unknown is how much of a share of the overall advertising pie will shift to online advertising generally and search advertising in particular. It's been a bumpy road thus far, but the future looks promising.

According to the 17th Annual Global Marketing report in *Advertising Age,* worldwide media spending increased to $74.2 billion in 2002, which was not only a 7.1% rise over the previous year, but also marked the reversal of a 2.6% decline that had been charted by the group in 2001. Total U.S. media spending was $37.31 billion, which was not only up 7% over the previous year, but also represented 50.2% of the Top 100 total. This compares with $23.06 billion in spending in Europe, which was up 12.2%, and $9.87 billion in spending in Asia, which was up 0.5%. Also, U.S. marketers accounted for 49 of the Top 100 rankings. The three largest advertisers were Procter & Gamble, Unilever, and General Motors, spending $4.48 billion, $3.32 billion, and $3.22 billion, respectively.[10]

Spending on Classified Advertising and Direct Marketing

Patterns of newspaper ad spending over the past 50 years or so are interesting to examine as part of the whole advertising picture. As a proportion of the entire newspaper ad spend and in absolute terms, classified ads grew rapidly, reaching a peak of $19.6 billion in 2000 before leveling off to their current $16 billion of the $44 billion total newspaper ad spend. The biggest spenders are in the automotive, real estate, and employment sectors.[11]

Depending on whom you talk to, direct-response advertising (of which direct mail is a subset) is another mammoth category. It's also commonly one of the media compared directly with Google AdWords. According to the Direct Marketing Association, total U.S. spending on direct-response advertising was $203 billion in 2003, which represented a 5% increase over the previous year. Total direct marketing–driven sales reached $1.7 trillion in 2003, and this was composed of $904 billion in lead-generation efforts, $635 billion in direct-order sales, and $212 billion in traffic generation.[12]

Disparities in the statistics for what the advertising industry views as "ad campaigns" (print, television, and radio combined), on one hand, and what direct marketers and sellers of classified ads measure, on the other, are a function of how these data are collected. It's probably fair to say that ad agencies and large broadcasters don't always think of classified ads when they think about the advertising business, given that these are self-serve ad programs that generate only a small number of dollars per transaction. And direct marketers have seemingly operated in relative anonymity through the years, even though the absolute amount spent is truly impressive. A variety of motivations are likely at work when it comes to how data are presented on aggregate spending on various types of ads or sales pitches. Who, for example, might speak for the makers of infomercials? If you work for a marketing or publishing trade association whose members compete directly with the makers of infomercials, you might have an incentive to trivialize this form of marketing.

Possibly the most telling way of assessing the relative weight of different forms of promotion might be to look at detailed financials from individual companies that are heavy advertisers on a number of fronts. Some financial institutions run a lot of television and print campaigns, while also investing heavily in direct mail, infomercials, and online campaigns. If we could examine the budgets for all of these programs, we would have a better sense of the proportions spent as well as the growth in the online component. Because I've managed a few online campaigns for such big-spending advertisers, I feel safe in telling you that while the absolute amounts of their online ad campaigns may seem impressive—in the millions or tens of millions of dollars—they're small compared to these companies' overall marketing budgets.

Since Google AdWords combines elements of a variety of traditional forms of print advertising, it can be useful to stack them up against one another. No matter how you measure it, the size of the online advertising business is still relatively small, but it is steadily making up ground.

Size of the Online Advertising Market

As the numbers presented in the previous section clearly show, offline advertising still eclipses online advertising by a wide margin. Since online advertising is still in its infancy, this is not surprising. To get a better feel for the future of online advertising, let's look at where it's been and where the experts believe it's headed.

Total Online Advertising Spending, 1999–2009

According to Jupiter Research, total spending on online advertising will increase from $4.3 billion in 1999 to $28.0 billion in 2005. In 1999, online ad spending in North America totaled $3.5 billion. Western Europe, which was the world's second largest market, accounted for $400 million (nearly nine times less), while in Asia, which was the third-ranked region, the total was only $200 million.

Some analysts believe that the strongest growth is expected to be in Latin America,[13] but recent rapid increases in online ad spending in Asia, particularly China, suggest otherwise. In addition, much of the available data on market size have failed to keep pace with the increase in online advertising, and the growth of paid search, in Europe.

A July 2004 report by Jupiter Research entitled "Online Advertising Through 2009" estimated that online advertising would increase to $8.4 billion in 2004 after experiencing tentative growth in 2003 and that it would nearly double to $16.1 billion by 2009. In fall 2004, a news release from the Interactive Advertising Bureau cited strong third-quarter revenues from "interactive advertising"—$2.4 billion, up 35% from a weak third quarter in 2003. The annual 2004 total spent on so-called interactive advertising was expected to eclipse the record total of $8.0 billion, set in 2000.[14]

Even though online ad spending amounted to just 3.5% of offline ad spending in 2003, this is expected to almost double to 6.5% in 2009, according to the Jupiter report. Furthermore, by 2007, online advertising is expected to surpass magazine advertising in terms of dollars spent. Internet advertising is also expected to be the fastest growing media category followed by cable and network television, which would signal its return from the dot-com crash in 2000.[15]

Many of these estimates now seem conservative, perhaps still influenced by the depressed mood that followed the online advertising crash and still reeling from a weak post-9/11 advertising environment. Analysts are now beginning to revamp estimates to more optimistic projections based on the recent turnaround. Recent quarterly results from a variety of companies in the sector are providing a solid foundation for healthier projections for the coming years. Even struggling Doubleclick has come in ahead of estimates of late. There is also a growing realization that phenomena such as local search might create a more rapid migration of offline dollars to online channels than previously expected.

There are structural reasons why some large companies might dismiss online advertising. If the size of the budget earmarked for online ads is small due to the fact that finding a large enough amount of ad inventory online is impossible, this can color corporate priorities for years. Assigning a team to manage a small budget may not seem cost effective once you factor in salaries, infrastructure, software, and so on. Putting a junior person in charge of such an "insignificant" budget might further marginalize the image of online advertising within the corporate power structure. However, as competitors (especially the fiercest online competitors, Internet "pure plays") make more use of the medium, and as tales of online ad effectiveness spread, even the most conservative companies have begun to study a variety of avenues for increasing their online presence.

> NOTE   *An Internet "pure play" is a company whose revenues are exclusively (or nearly exclusively) derived from online transactions, be they referral commissions from online travel bookings, e-commerce sales, or advertising-related income. Examples include Travelocity, Careerbuilder.com, E-Trade, and Amazon.com. A "pure play" is a financial industry term coined by analysts to describe companies that might be suitable investments for those seeking to "bet on" a particular industry or industry sector without any exposure to other industries.*

For now, the mere fact that General Motors spends over $3 billion annually on offline advertising may, to General Motors, be all the justification it needs that offline advertising is effective. As online opportunities like Google AdWords gain a greater foothold and historical track record, however, corporate ad executives in charge of such large ad budgets will most likely decide to plunge into online advertising with more enthusiasm.

It's been difficult to avoid the many feature articles about Google in major business publications in the past couple of years, especially since the company's initial public offering. Therefore, more business owners and advertising executives are becoming aware of the effectiveness of the medium. As large and small businesses alike begin to spend ad dollars online in amounts more proportional to what they're spending elsewhere, growth in the sector may require analysts to hastily adjust previous forecasts.

Moreover, the distinction between online and offline advertising will blur as media converge and as more of the world becomes digital. Microsoft CEO Steve Ballmer stated in a speech in March 2004 that in ten years, all media dollars will wind up online because the separation between televisions, mobile devices, and PCs won't exist.[16] Because the search sector is now seen as a growth area, Microsoft has regained its keen interest, releasing its own MSN Search technology to replace a previous mix of third-party products.

And what's to say a newspaper company won't offer an automated online auction system to sell part of its advertising inventory? (Or perhaps they'd begin with selling print classifieds through an online interface.) When this begins to happen, some advertisers might begin using centralized online control panels (similar to Google AdWords, perhaps) to manage both online and offline ad campaigns. So far, one newspaper, *The Boston Globe*, has tried a pilot project of this type. (In fact, they made the announcement just a few weeks after I first drafted this paragraph!) A popular half-page ad space which normally sells for $50,000 was auctioned online with a starting bid of $20,000. Stay tuned: we'll be seeing lots more of this.

The allocation of advertising dollars, at least between offline print ads and online ads of various types, depends in part on how consumers spend their time. We already see marked declines in newspaper readership among young people and marked increases in time spent online. A recent survey of "business decision makers" showed that most spend more than two hours a day online (excluding email), and that a significant reduction in television watching was the main price paid. The Internet is the main medium by which such decision makers access news and information while at work.[17] It may take time for media buyers to fully understand and adjust to these changing sensibilities and information consumption patterns.

Types of Online Ad Formats

Now that advertisers track the return on investment of their online campaigns quite carefully, anecdotal evidence abounds about the effectiveness of various channels and ad formats. Adware companies like Claria Corporation (formerly Gator) have plenty of data to prove that pop-up ads, for example, are effective (mostly, by indicating that consumers click on the pop-up ads more often than ordinary banner ads). But many advertisers now want to avoid the most annoying ad formats on principle. Ironically, certain large corporations have been outraged by Claria pop-ups for competitors being served to users visiting their websites, until they find out that their own marketing department is also doing business with Claria!

Unfortunately, reliable aggregate data about campaign effectiveness in various ad formats can be hard to come by and in any case, won't help the individual advertiser very much, as results vary widely from case to case. Mainstream advertisers continue to be content with measures proving *brand lift*—an impact proven to be significant for all forms of online advertising, including search.[18]

In this book, I focus more closely on the directly measurable return on investment that is a hallmark of paid search advertising.

Reality Check: Traditional Online Ad Networks No Longer Dominate

The first big wave of Internet advertising focused on banners and email ads. Major portals like Excite, Yahoo, and AOL, and ad-serving middlemen like Doubleclick, earned their keep largely by buying and selling overpriced banners. In the Toronto Google sales office, of the three main people I deal with, two formerly worked in ad sales for Doubleclick, and one was an account manager with Excite. This provides a snapshot of the recent history of the online ad business.

Because the online ad sector focusing on banners and email received considerable funding and enjoyed a financial heyday, assumptions about the relative importance of banner and email ads lingered past their expiry dates. Today, although the exact number is difficult to pinpoint, search advertising revenues are approaching 50% of all online ads. Leading search advertising providers (Google and Overture, primarily), have branched out and now serve text ads all over the Web, where blinking banners used to be. They're also fanning out into email ads and may begin to serve ads in all formats. In other words, the search advertising providers are essentially the brokers for the second wave of online advertising.

The bottom line? Don't underestimate the importance of search advertising. It's this sector that rescued the online advertising sector as a whole and continues to drive its growth.

The fate of first-wave ad network Doubleclick tells the tale of the rise and fall of the traditional online ad business. Once a powerhouse, Doubleclick's June 2005 market valuation of $1.05 billion (in spite of considerable diversification through the acquisition of a variety of smaller, profitable companies) is dwarfed by Google's $78.5 billion valuation. The once-tiny search engine company is now the Internet's leading ad-serving company, now 78 times as valuable as the former powerhouse. Another ad-serving company that experienced both the boom and the bust of the online advertising industry, 24/7 Real Media, is valued at only $159.0 million in spite of an improving outlook for online media buying. Aquantive, another online ad industry player that combined smaller ad networks and related technology units to form a sizeable force in the sector, is valued at $1.02 billion. Combined, these three traditional online ad brokerages are worth less than $2.2 billion compared to the $130 billion combined valuation of their key competitors, Google and Yahoo.

Second-tier paid search provider FindWhat (now renamed Miva) has struggled to keep pace with the leaders, and has dropped off to a $164.2 million valuation. In recent months, FindWhat has fallen well behind Aquantive, likely because the market is concerned that FindWhat may face serious threats to its viability due to a patent dispute with Yahoo's Overture division. (Google settled with Yahoo over the same patent issue, so that issue is behind them.) In the relatively near term, Doubleclick will probably be sold off or broken up, as its management has announced that it's exploring "strategic options." Additional merger and acquisition activity might result in an Aquantive or a 24/7 Real Media being subsumed as part of a larger media or technology company, or joining forces with a company such as FindWhat. In light of these trends, a reasonable conclusion is that a new era is upon us, and that Google carries the banner (so to speak) for online advertising today.

The Growth of Search Marketing

Two things we know for sure are that email is the most popular online activity and that search is second. But how does this translate into time spent viewing advertisers' messages? What levels of ad revenues are being generated by the activity? Let's look at how visits to websites are measured.

Search Engine User Growth

Until relatively recently, an observer would have been hard pressed to get a solid handle on the popularity of various search services. One statistic common to many industry reporting formats has been *reach*. A *web property* (typically a conglomerate or portal that owns many websites and interrelated services) might get credit for reaching a user if that user visits the entire network at least once in a month.

More recently, panel-based web measurement company comScore Networks has been doing more to specifically break out search data, releasing useful reports on monthly "share of searches" and the like. The information is only occasionally made public; most of the detail is buried in custom reports for corporate subscribers. Simply put, *share of searches* is a measure based on how many times a specific user performs any type of search in a month. If hypothetical user Jill used the same search engine to perform 20 different searches in a day, the count would be 20, or if she performed only 1 search on a different day, the count would be 1. Let's say Jill performed 100 searches in a month, where 50 of them were on Google Search, 36 on Yahoo Search, 7 on Ask Jeeves, 5 on Metacrawler.com, and 2 on MSN Search. For Jill, Google's share of searches would be 50% for that month. This is a useful way of measuring the popularity of a search engine, but for some reason, the data haven't always been reported this way in the press.

Nonetheless we do have access to some recent numbers. U.S. Internet users performed 3.6 billion searches in April 2004, compared with 575 million searches by Canadian users. The average Canadian searches more than the average American in a given month, 40 searches to 35. comScore reports that *search penetration*—the number of Internet users who actually use search engines—is higher in Canada than it is south of the border, at 85%. Amazingly, in their study, only 73% of U.S. Internet users performed any type of search. In the coming years this penetration will no doubt reach close to 100% in most countries.[19]

NOTE   *comScore is working on rolling out its qSearch panel studies to other markets throughout the globe, but the process is expensive and thus far has only been launched in a few countries (for example, UK, France, and Germany).*

comScore also releases market share numbers on the share of monthly searches, and such numbers have been picked up by Wall Street analysts to emphasize Google's dominance. In Canada and many other countries, Google maintains a commanding 60%–70% market share in "share of monthly searches." In North America and a number of other markets, Yahoo is in second place, and MSN Search in third, with "all others" making up the remaining 10%–15%. comScore's May 2004 release had Google with only a slight "share of searches" market share lead over Yahoo in April, at 36% to 30%. By November 2004, the gap had narrowed even more, with Google garnering a 34.4% share of searches and Yahoo coming in with 31.8%. Time Warner, which encompasses AOL Search as well as Netscape.com, Compuserve, and others, continued to erode badly, from 12.8% in May 2004 to 9.0% in November 2004. MSN has begun to show a serious rebound in the wake of releasing new search technology and based on the growing buzz that it wants to become a player in the search engine market. MSN's share of searches rose from 14.5% in May 2004 to 16.5% in November 2004.

It's all too easy to take these numbers as gospel. While the share of searches data are better than reach numbers, statistics agencies have a bad habit of focusing on aggregate numbers that make large clients like MSN and Yahoo look good. Not all searches are created equal, and not all are conducted on search engine pages like Yahoo Search, MSN Search, or Google.com. Users are beginning to search from browser toolbars and within operating systems, as well as in wireless devices. They're performing more news and image searches and *site searches* (searching once they arrive on a destination website). Is searching your Yahoo Mail, Gmail, or Outlook folders a search? What about searching your computer desktop or your corporate intranet? I tend to think so, because if it works well, it reinforces loyalty to a particular search engine or software brand. So much of current search activity remains poorly understood and misleadingly reported by statistics agencies.

Those running actual search marketing campaigns have a better feel for whether consumers are really searching and finding them through various channels. Nearly all would argue that Google's lead over Yahoo is wider than the comScore numbers suggest. In addition, insofar as Google Search powers searches for AOL Time Warner, and AdWords powers sponsored listings at both AOL Time Warner and Ask Jeeves, the combined 14.5% share of searches for these latter two companies for November 2004 can be understood, for now, partly as a consumer endorsement of Google.

A number of recent news articles and Wall Street analyst comments seem to indicate that Google's share of searches is above 50% in the United States just as it is everywhere else. This likely means that Yahoo's strong second-place showing is routinely overstated and will someday be adjusted downward to take account of more rigorous "apples to apples" comparisons of what counts as a search. How can it be that comScore is content to report share of searches for Google of 60%, 70%, 80%, and more, in a variety of major international markets, but now has Google's U.S. share at only 34.4%? It defies explanation.

As a counter-check, many webmasters look at their own site server logs or at press releases from statistics companies such as WebSideStory that have access to search referral data for a large number of clients. These releases typically confirm the so-called Google Domination Factor,[20] whereby Google refers over 50% of search traffic to most websites whose owners measure these things. Anecdotal note sharing on the Google Domination Factor is a staple of discussions at online search marketing industry forums such as Search Engine Watch Forums.

Types of Search Marketing

Marketers have recognized the benefits of search engine visibility for over a decade. The constantly changing rules of the game of getting seen in or near search results have made it difficult to stay abreast of key trends. Many unscrupulous operators continue to take advantage of business owners' naïveté in the field, selling them services they may not need, or scaring them with "ranking reports" that may obscure more than they reveal. As time consuming as it may be, you should try to keep up with the trends. Now that you know that the top three search destinations in the United States (Google, Yahoo, and MSN) make up as much as 90% of all search traffic, you're already more informed than many. Then again, if you're reading this, chances are, you're already aware of the Google Domination Factor and simply want to know how best to exploit it to your business advantage.

Optimizing for "Free" Rankings

So-called search engine optimization (SEO) has been about as widespread and controversial a practice as baseball players taking steroids. Fed up with the overblown claims of search engine ranking "scammers," Seth Godin ranted on his blog: "Lucking into (and it is luck) the top slot of a great word on Google is not a business plan. It's superstition. It's blind faith." He went on to praise Google AdWords for being the opposite of luck: "If you can figure out how to BUY (not luck into) keyword searches that bring you X number of visitors, and then you can figure out how to design your site so that Y% of those visits turn into customers, you win. And nobody can stop you from growing all you care to grow."[21]

It goes without saying that strong placements in the regular, or free, search results are important. For some, it's a full-time job. Unfortunately, the quality of the work performed by many search engine optimization professionals has often left much to be desired. MarketingSherpa, a leading publisher of online marketing information guides, publishes a comprehensive review of search engine marketing firms. Depending on the edition, the Sherpa researchers have attempted to rate the firms' performance and to discuss best practices. The effort has had mixed results.

I myself discovered that it was easy enough to get a high ranking (in the first edition of the SEO Buyer's Guide). One of my clients achieved a very high ranking on a commercially lucrative search phrase, with my help. Of course the client's success story proved temporary, but it was enough to give me a four-star rating as a barely trained one-man search engine optimization "company" in 2001. In general, the causal impact of an SEO consultant's work can be difficult to prove. If you land a Fortune 500 client with a content-poor, poorly designed site, the mere act of bringing the site up to its potential by employing standards-based web design and basic SEO tactics (like clearly written page titles) can make you look like a genius.

Many of the SEO tactics commonly employed by experts are the types of things that might be advisable to do even in the absence of search engines. For example, encouraging partners, suppliers, fans, or journalists to link to your site is something you might want to do anyway, even if Google didn't also reward such activity with the PageRank component of its search ranking algorithm. Self-described "link mensch" Eric Ward has been implementing such *linking campaigns* for a decade now, beginning with a successful campaign in 1994 for a company you might have heard of: Amazon.com.

If you want to come up to speed quickly on the field of search engine optimization, it's worth consulting a couple of the leading books on the subject.[22] After you read this one, of course!

Paid Inclusion

There are essentially two kinds of paid inclusion today. The first is a fee-based directory listing. The best-known of these is a Yahoo directory listing, which costs $299 per year. The second kind of paid inclusion requires you to pay a fee to have your site included in (but without any guarantee of rankings in or traffic from) a popular search index.

Inktomi (later acquired by Yahoo) was the first major web search index to adopt a paid inclusion model. Webmasters could submit a number of URLs to the index to guarantee inclusion (not ranking). Later, certain benefits of the inclusion programs were trotted out in an attempt to justify them. Webmasters were told that paid-for pages would be "re-spidered" every 48 hours. The Inktomi paid inclusion program was never clearly thought out. Rather, it was something of a panic-button reaction to the growing proliferation of index spam (paid inclusion would help weed out junk pages submitted by marketers hoping to capitalize on the free nature of the index), and an early experiment in how to defray the costs of running a search engine. Inktomi, like many search engine companies, never stumbled on a successful business model.

Others began to experiment with this methodology as well. AltaVista (also later acquired by Yahoo) famously lost credibility when its salesperson offered a marketer higher rankings in exchange for paid submission. AltaVista's public relations department quickly distanced itself from this nod-and-a-wink "rankings for cash" sales tactic, claiming it was an isolated mistake by an individual salesman and that the "trusted feed" payments guaranteed only prompt inclusion in the index.[23]

Today, Yahoo offers the best-known example of paid inclusion, now named Site Match. Costs vary, but the model is a somewhat confusing hybrid of a flat fee for inclusion and a cost per click once listings are included in the Yahoo Index. (Confused yet?) Larger companies may cut bulk deals and pay only for clicks, depositing a certain amount in advance against a minimum total click charge. Because consumers may be unaware of the nature of these paid inclusion programs and what, exactly, distinguishes "real" search results from the sponsored listings, numerous observers have been critical of paid inclusion programs.[24]

Nonetheless, the programs represent good value, particularly for retailers aiming for reliable bulk inclusion of catalog pages in a search index. There continue to be questions as to whether the reliability that larger listing clients are paying for is at the expense of smaller participants in the paid inclusion program who cannot afford to flood the system with pages, and who may not be given special behind-the-scenes consideration in ranking algorithms.

There is no way to guarantee or pay for placement in Google's regular, "organic" index listings. In other words, they remain free. With its newly designed MSN Search, Microsoft has gone a similar route.

Because paid inclusion of a large number of listings can be difficult to manage, third-party software companies and resellers have sprung up to help large companies with so-called feed management. Such facilitators typically also help large retailers get their catalogs included in shopping search engines such as Froogle, Shopping.com, and Shopzilla. Decide Interactive (a division of 24/7 Real Media) and Position Technologies are two leading feed management providers.

Keyword-Based Advertising, or Sponsored Listings

And then there are pay-per-click ads near search results, the subject of this book. When analysts talk about total expenditures on paid search, they tend to combine all forms of paid search—paid inclusion, pay-per-click listings near search results, and even so-called contextual listings served around the Web by companies like Google and Overture.

What Is an Organic Index Listing?

Over the years, a number of terms have been invented in an attempt to distinguish paid from unpaid search listings. What such terms have in common appears to be a recognition that the average search engine user in the 1990s developed a strong trust for web index search results, believing them to be "scientific" and "unbiased." Industry discussions are peppered with references to "scientific" results, the "real" results, "unpaid search indexes," and so on. There is some debate as to who coined it, but the term that really stuck to distinguish unpaid, algorithmically generated results that appear on sites like Google Search or Teoma.com, is *organic* listings. No preservatives added. Whatever its origins, the term has been adopted as a favorite by search marketing professionals to distinguish the unpaid results from various forms of sponsored listings that appear near those results.

Safa Rashtchy, an analyst with investment bank Piper Jaffray, is perhaps the best-known Wall Street commentator on the contemporary search business. Before Google's initial public offering (which required the formerly private company to finally disclose its financials in public filings), many had been speculating that Google's 2003 revenues were going to be revealed as coming in around $300 million. When Rashtchy, followed by a few others, began to peg the number at something closer to $800–$900 million, it looked like something big was in the making at Google, and indeed it was. The actual 2003 revenue number blew away even Rashtchy's bold estimate: it was $1.46 billion.

Rashtchy's recent projections for the paid search sector as a whole are worth noting. At the October 2004 ad:tech conference in New York, he predicted that total paid search spending will rise to $13.5 billion by 2007 and $23.2 billion by 2010, enjoying rapid growth from its humble beginnings (only $369 million as recently as 2001). He noted that these figures were approximately twice his firm's estimates made only a year earlier. The rapid growth of the sector has caught even the closest observers off guard.

According to estimates by Hoover's (a research company that maintains a database of information on 40,000 public and private companies), Google's revenues as a private company grew from a mere $50 million in 2000 to $125 million in 2002. The real 2002 number was actually a lot better than the outsiders' estimates: according to public filings, it came in at $439 million! As one who had a front-row seat working with excited new advertisers eager to try the new pay-per-click AdWords program after its release in February 2002, I wasn't surprised. Nor was I particularly surprised that 2003 revenues topped $1 billion. Back-of-the-envelope calculations of typical AdWords account sizes multiplied by a reasonable estimate of the number of active Google AdWords accounts gave careful observers good reason to believe that Google's 2003 revenues were in excess of $1 billion, not the $300 million or less that was commonly estimated by the news media.

Two major events caused Google's revenues to explode to their current levels (in excess of $800 million in the third quarter of 2004 alone). First, the shift from an unsuccessful flat-rate "cost-per-thousand-impressions" (CPM-based) ad program to a dynamic pay-per-click auction model. This attracted new interest in Google's ad program, leading to a rapid uptake of the AdWords program and bidding wars for traffic tied to popular keywords.

Second, Google expanded its reach to begin placing text listings near relevant content on partner websites through its AdSense program in summer 2003. The AdSense program grew at a breakneck pace. Of the approximately $2.12 billion in advertising revenues earned by Google in the first three quarters of 2004, just about half of that was generated by ads served on non-Google-owned sites. In addition to "content" ads, the third-party revenues come from search network partners like Ask Jeeves and AOL Search.

Another big part of the story for 2004 was the many content publishers who began displaying the AdWords ads, making Google a force to be reckoned with as an advertising network, with larger ambitions sure to be lurking not far under the surface. With 98% of its revenues generated from advertising, this "search company" could also be referred to as an "ad-serving company."

Yahoo, too, depends heavily on search advertising revenues, though less so than Google. According to public filings, Yahoo's Overture division (pay-per-click ads) is responsible for as much as 40% of Yahoo's advertising revenues, and this may well increase to 50%. But Yahoo, burned in the dot-com meltdown, has diversified to fee-based services (such as paid content, premium email, games, and so on), so it isn't completely dependent on advertisers. If Google is wise, it will begin to diversify its revenue base as well.

Why Pay for Search Traffic? Isn't It Free?

If you're actually a visitor from 1997 and have just emerged from your time machine, you might be under the impression that it's enough just to wait around for search engine traffic to reward your business with all the traffic it needs, at no charge. This probably isn't going to happen. Most marketers believe in a healthy mix of paid and unpaid search traffic. Presumably, that's why you've decided to consult this manual. There are several reasons why incorporating a paid listings strategy into your online marketing mix is essential.

Screen Real Estate, Location of Listings

At search destinations like Yahoo Search and AOL Search, more and more of the available screen real estate is taken up by paid listings. Although the sponsored listings served by companies like Overture/Yahoo and Google AdWords are generally marked to separate them from the organic search results, many users click on the most visible listings without pausing to contemplate the distinction between what is and isn't paid for.

Aggregate figures for user clickthrough rates on top-of-page sponsored listings compared with the search listings just below them are typically not shared by the portals, but we can assume that companies like Yahoo have tested various page configurations with an eye to revenue maximization. The bottom line is that sponsored listings, especially the top two or three, are very prominently displayed and can cut into the amount of traffic received by websites that appear in the first page of regular search results in a given category.

Therefore, the wise course is to pursue a mix of both paid and organic search traffic. In fact, there are some clear advantages to paid search. Advertisers use paid search because they want to, not only because they're "forced" to. Who ever said traffic was supposed to be free?

Some Ads Are More Relevant

If sponsored results were never judged relevant by users, no one would ever click them. The fact is, every so often (about 15% of the time, Google staff have stated informally), a user decides that an ad result is more relevant than any of the search results on the page. This is particularly so, of course, for search queries that are commercial in intent. An advertiser who knows just how to present the right ad message to the right user will get noticed (and clicked).

Post-Florida Fallout: Algorithmic Changes

To keep ahead of the crowd of *optimizers* and *index spammers*—those who attempt (ethically or unethically, on a wide continuum) to reverse-engineer search engine algorithms so they can flood search results with commercial listings and thus profit from free traffic—Google periodically tweaks its ranking methodology. It changes weightings of various factors that affect how high pages are ranked for a given search query. Sometimes, sites using known optimization or spam techniques are penalized or banned from the index. Historically, sites would be banned for obvious spam techniques like *keyword stuffing* (repeating keywords nonsensically to try to get a higher ranking on a search term).

Google stayed ahead of a lot of early spam techniques because its PageRank methodology was fairly sophisticated. It measured the authority of a site based on how many other authoritative sites pointed to it. PageRank proved vulnerable, however. Some optimizers set up *link farms,* or premeditated interlinking schemes, with the express purpose of increasing free search engine traffic for members. Google periodically banned entire networks of sites participating in link schemes, but the tactics are difficult to stop entirely.

In fall 2003, a most unusual reindexing initiative emanated from the Googleplex, just in time for the holiday season. Suddenly, tens of thousands of commercial websites that had been playing by the rules found their rankings plummeting. Whether it was because it felt like a hurricane, or because the webmasters affected demanded a recount, the reindexing was nicknamed "Florida." Wild theories flew around in an attempt to describe what was going on. Some webmasters talked of a filter that Google was applying on top of its normal algorithm—an additional test that would recognize common patterns of over-optimization. Those who optimize websites for a living can be paranoid, but it turned out their fears were not so far from reality.

What was happening was really just a continuation of an ongoing commitment by Google to what it refers to as "search quality." Peter Norvig, a vice president in charge of search quality, went on record describing some of the tendencies that Google "might" be trying to reward in ranking pages on a given query. Google had decided to emphasize more than ever that the organic search results should be for informational queries, not commercial queries. Even within the commercial,

What Is a Googleplex?

Googleplex is the nickname for Google's headquarters in Mountain View, California, which opened in 1999. Google completed a move to a new, larger facility in early 2004. The name Google is a misspelling of the word *googol* (a word coined by a mathematician in 1938, which means a very large number—1 followed by 100 zeros). *Googolplex,* as it happens, is the name for an even larger number. Visitors to Google's now-legendary headquarters will come across colorful graphical depictions of user search behavior, a fully stocked game room, a large dining area, and other quirks, such as machines that dispense M&Ms. As public scrutiny of the company has increased, puns, practical jokes, and sly references to pornography searches have no doubt been toned down, but Google is unlikely to ever shed its culture as a company that works endlessly and plays together. When I had my first tour of the first-generation Googleplex in August 2002, Sergey Brin's office was pointed out to me. Inside was a large metal waste can containing several hockey sticks whose blades were worn down to a sharp point from Brin's frequent participation in company road hockey games. As I wrote this in January 2005, most of the company (including the customer service department) was off-site at a ski retreat.

Norvig implied that Google might attempt to make distinctions between what we might call "informational commercial pages," such as company histories, and "solely commercial pages," such as catalog pages. Left unsaid was their nonetheless clear message: commercially oriented pages are most suitable for the AdWords program. Those who want to reach customers should pay for targeted clicks and optimize their paid search campaigns for the best possible results.

Nate Tyler, a member of Google's public relations department, was uncharacteristically candid at this time, telling me in an interview that site owners need to be aware that "Google Search was never intended as a service whose sole purpose was to generate traffic for commercial sites." He came very close to saying if you don't like it, use the AdWords program. Google was accused of deliberately shaking up their free rankings to send a message to website owners that they needed to buy paid listings from Google. By not vehemently denying those charges, Google seemed to be tacitly admitting that it was not above manipulating its search algorithms in ways that "reminded" webmasters to focus more of their time on paid search campaigns if they wanted their search referrals to continue.

In spite of its push for AdWords participation, there is no relationship I'm aware of between buying paid listings and getting better free rankings on Google. The two remain unrelated in any way. Website owners should participate in the AdWords program because it's a good opportunity for prime exposure on search results pages, not because they assume they'll be getting special consideration for sending Google a "bribe."

Many hard-core optimizers (those who make their entire living from gaming search results, with no provision for paid traffic) want to believe they can still beat Google's algorithm. You'd better be very good at optimizing if you want to act as if you didn't hear what Google was saying in fall 2003, however. Many ordinary business owners, formerly enamored of their SEO consultants' omnipotent powers to generate high rankings in the free index, now realize that Tyler and Norvig meant exactly what they said in the days following the infamous Florida update: Google is going to reduce the proportion of commercial websites that rank well in search results. While some lucky ones may continue to do well, it will be a bumpy ride for most anyone who relies solely on unpaid traffic.

Yes, commercially oriented websites will continue to reside in the Google index, and many formerly high-ranking pages have a good shot at continuing to rank reasonably well. But it seems that a great number of informational pages such as discussion forums, weblogs, university professors' home pages, public radio transcripts, magazine articles, and the like, are now dominating top rankings on many search queries. As a result, those who relied on those top rankings for revenue-producing traffic will need to diversify their approach.

Observers may note that on certain types of commercial queries, such as those referring to brand names, the organic results may remain full of commercially oriented websites. However, even here, webmasters sometimes report troubles getting good rankings. At the very least, there seems to be more volatility in rankings than there once was.

It's unwise to become too complacent about the status of organic listings. Even a very popular commercial phrase—**coca-cola**—doesn't give Coke unfettered access to consumers' eyeballs. On this query typed into Google Search, Google actually places two results from Google News above the first web index listing (which is indeed for the Coca-Cola home page). In other words, news stories about Coca-Cola will likely be seen first by many users.

At Teoma.com, the first web index result on a query for **coca-cola** is also the Coca-Cola home page. But the versatile role played by web search as a social and educational tool is clearly illustrated in this case by the fifth-ranked site on this Teoma query, killercoke.org, a critique of alleged crimes connected with Coke bottling plants in Colombia. If users feel that one search engine has suddenly stopped telling them the truth, they may switch to a different search engine. For this reason, we are likely going to see major search engines finding ways of ensuring that the organic results aren't dominated by commercially oriented listings. (For the record, killercoke.org ranked 13th on Google when I checked.)

Control Over Message, Navigation, Timing, Exposure

What could be seen as forced diversification into paid search might be the best thing that ever happened to many search marketers, because it compels them to run more disciplined marketing programs. Getting your pages indexed in a search engine is pretty haphazard. The description the user sees might not be what you want. The page the engine decides to index might not be a carefully tailored offer page. With paid search, you decide on the ad title and ad copy. You tell the system which landing page the user should go to, and install tracking that will confirm for you whether a given paid click resulted in a sale.

You can also control the delivery of a paid search campaign. Different offers and specials can be featured at different times of the year. You can turn campaigns off on weekends if you wish. You can turn off the half of your campaign that performs poorly, while leaving the rest running. Paying for traffic gives you a greater degree of control over your message and the timing of that message.

Furthermore, you can, to a considerable extent, control where your message is displayed. If you want AOL and Ask Jeeves users to see your ad, you can expand your ad delivery to Google AdWords network partners. Or you can just buy exposure on Google only. Now, even more micro-targeting is possible with Google's regional targeting feature that allows you to show your ads only to designated metropolitan areas or geographic areas specified with a latitude-and-longitude tool. You can also specify which countries see your ad. If you're ambitious, you can run ads in different languages.

Noncommercial Sites and the Organic Results

There are some good reasons why certain kinds of informational, content-rich sites do well in search engines, and conversely, why sales-oriented sites don't always do well. Search engines were built to discover topical content—to index text. If your site is not text rich, why try to impress search engines with a lot of content you don't genuinely feel is of interest to your target buyers? By purchasing paid listings, you can quickly skirt the problem of being content poor.

Another element of many search engine algorithms today, most famously Google's, is analysis of inbound links. Sites with many inbound links from other authoritative sites get better search engine rankings, by and large. But if you're a local paint store, it's not particularly realistic to expect hundreds of other websites to link to you, no matter how great your customer service might be. Some categories of business do attract a lot of links by their very nature. Hotels, for example, are often linked from the websites of businesses, trade shows, and associations who may be meeting at the hotel for a conference. Restaurants may garner recommendations from magazines and bloggers who might decide to link to the restaurant's site as a sign of their approval. But some businesses face tough sledding when it comes to getting inbound links beyond the ones that are easy to pay for (such as the Yahoo Directory). Linking campaigns are portrayed as an integral part of a search engine optimization strategy by some service vendors. But these campaigns have become more difficult to conduct, especially for smaller businesses that would have to bother strangers to ask them for a link. When you're selling something and people know you are, a lot of them will be stingy with links, since many website owners now understand that links confer authority.

The best way to get a lot of authoritative websites to link to your site, of course, is to follow Seth Godin's advice from the *Purple Cow* book: create a remarkable product or service; say something remarkable; do something remarkable; *be* remarkable. Or, you could join a link farm and hope Google doesn't ban your site from the index.

Or, you could integrate a paid search campaign into your strategy. A successful paid search campaign doesn't know if you have 200 pages of quality content on your website and doesn't care if not a single other website links to yours.

Organic and Paid Search Strategies: Not Mutually Exclusive

I can't tell you precisely how to allocate your time and resources when it comes to pursuing paid search traffic as opposed to better organic listings. As you embark on your paid search campaign, you'll develop useful new skills and knowledge related to your customer base. More importantly, you'll probably gain customers you never would have seen had you sat around hoping for unpaid search referrals to turn into business. You'll gain a level of control over your message and the pace of delivery that is simply impossible with unpaid, "stumble-in" search traffic. Paying for clicks is not admitting defeat, as some SEO consultants seem to believe. Unpaid traffic is no one's birthright. Paid ads, on the other hand, are an opportunity for growth available to anyone interested.

Whether the traffic is paid or unpaid, companies of all sizes are beginning to appreciate the unique qualities of search marketing. Google's widely reported business successes have given the whole idea of paid search the credibility it needs to become a real force in the advertising industry as a whole. As this chapter has shown, search advertising is still a small industry when compared to direct marketing and media buying as a whole. But with its superior targeting and noninterruptive format, the planets may well be aligned for continued rapid growth.

Endnotes

1. Jakob Nielsen, "The Most Hated Advertising Techniques," *Alertbox*, December 6, 2004, archived at useit.com.

2. Seth Godin, *Permission Marketing: Turning Strangers into Friends and Friends into Customers* (Simon & Schuster, 1999).

3. In a moment of weakness, a respected business publication allowed me, a small voice in the wilderness, to publish on op-ed piece on the subject of corporate spam: "Corporate America - Stay Out of My Inbox," *The Globe and Mail Report on Business*, September 12, 2000.

4. Godin, *Purple Cow: Transform Your Business By Being Remarkable* (Portfolio, 2003).

5. Godin, "In Praise of the Purple Cow," *Fast Company* 67 (February 2003), 74.

6. Featured as a case study in Emanuel Rosen, *The Anatomy of Buzz: How to Create Word of Mouth Marketing* (Currency, 2000).

7. "Relevant results: Jeeves vs. Google," Traffick.com, October 18, 1999.

8. Source: SearchEngineWatch.com, "Search Engine Sizes." Google's index has been overtaken in size at times, but generally regains the lead.

9. 10-Q quarterly report for Google, Inc., summary table citing nine months ending September 30, 2004.

10. Craig R. Endicott, "Top Marketers Spend $74 Billion; Annual Ranking Shows 7.1% Increase with P&G, Unilever Leading the Way," *Advertising Age* 74:45 (November 10, 2003), 26.

11. Source: Newspaper Association of America.

12. Richard H. Levey, "DMA Study Shows Industry May be Rebounding," *Direct Marketing Business Intelligence Magazine*, March 1, 2004.

13. Michael Pastore, "Reports Predict Web Ads Have a Future," ClickZ.com, June 21, 2000.

14. Interactive Advertising Bureau, "Q3 2004 Interactive Advertising Revenues Total Over $2.4 Billion Fourth Record-Setting Quarter," November 15, 2004, archived at iab.com.

15. "Web Ad Spending to Double," *iMedia Connection*. July 28, 2004.

16. Stefanie Olsen, "Ballmer: We Fell Down on Search," CNET News.com, March 25, 2004.

17. eMarketer, "The Elephant in the Room: The Online At-Work Audience," February 2003 (PDF). Archived at iab.com.

18. Kevin Lee, "Yes, Virginia, There Is SEM Brand Lift," ClickZ.com, Parts I and II, July 16 & 23, 2004.

19. comScore Networks, "Canadians Are More Active Online Searchers Than Their U.S. Counterparts," press release, May 13, 2004, archived at comscore.com.

20. Thanks to Mikkel deMib Svendsen for coining the term and leading online discussions about it.

21. Seth Godin, "The Problem with Search Engine Optimization," *Seth's Blog*, July 1, 2004, archived at sethgodin.typepad.com.

22. In particular, I recommend Shari Thurow, *Search Engine Visibility* (New Riders, 2002); Mike Grehan, *Search Engine Marketing: The Essential Best Practice Guide, 2nd ed.* (e-book, available at search-engine-book.co.uk).

23. Stefanie Olsen, "Is AltaVista Searching for Top Dollar?" CNET News.com, October 1, 2002, archived at news.com.

24. See for example Danny Sullivan, "Yahoo Reawakens the Paid Inclusion Debate," *SearchDay*, May 18, 2004, archived at searchenginewatch.com.

Chapter 2

A $4 Billion Afterthought: How Google Entered the Advertising Market

Google did not just appear out of thin air. It was conceived out of the efforts (and stumblings) of a number of precursors, each adding another stepping-stone upon which Google climbed to the top of the heap. As an online advertiser, you will benefit from understanding how and why Google developed and what it took to get where it is. That is the purpose of this chapter. When we're done I hope you'll understand why an AdWords campaign is the best bet for your advertising attention and dollars. You'll also pick up some insight into Google's unique culture, which will not only help you interpret official and unofficial Google policies, but also help you do a better job of dealing with problems and foibles in AdWords as they crop up.

AdWords Gets Its Start

In March 2002, when I first started advising clients on how to use Google's new advertising program, there was much skepticism surrounding this upstart's efforts. It all felt rather unfamiliar: an automated self-serve advertising platform with many restrictive rules and yet rather limited customer support. Complaints were common because few businesspeople had yet come to grips with what type of company Google was. A fair number of Google's first advertisers had learned the ropes on Overture, which structured its program differently. Others were completely new to search advertising. They were Google Search users and were attracted by Google's strong brand. "Hey, we can advertise on Google now! Let's try it!" was the typical thought process. Google invested nearly nothing in marketing the new ad program, focusing most of its energy on technological innovation, as usual.

Overture had a serious head start on Google AdWords, but AdWords caught up so quickly it took everyone, including Google, by surprise. Overture's advertiser base had reached 21,000 advertisers by the end of 1999, 37,000 by the end of 2000, and 60,000 by April 2001. By mid-2003, scarcely a year after the pay-per-click version of AdWords was launched, Google's advertiser base had already surpassed Overture's, reaching 100,000 advertisers. Strong global expansion pushed this to 150,000 by September 2003. By the end of 2004, Google boasted over 280,000 advertisers worldwide.

Playing the Middle Man

In the early days, I found myself acting as something of a translator, explaining to novice advertisers that there were actually key advantages to Google's heavily automated approach and passing along advertiser concerns to staff at Google whenever they would listen. Some of the things that seemed obvious to entrepreneurs muddling along out there in the real world of business evidently didn't occur to Google at all. For example, the tone of many automated editorial disapproval messages struck me as insensitive. Although the messages weren't meant that way, email is a brittle medium at the best of times, and repeated messages of what sounded like disapproval from a company that was supposed to be eager for your advertising business were discouraging to a number of advertisers. It wasn't uncommon at that time for advertisers to give up in frustration with disabled keywords, editorial disapprovals, and the steep learning curve required to achieve a positive return on investment (ROI).

As it turned out, Google was never all that eager for those advertising dollars. A closer inspection of the situation reveals that Google must juggle the demands of many stakeholders and must weigh many variables in deciding how to deal with its advertisers. It's that very lack of overeagerness that has provided such a solid foundation for Google's growth as a favorite destination for search engine users. It has built its brand around balancing the needs of users, advertisers, investors, employees, and other stakeholders.

Google Responds

In an effort to build and maintain its reputation, Google has always consulted its users, advertisers, and a variety of experts in the design of its ad program. Its public relations department regularly facilitates dialogue with those who might be able to provide the types of feedback that will help improve the service. The presence of Google staffers on discussion boards frequented by web geeks has been especially impressive. WebmasterWorld.com, in particular, has been one source of constant feedback for Google. Its reps (dubbed GoogleGuy and AdWordsAdvisor) have actively solicited detailed grassroots feedback on features of the search technology as well as the advertising platform.

Here's one particularly memorable example of Google's brand of responsiveness. The second-generation (pay-per-click) version of AdWords had begun life in February 2002 with a quirky pricing system. Although the official minimum cost per click was set at 5 cents, many keywords were arbitrarily assigned higher minimum prices. Let's say you had bid 25 cents on a keyword, but its Google-assigned minimum was 55 cents. You'd see that minimum displayed in red, and your ad wouldn't show unless you increased your bid to reach the minimum for that keyword. Talk about frustration.

According to Google, this was based on their study of demand for keywords in its earlier version of the program (also called AdWords). Notwithstanding this supposed market data that implied heavy market demand for the keyword ("derivatives"; likely to be typed by a sophisticated investing audience), there were no advertisers willing to pay Google's enforced minimum of 92 cents. But that didn't mean the keyword had no value. My client, for one, expected to break even if they could bid around 48 cents. So much for market demand! Google's approach to pricing was inefficient to say the least. AdWords, back then, wasn't yet popular enough for Google to force advertisers out of the market-based auction by inventing its own above-market pricing. The program needed more "floor traffic." Just as a house going on the market may sell more if priced lower because more people come to look at it and subsequently engage in a bidding war, I felt that Google would ultimately benefit by lowering its prices on the click auction. By enticing new advertisers to enter the auction at the 5-cent minimum price, Google would ultimately benefit from bidding wars.

At the time, I wrote a couple of complaints about this in my newsletter, and a number of advertisers kept the heat on. Eventually, Google just scrubbed the whole idea of inflated minimums. They had (after spending considerable time pondering) listened to reasoned arguments and to the pleas of their advertisers. The minimum price for a click remains five cents.

More recently, Google listened to many complaints about the "contextual" advertising program (where Google serves ads on partner websites known as AdSense publishers). I had argued in a couple of conference presentations that although wholesale changes to the level of advertiser control over this program might be too data intensive and too much to ask of Google, one thing they could offer advertisers would be a way to exclude sites they didn't want their ads appearing on. That way, advertisers could weed out publishers they thought might be inappropriate for their needs. I was surprised to hear, less than two weeks after I'd made this argument at a conference in December 2004, that Google was releasing the "publisher exclude" feature on a beta-test basis. Subsequent to that, an even more extensive overhaul of contextual advertising was announced, giving publishers more control over placement. This remains at a very early stage.

Is it a question of the squeaky wheel getting the grease? To some extent. But Google listens better to squeaky wheels who make specific, doable suggestions for changes to their program. The publisher exclude option is an example of a feature that was probably going to be part of a more comprehensive revamp of the AdWords interface anyway. The timing of that particular feature's release may have been moved up in response to criticisms of the contextual ad program finding their way into press reports.

A couple of key points are as clear to me now as they were three years ago. First, a general principle: to understand how to deal with a unique company like Google, you must understand its culture and its power structure. Complex organizations tend to arise under the control of a dominant coalition, and internal power struggles are typically won by that coalition.[1] These patterns will tend to dictate how decisions get made.

Google is rare in that its engineering culture is particularly strong; so much so that even after hiring a large sales force and taking on public investors' cash, the founders still professed a wish (in the prospectus for the initial public offering) to pursue long-term goals rather than chase short-term financial targets. Beyond that, the work habits and characteristics of the people Google hires have lent a certain flavor to day-to-day operations.

Google is stacked with PhDs, and even for the nonengineers who work there, the hiring process is stringent. By all accounts, new hires are judged largely on a combination of raw intellectual talent and the likelihood that they'll fit in with the values and habits of the "well-meaning geeks" who already work there. This isn't particularly remarkable for a technology company, but it certainly contrasts with the sales culture we might expect from a firm that generates nearly all of its revenues from ads.

The second, more specific principle to keep in mind is that Google's entry into the advertising business was an afterthought to their search engine business. A billboard is a billboard—it serves no other purpose but advertising. The same goes for the Yellow Pages—you don't use it for any other reason except to look for a local business. Google Search, by contrast, is still first and foremost a search engine that is intended to help people find information of various types, especially noncommercial information. No one forces users to visit Google's website. To become preeminent with users, Google's goal has always been primarily to build the world's best search technology. In spite of the fact that 98% of the revenues of this company come from ads, and as difficult as it might be for me and you (as advertisers) to accept this, you can only understand Google if you're willing to see the ads as secondary.

Predecessors and Competitors

Google wasn't the first web search engine, and it wasn't the first pay-per-click listings service. What it has been is the most successful company ever in both of these areas. While this overview is not intended to be a substitute for a full history of search engines and online advertising, it should help put things in context for those unfamiliar with the evolution of the field.

Major Predecessors in Search

The history of web search engines is woefully underpublicized at present, possibly because those involved were (and many still are) too busy building powerful companies to bother chronicling everything they were up to. As such, some of the best resources out there are actually quite limited.[2] Increasingly, web enthusiasts and pioneers are sharing anecdotes in public forums, on weblogs, and so on.

Yahoo Directory

Founded in 1994, the Yahoo Directory proposed to simplify the nascent process of finding useful pages that resided on the young World Wide Web. At first, it was little more than a collection of favorite links compiled by two graduate students, Jerry Yang and David Filo. Both were studying electrical engineering and had virtually no training in information retrieval technology. Although it eventually got around to hiring people with some background in subject classification, the company has arguably never been a powerhouse of search technology. By calling its staff "ontologists" (a term from library science that implies advanced background in categorization), Yahoo may have appeased a few diehard information scientists, but the reality is, these were mostly entry-level positions. As Yahoo grew in the mid-to-late 1990's, search and information retrieval expertise often took a back seat to business objectives and the imperatives of financial markets.

The company's success in going public as one of the early dot-coms (before they were called dot-coms) gave it the cash and the profile needed to build and acquire additional services, including email and personalized home pages. Yahoo soon became a diversified destination site known as a *portal*. Massive sponsorship revenues enjoyed during the online advertising boom provided the company enough momentum to survive the subsequent advertising crash. Yahoo has become a leading and profitable global Internet brand.

Yahoo (as with competitors such as Excite) did not always realize how important the search experience was to its users. To augment its popular human-edited directory, Yahoo made deals with a number of successive third parties to provide web index search results: Open Text, AltaVista, Inktomi, AltaVista again, and Google. Finally, it decided to get serious about search (and stop helping its competitors). In 2003, Yahoo terminated its partnership with Google Search and acquired Inktomi and Overture (at the time, the latter owned two struggling search engines, FAST and AltaVista, which meant that Yahoo now had access to personnel from three major, but declining, web indexes). Its technology team now bolstered, Yahoo set about releasing its own search index. Today's Yahoo Index is arguably just another generation of Inktomi technology. The paid inclusion model for listing clients is also similar to what Inktomi (and later, AltaVista) had offered.

The Overture acquisition also brought 100% of the pay-per-click search listing revenues into the Yahoo fold. Overture, a pure "sponsored listings" vendor with no search engine traffic of its own, relied entirely on partnerships to serve its ads and was vulnerable whenever the time came to renegotiate deals with major portal partners. The deal turned out to be beneficial to both companies. Overture would have been at risk of being squeezed, and the deal gave Yahoo ready access to Overture's huge list of advertisers and 100% control over what turned out to be a growing revenue stream. At the time of the acquisition, many observers thought that MSN, a major Overture partner, would terminate the relationship, but this hasn't proven to be the case. MSN renewed its deal with Overture through 2006, providing a nice ongoing revenue stream to Yahoo. However, MSN is now putting the finishing touches on its own paid search advertising program, and soon there will be three major paid search vendors—Google, Yahoo, and MSN—when there was once two. In the meantime, Overture has aggressively expanded its pursuit of advertising partnerships, particularly in its Content Match program. Thus, like Google, Yahoo has quietly become a powerhouse in serving online advertising in various formats on a wide range of partner sites, a business once dominated by traditional online advertising networks. Both companies wait anxiously for Microsoft to join the party in earnest.

From the standpoint of search user market share and search-related revenues, Yahoo is Google's main competitor today. As some of us predicted during the height of dot-com mania in 1999, the portal wars proved very real. Consolidation occurred as users chose the best online services and let the rest die. Competitors like Excite, Lycos, Go2Net, Infoseek, AltaVista, Snap, and many more went out of business or were acquired for a pittance. In the North American market, only the four leaders—Google, Yahoo, MSN, and AOL—seem worth discussing. The picture is different in other parts of the world, but overall, consolidation has been the name of the game everywhere.

Back When Many Crawlers Roamed the Web...

Search marketing strategies evolved during a time when there existed numerous web indexes, supported by *crawlers,* which would index as many web pages as possible. In the mid-to-late 1990s, as many as eight of these indexes were in play and being actively updated at any given time. The number of web pages available for indexing was relatively small; thus a web crawler project could be supported by limited funds (typically university research projects).

Different indexes had varying degrees of coverage of the Web, and they all ranked sites differently. Because it was often hard to find good information on one search engine, many searchers would try several. This lent the medium a feeling of slight chaos and led marketers to believe that they needed to be "on all the search engines" if they "wanted to be found." Because search usage data was limited, it was tempting to fixate on how high one *ranked* on the various search engines for a given query. The makers of rank-checking tools like Webposition Gold profited handsomely from the presupposition that high rankings were vitally important. Search engine optimization companies convinced clients that they had specialized expertise that would help them rank well on several different engines. Many site owners got so caught up in the rankings game they forgot to build viable businesses.

Arguably, then, the information provided by early search engine optimization experts such as Fredrick Marckini (author of an early book on the subject, and a founder of the leading search engine marketing agency i-prospect) and Danny Sullivan (founder of SearchEngineWatch.com) was geared towards an audience of webmasters and cutting-edge marketers who needed to know not merely general information about search engines, but specific information about how the different search engines were ranking pages.

Resources put together by research experts like Greg Notess (SearchEngineShowdown.com), Tara Calishain (ResearchBuzz.com), and Chris Sherman (formerly with About.com Guide to Web Search, today associate editor of SearchEngineWatch.com) also seemed indispensable to anyone trying to understand this cluttered landscape of search tools.

The various search engine comparisons and updates would not have found an audience if not for the apparent importance of a confusing assembly of viable and distinct search engines in the second half of the 1990s. Marckini's first book, for example, received many favorable reviews, but they seem to have dried up around 1999. Coincidentally, shortly after Google's founding in 1998, many of the formerly active search engine indexes stopped being regularly updated, got acquired, changed business models, or simply went out of business. This left a very different (consolidated) landscape: fewer unpaid search indexes, less need to "submit" your site to the various search engines, and fewer optimization techniques to worry about. Techniques like those Marckini had been lauded for explaining were fast becoming obsolete. Even seemingly obvious advice, like marking up the HTML pages on your site with keyword and description *meta tags*, was no longer useful.[3] Marckini's consulting company, like many, began offering an increasing proportion of paid search campaign management to its corporate clients, as was evident in Marckini's shifting focus in columns posted at ClickZ.com.

As the Web grew, and as search technologies became more susceptible to spam, the costs of running a web index had grown significantly. At the same time, venture capital and public investor dollars began to take chances on any company that might become the "next Yahoo."

Companies like AltaVista, Lycos, Infoseek, Excite, Snap, Go2Net, and Inktomi had their dreams of dominance fueled by varying levels of investor support. But in spite of their ambitions, they had few good ideas about how to make revenues from running a search engine. Some felt certain that banner ads would be the ticket. Others saw Yahoo become a portal and decided to follow suit, adding many related services to capitalize on their brands.

Excite was a classic example of a me-too portal strategy inspired by Yahoo's marketplace successes. As a user, I found this "#2 portal" exciting indeed, because some of the features it came out with (such as an early intranet platform for the masses called Excite Communities) were more full featured than anything Yahoo had on offer.

Building on its early popularity as the well-respected search engine, Architext, Excite kept adding services and advertising over the years, finally merging with cable Internet provider @Home in a promising, but ultimately ill-fated, partnership. A variety of large media companies followed the path of acquiring search engine companies, sometimes to capitalize on inflated stock market valuations. Disney Internet Group acquired Infoseek and launched a portal called Go, in the process building a volunteer-driven directory called Go Guides. NBC Internet went public and snapped up hot Internet companies with names like Snap and Xoom. These efforts turned out to be short-lived. At the height of the boom, Yahoo wannabes like TheGlobe.com went public on scant revenues, making them some of the most overvalued publicly traded companies of all time.

For the most part, the portal model was once again built around banner ads. In most cases, the costs of building these companies exceeded the revenues they brought in. The advertising model failed as banner ad prices plummeted, in large part due to the poor response received from these ads, and in part due to the collapse of a pyramid scheme of sorts—a weakening of demand for the ads from unstable dot-com companies that were going under.

Perhaps the most prominent memory of this wave of search engine technologies is that of their failure to foil relatively simple efforts by porn and gambling sites to reverse-engineer their algorithms and flood the indices with spam. AltaVista, at one time widely considered to be the world's leading search engine, staggered midway through its life when the quality of its results seemed to degenerate badly. Although the technology improved, the public never fully regained its trust in this mid-1990s generation of search technologies. Search engine users would need to hear new ideas if they were to regain their passion for search technology.

The other thing that left the public disillusioned—and again, AltaVista was in the middle of it—was the fact that the search engine companies couldn't seem to focus. People really just wanted to search for information, and yet they were being forced not only to look at intrusive ads, but pages full of clutter and information that they didn't care about. To be sure, the notion of a personalized home page full of news and features like calendars and weather was attractive to many. But few companies other than Yahoo, AOL, and MSN were truly skilled at creating a diversified information service. AltaVista released a decent web-based email product, for example, but couldn't handle the demand on its servers. In the UK, AltaVista claimed to be developing a free, ad-supported dialup Internet Service Provider business, but was later forced to back down from its claim that 100,000 "trial" users were on board. (The real number was zero, and the managing director of AltaVista UK resigned in shame.[4]) AltaVista users, typically a serious bunch, would have been much happier had this company stuck to what it knew best—search.

Inktomi, LookSmart: The "Portal Suppliers"

All the while refining their technology, Internet search engines struggled to find the best approach to turning a profit from the exercise. One school of thought had it that pure search technology companies could supply large portals to those who did not want to develop these technologies in-house. Some have called this the "wholesale search market."

Fortunately for companies like LookSmart and Inktomi, it wasn't necessary to be profitable in the early days. Venture capital, and later, public stock offerings, filled the company coffers with cash. Lofty valuations based on nonfinancial criteria eventually gave way to the harsh realities of profit and loss statements.

Inktomi, founded in 1996 out of a research project by computer science professor Eric Brewer and grad student Paul Gauthier, was widely hailed as an up-and-coming superstar in the field of web search. Initial rave reviews in the press did little to endear Inktomi with end users over the long term. It isn't hard to see why: by acting as the behind-the-scenes engine powering high-profile search brands like Hotbot.com, users were unable to literally "search Inktomi," so they never got behind the company. And advertisers had little direct relationship with "Ink." As Inktomi began to struggle more with the volume of spam, the decision was made to move to a paid inclusion model. Sites that paid for inclusion in the index would get guaranteed inclusion (but not guaranteed rankings); those that did not pay were not removed, but it was implied that they might be. This revenue model was interesting, but proved to be too little, too late, to save Inktomi from irrelevance.

Amazingly, an abstract of a speech on the history of Inktomi given by Eric Brewer in June 2004 suggests that "despite having real value, Inktomi was pulled down—not by the 'dot coms,' but by the collapse of the telecom sector...." Were it judged through any normal assessment of revenues and profitability as measured against business risk, Inktomi did not, in fact, have as much real value as its proponents believed. Its briefly profitable period was bestowed upon it by portal partners like Yahoo and MSN, who have proved repeatedly that they are apt to "taketh away" the privilege of supplying them with search results. Inktomi saw its market value plummet and was ultimately acquired by Yahoo in 2003 for relative pocket change ($235 million) because it (like many others) was surpassed by Google as a technology leader and as a favorite search destination by end users. Inktomi had good technology, but it proved conclusively that good technology alone does not make for a viable business.

The problem with the portal supplier strategy, as it turned out, is that by ceding their direct relationship with the public to their big-brand clients, search engines like Inktomi and directories like LookSmart faded from public view and lost leverage in the marketplace, since they no longer had ownership of traffic flows. Inktomi, perhaps out of loyalty to the companies it supplied, didn't even allow searches at its own website. LookSmart eventually followed a similar strategy, downplaying their own website as a destination for users. This proved to be a fatal error. When portals began to squeeze the suppliers on price (easy to do, since numerous suppliers existed, and licensing the Open Directory was free), these suppliers lost whatever independent brand loyalty they'd developed in their formative stages. With lackluster cash flow, Inktomi and LookSmart lacked the momentum to improve their technology. A downward spiral ensued.

Portals like MSN began to employ larger teams of search product managers, whose job it was to work with listings suppliers like Inktomi, LookSmart, and Overture in order to customize search results for their users. In addition, a variety of hand-tweaked editorial results and directly sold ad results had been folded into the mix.

Contemporary thinking at companies like MSN and Yahoo is now that search is so lucrative and pivotal a user activity that it needs to be taken in-house. AOL is the lone major holdout in this regard. Recognizing that it has little to gain from forging its own path with a second-rate search offering, AOL uses Google for both index results and sponsored listings.

The Open Directory Project (dmoz.org)

Beginning life in 1998 as GnuHoo and then NewHoo, the Open Directory Project (ODP) was conceived as a competitor to the Yahoo Directory. The work was to be done by volunteer editors, and the end product was to be licensed to any portal or site that wanted to take advantage of the information. Doesn't sound like much of a business? Well, it turned out to be a pretty good deal for the founders. The directory's popularity led to its acquisition by Netscape, which was later acquired by AOL.

AOL became the Open Directory's major distributor, but the directory was also licensed (at no charge to the publisher) in many other places around the Web. Google began using ODP data fairly early on, calling it the Google Directory. An innovative feature was Google's use of an "overlay" technique, ranking results in a given ODP category in order based on the site's Google PageRank score. This was illustrated with a green bar (on a scale of 0 to 10, similar to the way the info is displayed by searchers using the Google toolbar). This could have been a very useful feature indeed had there been more consistency to the underlying content in the directory. The so-called Google Directory still exists.

A couple of key Open Directory players, founder Rich Skrenta and marketing exec Chris Tolles, have now moved on to a new venture: Topix.net, a sophisticated news search engine that competes directly with Google News.

I was an early critic of ODP for the lack of professional standards in editing and its constant struggles with editorial corruption. The lack of transparency of submission procedures to the public and the huge variations in the degrees of disclosure of editors' biographical information meant, for me, that this so-called open directory was far from it.[5] The construction of a high-quality human-edited directory remains an elusive task, especially as directories like Yahoo have become so commercialized.

The Google Difference: A Third-Generation Algorithm

If Google hadn't moved to fill the void left by its struggling predecessors, someone else would have. Scientists in various research projects were working on new ideas about how to rank the importance of web pages vis-à-vis a given user query. What Google did was to popularize some of the best emerging ideas about how to design a large-scale search engine at a time when others were losing momentum. Some of these ideas are so central to the task of ranking pages in today's web environment that they were adopted in some form or another by all of Google's main competitors (including Inktomi, AltaVista, and FAST).

The working paper that explains Google's PageRank methodology, "Anatomy of a Large-Scale Hypertextual Web Search Engine," is frequently cited.[6] But the field of information retrieval technology is rich with ongoing experimentation by hundreds of well-funded scientists, some well known, some not. Some scientists take a slightly different approach to the problem tackled by Page and Brin, organizing the Web into topic-based "communities." Teoma, a search engine owned by Ask Jeeves, is the most public example of this approach.[7] The two approaches tend to provide somewhat different results, but they are clearly cousins of a similar generation of thinking about the "hyperlinked environment," and both have been a boon to researchers seeking that elusive piece of information online.

The idea behind PageRank is brilliant and intuitive. The governing principle revolves around a map of the linking structure of the Web. Pages that have a lot of other important pages pointing to them are deemed important. "PageRank can be thought of as a model of user behavior," wrote Brin and Page. "We assume there is a 'random surfer' who is given a web page at random and keeps clicking on links, never hitting 'back' but eventually gets bored and starts on another random page. The probability that the random surfer visits a page is its PageRank."

This was a significant advance over previous generations of web search. Although most major engines had experimented with a variety of ranking criteria, many of them had depended heavily on basic keyword matching criteria. Not only did this make good information hard to find because so many pages were locked in a virtual tie for first place, it made it easier for optimizers to feed keyword-dense pages into the search engine in a bid to rank their commercially oriented pages higher. Although this game of keyword optimization is quite effective to this day in ranking pages well on unpopular queries (even on Google Search), it seems to work rather poorly on common queries.

The ascendance of PageRank means that on a Google Search for **auto insurance comparison**, for example, it's likely that a well-known site will rank well here rather than some random site that just happens to contain those keywords. When I tried the query, I got insweb.com as the #1 result. This site is cited as a "Forbes Magazine favorite." This dovetails with the notion that authoritative recommendations do indeed confer authority as far as Google's algorithm is concerned.

The ability to break these "virtual ties" among similar queries is a breakthrough for search engines. Almost all major search technologies today are significantly more sophisticated than those from the mid-1990s. I recall a time when many websites used a free licensed version of Excite Search for their internal site search. The technology was weak, often providing a clutter of irrelevant results. If search was this bad in closed corporate environments, it was definitely in need of improvement if it was to help users sort through the enormous clutter of pages available on the Web.

The calculations involved in determining PageRank are just the beginning when it comes to determining how high a page ranks for a given user's query on Google. Brin, in a "keynote fireside chat with Danny Sullivan" (complete with fake fireplace projected on the wall) at a conference in San Jose in August 2003, noted that there are "more than fifty" factors in total that might determine how well a page ranks in Google for a given query. PageRank, one suspects, has become easier for optimizers to game. As predecessors such as AltaVista found, the integrity of a search ranking algorithm is more difficult to maintain when the engine becomes a leading source of commercially viable referrals.

The technology alone isn't what vaulted Google to its status of the world's favorite search engine, but it played a big part. In addition to the search results being more pleasingly relevant than what was available elsewhere, many users found the Google Search website to be faster and less cluttered than competitors' sites.

Google Search is far more than PageRank, then. Early innovations included theories about computing power that led to massive increases in processing speed. Search engines must innovate on a variety of fronts. Recently, when Google announced yet another leap in the size of its index (to over 8 billion pages), a company rep told me that part of the increase could be attributed to advances in crawling technology (how Google's spider, Googlebot, finds pages by following links on the websites it already knows about). More recently, Google surprised observers by releasing a standardized protocol called Google SiteMaps. This protocol allows webmasters to submit a file to Google that includes a listing of all important pages on the site, so Googlebot doesn't have to find them on its own or guess what pages are important to the site owner.

The fact that Google did well early on meant that it could tackle many small details with gusto, because it was attracting some of the world's best technical talent. Google kept impressing experts with quiet improvements such as its ability to index various file formats (PDF, ASP, JSP, and so forth). Just when things seemed to be settling into a groove, Google would come out with something new, like Google News, that just seemed to work better and faster than whatever else was out there.

The "Anatomy…" paper by Page and Brin shows them to be thoughtful and forward thinking when it comes to the business of search, too. In two short paragraphs ("Appendix A: Advertising and Mixed Motives"), the Google founders provide an insight into search engine bias: "Since it is very difficult even for experts to evaluate search engines," they write, "search engine bias is particularly insidious."

Noting the uproar that ensued when Open Text experimented with a paid placement scheme in 1996, Brin and Page worry that the public may well tolerate less obvious forms of search engine bias. "For example," they knowingly point out, "a search engine could add a small factor to search results from 'friendly' companies, and subtract a factor from results from competitors." Worse still, they argue, poor-quality search results could make advertising listings look better by comparison, providing leading commercial search engines at least a short-term incentive to provide lower-quality results. Over the years, critics have sometimes accused Google of adopting the very tactics the founders criticized in their early paper.

The question of improved disclosure of paid search listings has come up repeatedly in recent years, to the point where the Federal Trade Commission and Ralph Nader have taken an interest in potential harm to consumers caused by poorly labeled paid search results.[8] As Overture's fortunes improved in its early days, for example, it inked deals to display listings on partner sites. Depending on the partner, listings were either poorly labeled or even labeled in such a way to suggest the sponsored listings were particularly important ("featured listings," for example). These ill-advised practices made Google's strict labeling policy stand out even more and no doubt solidified the company's already solid reputation as a straight shooter.

Google's proactive approach to separating search results from sponsored listings is clearly based on their early thinking about the problem of search engine bias. This separation, above all, is the cornerstone of Google's tongue-half-in-cheek credo that "you can make money without being evil." Perhaps unknowingly, the Google founders were heading down a path that had been traveled by media barons of days gone by. No doubt the company will continue to face difficult dilemmas in its attempts to keep "search" separate from the business of search.

Major Predecessors in Paid Search

Google enjoyed something of a late-mover advantage in the field of paid search listings sold on a keyword-triggered basis. Even its own AdWords program floundered in its first 16 months of existence, before being re-released in its current pay-per-click auction format. The idea of paid search was first seriously entertained in 1996, making this a young field indeed. GoTo actually began building a business around it in 1997, but had no customers to speak of until 1998.

Open Text, AltaVista, Metacrawler: Coulda Shoulda Woulda

Open Text, a high-quality search index that came out of research projects at the University of Waterloo (Ontario, Canada) should be lauded for its hard-nosed decision making. It saw before many others did that the search engine market was getting crowded, and that only the innovators would survive. Instead of believing that investor handouts or partnerships with the likes of Yahoo would last forever, Open Text decided to try charging for "preferred" listings on its search engine. It was ahead of its time, unfortunately. The backlash against the move was too strong.[9] Experts and journalists (and to a much lesser extent, members of the Internet-surfing public) wondered about the ethics of promoting search results as "objective" while accepting money from companies willing to pay for prominent placement. Marketing staff at Open Text defended the practice, suggesting that it was largely driven by the steady stream of inquiries as to how a company might appear in the listings, and comparing the service to the Yellow Pages.

The Yellow Pages analogy was one that would be used repeatedly by proponents of GoTo/ Overture in years following its founding in 1997. Investors on discussion boards like Yahoo Finance frequently invoked the analogy of print directory listings to comfort themselves that they were onto the Next Big Thing, but a Big Thing that wasn't too unfamiliar.

Cowed by the controversy, and seeking a stable business model, Open Text subsequently shifted gears, becoming a successful enterprise software company, exiting the crowded web search field as other also-rans lingered too long after the party was over.

AltaVista was the next sacrificial lamb in the process of gauging public reaction to sponsored listings in or near search results. As if it didn't already have enough to worry about, the company floated the idea of selling sponsored listings in April 1999. Like Open Text, AltaVista backed down when the public reaction seemed too severe measured against the effort it might take to build and pioneer the concept in-house.[10] Arguably, AltaVista was more susceptible to user complaints about search engine objectivity because its constituency was made up largely of longtime Internet search enthusiasts who were accustomed to the 'Net being conceived almost as a public utility. Soon, AltaVista would be acquired by dot-com holding company CMGI, its third owner (after Digital and Compaq). This provided only a short-term financial cushion. AltaVista was dealt body blows by subsequent public relations gaffes. The failure to complete an initial public offering in late 1999 was the death blow. AltaVista never got the hoped-for second chance at going public. Market conditions deteriorated for Internet stocks and didn't recover until Google's IPO revived the market in mid-2004.

AltaVista might have been better off forging ahead aggressively with a plan to sell sponsored listings on one hand, and a plan to improve its search technology on the other. When it eventually took steps to monetize its traffic through paid inclusion and an Overture partnership, and to court search enthusiasts by launching Raging Search—a "clean interface" search engine site modeled after Google—it was too late. Late in its life, AltaVista finally figured out how to make money on its search traffic, but fewer and fewer people were using AltaVista. Googlemania—along with the ongoing strength of AOL, Yahoo, and MSN—was cutting severely into AltaVista's share of search engine users.

My memory is hazy on this one, but in 1997 or so, I recall doing some research on a new program offered by Metacrawler, a popular tool that returned results from a variety of search engines at once. Metacrawler got into the business of selling listings by keyword, in a crude way that only covered very popular keywords, only when advertisers dealt directly with their sales department. Some hazily recalled email exchanges with that department involved them quoting prices on particular keywords. Incidentally, I discovered they weren't averse to selling ads near trademark-related keywords like **yahoo** and **coke**. This experiment didn't last long, mainly because Metacrawler wound up partnering with Overture and other paid listings vendors who could do the same thing more systematically.

The bigger picture is that the period 1997–2000 spawned scores of venture-funded schemes that proposed to offer increasingly targeted forms of online advertising. Far too many dollars and column inches in magazines like *Business 2.0* were chasing after the notion of online targeting. Yet the eventual winners in the race to find a targeting model that truly worked—GoTo/Overture and Google—were not fast-talking advertising industry veterans sporting $500 eyeglasses and wielding convoluted flow charts. GoTo was a modest little company building a relatively simplistic experiment. Google barely gave the idea of selling ads a second thought until the money from its experimental ad platform started rolling in.

GoTo.com/Overture: Pioneers of Bid-for-Placement Advertising

If you judged it by its early financials, you would not have expected big things from GoTo.com, which later changed its name to Overture. A venture-backed experiment of Bill Gross's Idealab, GoTo had few users and few advertisers in the early going. While it might have dreamt of licensing its results to a large portal, at first it had hardly any partners, so it had to rely on becoming a user destination in its own right. It achieved only moderate success in that regard, rising to #28 in the Media Metrix rankings of web properties in 1999—an important caveat being that this ranking was probably related to advertisers checking on their listings! In the quarter before its initial public offering (ending March 31, 1999), GoTo.com raked in a trifling $1.4 million in revenues and posted a loss of $7.4 million.[11] Somehow, it managed to complete an initial public offering valuing the company at an imprudent 90 times revenues. The cash from that, and a later follow-on offering, gave GoTo the cushion it needed to aggressively pursue advertisers on one hand and distribution partnerships on the other.

Regardless of the challenges it faced, curious onlookers[12] saw some potential in GoTo.com. Little did we know just how well the company would do in such a short period. By 2003, the smashing financial success of Overture had rescued its founder and investors from some of their other dot-com failures and had made key company executives wealthy.

GoTo.com to Overture: From Small Fry to Legitimate Portal Supplier   A key means of distribution in GoTo's early days was to allow small webmasters to put a GoTo search box on their sites.

The resulting traffic, from an advertiser's standpoint, was often abysmal. Soon, the program became susceptible to rampant abuse. I can safely say that click fraud was born shortly after GoTo began sending healthy checks to small webmaster partners. GoTo's record in this regard was not pristine. Indeed, it almost seemed to be catering to these questionable partners.

Today, Overture takes a different approach to partnerships. Although it still signs up smaller partners as part of its Content Match program, it's arguably more stringent than Google in terms of its criteria for partnering with content publishers.

In 2000, GoTo began to dig itself out of a hole when it inked listings distribution deals with big-name partners such as Earthlink, MSN bCentral, and Netscape.com. The more quality traffic it began to send to its advertisers, the more its reputation would improve, and the more interested advertisers became in the opportunity. As it relied less and less on small-fry sites to distribute its listings, it was actually able to begin cracking down on lower-quality partners, in many cases terminating those partnerships.

Then again, Overture has never quite managed to shed its early, scrappy self-image. How else to explain its continued eagerness to make deals like that with Gator (now Claria), a controversial company that shows listings on pop-up ads?

The biggest jump in legitimacy, of course, came in September 2000, when Overture (it would still be called GoTo.com until September 2001) inked a deal to distribute sponsored listings on AOL Search. The exact financials of the reported "$50 million deal" (the figure is relatively meaningless) were not disclosed, but Overture probably needed to guarantee AOL a minimum cash payment based on a projection of the revenue share from the deal. It appears, nonetheless, that Overture did very well financially from this deal, as bidding wars for listing positions exceeded anyone's expectations. The AOL deal led to rapid company growth for Overture. Other partnerships, including an important one with MSN Search, followed.

Globally speaking, Overture and Google AdWords have played musical partners to an extent, emphasizing the power that traffic owners (portals) wield over third-party listings vendors. In May 2002, Google formed a partnership with AOL to provide search listings to AOL users and users of other AOL-owned services like Compuserve and Netscape.com. At the same time, AOL also began phasing in Google AdWords throughout its various properties, replacing Overture as its preferred paid listing partner. But it wouldn't all go Google's way. When Yahoo decided to stop using Google for index results, it also dropped AdWords in favor of Overture.

How Bidding Worked   For advertisers, GoTo made available a now-familiar bidding process. Advertisers would bid on words or phrases, and user searches would trigger a list of results in the order of how high the advertiser had bid. For quite some time, the price paid by the advertiser was prominently displayed next to a listing. This is no longer done.

Relevance was always part of the mix at GoTo. Editors vetted every submission by hand, looking over each proposed keyword, rejecting or allowing new keywords depending on how relevant they were to material contained on the landing page. Today, one wonders how efficient this method can possibly be given the growing trend towards building large accounts with thousands or even tens of thousands of phrases.

In the early days, editorial practices were particularly uneven. Inexperienced editors sometimes failed to grasp the meanings of industry-specific terms. This supposedly cutting-edge advertising company behaved similarly, in some respects, to the way directories like Yahoo and LookSmart behaved before you could buy your way in. There seemed to be a belief that paying advertisers needed gatekeepers to ensure relevant sponsored listings. Unfortunately, the average editor was often poorly qualified to make relevancy determinations. As we'll see, AdWords offered a major advance on this editorial-centric model.

Inktomi: Paid Inclusion Index

Inktomi, portal supplier extraordinaire, is the search engine most identified with the hotly debated concept of paid inclusion. The idea was that companies could pay to guarantee inclusion in the index, and this would help Inktomi defray the costs of running the engine and help it to weed out search index spammers. Inclusion would not guarantee placement. The ranking algorithm would still aim to present the pages that were most relevant to users in the most prominent positions on the page.

The practice of dealing with paid inclusion programs became more sophisticated over the years. Companies like Marketleap, Position Technologies, and Decide Interactive offered dedicated paid inclusion consulting and "feed management" services to help companies who had a high volume of URLs they wished to "bulk include" in the index.

The need for bulk inclusion led Inktomi and its partners to adopt a pricing model that would improve on the economics of the "$x per URL submitted model," which would not scale well past 50 or so submitted pages. Instead, larger companies would put down a minimum deposit of, say, $1,000 or $5,000. They would then pay only for clicks incurred, based on a flat per-click fee (this varies, but 25 cents is typical) charged against the initial deposit. Yes, that's right, paid inclusion is now charged largely on a pay-per-click basis, but it's not an auction, of course. The search engine algorithm still determines where sites show up on a given query.

The details of the programs change, but that's the basic idea. These models have been essentially replicated with the new Yahoo Index, which offers bulk inclusion through a program confusingly called Overture Site Match (although it's modeled on Inktomi's previous efforts).

LookSmart, Yahoo: Paid Inclusion in Directory…(and Then, Pay Some More?)

Yahoo and LookSmart both began life as human-edited directories that employed editors to sort out relevant and useful websites from bad ones. These opinionated categorizations were exciting because they promised to save web searchers time.

Business owners soon recognized the value of these listings. In the meantime, Yahoo and LookSmart, like all Internet companies, were looking for ways to raise revenue. All the relevant dates and policy changes would be cumbersome to pin down, because both Yahoo and LookSmart phased out their free submission options gradually (not unlike Inktomi's early claims that paying for inclusion wasn't "necessary.") In any case, the major changes began happening in 2000.

The evolution of the pricing models was vexing to many listing clients. At first, the submission fees were "one-time-only," and then they went to annual fees. Yahoo's annual fee is now $299 (higher for adult sites), though this figure seems hardly relevant today given the range of other ways you'll pay to be seen on Yahoo, including "category sponsorship" fees that guarantee you a better-looking spot.

Repeatedly, LookSmart and Yahoo appeared to violate unspoken social contracts with existing customers—and likely, the terms of written contracts. LookSmart, for example, wound up paying its advertisers a settlement in response to a class-action suit that charged the company with poor disclosure of impending changes in the terms of its advertiser relationship. Yahoo did not do right by those who had paid for directory inclusion, either. At a certain point, the prominence of the directory listings in Yahoo Search results was sharply reduced to favor the index results and sponsored listings, but of course, no refunds were forthcoming to those who had already paid for their coveted directory spots.

In fall 2003, LookSmart went one better (or worse, in the advertiser's mind) by instituting a pay-per-click inclusion program. Sites would still pay to be included in the directory, but would be unlikely to appear on major partner sites like MSN unless they participated in a pay-per-click auction as well, triggered by relevancy keywords that would potentially help the site rise higher in MSN Search results (which were, at the time, a mix of Inktomi and LookSmart results). Site owners could only look on in bewilderment at a struggling search company laughably asking them to "pay, and then pay some more" into a confusing paid visibility scheme.

Essentially, LookSmart was reinventing itself as a pay-per-click listings middleman to compete directly with Overture and Google AdWords. Financially, this was a sound move, but as so often happens in the business of paid search, it was too late. As advertisers discovered, LookSmart didn't lack for technology, and the bidding platform worked fine. It did, however, make the mistake of designing its program around flat click pricing, and then multilevel flat click pricing. Apparently LookSmart didn't learn from Google's mistakes with Soviet-style economics.

What LookSmart did lack was quality distribution partnerships, vital to the company's survival since it had long ago given up on the idea of being a destination search site in its own right. LookSmart's one remaining major deal, with MSN, was not renewed in October 2003, so (as had been rumored for some time) it was left only with minor partnerships. To make up the revenue, LookSmart positioned itself as a second-tier pay-per-click listings provider (in other words, it was no longer a directory at all) amenable to partnerships with a variety of small publishers, some aboveboard, others not.

The supremacy of Google AdWords and Overture was cemented by this development, with FindWhat remaining in reasonable shape in third place following its merger with European pay-per-click stalwart Espotting. (In June 2005, the four main divisions of FindWhat—FindWhat.com, Espotting, Comet Systems, and Miva Merchant—were all rebranded under the "Miva" name. The company is now simply called Miva, Inc. and trades under a new ticker symbol, MIVA.) LookSmart dropped off most advertisers' radars, and it will remain off until it lands a major partner.

After defying gravity for awhile (it was valued at $238 million in late 2004), LookSmart is nearly out of gas now, with a market valuation of $81 million. A succession of caretaker CEOs have come and gone in the past three years. Further downsizing will be necessary if LookSmart is to operate as a going concern.

Those Who Own the Traffic Control the Dollars

The fates of paid search also-rans like Inktomi and LookSmart, compared with powerhouses such as Yahoo and Google, illustrate a key principle. Even the former category leader, Overture, saw the handwriting on the wall and allowed itself to be acquired by Yahoo at an opportune time.

The fact is, although the pay-per-click listings services do differ somewhat in their feature sets, probably 80% of an advertiser's decision about which service to use (and how much to use it) comes down to distribution, or reach. A cool online listings bidding platform is worthless if it gives you access to only a handful of potential customers.

The search business is behaving rather like other consolidating industries have in the past. The biggest online destinations (today, these are Google, Yahoo, MSN, and AOL) can attract users by releasing better search technology. They can also retain them by controlling other aspects of the user experience and by behaving as monopolists do.

As Google has shown, the notion that search isn't "sticky" is a myth; its user base has a serious daily Google habit. Who would you rather be—a godlike economic force who owned all the railroads or asphalt roads at any given point in history, one that was able to pick and choose its preferred vendor of billboard technologies and allowed to charge tolls on usage, or merely one of a number of able vendors of tollbooths or billboards? When you look at it this way, it seems like the future of companies like Google is secure, whereas the chances that a vendor like LookSmart will make a permanent comeback are slim.

The Growth and Evolution of AdWords

AdWords is now, and always has been, a work in progress. Let's look at how it grew from a relatively minor experiment to the force it is in today's global advertising business.

Early Version Challenges

The first version of Google AdWords is rarely discussed today. Launched on October 23, 2000, Google AdWords didn't exactly take the world by storm. An opt-in Google Friends newsletter issue on November 22, 2000, covered a number of developments at Google, including the release of a beta toolbar, some magazine awards about the search quality, and instances of Halloween spirit at Google. The mention of the new ad program was included as a brief item. It was almost as if the advertising service was an interesting little hack that would help Google to defray its operating expenses.

Observers still didn't think that Google would earn much more than 25% of its income from ads; it was expected that advertising would be a sideshow to the real business of creating a powerful technology that would somehow be licensed to corporations and power users. Given the time it would take Google AdWords to begin dealing with issues like billing and customer service on an "adult" level, it's safe to say that few in the company knew how much money Google stood to make from its advertisers over the next four years.

The main trouble with the initial version of AdWords was its pricing model. Overture had enjoyed unexpected success with a pay-per-click auction model that created bidding wars for top listing spots, while allowing small-fry advertisers to stay in the game at a low cost.

Google inexplicably decided that it could dictate the terms of its relationship with advertisers by setting traditional fixed prices for ads. A maximum of three ads would be shown on a search results page, priced on a cost-per-thousand-impressions (CPM) basis: $15 CPM for top spot, $12 for second spot, and $10 for third position.

This model didn't take into account the wide variation in advertiser demand for, and the disparities in the potential profitability of, different search words and phrases. Furthermore, if an advertiser really wanted to be visible at the $15 CPM level, there was no way to lock in the position. Ad space would simply be rationed across all advertisers.

So, if a $10–$15 CPM rate was far too expensive for some keywords, Google wouldn't be able to sell that inventory to anyone, leaving too many unmonetized page impressions to earn Google the kind of money they'd need to expand their growing company. Worse (and this happened within a few weeks of Google's launching the program), word would begin to spread that Google's ad program was overpriced and didn't work. By contrast, if that same ad rate was a screaming bargain (priced too low) for some popular commercial keywords, this early version of AdWords left advertisers with no way of competing for maximum exposure. Instead, they'd be apportioned a relatively small number of impressions, being forced to share the slot with others—a recipe for advertiser dissatisfaction.

The worst sin of this fixed-price method, then, was that it left Google no room to raise prices on high-demand keywords. The pricing model Google chose couldn't have been more inefficient. There were clear advantages to Google's "new take" on the online advertising business, however. Google's hacking, experimental, software-driven attitude is still reflected in the many small differences between AdWords and Overture today.

Although Google's *pricing* method was at first inefficient, the way it chose to operate the program screamed scalability. It was a big plus that advertisers could get up and running in a few minutes by entering a few parameters into the interface. Overture had more human editorial oversight than Google AdWords. Close observers began to suspect that Google was up to something. If it could keep growing and taking in advertiser dollars while keeping a lid on hiring, this increasingly popular search engine could generate fat profit margins indeed. Investors, among others, quietly took notice.

Nonetheless, the program failed to catch fire because advertisers didn't like the pricing model. CPM-based advertising had been badly tarnished in the dot-com collapse, and many advertisers probably had a visceral reaction to the notion of paying $10–$15 CPMs when $1 CPM ad campaigns had failed for them in the past. Overture had done a great job of training advertisers to want *clickthroughs* on paid search listings, not mere eyeballs.

Google's next big move, on February 20, 2002, paid considerable homage to Overture's superior pricing model. After digesting the market feedback on the first version of AdWords for a full 16 months, Google released a new version of the ad program, called AdWords Select, that mirrored Overture's pay-per-click auction in important respects, while diverging from it in others.[13]

The press release announcing the new "Google AdWords Select" program (the name has now been shortened back to Google AdWords) treated this as an incremental change, as "new pricing for [the] popular self-serve advertising program." If you talk to anyone who is keenly interested in search marketing nowadays, though, it's more likely that they consider this as the day that the "real" Google AdWords was born. Advertisers adopted this program quickly, though not without various complaints and more than a little head scratching.

In forthcoming chapters, we'll examine specific examples from the AdWords interface, which has undergone at least a couple of major overhauls since its inception. To keep the momentum going, Google continues to make minor improvements on a regular basis.

Google as Referee: Complications of Multiple Stakeholders

As Brin and Page themselves implied in their early paper, search engines' stock in trade is legitimacy. As a former political scientist, I always grasped this instinctively. Analysts of the 20th-century "welfare state" (the New Deal) often pointed out that a capitalist economy would be most likely to thrive when all participants (including the weaker members) believed that the system was in the best interests of everyone. Government policies needed to support "capitalism in general," rather than particular companies' interests, if the most efficient path to economic development were to be found. In the worst-case scenario, governments that were seen to be interested only in helping those with money would lose face completely.

Is a search engine really that different? People loved the Internet because of the freedom and power it provided. They loved search engines because they were great ways of acting independently, searching out alternative sources of information, and avoiding biased messages. The objectivity of search engines, much like that of libraries, was something held sacred by many Internet users throughout the 1990s.

We saw what happened when some search engines sold out. Users did anything they could to avoid the clutter and deceit that awaited them on portals like Excite.com and AltaVista.com. The clean, fast, useful Google Search interface came along just at the right time. Google was the Internet's New Deal. Immense user loyalty was the result, and it continues to this day, though not without some reservations.

Advertiser Needs vs. User Needs and the Public Interest

Advertisers, of course, have had their own ideas about what they should be getting for their money. These ideas have often been ignored by search companies at the same time they were busy ignoring users' needs. Wouldn't it be a good idea for a company that derives its revenues from search advertising to pay closer attention to the needs of *both* their tens of millions of users and their hundreds of thousands of advertisers? Don't be so sure.

Advertisers typically request more prominent exposure for less money. Depending on the prices of the ads, they don't always care that much about relevancy. Targeted advertising is nice, but not all advertisers feel it's their job to worry about targeting if they can get their brand out there. Indeed, during the online advertising boom, big advertisers were eager to overpay for advertising as long as they could buy a lot of it. Plenty of big-brand advertisers remain dissatisfied with Google as an advertising medium because Google won't sell huge amounts of untargeted inventory to the highest bidder and won't offer big graphical ad formats.

Not only that, but as the history of paid search again shows, many advertisers would love it if their listings were embedded right in the search results, or confusingly labeled (for example, "featured listings") so as to induce users to click more often.

That's exactly what Google felt they needed to guard against when they designed the look, feel, and rules of their ad program. From the early days, I was impressed by Sheryl Sandberg's frequent use of phrases like "long-term viability" and "long-term interests of all advertisers" when explaining the emerging AdWords policies.

To protect the public, Google knew it needed to clearly label its sponsored listings. It also wanted to make sure that users wouldn't flee Google because the ads were too big or too bold. A muted, understated text-ad design was chosen. Google no doubt benefited from internal discussions as well as external advice from web usability experts such as Jakob Nielsen, who joined the company's technical advisory board shortly after its founding in 1998. In a discussion with Nielsen in 2003 about the AdWords program, I discovered that he remained "unsure" about the program, which to me suggested that he worried even more than Google staffers about the potential for users to become "blind" to the ads.

Moreover, Google decided to build relevancy requirements right into the design of the bidding platform, as we'll explore in more depth later. The final step to ensuring that the public was not turned off by what they were seeing was a wide range of strictly enforced editorial policies. Some of these policies were content related, but others related to form. Google prohibited things like repeated exclamation marks or other gimmicks intended to grab the user's attention in ways that might dissuade users from returning to search on Google.

Rules against excessive capitalization and inaccurate claims in ads were developed not only to protect the public, but to protect advertisers from one another. Clearly, Google's "New Deal" for online advertising would have the best chance of succeeding long term if it took a hard line against those who used unscrupulous means of inducing users to pick their ad over another appearing nearby. Of course, the practice of optimizing an ad's text to maximize response rates (as long as such testing is done within the program's terms of service) is vital to a successful campaign.

Addressing User Needs

Presumably, search engine users still expect certain kinds of search queries to be largely unfettered by sponsor listings. If no ads at all are relevant to a given query, Google simply shows no ads.

On commercial queries, many of the ads might be at least as relevant as the regular search results. Scratch *might*. I know they are, having worked with so many advertisers who have gained so many customers from these tiny ads. AdWords campaign data, and ongoing feedback from new customers gained by my clients, prove it: the Google ads are often relevant, regularly attract interested prospects, and do not appear to annoy too many people. As for nonprospects—those who are unlikely to be interested in an ad—Google has not yet seemed to alienate its user base, as its market share remains strong.

Whether ads appear on a page or not, Google's users expect the mix of results to be as relevant as possible. Clearly, that balance isn't an easy one to strike. To help users find specific types of information that they might want, but wouldn't be likely to go hunting for unprompted, search engines are now experimenting with what Danny Sullivan has referred to as "invisible tabs." A query that might appear to be "newsy" in nature might trigger a couple of Google News results at the top of the page in addition to the regular search results. Google has also experimented with prompting users with a couple of teaser results from its Froogle shopping search engine and its new Google Local feature; again, it depends on the query.

Taken in this light, then, it's not implausible to expect that AdWords, folded into the mix of information served to Google Search users, might actually lead to an increase in the perceived relevancy and helpfulness of pages of results. Some queries, after all, truly are commercial in nature.

Others may be mildly commercial or might at least be related to the subject matter of publications (earning revenues from subscriptions and ads), which themselves might find it profitable to advertise in the margins of search results using AdWords.

Indeed, I expect that by early 2006, Google will make it easy for users to search just the advertising associated with their chosen keywords. That would be "back to the future," since that was exactly the format of (then unpopular) GoTo's site when it launched in 1998. The consumer's degree of acceptance of advertising today exists on a continuum from extreme aversion to extreme obsession. There are people who deliberately watch ads and deliberately tune into the Shopping Channel. Millions of readers of auto magazines and fashion magazines are buying them partly for the attractive advertising pitches. Google has the option of keeping its regular Google Search site relatively unchanged, while making Google AdSearch a separate experience for those who are simply seeking vendors. Down the road, no doubt, they could release Google Trailer for those wanting to watch movie previews, and Google Infomercial for people who want to spend a long time considering the purchase of a Bowflex. The sky's the limit as media converge. A new media company can, if it wants, cater to all tastes.

Google's Profit Motive

Back to the text-based reality of today's Google Search. Google isn't a neutral observer in all of this. A very simple formula at least theoretically drives business objectives at a search engine company. Assuming x number of search engine results pages (SERPs) shown on a given day, the goal is to maximize the revenue per page of SERPs. As great as they may be for legitimacy, pages devoid of ads are a drain on the search engine company's budget. Pages that contain ads selling for a discount price are also not pulling their weight when compared to pages full of fully priced (or overpriced) ads.

The pay-per-click auction model, broken down by keyword, is so brilliant because it allows ad pricing to adjust nimbly to the forces of supply and demand. The boom-and-bust cycle of the online banner advertising marketplace happened in part because the pricing and media buying models were so inefficient. One day, everyone was jumping all over overpriced advertising inventory. Seemingly overnight, no one wanted any of it, so prices simply plunged across the board. This won't happen with pay-per-click keyword auctions because the demand for different keywords is so varied, and the bidding platform has so many potential buyers lined up at any given time. Most of all, the majority of today's pay-per-click advertisers are carefully tracking their results, so they won't be making rash all-or-nothing-style media buying decisions.

Keyword Inventory and the Auction Model   What's so interesting about Google's massive "keyword inventory" (the wide variety of search results served on a given day) is that huge parts of this would go unsold if it were priced on a fixed basis. This is certainly what happened with Google's first crack at AdWords. Now, with less-popular inventory available for as little as five cents a click, Google can make at least some money by selling off this vast secondary ad space for low prices. Google's wish to sell off remnant inventory at a discount can be to your advantage as an advertiser. One important task for all advertisers is to seek out the bargain-priced inventory.

What has made Google and Overture really rich, though, has been the serious bidding wars that have erupted on popular keywords. When 20 advertisers are desperate for exposure on a commercially viable keyword, the cost for a click can be driven up quickly in the auction process. The inflated costs of keywords like **mesothelioma** and **personal injury** are often reported in the press. But even in relatively humble fields like enterprise software, $10–$15 per click is not uncommon for the most commercially valuable phrases. Avoiding such bidding wars is an important goal for you as an advertiser. Where they can't be avoided, you'll need to at least be paying careful attention to advanced testing and tracking methods.

Revenue Maximization   As we'll discuss in upcoming chapters, Google injected relevancy criteria into its ad program in part to maintain the legitimacy of Google Search and to foster a good user experience. But it's also the case that by rewarding advertisers with relevant (frequently clicked) ads, they're basically ensuring that advertisers who generate the most revenues for Google are prominently displayed on the page.

Another important advance of AdWords when compared with its main competitor, Overture, was matching options. At the time of AdWords' release, Overture advertisers had difficulty achieving wide keyword coverage, since it treated every phrase as an exact match. AdWords, by contrast, allowed broad matching and phrase matching. This gave advertisers wider coverage with less work and, perhaps just as important, allowed Google to sell more of its keyword inventory without relying on advertisers to dump huge files of keywords into their accounts. Overture later added matching options.

Investors, Not Just Founders, Influence Direction   No matter what you read, it seems likely that a sales culture began to grow at Google as it hired more salespeople. It is clear that Google has worked towards goals that involve squeezing more ad dollars out of the daily flow of search traffic, and taking paid search market share away from rival Overture. Certain decisions along the way have seemed suspect in the sense that the balance between advertiser control and revenue maximization was skewed in favor of the latter, however temporarily. For example, Google released a feature called Expanded Broad Matching similar to an Overture feature called Match Driver. Ostensibly, this would show your ad on obvious variations of keywords in your account, such as plurals. However, the feature expanded to cover "semantic variations" and did not work very well at first. Some advertisers' costs went up while performance dropped. Google has learned from such experiences that it can only take so many liberties in the name of revenue maximization before advertisers begin balking.

Another case of revenue fever, it seems, has been the contextual advertising program (AdSense). Google was uncharacteristically quick in ramping up this program (*reckless* might be a better word). I presume that a certain rivalry with Overture and legacy ad networks like Doubleclick had, by this time, become ingrained at Google The Advertising Company, and the race was on to crowd competitors out of ad inventory all over the Web.

Although Google's relevant text ad was certainly an improvement in the user experience at many participating publisher sites, advertisers' needs seemed to be forgotten at times. Whether they admit it or not, the fortunes of Google as it hurtled towards a lucrative initial public offering of stock became increasingly tied to its fast-growing AdSense program. The vociferousness with which Google staffers defend the program to this day suggests that with so many mouths to feed, Google has become addicted to the content-targeting revenue. Why would a search engine company be so adamant in its pursuit of content-targeted ad-serving business? Perhaps Page and Brin would get a laugh today if they changed the company motto to "you don't have to be evil to run a search engine company, but it helps." What? Why aren't you laughing?

How Google's DNA Influences the AdWords Game

Let's turn to an overview of idiosyncratic policies and attitudes that will become familiar to you as you play the AdWords game. Many of them stem directly from the values of the founders and their immediate circle. On the whole, though, a certain kind of attitude permeates the company. If I had to boil it down, it might be "never forget the user experience," which in the case of a search engine company means "don't intrude, just help people find what they're looking for." A generalized wisdom also prevails: "don't forget why we're here and AltaVista isn't—don't be dot-com road kill."

Editorial Rules and Banned Items

Any publisher (online or off) is going to have guidelines for the types of products that they accept advertising for. Google is no different. They must ensure, of course, that ads comply with applicable laws. But they also go beyond the law in areas they worry could become controversial and alienate the general public.

Google has sometimes reminded advertisers that it does not censor search results. Whereas an ad may be banned for something like hard liquor or a certain type of knife that might commonly be used as a weapon, this does not preclude pages about these items from showing up in the regular search results.

In short, Google's ad policies are its prerogative. In gray areas, advertisers are advised to contact Google and request a clarification from a policy specialist. Some observers would prefer that Google would make their policies and lists of banned items more overt. This may still come to pass, but likely not without considerable pressure.

If you're curious, https://adwords.google.com/select/contentpolicy.html offers a list of basic content policies. It wasn't published until November 2004. It does not give much detail, and many gray areas are still left up to editorial discretion.

Pop-Ups

Since both Overture and Google reserve the editorial right to ban any ad just for pointing to a page they deem irrelevant to the ad, it's not surprising that Google has also taken the initiative in banning ads that point to pages that they deem to provide a poor user experience. Want to show your ad on Google? You won't be allowed to point it to a page that serves users an annoying pop-up ad.

NOTE   *Ironically, this very policy led some entrepreneurs to come up with pop-up-like technologies that were different enough from pop-ups that they passed editorial muster with Google.*

Privacy Policies

It will be interesting to see just how far Google The Advertising Company is willing to go to collect demographic data on users as competitors attempt to do the same. Google, for now, has relatively strict privacy policies and does not know much about the individual surfer using the Google Search tool, although it does look at the user's geographic location (IP address). Google's history might suggest that it will go slow on offering advertisers advanced demographic targeting, while its competitors forge ahead with more intrusive schemes. This will be interesting to watch.

Erratic Enforcement of Inconsistent Policies

The problem with some of Google's policies is that they aren't grounded in any solid principles and are at times nearly unenforceable. One quagmire is the quiet but rarely enforced prohibition on "double serving." If you think about it, an unscrupulous advertiser could open ten separate AdWords accounts and blanket the page with ads for the same product or service, crowding out competitors. Google prohibits such behavior, but it's not uncommon for exceptions to slip through. There are too many gray areas where it actually makes sense to have two ads showing on the same page from the same company on the same keywords. A large company like IBM might have separate divisions that are both likely to benefit from rather different ads on keywords that sometimes overlap.

Policies, procedures, and lofty principles are one thing, but the reality on the ground is that editorial and other policies must be enforced by error-prone humans, some of whom may be having a good day, and others whose dogs just died the same day. Some rules, like those against excessive punctuation, are cut and dried. Others, like the requirement that the display URL match the URL of the page users land on, may be bent (in this case, based on reasonable grounds that an advertiser may have, such as the need for ROI tracking on a different URL).

Tight Control of Information Flow

Despite its democratic, fun image, Google is a serious business entity that holds its cards close to the vest. It employs a degree of secrecy that many consider excessive. Some recent political reading that equated undue government secrecy with a deficit in democracy made me sit up and think hard about just what was going on over there at the Googleplex. Google staffers have always told me as much as they possibly can to help me understand AdWords features. But the company's secrecy often precludes them from telling the whole story.

The pressure on Google seems to have abated some now that the nail biting over their IPO is done. (The first trade of Google shares under the ticker symbol GOOG went through at 11:56 A.M. ET, on August 19, 2004, for $100.01, well above the offer price of $85.) In the pre-IPO quiet period, most everyone in the company was terrified of giving away material information or being perceived to promote the stock, since even the suggestion that Google might be a good investment would have violated SEC regulations and led to delays in the IPO. Delayed IPOs, as AltaVista found following 1999, are not good karma for search engine companies.

All Search Engine Companies Are Secretive about Algorithms   Much of the secrecy employed at Google is absolutely necessary. Search engine companies cannot share much about the "secret sauce" of their methodologies on a month-to-month basis, since millions of website owners are jockeying for high rankings in the free results. In this regard, Google is not alone. Its cryptic commentaries about its search engine ranking methodologies are in keeping with the demands of its ongoing battle with index spammers.

Concealing Details of How AdWords Functions, for Competitive Reasons   An unusual quirk of AdWords is that many features are a lot more complicated than similar features offered by competitors. Add to this the engineer-speak combined with public relations spin and you've got some features that are downright befuddling.

From the beginning, Google employed a sliding scale to measure the exact minimum threshold of clickthrough rate (a relevancy requirement) that advertisers were required to meet to keep keywords enabled. (Don't worry, we'll come back to this.) Officially, the cutoff was 0.5%. But Google emphasized that this was actually "0.5% normalized for ad position." This means that the relevancy policy, as measured by clicks on your ads, is relaxed as your ad moves down the page to a less visible position.

It's always fun to watch a Google representative explain that situation in public, because often, the public faces of Google are no more sure about the exact numbers to give as examples of a "normalized clickthrough rate cutoff" in ad position 7 than you or I would be. So they'll come out with something like "let's say it's 0.3%." Some product managers and engineers probably know the real numbers, but no one's saying.

In fall 2003, Google claimed to be raising the cutoff to 1.0% on some keywords in some situations, but the explanation for that was so confusing that virtually no one understood it. We can assume the 1.0% cutoff formula, whatever it was, was quietly dropped.

Google policy gets a lot more complicated than that. Many features have not been amenable to straightforward description because they're based on proprietary algorithms and predictive formulas. Pricing on content targeting, for example, is now subject to a so-called Smart Pricing formula, where Google's software determines the cost of a click (subject to your stated maximum bid) based on a predictive or actuarial formula that looks at which kinds of pages online are more likely to return a higher conversion rate to sales.

Listening to explanations of how Google's programs actually work sometimes feels a bit like being a grade-schooler hearing a lecture on quantum physics. Ultimately, though, you can get a knack for using a system (like driving a car) even if you don't have a good feel for how it actually works inside. You can "make it go" without being well versed in how everything under the hood works.

Three motivations have governed these elaborate feature designs. First, the brilliant Google engineering team always wants to take a stab at solving a problem through software. Second, Google wanted to design AdWords as an elaborate, proprietary system to muddy the waters in its drawn-out patent dispute with Overture. Finally, the more difficult Google made AdWords to copy, the less likely competitors would be to ape them. Certainly, Overture and FindWhat moved quickly to duplicate some of the most compelling features of AdWords—particularly matching options. But they'd be hard pressed to copy the more arcane features. Is *feature* even the right word for a formula based on complex interrelationships among a host of variables? Google AdWords is not only multifeatured, it's multiformulaed.

Not Disclosing Details of AdSense Program   Content targeting has been an ongoing source of concern for advertisers. Like Overture, Google is content to boast of major publishers and certain "poster child" publishers who have participated in its AdSense program. But there is poor disclosure of not only the full list of participating publishers, but many other details of the AdSense program, such as how pricing is determined, what the revenue share is, and more. Advertisers see click costs, and publishers see basic reports and receive checks in the mail, but a lot of detail is missing.

Failure to Break Down Reporting of Ad Spend by Country of Origin   My eyes opened wide when one staffer at an international Google sales office conceded that Google AdWords is a mysterious "black box product." If that's the way the sales team feels, imagine how we feel! Anyway, one thing I always found curious was that Google will let you choose which countries you show your ads in, but the reporting interface doesn't break down your click costs by country. I'm sure that's one feature Google has on its to-do list, but it does stand out as an example of an area of nondisclosure that was left to linger too long. There have been numerous others.

Technological Fixes vs. Service Orientation

In Google's mind, if flaws in its AdWords service are amenable to a software fix, so much the better. If changes require extensive human capital, on the other hand, they might meet with more opposition in Google's engineering-dominated culture. But that's really no different from any major corporation today. Most large companies try to keep customer service costs as low as possible.

Google Underestimated Need for Customer Service   At first, by using software to facilitate editorial review, Google assumed that it was onto something big: a business model that could reap revenues even greater than Overture's, while spending far less on human support. As the program grew, it became difficult to ignore the huge gulf in service. Google became aware that advertisers need a lot of hand-holding, and the pace of hiring accelerated. Today's attitude towards service appears to be nearly a 180-degree reversal from the early don't call us, we'll call you approach. Because Google can attract good people and is so stringent in its hiring process, their new commitment to service could make it tough on the competition.

Advantages of Greater Automation   Humans can do their jobs better if given the right tools. Google is constantly working on software that will help editors do a better job. For new campaigns, innovative features that check the spelling of ads and check whether landing pages are working *before* ads are accepted into the system reduce the editorial load. As the program's growth slows, Google will be dealing with more experienced advertisers, so they may find that problems facing their advertiser base become more routine or incremental in nature.

Inconclusive Direction on Rewards for Good Customers   Google continues to grapple with the problem of how to provide a higher level of service to agencies and advertisers who spend more. It's not a frivolous concern. Those who spend $500,000 a year expect some kind of dedicated support. Unfortunately, Google took a long time deciding on whether it should have any formal means of providing enhanced service.

Enhanced service can be self-serving. If Google staff are dealing with several manufacturers of pillows, let's say, do they help them all with the same keyword lists, similar advice, and so on? In an auction process, Google has a financial incentive not to tell the whole truth to advertisers. And from a legitimacy standpoint, Google actually might also have an ethical or legal responsibility to hold back on the amount of service it gives to a particular client lest others feel mistreated.

Uncertain Relationships with Advertising and Marketing Agencies   Third parties often advise clients on how to use AdWords. (That's what I do, for example.) Observing Google's progress in dealing with the environment of marketing and advertising agencies, they have never fully given up on the idea that advertisers really should be coming directly to them for advice. However, this situation appears to be improving.

A Google Advertising Professionals (GAP) program, launched in November 2004, seems to be a way of sorting out qualified from unqualified AdWords campaign management practitioners. The first version of this program was relatively limited and recognized only those deemed by Google to be qualified *individuals*, providing them with some recognition but little in the way of benefits. Google is adjusting to the idea that it must recognize the contributions of *agencies* and consulting *companies*—not just individual professionals and webmasters—as entities worthy of partner status, if it expects to count on having strong allies in the marketing ecosystem in the future. Traditional high-tech companies have always had formal reseller relationships, after all. Arguably, companies like Microsoft have cemented their status as leaders by working closely with their global force of third-party evangelists. This is a more delicate process than it appears.

A new version of the Google Advertising Professionals program, launched in April 2005, takes two important steps forward. First, it offers some benefit to those who qualify under the program: advertising credits that can be applied to clients' accounts. Second, it recognizes a separate "company" level of qualification. Third parties who have five qualified Google Advertising Professionals on staff and who meet a minimum requirement of $100,000 in aggregate client spending over a 90-day period qualify for "Qualified Company" status. Qualified companies receive more in the way of free advertising credits for their clients, but no doubt will also receive additional benefits down the road in terms of consistent points of contact and more continuity in case management that can help to get problems solved more quickly. This seems to be the beginning of a stronger relationship with the agency world. For more information, see https://adwords.google .com/select/ProfessionalWelcome. From an agency standpoint, a key drawback of forging formal ties with Google through this GAP program is that Google might take inventory of your clients and decide to poach the best ones. For the time being, many third parties are wary of asking for Google's help with a client account, lest that help translate into an adversarial relationship.

In its formative years, having the right attitude at the right time was a big part of what made Google into a global powerhouse. Some critics predict that this same attitude could be its undoing. Experts believe that the degree of Google's cooperation with the developer community (and I would add, the marketing ecosystem) will be the difference between the company having the staying power of Microsoft, or being eaten alive like Netscape.[14] Those same experts stress that the marketplace as a whole is not cooperative, and cast doubt on whether giants like Microsoft and Google can coexist peacefully. Google's survival may well require it to be more secretive, not less so, while becoming more open in the ways that matter to partners. As it enters adulthood, it might need to shed its laid-back attitude and become more strategic in forcing users and advertisers (and welcoming reseller partners and application developers) into proprietary, but widely shared, information technology architectures.

Recent developments, such as the introduction of the AdWords Application Program Interface (API) and the enhanced version of Google Advertising Professionals, are promising insofar as they signal a heightened commitment to cooperate with third-party developers and agencies. But Google will likely need to create more formal partnerships in the future, and invite more developers and agency types into ongoing dialogues about features and business relationships. In the past, such dialogues often appeared to be limited to select groups of beta testers and informal chatter mediated by the likes of GoogleGuy. These means of communication did little to forge long-term adult relationships with Google's advocates, resellers, and technology partners. This has begun to improve, which augurs well for Google's long-term survival.

Internally, Google may also begin to face disconnects between its rank-and-file sales force and core technical talent as revenues continue to surge, with each group feeling responsible for the rapid growth. If these two camps lose the ability to communicate, it will become even more difficult to translate Google-speak into a language its advertisers can understand.

Google's unique culture is shaped first and foremost by its founders, tempered by CEO Eric Schmidt. The company's ability to focus depends heavily on the ongoing involvement of top management in steering what has become an increasingly diversified enterprise. Vice President of Product Management Jonathan Rosenberg must face a weight of responsibility as he oversees development of Gmail, Orkut, Blogger, Groups, and other disparate experiments. To paraphrase the "risk factors" sections of the company's SEC filings: If Google should lose the services of Larry, Sergey, or Eric, it could be in big trouble. Time will tell, but there is no reason to believe that Google's top people have anything in mind other than overseeing its continued breakneck pace of growth and change.

Endnotes

1. A useful primer on such matters, covering the whole range of contemporary administrative theories, is Charles Perrow, *Complex Organizations: A Critical Essay (3rd ed.)* (McGraw-Hill, 1986). Chronicles of dot-com startup desperation, greed, and excess such as Po Bronson's, *The Nudist on the Late Shift: And Other True Tales of Silicon Valley* (Broadway, 2000), don't seem appropriate to grokking the Google work culture, which has always seemed relatively settled and self-confident as opposed to chaotic. As nerdy and unconcerned as Google employees may appear to be about the traditional goals and structures of large corporations, keen observers (see David Vise, "Following a Rich Tradition: Under the Avant-Garde Veneer, an Old-Guard Startup Strategy," *Washington Post*, June 24, 2004, E01) have argued that this powerhouse is very much a traditional Silicon Valley "insider" company. Key early investors and

advisers—including Jeff Bezos, John Doerr, and Michael Moritz—were all seasoned members of the Silicon Valley elite, and the hiring of Eric Schmidt as CEO introduced a degree of settledness to a group that was already arguably mature beyond its years. Of course, some sensationalistic press reports have suggested otherwise.

2. For example, Danny Sullivan, "Where Are They Now? Search Engines We've Known & Loved," *Search Engine Report*, March 4, 2003, archived at searchenginewatch.com.

3. See Danny Sullivan, "Death of a Meta Tag," *Search Engine Report*, October 1, 2002. This is not to say that metadata are unimportant, just that webmasters were still worrying too much about keyword tags in particular, when Google likely ignores them. Description meta tags are still visible in many search results and are therefore worth using. A proper discussion about the future of metadata would fill a book.

4. Claire Woffenden, "AltaVista MD Resigns Over Unmetered Fiasco," vnunet.com, August 30, 2000. The credibility of AltaVista's claims had been challenged by a technology "critique" site, *The Register*. See Kelly Black, "AltaVista's Unmetered Access Hoax," InternetNews.com, August 22, 2000.

5. "Why the Open Directory Isn't Open," Traffick.com, March 30, 2000.

6. Sergey Brin and Lawrence Page, "Anatomy of a Large-Scale Hypertextual Web Search Engine," Stanford University Department of Computer Science, 2000. Jon Kleinberg, widely considered to be the leading contributor to this generation of search technology, has published many important papers on search, including "Authoritative Sources in a Hyperlinked Environment," 1998.

7. For a user-friendly overview, see Mike Grehan's interview with Paul Gardi, "Inside the Teoma Algorithm," July 2003, archived at e-marketing-news.co.uk.

8. For those interested in such issues, Danny Sullivan, "The Bumpy Road to Maximum Monetization," *Search Engine Report*, May 6, 2002, archived at searchenginewatch.com, is a must-read.

9. Nick Wingfield, "Engine Sells Results, Draws Fire," CNET News, June 21, 1996, archived at news.com.

10. Jim Hu, "AltaVista to Auction Premier Ad Placement," CNET News, April 15, 1999.

11. Steve Harmon, "GoTo.com IPO set to go this week," InternetNews.com, June 16, 1999.

12. "Paid Search Is Here to Stay," Traffick.com, March 27, 2000.

13. Indeed, the formats were similar enough that Overture contended that Google violated key Overture patents. Following Yahoo's acquisition of Overture, the two companies settled the ongoing dispute out of court. In August 2004, on the eve of its IPO, Google awarded Yahoo 2.7 million shares of Class A Google stock as a lifetime license payment covering any relevant patents for the pay-per-click auction model.

14. Charles H. Ferguson, "What's Next for Google," *MIT Technology Review*, January 2005.

Part II

How to Play
the AdWords Game

Chapter 3

First Principles for Reaching Customers Through AdWords

This chapter is intended to describe as plainly as possible what Google AdWords actually are and how they fit into the typical user's journey in a given online search session. Even if you're well versed in online advertising, this chapter is worth reviewing. In the effort to master the finer points, it's easy to lose sight of the basics of how and why people are using Google Search, and what you can realistically expect them to do when they come across your ad. It's also easy to make stereotypical assumptions that there is one way of searching the Web, or one typical model for making sales to online audiences. The examples I'm about to give are intended to convey a sense of the diversity of this medium. There are many different ways to succeed, and also many ways to fail.

In addition, I'll briefly review recent developments and happenstances that have conspired to put Google and its AdWords program in the leadership position they enjoy today. Google's visionary path towards search market dominance has created special opportunities for advertisers, but the medium also poses some difficult challenges.

From Search to Buy: How Real People Use Google

For millions of Internet users, search is an habitual activity, performed daily. Accçording to recent figures from comScore Networks, the average U.S. user performs 35 searches per month. The average Canadian user is a bit more active, at 40 searches per month. Keep in mind that these are averages; many users search much more frequently than that.

The detailed data about user behavior gathered by panel-based web measurement companies like comScore are not actually all that easy to come by. comScore has a proprietary dataset it calls qSearch. To get access to all of the information about the complex daily patterns of search behavior, you would either have to subscribe to comScore's premium info service or have direct access to the same search data that some employees of companies like Google and MSN do.

The point is, we don't always know what is running through a user's mind when he or she undertakes a web search, so stereotyping or prejudging is unwise. But we do know that the purchase process is all about navigation and usability. Usability experts such as Jakob Nielsen write articles, convene at corporate seminars, and do in-depth studies to assist companies in their efforts to make it easier to navigate through the website to the point of purchase. But what we as search marketers need to do is to extend the thinking about the user experience back one step, to the very first stage of finding your site listed in a search engine. Users can't use what they can't find, obviously. And how they encounter your listing makes all the difference in initiating a positive contact with them.

To provide a feeling for the process, I'll offer a couple of straightforward examples of a typical search-to-purchase scenario.

The prospect of sitting in the same place long enough to write a book brought back painful memories of graduate school, eyestrain, and lumbar pain. A new monitor took care of the eyestrain, though I've already vowed to acquire a much bigger and nicer one after this book sells its 50,000th copy. But oh, my aching back! I decided I'd put off my purchase of an Aeron chair long enough, but I also wondered if there were any alternatives to Herman Miller's pricey design. Surely I could get a chair of the same quality for less with just a few minutes of research and a little shopping around.

What to do? As I and millions of others do every day to solve such problems, I went to Google.com and performed a keyword search. The first query I tried—**aeron-like**—could have been too clever for its own good, but it turned up a fair amount of useful material.

I suppose one of the wondrous things about searching the Web for information using a tool like Google is that nearly anyone can do it without a lot of specialized instruction. Google has advanced features, but no one is forced to use them. Arguably that's a big reason why search has spread so quickly throughout the population. It's easy. With a few keywords and a couple clicks of a mouse, ordinary users find even the most unusual information quickly, a scenario that would have been unthinkable a few years ago.

As you can see, a number of relevant results appear (Figure 3-1). The left-hand side of the page contains what are commonly known as *search results*. I often call these *Web index results* because they're pages drawn from an enormous database of pages created when Google's spider, Googlebot, crawls the entire Web. These are the pages that Google's technology deems the most relevant to my query.

NOTE   *Google's searching technology uses an algorithm that uses several weighting factors. Early versions of this algorithm may have drawn on PageRank—a complex analysis of which important pages on the Web link to other pages, about which topics. (But some speculate that Google no longer uses PageRank per se.)*

None of the search results are paid for by advertisers. There is no way to pay your way to the top of the regular search results, or even to guarantee that your website is included in them. Google currently maintains an index of 8 billion web pages, and on any given keyword query,

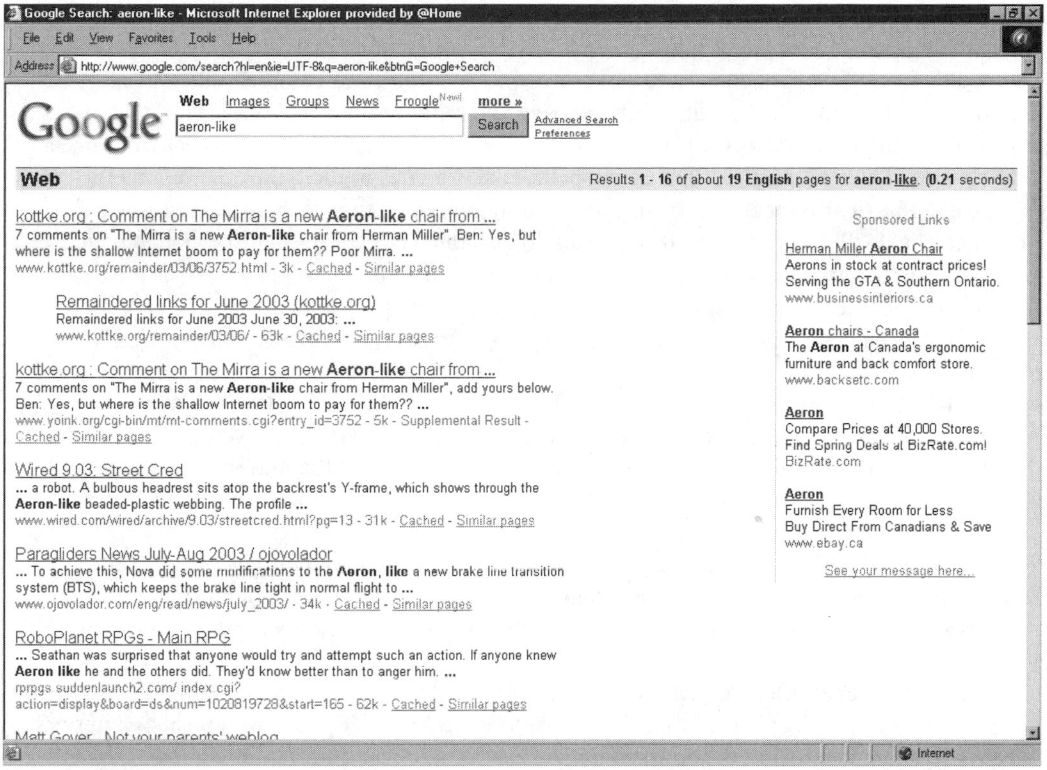

FIGURE 3-1   Typing **aeron-like** into Google Search yields a list of useful and interesting results.

Google will determine how many pages match. On popular keyword queries like **new york hotel**, there are thousands of matches. In fact, on **new york hotel** (without quotes), there are about 7.8 million matches. On **"new york hotel"** (with quotes to denote an exact phrase), there are about 870,000 matches. Good luck getting your website onto the first page of results there! Anyway, since my query, **aeron-like**, was so quirky, it turns out that only 16 pages matched.

One interesting thing that Google has been doing recently, some believe, is ensuring that a higher proportion of the search results are informational, educational, or governmental in nature. Google may be treating obviously commercially oriented pages differently when it comes to its ranking algorithm. A major reindex in fall 2003, now dubbed "Florida," elicited howls of protest from webmasters on discussion forums and was covered in the technology press such as CNET as well as in the mainstream press.

It does make sense that the average user—even someone looking to buy something—is using the search engine to look for information, not just a product catalog. In an interview for an article published on my own site, Traffick.com, Google's director of search quality, Peter Norvig, confirmed that Google might attempt to assess not only the degree of commerciality of sites, but different types of commercial intent (a catalog page versus an "About Us" page) and rank pages accordingly. It might even, Norvig told me, look for data such as how long a company has been in business, or how long a website has been operational, for cues to the quality or reputability of a given page. Practically speaking, this may be putting more pressure on commercial sites to use the pay-per-click AdWords program if they want to generate targeted traffic. Some merchants, though, have come through the Florida "storm" just fine and continue to get plenty of free search referrals from Google. It probably depends on the actual keyword query.

There has been endless speculation about which factors are most important in Google's algorithm. Most recently, some search scientists, such as the chief scientist at Ask Jeeves, have argued that Google no longer uses PageRank. That Google uses some form of link analysis seems unquestionable, but like most leading search engines today, Google's means of ranking websites goes beyond published formulas. Search engine ranking methodologies are a moving target—deliberately so, as marketers try to exploit knowledge of algorithms to achieve the best possible "free" rankings.

In any case, this book is *not* about getting your website well ranked on that elusive left-hand side of the page. It's about paying to place your advertisements in the right-hand side of the page *near* those search results so that you might grab the attention of customers typing in relevant keywords.

On my query, **aeron-like**, you can see (Figure 3-1) unobtrusive-looking text listings in the right-hand margin. These are clearly marked as "sponsored links." The ad from businessinteriors. ca caught my attention, as did the ad from Backs, Etc., which has a strong local reputation and a convenient showroom on Eglinton Avenue in Toronto.

I didn't click on any ads at first, though. I read a couple of the articles I noticed in the regular search results. I also noticed that the very top link in the search results was to a page describing a new, less expensive, stylish Aeron-like chair from Herman Miller called the Mirra. That's about as close to the definition of **aeron-like** as I could come. Is Google clairvoyant? Anyway, more research was still needed. I had three choices: spend all day reading articles about Aerons, zip directly to an online store and order one right away, or something in between. I chose the middle path: do just enough research to decide which chair was more or less right for me from the standpoints of form, function, price, reliability of retailer, and convenience of purchase. Once I got those issues settled, I fully intended to make my purchase in a physical store because I feel more comfortable making some purchases in person.

I point all of this out to show how easily a businessperson and an advertiser can fall into the trap of making assumptions about how people search and shop.

Above all, you can get lulled into believing that everyone is naturally going to do what you want them to do: buy your stuff online at the price you're asking, seconds after seeing your offer.

This might be nice, but it doesn't always happen. You can't control how people behave, and often, unless you're a large company with plenty of reliable data on hand, you can't even guess very well about what motivates them to act on your offer. Don't get too narrow in your thinking; just realize that your target audience—as my Aeron-like chair example shows—may behave in a reasonably orderly but ultimately untidy, unpredictable fashion. In particular, it's safe to say that many purchase decisions take time. Consider that a sales cycle—be this a week or a year—is a normal part of doing business online, and that repetition and consistency, along with targeting, are the bedrock of any online advertising investment.

If you're looking for some confirmation of this latter point, consult Jay Conrad Levinson's *Guerrilla Marketing*. It's the bible for the fundamental principle of repetition in advertising. More recently, Mark Stevens, in *Your Marketing Sucks*, explores marketing and advertising as "investments" that should produce a measurable return. In their own way, each provides helpful antidotes to the "overthinking" and "underthinking" of marketing and advertising that can cause businesses to fail. Examples of overthinkers are some of my clients who haven't paid sufficient attention to Levinson's key point: you must advertise consistently and confidently. AdWords makes it possible to optimize and improve your campaign, but don't try to squeeze every last inefficiency out of a campaign lest this overthinking cause you to advertise too little, or to become overly suspicious of every dollar spent. Stevens, by contrast, argues that many companies, especially large, complacent ones, fail to measure marketing success and fail to develop a comprehensive marketing strategy that can maximize the revenue potential of each ad dollar spent. What would be the point of doubling your advertising spend, for example, if your organization did a poor job of generating repeat sales from its best customers? So it's not just a question of overspending or underspending. A balance needs to be struck between over-planning and under-planning. Smaller guerrilla marketers cannot afford to over-plan. They just don't have the staff resources. Larger companies who fail to maximize their marketing dollars, however, don't have that excuse.

What Levinson and Stevens share is a bullish attitude towards clever, targeted advertising and a wariness of arbitrarily defined budgets and false economies. To succeed with online advertising you must, at a minimum, *be bullish about advertising* and understand why you advertise.

Although you can't totally control or predict your target customer's behavior, you *can* control many aspects of your AdWords campaign, which is what makes an AdWords campaign so different from traditional advertising. Here, you can analyze your data with reasonable degrees of precision. But don't be a slave to every single data point or day-to-day fluctuation. Avoid thinking in absolutes such as "no one shops at night," "they're not buying because the ad copy isn't exciting enough," or "everyone is looking for the lowest price." Relax. If you need to have one absolute guiding principle on hand at all times, try this one: advertising works. (Of course it works much better if you do it right, and it won't work at all unless some people really do want to buy what you're selling.) It often works best if it's repeated over a long period of time, however. My interest in the advertisement from local retailer Backs, Etc. was in part fueled by my knowledge of their long history of newspaper advertising over the years.

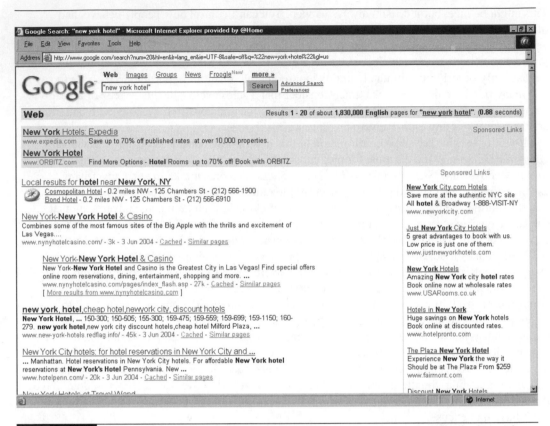

The phrase "**new york hotel**" attracts many advertisers. Google displays ads at the top of the page, above search results, as well as in the right-hand margin.

Back to the Google search results screen. In addition to the text listings in the right-hand margin, advertisements appear in one other place on Google Search. Depending on the query, how much you bid, and other factors (Google doesn't completely disclose these, nor many other details of their formulas), Google AdWords may also appear at the top of the page in bold text on a colored background, as you can see with the "**new york hotel**" example query in Figure 3-2 (above). These ads are not treated any differently from the ads on the right-hand side. Your ad might show up in these spots in the normal course of your AdWords campaign. This position is all part of the same price scheme. These top spots had been considered premium spots reserved for high-spending corporate advertisers, but the Premium program was discontinued on December 31, 2003.

When I originally searched for **aeron-like**, some of the ads that appeared on my screen applied to Canada only, as shown in the following illustration.

Sponsored Links

Herman Miller **Aeron** Chair
Aerons in stock at contract prices!
Serving the GTA & Southern Ontario.
www.businessinteriors.ca

Aeron chairs - Canada
The **Aeron** at Canada's ergonomic
furniture and back comfort store.
www.backsetc.com

Aeron
Compare Prices at 40,000 Stores.
Find Spring Deals at BizRate.com!
BizRate.com

Aeron
Furnish Every Room for Less
Buy Direct From Canadians & Save
www.ebay.ca

See your message here...

A different set of ads, however, would have appeared for my **aeron-like** query to a user in the United States:

Sponsored Links

Aeron Chairs - $849
Fed-Ex Delivery - Quick Shipping
Financing Available On All Aerons!
www.healthyback.com

Aeron Chairs- On Sale Now
All 2004 & Classic Colors Are In
Stock. Free Shipping Via FedEx
www.OfficeDesigns.com

Aeron Chair Sale
You Deserve It - Floor Model Sale
12 Year Herman Miller Warranty
UltimateBackStore.com

Aeron
Herman Miller Classics. Over 12,000
items online. Free Shipping
www.unicahome.com

Aeron
Compare Prices at 40,000 Stores.
Find Spring Deals at BizRate.com!
BizRate.com

Different sets of ads are shown to users in different countries because advertisers have control over which countries their ads show up in. (A new optional Google AdWords feature called "regional targeting" also allows advertisers to limit their ad display by metropolitan area. This is currently available in the United States and nine other countries, including Canada and the UK. Regional targeting is a great opportunity for local retailers, restaurants, and service providers who want to attract local business by spending money only on ads that are shown locally.)

At the conclusion of my research, Backs, Etc., a Toronto-based retailer, seemed to have gained themselves a customer. I'd say this was based on a combination of a relevant, timely AdWords campaign and their status as a trusted local store serving discerning customers for years. Many consumers might go strictly on price, but my inclination is often to go to a retail store that offers good service with sales reps who can answer product questions. Different consumers have different motivations.

Finally, I followed up on one of the articles I'd run across, which was actually a product review on Wired.com for an Aeron-like chair, the Ypsilon. As directed by the article, I went to the vitra.com website to find out more about the Ypsilon, but found it difficult to navigate, and returned to Google to search under the phrase **ypsilon chair**. The first thing I learned, after poring over a few regular search results, is that the "real" Ypsilon chair is an avant-garde wooden chair designed in 1950 by Hans Wegner. A reviewer declared it to be without "faults or mendacious pretenses." Possibly the only surviving example is in the Trent University Archives.

The high-tech 2005 type of Ypsilon chair, on the other hand, is widely available and, at a retail price of $900 all the way up to $3,000, must generate fat margins for the designer and retailer alike. But when I typed **ypsilon chair** (Figure 3-3), only two or three advertisers typically

FIGURE 3-3   Few advertisers took the trouble to show up on the query **ypsilon chair**—an opportunity missed, since such an ad would likely attract a high-income customer.

showed up for the U.S. market. This will vary over time, especially depending on how many advertisers can keep their ads enabled on the broad match for the word **chair**. In Canada, there are still no advertisers on this term. No doubt this search results page will eventually fill in with more advertisers. But the point is, when potential ad spaces go unfilled on such a high-margin product, especially when you consider that advertisers don't pay for the advertising until the user clicks on their ad, you can bet someone is missing out on an opportunity. And if you're reading this book, that's the kind of void you'll be looking to fill. There are many such opportunities on Google AdWords if you know where to look.

Do People Really Look at the Ads on Google?

In conversation I frequently hear observations like, "I never look at the ads when I do a Google search." The observer will then typically generalize his own experience to conclude that search engine advertising is a waste of time and money. Of course, proving that people not only look at the ads, but also click on them, and then move from click to purchase, is not difficult. They don't always do it, but they do it in predictable ratios day in and day out. Advertisers can increasingly measure the direct impacts of each ad on sales; so if ads truly aren't performing in today's data-centric environment, they won't last very long—or at the very least, prices will fall.

The incontrovertible proof of people not only looking, but also clicking on ads, is found in data from any given Google AdWords campaign. I've had the opportunity to access data from more than 200 client campaigns and to peek in on at least as many again. I can tell you that users are clicking on these ads, usually at a consistent rate somewhere between 1 and 5%. That is, for every 100 times a client's ad appears next to the search results for a given phrase, it will typically be clicked between one and five times. That's not bad considering that users usually see between 10 and 20 search results on their screen, and as many as ten text ads. For them to click on something that is clearly marked as a sponsored link even once out of a hundred times is something of a small miracle.

Google claims that its ads are clicked on 10 to 20 times more often than the typical online ad banner, even though such banners are becoming increasingly large and obtrusive. The disparity between search ads and banners might be even greater than that. Recent figures from Doubleclick put average clickthrough rates (CTRs) on banner ads at under 0.5%, whereas at least one of the ten Google ads that appears on a page of search engine results pages (SERPs) might be clicked on something like 15% of the time. That's 30 times more often than banners.

Looking at data from some of my clients' banner ad buys, or at past CTRs on banners appearing on sites I own, the picture often looks even worse than that for banners. CTRs below 0.1% are not uncommon. I wouldn't be telling tales, then, if I told you that a Google AdWords campaign will often perform "a hundred times better" than a banner ad campaign. Banner ad prices have come way down, but it looks like the return on banner advertising investment is now often so poor that they have room to fall even further.

Even the question of where people's eyes are looking when they're scanning a page of results can be answered with some degree of certainty. Some major search engines and portals, including Google, maintain usability labs that can graphically display where users' eyes go on a screen and how long they maintain their gaze at any given place (see Figure 3-4 for an example). What users are typically trying to do is to find whatever most closely matches what they're looking for.

Different eye-tracking studies may show different results, and these are nowhere near as important as the actual clicks on your ads, along with data that tell you whether there is a return on investment on those clicks, at reasonably high volumes. I don't need to make abstract predictions about whether a fifth- or sixth-position ad on a popular term will be seen or clicked, or whether this translates into a respectable return on investment. I see account data and financial data for a couple of my Fortune 500 clients that clearly show even the fifth or sixth ad position is big business and generates many leads at an identifiable cost per lead every day.

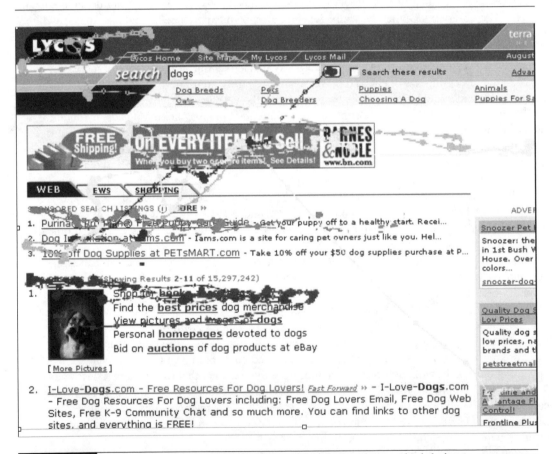

FIGURE 3-4   A study by Lycos outfitted users with a device that tracked their eye movements when viewing a page of search results. This screen shows a typical result.

The question of whether users pay attention to the ads is no trivial matter and is so important to Google that they've paid attention to it with a fervor sometimes approaching paranoia. The history of online advertising seems to follow a pattern: first, a high degree of user interest and attention to advertising presented in new formats; then, a phenomenon of unconscious ignoring (sometimes called "banner blindness") takes hold, and clickthrough rates (the number of times a user decides to click on an ad divided by the number of times an ad is shown) begin to plummet to levels approaching zero. As this happens, advertisers eventually move to devalue the advertising. As demand dries up, ad rates plummet, and publishers—especially large publishers like AOL, Yahoo, and Google who depend heavily on advertising income—find themselves in trouble. This happened following 1999 as the dot-com honeymoon ended. As ad revenues plunged and hopes of growth for online media companies were dashed, stock values plummeted.

In the past year or two, fortunately, companies like Yahoo have enjoyed an impressive recovery in advertising revenues largely owing to their discovery of—you guessed it—pay-per-click search advertising. Ads served by Overture, Google's main competitor in the pay-per-click advertising business, appear near search results on Yahoo. Overture was acquired by Yahoo in 2003. Recent financial filings by Yahoo show that 40% of the company's revenues (and growing) come from search listings (mostly Overture pay-per-click ads). That's huge, but not nearly as large as the 96% of Google's revenues that were derived from the AdWords program in the first quarter of 2004. The bottom line here is that Google depends heavily on the advertising program, and they are watching closely for signs that users are becoming "blind" to these ads. So far, this hasn't happened, but it explains why Google puts so much emphasis on relevancy and the user experience.

In his Alertbox column ("Will Plain-Text Ads Continue to Rule?" April 21, 2003), Web usability expert Jakob Nielsen wonders if banner blindness will give way to text box blindness. He argues that the low-tech text ads are currently enjoying the same novelty effect that previous advertising formats did, but that they "are not guaranteed a bright future outside of their native search engine habitat." But Nielsen does admit that the low-tech format that requires advertisers to be highly relevant *might* be able to hold user interest for the long term.

Thus far we are not seeing any major drop-off in clickthrough rates on search ads. In part, this is because of the uniqueness of the search medium—the fact that the ads are often exactly what the user is actually searching for. It may also be due to the care Google has taken to design the AdWords program so it doesn't turn users off. If people stop looking at the ads; or worse, if they stop using Google, then Google goes out of business, and advertisers no longer have such a great place to advertise. So if it seems like AdWords is structured and sold to advertisers in a far different way from any other kind of advertising, that's the explanation. Google is terrified that history could repeat itself.

Why Users Love Google

Google continues to report (for example, in a statement by Sergey Brin in a March 22, 2004, feature in *Newsweek*) that the total number of searches performed daily on Google exceeds 200 million. In terms of market share for pure search, Google is unquestionably the #1 search destination in the world; but the reality is that outside of major markets, data collection on Internet user behavior is spotty or suspect. Even relatively plentiful North American data can be difficult to interpret.

Search engine market share can be measured in different ways. Panel-based measurement services, such as comScore Media Metrix, report that Google leads the U.S. market for search, but not overwhelmingly so. comScore's release of user behavior data for the United States in April 2003 shows that Google had a 36% "share of searches"—Google's proportion of the total number of search queries performed at top search engines that month. Yahoo was close behind at 30%. There is some question about the accuracy of this data, however. comScore could be including some "channel" searching within the Yahoo site in their total for the number of "searches" performed on Yahoo. I tend to believe that this inflates Yahoo's number.

comScore's share-of-searches data for Canada (April 2003) may give us a better appreciation of the real market share Google has: in Canada, Google commands a 62% share of monthly searches, with Yahoo at 15%, and MSN at 13%. These are new data produced by comScore's new qSearch initiative, formerly unavailable for Canada. In the past, we were led to assume that major brands such as Yahoo and MSN were in the lead, but looking specifically at search traffic and not portal usage in general, we can now see that this is far from the case.

As more serious efforts are made to measure searcher behavior around the globe, it will be interesting to see what comScore's qSearch data show us for other major markets such as Germany and Japan. Clearly the picture varies around the world. Yahoo is the leading web property and leading search destination in Japan, for example, but unlike the U.S. situation, Yahoo Japan still maintains a partnership with Google and Google AdWords for search results and pay-per-click text ad listings.

Other measurement firms, such as WebSideStory, use a different methodology from comScore's panel-based approach. WebSideStory looks at the server logs of website owners who are users of WebSideStory's popular HitBox analytics software. Such studies typically show that Google has a commanding lead in search referrals, with a market share in excess of 50%. (*Search referrals* are the number of visitors to a website who found a site and surfed in by typing a search query into a search engine and then clicking on a search result in the "main" search listings.) After poring through the available data, I conclude that Google currently has a commanding lead in the race for search engine user loyalty, even more so than many media reports would indicate.

In terms of pay-per-click search advertising referrals, the picture is clearer. Google and Overture are the two largest players in North America and several other major markets, with most other players trailing well behind. FindWhat (which has merged with Europe's Espotting and more recently, changed its name to Miva) is a reasonably competitive third-place contender for pay-per-click advertising dollars.

The current landscape of search partnerships and pay-per-click "feeds" is important for marketers to understand. The four leading search destinations in the U.S. market are Google, Yahoo, MSN, and AOL. The former so-called fourth portal, Lycos, continues its slide into irrelevance. Ask Jeeves and Infospace, which own various secondary search engines, are also reasonably strong contenders, although their market shares remain in single digits.

As discussed earlier, you need to understand which advertising services, and which search technologies, power the offerings at the major search destinations. Many large portal companies such as AOL, MSN, and Yahoo have typically used third-party providers for their search technology. Yahoo has, over the years, used Open Text, AltaVista, Inktomi, and Google to generate web search results, before finally developing its own technology in-house (following its acquisitions of AltaVista, Overture, FAST Search, and Inktomi). AOL is currently using Google for its web search results. MSN has in the past used a mixture of Inktomi and LookSmart results and is now in the midst of a much-ballyhooed in-house search technology development process. Ask Jeeves' web index results are mostly powered by Teoma, an advanced search technology not dissimilar to Google's. Such partnerships make it difficult for marketers to stay on top of the game. Bruce Clay maintains a frequently updated chart representing the partnerships among major portals and providers of search technology and pay-per-click advertising results. It's available at BruceClay.com. Even Clay's data can be out of date or confusing, though.

For the present purposes, Google's strength is worth noting again. For now, it has managed to maintain some external partnerships to augment its reach. For example, Google Search and Google AdWords power AOL Search. Google AdWords currently powers Ask Jeeves pay-per-click results, too.

Google's main pay-per-click advertising competitor, Overture, is now a wholly owned division of Yahoo and has indeed been renamed Yahoo Search Marketing. As it's now owned by a leading portal, many of Overture's external partnerships with Yahoo's competitors will dry up at the same time that it becomes an increasingly important part of Yahoo's revenue picture. Several aspects of advertising on Yahoo are now managed under the Overture brand. Advertisers must use Overture to bid on pay-per-click search ads near Yahoo Search results. Overture now also operates the paid inclusion program that helps webmasters ensure that their sites get into the new Yahoo Search index. But that's a bit outside the scope of this book.

There is a big drop-off in usage once you look past the market leaders. Marketers should focus first and foremost on the top user destinations and less so on second- and third-tier search properties. Even Ask Jeeves, which has worked hard to stay on the map in this business and has recently grown through acquisitions, has a search usage market share below 10%. Flavor-of-the-week search engines, such as publicly traded Mamma.com, are typically more spin than substance, and marketers shouldn't waste their time on them until the user behavior numbers warrant. (Mamma.com saw its stock price soar in 2004 in spite of its market share being nowhere close to even 1%.)

Amidst this ever-changing menu of possibilities for users, why do so many users flock to Google Search in the first place, and why do they seem likely to continue doing so? In my view, it's what Google Search *isn't* that has attracted so many users to it. The clean design and singular focus is what people want. When they want search, Google gives them that, and nothing else.

In the portal era, emboldened by inflated stock market valuations, every search company wanted to become the next Yahoo, which had grown from a small directory service to a large media company with many offerings. Unfortunately, also-ran portals were not compelling to users.

They were simply ad-cluttered, unfocused messes. Taking advantage of the Wayback Machine at archive.org, you can look at old screen shots of Excite.com (Figure 3-5) and AltaVista.com (Figure 3-6) and understand why these companies didn't win the search wars. (These screens actually fail to do justice to how banner-cluttered many pages on these networks became, and they predate by a couple of years the desperate shift by online ad agencies and publishers to oversized, page-dominating banners.)

As other search sites admonished beleaguered users to shop until they dropped, Google quietly entered the fray in 1998 and gained momentum in 1999–2000 with a simple search box and new-generation search technology. AltaVista, one of Google's chief rivals at the time, lost market share quickly. Evidently, it had changed courses too many times. What a terrible time to give up on search! Google filled the void and soon took over as not only the leading search engine, but one of the world's best-loved brands.

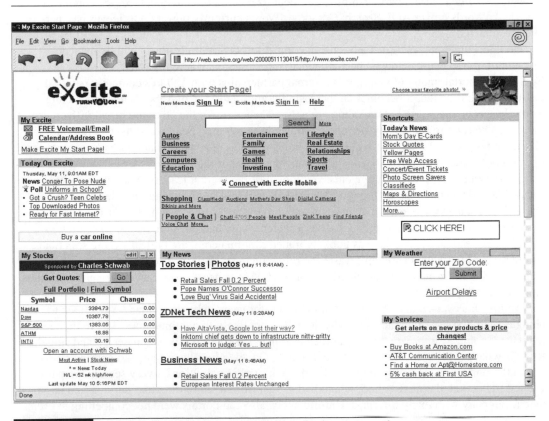

FIGURE 3-5   Excite's home page got too exciting for its own good.

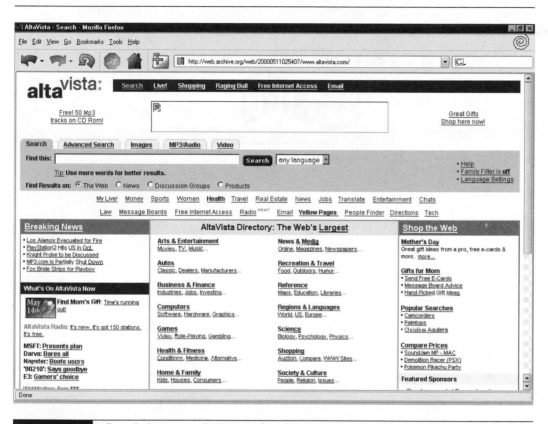

FIGURE 3-6   Portal clutter got the better of search specialist AltaVista.

In May 2000, AltaVista tried to copy Google's simple layout with a new, standalone site for "search enthusiasts" called, of all things, Raging Search (Figure 3-7), but it was too late. Google had already won too much mindshare.

Users flocked to Google's oasis of simplicity and relevancy for good reason: they wanted to search, not be shouted at. As a marketer, you need to understand that psychology and to be respectful of users' sensibilities in this unique medium. If an advertiser shows up near the search results and delivers something that's at least as relevant, users seem to see that as a fair compromise. But Google has never taken this for granted. The founders of the AdWords program had the vision to forge that compromise from scratch, taking Google from a company with virtually zero revenue to one raking in close to $4 billion a year from advertising without alienating that notoriously fickle user base. In my view, you can expect Google's strength in this sector to last for the next several years, in spite of the current faddish media analysis that the "big, moneyed portals" will eat their lunch.

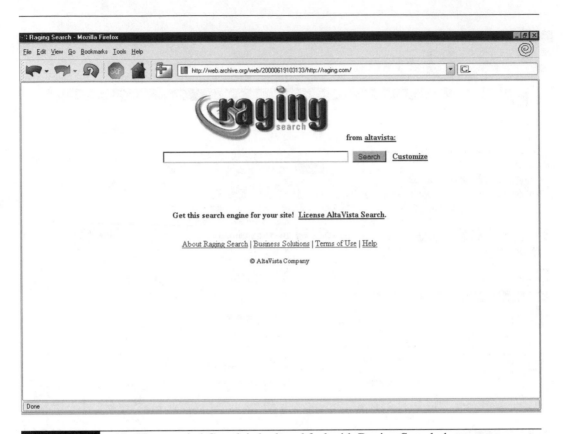

One of Google's main competitors, Microsoft, has been paying close attention to the user response to advertising near search results. On March 22, 2004, they announced that they'd begin displaying the Overture paid search listings less prominently than before, and would begin labeling them more prominently. Microsoft is developing a new MSN Search in-house and, with this announcement, may be signaling that they understand that users want a cleaner-looking search page with fewer inappropriate advertisements. Time will tell if Google's competitors have learned enough to avoid the fate of others, like AltaVista, which succumbed to the lure of intrusive clutter.

Different Types of User Intentions

Users are typing a lot of different keywords into Google Search, but user intentions vary greatly from search to search, even on identical sets of keywords. And needless to say, not every query typed into Google Search is commercial in nature. Arguably, the majority of web search queries—a teacher asks her elementary-school class to search for information about ichthyology, for example—are *not* commercial. A fair number of search sessions fall somewhere in between. Even a search that's informational in nature can ultimately result in a commercial transaction. A computer user hears through the grapevine that Windows XP has a security vulnerability whereby any user with an old Windows 2000 CD can circumvent the admin-password-protection on Windows XP. Is it true? She searches on the term **windows password vulnerability** to find out. In the midst of her research, an interesting, free "Windows tips" newsletter, Brian's Buzz by Brian Livingston, is advertised (Figure 3-8). She clicks on the ad and signs up for the newsletter. As it happens, Livingston's subscribers are typically so delighted with the free information that a predictable percentage of them turn into paying subscribers. Advertising near search queries that are largely informational in nature nonetheless produces a measurable return on investment for BriansBuzz.com.

As mentioned in Chapter 2, Danny Sullivan, editor of SearchEngineWatch.com, coined the phrase "invisible tabs" for emerging search technologies that attempt to guess at user intentions from the content of a query. Instead of expecting users to click on visible tabs on top of the page to tell the search engine whether they're interested in news, products, books, or opinions, (many users are too lazy or just unsure), the mix of search results may be adjusted by the search engine's using invisible tabs. For example, if a query seems news oriented (such as **jacko bankruptcy**), Google might automatically display news items from Google News more prominently at the top of the page. If it's clearly a product name being sought (**ricoh camera**), Google sometimes (not always) displays a few results from its product search engine, Froogle, at the top of the page. If a user seems like he might be looking for weblog commentary (**blogs about fashion**), the search technology might conceivably decide to highlight more pages that are identifiably structured as weblogs or commentary.

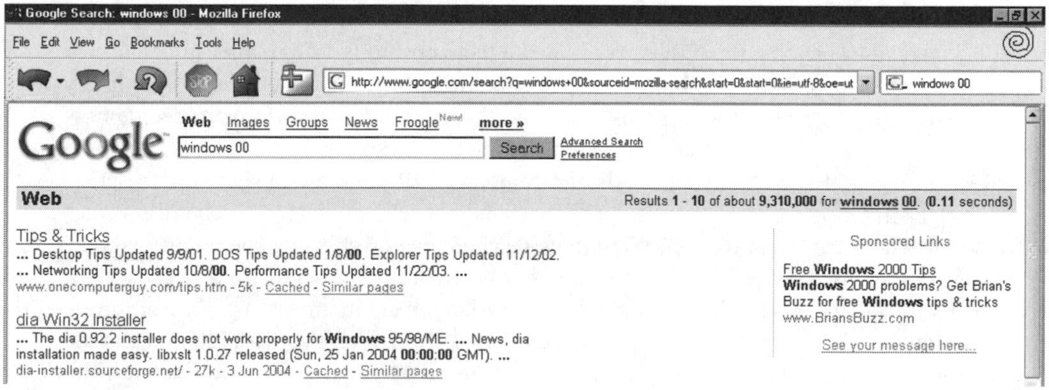

FIGURE 3-8 Official Microsoft bulletins appear prominently in the main search results for Windows-related queries, but some searchers are eager to receive a third-party viewpoint, so they click on the nearby ad for Brian's Buzz, a biweekly newsletter about Microsoft Windows.

But put more simply, several search engines, and reputedly Google, have attempted to parse search queries to serve a different mix of results depending on whether a query falls on the commercial side of that great artificial divide between commercial and informational. One of the first companies to do this was Infospace through its metasearch engines Metacrawler, Excite, and Dogpile. More recently, the new Yahoo Search has been explicitly designed, when encountering a product-related query such as **gummi bears**, to increase not only the number of commercially oriented results in the regular search results, but also to add more sponsored links as a proportion of total results on the page. (This changes from time to time.) Google, by contrast, has been accused of bending over backwards to rank informationally oriented results higher on a wide variety of queries so that advertisers will be forced to pay for advertising if they want visibility. There may be something to this, but I can't be sure.

This might all sound rather distasteful, except for one thing: on educational, informational, and governmental inquiries, users are often able to search without encountering advertising. On commercial queries, they will see more advertising, but might actually welcome it. Search engines are experimenting with the mix. Given Google's experience of winning with clean, uncluttered search, more search engines are erring on the side of conservatism when it comes to how much advertising they show. This can pose a challenge to many advertisers who won't be getting the volume they'd like to see.

In any case, when it comes to invisible tabs, there appear to be barriers to this type of technological "guessing." User intentions are often hard to discern from just a couple of words. And the concept of breaking billions of pages into types is far from new—this is what metadata protocols were supposed to make possible. In spite of smart metadata schemes being debated in ivory towers, the public Internet has yet to achieve, and will likely never achieve, "categorization nirvana." Imposing common standards on publishers and policing the accuracy of the way publishers label their pages is just too difficult.

Ultimately, what search engines like Google seem bent on doing more of in the future is to impose *de facto* labels on pages as third-party "meta-analysts" of page content. (Sort of a "calling it as we see it" method as opposed to a publisher-defined "tell us what type of page this is" approach.) Instead of trusting the publisher to label a page correctly as the "investor relations page" for a company, for example, imagine Google having a formula to determine how likely a certain page is to be an investor relations page, and then also using a formula to decide how likely it is that a given user typing in a company name might be looking for that company's investor relations information. Based on that analysis, the company's IR page might show up, in, let's say, position 12 in Google Search results out of thousands of relevant pages. Such efforts can only go so far. The very openness of the Web (anyone can have a web page, and no official body polices page content, page titles, descriptions, and so on, for accuracy) lends itself to deception and chaos in search and navigation, as argued by Cory Doctorow in an August 2001 article entitled "Metacrap." Users will have to be good enough to find what they need in this chaotic environment, even if the search engine can't read their minds. For you, the advertiser, a little chaos isn't such a bad thing. It gives you a chance to catch prospective customers when they're still in search mode, before they've made up their minds exactly what it is they *are* looking for.

Measurable and Nonintrusive: The AdWords Difference

AdWords is such a different environment from what advertisers have traditionally encountered that many have had trouble adjusting their strategy to suit this new medium. Here I'll outline what makes it so different and groundbreaking.

Request Marketing

The idea of customers finding you after searching for something related to your offering turns traditional media and advertising metaphors on their heads. Seth Godin's 1999 classic *Permission Marketing* alerted marketers to the difficulty and rising cost of reaching consumers amidst the cluttered landscape dominated by old forms of "interruption" marketing. However, his proposed solution to the clutter problem, developing relationships with customers through opt-in email marketing, still rests on the assumption that a company will broadcast messages to large numbers of people. Such marketing is getting much tougher to do effectively now that the inbox has become another site for clutter. And the problem remains: how do you get users to opt-in in the first place? Godin envisioned contests and incentives run by companies with fairly large marketing budgets, or perhaps he simply assumed that a lot of free search traffic would generate visitors to sign-up pages, and people would be eager to sign up. Those assumptions are no longer valid ones. Only six years later, consumers are worn out from being permission-marketed to death. The theory of permission clearly had a few holes in it and was too easy to abuse, as Godin now acknowledges.

Godin's recent book, *Free Prize Inside!: The Next Big Marketing Idea* (Portfolio, 2004), takes the argument against interrupting people to a new extreme. He lauds companies like Amazon.com who have eliminated their television advertising budgets in order to spend the money on product improvements or features that would generate excited word of mouth among consumers. (In Amazon's case, they used the money to offer free shipping.) Clearly, marketers are trying to find a happy medium between not spreading the word about their company at all, and wasting money annoying people who are not interested. That's what makes search marketing such a good compromise: you're advertising, but you're doing so in a way that seems relevant to the recipient. And the minute it stops showing a *measurable* return on investment, you can choose to shut it off. More to the point, you can keep it showing to the prospects who are likely to be interested, while showing nothing at all to those who aren't. Not only will that help keep you in business, but superior relevancy means people will keep coming back to Google and paying attention to the results they find there.

Jakob Nielsen, in an October 2000 article called "Request Marketing," made a seemingly radical statement:

> The Web and permission marketing work in opposite directions. Whereas permission marketing is business to user, the nature of the Web is from the user to the Website. It is the ultimate customer-driven medium: He or she who clicks the mouse controls everything. It is time we recognize this fact and embed it in Internet marketing strategy.

Request marketing basically means that customers ask the company for what they want. You can't get more targeted than that. You can't generate hotter leads. And, from a usability perspective, request marketing entails a design that works with the Web's fundamental principles, not against them.

What foresight! This is the kind of thinking that governs today's most successful pay-per-click marketers. Users have choices. To fight this reality is not an option if you want to succeed in search marketing.

Google Calls It "ROI Marketing" (Not "Spend and Hope")

With pay-per-click advertising, almost everything is measurable. Advertisers don't have to be content with a lot of traffic that might or might not be good for their business. (If it doesn't convert to sales, you can measure that and stop it.) Advertisers don't have to console themselves with "exposure." (That's spending money, not making money.) Mark Stevens, in *Your Marketing Sucks* (Crown Business, 2003), offers a powerful argument against the typical company's approach to marketing: earmark *x* amount, and then "spend" it. The opposite of spending money is actually making a positive return from your investment, thus paying for the marketing costs in a short time period after they're incurred. Make no mistake: this is revolutionary. Ad agencies and television networks have a lot at stake when it comes to defending the presence of million-dollar Super Bowl ads that may or may not pay for themselves. Big ad agencies pushed Google to develop a premium program so that agencies could swoop in with expensive media buys for their large clients. After all, the larger the buy, the larger the agency commission.

In summer 2003 when Google made the decision to put an end to the premium sponsorship program, their spokespersons told me unequivocally that they felt that the advertising community had not been quite ready for pay per click at first, so the CPM-based (cost per thousand page views, or impressions) model had been used as training wheels for ad agencies and large interactive agencies (to placate them so they'd spend their clients' dollars with Google). But, they continued, now that large and small advertisers alike see the benefits of "ROI advertising," the Premium Sponsor program (at CPM rates as high as $100!) is no longer needed. Above all, then, you shouldn't view this process as one of spending money. Many companies do lose money in the early learning phase, but there are so many ways to optimize an account in this medium that there is no time for hand-wringing about spending too much (or whether you should recommend to the boss that more be spent): there's too much work to be done to turn things around so that you're seeing a positive return as soon as possible.

Fast Feedback Cycles and Rapid Evolution

Google AdWords provides you with a powerful tool to reap competitive advantages from rapid feedback cycles. Advertisers who religiously implement a half dozen or so of the most important checklist items for optimizing their accounts, and do so repeatedly, can find themselves zooming ahead of their slower-reacting competitors.

It's not really all that difficult a concept to grasp, when you think about it. Think about golf clubs. Over the past 20 years, the average driving distance in pro golf has increased by 40 yards, making mincemeat of formerly formidable golf courses. Even the average player is hitting the ball farther today with the help of better clubs and balls. Because distance is generally seen as a good thing by buyers of golf clubs, manufacturers have bent over backwards to add yet more of it each year within the limits of golf's rules. So they've tested hundreds of small influences of materials and construction on the ball's flight, making changes to their technology every year to squeeze out that extra bit of performance. Companies that chose not to do this would have been selling measurably inferior equipment. It's pretty hard to argue with a tape measure.

In addition, advanced players now take on more of the responsibility for the process of equipment refinement. They actually match their equipment to suit their own unique swing patterns and ball flight as measured with increasingly sophisticated instruments. Senior tour players employ personal trainers and undergo deep stretching exercises to maintain their edge. Better use of available research has also exploded old myths about the types of club lofts and shaft flexes that are likely to maximize performance for the average player. In a world of rapid improvement, those who stand still find themselves falling behind.

Playing the AdWords game involves a similar process of refinement with the aid of a rich set of data that is available to you nearly instantly. Instead of having to measure hundreds of campaign elements, though, you might get away with periodically reviewing ten, or even a half dozen, key elements. You'll have to assess and then reassess your bidding strategy, keyword selection, ad wording, and other major determinants of campaign performance. If you do so on a reasonable schedule, you'll evolve into a superior being that survives as slower-learning competitors perish.

Companies that take care to consider these elements not only at the outset, but iteratively (again and again) as part of a process of ongoing adjustment, may beat the competition not just in narrow AdWords terms, but in the marketplace. Seth Godin, in a management theory book called *Survival Is Not Enough: Zooming, Evolution, and the Future of Your Company* (Free Press, 2002), teaches larger companies how to manage change by learning to "zoom." A summary of the ideas is contained in the April 2002 edition of *Optimize* in an article entitled "Chief Change Officers." In essence, Godin argues that too many companies generate mountains of data, but don't give the chief information officer the authority to act on it quickly enough. So, the competitor with a reactive culture—the one that zooms—starts to open a performance gap over the slow-moving company, until it's impossible for the slow mover to catch them. In Godin's words:

> Generational length is a powerful thing. If Project X resets every six months and Project Y resets every two years, X will produce eight generations of feedback in the time it takes Y to yield two. It's up to you to figure out how to dramatically increase the pace of change within your organization by making every generation of information of shorter duration than the last.

Google AdWords offers you powerful feedback as long as you're willing to use it to its fullest by creating a smart campaign, testing its performance with a decent monthly ad spend, and then reading and reacting. Your competitors are testing and improving their campaigns. So must you.

AdWords Campaign Strategy Checklist

The following checklist should give you an idea of the things you need to watch to keep your campaign in balance and improving steadily. Some of these are big-picture items, so this shouldn't be seen as any kind of detailed blueprint about when or how to do every small task.

- Do you have your campaign settings set appropriately for your business? This includes daily budget, language, country, region, and ad distribution options.

- Is your campaign well labeled and organized logically?

- Have you figured out how to measure success? Sales? Leads?

- Where sales are infrequent, can you measure a proxy such as whether people requested more information, or whether they arrived at a certain page on your site?

- Do you have a plan for systematically testing ad copy?

- Are you following Google's editorial rules and other terms of service? Do you take a passive or active approach to disapprovals and other hurdles?

- Are your bids too high or too low? Do you have a reason for bidding high or low?

- Have you a plan for ongoing keyword discovery?

- If keywords are being persistently disabled, are you doing enough to rectify this?

- Are you tracking ROI not just on your campaign in general, but on specific ad groups or keywords?

- Are you adjusting your campaign based on the ROI data you collect?

- Do you know how aggressive you want to be? Are you all about growth, all about profitability, or somewhere in between?

- Do you keep a consistent message from your listing through to the desired action on your website, in order to reinforce your brand?

- Is the process from clickthrough to the user leaving your site smooth, so as not to annoy, confuse, or distract users from the main goal of your site?

Let's turn to a deeper exploration of pay-per-click advertising. Advertising methods and pricing models for advertising have always been in flux. If you at least understand what you're paying for and how the online advertising industry got to this point, you may be better prepared for not only the current generation of paid search, but whatever comes along next year.

Online Advertising Pricing: Why Pay per Click?

No pricing model for online advertising is totally satisfactory to all parties in the transaction. This young industry has been through various fads, and I like to think it's learned something. The dominant model for online advertising pricing—both in email newsletters and banner campaigns—was, until recently, CPM, or cost per thousand impressions. This presupposes a certain value in "eyeballs." This model was touted in mostly self-serving fashion by portals like Yahoo and AOL that wanted to portray themselves as networks, as big media companies that can help advertisers broadcast their messages to a mass audience. They're still clinging to this image, but have also experimented with a wider variety of revenue models.

The problem with CPM is that it doesn't guarantee any type of performance. If an ad is shown, the advertiser is charged for it even if hardly anyone ever clicks on it to find out more. To put it mildly, many advertisers concluded that this type of pricing was a rip-off. But it hasn't vanished entirely, so it must be performing for someone. Either that, or hope springs eternal.

At the opposite end of the spectrum from CPM is cost per acquisition or cost per action. This is the purely performance-driven model: a commission is paid on a sale or lead that can be traced back to the user's visit to the publisher's site. What is the problem here? What self-respecting publisher wants to be reduced to a commissioned salesperson or affiliate for their so-called advertisers? This might be fine as incremental income here and there, but large publishers have principles to uphold, so they can't afford to give advertisers too much of an upper hand by agreeing to too many CPA deals. Neither side should be allowed to offload all of the risk onto the other party. Presumably, quality content (and pages of search results) are in short supply, so publishers should be able to set some of the terms of the advertising transaction. Enter cost per click: advertisers pay whenever a user sees the ad *and* clicks through to the advertiser's website.

How, typically, have search engines envisioned charging advertisers? They've tried a number of ideas, but the fact is, paid search hasn't been around very long, and no one, until recently, had any idea that it would even work at all. Search companies have experimented with paid inclusion as well as targeted ads near search results. (As discussed in earlier chapters, Inktomi, AltaVista, LookSmart, and the new Yahoo Search have charged websites anywhere from $10 to $299 per URL to be listed or included in search indexes or directories. Today, Yahoo Search offers paid inclusion that charges a flat fee *plus* a per-click charge, and that does not even guarantee your website will be ranked well in the search results.) Metacrawler, a metasearch engine, was selling advertising on a CPM basis near certain keyword search results as early as 1998.

Paid search itself had no precedent, and until recently, few publishers even believed in the model, let alone espoused a particular pricing system as the best. When Yahoo moved from free inclusion in its directory through various phases of paid inclusion ($149 one time, $299 per year), the message was something along the lines of "pay up or else." Little rationale was given other than the need to pay editors for their time. Those who had paid for inclusion weren't too thrilled, either, when Yahoo moved to downgrade the prominence of directory listings in their overall search mix. This directory inclusion model, then, is an example of an imperfect model that didn't seem to work well for the advertiser, yet didn't allow Yahoo to maximize its revenue from its advertisers without completely alienating many of them.

What really got search and portal companies interested in charging advertisers on a per-click basis seems to have been the wild success Overture had with the model, especially as bid prices rose on popular keywords. Even here, it took several years for the industry as a whole to catch on, as discussed in Chapter 2.

The reason pay per click caught on is likely because it presents a sensible compromise between purely performance-based ad models (these would make the publisher simply an agent of the advertiser, a degree of risk to which many publishers wouldn't stoop) and irrational, often-overpriced CPM-based models.

Google itself piloted the first, CPM-based version of AdWords beginning as far back as October 23, 2000, following the launch of a premium sponsorship program in August of the same year. That so little was written about the program in the ensuing 16 months, and the fact that advertiser uptake was so slow, says a lot about how ineffective and irrational the CPM-based AdWords program was for the advertiser. The feature set of the old AdWords was weak, and prices were fixed, not fluid. The program limped along, generating limited revenue for Google, and limited fanfare. This program was no threat to the leader, Overture.

When the new version of AdWords was launched on February 19, 2002, this all changed. The cost-per-click model "clicked" with some advertisers right away, although many found Google's rules and procedures too clever by half. Ultimately, as time wore on, it became clear that the pay-per-click auction model was remedying many of the inefficiencies seen in the online advertising business. Fixed pricing and the need for negotiating an ad "buy" were eliminated and replaced with market-demand pricing and a self-serve model. Friction in the market for targeted exposure was drastically reduced. This model became so successful that the major portals began deriving a high percentage of their total ad revenues from pay-per-click keyword advertising. Although banners and big interactive agencies were far from dead, "search"—and more to the point, keyword-based advertising—had come of age and became a dominant, driving force in online advertising. Yahoo was so convinced of the importance of pay per click to its future that it acquired Overture in 2003 so that it would no longer have to share pay-per-click revenue with this partner. Google, for its part, enjoys a situation whereby it keeps 100% of the revenues from its lucrative AdWords program.

Self-Serve, Pay as You Go, and Self-Learning

The whole notion that an online ad program could be self-serve, and allow advertisers to choose their own pricing, campaign duration, and a host of other campaign elements while sitting in their pajamas at 2:00 A.M., seemed to pique the interest of the early adopters. Some of these were true Internet pioneers, like Bob Ramstad, who has operated Condom.com (also known as Condom Country) since 1996, making him one of the world's pioneering online retailers. When I first corresponded with Bob in summer 2003, he had already developed an extensive keyword list for his Google AdWords campaign and had generated plenty of data about the return on that particular marketing investment.

Thousands of forward-thinking entrepreneurs like Bob were all over pay-per-click advertising from its earliest days. People like Ray Allen, a former advertising executive who founded a wildflower seed company called AmericanMeadows.com, Jimmy Hilburger of Switchhits.com (he sells switch plates), and Stephanie Leader of LeaderPromos.com (corporate promotional products), have been able to grow their businesses with pay-per-click ads by tapping into a degree of flexibility and cost-effectiveness that usually isn't available to the small to midsized business. Many others are now catching on, which reinforces the need to develop a sound strategy to deal with an increasingly competitive keyword auction.

No haggling with the ad department over prices; no scheduling the campaign according to availability. Instead, we get to play with a cool little ad-serving machine built by Silicon Valley engineers. Google AdWords' designers created a little universe for the entrepreneur to play in. "Knock yourselves out," they seemed to be saying. The true entrepreneurs among us loved the idea that you could change your ad copy on the fly, if it wasn't performing well or if you simply didn't like it. Don't want to run your campaign on Saturday? You can pause it. Want to change all your bids, or pause or delete just some of your keywords? You can do so instantly. How about ensuring that your ad is only shown in certain countries and not others? That's part of the campaign setup process. No problem. While AdWords can be complicated, and actually now does come with a larger human editorial and service staff complement than Google once envisioned, it can be very simple to operate. Paradoxically, there can be as much complexity to the process as you like, too, since the interface offers an incredible level of control. It's that control we find addictive, since without it, we don't make as much money. For the reasonably advanced AdWords advertiser, control really does equal profit.

One important aspect of this control is the money part. Advertisers enter their credit card information but are only billed after they've incurred a certain dollar value worth of clicks. Since reporting is real time (with typically only a two-hour delay in detailed statistical reports), you can usually step in and take action quickly if things aren't going well. With a tiny outlay of cash (under $50), then, advertisers can get started with their AdWords experiment.

Increasingly, services like AdWords want to make their systems easier to use for advertisers who don't want to fiddle around too much. As we'll see later, AdWords has a number of rules such as a stipulation that your ad must meet a minimum clickthrough rate requirement, indicating sufficient user interest or relevancy. That's less frightening than it sounds. If you have a large number of phrases in your account, and a few aren't performing well from the standpoint of Google's rules, the delivery of ads on those keywords is simply slowed and, if the nonperformance persists, stopped. You can rarely "break" AdWords, and in many ways, the rotten parts of campaigns take care of themselves—they simply wind up being shut off. There are a number of other training-wheel-style features in AdWords. Advanced advertisers will want to disable some of them, as we'll discuss later.

A Sales-Generation Machine That's Yours to Keep

Seth Godin (in *The Big Red Fez: How to Make Any Web Site Better,* Free Press, 2002) has likened a website to a Japanese game called Pachinko—a game that involves dropping a disk at the top of a game board full of pegs. The disk bounces around and hopefully, if you're lucky, lands in one of the scoring areas. If you consider that disk as your prospective customer, Godin argues, you want your website to get the customer from the top of the game to the scoring area with a minimum of bouncing around, to increase the odds that he or she will actually take action while on your site as opposed to leaving. The good thing is, of course, that you don't have to let some random arrangement of pegs dictate whether you score or not. Here, we can rely on some known issues about website navigation, some of which Godin outlines in his book.

Better, though, is the fact that the game—both your and your prospect's participation in it—do not begin when your user arrives at the website. It begins when the user first types a query into Google and sees the first page of search results. For you, it begins in your construction of an orderly, compelling AdWords campaign: keyword selection, campaign organization, bidding strategy, advertising copy, tracking URLs, the selection of appropriate landing pages, and more.

This is very different from the typical ad campaign because you have so much control over the minute adjustments needed to get the "machine" well oiled. Imagine running a local television campaign and calling up the TV station in mid-campaign to ask whether they'd be willing to run a split-test to determine whether you sell more product when the pitchman wears a red sweater as opposed to a yellow one. Good luck!

Indeed, such testing became the norm in avant-garde direct sales companies such as QVC, the home shopping channel. Jim Novo, formerly a vice president with QVC, now runs an online measurement firm called drillingdown.com. "If our data showed that people were more likely to buy microwave ovens between 3:30 and 4:00, then we'd sell microwave ovens between 3:30 and 4:00," Novo remarks dryly. But such testing capabilities have rarely been available to the small to medium-sized enterprise. In the case of large advertisers, many ad agencies actively discourage such quantitative methods, instead touting softer "branding" benefits.

Some think of direct marketing methods such as direct mail as most analogous to Google AdWords, because considerable testing can be done to measure the effectiveness of different elements of the direct mail offer right down to the envelope color. Successful direct marketers no doubt feel that their carefully honed, carefully timed mailings constitute a "system" or even a "sales-generation machine." But consider this: Google AdWords allows you to do the same kind of testing, but on a much more rapid cycle. Direct mail campaign feedback can take weeks or months and will cost several thousand dollars with each mailing. With AdWords, you have useful response data typically within 24–72 hours, and can make many small improvements at low cost.

The best thing about it is that once this machine is built, it's yours to keep. You or your company do not need to pay any third-party company to create those results. Indeed, many "lead-generation" companies—those that sell targeted leads to companies seeking customers in, say, the mortgage, real estate, tax planning, or insurance businesses—use Google AdWords to generate those leads and then simply sell them at a premium to companies who are hungry for them!

The fact that you are building not just a one-off "campaign," but a sophisticated lead-generation or sales-generation machine that weeds out the worst prospects and sends you the best ones at the lowest possible cost should justify your time investment in Google AdWords. The knowledge gained here can carry over to future campaigns in other media, as well. Because your prospects are coming to you based on a search for certain keywords, it's a great way to learn what's going on inside the minds of your customers.

What about Pop-Up Ads?

Like many forms of graphical online advertising, pop-up ads have gotten a bad name for annoying users. Some browsers and Internet service providers even block them. More importantly, users tend to develop banner blindness when a form of advertising is consistently too intrusive, which leads to plummeting ad effectiveness. Google AdWords text ads have been politely relevant to users' needs and appear only when users are in active search mode. They're everything that pop-ups aren't.

In my view, there are three primary reasons to avoid pop-ups—(1) if you can prove they aren't effective for you; (2) if their use will hurt your brand; and (3) if they depart so far from expected user navigation conventions that they violate your sense of what the Web is all about.

Personally, I don't like them for all of the above reasons. But some individual businesspeople have no problem doing the needed soul-searching and fact-checking to determine that pop-ups are, in fact, right for them.

However, I also believe there's a community responsibility to err on the side of nonintrusiveness, due to the classic Tragedy of the Commons problem. This is the old economic argument based on a common pasture with a few sheep grazing in it. There is individual incentive to add more sheep and reap higher profits, since additional usage of the pasture costs nothing. But, if everyone did this, the pasture would be grazed out and all the farmers would lose. Costly sheep would starve, or would at least need to subsist on feed that had to be purchased. In this scenario, a sense of collective responsibility, if upheld, is rational even on an individual level (unless you know where to find more free pastures). It's the same for the Newfoundland cod fishery. Individual trawlers have no disincentive to vacuuming up fish as quickly as technology allows. However, depletion of fish stocks leaves no fish for anyone.

User attention is like the fish stocks or the pasture. The example of email shows just how averse the user can become to being contacted in certain online formats. Individual corporate marketers may protest that their correspondence is legitimate, but too many have gone just over the line and communicated with customers too often, or on terms that were broader than those the customer agreed to. The result: people overcompensated. They started ignoring and filtering their email. Email marketing performance—measured in terms of open rates—declined as a result.

The same has happened with pop-ups. Today's Internet user doesn't particularly care that some marketers find them measurably effective, or that some are less intrusive than others. What they know is that they "hate pop-ups." So while many pop-ups continue to be served, many others are blocked by technology asked for by consumers. And companies that continue to profit from them—both publishers and advertisers—run the risk of alienating people and destroying brand equity built up over decades or centuries. I'm always surprised to see pop-up ads on a site such as globeandmail.com. Canada's national newspaper is obsessive about its image, but apparently this doesn't always translate over to its online division. It's not only the intrusive nature of the pop-ups that might turn off Globe readers, it's the type of offer! Forcing users to look at "cheesy" ads is not in the best interests of many publishers, as they're now beginning to realize.

At the very least, it's important to distinguish among *forms* of pop-ups. The most intrusive ones come about as a result of spyware that has somehow gotten installed on your computer. Others pop up in the form of advertising as you navigate a website. Annoying, but some don't mind.

An "entrance" pop-up is different from an "exit" pop-up. Sites that serve pop-ups as you leave the site are not harming their own chances of making a sale or having you read their content, perhaps (at least not this time). But they are slowly grazing out the common pasture of user attention.

Sometimes, when you click on a link for more information about something, a new window opens in a smaller size. That shouldn't necessarily be considered a pop-up. It's actually a new browser window, requested by you by clicking the link.

That's the crucial distinction from a usability standpoint: did the user request this form of interaction? If advertising is part of the user experience, is it in a format that they might reasonably consent to? By visiting a website, you are not giving the site owner tacit permission to employ intrusive or unexpected navigation conventions on you. (That's why even a musical theme playing on your website is considered tacky. What if the user's baby is sleeping, or what if they're at work, on the phone with head office?)

Occasionally, you'll see a marketer using a "pop-in" (similar to a pop-up, but embedded in the page) to highlight a special promo, as you scan down an article. I consider that to be a legitimate tactic if it's done after the user has already read a couple of pages on the site or spent fifteen or more seconds reading. But as with all tactics that depart from the navigational standards that users have come to expect, they should be used sparingly, if at all.

Ad serving companies sometimes resort to the defense that pop-ups are "relevant" to what the user wants. (How do they know? Well, they know what site you're looking at, for starters. Some spyware services know even more about you.) That argument doesn't wash, because relevance doesn't confer *carte blanche* to break all manner of social conventions. An Audi A3 is highly relevant to me, but I don't want to be run over with one.

Advertisers all too often buy pop-ups and a range of media options from third party ad brokers without inquiring as to the appropriateness of the sources or the nature of the technology used. If the ad serving company is violating privacy policies, making a mockery of online navigation conventions, and angering users, ultimately it becomes your problem. It can turn into a public relations nightmare.

Before You Start: Planning, Third-Party Tools, and a Reminder

Dynamics will differ depending on how many stakeholders are involved in managing an account. Whether a succession of marketing managers over a couple of years, just the boss and one staff member, or a third-party pay-per-click management firm or agency, in many cases there will be multiple people working on an account and trying to pull data from it. Therefore, it makes sense before starting that you step back briefly and resolve to make sure the campaign is tidy and orderly. Don't overplan, but don't just wade in and make a mess, either.

Will Third-Party Tools Be Needed?

Most beginners at pay-per-click advertising will have heard sales pitches for bid management tools and other types of software that they might need in order to do a good job at this task. Again, step back briefly before plunging in (and review the material on third-party tools in Chapter 6). I've found that many companies let the software dominate their process even before they understand the first principles of what they're doing. In short, if you rely too heavily on a superfluous or complicated third-party tool, you may find that the tail is wagging the dog. Don't create mountains of data for their own sake; you'll have enough data to contend with.

As mentioned earlier, AdWords is meant to be self-serve. Many of the bid management features and campaign reporting options give you everything you need. Google even has a tool to track sales conversions after the click. I don't recommend that particular tool, but the point here is this: take care before you get caught up in some third-party vendor's priorities.

But you will probably need to know this much: most systems that will help you track sales back to their exact source will require you to tag your ads—specifically, the "landing URLs" that tell AdWords which page on your site to take users after they click—with special tracking codes. You can also do this at a precise level, tracking sales by exact keyword or phrase; but it is possible to plan for more detailed reporting than you can ever use, to the detriment of sound analysis.

At the very least, make sure you do *not* build a large campaign with thousands of phrases and dozens of ads with the wrong tracking codes; do *not* build a large campaign with tracking codes designed to suit the needs of an inferior tracking tool that you'll need to change later. It can take a full day or two of work to reformat everything with correct tracking URLs should you set this up incorrectly from the start.

So yes, you are probably going to need to decide which post-click conversion tracking software is best for you before you begin. (A discussion of services to help track ROI and campaign performance is in Chapter 10.) If you already have something installed, or your IT department tells you they already have back-end systems that "work fine" and "track everything"—don't let that dissuade you from doing more due diligence to ensure that what you do have can actually give you the data you need in a format you can use.

Another common type of third-party tool you may need is *keyword research software*. It's less crucial to decide on this right away, but I want to emphasize this much: vendors of software have everything to gain from overselling the role such software may play in the success of your campaign. Keyword research is important, but don't let a software vendor confuse you into believing that it's the only determinant of success. The methods I'll teach in this book typically outdo one-sided software-driven efforts that rely on brute-force lists of thousands of phrases. Also, be aware that Google's own keyword suggestion tool is free, and it can be a very helpful adjunct to your own commonsense keyword selections. Google has continued to improve the keyword suggestion tool, particularly for advertisers setting up new accounts. Take advantage of this in the setup phase.

Real-Time Auction on Keywords and Phrases

As discussed earlier, a traditional media buy might involve constructing a few campaign elements, negotiating a price, and then broadcasting a campaign, which will hopefully achieve desired results. In this model, advertisers don't have much control, but they may have a stronger sense of how much they're paying, for what type of exposure.

AdWords is different. Prices fluctuate constantly depending on the presence of other buyers. Much of your strategy—and your good and bad results—will revolve around the fact that this is an auction-based environment. You're not just bidding for exposure across the board, though. As we'll explore further in the next two chapters, each keyword or phrase is treated separately, and the positioning of your ads on the page is determined in part by the amount you bid. Obviously, fluctuating prices create budgetary uncertainties, but the benefit is, the pricing model is more efficient and creates economies for the advertising community as a whole.

At the most obvious level, then, you'll soon become aware of the high prices on certain keywords and phrases. To achieve prominent placement (ad position 2, let's say) on **new york hotel**, for example, you'll need to bid as high as $3 per click on Google AdWords or Overture. In a business with thin margins, that's a steep cost to pay for a click unless a high percentage of those clicks convert to sales. Clearly, then, you have your work cut out for you if you plan to advertise in a competitive industry.

Let's move on to the nitty-gritty.

Chapter 4

AdWords Basics

Unlike most other forms of advertising, AdWords can be a self-serve process. Most of the basic instructions you'll need, and answers to common questions, are contained in the help files and FAQs freely available on Google's website. This chapter, rather than duplicating Google's own material, is intended to alert you to the most important issues and potential pitfalls.

Where Your Ads Will Show Up, and Why

Before we get into the mechanics of AdWords accounts, I'll give you an overview of how AdWords works and some of the theory behind it. Understanding how Google determines ad placement will help you make the most of your advertising dollars.

Where Sponsored Listings Appear on the Search Engine Results Page (SERP)

On Google Search, there are ten ad positions on a given search engine results page (often called SERPs). The first two positions are the bold links that sometimes appear at the top of the page and stretch across the whole width of the page. Based on yet another proprietary formula, AdWords might choose to show two, one, or no ads in the top-of-page position, so the *maximum* number of sponsored links that appears on a page is ten. Below these top-of-page ads the regular search results usually appear, although Google might also choose to insert teaser links to some Google News or Froogle shopping search listings. The next eight ad slots are the familiar text listings that appear in the right-hand margin, labeled Sponsored Links.

How Ad Position Is Determined

Where will *your* message show up? AdWords works on an auction system to determine how high on the page your ad will be shown, but it's not a "pure" auction. The maximum amount you're prepared to bid (called your *maximum bid*) on any given keyword, phrase, or group of phrases, is multiplied by the *user interest* generated by your ads on those keywords. In other words, Google will measure in real time how interested users are in your ad, and factor that into the determination of your placement on the page. This user interest, or relevancy, score is not subjective in any way. It's based purely on a measurement of clickthrough rate (CTR), which is the number of times a user clicks on your ad divided by the number of times your ad is shown. I'll elaborate at length on this odd formula (shown next) because it is unique to Google AdWords and creates special challenges and opportunities for advertisers that exist nowhere else.

Ad position on a given phrase = [your CTR on that phrase] × [maximum bid]

In other words, your ad position is determined by your score relative to other advertisers based on a calculation of your CTR multiplied by your maximum bid.

Let's take an example. Let's say your company is called Bunky's Bikes, and your ad is showing up near search results whenever users type **bicycle tires**. Your maximum bid per click is $1.08. Your CTR on that phrase is 2.0%. For our purposes, this gives your ad an "ad rank" score of 1.08×2, or 2.16. Now let's say one of your competitors, Mike's Bikes, is bidding considerably higher than you, at $1.53, but only has a CTR of 1.4%. Not bad, but still, their ad rank is only about 2.14, slightly less than yours. It's very close, but in terms of positioning on the page, your ad would rank slightly higher than Mike's in this particular case.

Now let's say a third advertiser, Dread's Treads, is vying for placement on this same phrase. Dread's comes in with a maximum bid of only 48 cents, but their ad is so effective, users click on it 4.7% of the time. This advertiser outranks you both, with an ad rank score of 2.26, which puts Dread's above both yours and Mike's ads. Finally, let's consider the efforts of a fourth, novice advertiser in this space, Spunky Spokes. This advertiser unthinkingly sets their maximum bid at $4.30, which is probably irresponsibly high. Spunky proceeds to write an ineffective ad that only gets clicked on 0.5% of the time. In spite of the much higher bid, Spunky comes in with an ad rank score of only 2.15, which puts them below you and Dread's, but still high enough to be ahead of the fourth-place contender, Mike's. Table 4-1 summarizes the company standings. (I've added some also-rans, Spike's and Handlebarz, for added realism.)

Advertiser	Max Bid	CTR	Ad Rank Score	Rank on Page
Dread's	0.48	4.7	2.26	1
Bunky's	1.08	2.0	2.16	2
Spunky	4.30	0.5	2.15	3
Mike's	1.53	1.4	2.14	4
Spike's	0.74	0.5	0.37	5
HandleBarz	0.20	1.4	0.28	6

TABLE 4-1   Rankings Based on the Google Formula

Just to make things interesting let's throw in another variable. The high-bidding advertiser, Spunky, uses the AdWords daily budget tool to set their daily budget very low to compensate for the fact that they pay more per click than they can afford. As a result of the low daily budget and AdWords' attempt to keep this advertiser within that budget, for a considerable portion of the day, Spunky's ad is not even shown. Spunky's sporadic ad serving is a bonus for the rest of the advertisers, who get to climb higher on the page in Spunky's absence without having to bid any higher. Over time, the majority of the advertisers on this page will probably generate a satisfactory return on their investment (assuming their business models are sound), in spite of heavy competition, because they understand Google's rules and have worked to optimize their campaigns. Spunky, by contrast, is doing a number of things wrong and will make a poor return on their investment, if and when their ad shows up at all.

Google's Love Affair with CTR

As you can gather from the previous example, advertisers who try to use high bids to compensate for badly written ads or poor targeting will often fare poorly. This is because Google has chosen to make CTR a primary criterion for ranking ads on the page.

Google's Zeal for Relevancy

Google wants ads to be relevant for two reasons. First and foremost, Google is a search engine, the primary purpose of which is to provide users with relevant results, whether in the regular search results or in the advertising section of the page. Basically, the goal is to reinforce user confidence in the quality of results.

The second reason is purely financial. Nonrelevant ads will produce fewer clicks, and fewer clicks mean less income for Google. The formula that rewards advertisers with higher CTRs is designed to maximize Google's revenue per page served. This eliminates the problems faced by other pay-per-click (PPC) models, such as Overture, that resulted in lost revenue. Some Overture advertisers were quite clever. They would write their ads so that few users would click, or they would advertise on broad keywords, which were only semirelevant to the actual ad shown. These advertisers would enjoy a branding benefit, or the economic benefit of putting out an extremely targeted offer to an overly broad audience, at Overture's expense. Overture shows tons of ads, but doesn't have a mechanism for inducing all of its advertisers to generate high CTRs. In response they've introduced a warning system called the Click Index. Nevertheless, Google is still far ahead on this front.

Think of it this way: if Dread's Treads were bidding $1 per click, and users clicked on the ad from Dread's Treads nine times more often than Spunky's ad, Spunky would have to bid $9 per click to make Google the same revenue. We can talk about the merits of the user experience all day long, but cold cash is changing hands here too. Google's formula is clearly calculated to maximize its profit from the PPC model. It certainly does help, though, that this profit is being earned by delivering search engine users more of what they're looking for more of the time. It's a model that makes everyone a winner.

AdWords Rewards Higher CTR and Punishes Lower CTR

Evidence that Google's formula isn't based on pure profit maximization is the fact that any keywords or phrases that drop below 0.5% (that is, a user clicks on your ad at least once for every 200 times it's shown in conjunction with a given word or phrase) are first slowed, then disabled, if you fail to improve your ads or take other steps to improve the performance of your campaign. To be more precise, Google pegs this cutoff as "0.5%, normalized for ad position," which means essentially that the cutoff becomes slightly more lenient in less visible ad positions. (Google doesn't disclose the scale, but as they might put it, let's say that it's around 0.5% for ad positions 1 through 3 on the page, and 0.4% for ad positions 6 and 7, and so on.)

In Figure 4-1, you can see AdWords reporting for someone trying to sell MP3 players and accessories. The status of the various keywords and phrases is highlighted in green, yellow, or red. A phrase that is above the CTR threshold is reported as "Normal." The yellow "On hold" and "In trial" notations are recent developments. Google introduced these as a response to

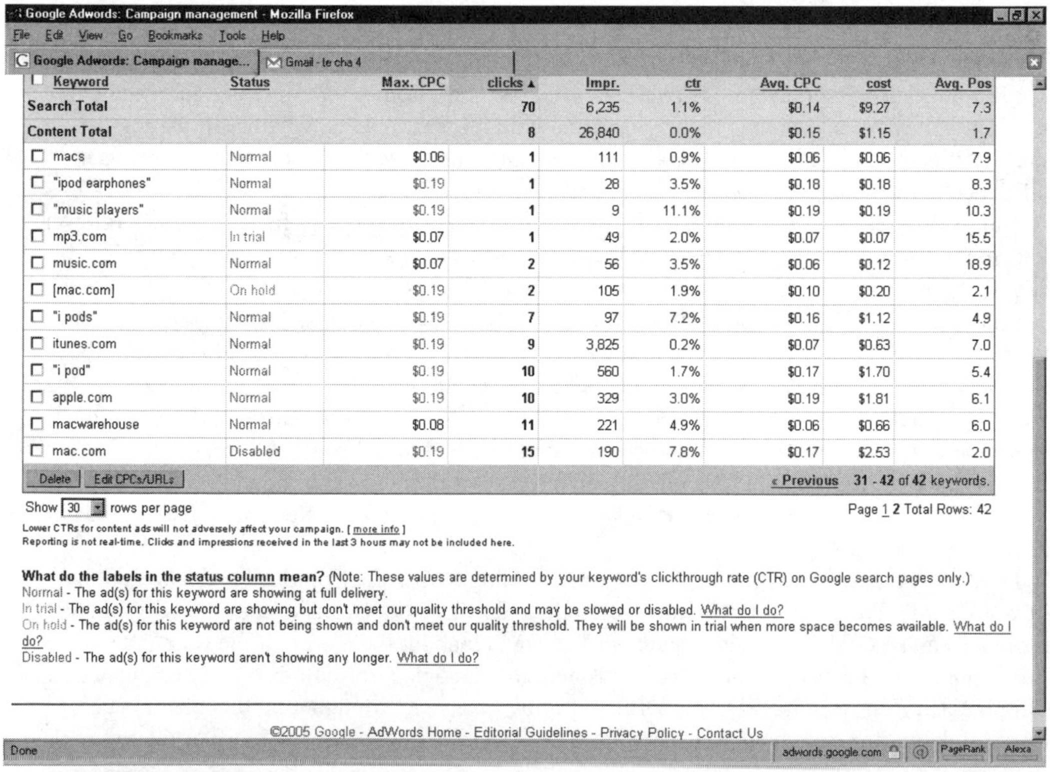

☐ Keyword	Status	Max. CPC	clicks ▲	Impr.	ctr	Avg. CPC	cost	Avg. Pos
Search Total			70	6,235	1.1%	$0.14	$9.27	7.3
Content Total			8	26,840	0.0%	$0.15	$1.15	1.7
☐ macs	Normal	$0.06	1	111	0.9%	$0.06	$0.06	7.9
☐ "ipod earphones"	Normal	$0.19	1	28	3.5%	$0.18	$0.18	8.3
☐ "music players"	Normal	$0.19	1	9	11.1%	$0.19	$0.19	10.3
☐ mp3.com	In trial	$0.07	1	49	2.0%	$0.07	$0.07	15.5
☐ music.com	Normal	$0.07	2	56	3.5%	$0.06	$0.12	18.9
☐ [mac.com]	On hold	$0.19	2	105	1.9%	$0.10	$0.20	2.1
☐ "i pods"	Normal	$0.19	7	97	7.2%	$0.16	$1.12	4.9
☐ itunes.com	Normal	$0.19	9	3,825	0.2%	$0.07	$0.63	7.0
☐ "i pod"	Normal	$0.19	10	560	1.7%	$0.17	$1.70	5.4
☐ apple.com	Normal	$0.19	10	329	3.0%	$0.19	$1.81	6.1
☐ macwarehouse	Normal	$0.08	11	221	4.9%	$0.06	$0.66	6.0
☐ mac.com	Disabled	$0.19	15	190	7.8%	$0.17	$2.53	2.0

Delete   Edit CPCs/URLs   « Previous   31 - 42 of 42 keywords.

Show 30 ▼ rows per page   Page 1 2 Total Rows: 42

Lower CTRs for content ads will not adversely affect your campaign. [more info]
Reporting is not real-time. Clicks and impressions received in the last 3 hours may not be included here.

What do the labels in the status column mean? (Note: These values are determined by your keyword's clickthrough rate (CTR) on Google search pages only.)
Normal - The ad(s) for this keyword are showing at full delivery.
In trial - The ad(s) for this keyword are showing but don't meet our quality threshold and may be slowed or disabled. What do I do?
On hold - The ad(s) for this keyword are not being shown and don't meet our quality threshold. They will be shown in trial when more space becomes available. What do I do?
Disabled - The ad(s) for this keyword aren't showing any longer. What do I do?

©2005 Google - AdWords Home - Editorial Guidelines - Privacy Policy - Contact Us

FIGURE 4-1   AdWords reporting labels show you the delivery status of your keywords.

advertisers, especially affiliates bidding near the minimum, who were taking advantage of the opportunity to stuff their accounts with all kinds of irrelevant keywords, just in case something panned out. If Google's back-end data indicate a high probability that a newly added keyword will stay over the CTR threshold, it goes to normal status immediately. If not, it may go in trial, which means its delivery may be slowed. Advertisers can only have so many keywords in trial at one time, so words that are added may wind up going on hold (very slow or no delivery) until a keyword that is in trial either goes to normal status or is disabled.

This is obviously a bit complicated, but for our purposes it doesn't force you to do anything. Consider in trial and on hold like a sifting function. Eventually the keywords you put into your account will be evaluated and wind up either normal or disabled. The length of time this takes depends entirely on how many keywords you try to cram into your account at once, but typically it won't take longer than 2–3 days to come out of the on hold/in trial waiting area. Finally, then, if a keyword or phrase falls below the acceptable CTR, Google may disable it and mark it "Disabled" in red. I've noticed that disabled keywords may sometimes be shown very sporadically by Google.

It is maddening to deal with disabled keywords, but it happens to everyone, especially in the beginning. There's nothing wrong with experimenting with various keywords to see if they pan out; some will, some won't.

The CTR cutoff is something that keeps many advertisers awake nights, especially in the early phases of their campaigns before they've had a chance to perfect their ad copy. High-volume, untargeted keywords (such as **boats**, **travel**) risk being disabled very quickly for low CTR.

Some advertisers run careful, targeted campaigns on very narrow keywords such as **aluminum siding cleveland** and manage to avoid this problem. Ambitious advertisers, though, will inevitably want to experiment with how broadly they can target, especially since some broad keywords can be quite inexpensive. One of the biggest moneymakers on AdWords, indeed, can be playing this particular game: keeping your ads running on broader keywords and phrases that no other advertiser has been able to keep above the 0.5% cutoff. This may be why, when you type certain broad keywords like **fashion**, or words that are usually noncommercial such as **arboretum**, into Google Search, you won't see too many advertisers. The ones that do appear are usually from brand-name advertisers who apparently interest enough users on their own merits that they attract the requisite number of clicks. Some are brand-new ads that are on their way to being disabled: here today, gone tomorrow.

Sometimes, one of Google's heavy advertisers will show up on such a term, evidently with an untargeted ad that is simply using a "dynamic keyword insertion" feature with just about every word in the dictionary. This type of message has always been annoying to users, and Google largely moved to phase this out when they eliminated the premium sponsorship. Is Nextag really getting a 0.5% CTR on the word **arboretum** with an ad offering discounts on, um, an arboretum (a product Nextag surely doesn't sell or provide any helpful recommendations on whatsoever)? The first time I tried this query in April 2004, Nextag appeared, but more recently, they didn't (Figure 4-2). The more irrelevant examples of these may become less prevalent as Google takes steps to put such keywords "on hold," dissuading advertisers from trying too many of them.

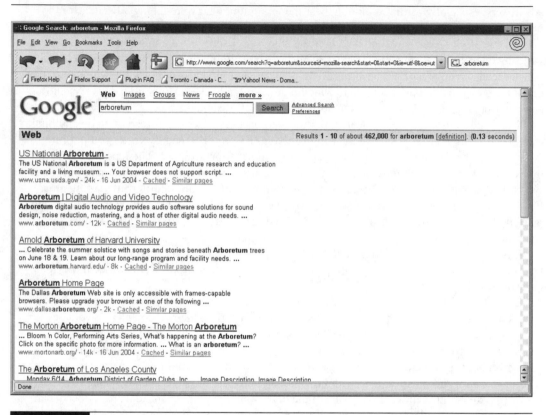

Most of the time, no advertisers show up on broad keywords, for example, arboretum.

Nextag still shows up with quite generic or misleading ads on terms like **schnauzers** (Figure 4-3). To be sure, they might help users buy books about schnauzers or pillows with schnauzers on them, but the widespread use of the "keyword replace" function does tend to lead to some ads that just don't look quite right. Big advertisers like this are doing their best to show up on as many search queries as possible by using automated methods.

Improving your CTR is a vital skill for a couple of reasons. The first is that high CTRs can create excellent campaign economics, allowing you to bid less per click while maintaining a visible ad location, as the example of Dread's Treads showed previously. The way I like to think of it is that a really well-organized, well-targeted, and carefully tested campaign actually makes a small bid bigger. Careful advertisers are rewarded; sloppy ones are punished. The second reason you must take care to generate a high CTR is that fairly untargeted, but lower-cost, keywords can be rescued from being disabled if you organize and test your campaign properly. Having a large proportion of your potentially profitable click volume disabled is something you want to avoid. Specific tactics for increasing CTR revolve around sound campaign organization, keyword selection and matching options, testing ad copy, and more.

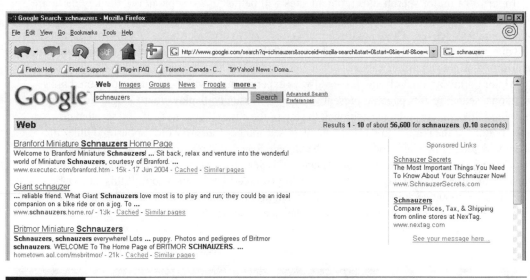

FIGURE 4-3   The "keyword insertion in title" method used by some advertisers tends to generate generic-looking ads.

CTR Calculation Is on Google Search Only

Just in case you thought you were starting to get a handle on the CTR situation, let me introduce a new wrinkle. Although the CTR *reported* in your account includes the aggregate CTR of your ads on Google Search, plus any search network partner sites like Ask Jeeves, that's not the CTR used to determine your ad rank and viability of keywords. The CTR used to determine these two items is drawn from user behavior on Google Search only. This can be quite confusing, since you may see a strong-looking CTR of 1.4% in the reporting on your account for a given keyword, yet Google might label it "at risk," because based on Google data only, it's not performing well. Many advertisers dislike this, but for now, until Google improves the reporting to provide a better breakdown of how well ads are performing on Google versus Google's partner sites, it's a fact of life.

Distribution Beyond Google.com

For most advertisers, the main reason to use AdWords is for visibility on Google Search results pages. Optionally, however, these same ads are distributed on other sites as well. Google does not do a particularly good job of maintaining a current list of search partners in its ad network. For example, as of this writing it still lists Sympatico (Canada's largest portal), but that partnership was lost to Overture.

In terms of major search sites (content sites will be discussed separately), the key partners that you receive exposure on by enabling search network partners in your account are AOL Search and Ask Jeeves. There are three main questions to consider here. One, is this desirable for your business? Two, how do your ads look on their pages? And three, how is ad positioning determined on these partner pages?

Major portals and search engines are always experimenting with how many sponsored links to put on a search results page. At present, AOL Search usually displays four Google AdWords sponsored links in a prominent position at the top of the page (Figure 4-4). If you scrolled down to the bottom of the page, you'd also be likely to see another four AdWords sponsored links after the unpaid "matching sites" (powered by the Google Search index), and even some comparison shopping results. On my query for **ford truck**, AOL Search also shows a "recommended" site, which is an informational page about Ford trucks powered by Edmunds.com. If this looks a bit different when you check it out, it's because search product managers at portals like AOL are always studying what users want. From time to time they may release new layouts with more or fewer ads.

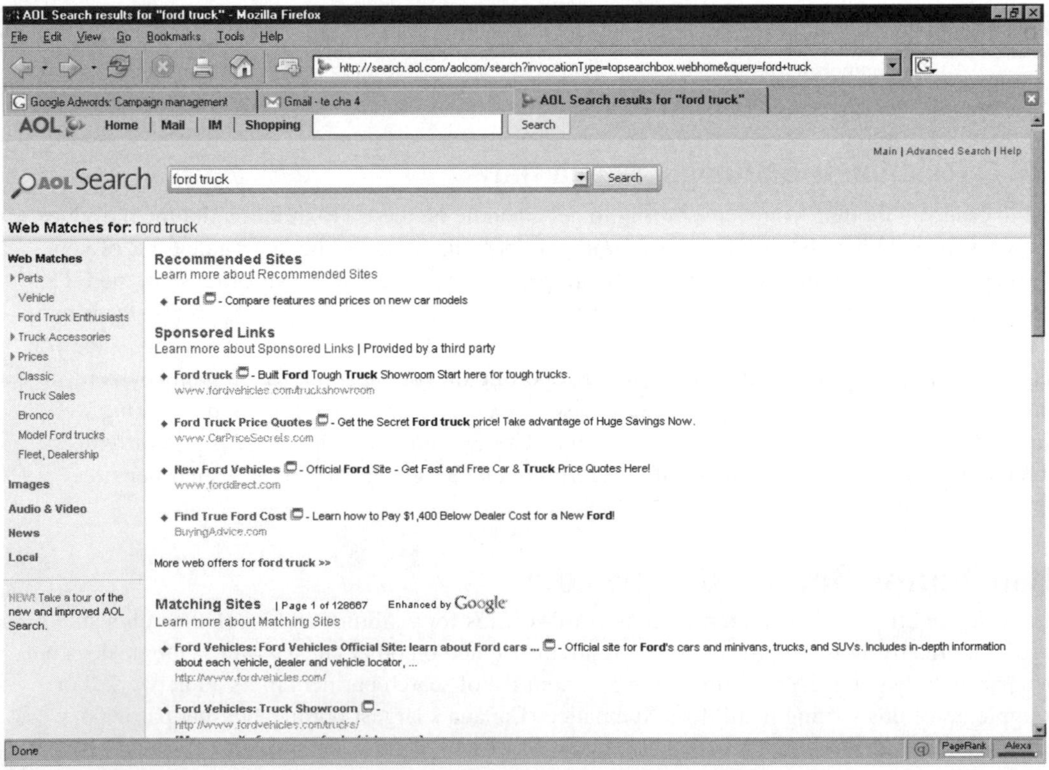

FIGURE 4-4   AdWords powers sponsored listings on AOL Search.

The limited number of sponsored links on partners like AOL has been debated by marketers for some time. When there were typically only three sponsors shown in the most prominent positions on sites like AOL and Yahoo, there was something of a "pig in the python" effect, whereby advertisers felt the need to bid heavily to squeeze into the top three ad positions so they could gain this portal visibility. This all-out panic to be at least #3 is no longer warranted. Depending on where the user's eye falls, there is nothing particularly wrong with sitting in fourth, fifth, or even eighth spot; all will buy you some degree of visibility.

Popular search engine Ask Jeeves (ask.com) is another major Google partner. Unlike its sister site, Teoma.com, which often shows only one or two sponsored results, Ask Jeeves is one of the most ad-cluttered sites out there, especially on commercial queries. It has recently taken some small steps to rectify this situation, however. Until recently, Jeeves showed as many as ten sponsored links above the web results, which could fill up the user's entire screen. A more recent version of the Ask Jeeves search results page can be seen in Figure 4-5. Although there are usually fewer than ten ads now, as shown here on a highly commercial query (**wi-fi industry**),

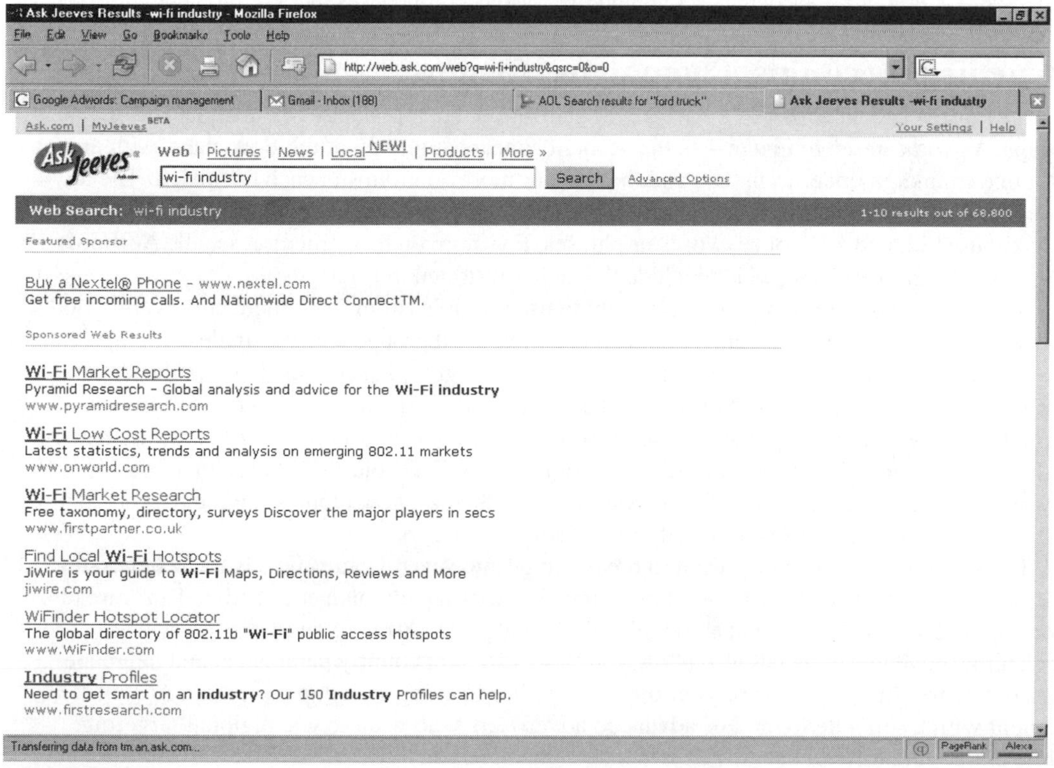

FIGURE 4-5   AdWords-powered sponsored links dominate the user's screen at Ask Jeeves.

the featured sponsor plus six sponsored links still fill up the entire visible area above the fold! It has been my experience that ask.com refers a steady stream of buyers at least commensurate with the company's market share in the search industry. This leads me to believe that many users either don't know or don't care about the difference between sponsored links and search results.

Since you'll be given the choice to opt out of these search partner sites, you need to ask yourself if your ad should appear on these sites, or just on Google? The majority of advertisers will find the traffic targeted enough on Google's partner sites that they will want to enable it. In the case of retail business-to-consumer offers, AOL Search can be considerably better than Google (unfortunately, you can't opt out of Google traffic). But like everything else related to AdWords, the only way to be sure is to do your own testing. Try it both ways. If you still can't tell, consider installing tracking software that can help you learn more about the economics of that traffic as it applies to your business.

Account Basics

Now that you've got the theory down, let's work on the practice. The first thing you need to understand is how your account is set up and the various components that go into it.

Structure: Accounts, Campaigns, Groups

Your AdWords account consists of two key organizational components—campaigns and ad groups. As you can see in Figure 4-6, the account appears at the top of the flow chart, with at least one campaign underneath that, and then one or more ad groups in each campaign. The ad groups, which are the basic building blocks of your campaigns, consist of one or more ads, a maximum bid, and a list of keywords or phrases. For more on this structure, see the AdWords FAQs on Google's website, which include the table illustrated in Figure 4-6.

If you're wondering why you would want to use multiple campaigns, there are several good reasons. The first is simply organization. Having all your ad groups under a single campaign can get chaotic and confusing, especially as the number of ad groups increases. For simple accounts, two or three campaigns is often sufficient, because the AdWords interface is now designed well enough to allow data to be accessed quickly no matter how many groups of keywords are listed under a single campaign. More campaigns become essential as your product list increases or if you want to keep a clear separation between certain themes, geographical target markets, content-targeted ads, or the work of different account managers.

The second reason you may want to break things into several campaigns is for better control over budgeting. You can have a "go-slow" campaign with a daily budget of $15 and an "already working, full speed ahead" campaign with a daily budget of $800, if you like.

Third, separate campaigns also allow you to set different country parameters and language parameters for different parts of your business without having to set up a separate AdWords account with a separate login. For advanced advertisers who want to use regional targeting, while employing different keywords, separate campaigns can also be useful.

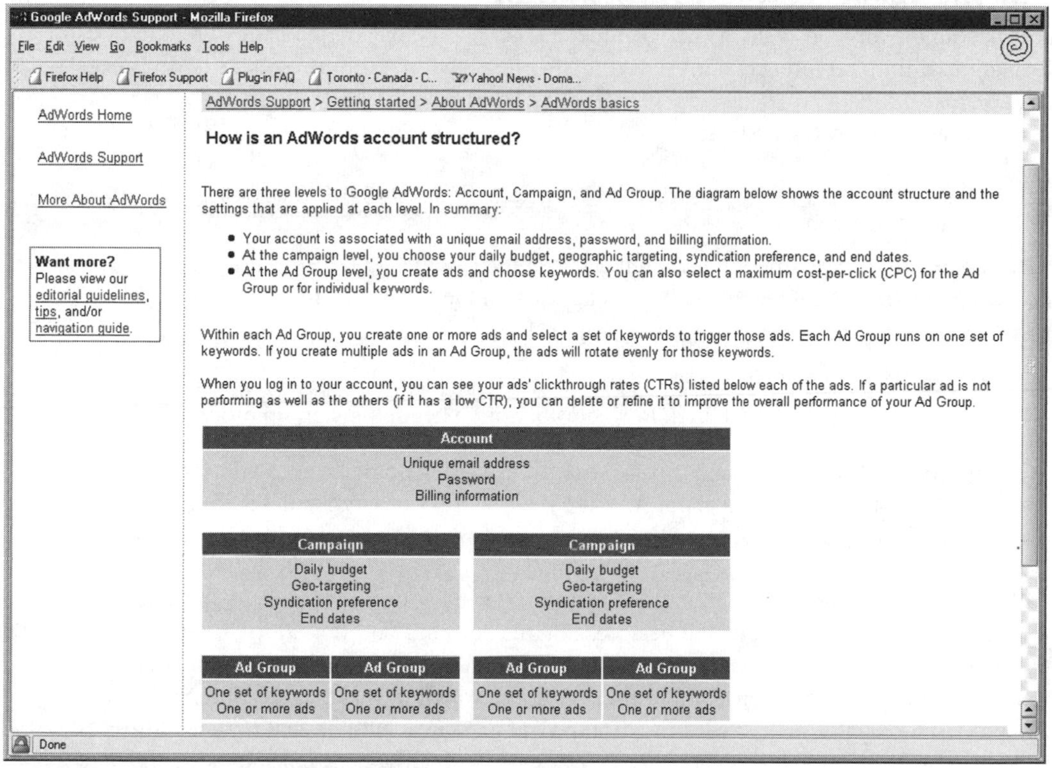

FIGURE 4-6 Google provides an overview of the account structure.

Advertisers who advertise in multiple countries will find that this can save them money. In Canada, for example, some keywords are much cheaper than they are in the United States. Instead of showing a single campaign to both countries, having a separate Canada-only campaign might allow you to bid very low on some fairly popular keywords.

You can also name campaigns. I used to prefer numbered campaigns (Campaign #1, Campaign #2, and so on), since I use campaign numbers and ad group numbers as the foundation for my tracking URLs. But increasingly as I work with various companies and employ their tracking code protocols, which are frequently more descriptive, I see the benefit of such protocols. Descriptive names for different campaigns can refer to different product lines or different account managers, making them much more readily identifiable. This is especially true if you're tracking a large number of campaigns.

Ad groups, the basic elements of an AdWords campaign, are the key to sound organization and strong performance. They're covered in depth in Chapter 5.

Entering Basic Account Information

At the account level, you'll set the key parameters of who you or your company are, credit card information, billing preferences, and so forth. Of course, the first thing you have to do is access the AdWords site.

To get there follow these steps:

1. Open your web browser and access the Google website. (For U.S. users, this is www.google.com.)

2. Click the Advertising Products link to open the Google Advertising Programs page. Information about Google AdWords appears on the left-hand side of the page.

3. Scroll down to the Apply Online section and click the Learn More link to open the AdWords login screen.

4. Click the Sign Up Now (Click to Begin) button to begin the sign-up process.

The basic setup is self-explanatory and straightforward. Google offers a sign-up tutorial as well as additional information about AdWords. If you have any problems during the setup, you can take a quick look at the tutorial before moving on. If you need more help, call 1-866-2GOOGLE.

One important thing to keep in mind is that you'll need a username and password to access your account. If multiple people will be accessing the account, you'll need to provide them with your login information as soon as you set it up. Your username is actually an email address. For now, accounts are based on a single email address, which means that any automated email messages from Google, such as editorial disapproval messages, will be sent to that address and that address only, so choose this carefully. If you work with an outside consultant or colleagues, make sure you forward them pertinent messages from AdWords Support so they're kept in the loop. There's nothing worse than one person receiving an email indicating some ads have been disabled while the person actually responsible for managing the account is unaware of this for several days. Hopefully, Google will improve on this in the future by offering the ability to have messages or alerts sent out to multiple locations.

Key Campaign-Level Settings and Possible Opt-Outs

Many important settings are determined at the campaign level. You'll find yourself frequently returning to the Edit Campaign Settings screen (see Figure 4-7) to check on things like daily budget, ad distribution, and more. This will be a staple of your account. Review your options carefully as you get started. Initially, you may want to accept the default settings Google offers, to simplify your setup. As you gain experience, however, you'll probably want to take more control of your campaign. Therefore, I'll discuss some of the more important options in detail.

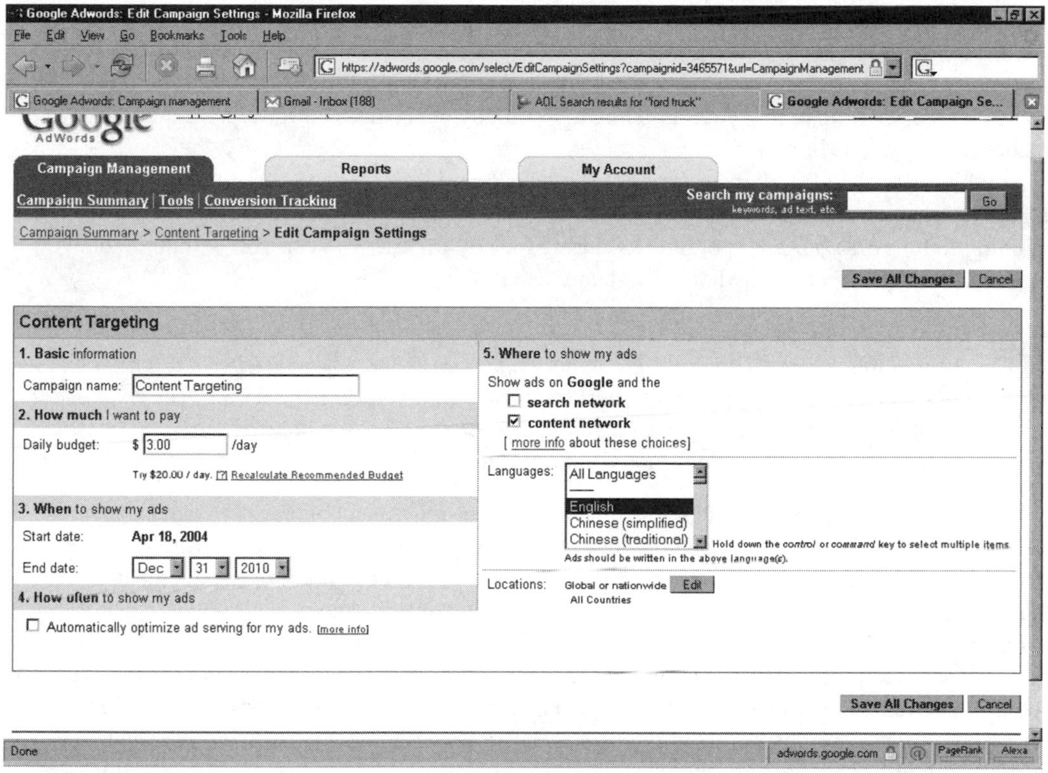

FIGURE 4-7   The Edit Campaign Settings screen is your ad campaign headquarters.

Daily Budget Setting

Understanding how unusual the daily budgeting feature is will help you to use it properly.
Because it doesn't necessarily work in a way that's intuitive you can easily misuse it and end
up wasting both money and time.

In addition to enabling you to enter a specific dollar amount in the Daily Budget option,
Google also has a tool that provides you with a recommendation. Click the Recommended
Budget link below the Daily Budget box and wait for AdWords to calculate your "recommended"
budget. If you already have it set high enough that Google considers your amount to be "maxed
out," it will return the message "Budget is OK." Google might also suggest a dollar amount that
will ensure full delivery of your campaign (as shown in Figure 4-7). Pay attention to this
amount and consider simply entering that as your daily budget. If the number of phrases in your
account, or Google's distribution network, grows in the future, that amount could become too
low. You should recheck this setting periodically.

But what does "daily budget" actually mean, how does it work, and how should you proceed? The first thing to understand is that Google is looking at the keywords and bids you have in your account, along with settings like country and distribution preferences. Using these parameters, it estimates how much you'll need to budget to ensure full delivery of your ads. By "full delivery," I mean that your ads show up virtually every time a user types a query that matches the keywords in your account.

Anything less than full delivery means your ad is only being shown sporadically. If your budget is set anywhere below Google's recommended amount, AdWords might respond by beginning to turn off your ads sporadically during the day in order to keep you within the budget; you might even find them turned off completely late in the day.

NOTE *If AdWords fails to keep you inside your daily budget limit, you may or may not be entitled to a refund. Officially, Google promises only that you will receive a refund on click charges if you spend more than your daily budget multiplied by 30 over an entire month's period. However, if you feel that a particular daily spike was too far over your daily limit, you might convince them to offer a refund anyway.*

When you're just getting started, it isn't such a bad idea to set a conservative daily budget. This will limit how quickly you spend money while you get up to speed on how well your account is performing. But you don't want to spend too slowly, or you won't collect the data you need in order to improve your account based on market feedback. And there is a whole list of reasons why the low daily budget is a poor strategy.

As I discussed in the earlier example of the bicycle store Spunky Spokes, allowing your ads to be apportioned by setting a low daily budget takes control out of your hands and may help your competitors save money. One of the biggest mistakes novice AdWords advertisers make is bidding too high on a hastily constructed set of keywords and then, in a panic, drastically reducing the daily budget to compensate. The problem with this strategy is that it doesn't improve performance—it just keeps your ads from showing as often. You're not saving money on a per-click basis with this strategy, and your return on investment (ROI) does not improve. You're simply doing less of what you came here to do: advertise.

In the case of a money-losing account, all a low daily budget does for you is to help you lose money slowly, which means you waste not only money, but time. Running your account as if it were a "slow leak" helps you put off making important decisions, and that can cost you. To create value with AdWords, you'll want to implement a range of sound targeting techniques and bidding strategies. Instead of using the daily budget to fix a problem account, I recommend turning down your bids, tracking your conversions, and optimizing your ad copy. There are many ways to change the economics of your account. Learn how to use the power of the tools available to you.

While it's true that Google's recommended amounts can be quite scary looking, more often than not the final tally is substantially less. That's because of the wide range of variables involved in predicting daily amounts. Remember, you're paying for something you can't control: thousands of users typing in queries that match your keywords and then deciding to click on your ad. Your competitors are bidding against you, and they might be changing their bids. User behavior fluctuates day to day and seasonally.

As a result, it's not uncommon for you to actually wind up spending less than 25% of the recommended budget. So when Google tells you to set the budget at $500, you'll be spending a lot less in most cases. It's really more of a worst-case number that ensures your ad delivery will be turned on "max" regardless of what users and competitors do. Now, having said that, there is always the possibility that the worst-case scenario will turn out to be the one that you encounter. Therefore, you must monitor your campaigns and make necessary adjustments before you run up a large bill that you're not anticipating.

Since my experience has shown that the actual spend is often much lower than the recommended spend, I recommend that advertisers max their budgets as soon as they feel comfortable doing so. The old adage that you get what you pay for is true in this arena as well. If you're going to be obsessed with spending less in this medium, you'll probably achieve less, too. By all means run cautious tests at first. But as you grow more experienced, you'll more than likely want to spend *more*, and spend *better*, not spend less. Once your account is profitable, or even on a trajectory *towards* earning an ROI of 100% or better, it's generally best to go full steam ahead with a maxed daily budget.

Ad Rotation Optimizer

Also adjustable at the campaign level is a tool that Google uses to automatically show the ads that are your best performers. We'll get to ad rotation and testing later in the book, but for now, you should be wary of using this feature. Since Google allows you to show multiple ads "in rotation" in relation to a given ad group, this tool automatically shows the ads that generate the higher CTRs. In some ways this helps you, especially if you don't plan to manage the account actively. But for those advertisers who actually want to run extended tests of their ads to look not only at CTR data but sales conversion data, this "optimizer" can take control out of your hands, making it difficult to run an informative experiment. You'll find this feature on the Edit Campaign Settings page. It's the Automatically Optimize Ad Serving for My Ads option located in the How Often to Show My Ads section. If you plan to test ad copy over extended periods, you'll want to leave this option unchecked, as shown earlier in Figure 4-7.

Search Network

As mentioned earlier, search network partners include Ask Jeeves, Infospace (Metacrawler and Dogpile), and AOL Search. Advertisers usually find this traffic to be beneficial, since it does come from brand-name web properties with wide distribution. Therefore, even though it's optional, I recommend you keep this box checked.

Content Network

Content targeting, on the other hand, is another matter entirely. This program places your AdWords ads on pages of publishers' websites, ranging from large publishers like CNET, the New York Times, and About.com to smaller content sites published by small independent publishers of high-quality content—even on weblogs. Due to the improving quality of the content network, and its continued growth, it offers an opportunity for advertisers in terms of both quality exposure and additional reach. Many advertisers put considerable effort into researching and building their accounts, and into ongoing bidding strategy and analysis of results, so the added reach is always a good way to make that effort worthwhile. You should be aware however that content targeting is quite different from search-based advertising. It should be treated more like banner advertising, even though the ad displays are triggered by the keywords in advertisers' Google AdWords accounts.

You may hear the term AdSense used interchangeably with "content targeting" (or a term that others have used, "contextual advertising"). AdSense is the name of the interface that publishers use to place the Google AdWords ads on their sites to receive revenues from Google (ultimately from you, the advertiser) when users click the ads. Figures 4-8 and 4-9 provide examples of the different ad formats used on content sites. Google actually offers a variety of ad display options. Most revolve around the clean, text-based look of AdWords. However, they've recently begun allowing static image ads for publishers and advertisers who want to test their effectiveness.

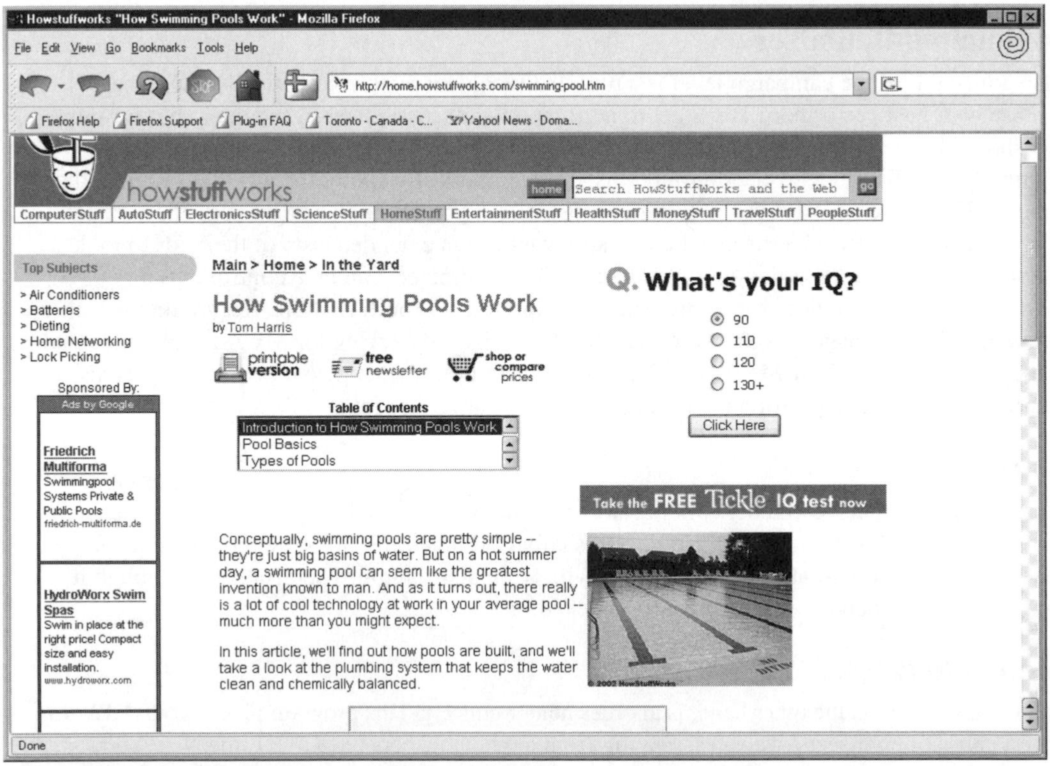

FIGURE 4-8 A typical AdSense publisher, HowStuffWorks.com, displaying text-based ads in the left-hand margin. These ads are served by Google AdWords.

Pricing for content targeting is based on proprietary semantic matching technology developed in-house that actually determines which ads to show on the fly as a page loads. The key criteria are how closely the meaning of the content on a page matches the keywords you're bidding on in your AdWords account, and, we can presume, your maximum bid.

CTRs for content targeting are typically much lower than they are on search ads; however, these CTRs are *not* factored into the CTR that determines your ad rank score for the purposes of ranking you on the page. Nor are they considered in the calculation of whether or not a given phrase is disabled. In other words, don't worry too much about these low CTRs in spite of how bad it makes your stats look.

In spite of the lack of negative consequences attached to these low content-targeting CTRs, some advertisers will see cause for worry when they attempt to interpret their stats for periods when content targeting is turned on. In statistical summaries for given ads, periods of content-targeting usage will frequently drag down the aggregate CTR number. Thus the strong performance of an account may not be immediately evident without scrutinizing the data more closely. Also, turning

FIGURE 4-9   Google AdWords ads for golf-related products show up in a text box in the middle of this article on the About.com Guide to Golf.

content targeting on and off can make comparing the CTR performance of ads difficult. Newer ads that were showing during periods of heavy content-targeting use are difficult to compare head-to-head over, say, a month-long period, when pitted against ads that were showing with content targeting switched off (or simply left on for a shorter duration). Until Google improves this reporting, you can be easily misled about ad performance unless the ads you're comparing have been running with the same settings applied to all. Keep this in mind when testing ads. Don't mistakenly stop an ad that may be doing well, but appears to be a slow performer due to content targeting.

Ads near content perform differently than search ads, because user behavior and expectations are usually different when they're casually reading articles rather than actively searching. Thus the economic worth of content ads to advertisers may be lower than what we see from ads placed near Google Search results. Since the inception of content targeting, Google has maintained that conversion rates on content ads are comparable to that on search ads, even if CTRs may be lower, so the value should be about the same.

In April 2004 Google introduced something called "enhanced smart pricing" for content targeting. Many advertisers had asked if they could bid separately on the content-targeted ads (something Google's main competitor, Overture, allows) or even create separate ad copy for content targeting. Although this smart pricing stops short of those demands, it does use a formula to adjust click prices based on their expected value to advertisers. This expected value is based on information Google may have about the probabilities that certain types of pages (say, a page containing reviews of digital cameras, as opposed to a feature-length article about the history of photography) have of converting to a sale for the advertiser. Google says it uses "all possible pieces of information" to determine the expected value.

The bottom line is, content targeting is a different animal from search targeting. If you're unsure, opt out of it for the time being by leaving the Content Network option unchecked at the campaign level. As you become more experienced, you may decide to try experimenting with it, since it can significantly expand the reach of your existing campaign. It's certainly far easier than negotiating ad buys with individual websites or traditional ad brokers.

Country and Language

Many of you will be focusing most of your efforts on the original and largest AdWords market, the United States, in English exclusively. Unfortunately, running campaigns to attract viewers who are using Google set to display other languages is not an automated process. For each language, you would have to run a separate campaign, choose different keywords, and write the separate ads.

By and large, you'll find that displaying ads to all countries is a money-losing proposition. Your mileage may vary, but not all English-speaking markets are equally responsive from an economic standpoint. More importantly, of course, your company might only ship its products or perform its services in the United States, or the United States and Canada. Unless you're prepared to do business in other countries and you know your product is marketable in them, you might want to take a cautious approach and go with the United States only, or United States plus Canada. For those who want to branch out a bit further, a typical approach seems to be to add the UK (one of the largest AdWords markets), and perhaps Australia and New Zealand, to the mix.

For business-to-business and professionals as well as midsized to large companies (especially those with a strong international base), it may make sense to run ads in English in a variety of target countries in the hopes of influencing decision makers in those markets. As a general rule, though, such efforts can be a waste of money, and my instinct (honed by client anecdotes from the past) is to be cautious.

Billing

Google's billing method is to bill you only after you generate a set dollar amount of clicks. This billing increment might escalate from $50 to a recurring charge of $500 or more depending on your spending pattern. Customers can be billed in a wide variety of currencies, but you can't change the currency you're billed in after you establish an account. If you decide to change currencies, you'll have to start a new account in the currency of your choice. Therefore, set up your billing preferences with care. Depending on the size of your account and your account history, you may be able to apply for credit terms. Currently $7,500 per month over at least three months is the standard for allowing credit, although Google's finance department may relax that standard at its discretion. Since policies change from time to time, you should check the Google FAQs for the most current information.

Make sure you keep your billing information up-to-date to avoid problems. For example, if your credit card is declined (account closed, expired, and so on), your AdWords account will be suspended. Google will send an email to the primary contact, but you will still lose a certain amount of exposure until you can remedy the situation. Google is working to provide more flexible payment options in the future.

Key Metrics and Terminology

Since your success will be measured based on key metrics generated in the course of the AdWords campaign, I'll review some of the Google terminology along with how certain statistics are calculated. You'll notice that some of these stats are best interpreted in terms of averages or aggregate totals. For example, your ad's position on the page might fluctuate during the day depending on what your competitors do, whether you've changed your bids, how relevant your ad is, and so on. So at the end of the day you'll be able to look at the stats for that day and see your *average* ad position—something like 2.4 or 5.1. Recall that this is not a typical media buy, but rather a dynamic environment, so the stats can look a little unusual to the new user, but most get up to speed quickly.

Impressions, Clicks, and Clickthrough Rate

If you're advertising on popular keywords, you should notice early on that your campaign generates a high number of impressions each day, possibly in the hundred thousands or more. Don't get too excited by those numbers. Remember, the number of people who see your ad is not what counts, but how many are motivated to take action when they see it. The majority of people who see your ad are probably not your customers and probably never will be. In some ways it's a brutal numbers game, but fortunately, it can be a consistent numbers game that yields an unusually devoted customer base when all is said and done. An *impression* is counted whenever your ad is shown, regardless of whether a search or a content page serves it up to a user. Although you aren't billed for impressions, they are part of the calculation of clickthrough rate (CTR). When a user clicks on your ad and comes to your site, that's a *click*. You will pay no more for that click than your maximum bid on that ad group or on that specific keyword.

As you saw in the example earlier, your clickthrough rate is determined by a simple formula:

CTR = clicks/impressions

Therefore, if your ad receives eight clicks after 100 impressions, your clickthrough rate is 8% (8/100).

Note that some statistics programs may interpret the measurement of a click differently. Whereas the company charging you for the click (for example, Google) might feel they've earned the right to charge the advertiser as soon as the user has seen the landing page beginning to load, your stats program might not count it unless the whole page loads. If a user leaves very quickly, then, that user might not be counted at your end. It's not uncommon to see discrepancies of 5% to 10% in the number of clicks counted by Google and those counted by your analytics package. And different analytics services will show discrepancies among themselves, as well. Also, Google doesn't charge you for every click, and clicks that aren't charged may not be counted in the AdWords stats. Their antifraud technology looks for duplicates and other anomalous click patterns in an attempt to charge you only for bona fide clicks. Your web analytics package, on the other hand, will count most of these as clicks.

Cost per Click, Maximum Bid, Bid Discounter, Total Cost

As you've no doubt already figured out, each time someone clicks your ad, you pay. Your *cost per click (CPC)* is calculated on individual clicks in real time, and when those costs are added up, that's the total amount you'll pay Google.

As you interpret your data, you'll typically be looking at *average* CPCs in relation to various parameters: the average CPC on a particular phrase, the average CPC for a particular ad group or ad within that ad group, the average CPC on a campaign, and so on. You might pay the *minimum* CPC of .05 on any given click, or you could pay several dollars. This depends totally on your bidding strategy and the market competition for any given word or phrase.

Don't ask what a normal CPC is, because there is no such thing. Yahoo and Google have become increasingly cautious about providing such information, even in their quarterly and annual SEC filings. Some time ago, shortly before being acquired by Yahoo, Overture was reporting averages in the 35–40 cents range, but this number is outdated and in any case means little given the wide range of business models that support different bid levels.

Fathom Online, a pay-per-click consulting firm, has begun publishing a keyword price index (KPI) that looks at the average price for a click in a variety of hot sectors. The methodology used to produce this study isn't entirely clear. But to provide you with some examples, in their December 2004 study Fathom claimed that the average cost for a click in consumer retail was 58 cents; travel and hospitality, 97 cents; automotive, $1.41; investing, $1.76; mortgage, $4.79.

They also show that click prices continue to rise, but not as quickly as in the past couple of years. My clients' average CPCs across whole campaigns range from 6 cents to $6. I've worked on campaigns that include the odd click in the $12–$14 range, but that is rare. Google's maximum bid per click is $100, in case you're curious. When you work on your own account, you'll see that some keywords are much more expensive than others. If the average price in your sector seems too high at first, you can beat the game by playing it better than your competitors.

The best explanation of variations in click pricing is that since this is a competitive auction, some keywords are more valuable in the marketplace than others. Clearly, **colocation hosting** and **insurance broker**, for example, are commercial words that are subject to hot competition. Less commercially relevant keywords like **arboretum** don't seem to have as much commercial value, although certainly a local museum or public facility such as an arboretum could do worse than to advertise on this term if they're looking for local paying visitors, tourists, or even donors. For now, few advertisers show up on words like **arboretum**.

Some words, like **cure**, are difficult to generate enough user interest on because they're too ambiguous, even though they might have huge commercial potential; so the ad space next to searches involving those words lies dormant, or as some in the online advertising industry would say, "unmonetized." By contrast with **cure**, a similar phrase, **the cure**, attracts the odd advertiser because it's the name of a popular 1990s band, and **cure for cancer** attracts several advertisers.

Sometimes, specific phrases cost more than general ones because advertisers have decided (sometimes using their sales data) that the person typing **colocation hosting seattle** is usually a better customer than the person simply typing **hosting seattle** or **colocation hosting**, so they bid more on the more specific term. More obviously, **buy lobster online** or **lobster delivery** will attract a higher bid than simply **lobster** or **lobster recipes**. Phrases with which the user is signaling an intention to make a purchase are frequently referred to as *buy-words*. Buy-words might be worth five to ten times as much as a generic word unadorned with clear commercial intent.

Like keyword searches themselves, click pricing is very *granular*, a term which is often used by search marketers to convey a sense of getting into the nitty-gritty. Search engine users can be considered granular because they sometimes type very specific queries. When LookSmart was a new, educationally oriented directory with many subcategories, they boasted of the granularity of the information they provided. See Figure 4-10 for a depiction of that old LookSmart directory, drilled down to display several subcategories. You'll do better if you understand what it means to "get granular" with your AdWords account.

AdWords advertisers need to be granular, too. Some go to great lengths to bid separately on every keyword and to set up their campaigns carefully in a granular, orderly fashion much like that old LookSmart directory. They treat different customers and different keywords like they're grains of sand.

The point is that you needn't be discouraged even if you're in an industry where clicks appear to be expensive, because prices vary a lot even within your own list of keywords, and you can always discover cheaper ones. If you plan to do a lot of keyword research in the hopes of uncovering words that other advertisers have missed, you'll discover a rewarding fact of life: the less-traveled keyword inventory is also less expensive. So when it comes to keywords, the idea is eventually to "go broad" to develop a larger list of keywords and phrases to advertise on. This will enable you to mix a lot of those 5-, 10-, and 20-cent clicks into the average. By doing this,

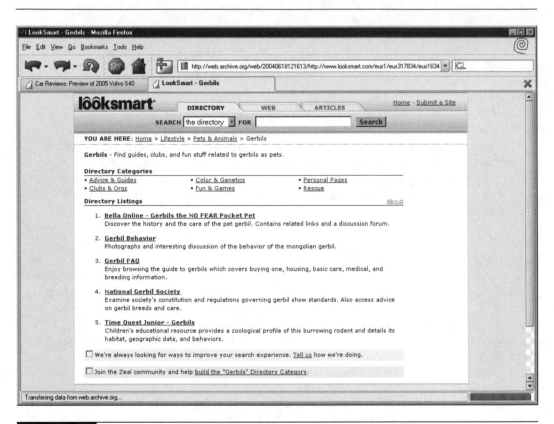

FIGURE 4-10 **FIGURE 4-10**   LookSmart was a granular directory. That's the nature of search: it gets very specific.

in no time an average CPC of $3.00 can be whittled down to, say, $1.80, even assuming that you're shooting for a comparable degree of targeting on the whole. Less expensive traffic isn't better in and of itself, of course; the goal is to find less expensive keywords that provide a solid return on that investment.

Be aware that Google, like several of its competitors, uses a *bid discounter* so you never pay more than you have to for a click. Let's say you're in ad position 2 with a bid of 0.95 and the advertiser in position 3 is bidding 0.90. If a user clicks on your ad, you only pay 0.91, one penny more than the next advertiser's *maximum bid*. Here's the best part, though. What if that third-position advertiser decides to shut down the account and the fourth-position advertiser only bids 0.15? Without the discounter, you'd have to monitor your account constantly or use third-party software to "close the gap" so you didn't pay the 95 cents of your bid. With AdWords, you will simply pay 0.16. That's why your average *actual* CPC will typically be significantly lower than the amount of your maximum bid. That's also why the steady, persistent advertiser may pay less than expected to stay listed all the time.

When all of your click charges are added up at the end of a given day, week, or month, that's your *total cost*. Total cost figures taken in conjunction with your sales data (or other post-click data) will be used in measuring return on investment and other metrics such as cost per action, cost per lead, cost per order, and so on. Using your total cost in conjunction with the number of impressions of your ad served over a given time period, you could even measure your CPM (cost per thousand impressions) to compare how your AdWords campaign is priced in the "old math" (how banners were typically priced in the past).

Unless you know how much money you're making from the campaign, there really is no good way of determining what counts as a high or low CPM or CPC. It's those cost-per-acquisition (CPA) and ROI numbers you'll be focusing on.

The Campaign Summary view shown in Figure 4-11 will quickly become familiar to you. It provides a bird's-eye view of the key aggregate stats for an AdWords account, including average ad position, total cost, average costs per click, and so on, all broken down by campaign. You can get much more specific information than that, by navigating to different screens that show ad group performance broken down by keyword, by ad, and so forth.

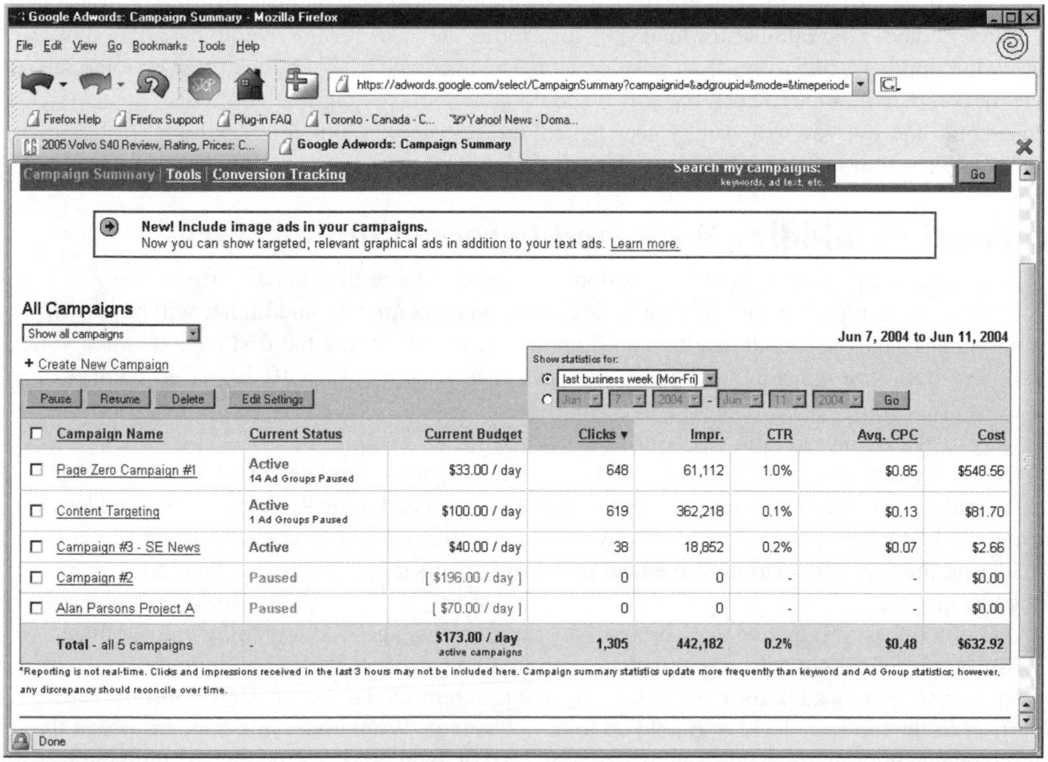

FIGURE 4-11 Aggregate account data—most advertisers will be paying close attention to total cost.

Be sure to adjust the date range of the stats to display the information that will be most helpful to you. You can choose the exact dates or terms such as Today, Yesterday, Past 7 Days, Last Week (Mon–Fri), This Month, Last Month, or All Time in the drop-down box. Often, the numbers for a single day (especially Today, because stats reporting may be delayed by up to two hours) aren't as helpful as the stats for Yesterday or Past 7 Days. Also, don't let your All Time stats be your sole gauge of performance. What your account has done in the past week or month probably tells you more than the all-time performance, particularly in cases where the first couple of months of experimentation were costly. One of the most common mistakes new advertisers make is to look at just one date range (particularly, the All Time stats). When I'm trying to come up to speed on an account's performance I might look at the Past 7 Days statistics to see what the account has done for me lately as compared with the same week in a prior month. Or I might compare entire single months six months apart, or look at trends month to month for several months in a row. This would be an informal means of quickly assessing account performance. I'd rather assess trends that include recent data rather than just looking at averages for the life of an account. (For more formal-looking reporting, you'll probably need to use custom features in third-party web analytics software, or at least download custom reports from the reporting area of the AdWords interface.)

For many advertisers, the number they'll be looking at most closely every week, and some, nearly every day, is the number for total cost, as it forms the basis for the overall calculation of ROI. Other numbers, like average ad position and even average costs per click, may be relatively trivial in comparison to total cost. By now it should go without saying that you'll also be heavily focused on CTR, but you will usually need to drill down further to look at breakdowns of CTR by keyword to see how the account is truly performing.

Ad Position, Bidding Wars, and Reverse Bidding Wars

On Google Search pages there are ten positions to a page. If more than ten advertisers are bidding on a particular keyword or phrase, ads falling into position 11 and higher will be shown on subsequent pages of search results. You'll know you're not making the first page if, when you check your stats, you see your ad page reported as a number higher than 10. Experience tells us that most users don't get beyond the first page of search results. Therefore, you're not going to get many clicks if your ad falls into a position beyond 10.

While ad position is clearly important, it is not the only factor you need to consider. One of the misconceptions many new advertisers fall prey to is the need to be #1. While it is considered by many to be the optimum position, it is by no means a guarantee of success, especially considering the financial extremes to which many advertisers go to ensure that their ad appears in the top spot.

One of the least productive exercises an advertiser can engage in is a bidding war for that #1 position. A typical scenario might include a group of advertisers content with modest bids on a given phrase. A new advertiser enters the fray and is determined to be #1. Unfortunately, the advertiser in the top spot decides to hold on to his advantage. What invariably happens is that the two bid one another up to an outrageously high bid, 10 or even 20 times the modest high bid of the remaining bidders.

The result is that the two competitors spend an unnecessarily inflated amount for the advantage of appearing in the top slot. Since many advertisers claim to get better results with lower ad positions, this is at best a crapshoot. Eventually one of the high bidders will relent and settle for second place, which costs only a fraction of the price that the top slot commands due to the bidding war.

When cooler heads prevail and both top competitors begin to realize the cost savings of settling for second place, a new bidding war may take place, only this time for second place. The reverse bidding war continues until the top bids approach the former modest bid range; however, they generally remain somewhat higher than they were before the original bidding war started.

Usually, Google is the real winner in bidding wars. So, my advice is to stay out of them and let the others battle it out while you keep your eye on the primary issue—making money! When I set up accounts for advertisers, I shoot for a slot somewhere between ad positions 2 and 5. Bidding strategy is an important topic that I'll address in more detail later in the book.

Conversion Rates

Conversion rates, which can be measured in a number of different ways, are a pivotal measure of a campaign's success. Let's start with a basic definition and the typical method of measuring conversion rates. The *conversion rate* is the percentage of clicks that result in either a sale or some other direct action that the ad has been created to induce. If your ad is selling a product, your conversion rate formula is as follows:

Conversion rate = number of sales/total clicks

Therefore, if you make three sales on 200 paid clicks one day, your conversion rate on those clicks is 1.5%. To ensure that your conversion rates are accurate, you need to be able to verify that those sales resulted from your AdWords ad rather than a customer who just happened to stumble onto your site. You can use tracking URLs or third-party tracking software to identify those sales generated by your Google ad.

Of course, sales aren't the only type of action that can provide a meaningful conversion. Some advertisers measure application forms, new subscribers to a free newsletter, and so on.

As with other metrics, there are no hard-and-fast benchmark conversion rates for a given industry. In reality, conversion rates are often quite low. I see 1% or less more often than I see 5% or more. The best advice I can give you is to keep your conversion rate goals subservient to your long-range goals. Don't set a conversion rate target and follow it blindly.

You want your own conversion rates to improve, to be sure, and you certainly won't make money if nothing's converting. However, aggregate conversion percentages can be misleading if they don't take into account the cost of the traffic.

Return on Investment (ROI)

ROI, while simple to calculate—total revenues divided by total cost—is not a short-term measurement. By that I mean you can't calculate it on a daily basis and worry (or celebrate) based on the numbers. Give your ad(s) a chance to perform before you start to panic. Smart marketers know that you need to spend on marketing up front to see benefits down the road. They also know that repeat business is important and that acquiring a new customer is worth a certain amount, no matter how little that customer spends at first.

As for the formula, total cost is the total cost of your AdWords campaign over any given time period. Total revenues is the total dollar amount of the sales that can be attributed directly to your AdWords campaign during the same period or some reasonable period of time after the initial click. As you may have deduced, this isn't an exact science.

For example, if you spend $300 over three weeks on AdWords to attract new subscribers to an information service, and by week three, you've converted two of the free-trial subscribers to paying status for total revenue of $150, your ROI thus far would be 50%. That technically means you're losing money, but as I mentioned, you might be on the right track if you're patient. Some of the free-trial customers generated in the initial three weeks might convert to paying subscribers next month, bringing the total revenues attributable to that first $300 worth of clicks to $375. Thus the ROI for the initial period would have reached 125%—in other words, a positive ROI. Your campaign would already be in the black. And that wouldn't even be factoring in the lifetime value of each customer—the possibility of advertising revenues, consulting income, sales of related products to the subscriber base, or next year's subscription.

This is the way in which smart businesses make the most of the clicks they're paying for. Those who rely heavily on initial sales to turn a profit, and who have a poor capacity for repeat sales, will find it more difficult to afford AdWords as the average cost per click rises.

Some campaigns really do pay for themselves as they go—revenues always exceed click costs on any given day. Some have referred to this as a "self-funding campaign." A positive ROI from the get-go means you're "playing with the house's money" and may give you incentive to aggressively search for ways to widen the distribution of your ads.

Chapter 5

Setting Up Ad Groups

For various reasons, some new AdWords advertisers launch themselves into the setup phase using methods that I personally wouldn't recommend. To put it bluntly, they're doing it wrong!

There seem to be a few common patterns here. Most revolve around a couple of tendencies: first, the desire to create an enormous list of keywords at the beginning rather than a smaller "beginner set" of keywords that fit logically into groups; and second, an interrelated belief that with the right amount of effort in the planning (prelaunch) phase, the campaign can explode out of the starting gate, generating huge numbers of customers right away. Small problem with the "explode out of the gate" mentality: Google has 280,000 advertisers. Lots of them already exploded out of the starting gate, and you'll be competing with them. You'll need to ease into this process at first and then build on your early discoveries. This process rewards smart "guerrilla" advertisers who can learn from feedback, not just those with a bigger marketing bazooka.

Where these notions come from I don't always know, but I can speculate. Some advertisers are still thinking in terms of a media-buy model (as mentioned in Chapter 3). I'll be honest—in some cases, that media-buy analogy really does work. But it's not always appropriate at the start, when you're building the little machine (your AdWords account) that will do the "buying" for you intelligently on a daily basis. At the extreme end of the media splash mentality is the Really Big Super Bowl Ad. Wrong analogy, so get that notion out of your head. It doesn't need to be exciting or dramatic. Stay the course and you'll build something relatively permanent for the long haul.

There are some historical reasons why many pay-per-click advertisers seem bent on doing things in a certain way (the way that I consider to be "wrong" for AdWords). Advertisers who had experience with Overture became accustomed to the idea of large numbers of keyphrases. One reason for this was that Overture didn't offer broad matching options in the past; so unless your keyword or phrase matched the user's query exactly, you didn't show up.

There is nothing strictly *wrong* with using every possible word combination of hundreds of words, culminating in a file of five thousand or more phrases. But the reason for doing it was initially because you couldn't capture enough search volume without wild-card-type matching options. Those who overdo it on the keyword generation front today should keep in mind that they're probably making too much work for themselves and for anyone else who might be working on the account and interpreting the results.

Another driver of keyword overkill today seems to be vendors of the latest keyword generation tools. One problem is that these tools are typically not that good; the second is that this push-button approach doesn't help you if others are mindlessly pushing the same buttons.

Another historical reason for large keyword files was that Overture's early interface was a first-generation utility with limitations in the usability department. The cumbersome process of dumping large files of keywords into the account without any really convenient or intuitive way of then managing or editing them seemed worth it to early Overture advertisers who felt like they were getting in on the ground floor of something exciting. It certainly delighted the makers of third-party account management software. I never much cared for it. When Google AdWords came along, it gave advertisers better tools for keeping everything straight—most of all, an intuitive way of grouping keywords. In any case, the result of all that history is that an orthodoxy sprang up whereby marketers felt they could impress one another (and all too often, me) by sending each other gigantic Excel files of keywords.

Let's take some time to explore *ad groups*, then, which I consider to be the core of Google AdWords.

Why Grouping Keywords Makes So Much Sense

When my colleagues and I use software to track what users are doing after they click through to a client's website, we don't overanalyze. We often prefer to track no finer than the "ad group and specific ads within those groups" level, because, if the groups are designed logically, tracking the results by group actually provides highly actionable and meaningful data. Sometimes we track everything right down to the return on investment on individual keywords and phrases, but this is not always necessary or even beneficial. This view is in sharp contrast to what most "analysis junkies" will tell you, but I'm confident that the stripped-down approach to analysis is most appropriate to the scale of most advertisers' tasks. There is nothing more frustrating than being bogged down in data and lengthy preparatory planning processes for, say, a small medical supplies company with annual sales in the $2 million range. This isn't NASA; you're just selling stuff. More to the point: the benefit of a streamlined approach to tracking becomes apparent at the "let's make sense of this" phase—in my case, it might be an interim or final report for a client suggesting how to proceed based on market feedback. Even a small amount of data often require a lot of commentary and timely responses.

Think about the analogy of a football playbook with 500 or 1,000 plays in it, grouped according to different types and situations. The quarterback and the coaching staff need to have these mastered and memorized so they can deploy them correctly at the right times. Even these are difficult to digest for many quarterbacks—hence the tiny crib notes you see written on many quarterbacks' wrist guards. With the play clock ticking, it wouldn't help that quarterback at all to receive a giant Excel file of new plays, or an even larger file of past and probable outcomes for 10,000 other plays. Not only must coach and quarterback choose among a relatively small universe of courses of action in calling the next play, but once the quarterback steps up to the line of scrimmage, he must have the ability to call an "audible" (a new play based on the defensive formation he sees). The number of possible audibles is typically tiny—there might only be two or three alternative plays to choose from. I don't think the analogy is so far-fetched. Most businesses will do better with a smart coach and a smart quarterback calling plays based on a manageable universe of data. A supercomputer won't help.

Ad groups give us that manageability. I tend to believe that each *group* of keywords expresses an idea of something a user is searching for. That might be a big idea or a very narrowly conceived idea. The idea could require only one keyphrase to express (let's say the exact match for **goat cheese**), or it could require 250 phrases covering a long list of low-volume but highly targeted industry jargon words. So, when someone asks me how many keywords is a lot, I usually avoid that question because I believe campaigns need to be thought of in terms of ad groups. I sometimes think in terms of this analogy: putting just a few of the most obvious keywords in a few groups is OK at first, because you'll find the process of expanding to more words within those groups quite natural. They'll almost multiply like bacteria (icky, but that's kind of how it works). Actually, you'll be using your own brain and keyword suggestion tools, but the basic idea is that ad groups often start off small and grow larger over time.

This can be an intuitive process, because you'll also give names to those groups within your account; so you'll be able to glance at them quickly and say something like, "I see the 'Last Minute Travel' group is generating a higher than usual number of clicks today," or, "The 'San Jose Sharks apparel' group is generating a low CTR lately; better figure out why." For my money, that's better than poring over huge files of keyword-specific data, because the intuitiveness of groups with sensible names allows you to read and react steadily to changing conditions. If you structure your data analysis task so that it's more daunting than that, you might find yourself putting it off for weeks and months, and that'll cost you.

Think of this as a kind of sorting or filing. The database-driven nature of the AdWords application is actually not too far different from the idea of a directory, with multiple levels in a logical progression:

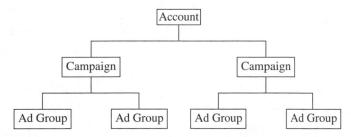

As librarians and search technology experts sometimes say, categorized directories (think of Yahoo or the Open Directory, or anything with categories and subcategories) possess an *ontology*. In other words, a professional categorization team needs to create a tree that breaks the world down into different levels of meaning. Your account won't be that comprehensive, but I hope the analogy helps you to understand that your job in creating a little "meaning tree" for your account will help you to do a better job of sorting out search users who see your ad after they've expressed meanings of their own by typing a query into Google Search. This structure will also make the campaign easier to make sense of down the road.

Ad groups express a thing (the "soup bowl group," for example) or an idea ("agricultural pesticides litigation" and 40 other ways to say that). Your advertising copy (or multiple ads) are *tied to* the keywords in that group. Different groups, different ads. Sure, you could use the same ad all the time, but it's best to write different ones, as I'll show later. Basically, whatever ad (or ads) you enter for, say, Ad Group #3 (or the "Tile Flooring Group"), will show up whenever a user's query matches one of the phrases in that group, assuming your campaign is active. That ad won't show up for your other ad groups unless you specifically create the same ad in those groups, as well. The AdWords interface allows you to control exactly which searchers are seeing which ads.

Once you've got a few phrases that all express something related to an idea or thing, you're on your way with your first ad group. It should be easy to set up several groups in no time as long as you aren't fussing with huge keyword lists. You can edit everything later as much as you like.

Not only will you write separate ads tailored for each group, you'll notice that you'll be bidding separately on each group. All the words and phrases in an ad group are tied to a global maximum bid. That makes it convenient to change the bid for the whole group, although there is also an optional feature called *powerposting* that allows you to set individual bids on keywords or phrases (more about that in Chapter 6).

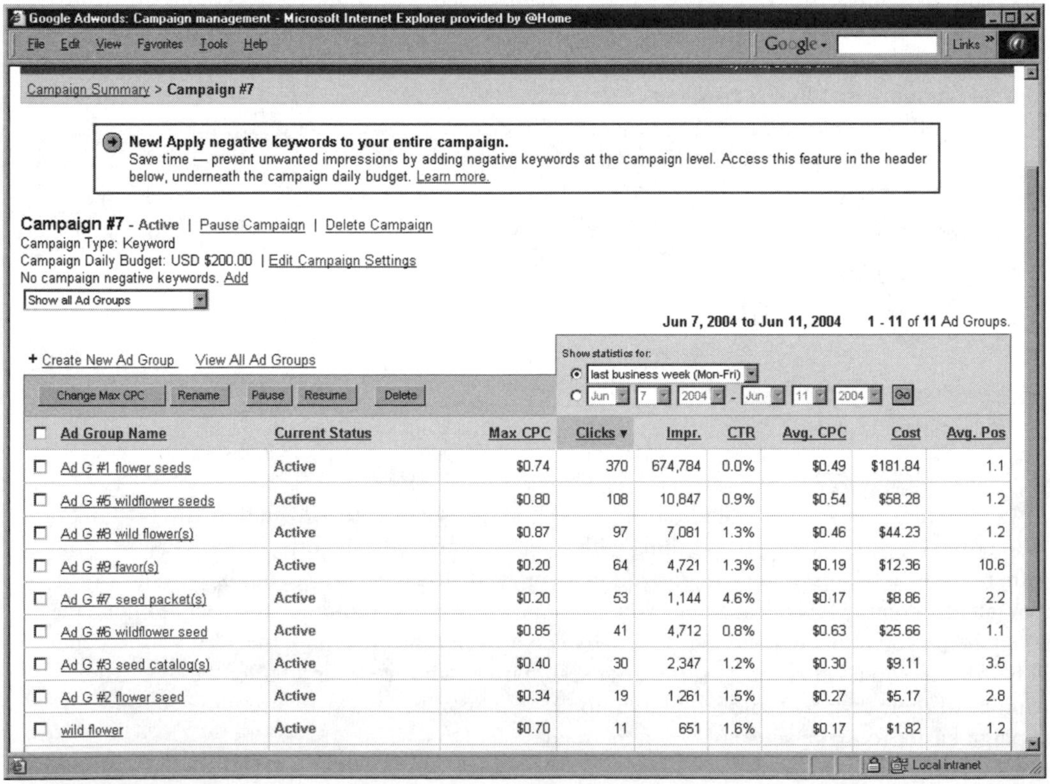

Ad Group Name	Current Status	Max CPC	Clicks ▼	Impr.	CTR	Avg. CPC	Cost	Avg. Pos
☐ Ad G #1 flower seeds	Active	$0.74	370	674,784	0.0%	$0.49	$181.84	1.1
☐ Ad G #5 wildflower seeds	Active	$0.80	108	10,847	0.9%	$0.54	$58.28	1.2
☐ Ad G #8 wild flower(s)	Active	$0.87	97	7,081	1.3%	$0.46	$44.23	1.2
☐ Ad G #9 favor(s)	Active	$0.20	64	4,721	1.3%	$0.19	$12.36	10.6
☐ Ad G #7 seed packet(s)	Active	$0.20	53	1,144	4.6%	$0.17	$8.86	2.2
☐ Ad G #6 wildflower seed	Active	$0.85	41	4,712	0.8%	$0.63	$25.66	1.1
☐ Ad G #3 seed catalog(s)	Active	$0.40	30	2,347	1.2%	$0.30	$9.11	3.5
☐ Ad G #2 flower seed	Active	$0.34	19	1,261	1.5%	$0.27	$5.17	2.8
☐ wild flower	Active	$0.70	11	651	1.6%	$0.17	$1.82	1.2

FIGURE 5-1   A list of various ad groups within this advertiser's "Campaign #7."

This advice, then, ties into advice given later in the book about how to write winning ad copy. There should be less mystique about how to write successful ads once you understand that your ads' performance will improve almost automatically by dint of the fact that you've written a variety of tailored ads that closely match or reflect the ideas or exact phrases in each ad group. The question won't be only "which ad works the best" across the board, but also, in many cases, "which ads work the best *with which groups of keywords*."

You'll want multiple ad groups for two key reasons, then. First, ad groups offer the convenience of tying your maximum bid (the highest you're willing to pay for a click) to all the keyphrases in a group, to save you the trouble of bidding individually on every keyword. Tweaking hundreds or thousands of individual bids is either impossibly cumbersome or requires third-party software, which can be expensive, time consuming, and unsuited to your particular needs. Ad groups solve this problem. Most of us use a mix of keyword-specific bidding and groupwide bidding. Figures 5-1 and 5-2 show two key views inside the Google AdWords interface: the summary view within a campaign showing a list of ad groups and a fairly typical example of an ad group.

| FIGURE 5-2 | A summary of AdWords campaign data for a week in the life of "Ad Group #5 Wildflower Seeds." |

The ad group shown in Figure 5-2 has a maximum bid of 80 cents that applies to all the phrases in that group, and as you can see, the 2 phrases in the group resemble one another. (Of course, 2 is an unusually small number of phrases to put in a group. It could just as easily be 5, 20, or 50, but this suffices for illustration purposes.) A single ad applies to this group of phrases, although this advertiser had previously tested multiple ads with this group to see which one performed the best. He has also made his ad timely, telling readers that the site contains specific information about planting tips for the month of June (not a common month in which to plant), which likely conveys freshness and expertise. This may be part of the explanation for the robust 10% clickthrough rate on this ad.

In this reporting summary, various performance data, including CTR, are broken down by keyphrase. Note that this advertiser is using the classic approach to bidding, using the global bid for the group so that all of these keywords have the same maximum bid. Many advertisers now make finer adjustments, adding specific bids to keywords within groups, which is often necessary to adjust bids to market demand. Still, there is a certain tidiness to the classic way of doing it.

A second, and not unimportant, reason that organizing around ad groups is helpful is to ensure that each group of keyphrases linked to any given idea is linked to an ad (or multiple ads) that closely targets users searching for whatever that idea or thing might be. The closeness of the match to users' interests, and those users' feelings of being catered to (basically, extreme relevancy in search), seems to improve campaign performance. If Google is giving us the ability to micro-target users with an offer that might really appeal to them based on what they're typing into the search engine, should we run a generic campaign that acts more like the traditional run-of-site banner ads? I don't think so. Groups remind you to target your ads more tightly to the user's query.

As I'll explain in more detail in Chapter 7, within an ad group you can run multiple ads at the same time. (Some call this "split-testing.") So even within a tightly focused area, you can still experiment with different ways of catching searchers' attention to find out what works best, and the independent impact of variations in ad title and ad copy will be measured accurately.

When called upon to improve my clients' campaign performance, I often proceed by reorganizing how the keywords are grouped. I often find that several somewhat similar words have been dumped into one large ad group. This might work fine, but in a competitive marketplace, you'll do even better if you break those up into their own groups. Even if the words are *somewhat* similar, they're not similar enough. And by breaking them out, your ad titles will be rewritten to be even more targeted to the user's query. That almost always improves user response (CTR), even if only slightly.

Let's say you can use six different keywords that mean something more or less the same as *fabric*, and you want to build commerce-friendly phrases around each (*cloth, pattern, material,* and so on). Make sure you use six different ad groups, each one revolving around a different way of saying *fabric*, and then build related phrases onto each. It also helps if your ad title contains that keyword. Your clickthrough rates are usually higher if there is an exact match between a word in your title and the phrase the user has typed in; even very close synonyms don't seem to do as well.

You'll probably want to write ad titles that are different for each group, for example:

Fabric for Less
Wholesale Cloth
Looking for Patterns?
Buy Unusual Material

Using a single ad title for all of the diverse keywords in the campaign usually lowers performance (CTR), and this can cost you money. The same goes for the written copy that goes with the title. It should be tailored as much as possible to the keywords in a logically sensible ad group.

Depending on your objectives, each of these ads might actually take the user to a different part of your website, or a different *landing page* (the target URL for the ad). When deciding on the target URL to enter with each ad, consider the user experience. Is the searcher's experience going to be intuitive and seamless? Does the "buy unusual material" ad take her to an appropriate page on your site, or just the home page? If you want, you can even test both to see which performs better. As a rule of thumb, this process is always about improving your targeting. Secondarily, it's a matter of usability and sensible navigation. Think carefully about targeting at each step of the process. Sales conversion rates generally go up when users get the exact information they were looking for right away rather than having to hunt for it.

Currently on Google.com, on advertising as well as regular search results, the search engine user's search words are being highlighted in bold, so this may also lead to higher CTRs (bold text is eye-grabbing) if you focus on making sure your ad titles and copy contain relevant keyphrases.

As I've discovered, advertisers use campaigns and groups in many different ways. Some advertisers have different campaigns for every product being sold—one small business I worked with was (unnecessarily) running 25 different campaigns. Google has worked hard to overhaul the architecture of their interface so that you can play around and use a large number of groups in one campaign if you like without huge problems with page load times. The bottom line is this: be granular in your campaigns. Break things up into logical groups and write ads that match closely to the keywords in each group. This is a fair amount of work at first, but once it's built, it becomes a superior machine for identifying and attracting targeted customers, and requires less maintenance than a lazily constructed campaign.

As you add keywords to groups over time, you might find your groups becoming too cluttered once more. Some phrases might merit being "hived off" and put in groups of their own. At that point, you may want to consider starting new groups revolving around such phrases, especially if you've discovered new ones that generate high volumes of clicks—new concepts or terms that might be worth building on in their own right.

Organize, Organize, Organize

A fastidiously organized account leads to faster AdWords success and prevents headaches later. Let's review four reasons for being careful about how you organize your campaigns, groups, keywords, and ads. The kind of organization I'm referring to here is basically what we discussed in the previous section: the idea of carefully piecing together a meaning tree within your account, with sensible labels on everything. Pretend you're the corporate librarian and assume that your job is to set things up so that the average person could understand where to find everything.

Multiple Persons Managing the Account

At the beginning, it might be just you managing the account, but that's rarely the case over the long haul. In many companies, a succession of people will be involved at one point or another. Even if it's just you, you'll find that things go much more easily if you organize carefully in the beginning. The "later-on you" might have real trouble figuring out where the "old you" put various keywords, or why certain bidding strategies were employed. Haste makes waste.

Post-Click Tracking

Depending on your goals, you will track clicks "post-click" to determine how well different ad groups and ads performed. Analytics can be a breeze when you've set up ad groups based on a logical structure of meaning, whether it be product line or different variations of similar words. What is going to be happening later is that you're going to discover that ad group #7 performed better than ad groups #1 through #6. But that discovery will be meaningless and random if you simply entered a pile of disparate phrases into various ad groups. If you set things up carefully, strong performance in a particular ad group is easy to interpret, and you can build on that knowledge.

Typically, then, you will set up tracking URLs to represent each ad group, or even every ad within every ad group. That should contribute to your success, because knowing which ad groups are converting to sales or desired actions can help you determine how much to bid on your keywords, or whether to bid at all. Cutting down on the wasted clicks will enable you to budget more money on keywords that promise a stronger ROI or, assuming that cash flow isn't unlimited, in other facets of your business entirely.

I strongly recommend figuring this out right at the beginning, because the setup of tracking URLs is busywork that can eat up the better part of a day for larger accounts. You don't want to have to do it twice. If you do nothing about tracking at the beginning, with a logical campaign structure, you can, at least, come back later confident that it will be easy to add different tracking URLs to represent each different ad in all of your groups.

Not all tracking solutions require tracking URLs, but don't choose your software on the basis of sheer convenience. Tracking URLs are not hard to enter and don't require any complex math or programming skills, just a numbering system (often one you invent yourself) that will help you keep score later. We'll come back to this.

Bottom-Line Performance (Ads Match Keywords)

Both Overture and Google will tell you this: their data clearly show that CTRs go up when your ad title matches exactly with the keywords typed in by the user. For the time being, there is no disputing this, although I think it's a little too pat. If that were the only secret to good copywriting, everyone would do it, and everyone would have the same ad titles on any given search query. Zzzzz. Taking the general principle to heart is the important thing. The better you organize your ad groups and the keywords in them, the easier it is for you to write a variety of different ads to achieve granularity. In other words, by writing differently worded and differently titled ads for each group, you'll wind up with ad copy that is closer in meaning to the keywords you're targeting. This almost invariably creates a higher CTR across your campaign. And with Google AdWords, there are at least two very good reasons to shoot for higher CTRs, as discussed in Chapter 4. First, you can bid lower to achieve the same ad positions because Google rewards high CTRs with higher ad positions. Second, you'll have fewer of your keywords disabled for falling below the CTR threshold.

By doing everything right from the standpoint of organization and granularity, your campaign will become easier to run and make you more money. This frees up your time to work on other things while your competitors are killing themselves managing their pay-per-click accounts. They might also be goaded into bidding too high, then wind up shutting their accounts down in a panic, because they don't understand one of the big secrets behind your high ad positions: proper campaign structure.

Avoiding the Horrors of Overlap

I'm often asked if you can put the same keywords and phrases into different ad groups or even different campaigns. The answer is yes, but the result isn't exactly as you might expect. If you sell eight different products that are all relevant to the same keywords, guess what, you can't have eight of your ads (or even two of them) showing up on the same page of search results. Google calls this *double serving*, and it's against the AdWords terms of service. As you can imagine, many advertisers would take advantage of this to crowd out competitors with multiple ads, and this goes against what the user is expecting to see in that space—a choice of different vendors. So, in the case of overlap (the same keywords in different ad groups or different campaigns), the AdWords system will choose to show a single ad from your account corresponding to only one of those keywords or phrases. How is that choice made? As with many such questions, Google is evasive on the point, preferring to emphasize the relevancy aspect over any messy talk about simply choosing the one where you've bid the highest. Likely, the ad chosen is the one from the group where that keyword or phrase has the highest ad rank, or the best combination of maximum bid multiplied by CTR.

So why do I speak of "horror"? After all, nothing breaks if you overlap. Your ad is shown. No problem. Usually it isn't a problem. If you happen to get forgetful and create some limited overlap, nothing terrible will happen.

But with significant overlap across different groups and campaigns, an account becomes virtually impossible to comprehend and manage, especially when multiple stakeholders come on the scene. You (or others) will find it difficult to interpret tracking data, to know which ads are going to show up, and to get a handle on how much you are paying for the keywords. If you're caught in an account that already looks like this, pause some campaigns and groups until you've built a cleaner campaign.

A typical example of what can happen with rampant overlap is the advertiser who decides she's paying too much for some of her keywords and wants to lower the bids on them by up to 60%. Her trusty AdWords consultant goes in and lowers those bids significantly, hoping the total daily spend will be slashed from, say, $800 to $400. It seems OK for a few hours, so the consultant takes off for the long weekend and the client thanks him for his help. Lo and behold, like those gag birthday candles that never blow out, the same keywords "pop up" in another campaign and start working to display ads for the same cost as before. The following week, it's discovered that some higher-volume keywords are hiding in no fewer than six campaigns, and they must be ferreted out and deleted. Yikes!

Various bad things happen with too much overlap. Avoid it, and build a clean campaign in which the vast majority of your ad groups have a clear purpose, with keyword lists that do not also appear in other ad groups.

Naming Campaigns and Groups

Just a friendly reminder: giving memorable labels to campaigns and groups is part of the process of staying organized. To go back and name or rename an ad group if you forgot to do it at the beginning, you'll drill down to the campaign level of your AdWords account to see the list of existing groups and click the check boxes next to the groups you'd like to rename. Then, from the gray buttons at the top of that list (Change Max CPC, Rename, Pause, Resume, Delete) click the Rename button.

To rename a campaign, go into Edit Campaign Settings and edit the first field, labeled "1. Basic Information—Campaign Name."

Your naming system should be one that will jog your memory later. It might be based on different product lines, different words (*fabric, material, cloth*), or even different AdWords strategies. I sometimes name groups "experimental," or even more specifically, such as "low cost experiments," "developer jargon," "competitor meta tags," "unconvincing AdWords keyword tool suggestions," after any number of nefarious strategies I might use to generate and test innovative keywords. The naming should dovetail with the structure as a whole—it should remind you to group similar keywords together, whatever *similar* means for you.

Writing Your First Ads

The first advertisements you write might not prove to be your best, but you do have to get them written to get things rolling. The AdWords interface will ask you to enter at least one ad right at the start. Later on, when setting up new ad groups, you'll simply drill down to the ad group level of the AdWords interface and click on Create New Ad.

As the interface will show, you have a very small space to work with: 25 characters for the headline, and 35 characters for each of two lines for the two-line description. The display URL (the web address that users will actually see below your ad) can only be 35 characters. However, the landing URL gives you plenty of leeway. It can be up to 1,024 characters. Some advertisers have very long tracking codes or complicated URLs for their catalog pages, so this helps.

A few tips on format first. For the *display URL* you'll typically just put in your home page URL. The user may be taken (by the landing URL) to a specific page on your website, but the URL displayed in your ad needs to be uncomplicated and, hopefully, should look trustworthy; for example, www.legumes.com. Sometimes I experiment with capital letters where appropriate in two-word URLs; for example, page-zero.com versus Page-Zero.com. I haven't seen any conclusive difference in user response. Google won't allow you to misuse capitals. You can't alternate caps manically just to grab attention (www.GiLoOLy.BiZ), for example. Not that you'd want to make a spectacle of yourself in this way, but you'd be amazed at what some folks dream up.

Choose the landing URL with care. You need to ensure that every ad you write uses a landing URL that gets two key things right: first, it must send users to the corresponding page on your site (this is preferably a targeted page that gets users to the information they need without an extra click); second, it must contain the correct tracking code based on whatever tracking nomenclature you've decided to use. I use a unique tracking code for each ad. We'll return to this in Chapter 10, but an example of a landing URL would be something like this:

http://www.legumes.com/lentils.asp?source=gaw&kw=23b

As for the ad itself: now the challenge begins. You have to squeeze your message into a small space. Some call it a haiku. But it's really no different from traditional classified ads, except that here, you have the ability to test response in real time. Once you've entered that first ad, a maximum bid, and a couple of keywords just to get the account set up and running with your first ad group, you're on your way—well, almost. Google has some fairly extensive editorial policies to contend with.

Editorial Review

No one has ever sent me a Google organization chart, but I've been fortunate enough to talk individually with several dozen Google staffers and executives at various levels of the organization and believe I have a decent feel for the company's internal workings (decent enough to doubt some of the sensationalistic press accounts insinuating internal chaos). Certainly, as with any industry, there is competition for good people. Google is one of the most prestigious companies in the technology world, and many want to work for the company. This works to Google's advantage. Competitors like Overture also have sufficient experience and prestige to attract top-quality editorial (and other) staff.

I point this out because customer service plays an increasingly important role at Google. Editorial staff are at the front lines, attempting to interpret editorial rules that aren't always cut and dried. While they may be fallible and make mistakes, they're smart enough to consider granting exceptions if you make a good case. But often this will be out of the editorial staff's hands. They may consult a "policy specialist" or other members of management in the advertising side of Google; clearly staff cannot and should not be making this up as they go along. If you've broken a rule, they'll have to enforce the policy. That said, I'll give you some tips on how to handle those "editorial disapproval" emails, what's important in the basic editorial style rules, and what Google's documentation doesn't tell you.

Responding to Editorial Disapproval

Inevitably, you'll find yourself receiving "editorial disapproval" messages by email, alerting you to the fact that one of your ads or keywords has been disabled. Don't get upset. Decide for yourself whether it's worth wrangling over. If you make it clear that you're familiar with the reasons behind Google's policies before you make your complaint, this can sometimes work in your favor.

To head off potentially condescending responses from editorial staff who may not fully appreciate your depth of knowledge about your own business and the advertising business in general, make an initial email contact (if you're experiencing problems) to identify yourself fully, possibly with a brief bio explaining your background. Politely explaining small distinctions about your industry or your campaign that staff may have overlooked may be required, too. With so many advertisers to deal with, staff might simply assume that your case isn't worth looking at too carefully, since many editorial disapprovals are fairly routine. You might have to remind them of your brilliance and convince them to squint harder at your correspondence. Unfortunately, this is a fact of life in dealing with customer service people who may be accustomed to receiving a large volume of inquiries.

Disapprovals for violations of minor editorial rules are common. Remember: if some of your ad copy or keywords are disapproved, it is never personal. Unfortunately, the online medium can lead to brittle communications, and there is no more uncomfortable feeling than receiving several warning emails that your advertisement has been "disapproved." Many of us have a deep psychological aversion to disapproval. If you work for a larger company, you'll probably be stunned that someone would nitpick you given your big ad budget. But consistent policies are obviously better for everyone concerned, even though they might be applied or interpreted too rigidly in some cases. So the best advice is to treat a disapproval as a minor setback, and either adjust your ads to make them conform to the rules, or politely appeal.

Why were so many minor editorial rules enacted in the first place? According to Sheryl Sandberg, an early director of the Google AdWords Select program, Google was from the beginning trying to set an industry standard for advertisers. Pressure to do this increased as Google entered negotiations to form a syndication partnership with AOL, a partnership that they won away from their rival, Overture. A standards-based approach was not implemented simply to appease AOL or imaginary consumers, though. It was also intended to protect advertisers from one another. (The concept is one of a level playing field for all participants.) If an advertiser breaks one of the editorial rules, it may be creating an artificially high CTR at the expense of one of its competitors. Google wants to reserve the right to disapprove ads for that reason as well as for reasons of quality control and consumer protection.

Quick Tips

The full list of editorial policies is at https://AdWords.google.com/select/guidelines.html.

Probably the most important idea is mentioned at the top of the guidelines list: "Use clear, direct language and avoid gimmicks." The targeting techniques I urge you to follow in this book in fact make gimmicks unnecessary.

Google does a good job of describing its own rules, so I won't duplicate everything they say; just a few words about them. Quite a few of the guidelines are basic matters of form—almost like the style guides reporters must follow when writing a news story. No repeated or unnecessary punctuation; don't use all capital letters for anything except an acronym; spell words correctly; don't capitalize the first letter of every word in your copy (that's incorrect spelling and looks unprofessional). Some guidelines are designed to prevent you from making misleading claims. Some forms of "come-on" might be disallowed—especially if they're clearly inaccurate. Phony low prices designed to induce clicks might be a waste of your money, so Google might actually be doing you a favor by asking you to reword your ad. Describe clearly what you have to offer without mind games. Save the high-powered sales techniques for your web site. After all, sales conversion rates are even more important than CTR. Accept a slightly lower CTR if you think the resulting traffic will be of higher quality.

Google has a set of policies aimed at affiliate advertisers. (An affiliate would be someone who sends referral traffic to, say, a parent company like eBay, receiving a commission if that traffic results in a purchase.) Some affiliate advertisers send traffic directly to the parent sites from their Google AdWords accounts, hoping to generate a profit on the difference. (This is not easy to do, by the way. The material in this book is not really aimed at affiliates, although it might be indirectly helpful.) As a result of too many affiliates crowding the page of sponsored listings on some queries, Google has enacted a rule that limits the number of advertisers appearing for a given display URL to one (so there won't be four ads for eBay.com on the same page, for example). There are few other policies governing affiliate behavior. Google lets the marketplace take care of itself in this area.

Although the press make much of every new keyword ban that comes along, I see the overall tendency going in the other direction. The rulebook is getting a little bit more flexible. In practice, Google has relaxed some of the rules, such as those disallowing repetition of words in ad text. It's also the case that advertisers are getting more experienced in this medium, and understand its culture better. Users aren't going to keep looking at the ads if they're littered with exclamation points, hype, and opportunistic, dishonest, or inaccurate display URLs, and most advertisers know this.

If you feel you've been the victim of a gray area ruling that goes against you, by all means reply to Google's support emails with a polite request for more information, clarification, and possibly an appeal of the ad disapproval.

NOTE   *Depending on your geographic location, your reply will be to AdWords-support@google .com, or if in the UK, AdWords-uk@google.com. Or just reply directly to the editorial messages you receive by email.*

My final word on this subject: don't spend your life swimming against the current or tilting at windmills. The efforts of advocates like myself and the many complaints of individual advertisers over the past two years have led to certain policies being reconsidered, to the extent that you'll probably be wasting energy getting into petty fights with the editorial staff. If your campaign's success depends on bending or breaking the editorial rules, you aren't in very good shape in the first place. Make your views known, to be sure; then, get back to work!

Time Lags and Special Rules

Some foibles in Google's editorial process are never explained in any documentation. There are certain background considerations that need to be kept in mind. In particular, you may find yourself tripped up by delays in getting ads running for new accounts, or new ads within an existing account, or even in unpausing an account that has been dormant for some time.

Google vs. Search Network Partners

A few of the odd editorial delays I encountered in the early days of the AdWords program were attributed by Google management to differential editorial standards at network partners such as AOL. For all I know, this continues to be the case.

Automated vs. Human Review

Many people assumed (based on how AdWords was marketed in the early days) that ads get "up and running right away." Indeed, many advertisers found it exhilarating that they could see their ads running nearly immediately and that editorial review mainly consisted of automated tests to see if ads broke any rules, followed by a *post facto* checkup by a live editor as Google's software deemed necessary.

Not so fast, though. While the process has often worked basically like this, Google has now deviated significantly from it, especially on popular keywords with many established advertisers. Although ads may be given a few token impressions and clicks (for what reason I do not know—to confuse advertisers further or to throw Google's competitors off?), it's been confirmed in support calls that new ads often sit in an editorial queue for up to a week. The most glaring example of this was over one Christmas holiday period, when some of my new clients' campaigns were built. Apparently, many new campaigns were built in December and turned on in January, leaving Google Editorial, which had worked with a skeleton staff over the holiday period, with a much longer than usual editorial delay of three weeks or more. Marketing projections were thrown off, clients disgruntled, and budgets not spent.

I've also come to suspect that (for reasons I can't explain) new accounts and new keywords undergo a "ramp-up" process (even taking into account delays in syndication through network partners or content targeting). They're served only partially at first, gradually increasing in volume, until one day, a week, or several weeks later, they finally reach full delivery. Again, no one at Google will confirm this, but plotting the number of daily ad impressions over a period of three to four weeks for any new campaign or ad group containing new keywords would offer some proof of this. As if it weren't difficult enough to project your monthly spend prior to launch, you may have difficulty getting any kind of consistent feel for how much you're spending until everything has been running steadily for a few weeks.

This could be happening for any number of reasons. Clearly Google needs to be more vigilant on the editorial side now that they're such a large, visible company. There are banned keywords, trademark issues, and consumer protection laws to contend with. Google likely uses lists and automated checks to speed the process, but they also have to have someone read your ads before they're approved, and that takes time.

So they've learned that automation can only take them so far. But the notion that—if you're looking for impressions on new keywords that you haven't used before—you should be slowly "fed into" the AdWords fray until finally reaching full delivery is a curious one indeed. I can't prove it's happening and cannot speculate as to why Google would do it. But I do recommend that you budget for at least a three-week ramp-up period, just in case. That means warning the boss that no matter what anyone says, Google AdWords now sometimes takes longer to reach full delivery than it once did. This might also affect you if you are pausing and unpausing campaigns, or using certain keywords for seasonal promotions. You need to consider turning on those keywords at least a few days before you really need them, and you should watch everything carefully to see if performance is as expected.

No Double Serving

As mentioned earlier, Google won't allow you to use multiple AdWords accounts to run several ads on the page at the same time on the same keyphrase. Of course, this has indeed happened, but it isn't supposed to. I recently watched a presentation by an IBM manager talking about different divisions of his company outbidding one another on Linux-related keywords. Because that's a pretty big company and different divisions can almost be like companies unto themselves, Google might have looked the other way. In this case, the project manager actually realized that this wasn't in his company's interest, and instructed various divisions to stop bidding each other up!

The principle here is simple: allowing companies to blanket the page with their ads by creating multiple AdWords accounts would be an abuse of the system, unfair to other advertisers, and a bad deal for users, who expect to see some choice in listings. The terms of Google's arrangement with advertisers do not, of course, include the right to buy up all of the screen real estate devoted to advertising. Evidently, Google prefers the competitive auction process because it provides users with more choice and drives up Google's revenues. Hey, they're the publisher and it's their website. So that's their right.

There may be exceptions, as in the IBM example, where different company divisions have good reasons to bid on the same keywords for substantially different products or services. When in doubt, ask.

I hope that Google redoubles its efforts to enforce this rule. Too often, we're seeing ads from multiple affiliates of a single distributor on the same keywords, and in general, advertisers seem to be exploiting more loopholes to get double-served on the page while pushing their competitors off the first page of ad results. I'm not sure this is what users want to see.

Part III

Intermediate-Level Strategies

Chapter 6

Keyword Selection and Bidding: Tapping into Powerful AdWords Features

Keyword selection and bidding are core features of AdWords. A clear understanding of how each feature works will help you use them effectively. At the most basic level, your keyword list is a list of words and phrases that you expect your potential customer to use in Google searches. When a Google user searches for any word or phrase on your list, your ad appears to the right of the search results, or occasionally, highlighted above the search results at the top of the page.

Bidding is the process by which you indicate how much you're willing to spend each time one of your ads is clicked. Your bidding strategy determines how prominently your ad is displayed when a user enters one of your keywords.

How Matching Options Work

Before delving into the theory and mechanics of keyword lists, let's look at matching options and how they work. Matching options provide the tools to fine-tune your keyword list and ensure that it focuses on your target audience. Without a clear understanding of how matching options work, you may be wasting a significant portion of your advertising budget either by casting your net too wide, or not wide enough.

Exact, Broad, and Phrase Matching

Many campaigns I've reviewed were not working well simply because the advertiser wasn't aware of the fact that the default setting of AdWords is "broad match." I've also seen plenty of campaigns hobbled by an advertiser determined to eliminate all nonproductive clicks by forcing ads to display on exact matches only.

As you can see in Figure 6-1, matching options are activated by the use of special punctuation in the keyword list. Notice that this advertiser is using two matching options within the same ad group: exact match and broad match. The exact match for the single-word query **seeds** is in brackets, and the broad match is listed without punctuation. Since this advertiser set aside this ad group specifically to test the performance of a popular single word along with the plural of that word, there is no need for a phrase match in this case. (A single word within quotes actually acts the same as if it were not in quotes—since there is no word order to worry about with a single-word query, phrase match would be treated the same as broad match.) Note that the broad match for the query **seeds** generates about five times as many clicks as the exact match. This illustrates how broad matching helps you cast a wider net without doing a lot of work.

So how does this work exactly, and what is the benefit to you? We'll get to how it works in a minute. As for the benefit, it is significant, especially in terms of ease of use and improved campaign performance. Recall that in the early days of Overture advertising, everything was an exact match, which meant that advertisers' ads would not appear unless the keyword list contained the exact word or phrase typed in by the searcher. So, if you wanted to get your ad in front of the user typing **mustang gt 2002 ford**—not an unimaginable query, just a very rare one—your

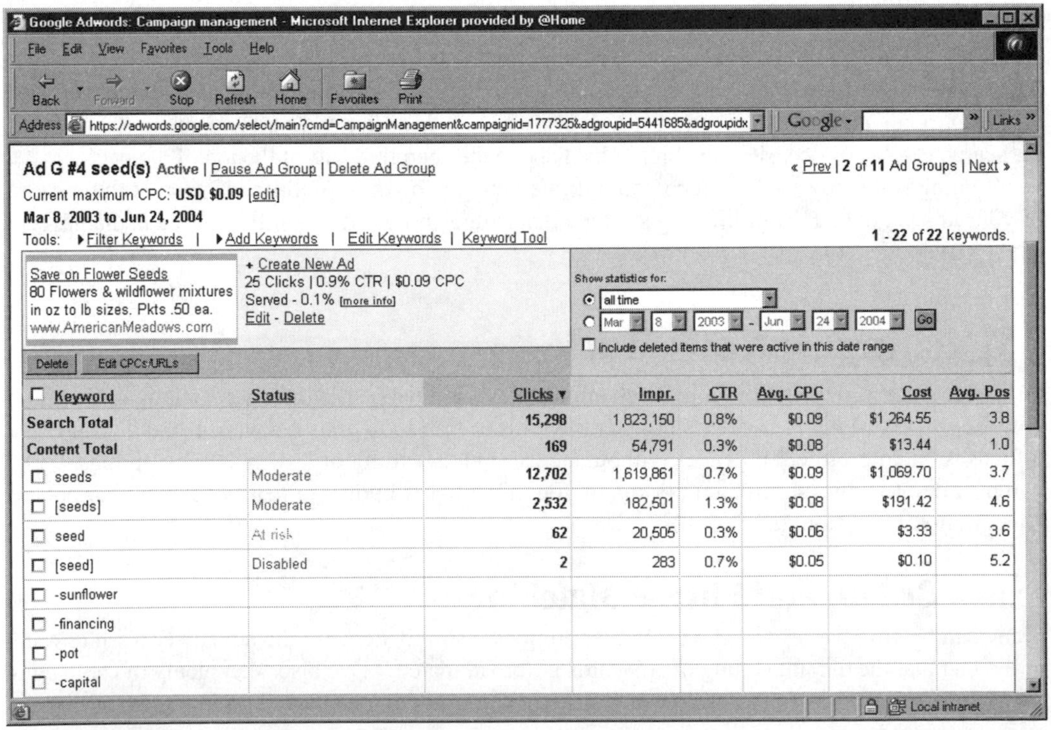

Keyword	Status	Clicks ▼	Impr.	CTR	Avg. CPC	Cost	Avg. Pos
Search Total		15,298	1,823,150	0.8%	$0.09	$1,264.55	3.8
Content Total		169	54,791	0.3%	$0.08	$13.44	1.0
seeds	Moderate	12,702	1,619,861	0.7%	$0.09	$1,069.70	3.7
[seeds]	Moderate	2,532	182,501	1.3%	$0.08	$191.42	4.6
seed	At risk	62	20,505	0.3%	$0.06	$3.33	3.6
[seed]	Disabled	2	283	0.7%	$0.05	$0.10	5.2
-sunflower							
-financing							
-pot							
-capital							

FIGURE 6-1   A short keyword list using both broad and exact match

keyword list would have to include that exact phrase. Since anticipating every conceivable phrase a user might enter is impossible, you ended up with an enormous keyword list and still missed some potential customers.

Google's introduction of matching options has made it easier for advertisers to generate a higher volume of clicks without being forced to generate huge lists with every imaginable keyword combination in them. Sadly, some advertisers are still churning out monster keyword lists, showing that they've either completely lost perspective on what will improve their campaign performance, or they simply don't understand how easy the matching options can make it for them. Even Overture now offers matching types similar to those in AdWords.

You might find substantial differences in your cost per click, and probably in the degree of targeting, among the three major syntax forms available on AdWords:

- **Exact**   The entry typed in by the user must exactly match a word or phrase appearing in your keyword list. Enclose your keyword or phrase in brackets to force exact matching.

- **Broad**   Keywords and phrases entered without punctuation will be interpreted as broad matching and will trigger your ad whenever they appear anywhere in the user's search query.

- **Phrase**   When you want a particular phrase to trigger your ad every time it appears, surround it with quotation marks. This is different from exact matching in that additional words can appear either before or after this phrase in the user's query.

> **NOTE**   *The use of negative keywords, which can also be considered a matching option, is covered in Chapter 9.*

Exact Matching

Exact matches are useful for controlling the number of clicks generated by common words and phrases. For example, if you distribute electric drills, saws, and the like, you might include the phrase **power tool** in your keyword list. However, left on its own (broad matched), the phrase would display your ad any time both words appeared, in any order, in a user's search query. The result would be a large number of uninterested users (and therefore not clicking) seeing your ad and lowering your CTR. The other alternative is equally bad—curious, but uninterested users clicking your ad with no intention of purchasing, thereby increasing your cost and reducing your ROI.

Exact matching enables you to eliminate both of these problems because your ad will display only when the user enters the words you've selected, in the order you've indicated. To create an exact matching keyword or phrase, enclose it in brackets—**[power tool]**. Keep in mind that exact matching, unlike phrase matching, does not trigger your ad if the phrase is part of a larger query. Therefore, **[power tool]** would not trigger your ad if the user entered **cordless power tool**.

> **NOTE**   *Exact matches and phrase matches are excluded from expanded matches, which include plurals and variations. Therefore, using the previous example, the **[power tool]** entry in your keyword list would not trigger your ad if the user typed **power tools** rather than **power tool.***

Broad Matching

The broad matching option is the least targeted and, depending on your competition, may be the hardest to make work, so you generally need to bid lower on broad matches. The other side of the coin is that it offers the widest reach for the least amount of effort. For example, if you use the word **tennis** in your keyword list, your ad is going to show every time someone types a query like **ticket prices for tennis tournaments**, or **history of tennis**. If you add other words but still use no quotes or brackets in your keyword list (for example, **tennis discount store**), you may capture a broader range of slight variations than you would get if you used an exact match like **[tennis discount store]**. Let's say someone types the phrase **tennis store discount** or **where do I find a store with tennis discount gear?** A broad match will still show your ad on these two searches, whereas an exact or phrase match would not.

While broad matching is not usually a good idea for common single keywords, it is great for specific terminology and names. The number of queries containing the word **tennis** is just so high, it's unlikely your clickthrough rate, or your sales conversion rates, will be sustainable if you use such an untargeted broad match. On the other hand, if you're in a niche industry selling Egyptian papyrus as a gift, your search volume on a word like **papyrus**, even used as a broad match, will be much lower, and you should be able to keep your campaign running without dropping below the minimum clickthrough rate enforced by Google, or blowing through your budget too quickly. For one word that actually means something really specific, like **aromatherapy** or **Caligula**, you might find again that the term is targeted enough that you can get away with broad matching.

Those rare advertisers who have been able to keep a one-word, popular, broad-matched term such as **tennis** alive (above 0.5%) have often improved their overall performance markedly. Think of the following scenario. While most advertisers can't keep their ad running on a particular term, you write an ad that's just a little more relevant. Then, you filter out a wide range of irrelevant words using negative keywords (see Chapter 9 for more on negative keywords). Between these two tactics, you manage to eke out a consistent CTR of 0.7%, and wind up paying an average of six cents per click on a high volume of clicks. Such a term can generate a volume so much higher than the rest of the phrases in your account that it can have a decisive impact on whether a campaign has a positive or negative ROI. And since one of the main problems with online advertising is too small a reach, many advertisers love it when they can connect with a wider range of targeted prospects while keeping the cost down.

That's why I'm ambivalent about that 0.5% CTR cutoff that Google enforces. I know Google is trying to enforce relevancy for good reason, but it's not written in stone that one-word keywords and broad matches don't generate results for advertisers because they're "not targeted enough." Sometimes they generate a strong return on investment (but, arguably, at the cost of annoying Google users who aren't interested in your ad). I have examples of client campaigns where one "make or break" keyword determines whether the campaign pays for itself or becomes a financial black hole. While the keyword is left running, the ROI is positive; when it inevitably gets disabled for temporarily falling to 0.38%, the campaign as a whole falters.

You will notice that the CTR-cutoff issue becomes more pressing when you start using broad matches. Whatever you do, don't be dissuaded from performing legitimate experiments just because the AdWords interface will sometimes label those keywords with designations other than "normal" (such as "on hold" or "in trial"). Marketplace anomalies and seasonal quirks in user search behavior might be as much to blame for "poor" (temporarily low-CTR) ad performance as the advertiser is. Also, factors that Google controls, such as the way ads look on the page (colors, bolding keywords, and so on), and even the relative quality of the main index search results, have had a lot of impact on CTRs over the past couple of years. I've seen CTRs go up across the board as a result of a cosmetic change made by Google, so conceivably, they might go down as well. Keep plugging away, and don't shy away from trying more broad-match experiments in the future just because you see those scary "disabled" notations in your account.

Phrase Matching

When you want a certain phrase (two or more words in a specific word order) to trigger your ad, all you have to do is enclose the phrase in quotes. For example, surrounding the phrase **landscape architects** with quotes (**"landscape architects"**) triggers your ad whenever a user types those words, in that order, regardless of what else the user includes in the query. So, adding the phrase **"landscape architects"** to your keyword list means your ad will display when users type queries such as these:

> seattle landscape architects
> landscape architects society
> east coast landscape architects who travel south for the winter

Many advertisers will discover substantial cost savings with better use of matching options even if they do nothing else to improve their campaigns. With some experimentation you will probably discover the combination of exact, broad, and phrase matching that works best for you.

CPCs on Different Matching Options

Many advertisers look at the differences in cost per click (CPC) and ROI that seem to occur with different matching options. It can be an interesting guide to user intent. Users who type three-word queries that include the words in the phrase match **"storm insurance"**, for example, might be more sophisticated on average than those simply typing the two-word query. Your bids might need to adjust upwards to reflect that, if these are better customers for you. Some advertisers seem to think that exact matching is "safer," or "more targeted," but it isn't inherently so.

Based on the assumption that exact matching is more targeted, one common question is this: are prices always higher on exact matches? If so, why? The answer is that it depends. There is nothing inherently "good" about exact match from a campaign economics standpoint. But sometimes exact matches—especially exact matches of three or more words—will perform relatively well from a CTR standpoint, perhaps because competitors using other broad and phrase matches are content with reaching a wider audience with an ad that is less relevant, on average, to any given searcher. If you really know the psychology of your user, you might find that you pull very high CTRs on long exact matches like **[research gay travel]** or **[apply for a student loan]**. Even if that exact match works great for you, you might not need to bid as high due to the CTR benefit you're receiving. So, prices are not necessarily higher on exact matches. Nor are you guaranteed a high spot on the page, as someone else might be bidding very high on broad or phrase matches that will trigger their ads so that they compete to appear on the same search results page as your ad.

If it were me, I'd probably cast a slightly wider net with a three-word broad match like **how vc funding** as opposed to a long exact match like **[how to get vc funding]**. It's just too much work to find every long exact match phrase when you can be nearly as targeted with multiple-word broad matches.

Keyword Research

One of the most important tasks faced by an advertiser is the generation of the core list of keywords used in a campaign. While there are many keywords that are obvious, there are probably just as many that aren't. Fortunately, a number of resources are readily available to help you in your quest for the most effective keyword list.

The Google AdWords Keyword Tool

While a large number of third-party keyword generating software packages have sprung up, the first tool you should explore is only a mouse click or two away from your AdWords campaign. The Google AdWords keyword tool is doing an increasingly good job of providing lists of suggested keywords to augment the lists that you may build yourself at the outset of your campaign. Begin by clicking the Tools link on the Campaign Management toolbar to display the page containing links to various AdWords tools. Click the Keyword Tool link to open the Google AdWords keyword tool. This excellent resource offers several pieces of information (see Figure 6-2). It seems to work best when you've already built an ad group with a few phrases.

All you have to do is enter your keyword or phrase in the left pane and click the Show Matching Queries and Alternatives button. The tool displays several useful lists. The first is the More Specific Keywords list on the left. These are the most popular queries that will show up on your keyword. For example, if I've elected to show my ad on a broad match for **search**, this tool alerts me that some of the most popular phrases containing the word include **executive search**, **code search**, and **google search**. Two out of these three are irrelevant to my business, so this might help me to refine my ad group by adding negative keywords (discussed in Chapter 9) to the ad group.

In general the keyword tool provides excellent info about user search behavior, although it does not give you data about the frequency of searches. Several other **search** phrases are popular (such as **strip search**), as it turns out, including dozens that I wouldn't have thought of, being too close to my own industry. Using the keyword tool can be a real wake-up call, reminding you of the fact that very few people typing keywords that include your word or phrase might be searching for what you offer, and that lack of targeting could be the explanation for why you are finding it difficult to keep your CTR high.

On the right-hand side of the screen, depending on whether you're using broad-matched terms, the keyword tool will show you any current "expanded broad matches." This, too, is discussed in Chapter 9; but the upshot is, when you use broad-matched terms, Google may sometimes use semantic technology to show your ad near similar words, even though you don't use this word anywhere in your keyword list. (You can avoid this by using only phrase or exact matches.)

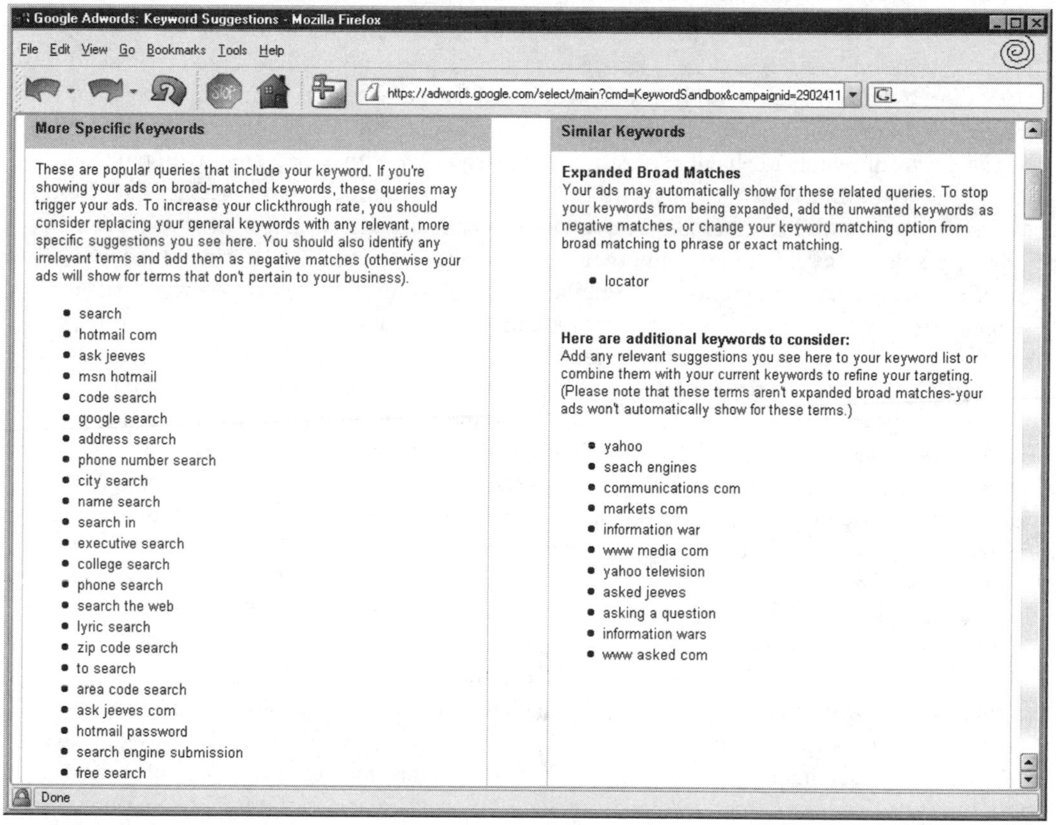
Google Adwords: Keyword Suggestions - Mozilla Firefox
File Edit View Go Bookmarks Tools Help
https://adwords.google.com/select/main?cmd=KeywordSandbox&campaignid=2902411
More Specific Keywords
These are popular queries that include your keyword. If you're showing your ads on broad-matched keywords, these queries may trigger your ads. To increase your clickthrough rate, you should consider replacing your general keywords with any relevant, more specific suggestions you see here. You should also identify any irrelevant terms and add them as negative matches (otherwise your ads will show for terms that don't pertain to your business).
search
hotmail com
ask jeeves
msn hotmail
code search
google search
address search
phone number search
city search
name search
search in
executive search
college search
phone search
search the web
lyric search
zip code search
to search
area code search
ask jeeves com
hotmail password
search engine submission
free search
Similar Keywords
Expanded Broad Matches
Your ads may automatically show for these related queries. To stop your keywords from being expanded, add the unwanted keywords as negative matches, or change your keyword matching option from broad matching to phrase or exact matching.
locator
Here are additional keywords to consider:
Add any relevant suggestions you see here to your keyword list or combine them with your current keywords to refine your targeting. (Please note that these terms aren't expanded broad matches-your ads won't automatically show for these terms.)
yahoo
seach engines
communications com
markets com
information war
www media com
yahoo television
asked jeeves
asking a question
information wars
www asked com
Done

FIGURE 6-2 Google's keyword tool provides valuable keyword suggestions and information about popular queries.

The more important information on the right-hand side is the list of suggested terms. You'll see a jumble of synonyms, misspellings, semantic variations, and related phrases, not all of which will be helpful. My advice would be to hand-pick the ones that seem valuable, add them to your campaign as appropriate, and ignore the others.

Of course, all the Google keyword tool can do is offer suggestions. You'll have to do a bit of extrapolating and exploring on your own to discover new keywords for your campaign.

Keyword Research Tools and Tips

As good as the Google AdWords keyword tool is, it may not be enough for your needs. In that case you might want to consider one of the many third-party solutions that are available. In addition, you can pick up ideas simply by reading the news and watching TV.

Use Third-Party Tools: WordTracker

WordTracker (www.wordtracker.com) is the best-known keyword research tool on the market. It offers subscription-based access to its extensive database of over 3 million search terms and provides search data on each term. It has been adopted by many search engine optimization experts for use in determining the frequency of certain search terms. WordTracker uses whatever data it can get from searcher behavior to estimate the frequency with which any given phrase is searched in a month. Since the folks at WordTracker do not have access to proprietary data from search engine companies like Google, however, they must extrapolate using their own methods. They don't disclose these, but they and other similar companies can forge partnerships with Internet Service Providers or metasearch engines who will offer data on user search behavior. These methods pale in comparison to actually looking in hindsight at real behavior confirmed by the stats from an existing AdWords account.

In addition to giving search frequencies, WordTracker uses thesaurus-type technology to suggest similar keywords. This can be helpful, but no more helpful than many of the free tools available in the marketplace. Nonetheless, it's worth trying WordTracker to see what it does, and a 24-hour trial subscription is available for under $10. Personally, I'm not a huge fan of WordTracker because they fail to disclose their methodology. More advanced technologies from companies like Quigo are coming along now, and of course Google's in-house capability is likely the most advanced of all.

Various companies come and go in this space, but few have made much of an impact. Given that search data on search engines like Yahoo, Google, and MSN are confidential, few third parties can offer reliable search behavior data. Most are just extrapolations of a small data segment (and thus not accurate). More promising are probably the lateral-thinking "vocabulary brainstorming" tools. Applied Semantics is one company that led in this area until being acquired by Google. Their CIRCA linguistic mapping technology has been one of the elements that Google has used to choose the ads that best match web pages published by participants in the AdSense (content-targeted listings) program.

Another player, Quigo, has become a leader in contextual advertising, serving targeted pay-per-click listings on the sites of publisher partners. They currently dominate certain vertical industry fields, such as automotive. Quigo has assembled strong technology and sales teams from the ranks of now-defunct search engine companies, and they say they are set to release a powerful new keyword research tool soon. Based on Quigo's track record, it should be worth a look.

Read the News

As you get closer to filling out your keyword list, you'll need to search for more insights and lateral-thinking opportunities. I find that a news article on a particular industry will often contain insights into key problems facing consumers and companies in that sector. Let's say it's credit problems. Where there is a sense of urgency, you'll likely stumble across new and unusual keywords that are commonly typed by your prospects. In the credit area, for example, let's say the article is about credit bureaus and FICO scores. As you read quotes from consumers and industry players, you may find additional real-life ways of describing consumer credit problems that your more formal research has overlooked.

The nice thing is you can use a source like Google News, Topix.net, or Yahoo Finance to look up archived news on a given topic or stock symbol.

Watch TV

No, I don't mean you should sit around watching *Leave It to Beaver* reruns. If you come across a television ad for a company in your industry, you might find certain buzzwords or promotions being mentioned that appear nowhere in your AdWords account. Picking up on these kinds of catchphrases is a perfectly legitimate way that you can leverage someone else's hefty TV advertising budget. Your competitor may be drawing attention to an issue and causing a spike in Internet searches for information related to that issue. Of course, if these kinds of words and concepts appear in a *60 Minutes* news feature, you shouldn't turn up your nose at them either!

The Bottom Line: Use Your Own Campaign

So far, this has a fairly unsatisfactory feel, doesn't it? It's because we're trying to generate projections based on user search behavior, which is in fact valuable data that search engines just don't publish for anyone to see. We're fumbling around and guessing. Keyword research tools can be helpful for brainstorming, but if you know your business well and build your keyword list first based on that knowledge, chances are, most of what the tools tell you will elicit a "tell me something I don't already know!" response from you.

Perhaps the most accurate and useful tools are available within the actual pay-per-click keyword advertising interfaces themselves. All three of the major players, Overture, Google, and FindWhat, offer their own handy keyword suggestion tools. Overture's will tell you search frequency in a given month (Figure 6-3), but that data could be skewed for the simple reason that popular commercial terms are searched quite often by advertisers checking their own listings! Therefore, be careful not to rely too heavily on these tools as projection aids.

So what can you trust? The data from an *actual Google AdWords campaign* that has been running in real time for the past week, month, or year! My experience has shown that the "ready, aim, fire" (extensive planning) approach to keyword research pales in comparison to a "ready, fire, aim" (generate real market data, then adjust and expand) approach. Let's walk through the kind of exceptional keyword data that are available to you after you've actually been *running* an AdWords campaign.

In Figure 6-4 you can see some fairly standard reporting for a typical AdWords campaign over the month of May 2004. By looking at the number of impressions of his ad on any given phrase, the advertiser, Ray Allen, now knows (assuming he kept his AdWords campaign at full delivery throughout the month) that 5,512 people in the United States searched for the phrase **seed packets** or some query including that phrase, during May. The number is slightly lower than the previous month's 6,587. That's not a projection, it's real, and it makes sense intuitively. People were more into planning for their gardens in April than they were in May. These patterns may vary from month to month, but it's a much clearer benchmark than the information provided by a third-party tool that has no way of knowing what real users are doing on Google. Moreover, this advertiser knows that 5.7% of the people typing that term into Google clicked on his ad, down slightly from the 6.7% in April. Pretty good. You'll never learn that from any "research" tool. The total cost of

Overture- Search Term Suggestion Tool - Microsoft Internet Explorer provided by @Home

Search Term Suggestion Tool

Not sure what search terms to bid on?
Enter a term related to your site and we will
show you:

- Related searches that include your term

- How many times that term was searched
on last month

Get suggestions for: (may take up to 30
seconds)

data recovery

Note: All suggested search terms are subject
to our standard editorial review process.

Searches done in May 2004	
Count	**Search Term**
94408	data recovery
10823	data recovery service
6666	data recovery software
6183	hard drive data recovery
4403	disk data recovery
3039	hard disk data recovery
2772	computer data recovery
2366	data recovery secure
2340	data recovery expert
2299	raid data recovery
2256	emergency data recovery
2085	data recovery tool
1930	laptop data recovery
1683	compact flash data recovery
1620	data recovery program
1543	mac data recovery
1542	data recovery specialist
1540	tape data recovery

FIGURE 6-3   Overture's keyword suggestion tool shows how frequently a term is searched in a given month. This is of somewhat limited value in practice.

running that advertising to learn this? About $50. Of course that wasn't $50 wasted—it was spent on advertising that also generated new customers.

You can get as specific in your analysis as you like once you have your campaign running. In this example, 143 people searched for **seed packets** on May 6, 2004. And 9.0% of them clicked on Ray's ad. Pretty tough to predict that without actually running a campaign.

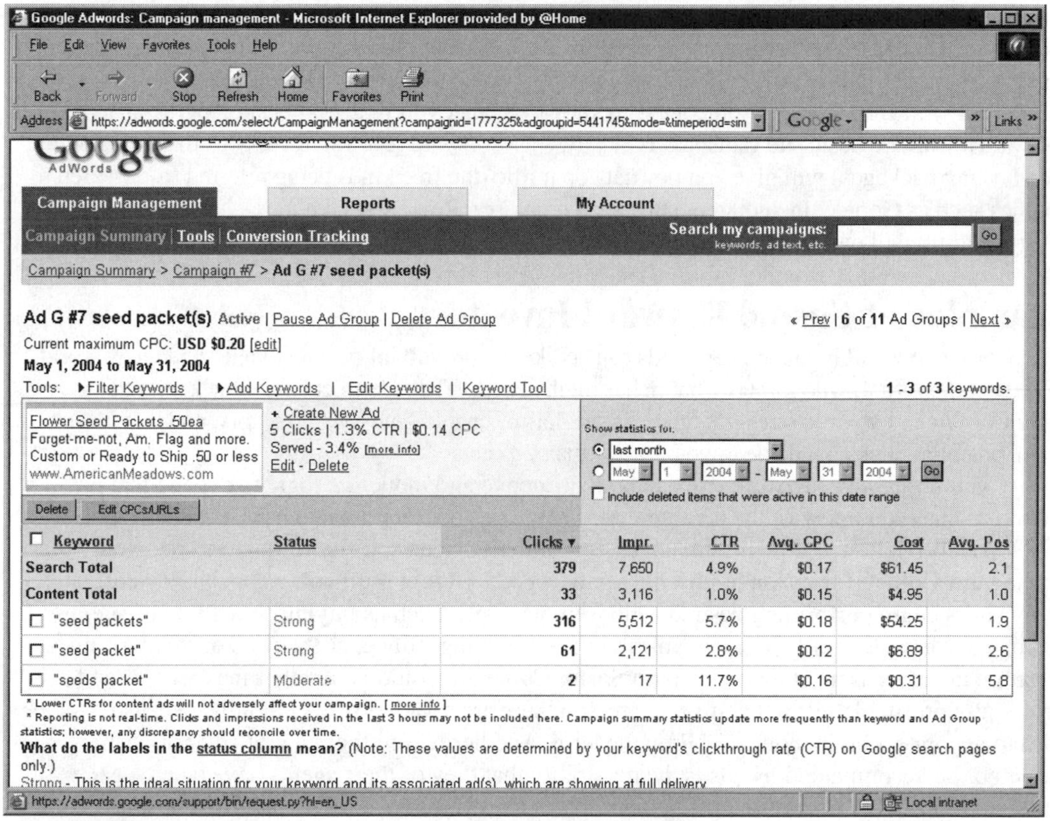

FIGURE 6-4   Ray Allen of AmericanMeadows.com now knows roughly how many people searched for the term **seed packets** in May 2004.

Keywords You're Already Using

For many of my clients, especially those in retail, generating an exhaustive keyword list is not terribly difficult, because most of this material is already on their websites. Articles and sales materials may contain much of the needed jargon that would go into a successful AdWords campaign. Product pages might contain product descriptions, product names, product attributes, or brand names. In light of this kind of information, coming up with the keywords is not always a major challenge. The real test will be to organize those keywords into logical groups with closely matching ads (as discussed in Chapter 5) and, if you're ambitious, to generate minor variations (misspellings, odd ways of saying things, and so on) that competitors may not have thought of.

If you want to be really exhaustive, review not only your website and your competitors' websites (including any keyword or description meta tags you might be able to see in your browser by viewing the HTML source of the competitor's pages), but also your website statistics (server logs) to see what kinds of search phrases are leading people to your site. If you're not familiar with server logs, you'll need to ask someone who knows whether you're already using logfile analysis software to capture basic site statistics. Typically, such software (even free versions that come with web hosting packages) will give you raw data on traffic (the free kind) being referred from search engines such as Google, including popular search phrases. Review such phrases in case they might trigger additional keyword ideas for your campaign.

Examples of Unsold Keyword Inventory

Discovering new and untapped keywords can be like the proverbial ocean voyage to the new world. If you get there first, who knows what riches might await? The race to colonize the keyword space is far from over. I want to stress that there is still lots of unsold keyword inventory, and that means many potential clicks available to you for less than 20 cents.

As you build your keyword list, use both deductive and inductive logic to expand that list based on what you know of the demographic profile of your target customers. In other words, develop a correlation you might like to test—whether you can sell figure skates to people who type **Sasha Cohen**, for example. If it hits (pulls a good CTR at high volumes with low cost, and site visitors begin performing desired actions on your site, such as buying something or signing up for your newsletter), you know you're onto something. Since, at the time of this writing, there are no advertisers at all on the term **Sasha Cohen**, it would be a rather inexpensive and potentially profitable test. Of course, the reason there are no advertisers might be because it's hard to generate a high enough CTR on the term. Another reason that a lot of celebrity names *might* not be accompanied by ads is the possibility that they or their agents have taken legal action to block advertisers from using their names as keywords.

To find an example of a celebrity athlete whose name does trigger ads on Google or Yahoo, you'd have to pick Annika Sorenstam. Hardly competitive, though—only one advertiser on Google (Figure 6-5) and two on Yahoo (using Overture). **Annika** by itself appears to be a common search query, perhaps because many users don't know how to spell Sorenstam. (The ad in Figure 6-5 was written by me when I did some work for a golf psychologist.)

What about inductive logic? If an ad for sporting equipment on phrases relating to a sports figure's name performs well for you, and you don't fully understand why, back up and try to figure out why. That will give you a new theory that you can use to generate new potential correlations. For example, if you successfully sold a book on skating techniques to people typing **Sasha Cohen** into Google, you suddenly have about 100 more names you might try adding to your campaign.

An easier technique is to target affinity-indicating phrases that don't attract many sellers of products. For example, pick a historical event that might be a common search phrase for people who also just happen to share the demographic characteristics that fit your offer, and bid on this phrase. How many are bidding on **Louisiana purchase**, **Gettysburg Address**, or **Battle of Versailles**? When I first began writing about this, no advertisers appeared. Now, ads from Amazon. com, or a research library like Questia.com, might show up, but that means you can still be visible here for ten cents or less.

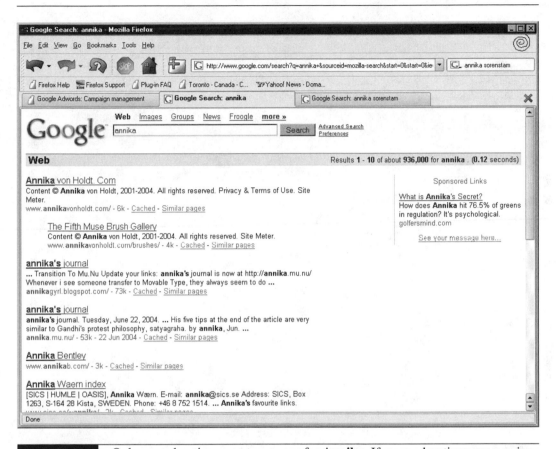

FIGURE 6-5	Only one advertiser next to a query for **Annika**. If more advertisers were using deductive logic, there would be more golf-related ads.

Even more focused terms like **Louisiana travel** are currently underused, though there are many more advertisers in that space this year than there were a couple of years ago.

So you don't necessarily even need to find creative phrases—just targeted ones. Depending on the type of travel or accommodations being sought, a local business might have a much higher CTR on its ads than some of the generic national advertisers would, and would therefore get a higher ad position for a low cost. Too bad few in the local Louisiana hospitality industry have yet to figure this out, though by the time you read this, more will have done so.

User search behavior is, in a word, wild. A fairly high percentage of all queries ever typed into a search engine are unique. (Over a several-year period, at AltaVista, the number was 25%, according to company officials at one conference presentation I saw in 2001.) That is to say, they've only been typed in once, ever, and never typed again! This "wildness" of user behavior means that you're probably missing out on reaching many of them because you can't predict what they're going to type. The range is fantastic. Using Metaspy (Figure 6-6), a tool that looks

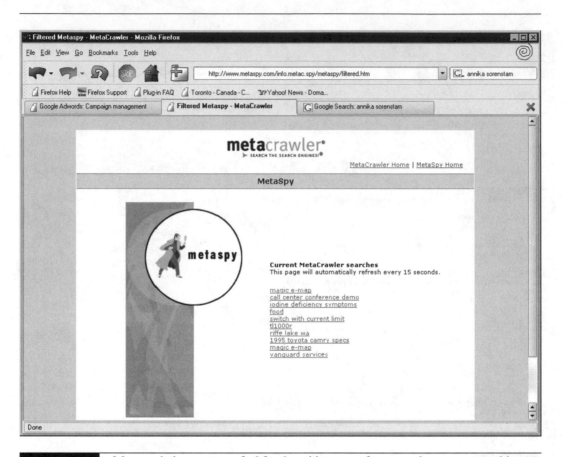

FIGURE 6-6   Metaspy helps you get a feel for the wide range of terms real users are searching on.

at a sampling of real-time search queries on the search engine Metacrawler, I can immediately begin to see what kinds of strange and wonderful things people are typing. (Google has a similar display of real-time sample queries running perpetually inside its Googleplex offices and has been known to project the same display on the wall at industry parties.)

My Metaspy session included these phrases:

hp bekas
exempt forensics
olanzepine
desert combat
olscer
veal scallopini
muppets and weezer
odometer rollback

I don't know what half these things are, but those users out there are looking for information, that's for sure—no doubt confounding the experts' expectations of what users seek. To be honest, the vast majority of searches (**muppets and weezer**?) are useless to your business. The good news is, you can make certain that you don't show your ads to those people, and only show them to the interested parties.

Few marketers are aware of how to tap into uncommon search phrases—which are actually, as you can now see, quite common. Well, some marketers are finally starting to catch on. I notice that the phrase **odometer rollback** is attracting a variety of advertisers: companies that will offer to "calibrate" or "replace" your odometer, and law firms that will help you sue a vendor who has illegally rolled back the odometer on a used car.

If I were giving you advice on how to get more "free" search engine traffic, the way to intersect with a wider range of relevant search queries would be to create more content on your site that might be indexed in the search engine and rank well in search results (if you're lucky). When you have a large volume of content on your website, search engines by definition have more pages filled with a variety of words to index, and this creates a wider net that helps you to snare visitors typing keyphrase combos that no one else has in their content. The problem with this, as many of you already know, is that many e-commerce sites aren't designed to be gigantic warehouses of articles; they're designed to sell one product or a line of products, and that's it! In fact, a search engine optimization consultant's recommendation to add tons of content to your site may conflict markedly with the principle of simplicity and smooth purchasing process that every online marketer should pay close attention to.

With AdWords, you can have a very simple website or landing page that is focused on closing the sale. You tap into user search behavior with your keyword list, not by building a website crammed full of content that contains those keywords. That's good news! When you're paying for traffic, a lack of content on your site won't hurt you at all.

Benefits of Being the Only Advertiser on a Phrase

In Figures 6-7 and 6-8 you can see two examples of search engine results pages that have only a single advertiser. The most obvious benefit to this is cost: if you're the only advertiser on the screen for a given term, you pay the minimum of five cents per click. The more of these phrases you have in your account, provided they're relevant, the better your economics will look.

The second benefit of being the sole advertiser may be branding and positioning. For many businesses it's not particularly desirable to have to prove that you're the best at something. The key to strong margins and customer loyalty is to have customers think that you're the *only* viable solution to their problem at a given time. When Ray Allen and I first discussed the idea of advertising on the Latin names for wildflowers, no one else was doing it. Ray has no doubt gained hundreds of new customers by showing up—in both the free search index and in Google AdWords listings—on botanical search terms that none of his competitors thought to highlight. The fact that many advertisers keep their campaigns turned off when their products are out of season might play into the hands of the advertiser Gurneys, who is showing up for a botanical term in Figure 6-8. After all, being the only advertiser there, a click would only cost five cents. Hardly a calamity even if some products are out of season.

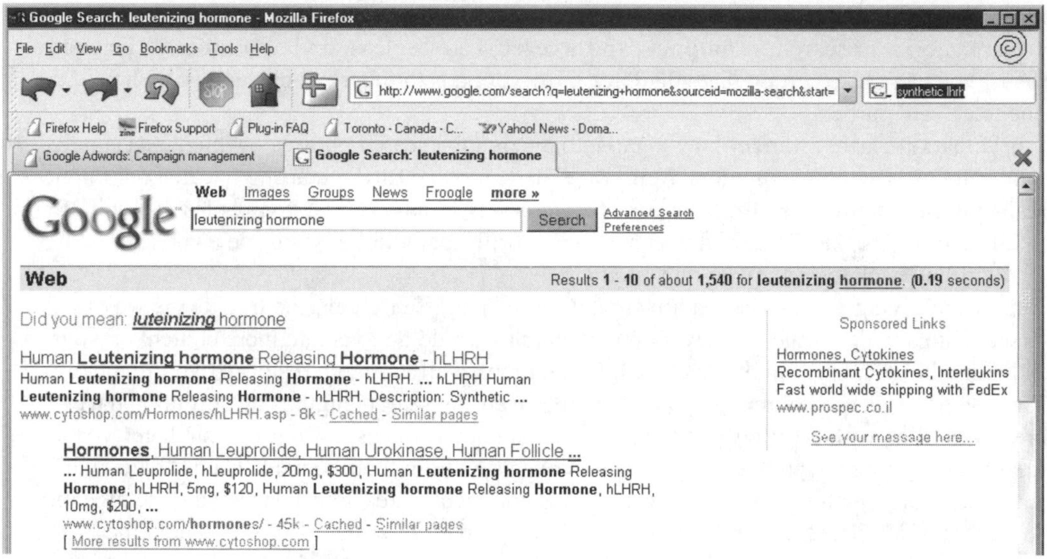

FIGURE 6-7   An Israeli company is the only one advertising on the misspelled niche term **leutenizing hormone**.

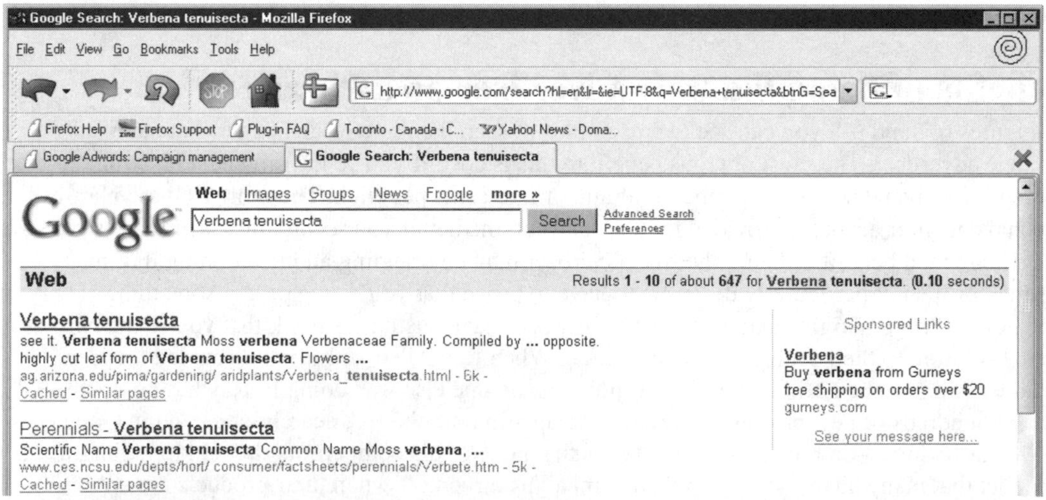

FIGURE 6-8   Here you can see that only one advertiser, Gurneys, shows up on **verbena tenuisecta**. There are 647 listings containing that phrase in the Google index.

One of the big challenges for online advertisers, especially with the advent of comparison shopping services such as Shopping.com and Froogle, is to guard against declining profit margins that result from exploding consumer access to goods and comparative information about those goods. Some consumers will compare on price alone. Others may run you ragged with questions about your products and services before they buy.

One way to fend off this pressure on profit margins is to build a trusted brand by making sure you're showing up in many different places online (paying for traffic in a variety of areas), building a word-of-mouth reputation, and doing things that no other company does.

But another great way to get around the comparison shopping problem is to be smart enough to be the *only* advertiser to "bother to show up" on a given search term. To achieve this, an ongoing process of keyword discovery is paramount.

Keyword Brainstorming: It's about *Them*

Keyword selection is pretty much synonymous with *targeting*. With broad keywords and broad matches, you're often targeting, well, broadly. But as you build a longer list of unusual phrases, you'll find that you're micro-targeting your ads to some very specific types of customers. You have the opportunity to get "in the face" of only a small subset of people. Therefore, one of the best investments of your time may be in brainstorming to come up with very targeted keywords and phrases.

Solve Your Target Market's Problems

Certainly, the best prospective customers are generally typing a search query that actually describes your product or service, but other searchers (and this doesn't mean they aren't potential customers) may be typing something related to the problem your product could solve for them. Let's think about problems for a second. There are many kinds of problems: broken windows, broken promises, broken relationships, broken laws, broken homes, broken legs, broken software, broken hardware, broken banks. And there are thousands upon thousands of businesses dedicated to patching up, fixing, solving, healing, or masking such problems—or just consoling or distracting people who suffer from them. People using search engines won't always type in words related to your solution, patch, consolation, or distraction, but they may have all kinds of ways of describing different aspects of their dilemma. Most will be searching for information and will not be in a buying mood. But if 1% click on your ad, you only pay for those clicks. From there, 2%, 5%, or 10% may buy. It's a numbers game.

Someone selling allergy medication might want to include **irritated nasal passage** and a host of other symptoms of someone suffering from airborne allergies, for example. (As usual, in spite of the fact that I've used this example in past writings, at press time I see no advertisers on this term, and there are 1,980 listings in the Google index containing these three words.) If your prospective markets exhibit many *symptoms* that would predispose them to your solution, which is designed get to the root of the problem, then you may be able to distract them (ever so slightly) from the information they *thought* they wanted. After all, people don't always know what they're looking for. People who believe that online search needs to be reinvented as some kind of product catalog, where people go in and drill down to the exact thing they need, must not have much imagination, either about what shopping is really like or about what it means to do online research.

If this dynamic applies to your business, spend an hour generating a long list of symptoms—be these caused by computer operating system problems, financial problems, health problems, or whatever—and think about how you might use them as keywords in your AdWords account. A computer crash could be caused by a virus or trojan. It wouldn't hurt, in this case, to try showing your ad for a personal firewall technology to people typing in very specific phrases related to computer errors and crashes they might be facing. It's nitty-gritty work, though. After you get past the obvious—**computer crash**, **computer infected**, **windows problems**—you'll have to dig deeper to come up with a more extensive vocabulary. The benefit of stopping your discovery process early is that it saves work and you'll probably be focusing on the most obvious words, words that are nicely targeted and have the best chance of creating a sale. Those of you who continue to add new groups of experimental words, though, will discover less expensive words. Some of these will *always* be less expensive because they're so offbeat and won't attract crowds.

It's not the specific example that matters here; it's the process. Once you've identified your target market or markets, the game becomes a strategic brainstorming exercise of imagining their online search behavior. You'll be asking yourself a slightly different question than a traditional media buyer might ask—"what magazines do potential buyers of our skateboards read?"—but then again, it's not so far off. What you're essentially doing with a keyword discovery process is buying exposure to a very specific target audience. Because there's never been anything quite like this in the history of advertising, you have to throw a lot of your traditional assumptions out the window.

Keyword selection should not just revolve around your perception of what are the exact, correct words for things. Many marketers seem oblivious to this simple truth. Knowledge can be the most powerful weapon in your arsenal—knowing more about how actual users' search engine behavior works, what keyphrases people are actually typing in, and in what volumes and combinations. Think about my friend Ray Allen of AmericanMeadows.com. I love to brag about the great keyword list Ray has. But half the time I type in a term expecting to see Ray there, it's a competitor, not Ray, advertising on the term. (Bad Ray!) It's just a matter of *doing* it—of maximizing the opportunity to advertise on that amazing Google keyword inventory—and even the best of us aren't doing it optimally. That leaves plenty of opportunity for all.

Unless you've been dealing with search engine marketing as a full-time job, you're bound to be lulled into making the classic rookie mistake—the same mistake most of us made when we thought we were optimizing our sites for "free" search engine traffic: focusing on a limited range of keywords, obsessing about them, and trying to put all of our efforts into attracting users who search for them. While it's true that the most popular search queries are indeed valuable commodities to the advertiser, it would be foolish not to continue searching for the incremental revenue that might be generated with further testing of unusual or highly specific keyword ideas.

This has become clear to me after spending considerable time refining client campaigns. I've often been lulled into thinking that I was compelled to bid high on certain keyphrases. But on those campaigns that started losing money and on which we were forced to perform radical surgery (lowering bids across the board in order to stop the bleeding), I made an interesting discovery.

The ROI of the campaign would improve as we stopped showing our ads on the more expensive, highly targeted words. Many of those secondary keywords were holding their own as revenue generators and weren't subject to creeping bidding wars. Although it might have been *nice* to be able to afford to pay top dollar for some of those supertargeted words, when that option was ruled out, it seemed that we were forced into creating a clever little lead-generation machine that had more permanency to it. And that modest success would propel us (or the client) to try to figure out what thought process we used to discover a few of the gems that helped us do so well. We'd add yet another unusual (but targeted) group of experimental words, then another. The process can become downright addictive.

After observing how dozens of client accounts went from being trapped in impossible bidding wars to being consistently profitable, I asked myself what the problem was with the first approach they had typically taken to keyword selection. The problem was often this: they were getting caught up in insider phrases and insider thinking. Insider thinking is endemic to corporate life, it seems, even if you're a small startup. Hold a meeting, even if only two people are present, and suddenly it's about "we this" and "we that." But what about *them*—the potential customers? Let's face it. Every person that might be predisposed to buy the services of a disaster recovery firm might not type the phrase **disaster recovery firm**. There is some art and some science to determining what such a person might indeed type in. If it's not **disaster recovery firm**, then what? Should we just load in words like **disaster**, **hurricane**, and **flood** and hope for the best? Of course not—too general. Millions of people use Google to search for information about disasters and hurricanes. A tiny few would want the services of a certain type of consulting firm, and Google won't show your ad if only a miniscule percentage of users click it.

Typing just about any query is good enough to show corporate arrogance in action. When I type **disaster recovery**, for example, in the advertising area on Google there are a range of IT firms screaming at me about "data disaster recovery." Indeed, for their own convenience, many appear to have talked themselves into believing that there is only one kind of disaster that can occur in the world—data loss disasters. Beam me up, Scotty... please.

We don't know, and probably won't soon know, all that much about user intention and how it breaks down among people typing ambiguous queries into search engines. But in determining what keywords to target and the likely response, it's probably worth taking a deep breath and trying to understand at a commonsense level what a user might be looking for when typing a term like **disaster recovery**. Let's say the searcher is a manager who is going to be charged with developing a disaster recovery plan for her company using a mix of in-house and outsourced expertise. She's in the preliminary research stage before having a meeting to determine the terms of reference. She wants some reading material on the main issues about disaster recovery and will also be looking around for some experts she can talk to who might be able to point her towards companies that might be helpful in an advising capacity.

The first thing this user comes across, listed first in Google's main index results, is something called *Disaster Recovery Journal*. She subscribes immediately, becoming the 60,001st subscriber. She then goes to lunch.

Luckily, you, as an advertiser, have also been reading this publication. Already, this gives you an extensive lexicon of terms that may be of interest to your target market! Hundreds, when all is said and done. Sometimes, your target reader will want to learn more about one of these subtopics and will head to, you guessed it, Google, and type in that term. If you're lucky (and yes, a certain amount of luck is surely involved), your ad, targeted to one of those nitty-gritty little industry phrases, actually appeals to him more than any of the other listings he sees on the page. If you're good at converting website visitors to leads, and leads to sales—and yes, that process can take anything from a few seconds to a year, and is a numbers game like anything else—then it will be mission accomplished. As obvious keywords become prohibitively expensive, more and more guerrilla advertisers will need to understand how to find customers through the back door by targeting secondary terms intelligently.

One of the things you immediately notice from studying the disaster recovery industry and its jargon is that there is quite a bit of talk about "business continuity" in the same breath as "disaster recovery" planning. So advertising on the phrase **business continuity** becomes a no-brainer, or at least you'd think it would. It gets better, though. If your tracking is set up right, over time you'll be able to determine the return on investment of that part of your Google AdWords campaign that focuses on **disaster recovery** and related keywords, and the part that focuses on **business continuity** and variations of that term.

You don't need to know this in advance. You simply go ahead and set it up as an experiment and let the market tell you what works best. Then you'll be able to tell people (those you trust) strange stories at cocktail parties: "We generate more disaster recovery white paper downloads on the disaster recovery words, so at first we thought it was the higher-performing keyword area, but as it turned out, the ROI on business continuity words turned out to be much higher, because web exposure in this area helped us initiate several relationships with Fortune 500 clients!... We know because we track things using this cool software..." Just be prepared for the victim of your minute analysis to make an excuse and head for the veggie dip. The life of an AdWords junkie can be lonely.

That's not a bad example, actually. A quick check of some bids on Overture showed that **business continuity** is a very pricey phrase indeed, with several advertisers running above $5.00 per click and the top bid approaching $10.00. Maybe it really is a magic bullet for a higher class of client, then. But phrases like **disaster plan** are going for as little as 25 cents, while **disaster planning** is in the $1.50 area. If it were me, I'd want to be trying them all out and tracking my results. You never know who's typing what, and you never want to base your keyword selection or your bidding strategy on gut feel or limited data. When you're in a business that might generate only one or two really large contracts a year while generating a steady stream of smaller service contracts and software sales, a "rational" look at the payback on certain keywords, especially if it were over a short time frame, might lead you to wildly underestimate their value—at least until that big client inks a deal, at which point you might reevaluate your suppositions about what a certain phrase is worth to your business.

NOTE   *I know nothing about business continuity or disaster recovery, and have no clients in this business, so my discussion is purely for the purposes of illustration. No letters, please.*

In any case, there often seems to be a subtle difference between advertising on terms that represent the kind of jargon and problems that might be fodder for your target market's search queries, and the preoccupations of the people who happen to work at your company or sit on its board of directors. Think about your market. Customers don't hold the same sacred views of your industry as you do—they're searching in an area that is new to them, after all. They are in a process of discovery. If you intercept some of them early in that process, you have a much better chance of being seen as uniquely able to fulfill their needs.

As branding consultant Rob Frankel wrote in an article entitled "Why Ads Are So Stupid" (http://www.robfrankel.com/dumbads.html):

> The fact is that the dynamics of advertising are different for everyone, at every level, in every business. Even looking across the street at your local competitor can be dangerous. I can't tell you the number of clients who tell me they run radio spots here or banner ads there because that's what their competition does. Oh yeah? Well what made the competition such media mavens? How do you know that they didn't follow someone else's misguided notions? Do they have more or less to spend than you do?

Keyword Variations: Plurals, Verb Forms, and Misspellings

When it comes to selling ads on keyword variations that might be considered trivial, such as plural forms, the industry is at a crossroads. The instinct of many large media buyers is that bidding separately on **ski boot** and **ski boots**, for example, is too complicated. But experienced advertisers know that no two situations are the same. While plural and singular forms might connote a similar meaning on one keyword, in another keyword area the differences in meaning from an advertiser's standpoint might be substantial. Moreover, many experienced advertisers have data that show one form of a word makes them money, whereas another form does not. What exactly is the reason that **pearl earrings** seems to be a more commercially viable term than **pearl earring**? I don't know for sure, but can speculate that the first person is more likely to be a shopper, and the second person might, at least some of the time, be looking for a photo, the name of a band, or who knows what.

None of this would matter so much if the advertising weren't based on an auction system, or if Google didn't create such strict rules around things like CTR. But the fact is, once you get used to the idea that you can bid less on a form of a word that converts poorly to sales, it can be tough to give up that control. Also, if Google wants advertisers to be relevant and enforces rules to that effect, it might be hypocritical if they began selling keywords in "bundles," taking away some of the granularity that advertisers have come to appreciate.

Overture was the first industry player to begin automatically using matching technology (it was called Match Driver) to save advertisers the trouble of listing both singular and plural forms in their accounts. This soon expanded into verb stems and common misspellings. If a user types **seattle hotell** by accident, wouldn't an advertiser for **seattle hotel** want to show up anyway? No doubt. But because this kind of technology is automated, there are all sorts of unforeseen outcomes. And at various junctures, Overture was pushing the envelope too far, showing ads on too many variations without regard for the advertisers' wishes. At one point, they began factoring in the ad title you'd written, along with the keywords in your account, to decide whether to show your ad on a related keyword. A ridiculous example was an old ad of mine that I'd all but forgotten about, running only on Toronto-related and Canada-related keywords such as **Toronto marketing**

consultant, **canadian search marketing**, and **search engine marketing Toronto**. The ad had a frivolous title: "World-Famous Consultant...from Toronto." Apparently, based partly on my ad titles, Overture's Match Driver was showing my ad on queries that had nothing to do with the keywords in my account, such as **famous Canadians**. A lot of people type that query, it seems. Hey, my title was a joke to get local companies to read my ad, but I'm obviously not Celine Dion or Peter Jennings. The kinds of people who clicked on the ad weren't prospective clients, needless to say.

In fall 2003, Google released a similar technology called "expanded broad matching," and it immediately began causing problems with campaign performance for some unlucky advertisers. Complaints on industry discussion forums, such as WebmasterWorld.com, were rampant. Some of my clients ran into major problems with increased spending for little return.

Google has been testing the technology ever since. It does work better now. At first, I feared that the new technology would render many of my favorite keyword tricks obsolete. But it did not. Google has backed off the expanded broad matching initiative to the point where many small variations are still performing quite differently in the marketplace, and are worth bidding on separately. You can often save money on some odd variations by using them explicitly and bidding less on them, which frequently generates higher ad positions for less money. You can opt out of expanded broad matching by making phrases into phrase matches or exact matches. This means that advertisers will continue to have the ability to maintain control over small keyword variations if they choose.

Let me run through a few of the major keyword variations you should consider adding to your account. The list is not exhaustive.

- Plural and singular forms.
- Verb forms, related nouns, related idioms (fix, fixing, fix up, fixing up, how to fix up, fix-it, fixer upper, fixer).
- Spelling mistakes or spelling variations (address, adress; email and e-mail).
- Numbers and codes (years, product numbers, other weird uses).
- Hyphenated and unhyphenated versions (soup ladle, soup-ladle).
- One word versus two words (teacup, tea cup).
- Abbreviations and acronyms.
- Phrases with who, what, when to capture readers who type a question into the search engine. (For example, **how do I repair a kite** or **how to launch a new business** might be common queries and might convert quite well.)

I've tinkered with many other tricks, such as using punctuation marks (**U.K.**) instead of just letters (**UK**). I'm not sure if they all work, since AdWords likely disregards certain punctuation marks such as periods. At certain points in time, these methods have worked, even if by accident. All I can say is, if conventional keywords aren't giving you great performance, try these tricks and any others you can think of.

Going Narrow

After achieving some success following a principle like "more specific keywords are often more profitable," many of us become complacent and stop exploring. Real estate, for example, is an increasingly competitive field. Many realtors have discovered the value of targeting home buyers and sellers in particular regional markets using phrases like **atlanta home values**. While working with one realtor I went a step further and made a suggestion that seemed obvious to me as a resident of a well-known area (High Park) that is sought by a percentage of home buyers: people are probably typing the names of neighborhoods into Google! Heck, for all I know, they're typing streets and the names of specific condo developments. So, if you've got a small campaign that's targeting buyers of Atlanta real estate, but find the keywords are getting too pricey, simply build out your keyword list. A realtor who wants more business should have no problem generating it for pennies per click just by thinking intuitively about probable search engine user behavior in the home buying field. In a hot condo market in many urban centers around the world, I find it amazing that so few realtors are buying AdWords targeted to the names of new buildings.

Whatever your field, make it your goal to double your click volume, targeting extremely targeted searchers, on keywords that should be priced at rock-bottom levels (due to other advertisers being too lazy to do what I'm suggesting here). In most cases, the return on your investment will improve substantially.

As you move forward, you'll engage in a process of extended keyword discovery. Once you master the art of keyword brainstorming and start using uncommon phrases along with keyword variations, you'll want to look at your account every month or two and attempt to revisit your keyword expansion efforts.

Keyword Troubleshooting

Google is always happy to advise you what to do in order to keep the keywords in your AdWords account activated: you should write more relevant ads and use sound campaign organization, as I've discussed thus far, to ensure you're getting as high a CTR as possible on all keywords. But what if they keep getting disabled before you've had a chance to experiment with various ads? What if you feel that a previously disabled keyword, due to a change in season or business conditions, might work now if you were to reactivate it? Here, I'll give you some tips on reactivating disabled keywords and what recourse you have when keywords are disapproved.

Rescuing Disabled (Low-CTR) Keywords

Disabled keywords represent a large pool of potential ad dollars that may be going unspent unnecessarily. Some advertisers may be on the verge of making certain high-volume keywords work, but fall just short of the mark. In such cases it's obviously worth knowing how to turn them back on. Unfortunately, Google hasn't thought this one out too well. For a time, it seemed that making any change to your ads in the group where the disabled keyword resided was a way to show that you were at least making an effort to optimize your account; so at one point, such actions would trigger a reenabling of disabled keywords. This is no longer the case.

What to do? Well, you can delete those keywords and move them to a new campaign or ad group—essentially moving the disabled keyword from one "place" to another. This seems like a pretty unsatisfactory way of dealing with the situation—advertisers who keep the shells moving, as it were, are more likely to wind up with a smaller proportion of disabled keywords than those who don't take such "reenabling" measures—but there you go.

You can also change the matching option on a keyword. If a one-word broad-matched keyword gets disabled, for example, you can put it in your account as a phrase match. A one-word phrase match works exactly like a broad match, but in this case it is being used to "fool" the AdWords system into thinking it's a different keyword. Often such workarounds will buy you some time, but then will wind up failing to clear the 0.5% bar as before, so don't get too excited about this cool tip.

If none of that works out, and if you simply feel that you have a special case that warrants special treatment, Google is usually pretty good at helping you out by turning disabled keywords back on, within reason. Rules are rules, though. In most cases, these keywords will continue to generate a low CTR for you (if they did before, they likely will again), so you'll find them disabled again. After a certain point, you may have little recourse but to throw in the towel and accept that you won't be able to make those words work for you.

Disapproved Keywords

Google doesn't allow advertising on certain keywords. I've run into prohibitions on liquor advertising and certain kinds of weapons, for example. From time to time, areas like casinos and online pharmacies are off limits, and using related keywords in your account might trigger an editorial review. If you run afoul of Google's keyword policies, they likely won't refer you to an exhaustive written policy to justify it; they'll simply send you a disapproval message, and there is likely little you can do. Policies on keyword prohibitions are set by senior people in the company, including the cofounders; editorial staff simply apply the rules. For now, the rules are not all that clear. In the future, we can only hope that they'll be made more explicit.

As with any decision, you can appeal to Google's editorial staff to reconsider, and sometimes your request will make it to a policy specialist for review. You have nothing to lose by trying, but some of these rules may be firm, so don't get your hopes too high.

Approaches to Bidding and Ad Position

Another fundamental variable in where your ads show up on the search engine results pages is bidding. As I've already discussed, AdWords determines ad position by multiplying your maximum bid by your CTR. When many advertisers are competing, you must either bid high, or have a high CTR, or some combination of the two, to appear near the top of the listings. Therefore, you need to develop a clear bidding strategy and not get caught up in the heat of the moment.

What Do We Know about Ad Position and Visibility?

Unfortunately, we know less than we'd like about how likely a user is to click on your ad, or whether users "see" ads that are sitting in the middle of the list around ad position 5 or 6. In the early days of AdWords, I (unsuccessfully) attempted to grill Google about such phenomena. I did gain a few insights by writing some things that were terribly wrong, and having them come out of their shell long enough to correct me! In any case, having a lot of campaign experience, I can help you avoid some of the major misconceptions and pitfalls.

The first misconception is that ad position is utterly decisive in determining whether you'll be visible. Users are smart enough to scan down the page to look for something that interests them. Don't get too worked up if you have lower ad positions. They generally don't hurt and can sometimes work in your favor.

One key problem with the Google bidding system is that you can't lock your ad into a certain position, even if you decide you prefer it. Let's say you find positions 8, 9, or 10 are bargains, but you prefer 10 above all. Short of using third-party bid management software, you'll have trouble staying in that slot. As a result you need to be flexible in your approach.

Ads are seen in all positions, and a good ad in any position can attain a good enough CTR to keep your keywords running. Be aware, though, that on some partner sites such as AOL Search, you might not be visible unless you're in the top three or four ad positions. This is one reason your volume of impressions and clicks can go up significantly when you up your bid to go from ad position 5 to 3, say.

We all have our likes and dislikes. I am partial to ad positions 2 and 3. Often but not always, ad position 2 will get you prominent placement above the results on Google Search, with a colored background. Ad position 3 typically puts you at the top of the ads in the right-hand margin—a personal favorite of mine. You pay significantly less than you would for positions 2 and 1, but you're still at the "top" of the right-hand listings, which looks good.

Others think about whether they're "above the fold" on the right-hand side of the page. Does your ad show on the user's screen, or would he need to scroll down to see it? That's not a huge worry, as many users' screens will show as many as six or seven ads above the fold. Indeed, it's starting to sound like lower ad positions can be a bargain, isn't it? For the small business on a limited ad budget, you can take a low-bid approach, sit in sixth or seventh position much of the time, and stay out of costly bidding wars. This reduces your risk.

Users' browsing habits vary so much that the benefits of one position over another are more a question of tendencies and averages than absolutes. On the whole, higher ad positions do generate more volume, and many "big spend" advertisers feel that they just don't get enough action in lower ad positions. Some swear that the cachet of a higher-position ad is better and thus convert to sales at a significantly higher rate. The jury is out on that one. Part of that might be the "AOL effect." Just showing up at all on AOL might help some business-to-consumer advertisers convert a lot better than they would on Google alone.

Google definitely does not disclose how CTRs fluctuate by ad position, but they do say that the CTR cutoff of 0.5% is "normalized" to take account of lower CTRs in some ad slots. So it may be a tad more lenient than 0.5% in some of those positions.

Do Your Bids Have a Sensible Purpose?

Your bidding strategy is important not only because it impacts the cost of your campaign, but also because it determines your ad positioning. When you look at the campaign summary or ad group view in your campaign management interface, you'll see the average ad position (Avg. Pos) reported over the selected time period. Since ad position fluctuates due to the nature of the auction system, the reporting tells you the average of where you showed up—say, in position 4.2 on the page—over that time period.

On the bidding front, AdWords defaults to using one bid for an entire ad group. While this may be a real time-saver, most advertisers generally want more control over their bidding and, therefore, ad positioning. To accomplish this, they use a granular strategy of bidding on individual keywords using Google's powerposting feature, which we'll discuss shortly. Fortunately, this is not an either/or scenario. Bidding individually on thousands of keywords would be counterproductive, but having the flexibility to bid and track some of your most important keywords separately is very useful.

When it comes to bid limits or ceilings, it's all about choice. Some advertisers feel that their budget is best spent by showing up in ad position 7 or 8. Some like 1 and 2. I'm partial to 2 and 3, but anything from 1.6 through 5 or so is acceptable. If you're seeing a lot of ad positions reported as 1.1 or 1.2, you may be overspending.

Although you don't have complete control of the exact position at any given time, you can maintain your desired positioning by developing a smart bidding strategy and monitoring the results regularly. Unfortunately, many advertisers don't have a strategy, which frequently results in poor decisions and zigzagging ad positioning.

Rather than winging it, you should establish a range that works for you and strive to keep your ads within the range. Whether it's 2 to 5 (my personal preference), or 7 to 12, just make sure it keeps your ad on page one. One thing's certain: if you're in ad position 23, you'll be waiting forever between clicks.

Set and Forget?

Many advertisers are concerned about the need to monitor their accounts. The key is to consider how much it's going to cost you to monitor bids closely. For smaller accounts, it may not be cost-feasible to pay a person to watch closely, or to invest in some of the third-party bid-monitoring services. With the recent advent of the AdWords Application Program Interface (API), we'll see more rules-based bid management technology being developed. But as an advertiser or software developer using the API, your usage of the Google AdWords interface will be limited by how much you spend (on a "token" system). Without going into too much detail, I want to point out that third-party bid management technology will be costlier if you have a large number of keywords and if you check and update your bids frequently throughout the day.

NOTE   *One third-party bid tracking service, PPCBidTracker, has a wide price range: as low as $50 and as high as $10,000 per month. The higher price is based on 10,000 keywords and 48 bid updates per day. The $50 price is based on 50 keywords monitored and updated 6 times per day.*

Most smaller companies will want to ensure that the costs of monitoring their bids are in line with their overall budgets. In most cases, there comes a point of overkill in monitoring, and every business needs to decide that point for themselves.

Remember that Google has a bid gap discounter that automatically charges you the minimum amount needed to maintain your current ad position. You can set your maximum bids fairly high and yet find that from day to day, the average actual cost may not differ very much. Some days, one of your competitors may take a holiday and you'll suddenly be getting cheaper clicks without having done anything with your bids. Because of this, it sometimes pays to look more closely at your actual costs than at your bids.

As PPC advertising has grown, the number of bid management tools available has grown as well. I'm sorry to say that I'm not particularly impressed with the current state of bid management software. Part of the problem is that most bid management tools were designed to work well with Overture in the days before bid gap discounters and other built-in features existed. Some features seem redundant today. Other features seem to foster mutually destructive behavior among advertisers. For example, several leading vendors offer a "punisher" feature to allow bidders to bid slightly higher to ensure that the next higher bidder pays more than they otherwise would after the bid discount is calculated. In my experience, the result of more automated "bidding to position" and "punishing" bid tactics on Overture has been an increase in destructive bidding wars and an unnecessary net transfer of wealth from advertisers to Overture. I'm wary of the same thing beginning to happen on AdWords.

To the extent that Google has now opened up the API and welcomes developers to invent new tools that synchronize with the AdWords interface, this state of affairs should be improving. But software developers can only do so much. It might be more difficult for them to create rule-based bidding such as "keep me in position 3 unless the bid required exceeds $3.00"—a common scenario when using such tools with Overture—because AdWords calculates position differently. I am nonetheless looking forward to any innovative new third-party aids that may come along in the next year or two.

Unlike competing services, Google AdWords does not let you see competitors' bids. Personally, I like it this way. It leads to less gamesmanship and less needless speculation about others' intentions and motivations. Worry about your own campaign, not someone else's.

How to Use Powerposting to Bid at the Keyword Level

Powerposting is a handy bidding technique that allows you to go into your existing ad groups and specify a bid for a specific phrase while leaving the "global maximum bid" for the group the same as it was. Let's say your max bid for the "lizards" group is $1.50. You want to bid higher on the phrase **buy lizards** but lower on the phrase **discount lizards**.

There are several ways to powerpost. The easiest is to access your list of keywords in AdWords, select the keyword(s) to modify, and click the Edit CPCs/URLs button that appears just above the keyword list. This displays an easy-to-use Change CPCs and URLs form. Simply enter the maximum CPC, enter a different target URL for this keyword if so desired, and click the Save Changes button.

If you prefer to do your own manual editing, you can access the keyword list, click the Edit Keywords link, and enter your own notations to signify different bids. The process is fairly simple. Just enter a pair of asterisks after the keyword, followed by a bid amount (for example, **"buy lizards" ** 3.05**). When you're finished click Save.

Let's say your global maximum CPC is set to $1.50. After you add powerposting notations to tell Google to bid something other than $1.50 on some of your phrases, the list of keywords in your ad group might look something like this:

lizards
"buy lizards" ** 3.05
kapuskasing
"discount lizards" ** .40
iguana

In this example, the maximum CPC for **"buy lizards"** is raised to $3.05, lowered to 40 cents for **"discount lizards"**, and kept at the default ($1.50) for **lizards**, **kapuskasing**, and **iguana**.

Powerposting has become a must for some advertisers, so they wind up doing a fair bit of this after-the-fact editing. For many of your keywords, you may want to bid only enough to keep your ad in position 2, 3, or 4 as opposed to 1, but if you're bidding high enough to keep your more expensive keywords visible to searchers, you'll potentially be bidding more than you need to on your "cheaper" ones, putting them in the #1 ad position when you'd be content with #2 or #3. If you're in #1 spot too often, that can be a red flag that you're overspending and may need to either lower your bid for the whole group, edit individual bids, or both.

In fact, there will be times when you get clicks for 5 cents in second or third position, but you'll pay something like 31 cents or 50 cents to get listed first. You may not want to be first all the time, and in cases like this, it can really mess up your average cost! At the risk of belaboring a point, this brings up a third reason to be tidy and organized in setting up campaigns and groups: it is easier for you to be thrifty. For many advertisers, the use of powerposting is like housekeeping to improve the effectiveness of their bidding strategies. You can go overboard with powerposting, though. Use it judiciously so you don't create mounds of difficult-to-interpret data and a lot of additional work in managing all those different bids.

Software Saves Time with Keyword-Level Tracking

Third-party software does have one major advantage: keyword tracking. Even if you don't use bid management software to actively manage your bids, it can be an indispensable aid if you're going to be tracking by keyword. A major problem with bidding by keyword is making sure you have the correct tracking URLs in your AdWords account so that you're also correctly *tracking* by keyword. You'll find it prohibitively time consuming to enter unique tracking URLs (another feature of powerposting, and a second set of asterisks followed by a URL) by hand for hundreds or thousands of individual keywords.

Fortunately, an increasing number of third-party tools allow you to tag every keyword with a tracking code and automatically insert all those codes correctly into your AdWords account in conjunction with powerposting. This is something you don't want to do by hand. Some examples of tools that assist with keyword-by-keyword tracking include Did-It Maestro, PPCBidTracker,

Atlas OnePoint, Decide DNA, KeywordMax, and IndexTools. ClickTracks has just released a new bid management tool called BidHero, which, based on the company's track record, could prove to be the most intuitive of the lot. These tools are likely to improve and be joined by a host of new ones, now that Google has formally released an AdWords API.

Dayparting

Some software vendors emphasize the benefits of rapid bid changes and the need for *dayparting*— the turning on and off of ads, or adjusting bids based on prior knowledge of time periods when customers are more or less likely to buy. As you gain more experience with AdWords, you'll probably feel the need to explore such advanced bidding strategies at some point. Large retailers may have no choice but to daypart, as their razor-thin margins make it crucial to generate revenues on as many clicks as possible, and not to waste money showing ads to nonbuyers (for example, in the middle of the night).

Many advertisers can safely ignore this for the time being. An argument can be made that you can out-think yourself. For example, it could actually hurt your company to reduce exposure with some advanced dayparting method when this exposure might actually be a cheap long-term brand-building method that compares favorably with exposure in other media.

One problem with dayparting is that ads do not always turn on and off instantly, especially on the sites of content and search network partners. So you can't be too exact with it.

Also, in an auction scenario, if everyone starts dayparting, the advertisers who remain should save money as advertisers drop out, thus canceling out the benefit of dayparting. It never hurts to consider ways of optimizing your account, such as turning the campaign off on Saturdays if you're sure that it's hurting your bottom line. But be careful not to be lulled into underspending based on faulty premises.

One of the main reasons some of my clients have been slow to adopt dayparting is that it's mainly offered by bid management software companies who also want to sell you on a whole range of additional features, so the process of choosing an appropriate solution was daunting for them. Again, let me point out that now that the API is officially available, more developers will be able to design applications that legitimately interact with your AdWords account; whereas in the past, the few developers who waded into these waters accomplished the same goals through unauthorized means. Now, if your needs are as simple as wanting your ads to appear only during the day from 9 to 5, it might be cost effective to hire a programmer to help you design a simple AdWords account scheduling application so you don't have to rely completely on human oversight. More off-the-shelf applications should become available as well. I'm betting a few of the simpler ones will even be free. I don't rule out Google building some simple dayparting right into the AdWords interface, either, but for the time being they appear to be standing pat.

Dealing with Foolish Competitors

The increasing cost of keywords is nothing new, of course, and every month brings new waves of advertisers testing the waters. Some will muck things up for you. But there's no need to panic just because some newbie comes in with both guns blazing, badly overbidding on your best keywords. You probably shouldn't be relying that heavily on those keywords anyway.

Advertisers shouldn't be goaded into bidding wars or overly discouraged by what seem to be high costs per click. Moreover, the proof is in the pudding. Wait until you receive a series of monthly reports with sufficient data to see a pattern. Things might not be as bad as you think! Look again at your data.

As much as CPCs may be rising in some areas, in others they might be dropping as advertisers pay more attention to their ROI data. In some fields we see reverse bidding wars taking place as some advertisers take a stand that they won't bid to position, but rather, to a certain cost per click that seems reasonable. So prices can rise, but they can also fall, and by taking action in lowering your own bids, you can contribute to that fall. When two or three of the top advertisers stop beating each others' brains out, you can see significant declines in CPCs in areas that were once thought to be cost prohibitive.

The various techniques I cover throughout this book should continue to insulate smart advertisers against foolish bidding wars.

Chapter 7

Writing Winning Ads

Since AdWords allows no graphics, colors, font styles, or other eye-catching elements, and even limits some powerful textual elements (exclamation points, symbols, caps, and more), your ad copy is the only thing you have to entice users to visit your website. Therefore, it has to catch their attention right from the start. In this chapter I'll provide pointers on writing effective Google AdWords ads. I'll start with some of the basic building blocks provided by great copywriters from the past and then move on to techniques unique to this particular medium.

Before delving into the mechanics of copywriting, you should be aware of two key principles of advertising on the Web, both of which target the user's experience as he or she makes the journey from a search query to a purchase on your site.

Targeting and Testing: Key Principles of Web Advertising

First, as you may have heard from various web pundits already, it's all about personalization. I can assure you, they're right! Regardless of whether you call it personalization, targeting, or micro-targeting, the harder you work to achieve it, the sooner you'll leave your competitors in the dust.

The fact that people are typing specific, interest-driven keywords into a search engine is part of an age-old phenomenon with a modern twist—the search for a solution to real or imagined problems. Advertisers who recognize this simple truth will, on the whole, enjoy better performance with their online campaigns.

What it boils down to is that the user who feels catered to will be a more responsive user. As soon as an ad fails to address the user's wants, needs, or expectations, there's a good chance that potential customer will move on to the next vendor. In Chapter 6 I mentioned Ray Allen of AmericanMeadows.com. Ray knows that it's not enough just to lure the potential buyer in. He keeps the personal touches flowing even after the user clicks through. This is why he includes things like the regularly updated, beautifully illustrated weblog found on his site (Figure 7-1).

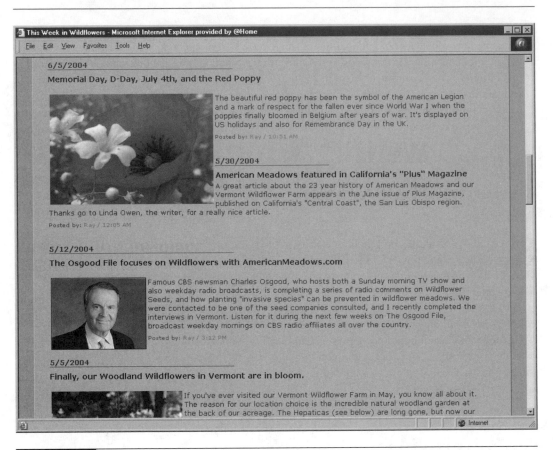

FIGURE 7-1   Ray Allen's frequently updated weblog, like his constantly changing ad copy, gives web surfers the kind of customized, relevant information they seek.

This kind of personalization combined with a passion for the subject matter, I am convinced, can make a difference in retaining customer loyalty in a fickle world.[1] Little wonder that, along with the rest of his marketing, Ray's Google ads look different from everyone else's. As a former advertising executive, Ray likes to draw on past experience and try out a variety of hooks: up-to-date special offers, seasonal information, and so on.

The second principle to bear in mind is that testing is the key to determining the effectiveness of your ads. Empirical data (results) matter more than anyone's opinion (including mine) about what kind of ad copy to write. The performance of your ads is so readily testable that your ad strategy should largely revolve around which elements to test as opposed to following some theoretical law of ad copywriting from the experts. When testing produces unexpected results, it can be an eye opener, and this helps you take a major step forward in understanding your audience's psychology and needs.

How Your Ads Look to the User

In Chapter 3 my goal was to convey a feeling for users' reactions to search listings and ads. Remembering that you're not creating a single ad to appear in a predetermined space is vital to understanding the variations you'll likely see in user response.

Impact of Media Type and Location

In the advertising business, the choice of media type and location (where the ad is placed) has always been a decisive factor in how an ad performs. The selection of media is, as much as possible, the selection of an appropriate target audience based on what we know about audience demographics. Since Google does not currently require users to register with personal information, we don't have direct clues about audience age, gender, income, and the like. Like everything else on the Internet, that may change in the future. (MSN Search has recently moved to offer advertisers more advanced targeting of this nature.) Even without such clues, the selection of keywords on which to advertise provides an opportunity to select an appropriate audience, albeit indirectly.

One key variable to be aware of is the placement of the same ad with different online services. A user who sees your ad as the result of an AOL Search rather than a Google Search may respond differently. It might be a simple matter of placement, such as the ad appearing in position 8 instead of position 1. Or it might have to do with the ad showing up in the middle of a keyword search as opposed to seeing it on the page where the user is reading an article, or beside a conversation in Gmail or other email account. Unfortunately, with limited data on hand, we are left to educated guessing at this point.

As you proceed, keep in mind that your ad will potentially show up in different contexts. It will, of course, show up in Google Search (and hopefully in the top ten depending on your bid/CTR ratio). One thing is certain, Google is a strong media brand and a good place to be showing up, which you no doubt already know, and is the reason you're reading this book.

Fitting Big Ideas into Small Spaces

If you're sitting there wondering how you're going to turn 95 characters (including spaces and punctuation) into killer ad copy that will sell your product or service, don't worry. Yes, it's true that the character limit is so strict some advertisers refer to Google ads as "advertising haiku," but this is not the selling stage and therefore doesn't require lengthy copy. Google ads are, or should be, qualifiers—the tools that sort, or prequalify, prospects, not sell to them, as I'll explain shortly.

After all, if you were able to write very long ads, and Google showed ten of them to a page, do you really believe that users would read them? Would you read them? Of course not. This system—short ads that people may read but can easily ignore if they wish—works well. The ad you write has to be relevant enough to induce action, but specific enough to limit that action to potential customers only.

| TIP | *Forget about cramming your whole sales pitch into your AdWords ad. You only have space for a clearly worded offer, plus one or two of the following: (a) a value proposition or third-party endorsement; (b) a call to action; (c) special wording that might weed out inappropriate prospects.* |

Remember, there will be plenty of space for detail on your landing page, after they've arrived on your website. You need to convey one or at most two concepts in your brief ad. Most importantly, the ad must be clear and unambiguous. Avoid using abbreviations, acronyms, and other devices that the target customer may not recognize. That doesn't mean you can't use them at all. If your potential customer should be familiar with them and they are relevant, by all means use them. Just make sure they're appropriate for the intended audience.

> **TIP**   *Clarity is a guiding principle of copywriting.*

Adopting the Right Tone

The correct tone for your ad is the one that best suits your audience. That may sound obvious, but depending on that audience, it may mean simple, exotic, mellow, wild, homey, sophisticated, or even technical to the point of being unintelligible to the average user. In the end, what counts is speaking the same language as your potential customer.

> **TIP**   *Setting the right tone for your audience is a guiding principle of copywriting.*

Bearing in mind that Google users are probably savvy enough to see through high-pressure sales pitches and other intrusive advertising, you'll want to avoid ad copy that focuses more on the cleverness of the writer than it does on the product being advertised. In reflecting on the general tone of the ads I've seen working well—and their general lack of cleverness—I've come to realize that the principles for writing effective AdWords are not so far from what some of the advertising industry icons of the 20th century, like David Ogilvy, have counseled (see the upcoming sidebar, "Giving Tradition Its Due").

What is different is that we're seeing more ads being written for a much wider variety of situations than ever before, and these ads are often being written by relatively inexperienced copywriters. Inexperienced copywriters should avoid the tendency to stereotype the process of writing ads based on what they've heard about contemporary advertising trends. Writing ads is a practical task and one that's unlikely to win you a major award.

As a Google staffer recently confided to a group of search industry execs at a meeting I attended, ad agencies aren't all that interested in search advertising today because they can't bill much for the service of putting together the ad "creative." Compared with the task facing agency creatives when putting together an expensive television or print campaign, Google AdWords basically requires "no creative," as this Google employee put it. You will likely find that there is not a great deal of magic to writing effective AdWords ads and that a range of approaches can work.

Nonetheless, working on a relatively narrow range of parameters, writing and testing AdWords ads *is* a science. Certain principles usually hold true, and violating them will waste time and money. For the time being, major ad agencies are relatively uninterested in this science because those billable hours aren't as profitable as other agency activities, like creating TV commercials and purchasing TV ads. More to the point, they don't have the analytical personnel who can do it

Giving Tradition Its Due

The great copywriters of old, such as David Ogilvy, did know a thing or two. Many of Ogilvy's admonitions in *Confessions of an Advertising Man* (Southbank Publishing, 2004), particularly the section about writing headlines, still apply to search advertising. He counsels directness over cleverness and offers suggestions such as ensuring that headlines appeal to readers' self-interest, for example. He says that copywriters must resist the temptation to entertain, and that their performance ought to be measured by how quickly they can foster the adoption of new products and ideas. Ogilvy's views on such matters seem to have great foresight considering that no one could have foreseen the flexibility of the Internet, the fragmentation of media, and the demanding and highly measurable Google AdWords environment.

properly. Insofar as such agencies are considering moving into search marketing, it's on the hope that their clients will begin to spend more on it, and agencies will get a percentage of that as part of a large online media buy. Anyone who understands that this is not so much a buy as an ongoing test can thrive even if large agencies begin to run campaigns against them.

Many of those who work in the ad industry today repeatedly ignore the wisdom of pioneers such as Ogilvy, preferring to create ads that impress peers.[2] But peer recognition isn't what we're after here. As Ogilvy aptly put it in *Confessions*, "juries that bestow awards are never given enough information about the *results* of the advertisements they are called upon to judge." Instead, they fall back on "their opinions, which are always warped toward the highbrow."

Fortunately, with all the data at your disposal, your opinion is the last thing you'll be forced to rely on when it comes to writing effective Google ads.

Trying to win an award in such a small space would be difficult, wouldn't it? Let's look at a hypothetical ad by Tad, a transplanted agency type who is so bored with writing search engine ads that he comes up with this ad to sell some enterprise software from a company called Reemar:

Reemar's App Kicks!

Reemar's slim shady is the PrSolvR.
Yo BigCorp: we're here to destroy u

Apparently, Tad thought this ad would be "triply ironic." No one would think anything like this would be cool, so by some convoluted logic, Tad believed this ad would imprint his "signature style" and really have them talking (not customers, but ad industry people and awards juries). The only thing that would probably happen is that the ad would confound users, they wouldn't click, and the advertiser's keywords would get disabled.

Not only does the previous ad fail even to hint at what PrSolvR does, or indicate any benefit whatsoever, it might violate Google's editorial guidelines. (Different versions of Tad's ad also had weird punctuation, in addition to the veiled threats against BigCorp.) The word *yo* would also be seen by the AdWords spell checker as a misspelling, and the author of the ad would then have to wait for Google Editorial to grant an exception. They might not grant it.

Now let's look at a non-Madison Avenue approach to Reemar's ad. Perhaps you believe that a more industry-centric ad would speak to your target audience, who, you think, are savvy in the extreme. So you try this:

Faster DWW Func in FWall?

GMUI modules 3X beat KLT security
"best pligtonferg of '04"-WRSS Mag

Well, maybe the people who read your ads are not that savvy. Or, like most average people, even savvy ones, they prefer not to read gibberish. This ad fails too. With the use of less jargon and more plain English you can turn the previous ads into a winner:

Easy & Powerful Firewall

Reemar ProblemSolvR beats BigCorp
Terminator by 74% in industry tests

This example uses the word *easy*, which tests out better than a few other adjectives describing your software. It says you're selling a firewall, which is exactly what you're selling and what that user typing **firewall product reviews** is probably looking for. And it introduces doubt about the quality of the industry leader (you have proof on your website). They happen to have 81% market share (you only have 6%, so comparing yourself with them is inevitable), but their product is rather expensive and difficult to use. This piques the interest of real prospects—enough to click on your ad—but because it's fairly clear about what you're selling (and mentioning BigCorp Terminator makes it even clearer, as it further "marks" this territory), you don't attract the confused or the curious. From here you can go on to test other ads that highlight affordability, or perhaps include a limited-time offer.

The bottom line is, sometimes plain and simple is the most effective ad copy to use. While every attempt may not be a winner, as long as you hit the tone right and write a clear ad, you'll know you're on the right track if your ad is attracting a strong clickthrough rate and, ultimately, if your post-click tracking shows these clicks converting to sales, leads, and registrations. Tracking users after they click is covered in detail in Chapter 10.

Here's another example that shows the difference in performance when you do a better job of understanding your target audience. The first ad uses a generic and somewhat hyped-sounding headline, with some impressive but unverifiable claims:

Hot Stocks Uncovered

Our portfolios were up 67%, 58%, &
34% for 2003. Free trial & report.
www.FindProfit.com

The second ad uses more specific jargon and touts the founder's credibility:

Short-Term Trading

New site from Raging Bull founder
RT commentary. Free report & trial
www.FindProfit.com

The first ad pulled only 0.5% CTR, leaving keywords at risk of being disabled. The second ad pulled a much healthier 1.3%.

A third ad was a hybrid of the two, using the short-term trading headline but sticking with the claims about portfolio gains. As you might expect, it performed somewhere in the middle, at 0.8%. The underperforming ads were dropped, and a couple of additional tweaks were then tried with the winning ad. Tone, directness, and credibility helped this new information service find its audience. Of course, we only know this in hindsight. No one could have predicted in advance that Bill Martin's and Matt Ragas' past experience in creating investment-related content at financial discussion site RagingBull.com would resonate so concretely with the target audience.

Bill and Matt gained some fame in the dot-com boom era as college students who founded a stock discussion site that grew rapidly from inception in 1997, attracted $22 million in investment from CMGI and CNET, and went on to be acquired by Terra Lycos in 2000. Many savvy online traders seem to know who Bill and Matt are because they remember trading stock information at Raging Bull. Based in large part on their paid search campaigns, the paying subscriber base of FindProfit.com has continued to grow throughout 2004 and 2005.

> **TIP**   *Credibility is a guiding principle of copywriting.*

Be careful not to obsess about ad copy so much that you change it when you perceive it to be stale. Remember the maxim that you should stick with a campaign as long as your accountant likes it.[3] Who cares if you're bored by a certain phrase or angle; who cares if your friends wonder if you're ever going to put up a new ad? If it ain't broke, don't fix it! Continue to test new theories; you may find something that works better. Just don't make changes simply for the sake of making changes.

One approach that withstands the test of time is the appeal to your customer's self-interest. Saving money, making money, winning at something, getting a deal, being able to make installment payments, alleviating an annoying headache, beating a competitor, making a friend—these are all reasons for most users to decide that what you have to offer may be the ideal choice for them. Sometimes, you'll be offering a product that is sold online (such as generic pharmaceuticals) that competes directly with high-priced brand-name items. In service industries, the same approach works. A local insurance broker might combine the idea of shopping for the best price with personalized service that can help the customer through this complex process. People can figure out for themselves whether their self-interest is best served by responding to your ad.

It's possible to go too far in analyzing the underlying motivations (money, sex, love, beauty, simplicity) that supposedly drive every purchase. At the extreme are the ads you see from time to time in technology magazines somehow trying to convince readers that supermodels will be impressed if they would just acquire the latest in RAID disk array technology. It would be funny if it weren't so prevalent. Surely there must be a better way to convey a product's benefits.

In some industries, exaggerated promises work. For a brief shining second, some golfers appear willing to believe that hitting a ball two yards farther is akin to conquering the galaxy. In almost any business, appeals to customers' rational side—to improve their communications skills by buying a book, tape, or hiring a coach, for example—often work. But what motivates someone to purchase seeds for a certain mossy perennial? They desire a beautiful garden, of course. Do we need to know why they want a beautiful garden? Probably not. I'm not sure I even want to know. Ideally, at a certain point, the process takes care of itself: users want what you have, and you sell it to them. I think it may be a blessing that Google advertisers can't gather detailed demographic information on Google users. I don't personally want access to the proverbial electrodes to the head that might reveal every motivation that drives purchase behavior. Having access to a narrower set of user data actually makes this job easier for the average business to deal with.

Addressing Multiple Priorities

Writing ads would be easier if you had a single goal in mind, but that isn't the case here. You must weigh a number of priorities. The two primary goals of an AdWords ad actually compete with one another. Sound confusing? It isn't really. On one hand, your goal is to encourage prospective customers to click your ad. On the other hand, you want to discourage inappropriate prospects from clicking on your ad so you don't waste money on clicks that have a low probability of ever turning into sales. But if all advertisers became extremely good at this filtering process, Google would be showing ads that got lower CTRs across the board, which would hurt them in at least a couple of ways. First, the perceived relevancy of Google ads would be in jeopardy, but more importantly, Google would make less money per page of search results served, because fewer users would be clicking on ads. As a result, as I already emphasized in Chapter 4, Google designed the system to *reward* you for a higher clickthrough rate (the formula whereby your ad position is determined by your bid multiplied by CTR).

All else being equal, you should test your ad copy with a view towards generating higher CTRs on ads. As CTRs improve, you can bid less and maintain the same ad position. I sometimes advise advertisers to "walk bids down," or decrease their bids little by little, as their ad testing process yields ads with higher CTRs. This is a key technique for decreasing your average cost per click without any decline in performance. By default, then, most of my recommendations for split-testing ads will be about searching for that holy grail of higher CTR. If your highest-CTR ads turn out to perform worse from an ROI standpoint, then you'd need to revert to the one(s) that offered the optimal trade-off between CTR and return on investment. That's a matter for experimentation with the help of post-click tracking data, discussed in Chapter 10.

Balancing CTR and ROI

You may be thinking that a higher ROI is the holy grail you're pursuing. But this is an oversimplification, given how vitally important CTRs are not only in keeping a campaign running (that is, not disabled) but also in allowing you to lower bids and ultimately improve ROI. Remember, you must encourage prospective customers to click your ad while discouraging inappropriate prospects from clicking on your ad so that you don't waste money on clicks that have a low probability of ever turning into sales. While ROI will be the ultimate arbiter of success, realize that in the early going, you'll probably need to move CTR higher up your priority list than you might expect, or wish to, because of the strong incentive system built into AdWords that favors high-CTR ads.

Other goals for your ads revolve around credibility. You might wish to use certain phrases or wordings to reinforce your company's brand awareness, regardless of how well the ads perform over the short term. Management has every prerogative to sacrifice short-term sales numbers for long-term strategic goals if they believe that to be their mandate. Sometimes, then, ads that aren't really about selling anything might pop up on AdWords.

To be sure, a sampler of searches for dozens of terms will turn up few big-brand advertisers, and even large advertisers appear to be drawn to AdWords mostly as a highly measurable, direct-response medium. For the time being, most of the "presence and awareness"-style ads are from government and nonprofit organizations. For example, a search for **pesticides** brings up an ad from the Natural Resources Defense Council stating that "NRDC studies the environmental & health impacts of pesticides." This ad contains no call to action, and the landing page is the home page, which is packed with information but does not aggressively funnel users into a sales channel. Although the ad no doubt attracts donations, it also serves a more diffuse purpose. It simply draws attention to the organization and its mandate. For the time being, this type of advertising is relatively rare on AdWords.

Some ads will have multiple roles, attempting to increase sales, but only indirectly, by changing consumer perceptions. What about a company like McDonald's, which recently underwent a successful turnaround from a declining purveyor of supersized calorie-laden meals, to a solidly profitable company that can convince people to buy $6 salads at a drive-through where they once bought a $2 burger? Many know about the salads now, but it wouldn't cost that much to add to this awareness with a simple AdWords campaign. Online promotions by large companies have often been obsessed with complex schemes involving coupons, loyalty, contests, and so on. They require high-powered thinking. But given the low cost of a pay-per-click campaign, a basic campaign merely alerting the public to the sea change in McDonald's product mix—for example, adding awareness of the quality and health benefits of their new salads— would be worth every penny, even if no particular tracking scheme were built on the back end. For all the money companies spend on expensive television and billboard campaigns "getting their message out," pay-per-click seems like an incredibly cost-effective way to achieve that goal, one highly targeted customer at a time. And those kinds of avid customers create word-of-mouth advertising, which is free. A campaign of this nature wouldn't need particularly clever ads— "learn more about our delicious new salads" or "50% off coupon to try our Mandarin Chicken salad—limited time offer" would be enough. It would be the power of the salad-related keywords and the fact that the clicks were so inexpensive to reach out to salad enthusiasts that would be the real driving force behind such a campaign, not necessarily the ad copy.

To give you a better sense of the current economics on such a campaign, let's say McDonald's managed to garner a million ad impressions on their AdWords ad at ten cents per click, for a cost of $1,000. A million impressions for a comparable television ad would cost significantly more. According to recent press reports, CPM rates on 30-second ads on network prime time are running at about $16. Shorter commercials in off-peak hours might cost 40% of that, but ads on specialty channels can cost significantly more. At a relative "bargain" CPM of $7, a 15-second spot for McDonald's would cost $7,000, or seven times more than the AdWords ad. This doesn't factor in heavy production costs for TV advertising, nor does it measure its relative effectiveness. Search ads are significantly more effective and measurable even than other forms of *online* advertising, yet on a lot of very targeted keyword inventory, you still don't need to pay an outrageous premium. Keep in mind that those "impressions" for a McDonald's spot are impressions of the ad by *anyone with their TV tuned to that channel*. Search ad impressions are restricted to people who have actively typed a query into a computer. The difference is difficult to quantify, but qualitatively speaking, the contrast is stark. Performance aside, the disparity in price between TV advertising and search advertising (7x in this example) is great enough that more big companies will find the opportunity worth investigating.

Some time after pondering this example, I did spot a special McDonald's promotion being tried in an AdWords ad for McDonald's Canada only (triggered by a search on the keyword **McDonald's**). The campaign didn't make much sense to me—coupons for low-end sandwich meal specials for different days of the week—but I was intrigued to see larger companies beginning to experiment in this way.

Larger companies needn't confine themselves to direct-response models. Even beginning to create a change in consumer perceptions about a product line (KFC is another major fast-food chain said to be planning a transition to healthier meal offerings) could create word of mouth that would pay major dividends. And while we're on the subject of healthy eating, the In the Zone Delivery meal service I used to save time while I completed the final draft of this book advertises in the newspaper, and on AdWords keywords like **zone diet**, but the broader words like **salad** remain relatively barren of advertisers. A combination of Google's tough relevancy rules and advertiser indifference to keyword inventory seems to be leaving plenty of these "open spaces" in the right-hand margins on Google Search. I doubt that this situation will stay static.

Currently, forward-thinking campaigns by large corporations concerned about protecting their brand image or sending a general message to consumers are relatively rare in the pay-per-click online ad space, which leaves many opportunities for nimble smaller companies.

Maintaining Accuracy

One of the most important pieces of advice I can offer is, be meticulous. The image of your company as a provider of quality at every level of the operation certainly won't be helped if you have misspellings in ads or use nonstandard punctuation such as capital letters at the beginning of every word in the main body copy. Some advertisers write their Google ad copy as if no one is watching. Obviously, just the opposite is the case. Don't make spelling and grammar mistakes!

> TIP   *Accuracy is a guiding principle of copywriting.*

You should also avoid false or unverifiable claims. Google Editorial might clamp down on you if you use unverifiable superlatives such as *best, cheapest*, or *longest lasting* anyway. But no matter what Google says, you must ensure that you do not shade the truth, misrepresent your product, or misreport your pricing. As an Internet marketer, you're under the microscope. "Accidentally" inserting *fresh* for a frozen shrimp delivery can land you in regulatory hot water.

If you're a consultant, or work in a company with a clear chain of command that requires approval of written materials, leave new ads on hold until the appropriate person approves them. For smaller companies, this offers another advantage. While the big guys are waiting for approval, you can beat them to the punch and test new ads at will.

Getting the Most out of Your AdWords Ads

Possibly the most consistently successful copywriting tactic is to write more ads, make them more personalized, and make sure that more of your ad titles and/or body copy match (or come close to matching) the keywords the user types in. This dovetails with the admonition to "organize, organize, organize" in Chapter 5.

Clearly, if you sell a fairly diverse line of (let's say) diamond jewelry, your performance won't be as good if your whole campaign relies on a single generic ad:

Diamond Jewelry Store

Earrings, bracelets, watches, more
Check out our weekly specials!

This ad might be fine for those searchers who have specifically typed **diamond jewelry**, but if they typed **diamond bracelets**, it would probably be outdone by a more specific ad run by a competitor. As I've said before, users gravitate towards the ads that match more closely to what they've typed into the search box. Both Overture and Google frequently state this at industry conferences, and the data I've seen from client campaigns usually bear this out. To improve on the performance of this ad, you'd simply write ads that are more targeted, such as this one:

Designer Diamond Bracelets

Diamond bracelets by top designers
Dazzling one-of-a-kind items!

The effectiveness of an ad depends on a large variety of factors. Your ad must inspire confidence in the user. As you ponder alternatives, don't overthink. Just plunge in and write an ad or two that you believe will attract your target audience, and test and adjust from there. In this case, I mentioned one-of-a-kind items to reinforce the image of designer jewelry so as to attract a higher-spending clientele.

Getting Help from the Experts

Can we learn about what works from professional copywriters, for example, Bob Bly and Nick Usborne? Having reviewed their work, I'd say yes and no. Consider that many AdWords advertisers (myself included) stumbled into the process with no formal background in writing marketing copy (but plenty of general experience in thinking, writing, persuading, and testing ideas). By all means, read the works of such authors—especially Usborne's *Net Words: Creating High-Impact Online Copy* (McGraw-Hill, 2001), which is particularly accessible and current. But keep in mind that some of their teachings about writing for the Web only apply to websites and e-newsletters, both of which provide considerably more room to develop your message. Unfortunately, an understanding of either will not be much help in writing AdWords haiku.

For other background materials that help achieve better bottom-line results from ads, more and more marketers are delving into the literature on "scientific advertising," which begins with a very old book by Claude Hopkins entitled (not surprisingly) *Scientific Advertising* (Chelsea House Publishing, 1984). It includes various split-testing practices that have been adopted by many direct marketers (direct mailers) over the years. A more recent book by Seth Godin, *Survival Is Not Enough: Zooming, Evolution, and the Future of Your Company* (Free Press, 2002), helped me understand the evolutionary process of more rapid testing and improvement that seems to be required in modern companies.

With so much material available, it's easy to get carried away. Not only have social scientists been writing about this type of thing for centuries, but since the "Total Quality Management" movement, the market has been flooded with books about testing and improvement of manufacturing processes. This carried over to other fields such as web design. More recently, buzzwords from the manufacturing world seem to be leaking into general usage to cover almost any situation, but they don't always apply. When your child's T-ball coach starts talking about Six Sigma swing improvement, it's probably time for a reality check.

In any case, writings covering the rapid technological improvements at companies like Intel and Netscape—and now, Google—have been a staple of the business bookshelves and have filled magazines like *Business 2.0*, *Wired*, and *Fast Company* in recent years. It's sexy to maximize performance and to "iteratively" improve your processes through a series of versions, just like chip manufacturers and software companies do. But even these companies understand that the point is not to improve on every single aspect of their operations, just the aspects that matter. Furthermore, unless you're a billion-dollar company, you'll have to scale back your ambitions when it comes to ad testing.

Six Rules for Better AdWords Copy

So far, I've discussed how principles of advertising and copywriting provide a foundation for writing AdWords ads, but one problem with following standard copywriting techniques is that Google AdWords are anything but standard. Since they are out of the mainstream of copywriting experience, a specific set of rules applies. Here are my six rules for writing better AdWords copy:

- Match the user's query as closely as possible.

- Send appropriate cues by speaking the same language your target customer speaks.

- Filter out inappropriate prospects.

- Get the prospect's "action motor" going by inserting a "call to action."

- Based on CTR and conversion data, pick the winning ads among several you've been testing. Occasionally, introduce new ads so the testing process never stops.

- Inject some flair or brand appeal in the process.

Pick any example ad, and these six rules should be enough to get you thinking about how to write winning copy.

Rule #1: Match Ad Titles to Searched Keywords

The example about diamond bracelets gave you an idea of the typical process of improving on a single generic ad by writing many more specific ones so the ad titles match query keywords. (The example is drawn from a client campaign, but the type of jewelry has been changed to protect the confidentiality of their data. My tests consistently proved the power of creating a large number of more specific headlines as opposed to a smaller number of general ads about the jewelry store. In most cases, the more specific headlines had significantly higher CTRs.) This isn't a rule that applies across the board, but in many cases where users are looking for a specific item that might be found in a retail catalog, such as a diamond brooch or a diamond pendant, ads that contain that exact item in the headline feel more personalized to the user, so they're more likely to click.

Working for clients like this, I'm often amazed at how well they can do against much larger competition simply because the other advertisers may have limited themselves to a generic ad covering, for example, diamonds or jewelry in general. Ads that have a "canned" feel to them— or more to the point, ads that don't seem likely to take the user to a page describing *exactly* what he's looking for—might not get clicked on quite as often.

Perhaps you're wondering if this tendency would continue if every ad on the page had exactly the same title. If everyone did this, and every ad contained "diamond brooch" in the headline for ads appearing next to searches for **diamond brooch**, it's possible that a different sort of headline might stand out and therefore be clicked more often. For the time being, this is still a strong rule, but like any user tendency, it's subject to change.

Rule #2: Send Appropriate Cues to Your Target Audience

A corollary to matching ad titles to searched keywords is *appropriateness* and sending cues to certain consumers, and that's a bit subtler. You might not consider the mention of "one-of-a-kind" jewelry items to be filtering out bad prospects so much as it is a kind of cue that you hope will resonate with a very specific type of customer because it literally speaks their language. Some car buyers will respond to "240 hp" or "6-speed manual"; others will assume the horsepower is in line with comparable vehicles and will actually respond better to "zoom, zoom." (I would like to state for the record that I am not one of those who would buy a car just because it goes "zoom, zoom.")

Consider using language and terms that will resonate with your target audience. Let's say you sell housewares and your target customer is female, moderately affluent, and seeking the latest style. You're not selling traditional dinnerware, and there's simply no better way to convey that than just to tell it like it is, by using words like *modern* and *contemporary* in your ad copy. Clearly, different demographics require subtly different wording in ads, which can be achieved with an adjective here, an expression there. For example, even though I'm a nonexpert when it comes to martinis, and I don't throw dinner parties, I knew that the ad copy "elegant martini misters for the discerning martini-meister" would work well for my client, KlinQ.com. I was speaking the lingua franca of the affluent, young, martini-drinking set. A light touch of tongue-twisting humor and a post-materialist (nonbasic, nondiscount) ethic were conveyed to give that demographic what they were looking for. The fact that customers quickly found what they needed, and felt that this retailer understood their needs (my ad was only a small part of that equation), quickly overcame any price sensitivity on the part of the *bon vivants* in the market for martini-ware.

Rule #3: Filter Prospects

The process of filtering out bad prospects begins with keyword selection and targeted phrasing. Make sure your keywords are not so broad as to cause your ad to appear in searches that are irrelevant to your product or service. For example, if you're offering loans for cars and title your ad "Low APR Loans," you'll get people looking for personal loans, mortgages, home equity loans, recreational vehicle loans, and student loans, most of whom are not your target customers. By adding the word *auto* ("Low APR Auto Loans") to your ad, you can eliminate a large percentage of those nonproductive clicks.

Probably the most common problem pay-per-click advertisers face is the bargain hunter who clicks on an ad seeking an inexpensive or free product. Sometimes it just doesn't pay to be subtle. One client from the UK was getting too many tenants applying for loans, even though the product was clearly targeting the home equity loan market and even though the ad made it seem reasonably clear that you'd need to be quite creditworthy. The problem was easily solved by making the first word in the ad copy: "Homeowners!" (A searcher would be hard pressed to misinterpret that.)

As pay-per-click advertisers, we need to be mindful that there are millions of noncustomers out there clicking away on our ads. We need to be particularly careful of those who are looking for something cheap or free. Unless you rely on a strategy of upselling people from an entry-level product or free offer, you might need to filter the low end of the market. I realize that advice won't apply to all of you, but the general principle of filtering does, and the "low end" (low-budget buyers, tire-kickers, and looky-loos) presents a formidable challenge for pay-per-click advertisers. Keep in mind, though, the difference between someone who is in the early phases a normal buying cycle (just not ready yet) and someone who is simply a poor prospect for you. They won't all buy immediately.

The classic example that's been given by companies like Google at seminars on this matter is the seller of graphics software who, due to poor ad copy and indiscriminate keyword selection, is inundated with clicks from people looking for free clip art. When I refer to the low end of the market, I'm really referring to a type of behavior that is endemic to search. Most of us constitute the low end (or "no end"!) of the market for advertisers on any given day, because we might be looking for free information, shareware, and so forth. If we click on someone's ad listing when we're in the "looking for free stuff" search mode, we usually wind up costing that advertiser money. Niche advertisers are looking for a relatively rare bird: a relatively warm prospect who is likely to convert to a customer.

Does this mean you should put your prices in your ads? You're welcome to test it, but it doesn't necessarily work. You can convey a sense of your positioning in a price range with verbal cues and brand names. Most folks have a general sense of where Pier 1, Holt Renfrew, Home Depot, Best Buy, McDonald's, Outback Steakhouse, and Target stand in the price spectrum just from their well-known brand names. If you're not well known, you can certainly choose your words carefully to convey a sense of price points. "Competitively priced data loggers" or simply "data loggers" might convey one message, whereas "industrial use data loggers" might convey another. Someone who is confused and seeking a speedometer gizmo of some sort for his bicycle, at the very least, is unlikely to be confused enough to click on the ad if you work in cues like "industrial." On popular terms, sometimes even stronger language may be required to deter the mass market from clicking on your ad for a niche product. One simple word might not be enough. Though it sounds redundant, "data loggers for business and industry" might be needed to weed out the wrong sorts of browsers if data logging for personal uses like sporting activities were suddenly very popular. When too many eyes are flitting quickly across ads, it may not hurt to hit them with a couple of really obvious prequalifying words (such as both "business" and "industry" in this example). Note too that such examples are not cast in stone, because search behavior is fluid. Spikes in search activity on certain keywords can be driven by shifting trends, news items, and consumer tastes. These spikes in the frequency of certain keyword searches can cost your business, so you need to be attuned to changing search patterns and filter more aggressively if you believe that you're paying for too many mass-market clicks that don't genuinely want what you have to offer.

I've worked with service-oriented clients, such as one in the web design business, who are upset that they receive too many low-budget inquiries from their pay-per-click ads. Unfortunately, though, shouting about a $5,000 price tag up front is no answer to this dilemma. After all, why deter potentially good clients? Some relationships take time to develop. To be blunt, I found it very hard to work with one client who only wanted me to "send him $5,000+ customers." It's all too easy to forget that there are many others competing for those customers (and advertising in the same space!), and that for these prospects, $0 is always the default amount that they plan to pay you until they get to know you a little better. When a potential customer is early in the buying cycle, you can hurt yourself by posting a price completely out of context, not least because a competitor can easily undercut you in the same space.

Ultimately, your whole business model needs to be examined when you are selling a high-end niche service by targeting popular keywords. For example, a low-cost tool or publication might be sold to people typing those words, creating a break-even campaign that later funneled some prequalified inquiries for the high-end service. There is no way of guaranteeing that you will only get inquiries from "$5,000+ customers." Certainly, it takes a lot more to position a business than simply listing a high price (or low price, in the opposite situation) in your ad.

Wholesale versus retail, and business-to-business versus consumer, are two other common filtering concerns. In wholesale and business-to-business, the number of target buyers is smaller. There should be no sugar-coating the fact that filtering out all the inappropriate prospects is difficult. Mostly, this should be done with keyword selection in your AdWords account. But when it comes to ad copy, you'll want to experiment. In certain industries, conventions grow up so that you can address the target audience with ad titles they'll understand. For example, in web hosting, an ad title like "Reseller Hosting" would be fairly well understood by your target audience.

Recently I was contacted by the principal of an agency providing public relations services to companies seeking to reach a Latin American audience. His target audience for this particular campaign was narrow: he sought to build new partnerships with public relations agencies rather than selling directly to PR-seeking companies. There is no magic formula for ensuring that only PR agencies will click on your ad, but certainly a plain-spoken ad with wording such as "solutions tailored for PR agencies" would be on the right track. Such a campaign would almost always be inadequate on its own. Direct mail, personal networking, and phone calls would need to be factored into the mix.

Rule #4: Insert a Call to Action

Google now recommends experimenting with calls to action, such as "download" or "shop and compare." Editorially they only reject a small percentage of calls to action. (As stated in their written policies, they prohibit universal calls to action such as "click here.") They've been a bit quieter about the related notion of an "offer," which is a staple of ad copywriting. If I had to guess at the reason why, I'd say they are concerned about their advertising space being littered with unverifiable claims. Nonetheless, ad copy with an offer must be tested against ad copy without an offer. The results may amaze you.

One client, for example, tried this ad that included a bland mention of their company name along with a product benefit:

ClearTone Acne Treatment

Finnish acne cream now available!
Clearer skin in as little as 7 days
foracne.com

A second ad contained a benefit and a free offer:

Get Clear Skin in 7 Days

European Acne Treatment now in the
US. Act now & get one month free!
foracne.com

The first ad pulled a CTR of 0.8%. The second ad pulled 1.7%. By generating a higher CTR, we were able to keep more keywords enabled, and we were able to lower bids and significantly lower average CPC while maintaining a similar ad position. This did improve ROI, though ROI could have gone down in the process of attracting more clicks. This is why it's so important that Google rewards advertisers with higher ad position when they do increase CTR.

We are hearing more now about testing calls to action such as "buy now" in pay-per-click ads, but what is not often discussed is the wide range of calls to action that are possible.

Such call-to-action suggestions should connect closely with the nature of your offer or with a larger marketing strategy that you're pursuing. One of my clients, a popular technology journalist, established a relationship with his audience by having them subscribe to a free newsletter about the foibles of Microsoft Windows as they affect the average computer user. It was his firm belief that the word *subscribe* sounded too daunting (he thought users would worry "would it cost money? would it mean an arduous sign-up process?"). He was adamant that we try the word *get* instead. As it turned out, those who saw the ad containing the word *subscribe* were slightly more likely to become subscribers than those who saw the ad containing the word *get*. The word *get*, evidently, did not explain to prospects what they'd be doing as well as the word *subscribe*. Moreover, the word *subscribe* did not result in unsustainably low CTRs. The concern over this word turned out to be much ado about nothing.

Rule #5: Run a Test, Keep the Winning Ads

Unless your marketing campaign consists of nothing more than a single AdWords ad, you'll need some method of measuring the effectiveness of your ads. With one ad, your sales either increase or stay the same. If the sales go up, your ad is effective. If the sales stay the same or, god forbid, go down, your ad is ineffective. If you're running a number of ads, and you should be, the only way to determine the effectiveness of your campaign is to do some testing. For a detailed look at testing methodology see the section coming up, "Testing Ads." After running a test, you'll delete the losing ads and keep the winners.

Rule #6: Inject Some Flair

Keep in mind that copywriting flair and writing catchphrases that cement brand awareness can be overrated in a realm where targeting and testing reigns. You might require more panache if your job is to write longer copy for the sales page on the website. Here, though, I am referring solely to your AdWords ads. For example, earlier I mentioned the example ad text "elegant martini misters for the discerning martini-meister." In many contexts, this ad would be too silly, but my test identified this ad as the winner, likely due to the whimsical tone. There are many more examples, however, of attempts to inject flair, whimsy, or style into an AdWords ad that simply fall flat. First and foremost, search users are trying to find their way around, not get a chuckle. In an ad for a website-building product aimed at novices, I tried the ad title "No Web Geek? No Problem." This didn't work; the ad got low CTRs. However, the factual ad text "no programming required" did work. Flair-driven advertising is still more the exception than the rule in AdWords copywriting, but you need to incorporate it as part of your repertoire of techniques depending on the target audience.

Testing Ads

Testing Google ads is best done through a split-test. The AdWords interface is set up so you can test the performance of ads "head to head." For ideas about what kinds of variables you'll want to consider testing, see the section "Ideas for What Variables to Test," a little later in the chapter. You'll be using special tracking codes to distinguish one ad from another. The subject of tracking is covered in considerable detail in Chapter 10.

In the broader marketing world, split-testing is an advertising methodology that has been perfected over the years by direct marketers, often at considerable expense. Sending two offers randomly distributed over two segments of a mailing list is one way of testing response. The marketer varies a key variable, such as envelope color or the copy in the introductory paragraph, and tests response rates. It might take many years to learn which combination of elements is optimal.

How Split-Testing Works

Fortunately, Google has made split-testing easy and cost effective. The ability to run two or more ads simultaneously against one another is actually built into AdWords. In any given ad group, you simply use the Create New Ad feature (see Figure 7-2), and presto, you're testing two ads

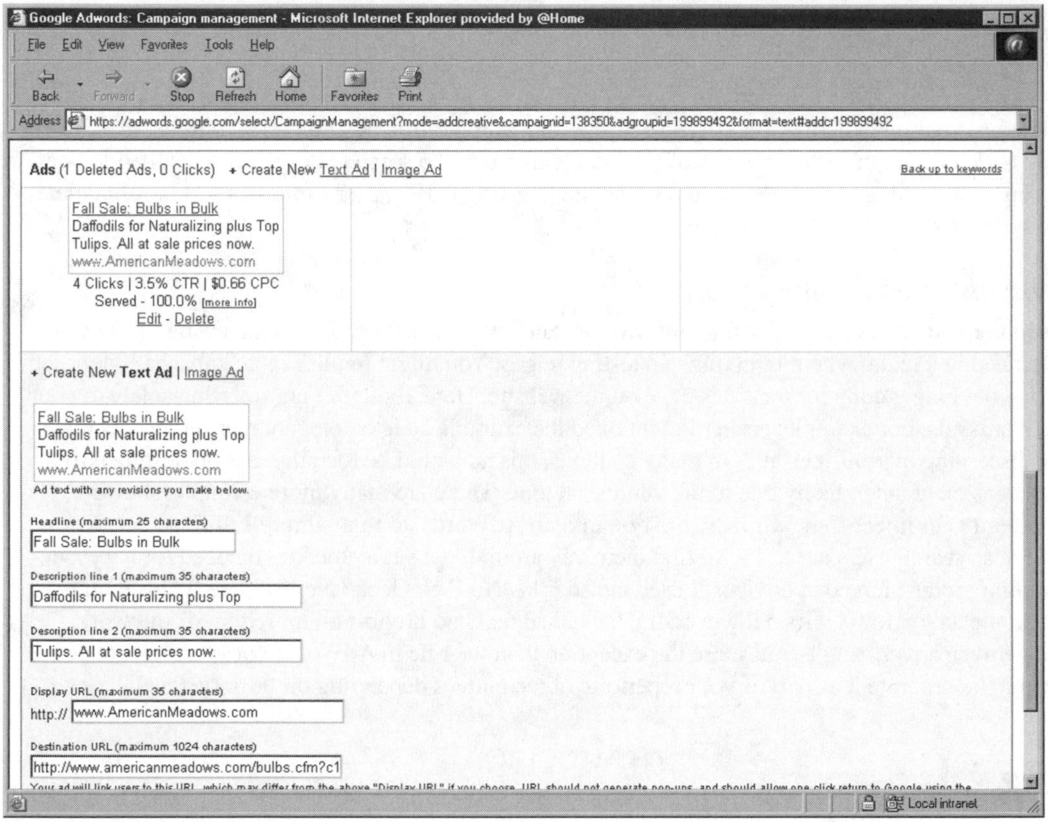

FIGURE 7-2   Click on Create New Ad, and presto, you've initiated a split-test.

against one another. The primary metric you'll be looking at is CTR, but if you're tracking by ad (using tracking URLs), you can also track conversion rates and ROI on each ad.

When you're running multiple ads in a single campaign, Google automatically rotates ads as "evenly" as possible. Therefore, if you run four ads simultaneously, each ad should be shown approximately 25% of the time. If your numbers do not show that to be the case, it might be the result of looking at a date range during which not all ads were running for the entire period. To make a reasonably accurate comparison you'll want to wait until all ads having been running long enough, and then choose a date range during which all ads were running. Unfortunately, you cannot adjust Google's automatic rotation so that some ads appear with more (or less) frequency.

> NOTE
>
> *To see the performance of your multiple ads, you'll need to scroll down the page past your keyword list when viewing at the ad group level. AdWords lists them all at the bottom, which can be misleading since the first ad on your list is also listed by itself more visibly above the fold.*

In an attempt to make the process as painless as possible, Google has another automatic feature, which is convenient, but makes testing less accurate. The feature has no formal name, but is referred to as the "ad rotation optimizer." It automatically crowds out your lower-CTR ads in favor of higher-CTR ads, which is great, if the only thing that matters is CTR. To get a true picture of the total performance of each ad, however, you need to disable this feature. To turn the ad rotation optimizer off, log on to AdWords, and open the campaign you plan to do the testing on. Next, click the Edit Campaign Settings link to view the options available for this campaign. Finally, uncheck the Automatically Optimize Ad Serving for My Ads option on the Edit Campaign Settings page seen in Figure 7-3. That's it. From this point forward, CTR will have no effect on how frequently the ads in this campaign appear.

The results of split-testing can be very educational. Even small changes in the ad copy can cause CTRs to vary significantly. For example, I discovered that the mere addition of a single letter had a profound (and unfortunately, negative) effect on one client's ad campaign.

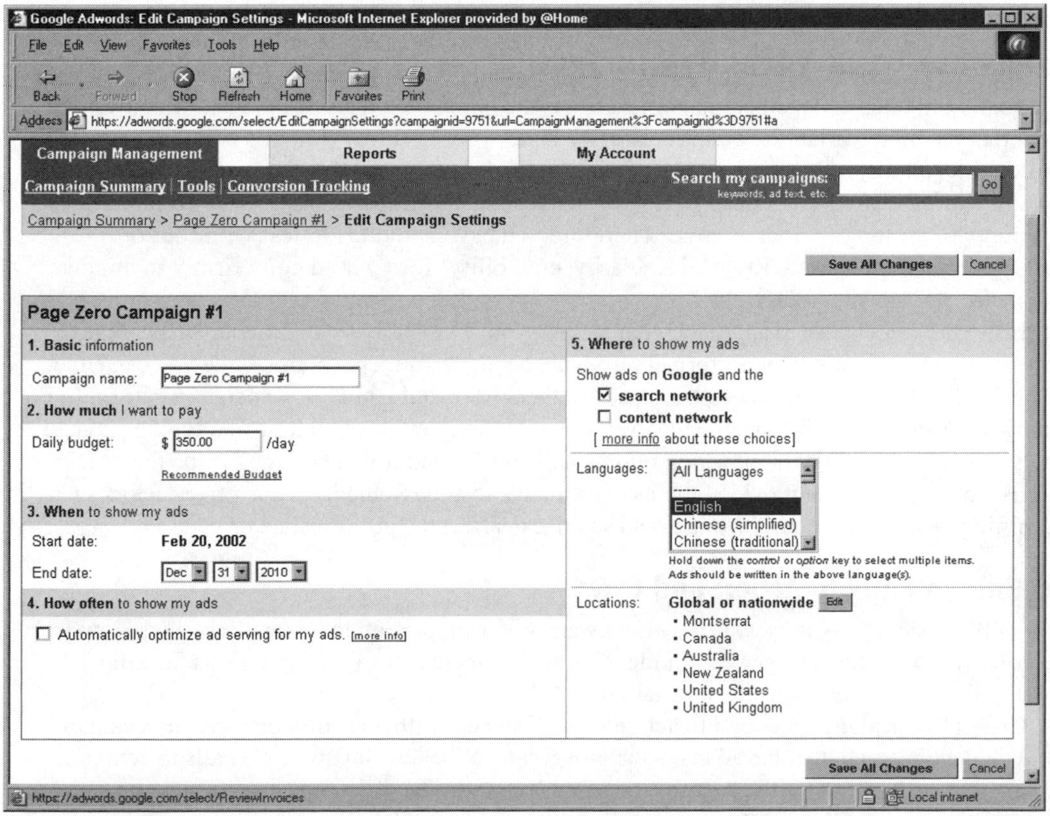

FIGURE 7-3   Uncheck the ad rotation optimizer, or AdWords will decide for you which ad is the "best performer."

This client sells a technical product that can be bought elsewhere in bulk, for a lower price. By changing the ad title from the singular "get your widget today" to the plural, "get your widgets today," I reasoned we could increase the average order size. What happened instead was that conversion rates plunged. It quickly became apparent that the singular ad attracted newbies, this client's most profitable customers, while the "plural" ad attracted savvy customers who thought they might find a new, lowest bulk price for this item. But when they didn't find that, they moved on without buying. The ROI on the ad that asked people to buy one of something turned out higher, in the end, than the ad that tried to get them thinking about buying more than one. Even though, ironically, the "newbies" often went in with the intention of buying just one, but wound up making fairly large orders once they were comfortable.

You'll have no way of making such unexpected discoveries unless you're looking not only at CTRs on ads, but also the revenues or actions converted by the ads you're testing. Some ads are effective at inducing the wrong kinds of prospects to click, which is generally a bad thing. Bear in mind though that Google does reward you for higher CTRs, so it will be relatively rare that you'll find that ROI is worse on an ad with a significantly better CTR, because you should be able to lower your bids on those ads.

Ideas for What Variables to Test

The first thing to consider when planning a test is the number of variables to test. Initially, it may seem that the more variables you introduce, the better your testing. While it's true that you could introduce an almost infinite number of modifications, keep in mind that the more variables you have, the more difficult it is to achieve conclusive results. Minor variables will eventually test differently over long periods of time. Therefore, the best method is to test with four or five possible *objectives* (brand, ROI, CTR, clarity, credibility) for your ad copy firmly in mind, in whatever proportion feels right.

However you choose to approach your testing, you'll probably find that your first couple of tests weed out the really poor performers from the better performers. At this stage you can either make drastic changes to the poorest ads and put them back in the mix, or just concentrate on fine-tuning the better ads in the bunch. However, there is a limit to the amount of fine-tuning you can do. Eventually, the law of diminishing returns will kick in, and it will be time to stop the tweaking and use the ads that have provided the most profitable results. Remember that other factors such as shifting tastes, randomness, timing, and so on, can affect the performance of your ads.

Testing on Calls to Action and Offers

One of the easiest things to test is the effectiveness of a simple call to action. In one ad, simply describe your product. Then create an identical ad, but include a call to action such as "Buy now!" "Try it free!" or some other variation.

Generally speaking, your call to action should connect with an action that's easily available from the landing page that the ad takes the prospect to. When testing multiple calls to action, be sure that each one takes the user to a different landing page. This is the only way you can accurately determine the effectiveness of the different calls to action.

Closely related are offers, which typically combine a call to action with a time limit or discount. Even without a call to action, an offer *implies* a call to action (purchase before a certain date to receive a discount, for example) and typically creates a sense of urgency. This real-life example should give you an idea:

Cool Birthday Gifts

For anyone! An amazing selection
of quality products. Delivered.
Uncommonlygifted.com

Cool Birthday Gifts

For anyone. An amazing selection.
15% discount for a limited time!
Uncommonlygifted.com

These two ads were tested over a relatively high number of clicks—in excess of 2,000 for each ad. Searchers clicked on the second ad more than twice as often (1.9% to 0.9%), allowing Uncommonly Gifted to bid lower on popular gift-related terms (average CPC was reduced from 17 cents to 12 cents) while maintaining visibility with a high ad placement on the page. The benefit continued after the click, as this ad generated a higher conversion rate to sales.

Testing on Syntax Variations

As I demonstrated in an earlier example in this chapter, minor variations like plural instead of singular can have a significant impact on the response your ads elicit. Since the ad space is so limited you'll be tempted to use abbreviations and symbols where possible. Remember that Google policy limits the use of symbols to their true meaning. Whatever you use, try testing both—the abbreviation and the full word or phrase, or the symbol and the word. For example, try using *and* in one version of an ad, and an ampersand (&) in another. See if it makes a difference.

Differentiation of Ad Copy from Other Ads on the Page

Frequently, many of the ads that appear for a given search will have very similar titles and copy (see Figure 7-4). If you find that to be the case, try setting your ad apart by using different copy or a totally different approach. The traditional approach to differentiation is to communicate your company's unique selling proposition or points of difference and focus on them; I'm referring to something a bit narrower here. As many advertisers will begin thinking alike about what creates an effective ad, you could try creative, unusual ad titles that might boost your CTR relative to the others. If seven ads say "pumpkin seeds" and yours says "premium pumpkin seeds" or "grow giant pumpkins," you might stand out just a bit.

Sell a Solution, Not a Product or Service, and Test It

If you were selling knee braces, you could have "Knee Braces" in your ad title, of course. But why not test an ad with "Knee Problems?" as the title and "knee braces" in the body copy? In general, ads that remind the consumer of their fears, problems, or concerns—"scary" ads—can

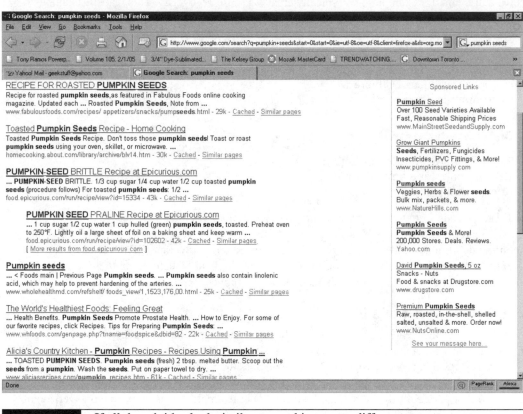

FIGURE 7-4   If all the ad titles look similar, try making yours different.

be effective if the product or service being offered in the ad resolves the prospect's perceived problem or fear. This approach is particularly effective in certain industries such as computer network security and insurance.

For example, "Is Your Family Safe?" is more likely to attract attention than "Carbon Monoxide Sensor." However, it might attract people looking for locks, alarm systems, and smoke detectors as well. The only way to know if it produces the desired results (higher ROI) is to test it.

Flair vs. Flat

As I've already pointed out, plain ads often work well in Google AdWords, but depending on your business, light humor and flair can help connect with the audience. For one client (KlinQ .com, a seller of designer housewares), I tested a fairly plain ad for teakettles against one for "whistling teakettles" that concluded with the hokey phrase "just whistle." The latter won out, much as the "discerning martini-meister" ad had performed well for another one of their products. This surprised me because such flair does not usually make a significant difference. The target audience in this case is obviously looking for the psychological lift that comes from purchasing "fun" kitchen items; they are seeking style, not merely basic need satisfaction or the best price.

In the realm of style, identifying a product with a celebrity might also be worth testing. Drawing attention to someone who endorses a product (a baseball player who wears an Indian Motorcycle jacket, an actor who wears a certain type of jewelry in a movie, a celebrity who has learned to drive a go-kart at a training facility) can provide context that reminds searchers of hot trends and also hints that the celebrity's glamour might rub off on them. If you use this technique, the content on your website needs to be factual in such cases to avoid potential liability issues.

The third-party endorsement falls under the general rubric of credibility. Rather than seeing this as merely a dimension to test, I believe that advertisers should always be thinking about credibility of this nature. "Voted best free content by PC World" or "USA Today recommends" are excellent endorsements that would stand out from other, similar ads on the page. However, it must be clear that the endorsement is real, as proven by the content on your landing page, or Google Editorial may reject it.

Brand Impact and Story-Telling

Consumers will look at the display URL before they decide to click. They'll also look for cues in the ad to decide if you're full of hype. So does this mean that you're facing an uphill battle if you're not a big company with a recognizable URL? Not really. To be sure, in some industries consumers will outclick a "familiar" ad by a factor of 4 to 1 over an ad from a company they've never heard of. But you can overcome the familiarity factor by capitalizing on your unique position in the marketplace.

Using familiar phrases, features, and benefits associated with your company, or emphasizing your long history, are things that should help you stand out from a crowd of wannabes. But if you don't have these, you need to invent something. You need to begin telling your own story and writing your own history. That doesn't mean misleading people! But your buyers often respond well to imagery and mythology. They want *you* to *create* this. "Diamonds are forever" isn't just a cheap slogan. Marketing campaigns by de Beers repositioned diamonds completely in the marketplace. They went from being just another precious gemstone, to the standard for engagement rings, with a suggested "two months' salary" dollar value attached.

Seth Godin reminds us that in the wider world of marketing, you don't get much time to tell a story. But if told consistently, encountering just a tiny sliver of the story later on can remind people of what you're all about. Godin shows an image of two-and-a-half letters of the Starbucks logo, and he's right: by viewing just a couple of letters and a single pointed shape from the logo, I immediately began to feel myself walking into the familiar Starbucks store layout. The other image he shows is a tiny drawing of the tip of an elephant's trunk. Just by glancing at a couple of circles and lines, the mind begins to evoke the majesty and beauty of this hulking beast.[4]

So you might consider your AdWords ad the "tip of the elephant's trunk." It can work in your favor whether you're a large company or a small one. But not if you haven't made the effort to invent a mythology to help your customers convince themselves about the experience of buying from you.

Some categories lend themselves particularly well to smaller players. A maker of fresh pastry shipped overnight—let's call her "Little Old Pastry Chef"—may do better than a large company whose brand name has already been associated with lower-priced products selling in supermarkets. Sometimes consumers are captivated by "small." Supermarket products aren't remarkable, but custom-made items are. If the smaller retailer seems dedicated to a niche like fresh pastry, consumers will be open to buying from it. Small companies with focused ads can beat large companies who run ho-hum, me-too ads. In some cases, it's the big guys, not the little guys, who look out of place. Unless you're really sure the recipient would like it, for example, you're probably not going to order a box of Dunkin' Donuts as a birthday gift.

The increasing consumer appetite for customization, and the growing adoption of local search, also gives smaller firms a potential advantage. Such trends at least don't appear to put the niche player at a significant *disadvantage*, as long as they're content to stay small. Larger retailers can also capitalize on such trends if they understand the psychology of their customers. A great example is Zingerman's (www.zingermans.com), which began as a deli in 1982 and today is one of the most successful online food retailers in the world. Zingerman's does so well by word-of-mouth and organic search listings that they don't need to advertise (or so they think!). But the remarkable thing is how few of their competitors are currently taking advantage of the wide-open keyword inventory on keyphrases like **online deli**, **cheeses**, and **specialty vinegar**. By doing so, someone could become the next Zingerman's. Can you build a brand online just with a sustained AdWords campaign using consistently worded ads? If the CPCs are generally reasonable in your field, what's stopping you? There's no sense worrying about the big guys. They're not as nimble.

In my view, a sense of physical place can be the biggest advantage going for the smaller retailer. A Canadian boutique called The Added Touch evolved into a mail-order (and now, online) sales leader. The company's brand was built largely around the Oakville, Ontario location of the original physical store, and customers are well aware of this. If Martha Stewart found herself in the Toronto area, you can imagine her making a beeline for tony Oakville. A live appearance at The Added Touch wouldn't seem out of the question.

Many online sellers today have a great story to tell, but they aren't telling it. Why not test ad copy—and website copy—that refers heavily to your physical location and humble origins against copy that emphasizes only product features and benefits?

Testing the Display URL

Speaking of the display URL, recall that this is prominently displayed at the bottom of every ad. Users may look at this for some cue as to the identity of the company they're dealing with. Some URLs, particularly short, readable ones, may inspire a more positive response than others. If your company name is two words, a typical thing to test is whether an all-lowercase URL gets a higher CTR than one with a capital letter at the beginning of each word—dolphinzone.com versus DolphinZone.com. You shouldn't uncover major differences in user response, but it's worth a look.

Because Google may allow you to include a directory name in your display URL, you may find that a keyword-rich directory name helps, provided you actually take the user to the appropriate category page. For example, you might test www.apple.com versus www.apple.com/imac.

Sometimes a client with a well-respected brand will want to test the impact of that brand in the display URL. A large financial conglomerate I worked with tried (generic examples given for confidentiality reasons) www.FinCon.com against a more generic site with the URL www.home-finance-savings.com. A second test pitted a longer but more targeted URL against the brand-name URL: www.FinConHomeFinance.com against the original www.FinCon.com. These tests are all premised on actually having websites at these destination URLs, or at least getting Google Editorial's permission to run the generic company URL as the display URL in cases when the destination URL doesn't match this exactly. (Usually, Google will accept this if you tell them it's a large company and the IT department has no other way of accurately tracking results for the time being but to send users to a separate site, but that you'd like to keep the main corporate URL as the display URL.) I can't tell you the results of the test, but I can tell you that it is worth testing if you're in a similar situation. By and large I recommend incorporating the brand name into your display URL, even if a particular campaign sends users to a slightly different destination URL. And this might require special permission from Google Editorial.

Keep in mind that you can't use all caps or odd capitalization in your display URL, but you can divide two-word names with a capital letter in most cases.

It's Not What You Say, but How You Say It

As we've all discovered at one time or another, your choice of words does matter. There's a big difference between *happy* and *ecstatic*, even though both describe the same basic emotion. Therefore, as you test your ads, try using different words and phrases with similar meanings. If you're looking for a catalog of suggestions for word variations to try, see Richard Bayan's 2003 book *More Words That Sell*.

Tracking Results

The best way to track the performance of your ads is to tag each ad with a unique tracking URL, usually using parameters dictated by your web analytics software, and a naming system that you find helpful. For example, you might refer to campaign 2, ad group 23, with the numerical code "0223," and to denote each successive ad you test in that group, you might use a letter of the alphabet. So a typical tracking URL for the first ad might be http://www.qvack-qvack.com/shirts .asp?source=adwords&ad=**0223a**. The next ad in that same group would have same URL, but end in the letter *b*, and so on.

Unfortunately, this system doesn't lend itself very well to tracking "by keyword." Therefore, many advertisers find themselves facing the choice of either testing for ad copy variables or for keywords, but not both. It can be a thorny problem, though not entirely insurmountable. Ultimately, you need better software or a better interface from Google to facilitate improved tracking. Unfortunately, few advertisers have access to particularly easy solutions from third-party vendors at this point. When in doubt, track by ad group and ad, and track by individual keyword only sparingly as needed. Again, for a fuller discussion of tracking, see Chapter 10.

Statistical Significance in Testing

Advertisers often wonder if there ever comes a point at which you can be confident that one ad will outperform another over the long term. Some statistical experts will say that as few as seven occurrences of the desired outcome (clicks or sales, in this case) provide enough information to be confident. While such claims are based on raw math, they assume that no other influences are at work in the experiment. In the real world, I have found it necessary to run tests longer than some experts suggest. Unevenness in ad delivery across different sources, different user behavior at different times of day, changing ad positions, comparison behavior by users seeing different competitors' ads at different times on different keywords, and numerous other factors make it difficult to trust the orthodox statistician's approach. Without a better way to describe it (I'm no math PhD), allow me to suggest that patterns can be "wonky" over the short term, but become very reliable over a longer period of time. That does not, of course, explain why previously solid patterns begin to reverse themselves so that black becomes white and up becomes down. But often you can chalk that up to changing market conditions, shifting consumer demands, and strategic behavior by competitors.

Since AdWords clicks are generally pretty inexpensive, I suggest that my clients run ad tests for a relatively long period to ensure the results are accurate. "Relatively long" plays out differently for different ad campaigns.

Practical experience has shown that ads may even out in performance, even though probability theory would have given them a 95% chance of continuing their gap in performance. It is beyond the scope of this book to fully explain why this is so, except to say that conditions change rapidly in this environment, and there is more randomness and volatility in small samples than there might be if you were flipping coins. Clicks and buying interest might flow in from one region all at once, for example, skewing results towards one particular ad, but only temporarily. Probability theory doesn't account for consumer enthusiasm, which might flood into this process and then vanish as quickly as it came.

So, as long as a campaign is within the normal range of attracting a steady number of impressions and clicks, I make sure not to jump the gun on interpreting split-tests. Instead of thinking in terms of numbers of clicks or sales, I often think in terms of a representative time period, such as two days or a week. My rule of thumb is to give tests time to play out fully. I'll look for 40, 50, or even 100 or more clicks on each ad, if I can get away with holding the test that long. As shown in the example for UncommonlyGifted.com, we generated over 2,000 clicks for an ad containing a time-limited discount offer to compare it with an ad that did not contain the offer. Our findings form the foundation for a long-term campaign strategy. We are surely not going to plan such a strategy based on some statistician's views (not directly suited to this complex medium) that seven clicks are enough to compare ad performance. After generating over 2,000 clicks on each ad, at 17 cents per click, we're rock solid in our belief that the ad with the offer works better. The $680 spent on that test is an inexpensive piece of market research, especially considering that they are making sales while conducting the test.

Moving from Ad Content to Campaign

So far in this book, I've addressed the short history of paid search and how it fits in with other forms of marketing. I've shown you the basics of how the AdWords interface works and introduced you to some intermediate-level campaign management concepts that should help you succeed over the long haul. And you've now gotten a taste of how easy it is to tweak your ad copy to improve performance. It's the world's fastest and cheapest market research!

Speaking of testing and market research, a lot of companies get a bit gun-shy when it comes to actually launching their AdWords campaigns because of the difficulty in forecasting results. Not uncommonly, paid search will have an advocate within a company, but this advocate may lack the support of senior management. Whether your company employs two people or two thousand, it's worth taking an in-depth look at how this kind of marketing campaign fits into your overall corporate strategy. Some corporate cultures still resist innovative marketing methods because they feel they're too unpredictable. In Chapter 8, I explore ways of convincing the boss (and yourself) that AdWords is a relatively low-risk, if unpredictable, marketing opportunity. I also explain how to shape your campaign from the beginning by identifying key campaign goals, carefully assessing your sales process from clickthrough to revenue generation, and asking where your business model fits in the context of other successful online business models.

Endnotes

1. Matt Ragas explores this phenomenon nicely in his book *The Power of Cult Branding: How 9 Magnetic Brands Turned Customers Into Loyal Followers (and Yours Can, Too)* (Crown Business, 2002).

2. For a recent critique that makes this point, see Bob Garfield's *And Now a Few Words from Me: Advertising's Leading Critic Lays Down the Law, Once and For All* (McGraw-Hill, 2004).

3. Jay Conrad Levinson, *Guerrilla Marketing: Secrets for Making Big Profits from Your Small Business* (Houghton Mifflin, 1998).

4. Seth Godin, *All Marketers Are Liars* (Portfolio, 2005), 70. For the counterpoint, which criticizes large companies and their advertising agencies for being propagandists, see Laura Penny, *Your Call Is Important to Us: The Truth About Bullshit* (Crown, 2005). Penny is an enemy of phoniness, especially phoniness in the pursuit of profit, but never makes it clear what authenticity would look like.

Chapter 8

Big-Picture Planning and Making the Case to the Boss

Before you launch your online marketing campaign, you'll need to make a number of strategic decisions. In earlier chapters I covered the pragmatic aspects of launching a campaign, since that's what most marketers are most interested in. However, if your job is as much political as it is operational, or if you're an executive trying to weigh the AdWords initiative among competing priorities, you'll want to pay particular attention to this chapter.

How Valuable Is Search Engine Marketing to Your Business?

First, you'll want to satisfy yourself that search engine marketing (SEM) in general, of which Google AdWords advertising is a subset, is a smart investment of your marketing dollars. I've attempted to set the stage for such decision making in Chapters 1 and 2. You might also find useful supporting materials at the website of an industry group called SEMPO (Search Engine Marketing Professionals Organization)—www.sempo.org.

Recent studies by the Internet Advertising Bureau (IAB) point to the effectiveness of search engine marketing. The first, a "sponsored listings effectiveness" study based on data from a 1.5 million-member panel compiled by comScore Networks, and containing a foreword by Kevin Lee of www.did-it.com, is available at www.iab.net. A more recent IAB-commissioned study, performed by Nielsen/Netratings, showed strong brand recall for companies who attained listings at or near the top of a search results page.[1]

You might also check out what Seth Godin, author of *Free Prize Inside!: The Next Big Marketing Idea* (Portfolio, 2004), had to say recently on his weblog (July 1, 2004). He noted that the South Beach Diet spends "more than $1 million per year on online promotion (keywords, etc.)." Godin calls this "marketing that pays for itself... no magic, no superstition. Just planning and measurement and hard work." That was part of Godin's critique of unscrupulous search engine optimization firms who want you to believe that success is easy if you can only luck into a #1 search ranking on Google. Don't let it be about luck.

In mid-July 2004, MarketingSherpa wrote a case study of Edmunds.com, the automotive information site. After having some success with optimizing the site for free referral traffic, but reaching the limits of that strategy, Edmunds now spends nearly $500,000 per month on keyword advertising with Google and Overture, employing full-time in-house staff to manage the campaigns. This initiative has made a multi-million-dollar impact on Edmunds' business, providing the catalyst for recent rapid growth.

Once you're satisfied that SEM is right for you, and Google is your preferred venue, the next step is determining what percentage of your search engine marketing budget should be dedicated to AdWords. Obviously, this proportion may vary depending on the opportunities you can discover in other forms of paid search, such as Overture and FindWhat pay per click, shopping engines, and paid inclusion in Yahoo's index. Because opportunities for keyword-based advertising are often fairly scarce, I've found that allocating 40% or more of your search marketing budget to AdWords is quite realistic.

Strange as it sounds, you may find it difficult to spend heavily on AdWords in the early going. Unlike the expensive TV and print ads that many advertisers are accustomed to buying, large chunks of AdWords exposure can't be bought in advance for a predetermined price. Those large media buys are the reason many larger companies have bloated advertising budgets. They know advertising works, and they know that it's more likely to work (at least from a top-line, market-share-maintaining perspective) if they throw more money at the problem. Putting together a media buy in such scenarios (either by outsourcing the job to an agency or negotiating a few large buys themselves) does a terrific job of "spending the budget." The big media buy is a no-surprises method that may keep everyone in a company happy because there are few internal planning questions left unanswered, except for the most important one, of course: "How can we measure and improve on the profitability of our ad campaigns?"

The rest of this chapter will serve as a reminder that the planning process for a Google AdWords campaign may be quite different from what many companies are accustomed to. But the risk of missing your "targets" is worth taking because the *material* risk is so minimal, and the potential upside is attractive: you may discover a new, high-ROI channel.

Many companies today need little convincing to embark on the uncertain path of experimenting with AdWords. The fact that their competitors are already highly visible in that space is enough to spur them to action. Increasingly, then, the boss might be all for it. If anything, I'm finding that marketing managers who are asked to plan an AdWords campaign may handcuff themselves unnecessarily because they overestimate the career risk of dramatically "underspending" the budget at first. No, the process won't be predictable, and at first you may not be able to give your boss those simple answers she might seem to want. But consider that many companies today are more entrepreneurial than ever before, and senior management might actually reward those who take chances, make mistakes, and champion unorthodox paths to growth.

Strategies for Small vs. Large Companies: How Different Are They?

There needn't be a radical difference in the way an AdWords campaign is developed just because a business is particularly small or particularly large. Campaigns tend to run on a basic premise that calls for gaining one customer at a time, one search at a time. Obviously, campaigns will vary quite a bit in terms of breadth and ad spend, but I see more similarities than differences in the general approaches taken.

Large companies will want to consider budgeting for more sophisticated web analytics software, additional staff time or full-time hirings, bid management software where appropriate, and of course, more money for clicks. Furthermore, additional time can be spent on usability testing, site development, ad testing, landing page tests, and so on. But the remarkable thing is that companies of all shapes and sizes are doing all of these things in much the same way, albeit at different budget levels. Because I've worked with a lot of small companies and midsized companies that are careful (but not unrealistic) with their budgets, I've developed a sense of what's essential and what can be safely ignored. Given that a typical AdWords sales process takes the user from a brief text listing to a tailored landing page (reminiscent of the ultrasimplistic "Pachinko machine" described by Seth Godin[2], which imagines the Web as the ultimate, super-simplified direct marketing channel), there is no reason why a smaller company can't make a big impact with limited dollars. Indeed, one reason that larger companies sometimes agonize so long over the decision to move forward with a pay-per-click campaign is that it can be so inexpensive and accessible as to seem insignificant. Surely there must be more to it than this! (Nope.)

One thing large companies will need to do is sort out who is responsible for what. Multiple stakeholders and long meetings are the norm in large companies, but this should be avoided wherever possible. Turnaround time is paramount. Somebody must be given the flexibility and authority to test and tweak as steadily as possible. This perhaps explains why more large companies are willing to pay substantial salaries to senior search marketing experts to manage affairs in-house rather than hiring junior trainees whose decisions must be second-guessed. Failing that, outsourcing the job to an integrated, multitalented marketing agency that can implement and understand various elements of the campaign strategy (business analysis, copywriting, keyword discovery, tracking, landing page design, and so on) will help to avoid slowdowns that inevitably crop up in situations where responsibility for project results is made too diffuse. You're not going to hand over your whole company to a third party, of course, but giving that third party more discretion and more freedom to achieve results is one way of signaling that the AdWords campaign is a high priority. Increasing the budget is another way.

Large companies with centralized IT systems or laborious processes of gaining approval for the release of website stats will also need to consider streamlining their procedures. In some cases, it's easier to set up a separate website for the AdWords campaign to allow direct supervision of the project by those who understand the need for quick response and hands-on control of landing page copy, tracking codes, and so forth. One of my clients, an international bank that offers an international debit card called ExactPay, runs the AdWords campaign through a separate site called ExactPayDemo.com. This makes it easier to deal with shifting priorities in marketing the product without undue involvement from various company managers. At the same time, senior management can remain quite hands-on in their supervision of the campaign results.

Another difference with large companies is that they can afford to "lose money" (or at least to bid so high as to seem to be losing money) on a campaign. By locking down exposure in a key channel, you can keep competitors out of that channel. Bidding high enough to be #1 or #2 on the page for popular search queries might be a high priority for a large company, whereas it could be suicide for a small company. Microsoft and McDonald's aren't just selling "word processors" and "hamburgers." They're also selling "not the competition." When McDonald's puts a franchise in a key location next to the service station on the turnpike, they're not only selling burgers, they're making sure the other guys aren't selling them. When Microsoft bids on keywords related to some small service provided by a small unit of their MSN subsidiary, they're not just selling that service, they're selling Microsoft in general, and bidding to make it tough for nimble small competitors to gain exposure on the page.

If you're smaller than Microsoft, there's not a lot you can do about that. Fortunately for you, if too few users click on Microsoft's ads, their ads will get disabled just like anyone else's.

If your company is particularly small, in spite of the increasing cost of keywords, AdWords is going to be a relatively comfortable environment for you because you can pause it anytime you don't like the way it's performing. You can monitor results on a daily or even hourly basis, if you want. I offer a couple of key pieces of advice to small companies. First, understand your limitations. You won't have the resources to hire staff to monitor and adjust everything constantly. And while you might already be in the habit of saying, "I'll do it myself," you won't be able to keep up that pace forever. So if you plan to do it yourself, be kind to yourself, and plan to do less. A simpler approach to campaign management and tracking is better than a convoluted one. Simpler does not just mean abdicating the role of campaign manager to some automated software.

To those special small business owners who really do have the energy and curiosity to spend hours every week poring over every detail of their campaign, I advise them to use those admirable energy levels to better advantage by not allowing themselves to become full-time AdWords junkies. Eventually, you'll burn out. Even if you don't, a fanatical obsession with squeezing every last ounce of productivity out of your campaign could be a symptom that you have more important work to do in other, more fundamental areas. It could mean you're in a dying industry, or need to change your overall marketing strategy. In terms of the amount of time you budget to spend working with AdWords for your small business, then, be realistic from the start. Work on your business, for heaven's sake, not just your AdWords campaign. If you want to play, crack out a nice game of online chess or fire up Pinball or Retro Galaga on your computer. Don't use AdWords obsession as an excuse not to visit your mother or water your plants. End of lecture.

What about Affiliate Marketing?

At the small end of the small-business spectrum is the aspiring affiliate marketer. This is someone who joins a parent company's affiliate program, receives custom linking codes that are used to credit them with sales, and then goes out and finds customers for the parent company. I've no doubt that for a clever minority, the math can work—attract targeted clicks by placing AdWords ads and hope enough of them convert to a sale to make you a profit. Just don't ask me for tips.

If I could tell you how to turn a passive profit in your home in your spare time, then why wouldn't I set up all those affiliate codes and keywords myself, shut down my computer, and take a nap?

Certainly, if you already have a following on your website or newsletter, affiliate sales can be a nice bit of residual income. Think about how many folks attach affiliate codes when they recommend a book that's available for sale on Amazon.com, for example, as part of the Amazon Associates Program. I'm not down on affiliate income in general, but I don't think much of the idea of individuals with limited business experience trying to turn an easy profit by playing affiliate roulette with no website at all by buying AdWords clicks and sending them directly to the parent company's site. Some such "marketers" have complained to me that my writings aren't "advanced" enough for them—they're looking for the latest get-rich-quick mumbo-jumbo, I guess. This confirms for me that many "top dogs" in the multilevel marketing area want you to believe that black is white and up is down.

There no doubt exist numerous opportunities for affiliates to profit from AdWords, but this book won't show you how to do it. I want to emphasize that the challenge is daunting for aspiring affiliate marketers in the pay-per-click auction. You'll be up against legions of others trying the same thing, and the room for error is tight because you're typically only making a few dollars on each sale. More importantly, you don't get the kind of detailed tracking data that can help you track a sale back to a specific keyword or ad in AdWords, so you're not given the tools you need to improve your campaign or gain insight into its performance. Yet another drawback: while the parent company can upsell, cross-sell, and repeat-sell to its client base, as an affiliate you never develop a client base. After making a few bucks on a sale, you're right back to where you started. Worse still, the buzz in the industry today is all about parent companies restricting affiliates' advertising efforts in the pay-per-click arena, because affiliates bidding on the same word as the parent company can create a bidding war for clicks and eat into the parent company's profits.

Promises of passive income are usually empty promises. Don't buy into hype. Follow your dream by building a business and selling your own product or service, as difficult as this may be on a tight budget.

B2B, Retail, Independent Professional, or Informational—What Is Your Business Model?

Campaigns are often run very differently depending on whether they're niche-focused business-to-business (B2B), or retail-focused business-to-consumer (B2C). A third category is the independent professional firm, which may fall on either side of the B2B/B2C divide, but which most often conducts its campaign and customer acquisition effort as if it were B2B. A fourth category is information publishing. There are many business models and they all have their quirks. The following discussion is an overview of a few things to watch for.

Business-to-Business

Business-to-business campaigns are some of the most profitable types of Google AdWords campaigns because the targeting is so tight, you won't often waste a lot of clicks. In planning such a campaign, be bullish about potential profitability but take heed that the biggest challenge—if you correctly micro-target your keyword list instead of reaching too broadly into generic search queries by the masses—will be to spend enough. If you're just targeting a few purchasing managers and C-level execs, you have to wait for them to type relevant terms into a search engine, and that may take months or years. You might generate very few clicks, but the value of those clicks could be high.

As a result, don't be alarmed when you see costs per click in the stratosphere for niche terms in your industry, especially not if a successful lead could be worth half a million dollars to your company! Costs per click of $2, $5, and $10 are not uncommon in some areas. You can lower the average by experimenting with the techniques offered in this book, of course.

The most appropriate model for a business-to-business campaign is often to request that interested parties fill out a contact form in exchange for receiving a valuable white paper or some other professional incentive. This is a lead-generation model and will help you operate the campaign based on a cost-per-lead metric.

Business-to-Consumer

Online retail seems to occupy the most real estate when it comes to pay per click. Campaigns can vary from a single product (acne medication), to a product line (contact lenses), to a diversified storefront from a major retailer carrying 10,000 or 100,000 items. As the scale grows, my earlier advice about meticulous campaign organization becomes all the more important.

In forecasting, begin with a test of one product or category before expanding the campaign, to get a feel for cost and performance.

Online retailers face special challenges. Margins are often slim and competition fierce. As a result, careful bid management, possibly even dayparting, is a must. Meticulous attention to tracking URLs and landing pages is time consuming. Depending on the size of the campaign you will need to write dozens, hundreds, or even thousands of different ads. To manage this task properly, large-scale retailers need to look carefully at available software and services to make the task more manageable, and some will need to hire full-time staff or a third party to handle it.

In consulting and auditing the progress of some large campaigns, I've been told that some very large retailers have been disappointed in the performance of third-party bid management tools, so buyer beware. Bid management and dayparting are inherently risky, especially the way ad delivery is currently handled by AdWords. Ads may not be turned on and off instantaneously. This is of particular concern on partner sites. Currently, there are technical limitations to what you can accomplish with "bid jockeying," so don't overestimate the effectiveness of constant motion.

Professional Services

Individual doctors, insurance brokers, accountants, realtors, lawyers, and the like, often have trouble with online marketing. After being dragged kicking and screaming into the modern world where small-town word of mouth and bus shelter advertising are no longer enough, they tend to reinvent the wheel and use overly complicated website designs more appropriate to large companies. A simplified campaign is what's called for in this instance. Landing pages should be clear and lead the user to a contact form in most cases. The upside is that geographically specific terms and regional targeting can be used, so you only pay for the most targeted clicks.

Perhaps it's just an occupational hazard, but these companies tend to be behind the times in technology. Seems all the lawyers I know were still using Corel WordPerfect long after everyone else stopped. Today's independent professionals tend to be outdated when it comes to the Web, too. Many spend a long time hunting around for web design firms, then overpay for outdated designs. When it finally comes to marketing the website, funds might be running low, so they try to get away with spending next to nothing, or they assign the task of "figuring out the search engines" to a receptionist. They've got it backwards. A website alone won't get you clients. Marketing is not synonymous with having a website.

Sometimes, when people lack savvy in a specialized area like web marketing, they make the mistake of overspending as opposed to underspending. Savvy online marketers understand that they need to avoid overpaying on any given component of a web project so that they can budget for everything that is needed. "Getting the Web," then, doesn't mean paying an exorbitant amount for a one-off site design, but rather, understanding the nature of the sales process. A simple yet effective site can be designed (without sacrificing an arm and a leg in sunk costs) to capture leads. That way, sufficient funds can be kept in reserve for the marketing effort, which might include testing multiple landing pages, ads, and so on, as well as monitoring ROI in detail.

The minority of professionals who "get the Web" can clean up. To do so, they must recognize that online marketing is an ongoing process, not a single event. It is not a matter of "how much" is spent, but "how" your budget is spent. If you get it right, there is enormous opportunity to succeed online in a professional niche.

Don't crowd too many priorities into the design of your website. If the main goal of the site is lead generation, you can probably limit the site's content to a landing page or two plus enough background information to provide credibility and context for your prospect. Every business is different, but when in doubt, start with something simple and straightforward. (That doesn't have to mean cheap looking.)

Increasingly, independent professionals will benefit from local targeting options offered by Google, Verizon Superpages, Yahoo, and several others. Unfortunately, as local search is rapidly becoming the "next hot thing" in search, a number of upstarts have come along to cash in. Not all of these new local directories offer value. If you're offered the opportunity to pay as you go, it might be worth advertising with a service like RedTO.com (a Toronto local listings service) or TrueLocal.com (a local search engine that attempts to list only businesses with physical locations, in beta right now). In a pay-as-you-go relationship (such as pay per click), your risk is limited since you can always track results; but if someone asks you for $500 per year up front for a "listing," you might wind up handing over $500 to a listing service that gets very limited user traffic.

Pay particular attention to Google's local offering. Local advertisers have recently been given the opportunity to list with Google by using something called Google Local Business Center. It's not yet clear what the value of a listing is, but for the time being, the service is free and therefore represents wonderful value. It will be interesting to watch it evolve. To sign up, visit https://www .google.com/local/add/login.

Information Publishing

Selling subscriptions or e-books, or driving traffic to an informative website that sells advertising in its own right, are natural online businesses, since, after all, "search" is inherently informational in nature.

Hundreds of interesting examples of how information changes hands for a fee come to mind. For example, when I was looking for models of self-publishing how-to information, I was stunned to see how much money even a modest self-publishing company like Self-Counsel Press was able to make. The founder, Diana Douglas, started selling divorce how-to kits in the 1970s, and her company took off from there. Recently, when I spoke to Ms. Douglas about the evolution of her business, she stressed that nearly all of Self-Counsel's revenues continue to come from print, not online, information sales. This is due in part to distribution agreements with the bookstores that carry Self-Counsel's titles. Although Self-Counsel doesn't currently disclose its annual revenues, and the founder is quite modest about the accomplishment, they deserve credit for growing from a single handbook title into a publishing business with hundreds of titles that has remained a going concern for 30 years. While Self-Counsel didn't reap its success online, the model is the same. Online publishers, indeed, may have more flexibility. Whether or not she'll admit to being a great success, the growth of Diana Douglas's Self-Counsel Press was an inspiration to me when I decided to distribute niche information online. The voracious readers in niche information markets, coupled with low overhead costs, make it an attractive risk for an online venture.

My colleagues at MarketingSherpa have built a business around selling specialized information that includes marketing reports, buyer's guides, email marketing data, and more.

On a grander scale, media giants like Bloomberg and Thomson are all about packaging and selling information. Thomson has divested itself of some high-profile mass-media assets, focusing on acquisitions of niche information providers you've never heard of in fields like medicine and accounting. Thomson is worth billions. For one example of a powerhouse B2B information publishing division of Thomson, visit TechStreet.com, which sells things like technical specifications and drawings. "Rules for Construction of Nuclear Power Plant Components" will run you $3,940.

You're limited only by your imagination when it comes to putting together an information product, particularly in consumer areas where much disparate information is available that has not yet been aggregated into a coherent package. Not only those who have proprietary information and big budgets can succeed, but so can those like Diana Douglas, who put together her first product, the do-it-yourself divorce kit, on the strength of personal experiences and research. The positives of information publishing as an online business model include low overhead, the ability to find highly specific keywords for low cost, ease of delivery of the product (digital), and plenty of examples online of companies that have created compelling landing pages for selling an information product.

How to Play with the Big Boys in Content Publishing

Danny Sullivan, the search marketing expert, has over 200,000 subscribers to his free newsletter, the Search Engine Report. You don't hear much about the newsletter as a business model for parent company Jupitermedia, perhaps because the company's focus is increasingly on the trade show business (including the shows Danny leads, Search Engine Strategies). Jupitermedia CEO Alan Meckler is fond of the content business, though, in spite of investing in a few content plays that failed. He has often commented about the positive sides of niche content plays on his weblog; his continued enthusiasm for content has been demonstrated by the company's acquisition of dozens of niche content sites. Most recently, the company has been making forays into the digital photography space, which is a kind of content.

As Meckler reminded me in an email, the company (when it was named Internet.com) actually started a venture fund to invest in content plays, so great was his estimation of content's potential. As a former advertiser in the premium version of Sullivan's newsletter, I can tell you that it has had as many as 5,000 subscribers. If only 5,000 people are paying for this $99 premium version, that's an extra $500,000 in annual revenues from a somewhat upgraded version of a popular free newsletter. Will this model work for everyone? Of course not. You probably need to have an avid following, as Danny Sullivan does. But ordinary people can achieve a great deal if they discover the right niche and serve it relentlessly.

These kinds of business models are quietly thriving in quite a few places. Bill Martin and Matt Ragas, whose ads I talked about in Chapter 7, are known as the cofounders of popular investment discussion website Raging Bull (acquired by AltaVista during its portal phase and later bought out by Lycos). Today the two publish an investing newsletter, FindProfit, that sells for $219 per year. Part of the strategy they use is a targeted AdWords campaign that lands sophisticated investors on a targeted landing page at FindProfit.com. Most prospects try the free trial first, but the rate of upgrades from trial to subscription is consistent and healthy.

I think a lot of small publishers "psych themselves out" of the business before they ever get started. To be sure, producing valuable publications isn't easy, and if you produce terrible work, your reputation will be ruined. That aside, though, more potential information sellers should just do it.

Some will watch the "big boys" and assume they need to price their material for the high end of the market. Ask yourself seriously, though—how successful are the high-priced reports sold by the big or even midsized consulting firms? Many are priced so high that their potential market is very narrow, which creates considerable risk as a business model. A business model that relies on 5,000 or 50,000 subscribers is a lot less risky than one that relies on 500 or so buyers. Companies like Forrester Research and Jupiter Media Metrix have had their share of bumps and bruises in the marketplace. Some have been quite unprofitable and have been rescued by sounder, more diversified companies buying them out. (Jupiter Media Metrix, for example, was acquired by Internet.com, which changed its name to INT Media and then to Jupitermedia, before selling the money-losing Media Metrix division to comScore Networks.) So beware of looking to them for guidance.

Panel-based web behavior measurement firms like comScore Networks and Nielsen/ Netratings appear be doing fine today, but I believe they would do even better if they worked harder to develop less expensive mass-market subscription products. Hundreds of thousands of professionals are interested in web statistics trends, yet these kinds of firms seem entrenched in their reliance on a small number of corporate subscribers paying top dollar. Not only does this mean their business models are unduly risky, but doesn't overreliance on certain corporate subscribers (for comScore, let's say Yahoo as a client) potentially skew the research or the way it's shared with the press? Imagine if comScore could figure out a way to sell a product that would be attractive to 100,000 readers, each paying $100 per year? Would the backlash from large corporate customers be too much to bear? Or would the trade-off be worth it? Wouldn't it also be possible to generate ad revenues and create additional upsell business (trade shows and special webcasts, for example) from that same large readership?

We've become accustomed to traditional industries being disrupted by web technology. Few observers today expect the music publishing industry to remain as it was, for example. Even those who value and sometimes pay for the advice of traditional stockbrokers may also have an online trading account so they can save money on a portion of their trades. Is the traditional business strategy used in consulting and publishing—at firms like Forrester and McKinsey, for example—another field that we can expect to be "flattened" by the dissemination of lower-priced, more accessible materials by online upstarts? Perhaps this flattening is already quietly taking place.

If you can successfully build a business around low-priced, broadly based subscriptions and report sales, you may find yourself in one of the lowest-risk, highest-reward professions on the planet.

The Kelsey Group is a company that specializes in informing a business audience about trends in the Yellow Pages and online local search markets. They sell $1,000 reports and costly premium newsletter subscriptions on the local search market. I've often wondered: how many can they sell? By positioning their price point higher, they're in neither better nor worse shape than companies that position themselves at the middle and low ends of the same market for information. Unfortunately, many entrepreneurs assume they cannot compete with the big guys. Don't think a competitor is formidable just because their price tag is $1,000! A information publishing company like MarketingSherpa can sell $129 reports and reach a wider audience based on price points, sales acumen, and accessibility. A company like mine could pick just

Keyword Arbitrage: Scam or Rational Business Strategy?

A current phenomenon is online publishers that have high advertising rates seeking to buy inexpensive keywords to drive more traffic to their sites. This is frequently due to the fact that their advertisers are willing to pay for more impressions than the publication can currently generate from name recognition, bookmarks, and free search referrals. One name-brand business magazine contacted me to discuss the tactic in connection with a growth plan for their website division. Some take a dim view of this "keyword arbitrage" and feel that only scammers are involved in buying ads low online and selling them high. Not necessarily. It's a perfectly rational strategy for a major business publication to remind people of their expertise in an area in order to build a long-term subscriber base, and failing that, to generate 20 cents in advertising revenues out of a 10-cent keyword buy. The fact that they can do it with 5- and 10-cent AdWords clicks is downright clever. If you're going to break even on a marketing initiative, I can't think of a better way to do so than to generate more mindshare for your magazine. Longer term, that's going to do better than break even. When keywords were as cheap as a penny on Overture's predecessor, GoTo, I sometimes used to buy them up for popular keyword searches like **Yahoo** just to drive traffic to my site so people would read my articles. Talk about vanity! Talk about a money-losing proposition! But I think that showed foresight, and it paid off in the long run. And yes, I'm slightly crazy.

one or two niches—perhaps competing directly with the two companies mentioned here, but not necessarily—and also sell $129 reports to a broad audience that requires timely marketing information. Most of this audience is simply not prepared to pay $1,000 for a research report. But they are willing to pay something.

Although the company is privately held, sources tell me that MarketingSherpa did over $1 million in report sales in 2003—pretty good for a small company. When you sell $50–$100 how-to kits, you're dealing with a mass market, as the many titles of Self-Counsel Press prove. Basically, I believe that there are many modest successes in information publishing worth noting and that we shouldn't be too impressed by the publishing lines of big-name consulting outfits, especially the unprofitable ones.

What's the bottom line? You have to deliver value. As long as your customers are making money or avoiding headaches by continuing to read your material, they'll gladly keep their credit cards on file with you.

AdWords isn't the only marketing device you can use to build a successful minipublishing empire. But it could be a great way to kick-start one—recall how much it's done for the South Beach Diet—and the risk is low.

To do more background research on what has come to be called the content business, check out Anne Holland's ContentBiz.com and subscribe to the newsletter. A professional association for newsletter publishers, NEPA (newsletters.org), is also a great resource.

Assess Your Sales Process

Knowing that you want to reach customers through pay-per-click marketing, unfortunately, does not automatically translate into a successful AdWords campaign that makes money for you like clockwork. Attaining decent conversion rates on targeted clicks depends on developing a solid game plan.

Most businesses today need to maximize their revenue per customer, especially as the cost of gaining a new customer in this channel rises. If you use a shotgun approach to your ad copy or landing pages, you're less likely to succeed than if you have clear, concise goals. First determine what type of customer relationship you want to establish. Equally important, think about how those relationships can be turned into additional revenues in the future. If your competitors are calibrating their bidding strategy to the lifetime value of a customer, and you're only looking at the immediate benefit, you may be underestimating the value of each click. You could wind up underbidding and letting competitors increase market share at your expense.

What's Your Goal: Retail Sales, Leads, Registrations, Buzz, Subscriptions?

Even where you have multiple goals for each customer relationship, you should make every effort to isolate a main objective for clarity of the sales process, as well as for the sake of benchmarking how well you're doing. From there you can expand to the other details and prioritize them in a sensible manner.

For example, if you know that making an immediate return of 100% or more on the ad spend through retail sales of items such as Lego toys is your goal, that's enormously helpful to understanding what can and can't be accomplished with your AdWords campaign. A further stipulation—that dump trucks and space stations are higher-margin items and thus worth bidding more on—might be helpful here as long you don't waver from a tight focus on gaining new retail customers. Finally, in this hypothetical scenario, you might want to remind yourself not to bid any more than 10–15 cents on the lowest-margin items (such as that long-forgotten "How to Remodel your Kitchen with Lego" book by Bob Vila). Remember, these are initial and primary goals for your sales process. You literally cannot function if you don't pick one primary campaign metric and one primary purpose for any given landing page, and use the performance of clicks driven to that page as a yardstick of campaign performance. That does not preclude you from selling other things to these customers or other customers, or from convincing them to become a member of your frequent buyers' club, or entering your contest, or... all of the other plans you have for your business. But you can't attempt to do all of this at once.

You should engage in, at least, a formal process of narrowing down your main general goals, and following that, you'll want to select campaign metrics like cost per sale or ROI and stick with them. In the informal narrowing process for the initiative, then, you might think "emphasize converting first-time visitors to buyers of high-margin products; failing that, get them to buy something else." Consider other goals as secondary. From this type of thinking you'll probably gain valuable cues as to whether your website is suitable to attaining your goals. If pages are cluttered with other things you're asking users to do, they're likely to go away confused or perform actions that are more like browsing than entering into some kind of relationship with your company.

Lessons from a Seafood Company's Campaign

One of my former clients, a global conglomerate that owns a popular supermarket frozen fish line, decided to test the waters for online sales of fresh lobsters in fall 2003. At the time, they were concerned that conversion rates might be low because consumers, trained by years of seeing their displays of low-cost frozen products in supermarkets, have trouble perceiving their products in higher-priced "fresh delivered" categories. In spite of assurances of special packaging to ensure freshness, this fear turned out to be well founded. Conversion rates were poor. This deep-pocketed company was being outbid on AdWords by owners of small boutique fresh lobster shops. By all indications, those boutique shops were converting more sales perhaps because the more tactile and "small feel" of their operations and brands reassured customers that they were getting fresh goods right out of the ocean, worth paying extra for. Since the campaign was based in the United States, some buyers possibly liked the idea of supporting a smaller local business as opposed to a Japanese-owned conglomerate.

Despite this shortcoming, as I saw it, the fish conglomerate's fresh seafood campaign objective was pretty clear: sell specialty fish products, especially lobsters and a couple of other rare, high-margin items. If they also tried to promote their frozen lines, build their brand, get consumers to join an email list, or enter a contest, I would have a harder time helping them out. From an AdWords standpoint, focusing on converting visitors to buyers of identifiable products would at least translate into a campaign that could be measured and improved. As I'll discuss later in the chapter, I had to debate this with the client. Sure, I think opt-in newsletters are neat, but do they sell fish? Do they sell enough fish to make up for the cost of driving people to the site? It's unlikely, especially given customers' increasing propensity to ignore email.

In the course of a comparable campaign dilemma with a site called UncommonlyGifted.com, I noticed that certain types of customers signed up for the newsletter, and others bought products. Given the prices we were paying for a click, we much preferred the buyers. You need deep pockets and faith to be satisfied with a free newsletter subscription alone, unless you already have a proven sales process built around that.

While I thought the fish company's primary campaign goal was worthwhile and achievable, I ran into a snag with the retail expert who'd been brought in to provide a second opinion. I suggested a streamlined shopping cart that got the customer to place the order before filling out the shipping and billing info. Experience has shown that with complex shopping carts and preregistration procedures, shopping cart abandonment rates are very high, thus preventing the initial transaction from occurring in too many cases. Clearly, someone on the verge of shelling out $100 for fresh mussels to be shipped overnight in special packaging (something that does require quite a leap of faith) would be a potentially lucrative customer to have. Therefore, to my way of thinking, you should do everything you can to avoid turning them off just before the successful completion of their first-ever transaction, especially since clicks aren't free and it takes as many as 50 to generate a customer on the relevant keywords.

As too often happens, though, the combination of a third-party web development firm that apparently didn't care about usability or revenues unless they were paid extra to do so, and a retail expert who seemed to be living in the 1950s and believed that a good way to develop loyalty was to bombard potentially valuable customers with to-do items instead of turning them into customers quickly, the shopping cart abandonment problem wasn't solved. Unlike every other online purchase I've personally made, this process required the hungry seafood lover to "register" before proceeding to checkout. The idea here was that forcing them to register would make it easier to check out next time. Good idea, if you're Amazon or Yahoo and can make that bold assumption of repeat business! But if customers don't buy now and try the product tomorrow, there's not going to be a next time. Not enough new customers, no buzz, no repeat business. What a shame.

In general, the shopping cart's seven steps to checkout were killing conversion rates. With each additional step to checkout, more potential customers fall by the wayside. This is simple, unwavering math. To make a sale online, reduce the number of steps wherever possible. Amazon didn't patent "one-click" ordering for nothing.

What's Going on Behind the Scenes?

In the case of the seafood merchant, something very simple was made into something complicated. This led to more questions than answers. Should we rehire the developers to fix this issue? What about a focus group? Are there any studies we can look at? Probably, but in some cases, a focus group of one or two people can tell you what's glaringly wrong. Why does the retail expert assure us that the extra step doesn't matter when it clearly does?

All that needed to be done here would have been to look at other checkout processes around the Web (some of them belonging to quite dinky-looking, but very successful, smaller businesses), and engage a web development firm that would implement a better checkout process as if usability issues and cart abandonment rates were their business, not just the client's problem. In this case, "check out without registering" should have been an obvious and easy option to implement by a qualified programmer. I sometimes think that many web shops are actually implementing canned solutions on a "white label" basis, and don't even understand the technology well enough to go out and find a different, more appropriate canned solution. As the overseas outsourcing fad spreads, this problem could get worse before it gets better. Not every inexpensive IT worker is qualified at problem solving and integrating disparate technologies.

Although the idea of not registering doesn't really save the user that much time, perhaps abandonment rates go up at this stage due to the personal affront of being asked to register for a website that the user may never want to come back to. In addition, it increases the already sky-high concern that maybe this particular retailer intends to abuse my personal privacy or send me unwanted emails under the guise of permission. Asking someone to take out membership in a retail experience before he or she has had a chance to sample the product or service, it seems to me, is presumptuous.

The only way to know for sure what users will do is to lab-test different checkout processes. Unfortunately that can be a chore (though made easier by the split-testing capability of AdWords). If you're working with a limited budget, you could be left to your own devices when it comes to championing usability and clean navigation on your website and when it comes to making judgment calls on specific features of the site. You might be forced to join an online discussion group or do a little background reading to interpret the latest findings on Internet navigation and usability from experts such as Jakob Nielsen (useit.com), Jared Spool, B.J. Fogg (Stanford University Web Usability Lab), Jeff Johnson (author of *Web Bloopers*), and Bryan Eisenberg (Future Now, Inc.). In this quest, you're not alone. Just don't hire someone who is stuck in aisle 6 of a 1958 supermarket.

Rather than getting caught up in outdated retailer-centric moralizing about what a typical customer should or should not do, today's online marketers must attack problems pragmatically and test responses iteratively. In the earlier example, we needed to focus on lowering cart abandonment rates so that the initial transaction could take place and the fish would get to the valued customer's door. Regrettably, since it wasn't clear that that was the primary goal, it was easy to forget about this and to gradually focus more and more on other, less quantifiable priorities.

The debates about the seafood site didn't end there. Another goal was to ask people to sign up for a free newsletter. This would contain free recipes and offers, and would either (a) help the conglomerate to build their brand, or (b) lead to an online sale (the one this consumer didn't complete in the first instance because he or she wanted something free instead).

This goal created new problems. How much is a newsletter subscriber worth? How much should we be bidding on keywords in order to attract the types of people who might not want to buy today, but based on feel-good communications including tasty recipe ideas, over time might become good customers? Which keywords should we be highlighting to attract those kinds of customers, as opposed to customers who might be expected to buy lobster today? Who do we contact to install the tracking software on the appropriate pages associated with successful newsletter sign-ups? Nobody knew right away, and answers were slow to come, since this was a secondary goal on its way to being a tertiary goal. It just sort of hung there as another thing to look at.

This opens up a much broader topic—the current cluttered state of permission marketing through email—but for the present purpose, marketers do need to clarify their customer relationship strategies. Most know in general they "need a newsletter" (because that's the conventional wisdom), but how aggressively should they pursue the effort of building up that subscriber base, and how much (if anything) should they spend on it? Many of us assume that emailing customers is a good thing, but is it? The exercise of thinking this through might lead some marketers to conclude that building this "permission asset" may not be worth the cost today. Take a hard look at the newsletter idea, which many marketers today just haphazardly fold into their thinking based on best practices that are five years out of date. Perhaps the act of asking customers if they'd like to join something like a newsletter should be reserved for the most enthusiastic subset of customers, or not undertaken at all.

One thing you can be doing when you allow a free newsletter option to interfere with your sales process (unless you really know what you're doing) is to pay good money for clicks to attract the world's worst customers! In some cases, those requesting free information are like gold. One client of mine is a popular doctor who sells a breath freshener product. Those who request free information convert to high-margin, paying customers at a spectacular rate. That aside, this particular site converts well in its own right. Eighty percent of the completed actions from our AdWords campaign happen to be sales of products; only 20% of them requested newsletters. These prospects generally knew what they wanted and didn't want to wait around for free information to help them decide.

Customer Relationship Strategies

For marketers looking to maintain relationships with a loyal customer base, it will pay to keep thinking about their needs in a cluttered world. Consider less intrusive formats than email, such as Really Simple Syndication (RSS)-based news feeds, weblogs, or a nonintrusive discussion group platform such as Google Groups 2 (currently in beta) that would be more welcomed by particularly loyal customers. Because other marketers have been abusing permission and creating a "tragedy of the online commons" situation over the past five years, you need to think ahead if you want to form lasting relationships with your customers. Don't assume that email is a must-have channel, in particular if your efforts to build out that channel are killing or confusing your online sales process.

Consider this: there isn't any law against using direct mail to send good customers offers. A postcard from a sunglasses retailer won't offend anyone. Believe it or not, phone calls from the suit salesman at Harry Rosen or the service department at Downtown Acura don't offend me (while the upsell calls from Rogers Cable do). Somehow, businesses struggled through and maintained customer relationships in the days before email.

Many of the retailer websites I visit force me to use my email address at checkout, and then they send me special offers. I'm not sure I like it. More to the point, the way many of them are doing it today might not be legal next year, or the year after that.

Few marketers think these things through, but they should. If you don't understand the current state of permission marketing or online subscriptions, don't dabble in them in tandem with your retail sales or lead-generation effort. (Note: I'm not telling you exactly what you *should* do about the customer relationship process and email newsletters, just reminding you that you need to have good reasons for what you do.)

Clean up your AdWords campaign strategy by streamlining your goals as they pertain specifically to the campaign. You're paying for every click, so you need to develop a goal that revolves around a specific success metric, whether that be cost per order, cost per lead, or cost per action, such as free newsletter sign-up.

Cost per Acquisition, Cost per Order: Two Brief Case Examples

Let's turn to an example of a fairly messy AdWords campaign experiment that nonetheless yielded a clear cost per acquisition (I also like to call it cost per action) metric within 60 days. Then we'll look at a case where tracking cost per order added a useful dimension to the analysis.

Brian's Buzz (Generating Newsletter Subscriptions)

Brian's Buzz (also called Windows Secrets) is a newsletter produced by a well-known technology author and consultant, Brian Livingston. *PC World* reviewed it and declared it good enough to be on their "best free stuff" list (one of the tags we tried out in the ad copy). But of course nothing in life is truly free. If you're paying for clicks, it had better not be!

Brian's business model was and still is too complicated for my tastes, but I am grateful for the wealth of ideas he brought to the campaign, some of which caused us to identify key flaws in the AdWords platform itself. Without giving too much away, the business model is a mix of free newsletter subscriptions, paid subscriptions, volunteer "thank-you" tips from free subscribers, and "other income."

Going into the AdWords campaign, the goal was to increase subscriptions to the free product and then to track voluntary donations. The hope was that the cost of the clicks would be recouped within a month or so (requests are made at the end of each newsletter, every two weeks), with any additional revenues being gravy. This would require a 100% ROI within 30 days—a timetable I felt, and still feel, is unduly restrictive, especially considering how well the AdWords campaign went. Certain keywords attracted high volumes of clicks, and conversion rates from clickthroughs to newsletter sign-ups were consistent if not stellar (13%–15%).

After two months, we came away from the exercise with an important piece of knowledge: what it costs to generate an individual subscriber. (This is often called *cost per acquisition,* or CPA, but at times I call it *cost per action*, the measurable action being a newsletter sign-up.) The cost per subscriber of about 60 cents seemed well below industry norms for such a filtered group. More importantly, the advertiser, Brian Livingston, has full control over delivery and can assess many factors in the process of attracting these subscribers. By contrast, many lead-generation services can be mysterious as to how they generate leads or subscribers for you, and the quality can be (put charitably) uneven or (less charitably) terrible.

The absolute number (60 cents) on its own isn't all that telling until you can determine the long-term value of a subscriber. The ROI after 60 days, focusing solely on the voluntary thank-you payments given by some subscribers (fewer than 3% chipped in, thus identifying a hole in the model that allowed 97% of readers to free-ride on the generosity of others), was only 40%.

That is to say, from about $2,000 spent on clicks, only $800 was raised from these donations. But over a one- or two-year period, if we could identify, say, an average of $3 in revenues per subscriber (through advertising, book sales, paid subscription conversions, and so forth), the ROI would probably look excellent—4x or better.

Some clients are shy about sharing their full revenue picture with me, preferring conservative disclosure to ensure we're careful about bids and budgets. Later on in discussions with Brian, I satisfied myself that his various revenue streams, which indeed included premium subscriptions, books, and speaking, would have made the average subscriber worth quite a bit more than he was letting on. Focusing on the thank-you payments only, and tying bids to the ROI on those alone, was an attempt to create a campaign that was self-funding from the beginning. But longer term, each new subscriber was clearly worth more than 60 cents—$3.00 or more is my educated guess based on further discussions with the client.

Even in the short term, the raw "60 cents per new subscriber" cost-per-acquisition metric is useful because it allows Brian to directly compare the effectiveness of the AdWords campaign with other lead generation sources: Overture, subscriber generation services, banner ad campaigns, and so on.

One subscription generator service that we were tracking in tandem with this AdWords pay-per-click campaign charged only 30 cents per subscriber, but as long as I was watching the tracking data, these subscribers subsequently contributed $0 in revenues to Brian's Buzz. Either these were just a bunch of recycled, infrequently checked Hotmail addresses being sold off to many other marketers, or these were the world's least responsive readers.

For my money, when someone charges you for bogus traffic or bogus "subscribers," this is unethical at best. Even when they attract sign-ups semi-legitimately with contests and incentives, something can get lost in the translation. If someone hoped to win a Ford Explorer and signed up to your newsletter to gain entry into a contest run by a third party, his interest in your newsletter might be minor at best. More than likely he'll never even open it.

When you track your results carefully, you can prove or disprove a lot of claims, as we did here. The people clicking on the AdWords ads were reasonably responsive over the short term. At least we were able to identify a pulse!

Brian's campaign was a qualified success. Although ROI goals were not achieved as quickly as he had hoped, the campaign did work well on several levels. It could not have generated useful data or moved closer to achieving its goals, though, had the primary goal not been identified from the start: *generating as many well-qualified free newsletter subscribers as possible* for the lowest feasible cost per subscriber. This goal coincided well with the ad copy and keyword selection, and the custom-tailored landing page (Figure 8-1). By being focused—by avoiding the trap of conflating a number of objectives—key metrics were established that should allow for sensible adjustments and progress towards solid profitability.

Iguana Corp.: Pinning Down an Allowable Cost per Order

Iguana Corp. (not their real name) sells a commodity technology service. It's an ongoing challenge for this company to achieve decent ROI from a pay-per-click campaign because many of the keywords are expensive. On their main keywords, large companies like Microsoft and

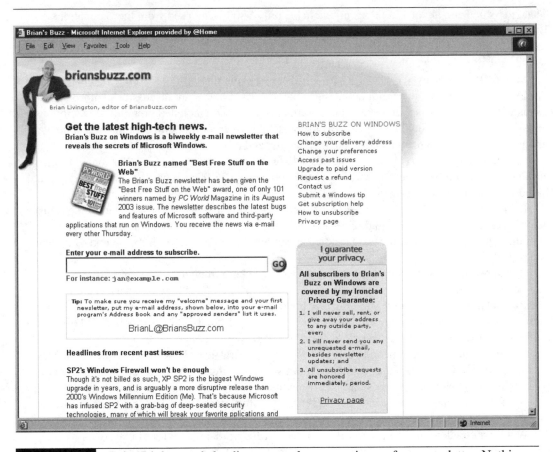

FIGURE 8-1   Brian Livingston's landing page asks you to sign up for a newsletter. Nothing complicated here, because the goal was well-established from the start.

Yahoo are bidding very high, presumably because this product is merely a loss leader in a whole suite of services the conglomerates hope to offer once they hook a new customer. By avoiding bidding wars and by tracking results, Iguana has been able to show steady improvement in their campaign performance.

In spite of Iguana's being a fairly recognizable brand name in their own right, and with plenty of brainpower resources at hand (over 150 employees), at first they were doing little if any meaningful post-click tracking. Because all company computing functions are centralized, I was told we could only get access to full stats reports on the 1st and 15th of every month. This makes it difficult to feel the impact of campaign adjustments, but with perseverance, it's been possible to make gradual progress.

The main bits of data that were sent to me every two weeks were the numbers of orders corresponding to specific ads or keywords in the Google AdWords and Overture campaigns, and the revenues associated with those orders. By plugging in the total cost for all clicks generated by those same ads or keywords, the spreadsheet summary I received would spit out a dollar figure for whether that part of the campaign (represented by a unique tracking URL that I created for each ad and/or important keyword in the AdWords interface) was in a "profit" or "loss" position. This reporting seemed problematic to me, because the more popular keywords generate a lot of new business at a slight loss. It makes these keywords look like culprits in an otherwise healthy campaign, because they generate a high volume of "money-losing" orders. (As it happened, these keywords really *were* culprits, but at a lower bid amount they might not be so expensive to warrant rejecting them entirely.)

If their click volume were lowered, these keywords might generate a smaller aggregate loss, and that would (possibly wrongly) be read as "improvement." Clearly, there is a point at which you may be losing too much money on each sale, but unless you know what that point is, the profit/loss methodology might cause you to abandon keywords that are excellent for acquiring new customers who will become profitable repeat customers within a year.

Therefore, I suggested that we also add *cost per order* into the reporting to give us a consistent feel for what it was costing to acquire a new customer, instead of looking only at a "loss" number that would escalate as you put more money into the campaign.

Unfortunately, Iguana's management remained vague as to the allowable cost per order. At around $15, I knew that Iguana was making money on the average first order, so clearly, that would be a safe figure. But we haven't been able to get some high-volume keywords much below $30—territory I still feel is profitable long term and worth mining given the high volume of new customers available through this route. Given the vertical integration of this particular tech space, I suspect a well-run company in Iguana's industry might have an allowable cost per new customer acquisition of up to $50–$60. Market share, not just pure profitability, is always a consideration in any cut-throat industry.

Unless you're prepared to review your operations to determine what really might be an allowable cost per order associated with your pay-per-click campaign, you might make poor assumptions. You can be sure that in the future, the competition will have made such calculations and will be bidding accordingly. There is no risk in being "too cheap" with some keywords over the short term, but there can be long-term risk to your growth prospects if your fiscal restraint results in less and less exposure and fewer and fewer new customer acquisitions. The irony is that Google AdWords campaigns can be pegged as too expensive precisely because they're easy to measure, but they are often less expensive than campaigns running concurrently in other media that aren't being measured at all.

While Iguana Corp.'s campaign objectives were not initially clear, they have become more so over time. By monitoring both the profit/loss metric and the cost-per-order metric, we get a balanced perspective on whether any parts of the campaign are performing unacceptably. In addition, we can compare the relative performance of Google AdWords versus Overture. But to date, no one at the company has proffered a specific number for allowable cost per order. This isn't uncommon, as many companies would rather protect the secrecy of their model, not even telling employees the details of where the profits really come from. Typically, then, marketing managers and consultants are simply asked to "do better" each month and to fix glaring campaign problems. Some strategic information might always be withheld by top management, in some cases because they don't have any better crystal ball for future market trends than anyone else.

Difficulties in Forecasting

Speaking of crystal balls, many marketing managers charged with the task of "costing out" a Google AdWords campaign may be facing an uphill battle because the cost really is difficult to predict in advance. It isn't impossible to come up with estimates, but they may be far rougher than you might wish due to the unpredictability of the relevant variables. The aggregate cost of a campaign will be hard to pin down due to the instability of a number of factors.

Forecasting Cost per Click and Click Volume

When adding new keywords or changing bids, AdWords offers an estimator tool that shows you how many clicks that bid level is likely to generate for you in a day, in what average ad position (Figure 8-2). Multiplying this by 30 gives you the estimated cost for a month for a given keyword or ad group. By now it's fairly common knowledge that you can't put much stock in these estimates.

There are several reasons for this. First, AdWords tries to predict how many searches the general public will perform on a given phrase, but this tends to be volatile. Search behavior is wild, and definitely outside of Google's (and your) control. Second, advertisers may enter and leave the auction. Third, the very fact that it's an auction means that prices are hard to predict, as advertisers may change their bids frequently. Fourth, your ad position is difficult to predict because it depends on how well you optimize your ads (and your competitors, theirs) for high CTR, which, along with your bid, affects ad position. Since ad position will affect visibility, and thus the volume of your clicks, this adds yet another element of unpredictability, which Google's estimator tool is hard pressed to deal with. Finally, the estimator likely does an even worse job of predicting patterns on partner sites like Ask Jeeves than it does for Google Search, and yet worse again for content partner sites.

Click volume is difficult to pin down because the early stages of a campaign should involve not merely deployment of a predetermined keyword arsenal, but rather, ongoing keyword discovery. You need some initial data to build on, but it's often difficult to tell how your efforts will progress week to week.

A more accurate method than the generator tool is to look at what actually happened in a given 24-hour period. Unfortunately, the first couple of weeks of your campaign (for reasons of editorial review, partner syndication, or other undisclosed technical issues with ad delivery) will not be a particularly good bellwether. New campaigns seem to ramp up over time before stabilizing at a more predictable ad spend pattern for any given day of the week.

For these reasons, then, costs can be difficult to predict. If solid budget figures are absolutely required, you will have to budget conservatively at first, while expecting a sharp increase in your spend (and hopefully, associated revenues) as the campaign progresses.

You may continue making changes and re-calculating estimates <u>below</u>.
When satisfied, please save your changes.

[Save Changes] [Cancel]

Traffic Estimates

Keywords ▼	Maximum Cost-Per-Click		Clicks / Day		Average Cost-Per-Click		Cost / Day		Average Position [?]			
	current	new	current	forecast	current	forecast	current	forecast	current	forecast		
"crawl space" (to be added)	$0.16 (default)	$0.16 (default)	-	8.5	-	$0.12	-	$0.94	-	4.6	find alternatives / delete
"crevice tool" (to be added)	$0.16 (default)	$0.16 (default)	-	0.1	-	$0.10	-	$0.01	-	4.1	find alternatives / delete
"human resources" (to be added)	$0.16 (default)	$0.16 (default)	-	170.0	-	$0.08	-	$12.43	-	2.3	find alternatives / delete
"invaders from outer space" (to be added)	$0.16 (default)	$0.16 (default)	-	< 0.1	-	$0.05	-	$0.00	-	1.0	find alternatives / delete
"outer mongolia" (to be added)	$0.16 (default)	$0.16 (default)	-	0.3	-	$0.08	-	$0.02	-	1.2	find alternatives / delete
"space invaders" (to be added)	$0.16 (default)	$0.16 (default)	-	18.0	-	$0.08	-	$1.38	-	1.6	find alternatives / delete
"tall ships" (to be added)	$0.16 (default)	$0.16 (default)	-	35.0	-	$0.08	-	$2.62	-	2.0	find alternatives / delete
"virus software" (to be added)	$0.16 (default)	$0.16 (default)	-	23.0	-	$0.13	-	$2.89	-	5.1	find alternatives / delete
[mustard] (to be added)	$0.16 (default)	$0.16 (default)	-	0.9	-	$0.13	-	$0.11	-	2.3	find alternatives / delete
best practices (to be added)	$0.16 (default)	$0.16 (default)	-	55.0	-	$0.10	-	$5.01	-	2.4	find alternatives / delete
road signs (to be added)	$0.16 (default)	$0.16 (default)	-	18.0	-	$0.10	-	$1.66	-	3.2	find alternatives / delete
single bounds (to be added)	$0.16 (default)	$0.16 (default)	-	< 0.1	-	$0.05	-	$0.00	-	1.0	find alternatives / delete
tall buildings (to be added)	$0.16 (default)	$0.16 (default)	-	2.6	-	$0.07	-	$0.16	-	1.3	find alternatives / delete

FIGURE 8-2   The AdWords cost estimator tool, for what it's worth

Forecasting Clickthrough Rates and Conversion Rates

I'm more comfortable predicting CTRs than conversion rates. Developing a series of ads that will pull pretty well is not particularly difficult, so it's fine to go ahead and estimate that you will achieve 1%, 2%, or 4% CTRs, depending on how confident you are and on how ultratargeted your keywords are. Then again, even if you do hit very close to the CTR you'd been expecting, this does very little to tell you how much you'll spend.

A strange thing with CTRs is that you can have very high ones and very low ones mixed together in the same account. Content targeting might garner a paltry 0.2% CTR, for example, or it might even be ten times worse than that! Again, the rate doesn't tell you much about the bottom-line impact. Recall that with content targeting, as opposed to the search component of a Google campaign, you aren't penalized for very low CTRs.

Recently, I've been seeing some high CTR figures reported that make me wonder if we're getting some weird feedback as a result of Google's new "improved ad relevancy" methodology. In yet another quirk of the ad delivery system, broad-match keywords are now being "selectively" disabled as opposed to completely disabled when they fall below the CTR threshold. That seems to mean that your ad may show for the high-CTR niches but not show for areas that Google AdWords has learned perform poorly for you. Whether a result of this methodology or not, from year to year, CTRs may jockey up and down for a number of reasons.

Recently, Iguana Corp. suddenly had some really high CTRs on certain keywords, on reasonably high volume. Should they be happy about this? Perhaps so, as long as the jump to a garish 20%+ CTR isn't shared by other advertisers. But it's really hard to know how to react to it, other than to say that forecasting CTRs in advance is a mug's game just like most other types of forecasting in this medium. Ultimately, we look at how the campaign performed group by group, and the dollars in and dollars out, seen in retrospect, are what really count.

The game of predicting how many visitors will turn into customers after they click (conversion rate) is also subject to such serious miscalculation that you probably shouldn't forecast. You can get rich quite easily on the back of an envelope. When I began selling my own information online, I had no idea how many copies I would sell, or what it would cost me to generate sales over and above word of mouth. I just hoped *someone* would buy! Today I suppose my conversion rate on AdWords is between 1% and 3% depending on the day. But that could easily be raised to 5% by constraining the keyword list to only the most highly relevant (and expensive) words, or lowered to 0.1% by going really broad with keywords (and paying less for them). A raw conversion rate number doesn't tell you much. It also doesn't tell you how many "walk-ins" your initial advertising might generate down the road. Although users are cookied by most common tracking services, and tracking can accurately attribute conversions from AdWords campaigns 30, 60, or 90 days down the road, people do switch computers, clear their cookies, and so forth. Insofar as tracking is imperfect, a recorded 5% conversion rate might be a real conversion rate of 10% or higher based on "nonattributed" sales from users navigating directly to your site in any given week.

One thing is clear: once you establish your approximate conversion rate, you want it to get progressively higher. You want to know about factors that create conversions when customers are waffling. But pulling a number out of thin air in advance, as if you're entitled to this revenue, never made it happen.

An Alternative to Forecasting: A $1,000 "Testing Budget"

Simply try this: put aside at least $1,000 and 2–4 weeks for a trial run on your AdWords campaign. This will help you generate benchmarks for CTRs, conversion rates, ad position, CPC, and so forth, which will be helpful in further forecasting. Lately, campaigns are slow to ramp up, so 6–8 weeks might be a better time frame. If a third-party consultant is implementing the test, the cost for their services will often be higher than the amount spent on clicks at this stage.

If that's too much, and you're a very small company, you can still generate 500 clicks at 20 cents per click for only $100. This will often be enough to give you a sense of where things are headed. Preferably, too, you'll make more than $100 back from the effort!

If $1,000 is too small and will make your colleagues laugh at you, forget we ever had this conversation, and up it to $5,000 or $20,000 as need be. A division of a financial institution I worked with in 2004 had a 90-day testing budget of about $300,000! Based on the learning from that successful test, the budget for the same period in 2005 was set at just under $1 million. The same logic applies regardless of company size.

In running your tests, try to start with very targeted terms that are more likely to lead to a sale. It's easier to build on a modest success—a few initial sales conversions—than to know which way to turn if you strike out completely.

As I've made clear, I prefer testing to forecasting. In many ways, the first six months of a pay-per-click campaign are like a lab experiment gathering valuable data. Building on that initial effort, campaign management should require less ongoing effort each month, even as its budget increases.

Endnotes

1. Janis Mara, "Search-Style Ads Lift Brand Awareness, Study Says," ClickZ.com, July 15, 2004.

2. Seth Godin, *The Big Red Fez: How to Make Any Web Site Better* (Free Press, 2002).

Chapter 9

Expanding Your Ad Distribution: Opportunities and Pitfalls

Probably the most common challenge I face in helping out "mature" AdWords accounts—either those that my company has been overseeing for some time, or new clients who come to us having reached an impasse in their efforts—is insufficient click volume. The problem is easy to describe: the advertiser loves the results so far and just wants more of them! "Great. We're at $28 a lead, comparing favorably with the $74 per lead generated by offline advertising. Now we need more leads!" might be a typical directive.

This can lead to some interesting judgment calls. Do we increase the average cost per lead of the whole campaign in order to generate additional volume (by, say, increasing bids to improve ad position)? Or do we hold firm on the cost per lead and search harder for ways to increase targeted clickthroughs at low cost? (The latter, obviously, is the bigger challenge. It's pretty easy just to go in and increase all your bids.)

Conventional wisdom suggests that when you've found the low-hanging fruit of inexpensive customer acquisition methods, you're forced to pay more for incremental customers. As discussed in Chapter 8, there are tactical and philosophical considerations that determine whether a company wishes to pursue market share or profitability at a given juncture. Marketers typically use terms like "aggressive" as shorthand for pursuing more leads or customers by raising average CPC and ad position. Those who can't afford to raise their cost per new customer too high, and want to squeeze the maximum ROI out of every click (or not incur that click at all), might refer to themselves as pure direct marketers, conservative or cautious, slow growth oriented, or ROI focused.

Even if you leave bids where they are, you can push your ads out in front of more prospects using AdWords. This chapter offers some suggestions for the most likely avenues to accomplish that, so you can implement an expansion plan with a minimum of fuss. This chapter also covers a couple of advanced topics in ad distribution: local targeting and ads appearing in Gmail.

I'll assume that you've already selected the check box that shows your ads on search partner sites, a first step in expanding distribution beyond Google Search, and that you've already thought about which countries are good places to show your ads and selected them accordingly in your campaign settings.

Getting the Most out of the Keywords You Know

You may be tempted to think that generating lists of additional keywords and throwing them into your AdWords account is a good way to make more money with your campaign. I'll cover that, but first, are you getting the best performance out of the keywords that are already there?

Rescue Your Disabled Keywords

Over time, sometimes through no fault of your own, some of your best words may be disabled due to low CTRs (Figure 9-1). You don't want to search for trivial new words when your bread-and-butter words aren't working for you! To reenable them, you can try a few things. Google's FAQs recommend that you start new ad groups or campaigns, or move these keywords to different groups or campaigns. The idea is that you should be continuing to experiment with new ads that pertain to these keywords to ensure that they're as relevant as possible—sound advice.

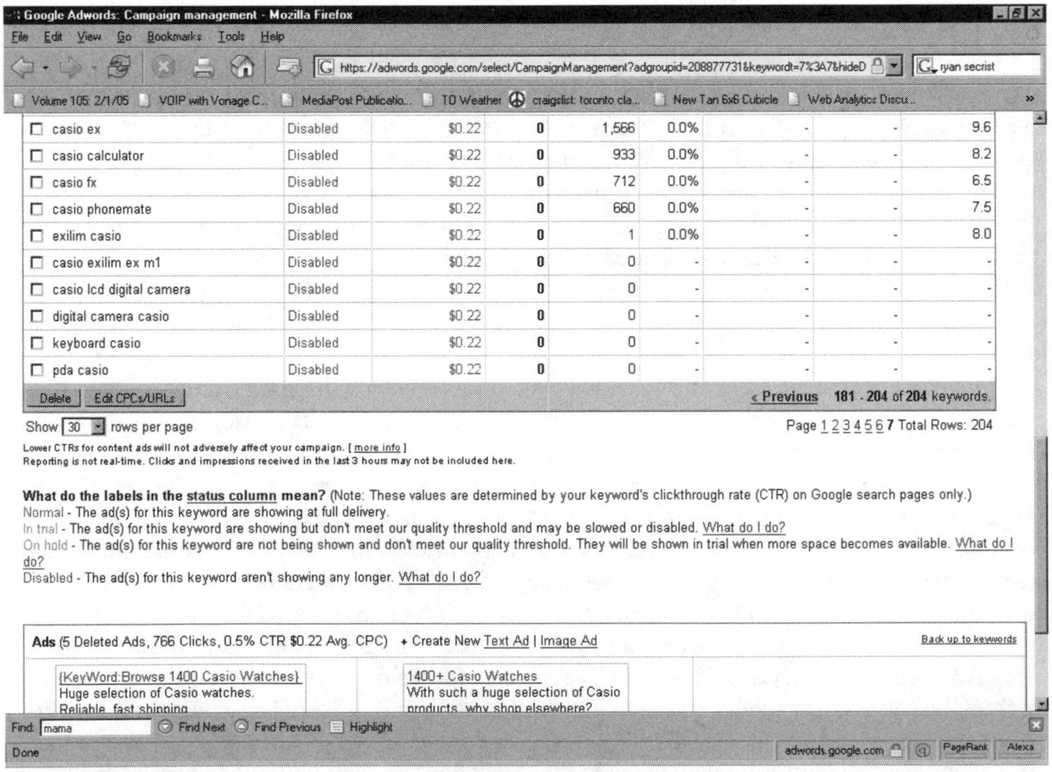

FIGURE 9-1   A list of keywords that have been disabled for poor CTR performance

TIP *On a public forum (Search Engine Watch forum), an AdWords representative recently reminded advertisers that they must take care to delete* all *instances of a disabled keyword throughout an account. Use the Search feature of AdWords to make sure you haven't left any instances of a disabled keyword active. Only after deleting all instances of the disabled keyword should you attempt to enter it into a new group with an ad you hope will perform better.*

Unfortunately, this advice doesn't always work in getting your keywords reenabled. If you're running into problems, contact AdWords Support. They may voluntarily reenable disabled keywords if you make a special request, but don't use them as a crutch.

Two-Word Broad Matching

Many conservative AdWords advertisers prefer to use phrase match and exact match rather than go "broad" with their keywords. But this can limit your distribution. To expand your distribution cautiously, choose one popular word and then enter 20–30 two-word broad-match combinations that include that word. This will show your ad to more users but at the same time will allow you considerable control over the types of queries that show your ad. The fact that the second word needs to appear in the user's query will reduce the potential distribution enough to make the ad highly targeted, without ruling out users who type in long, unpredictable queries that include any number of other words.

The additional advantage of the two-word broad match is that it can be fairly specific, so you'll probably generate healthy CTRs. As such, you can afford to bid less and generate a strong ROI. The same general logic applies to three-word broad matches.

Four-word broad matches are rarely worth bothering with. It's generally too much effort to use long strings of words in your campaign, except perhaps in special situations. For example, you might find that a fair number of users put questions to the search engine, such as **how to sell my timeshare**. Even here, a three-word broad match—**how sell timeshare**—would handle many possible combinations, as would the two-word broad match omitting the word *how*. You can experiment with various matches and combinations concurrently, of course. This might teach you a bit about performance, and will probably allow you to tweak your bids to lower costs somewhat, if you wish to be very meticulous.

Expanded Broad Matching: Disable Only if Necessary

An additional benefit of broad matching is that it invokes Google's expanded broad matching feature that may selectively show your add on similar phrases that include plurals, verb stems, and other close variations without making you do all the work of discovering them. Although at first, many advertisers saw expanded broad matching as worrisome when it was rolled out, Google has been careful to test the technology and to calibrate it conservatively enough that ads are not showing on all kinds of unrelated search queries. The way to disable expanded broad matching is not to use broad matching at all. If you wish, you can change all broad matches in a campaign to phrase matches by invoking this at the campaign level (Figure 9-2). I no longer see the need to be so cautious, however, as the feature now works pretty well.

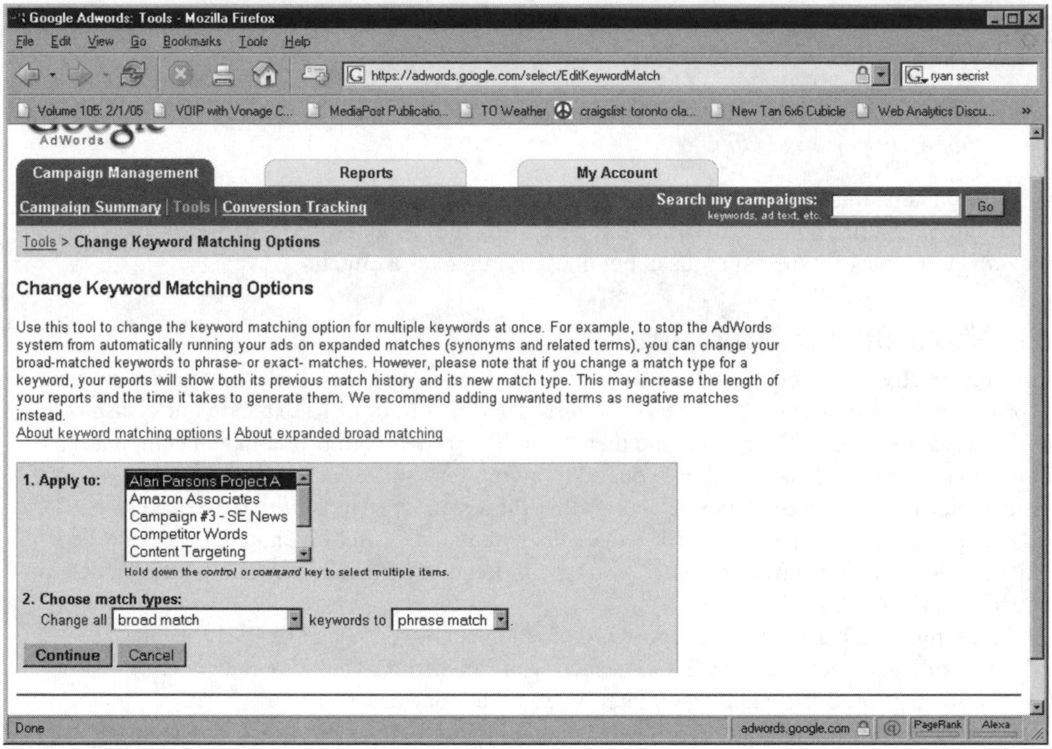

FIGURE 9-2 AdWords makes it easy to change matching options for entire campaigns with a single click.

One-Word Broad Matching + Negative Keywords

Many advertisers fear the one-word broad match with good reason. It can cast too broad a net, and paradoxically, because uncreative or deep-pocketed advertisers may be drawn to such words, prices can be too high.

The other reason that many ignore the potential of one-word broad matches is, it must be said, slavish adherence to conventional wisdom. Google does its part on this one. If you ask staff for advice on your campaign, they'll often recommend against such "untargeted" keywords.

As the imagination of the average advertiser is increasingly captivated by more targeted keyword choices, one-word broad matches may now be a relative bargain if you bid low enough. The other important benefit here is that they can provide your campaign with huge additional volume! And for most experienced advertisers, volume is where it's at. As long as the conversion rates generated by such words are keeping the cost of an order or lead in line with what you're getting from other parts of your campaign, you'll be fine.

The problem is that these words are often disabled because your customers come from a small subset of phrases that include the word in question; so only a few people click on the ad, and the resulting CTR is below Google's threshold. One effective way of keeping one-word broad matches alive is to enter long lists of *negative keywords* to ensure that the ad isn't showing on any popular queries that are irrelevant to your business. You can continue to discover and add negatives to solidify your CTR on the broad-matched term.

To discover what phrases including that word are popular of late, you can use the keyword tool (Figure 9-3). Then you'll enter a long list of those phrases as negative keywords (Figure 9-4). This is a lot of work, but it can help you outdo other advertisers in competitive fields and increase volume on a stalled campaign; so it can be well worth the few minutes a week you spend doing it.

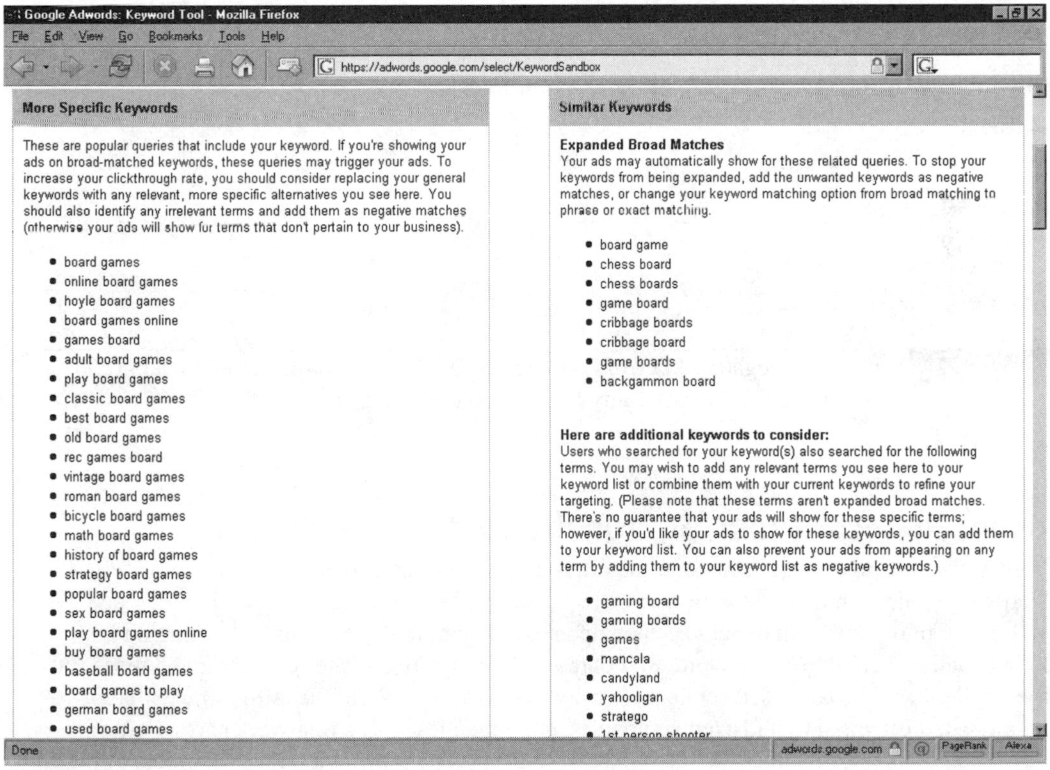

FIGURE 9-3   The keyword tool shows you popular searches, including some that may be irrelevant to your business.

| Toys & Games: Hasbro Paused | Resume Ad Group | Delete Ad Group | « Prev | 2 of 44 Ad Groups | Next » |

Current maximum CPC: **USD $0.20** [edit]

Aug 23, 2004 to Apr 7, 2005

Tools: ▶ Filter Keywords | ▼ Add Keywords | Edit Keywords | Keyword Tool

Add Keywords ✕

Enter one keyword or phrase per line:

```
-sex
-old
-dart
-used
-german
-skate
```

[Estimate Traffic] [Save] [Cancel]

To add or remove words by altering your current list, use Edit Keywords page.

1 - 30 of 60 keywords. Next »

| 2000+ Board Games
Huge selection of board games;
Trivial Pursuit & 2000 others. aff
www.amazon.com | + Create New Text Ad | Image Ad
1 of 2 Ads: View all below | ◉ all time ▾
○ Aug ▾ 23 ▾ 2004 ▾ - Apr ▾ 7 ▾ 2005 ▾ Go
☐ Include deleted items that were active in this date range |

[Delete] [Edit CPCs/URLs]

☐ Keyword	Status	Max. CPC	clicks	Impr.	ctr	Avg. CPC	cost ▼	Avg. Pos
Search Total			6,954	476,138	1.4%	$0.19	$1,261.22	6.4
Content Total			2,691	3,011,227	0.0%	$0.12	$307.09	2.9
☐ [board games]	Normal	$0.30	2,118	92,707	2.2%	$0.22	$452.45	6.2
☐ "board game"	Normal	$0.31	1,563	71,168	2.1%	$0.24	$370.16	6.0
☐ "mad gab"	Normal	$0.20	498	29,461	1.6%	$0.18	$85.75	5.8
☐ "trivial pursuit"	Normal	$0.27	233	17,341	1.3%	$0.23	$52.71	6.2
☐ "parker brothers"	Normal	$0.20	205	8,256	2.4%	$0.17	$34.75	4.3

Transferring data from adwords.google.com...   adwords.google.com   PageRank   Alexa

---

FIGURE 9-4   Entering negative keywords (indicated by the preceding –) into an ad group can help raise CTRs, especially on tricky one-word broad matches.

Advanced Technique: "Go for the Tail"

Lately, software and service companies have been moving aggressively into the pay-per-click advertising game, some armed with ambitious business plans and fueled by venture capital.

It's now fairly common to hear such companies advocating the benefits of bidding on 50,000, 100,000, and even a million keywords and phrases. Although this strategy might make sense for large retailers with broad-based catalogs, I'm always surprised when I hear this strategy being recommended for small to midsized companies, or companies with a relatively narrow offering.

The logic goes something like this. Most advertisers are ignoring the huge numbers of highly specific phrases that are typed by search engine users. By examining server logs for referral phrases coming from the regular index (or organic) Google results, we can see that in some industries, obscure phrases with only one or two referrals per month might make up 50% or more of overall visits to a website. By entering as many as possible of these phrases into a campaign, the argument goes, the average cost per click will come down, and return on investment will increase markedly. If the most obvious, frequently searched keywords form the "fat part of the curve" on a search frequency distribution graph, then the large number of infrequently searched terms can be called the tail; hence, to focus on these is called "going for the tail." I also call this the "keyword dump methodology."

I agree with the premise—indeed, the fact that a high number of unique queries are typed in by search engine users has been fundamental to my approach to AdWords since day one. But I don't necessarily think it follows that the average advertiser will see a significant improvement in performance by aggressively going for the tail using word-generation software. I believe such overkill can be a distraction from a healthy focus on a variety of determinants of success or failure of a campaign.

The first thing to remember is that by using phrase and broad match advertisers are reaching the tail anyway. That's the whole purpose of matching options. What proponents of the keyword dump methodology will now say is that the bidding process on AdWords may allow you to reach that tail *more inexpensively* than if you used phrase match. Perhaps this is true to some small extent, but it is all too often exaggerated. Advertising on exact phrases like **find me a good hotel near Houston**, because it showed up in your server logs as a search referral, or because some software generated this as one of a million variations, is certainly an option. But you'll still be competing for position with others in the hotel industry (for example, advertisers using a two-word broad match including the words *hotel* and *Houston)*, and you'll still find the CPC expensive. I personally do not see the advantage to such a strategy.

A real drawback to going for the tail so aggressively emerges in your tracking and post-click analytics process. If you decide to track everything by keyword, you'll be left looking through sheaves of results that show numbers of impressions and clicks in the single digits. Worse still, if you use an automated method that determines how long to keep a phrase running, you could be overanalyzing and turning good phrases off based on random user behavior on phrases with tiny sample sizes. The typical revenue associated with one of these phrases will be zero; every so often, there will be a purchase, possibly a large one, on a highly specific phrase. Who is to say that this highly specific phrase was actually the *cause* of this purchase? One purchase could lead you to overestimate the value of a certain phrase for months or years to come. That's why I think it's safer to think in terms of groups of related words.

Clearly one of the real drawbacks to using the keyword dump methodology is that the task of interpreting and acting on such fragmented results is too unwieldy for even a hard-working analyst. To this argument, tail-chasers will respond that they facilitate analysis by ensuring that similar keywords are grouped. Some will refer to patent-pending linguistic technology that helps them group words—without mentioning that Google's own technology in this area is likely to be offered to advertisers within a year or two (and already is, to the extent that the keyword suggestion tool shows related words that you might want to consider).

So we've really come full circle. By grouping keywords, and tracking based on those groups (assuming the software that attempts to automate these "groupings" actually works), we're back to the methodology I've been recommending all along: developing an AdWords strategy that revolves around groups of like keywords. To me it appears that advocates of the keyword dump methodology are chasing their own tails.

This is only worth exploring if you're an advanced AdWords user. I believe there ought to be a happy medium between extending the process of keyword exploration and looking for useful two- and three-word phrases, on one hand, and pointless overproduction of keyphrases. In my opinion, chasing the tail makes the most sense if you happen to run a company that creates keyword-spinning software. Venture capitalists enjoy investing in ideas like this, because for them it's "go big or go home." A million keywords sure sounds impressive, but is it appropriate for you? Will dumping them in your account improve performance? The jury is out, and further study is required; for now, I'm a confirmed skeptic.

Building on Success: Hypothesize, Extrapolate, and Profit

One of the easiest things you can do to increase profitable click volume is to look again at your successes and try to build on them. It's easier to do this if you've made discoveries that are based on testing a particular theory.

Defining the "Same" in "More of the Same"

I hope a couple of brief examples will give you the flavor of this kind of "determine what works, then do more of it" method of experimenting. Iguana Corp. and I are always pinpointing which types of online searchers are likely to be their most profitable customers. We don't have all the answers, but we have been able to make a couple of interesting discoveries using common sense first, followed by data analysis.

Recall from Chapter 8 that Iguana is in a hotly competitive Internet-related service business. One of the few differentiators we could identify with Iguana's service offering amid a sea of competitors was that they pride themselves on superior customer service. Since many advanced users view the service as a commodity to be bought as cheaply as possible, it was becoming rapidly evident that targeting these savvier customers—at least when we were paying a lot per click to do so—was a money-losing proposition. I proposed that newbies seem like their best AdWords prospects. These customers would be attracted by advertisements that promised integrity and more hand-holding as opposed to ads promising rock-bottom pricing.

To give that theory a solid test, I added more and more phrases that were the types of things that a confused, "unhip," new person to the particular technology in question might type into Google. I even tried certain very broad phrases indicating an interest in starting up a new web venture, such as **new web** or **start site**, and many others besides. Some of the terms, as advanced users might see them, would be considered mistakes or at least very awkward ways of expressing the "correct" idea. No matter. If a newbie typed it in, I wanted to show them this ad.

The theory proved correct. The cost per new order for these kinds of keywords was significantly lower than those on the rest of the campaign. That meant our work wasn't done. Since we had strong evidence that the newbie theory was correct, the trick was to go out and find more of them. Keyword discovery in this particular realm—"newbie words"—is ongoing.

Another area that we tested was various relevant brand names and trade names ("industry words" or "competitor words"). In spite of the ongoing legal controversies over the use of such keywords to trigger relevant ads near search results, we do know that they're often not only effective lead generators, but also less expensive on average than the more generic product words. Here again, the effectiveness of this group proved itself quite readily, so our job is to continue with keyword discovery as long as we can find new ones of this type.

If we find that performance begins to degrade in either of these groups, we'll take a hard look at recently added words that might be the culprit. As the groups get very large, it makes sense to subdivide them to test further distinctions and microtheories about what works even within this narrow realm. Keep in mind, this doesn't mean you have to track each and every keyword.

Upping the Bid to a Fulcrum Point

If some of your ad groups are performing at a significantly lower cost per acquisition than others, it doesn't make sense to keep the bids low on such groups just for the sake of frugality. If your average ad position is, say, 3.3 on one of these successful groups, you might want to find out how much more you need to bid to push it to 2.8, or 2.1, and whether raising the average position creates an unacceptably high cost per acquisition. You can creep bids up gradually and continue monitoring your ROI figures as you do so.

To keep bids too low means you're generating too few potentially profitable clicks. But at some point, you will have raised bids to the point where the additional clicks cost too much. There is no hard-and-fast rule for how to approach this, and results may fluctuate from month to month. But clearly, leaving one part of your campaign with very low bids if its ROI is particularly strong makes little sense. Generally speaking there shouldn't be vast disparities in ROI across a campaign. An ad group's ROI can indeed be too good. An ROI of 1,000% might simply be an indicator that your volume is too low in that part of the campaign and that you need to bid more to increase clicks.

Content-Targeted, or Contextual, Ads

As I explained in Chapter 2, at one time, online advertising brokers (or "networks") such as Doubleclick played an important role on the Web, allowing advertisers to place large banner ad buys without having to approach individual publishers and giving publishers access to more advertisers. Today, these first-generation online ad brokers are rapidly being displaced by the second wave: programs like Google AdWords, Overture Content Match, FindWhat, Quigo, and several smaller pay-per-click players. Some traditional-style ad networks, like Advertising.com, are going strong, but it's striking how dominant companies like Google and Yahoo (Overture) have become in the field of online advertising as a whole.

Ads Appearing near Content

Having regularly insisted they'd stay "laser-focused on search," Google surprised some observers in March 2003 by launching AdSense, an ad network that pays publishers for displaying ads that look very similar to standard Google AdWords ads. If you're an advertiser, the option to display your ad on these publishers' sites appears as a check box in your campaign settings area; you'll be asked if you want content targeting turned on or off (Figure 9-5).

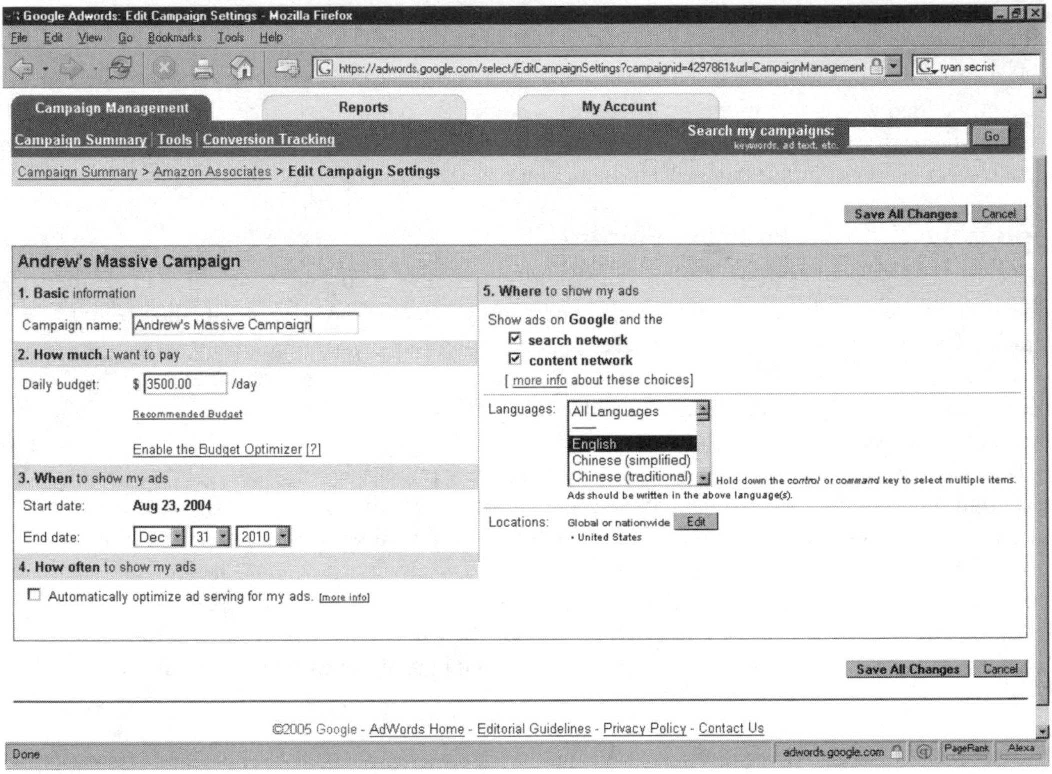

FIGURE 9-5   Under Where to Show My Ads, click Content Network "on" if you want to expand distribution.

You can be easily confused by the terminology since there are so many publishers out there these days noisily discussing the most profitable strategies for displaying "AdSense" ads on their websites. You're coming at it from the other side. You're placing those ads, and paying for the privilege. Remember, as an advertiser this is basically an extension of your existing AdWords campaign. There is so much ad inventory now being shown through this program all over the Web, its impact cannot be ignored. Indeed, according to recent public filings, at least half of Google's ad revenue is now generated through this program.

How does content targeting work? As with many things that Google does, the exact formula is proprietary. One thing's clear: it doesn't work the same as the ads appearing next to search results.

With content targeting (sometimes called contextual advertising), the keywords in your account still serve a purpose. Google's semantic matching technology uses these keywords, along with the amount you bid, to decide whether or not your ad is relevant enough to show on a particular page. The semantic matching technology "reads" pages for meaning; it isn't just pure algorithmic keyword matching. Ads—up to four at a time—are selected on the fly as the code on the publisher's page loads the Google AdSense ad creative. These *ad creatives* (*creative* is an online ad industry term for the size and shape of an advertising unit) can vary in size, but they take up the same screen real estate as the graphical ad banners that were once ubiquitous online. The need for site owners to place code on their pages to serve and track the ads is also similar. The key difference is that the ads are all text and look quite similar to an AdWords ad, with the notation "Ads by Google" placed unobtrusively somewhere in the ad unit. Online content is not restricted to any particular format. So-called contextual ads can be placed near discussion forum content, email messages, articles, or, as the example from the online photo sharing site Flickr (Figure 9-6) shows, thematically tagged images. As an advertiser, you'll need to be flexible in how you think about content, because chances are you'll have the opportunity to show your AdWords ads in a lot of different places in the coming years.

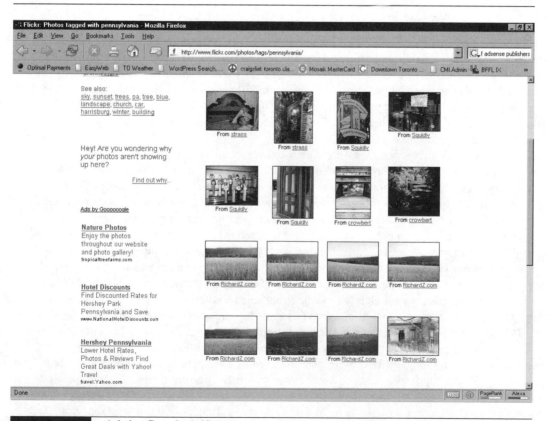

FIGURE 9-6   Ads by Google AdSense, appearing near photos on a content publisher's site

Google has provided more options over time so that publishers can customize the ads to what seems to generate the most revenue. Many choose to use the smaller ad sizes that only show two ads, but the units displaying four or five ads are not uncommon either. Publishers can also customize the look and feel of their ads so that, for example, the background color blends into the site or catches the user's eye.

Moreover, the price you pay isn't easy to pin down. It's not an auction in the same sense as the search ad program. You won't pay more than your maximum bid, but how much less than your bid you wind up paying can be determined by another proprietary Google formula called Smart Pricing. Google did a study and determined that certain kinds of pages (and presumably, some publishers) will produce a lower-than-average return on investment for advertisers. Instead of showing those publishers the door, Google has chosen to proceed with a pricing formula that simply pays them less per click based on an actuarial-style formula devised by Google. As an advertiser, Smart Pricing benefits you insofar as the prices on lower-quality ad inventory have improved; but this still leaves much to be desired, as the pricing is not transparent to you or the publisher.

Recently I received two pieces of evidence that Google is eager to expand the distribution of this type of advertising. First, they've begun aggressively approaching advertisers who have shut off their contextual ads and offered them rebates of up to $1,500 on their overall AdWords spend if they spend enough on another go-round with the contextual ads. To make room for the expected spike in ad demand that this rebate program will generate, Google then announced that they were permitting AdSense publishers to display up to three AdSense ad creatives per page where formerly only one was permitted. Google is also rolling out contextual ads in its new Gmail service, to be discussed shortly.

After having experimented extensively with contextual ads, to say nothing of studying the situation in depth from the publisher's standpoint, I can confirm that it does provide many advertisers significant opportunities to increase the profitable click volume in their AdWords accounts. But the big *if* here is this: it will likely prove profitable for many of you *if* you're able to bid much lower on content targeting than you do on your ads that appear near search listings.

There is no easy way to bid lower on content-targeted inventory at present. Since tactics and Google's rules may change frequently, I'll just leave you with the key principles to keep in mind.

First, you must have some way of tracking the contextual ads separately from your search ads. Many third-party tools have trouble doing this. One advantage of the free conversion tracker that comes with AdWords is that it clearly separates your sales conversion data (or other conversion data such as newsletter sign-ups) from search ads from the conversion data on content-targeted ads.

This kind of tracking is also not particularly complicated with a conversion tracking tool such as ConversionRuler, provided that you know how to use it. In addition, you'll have to devise a workaround in your Google AdWords account that creates a separate campaign with lower bids for contextual ads, duplicating keywords from your search-focused campaign. Tagging these ads with different tracking URLs would allow you to track that campaign separately. It's complicated, but it works well. Another thing I like to do with ConversionRuler is drill down on the "raw" data for converted sales or leads so I can "eyeball" the actual referral strings for each sale or lead

(Figure 9-7). Usually the leads that are coming from long referral strings that include something like "pagead2.googlesyndication.com" are from contextual ads. Additional detail, including the URL of the referring site, is frequently buried within that long string.

Typically, content targeting will perform poorly for you in competitive keyword areas unless you bid lower than you would for your search ad. This brings us to the second key principle: if your tracking shows the performance of content targeting to be terrible, you have two choices—shut it off completely, or find a way to bid lower (even if that solution might be a bit convoluted since Google currently does not make it easy to bid separately on content). Consider the latter. It can truly pay off, as several case studies have proven to me. One of the most successful examples was with Iguana Corp. By bidding much lower on content-targeted ads on expensive, popular keywords, they expanded their ad distribution and increased sales without sacrificing profitability.

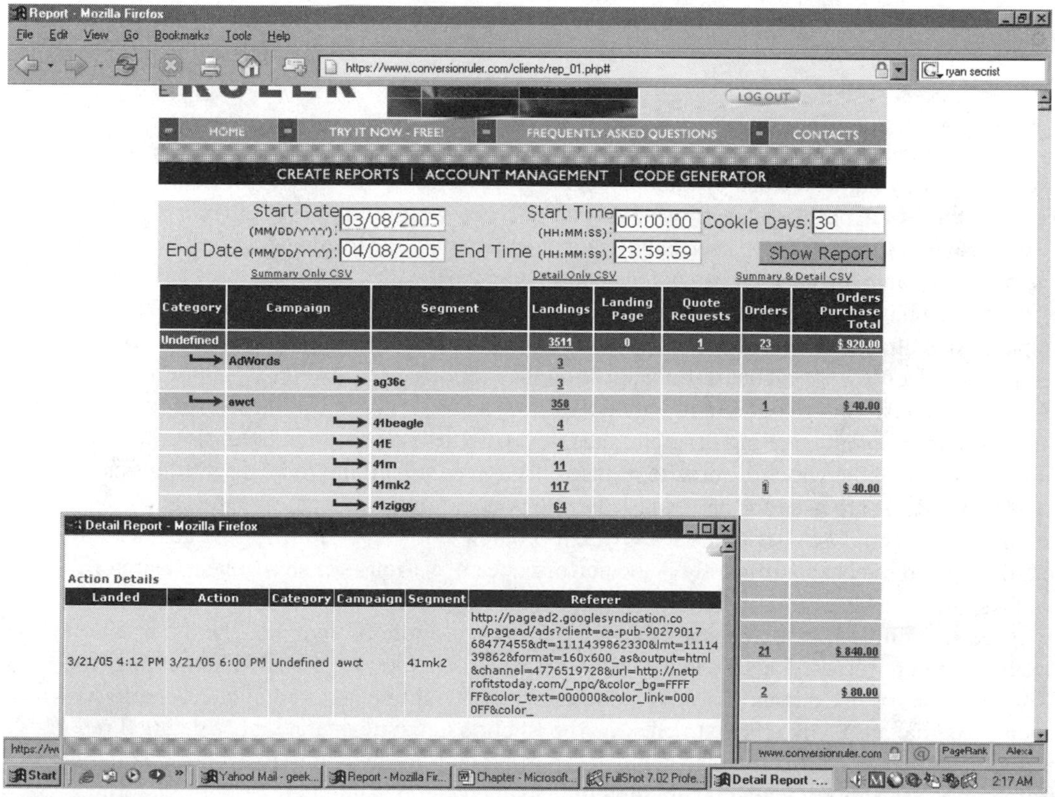

FIGURE 9-7   Raw referral data is clearly visible with a good tracking tool. This shows some leads generated by content-targeted ads.

Content Targeting Workaround

Until Google makes it possible to bid differently on content targeting, you may need to consider using what I call the "content targeting workaround" to ensure you're bidding much less—up to 75% less—on content targeting. The workaround has five basic steps:

1. Create a new campaign and keep content targeting turned on.

2. In that campaign, begin creating ad groups that mirror your best-performing ad groups in the original campaign. Keep building this out as usual, group by group, rather than dumping everything in a single group.

3. Turn content targeting off in the original campaign.

4. Bid much lower on the new campaign.

5. Monitor and track the new campaign separately by giving its ads unique tracking URLs. Both search and content campaigns should now work at different bid levels.

Another thing to keep in mind with content targeting is that CTRs will typically be much lower than with your search ads. Do not panic! AdWords does not count CTRs from content targeting against the performance of your account. So you won't rank lower on your keywords due to these low CTRs. Google uses only search ads (and only those appearing on Google Search) to calculate the ad's relevancy for ranking purposes.

When you have content targeting turned on, the aggregate CTR performance of your campaign will almost always be lower, because those who are seeing the ads aren't in active search mode. Don't worry about it. Recall that on the search side of AdWords, your rank on the page is affected by your maximum bid multiplied by your CTR. CTR is *not* used for ranking purposes in the content targeting program; thus, low CTR's don't hurt you here.

Unfortunately, the way AdWords reports results leaves something to be desired in this area. The CTRs as reported for particular ads give you aggregate percentages instead of percentages broken down between "search" and "content." If you're split-testing ads, usually what diverges the most significantly is the performance of various ads shown near search results, so that's what you'd want to test. With content targeting mixed into the reporting, you might see something like 0.2% across the board for two or more of your ads due to the diluting impact of content-targeted ads. In that case, to get a realistic picture of what's happening (for example, 1.1% for one ad, and 2.0% for another, which would be a more typical scenario on search-proximal ads), you'd have to click on the Reports tab and generate more detailed reports on your account's performance. The detailed reporting does allow you to isolate, for example, "search only." In short, having content targeting enabled can make it a bit harder to interpret data from split-testing different ads.

Special Case: Ads in Gmail

Did someone say Google isn't just about search anymore? They now offer Gmail, a fast, innovative web-based email service that offers two gigabytes of storage, with a clever campaign now hinting at unlimited storage. In exchange for a free account, users accept that Google will show ads in the right-hand margin of the interface. Below that, Google also displays "related links" drawn from the regular Google index. Most users find the ads to be nonintrusive, similar to the familiar AdWords ads near search results.

They're considerably tamer than the large graphical ads that formerly appeared in Yahoo Mail users' accounts. Yahoo, in response to the rollout of Gmail, has significantly improved its mail offering. Storage size has increased, features have been improved, and premium-paid users no longer see any advertising at all. All in all it seems that Gmail is already exerting a civilizing influence on the web-based email category.

Ads appearing in Gmail, like the contextual ads discussed previously, are matched with the content of emails based on a semantic matching technology Google doesn't disclose. One handy feature of Gmail is the threading of conversations, which makes it easier to refer back to previous emails in a series. I've noticed that as a conversation gets longer—as more emails back and forth start to pile up—the matching technology is more precise. Ads seem to get more relevant by the third or fourth email in the exchange.

In terms of effectiveness, as a general statement I'd probably rank ads in Gmail in the middle—somewhere between ads near search (more effective) and ads near pages of content (often less effective). Email-based ads may often be more effective due to the personal, interactive, and self-generated nature of the content. Email is the most-used online application (search is second). Users tend to linger over emails, leaving them open for extended periods. Particularly relevant ads in the margin do get noticed. I've already found myself clicking on both ads and nonpaid "related links" in the margins of my Gmail account.

For the time being, Gmail exposure is just considered a part of what you're enabling when you turn on content targeting in your AdWords account. This channel is a potential gold mine for some advertisers, particularly if Gmail usage increases or if Google begins deploying the same technology through partnerships with other email providers.

But the current setup is a double-edged sword. On one hand, because it's part of a network that Google builds, the appearance of ads in email via your AdWords account is a convenient way to expand distribution. However, you lack control. There's no ability to bid specifically on email (some might even want to bid higher). There's no option to change your ad text to be more suitable for that channel. Certainly, Google's entry into email ad inventory poses a significant threat to brokers and specialists in email marketing. For its part, Google probably feels like they're going to demonstrate that such firms' expertise is overrated. The specialists, on the other hand, will no doubt be critical of Google for generically lumping Gmail ads in with the rest of their contextual ad program, which is, in turn—insofar as the keyword lists, ad copy, and bidding are not separated—generically lumped in with the AdWords program as a whole.

To put this in perspective: as an advertiser seeking expanded distribution, I think you'd be better off banking on an expansion in Gmail exposure (thus leveraging the work you've put into your AdWords campaign) and other email exposure through AdWords than you would be by experimenting with email buys with lesser-known players and small-time ad brokers. The effort involved in developing those relationships, and the fact that low-quality inventory and shoddy practices are widespread in today's email marketing arena, mean that you'd be better off sticking with a known brand name like Google in spite of the current shortcomings of their offering.

Trademarks as Keywords ("Competitor Words")

Currently there is ongoing debate about whether it's legal to use a competitor's trade name as a keyword in your AdWords account in order to trigger your ad near search results on that keyword. But the status of this tactic is clearer today than it was a couple of years ago. GEICO lost a recent case, *GEICO vs. Google*, a lawsuit launched to stop competitors' ads from appearing near search results when users typed queries including the trademarked word GEICO. I see the judgment in this case as a vindication of the principle that AdWords—even when triggered by trademarked words as long as there is no reasonable likelihood of consumer confusion—can foster legitimate forms of comparative advertising similar to those that have long been legal in the United States. Most U.S. trademark experts agree that there is such a thing as fair use, and that whether the use of a trademark in advertising is illegal hinges on whether it causes consumer confusion. Google has, however, lost similar cases in France and is likely to lose them in some other jurisdictions. Eric Goldman, an expert in this field and a member of the law faculty at Marquette University, maintains an extensive blog on the subject of marketing and technology law. He is the author of a paper specifically dealing with recent cases like *GEICO vs. Google* and *American Blind vs. Google*. Goldman takes Google's side, marshaling considerable evidence in the attempt. Formerly the general counsel for Epinions. com, he has also defended WhenU.com, a company that uses pop-up ads to trigger comparative contextual ads. See http://blog.ericgoldman.org for a collection of resources.

Remember, you aren't typically using that competitor's name in your ad or intending to cause confusion, you're just using it inside your AdWords account to see to it that your ad appears in the advertising-earmarked area on Google Search should a consumer type in that term.

I've watched the debate closely and have watched the performance of campaigns that experiment with brand names and company names. What I can tell you is, in nearly all cases, these types of words outperform the other parts of your campaign, especially in a competitive industry with expensive keywords. Such keywords can be highly relevant, but they cost less because many advertisers fear legal action.

The second (requisite) bit of advice is, don't take my word for it. If you're uncertain about the legality of what you're doing, seek legal counsel. Also remember that trademark law in North America may be different from laws in Europe and other parts of the world.

Google owns the pages of search results they serve; trademark holders do not. Trademark holders have certain rights; so do advertisers. In a free society, the rights of all parties must be respected. Laws exist to serve the public interest, not solely to protect (for example) large companies' interests against smaller competitors' incursions. Free commercial speech is vital to providing consumers information they need. This free market in information can help the economy grow and provide consumers with better products and services. It simply needs to be done so fairly, without causing consumer confusion or "trading on" someone else's name.

If you try this tactic, you might want to create a separate ad group or campaign for such words (or even two or three for different subtypes) to facilitate tracking. You might use the names of companies, people, and publications, as well as product names, domain names, and so on.

Exporting Your Successful AdWords Campaign

Some observers have argued that AdWords works like a focus group, giving you valuable insight into your market. Once you've tested an AdWords campaign and achieved some success with it, there's no reason not to put some of that knowledge to work.

Other Pay-per-Click Services

What works on Google AdWords is likely to work on at least one other major competing service: Overture. It may or may not work on other such services. The question you'll need to ask yourself is whether it's worth the effort. In practice, after Google AdWords and Overture, it often isn't worth your time to set up accounts with second-tier services, with the possible exception of FindWhat and Business.com. Many of the smaller services have merged, been acquired, or shifted focus. In LookSmart's case, they've become a shadow of their former selves after losing the MSN contract. This instability is a further deterrent to examining the alternatives among second-tier pay-per-click providers.

Shopping engines are a separate subject. They also operate on a pay-per-click basis in many cases and are a must for retailers to investigate. From a Google standpoint, its Froogle engine hasn't gained that much traction yet and isn't yet out of beta. See Chapter 12 for more on Froogle.

Overture

You could take a few different approaches to using the knowledge you've gained on AdWords and transferring it to Overture. As a reminder, one of the main reasons for using Overture is to get exposure on Yahoo Search. For the time being, it also gets you on MSN Search. (Starting sometime in 2006, you'll need to buy paid search directly through MSN. It is probably worth exploring this option now as MSN, the #3 search property after Google and Yahoo, makes the transition to selling listings directly.)

I like to take the best-performing keywords (after running a test on AdWords for at least two months) and try just these on Overture. Because AdWords allows you to split-test ads much more easily than Overture, test your ad copy on Google first, and then use the top performers on Overture.

Overture has some key differences that might impact how you proceed, though. The first thing to note is that there is no particular advantage to sky-high CTRs. You can get keywords disabled for very low CTRs, but there is no high-CTR benefit.

Long keyword lists have long been seen as "the secret" to success with Overture. This dates back to when Overture's default (and only) matching option was exact match, which, fortunately, is no longer the case. The problem is that such lists can be unwieldy to track, so you'll have to decide whether the huge keyword list is something you really want to deal with. Although Overture doesn't allow you to set up ad groups nearly as intuitively as AdWords, you can set things up in categories if you wish. If you plan to manage only one or two accounts for your own business for a long time to come, the work you put into dividing keywords into categories will make for less work later. Some of us who manage many accounts often can't find the time to dither with categories, especially since we're often working with old accounts that date back to a time before Overture offered that feature.

Since you don't get an economic benefit from high CTRs, you might actually improve your ROI from Overture by working harder to prequalify prospects with jargon, price tags, and other filters that attempt to weed out nonbuyers by lowering your CTR.

Overture now offers all the same matching options as Google, including broad match and negative keywords, so you can cover a large keyword universe with a relatively small set of keywords. Again, because there is usually no drawback to a low CTR, it doesn't hurt here to cast a wide net by using plenty of broad matches. You do have to drill down within the interface to make sure broad matching is turned on, and possibly to bid separately on it. Unfortunately, it can be a time-consuming process. Since feature sets are evolving quickly, I won't go into too much detail.

Overture also offers Content Match, which is similar to Google's content targeting. You can and should bid on this inventory separately.

By and large, Overture and Google performance are often comparable. Exploring their minute differences could take up many pages. For the time being, let's just say that with a few minor adjustments, what works for you on AdWords should also work on Overture. Your biggest challenge, to reiterate, will be to come up with a tracking solution that isn't too complicated to manage for the long term.

FindWhat

About 80% of my clients find comparable success on Google and Overture. But for those who have tried both of these, probably only 25% have succeeded with FindWhat. Because bids are often lower, and volume is decent, FindWhat is worth a try. The quality of the traffic is generally lower, but not terrible. Some clients have generated a higher ROI with FindWhat than with the two leaders, though that isn't the norm. Again, use your best-performing keywords, bid less, and track your results. If you can't squeeze good performance out of this engine, don't constantly waste time monitoring it. Simply stop funding the account and leave it be.

You'll also need to be more vigilant with poor-quality traffic and fraudulent clicks, although FindWhat has improved greatly in the past couple of years on this front. If you'd rather not have the headaches, steer clear. Such problems are even more evident with the lesser PPC players in the second or third tier of the market. By necessity, they must take whatever publisher partners are left (the crumbs) after the top three players get their fill. That means a lot of inconsistency in traffic quality and fewer resources to fight click fraud.

Second-Tier Players

Business.com and IndustryBrains are useful for any company seeking business-to-business or high-tech clients. Both offer decent-quality, if low-volume, targeted traffic opportunities.

LookSmart still has some reasonable partnerships after losing the MSN contract, but the majority of the traffic today is of low quality. If you care to run a test to see if this traffic converts for you, great. But if you're short of time or patience, don't bother. As always, track your results to the source.

Enhance Interactive and Kanoodle have both made significant strides under improved ownership, and both offer solid campaign management interfaces and a range of features. But there are enough drawbacks to them that you'd have to be very eager to expand your distribution to spend money with them. If it were me, I'd wait until there was further consolidation in the industry before messing with these second-tier players.

Deciding whether to use these companies is a question of focus and time management. It's rather unfortunate to have to say this, because these companies sometimes offer features that Google does not. If they weren't around to push Google, it could slow its pace of innovation. But I'm not sure good features make for good economics. Without wide reach and traffic quality, cool features don't help the advertiser too much.

Below this level, there will be numerous third-tier players. Some will have very convincing sales pitches, but to investigate every pitch can, once again, be quite time consuming. Ask yourself if adding perhaps 2% to your overall sales volume (with considerable risk) is worth your time, when the known quantities could offer much more if you just follow some of the steps I've outlined in this chapter to expand your AdWords distribution.

Offline Marketing

The strange thing about search engine marketing is that it's a bit like "anti-marketing." You don't bother people—they find you when they're ready to look into a subject. Finding customers this way can help teach you a lot about what those customers actually want. Listen to them, and keep giving it to them, or develop new products and services to fill those needs.

So under the heading of "expanding your marketing offline," I'm going to tread a bit cautiously. Seth Godin, in two recent books (*Purple Cow* and *Free Prize Inside*), trashes most modern marketing, insisting that the product or service offering itself is what wins over savvy consumers. Marketing is ideally built into the product from day one. The idea that marketing professionals can simply be brought in at will to "put lipstick on pigs" and create demand for a new product is a myth. If your market is growing at a solid pace, or if it's really taking off, chances are that some underlying forces (the merits of the product, your personal reputation, changing market trends) are at work, not just the fact that you decided to shout louder.

Telling you how offline marketing works is outside the scope of this book in any case. But one (admittedly radical) approach to the subject of advertising and marketing offline is, do less of it, and plow the proceeds back into innovative products and features that will delight customers and make you stand out in the marketplace. Amazon.com, for example, slashed their television ad budget so they could offer free shipping. Great move. Your company might be better off investing in design software, customer relationship management solutions, or other forms of automation that boost productivity than it would be to invest in ads that create top-line growth of new customers who enter into the same old inefficient relationship with you. You must weigh your priorities.

For the less radically inclined, you can certainly transfer some AdWords learning over to your offline campaigns, but you'll probably need to retest. If certain ad text or sales copy on landing pages works well for you online, it can't hurt to try it offline. But these things don't always translate. In a perfect world, the direct mail people would talk over their findings with the online marketers. By sharing insights, marketing projects might proceed more quickly through the early learning phases, with fewer failed experiments at the outset. Time will tell if the integration of direct marketing agencies and online marketing consultancies will lead to a productive synthesis that can help more companies reach their marketing goals more quickly.

Above all, marketers need to be open to unorthodox ways of persuading consumers to try their products and services. Infomercials, for example, caught the marketing world by surprise just as AdWords is now doing. One unsolicited endorsement from a leading author, athlete, or celebrity could mean more to your business than a year's worth of magazine ads. Don't assume that because large brand advertisers are spending heavily on traditional television, billboard, or radio ads that you ought to do the same. Look before you leap.

Many advertisers try to generate traffic from a wide range of sources, making for unwieldy and chaotic marketing strategy. I've tried to argue here that you may be best served by taking simple steps to increase profitable click volume from your existing AdWords campaign before troubling yourself with a host of other online marketing experiments.

Part IV

The Next Level:
Winning the AdWords Game

Chapter 10

Tracking Users after They Click

To take your AdWords campaign results to the next level, you'll need to track what happens with your paid traffic after users click through to your site. To succeed, you must understand your business objectives, decide on your key campaign metrics, and figure out which tracking methods and tools are best for you.

The Google AdWords interface itself, as you've learned, provides a lot of campaign data. But CTRs, CPCs, and average ad positions won't tell you the whole story. Statistics like *return on ad spend (ROAS)* are becoming *de rigueur* in search marketing circles today, and to get a better sense of these, you'll need post-click tracking. Since covering the entire field of web analytics is beyond the scope of this book, I'll use this chapter to help you understand some of the main principles.

Take Control of Your Web Analytics

At the height of the dot-com bubble, Jim Sterne, a leading web analytics expert, made no bones about it: he believed that too much focus was being put on advertising, which is only a small part of the online customer relationship. Sterne thinks a true web marketer ought to focus more on what happens after the click and less on the message that is displayed to the prospect. "Advertising slays me. I laugh at Taco Bell, I cry at Hallmark," wrote Sterne. "If you create a banner that people remember you deserve an award. If you create one they click on you deserve a medal. If you create one that gets people to accomplish the objective set by the client you deserve large heaps of cash. If you can help your client or your boss figure out what their objectives are, you deserve sainthood."[1]

The current generation of search marketers has awakened to the power of web analytics for good reason: targeted traffic (what Sterne might have called "advertising" five years ago) has begun to increase in price as online advertising prices recover from the dot-com crash. The days of advertising (paid click) bargains are long gone. Everyone is beginning to understand the value of targeted clicks and that wasted clicks equal wasted cash.

The value of targeted clicks was routinely underestimated just a couple of years ago. Remember, the pay-per-click version of Google AdWords is still in its infancy: it enjoyed its third birthday in February 2005. In the past couple of years, the rapid growth of this marketing method has spawned a supporting industry of related tools and aids. Key among these is web analytics software or services that can help track the performance of a Google AdWords campaign after the click.

In the past, a handful of these types of tools existed, but many marketers ignored them, partly because they assumed they were aimed at larger companies. Today, a bewildering array of web analytics players are clamoring for attention.

Sterne's books (the most recent, *Web Metrics*, was published in 2002) and seminars convey a keen sense of a generational divide in how website stats are gathered and analyzed. A big part of Sterne's presentations is his historical overview, which explains why common ways of collecting and presenting web stats are not particularly useful to the marketing department.

Sterne offers some insightful history that attempts to explain the evolution of analytics through the lens of changing corporate practices and the changing roles of computing within large enterprises.[2] Sterne stresses the value of "centralizing web services" in larger companies as a reaction to the information technology (IT) decentralization that was made possible by minicomputing developments in the 1980s. In the "big-iron" (mainframe computing) era of the 1960s and 1970s, corporate computing was highly centralized. But as new forms of computing emerged, disparate departments managed their own information technology needs, leading to chaos. The ultimate culmination of such chaos was the experimental development of company websites by amateurs at different levels of large companies—what Sterne calls "skunk works enterprises."[3]

For the benefit of upper-level executives, Sterne argues that centralization is required to rectify this chaos. Most advocates of decentralized approaches (like me, or Gumby) would agree with Sterne on the merits of coordinating extremely messy, large, diverse web services at the biggest conglomerates (such as Motorola). But my goal is generally just trying to help a particular unit, division, or company achieve solid results quickly and to adjust its campaign iteratively.

Sterne has an unmatched practical grasp of some of the challenges that face today's companies in measuring their website success, but he is framing the problem for the benefit of a narrow group: top execs at Fortune 500 companies. To solve managerial issues at GE or Motorola is not in the average marketer's job description; it's a rather esoteric job that is best handled by an experienced management consultant. For those of us who have specific marketing objectives in mind, an experimental mind-set, or short-term targets to meet, decentralization is not a problem in itself; indeed, as the quasi-Darwinian evolution of corporate structures has proven in recent decades, it can be a great benefit. Moreover, the typical pressing "problem" in the average web marketer's eyes is not best characterized as an IT management or web services deployment problem, but as an ROI-seeking, marketing-driven problem. Forcing marketers to adopt a rigid chain of command, or asking them to defer to company engineers in the choice of analytics methodologies, allows nimbler companies (and divisions and subunits of companies) to adapt better to a changing marketplace. Fairly regularly, even dealing with smaller companies,

I've had the individuals responsible for the website refuse to install an analytics package because *they* couldn't see what the numbers are good for. Centralization of web services to the extent that campaigns are overseen by site developers and system administrators can really put the brakes on a marketing campaign.

If you're a small company, you'll likely want to view your analytical tasks more narrowly than an information junkie like Sterne would recommend. Indeed, I'd say that most available published work on the subject of web analytics is not tailored to small companies, and those who read such works too literally might even develop a misplaced focus.

I recently asked John Marshall, CEO of web analytics provider ClickTracks, for his take on the past decade in his field. How much have marketers' needs changed? As it turns out, a lot.

Marshall considers online marketers' analytics needs and wants "in terms of a bell curve," with the most frequently requested features and measurements in the middle of the curve, outdated, less-requested features and measurements to the left-hand side of the curve, and cutting-edge features and measurements over to the right-hand side of the same curve.

As recently as five years ago, the fat part of the curve—the information most often requested by website owners—was simply the absolute number of "page views" and "user sessions" occurring on their websites. A slightly more refined metric is "unique visitors" counted over the course of a given day or month.[4] Unique visitors in a month is a pretty good measure of audience size. Today, that type of information is taken most seriously by those who publish content sites— those who sell advertising based on those metrics—and is given a lower priority by those with business models that involve the sale of products or services.

If you're selling products or services with your website, the fat part of the curve today is measurements relating to the return on investment on your online marketing spend. Your web analytics need to measure that in some form or another. That's why simple logfile analysis, showing a lot of information about the traffic to your site but not much more than that, has been surpassed by today's ROI-focused conversion tracking.

Over to the right-hand side of the curve are more exotic measurements relating to user behavior. Marketers probably should be getting a better handle on the simpler ROI-related measurements before they tackle advanced matters like "propensity to repurchase" or following users around the site by viewing "click paths." In five years, more advertisers will be demanding such advanced analysis. Here again, I see no reason to centralize the approach to learning about customers using various measurement tools. No matter what size your company, there is nothing particularly wrong with letting different divisions or projects handle their own tracking and their own initiatives that relate to intimately understanding niche markets.

Make no mistake: although you'll hear anecdotes about companies who are tracking scrupulously, studies show that many aren't doing *any* ROI tracking. Recently I undertook such a study, albeit an unscientific one, to see what percentage of my newsletter readers were using conversion tracking tools. A healthy number of them cited tools like ClickTracks Professional or ConversionRuler, or at least Google's free conversion tracking tool. But 29% of this relatively sophisticated audience (all are AdWords advertisers) said they were using no tracking at all. If I were to look more closely (as I do fairly often when I perform formal written diagnoses of people's paid search campaigns), I wouldn't be surprised to find another 15% who weren't really actively tracking in spite of claiming to do so. By my estimate, then, 40%–45% of online advertisers still aren't tracking adequately.[5] You don't need to be at the right-hand side of the curve to improve your campaign. At least ensure that you get to the "fat part" of the curve. Start by doing a decent job of tracking key campaign metrics. You can always graduate to more advanced measurements later.

Measure ROI, Not Traffic

To put things in perspective, let's take a look at how companies *used to* track their website performance. About ten years ago, larger companies began building websites and taking the performance of those sites seriously. Typically, the administration of the site followed a command-and-control process, and where centralization initiatives prevailed, the IT department was put firmly in charge. Companies like WebTrends came to dominate the field for gathering data on website user behavior. In those days, a big-iron mentality still ruled the Web. There were "insiders" who helped put together web protocols and standards, and who ran the web operations at big companies. Many were pioneers and are responsible for the subsequent growth of the medium.

A *log analyzer*, or logfile analyzer, is a key type of analytics software and is often included with your web hosting package. A version of WebTrends, for example, is available for free with many hosting service offerings (Figure 10-1). This is not to be confused with comprehensive and costly web analytics suites available from the same company. Other popular and inexpensive log analyzers include 123 Log Analyzer and ClickTracks Analyzer. For years, logfile analysis was the only type of data gathering available to most companies with an online presence. Because log analyzers were not initially designed with direct marketers in mind, those who analyzed "web stats" became accustomed to slogging through huge piles of data about browser usage, referral traffic, time of day, and so on. Some of the data was very useful, some much less useful.

On the whole, the web stats reports of old were not actionable and did not tell marketers how they might better reach customers online. Worse, the data were released to the marketing department on someone else's timetable, in a format that someone else decided. The typical web stats report was particularly unsuited to the nimble startup or short-term direct marketing exercise.

Today's companies demand more out of their employees and often reward them for performance. People change jobs more often. Few of us today expect a 20-year career with the same company or even in the same profession. The marketer doesn't have the luxury of looking at inessential data; instead, she must hit targets quickly so the company or client can evolve in step with the marketplace.[6] A typical example of this is a midmarket financial institution my company helped, in collaboration with the company's Nashville-based direct marketing agency. Managers at this loan company were under intense pressure to hit short-term sales targets. This pressure flowed down to their direct marketing agency and to us as a subcontractor to that agency. If we had accepted the delays and compromises on tracking solutions that were put forward by the loan company's IT department, we wouldn't have been able to deliver the

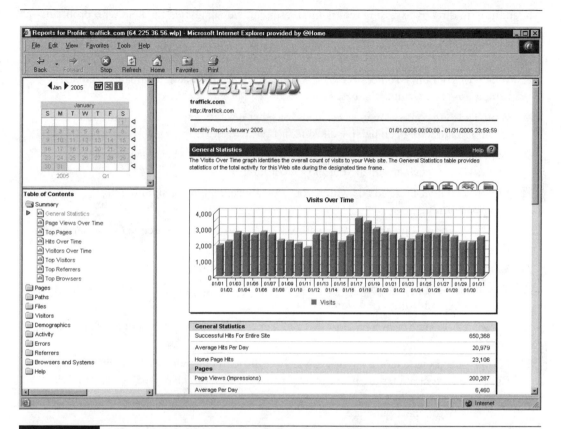

FIGURE 10-1   General website usage stats from a free version of WebTrends

online advertising ROI we were hired to achieve. As a result, we argued in favor of a more decentralized, simplified, and nimble approach to tracking the cost per lead on the pay-per-click campaign. Unfortunately, it also took too long to get suggested landing page improvements implemented, which hurt conversion rates during a busy season. IT centralization is certainly no friend of mine.

As corporate marketers demanded more, companies like WebTrends gradually improved upon their models. They began to offer report formats that did a better job of reporting on various items such as search traffic. Today, the major players like WebTrends compete for the web analytics dollars of large companies. However, for the small-business marketer, and even for many large companies seeking a more streamlined approach, the expensive newer-generation analytics packages offered by WebTrends and others don't offer the best value.

In addition to directly assessing return on investment, web analytics can help with problems like isolating low-quality partner traffic, and even recognizing patterns that may indicate fraudulent clicks. Specifically, analytics software can help you find out the following:

- Which of your click sources (Google AdWords, Overture, banner campaigns, email campaigns) is providing the best ROI.

- Which ads are converting to sales, leads, or other desired actions at a healthy rate, and which are attracting compulsive clickers or tire-kickers.

- Which keywords are converting well, and which aren't (so you can decide which to shut off, or so you can adjust your bids accordingly).

- Whether content-targeted ads within your Google campaign are significantly underperforming.

- Whether certain sources, like AOL and Ask Jeeves (AdWords' search network partners), are performing up to par.

- Whether AdWords ads in sources like Gmail are converting.

- The differential in performance between organic clicks (unpaid search engine listings) as opposed to paid listings (AdWords and others).

- Whether your paid search results have a higher ROI at different times of the day or on weekdays.

- For advanced marketers, analytics can answer difficult questions such as whether your ROI or conversion rates are better in ad position 1 (high on the page), 3 (farther down the page), or 7 (well down the page); or even fancier items like "repeat purchases" and "propensity to repeat-purchase."

The majority of clients I've worked with focus on as simple an analysis as possible. You've got to walk before you can run.

It's never too late. I sometimes encounter clients who resist tracking and specifically ask that I not bother with it "for now." I recently finished up an overhaul of an AdWords campaign for a local sauna retailer who absolutely depends on paid search traffic to generate five to ten sales per day, at an average order size of around $1,000. He was so impressed with the targeting offered by pay per click that his bids had grown to over $3.00 per click (as competitors continued to push their bids up).

A couple of years ago, this busy retailer had no reason to even bother tracking his paid search campaigns. His daily spend at an average of 5–10 cents a click might have amounted to $10 per day. Today, depending on how he sets his budget, he might be looking at $600 per day, so it makes much more sense to track. Of course, when someone resists tracking as this client did in the early going, it always goes against my wishes, but I must concede that it's considerably harder to track ROI for companies (like this particular one) that choose to close nearly all their sales over the phone. If your business approach involves talking to a customer and hearing them say something like, "I think I'll drop by the showroom tomorrow," I realize that you, like the sauna retailer, may find this chapter to be overly optimistic about the prospects for tracking. Not every website represents an online business. Many sites represent a business, period, where a small proportion of the sales may be concluded online. Nonetheless, there are a couple of simple ways to approach tracking offline business. For a brief taste, see the "Tracking Phone Orders" section later in the chapter.

But for the rest of you, back to the pep talk. In this increasingly competitive environment, advertisers who spend without tracking are basically trying to manage their campaigns based on myths and superstitions about campaign performance. They have no idea whether the campaign is actually responsible for sales, and cannot determine which parts of the campaign are wasteful. By taking control of your web analytics, you can optimize a campaign with correct bids and strategies. It's not uncommon to double or triple ROI by implementing basic conversion tracking.

One of the biggest problems with advertisers who don't track is that they frequently adopt a sporadic on-and-off approach to their campaigns without rationally determining the reasons for alterations in the pattern of ad delivery. Nontrackers will shut down their whole campaigns when they don't "feel right," or will double their bids when they "feel lucky." To be blunt, superstitious advertisers will soon be up against many competitors who have mastered the math. Those more analytical competitors will make the instinctive marketers look prehistoric by comparison.

Relevant Stats, Not Mountains of Data

If you're like many website owners, you have some experience with the range of reports that you can access with a free or inexpensive log analyzer. In my own experience with my content site, Traffick.com, I got hooked on poring over a variety of statistics on the users who came to the site. Some of the really interesting stats referred to which sources were the leading referrers, whether search engines or sites that had linked to us.

There are a ton of great things you can do with traditional logfile analysis. A webmaster can discover whether there are frequent page load errors, form fill errors, and many other things. And if you produce a lot of pages of content, you may have a lot of referral and user data to study. However, unless the revenues from your site are derived from advertising, or if you are a big retailer dependent on studying user patterns in detail, don't get too addicted to poring over these general site usage stats.

Today's conversion tracking software gives you both less and more. It allows you to focus on a narrower range of data that will tell you a lot more about the value of the clicks you're paying for. After all, what you really want to know is, how many clicks from your AdWords account converted to a sale today? You'll also develop more sophisticated questions as you get more comfortable. Some of these questions might be Which keywords are really performing well? Are certain ads better performers? Do some times of day seem to drain your budget? How often do your paid clicks convert into secondary actions like newsletter sign-ups?

TIP   *By adopting streamlined direct marketing models and tailored landing pages that lead users to a desired transaction, you can do yourself a huge favor. You can achieve the same or better results by examining a narrow range of actionable campaign statistics rather than poring over huge logfile reports.*

If your company already has a tracking solution that is generating the conversion data you need, you might be locked into a particular piece of software. No problem, if it gets you the info you need. Depending on how the interface looks to you, there may be implied pressure on you to pore through many different types of stats. With Omniture's SiteCatalyst, for example, you'll notice the availability of both modern "conversion" data like "revenue per click" and traditional info more common to the logfile analyzer generation. Resist the pressure to look at all of it. If you're allocating your time properly, you should be analyzing the data that will help you adjust your AdWords campaign and ignoring much of the other "nice to know, but not essential" reports.

IT vs. Marketing Politics

The "IT department versus the marketing department" turf war is far from new when it comes to corporate website strategy. Additionally, it isn't restricted to large companies, contrary to what you might think. Jim Sterne wrote an article on this subject as long ago as 1995.[7]

Bottom line: if there's no cooperation, you can't maximize campaign results, and marketing dollars are wasted. Providing limited or slow access to website stats prevents the marketing people from adjusting campaigns to get ahead of the competition, ultimately threatening the company's competitive position. If someone says it can't or shouldn't be done, find someone who will do it. In large companies, the challenges of sharing information and installing new tracking methodologies may be considerable. However, in small companies, there really is no excuse.

Don't Assume the Answers Are Obvious

Whether your campaign is making money or not can be a matter of interpretation, even if you're asking the right questions in the first place. While it's true that you should be zeroing in on key metrics like return on ad spend, cost per acquisition, or cost per order, you won't always be able to get 100% accurate readings on these. Don't assume there are hard-and-fast rules to tell you whether a campaign is successful or profitable. In many companies, deciding how aggressively they should continue to advertise is a matter of debate and interpretation. Don't assume you missed something in business class, or that the campaign needs to turn a profit in three weeks, or else. Ask others what they think. Be flexible.

You don't need to settle on a single campaign metric as your key. You may want to look at the return on ad spend, but if you're in retail, you'll need to factor in profit margins. You might already be aware of what it costs to acquire a customer or lead because you've run similar offline or online campaigns. If so, great. Weigh the merits of several metrics at once.

It's an inexact science. But by assessing the *relative* performance of different sources, keywords, and ads, you can always improve on your overall performance. If that improvement never gets you to a point where it makes sense from the standpoint of short-term or long-term profit, of course, you might have to shut down your campaign. But the answer to what is a profitable campaign looks different to different companies.

Imperfect World Case Example #1: Brookbend Outdoor Furniture

I'll repeat this point because it's quite important. It's not always possible to pinpoint exactly an *absolute* measure of success, but pursuing *relative* success is easy if you shape your tracking so it provides you with metrics that can be *compared*.

I'm definitely not talking about pre-click metrics like CTRs in this case. I'm often asked, "Is my CTR OK? How does it compare to others?" While this matters to a degree, it's a distraction from the real business of measuring ROI. A person who pats himself on the back solely for achieving an 8% CTR is probably a person who doesn't own a stake in the company!

Take the example of one of my clients, Paul Marcus of Brookbend Outdoor Furniture. Paul's color catalog has always been his best sales tool. He found that getting consumers to request the catalog through pay-per-click ads only cost about 25% of what it had been costing to achieve the same goal at home shows. This was a great result. But what if Paul had not had such a cost-per-catalog-distributed precedent going into his pay-per-click campaign? He might have erroneously assumed the wrong number to shoot for at first; what was actually a good result might have "felt like" a bad result. Since many such businesses have long sales cycles and different profit margins on different items, and a variety of goals such as clearing out excess inventory at a slight loss to maintain cash flow, the bottom line is not always easy to calculate day to day. A variety of pressures are typically being juggled by the small business. Paul's main goal when he came to me was indeed to clear out a large amount of inventory that wasn't moving quickly enough. In other words, at first his goal wasn't so much to maximize profitability as to cut his losses so he could start with a decent cash position the following year.

But while we worked to improve Paul's pay-per-click campaigns, what we could clearly strive for at all times was some sense of relative success. We learned that some AdWords keywords were worth high bids; that others were receiving comparable response at lower bids; and that still others were not worth bidding on at all. We also found that certain ad copy led to a rise in catalog requests. And we were able to clearly see that AdWords performed slightly better than Overture, so we allocated funds and effort accordingly. By pursuing steady improvement, the result turned out to be far better than the client had hoped. We might not have ever made it to the end goal if we had focused too closely on some arbitrary measure of success in the first couple of weeks.

Adding to the challenge of ROI measurement, as with many small retailers, was this client's preference to close sales, and upsell recent clients on larger new orders, with ongoing phone contact. When business is booming, it can be impractical for an understaffed entrepreneur like Paul Marcus to record everything and to track it back to particular ads. (Many prospective customers would lead in with, "I saw your ad on Google"—enough that he was satisfied that for a few pennies, he was attracting prospects who might spend anywhere from $75 to $2,000 on furniture. The occasional large custom order would be $5,000 or more.) In this "real world situation"—admittedly imperfect—a general knowledge that pay per click was working better than offline advertising methods on a cost-per-catalog-request basis, plus a commitment to examine and adjust bids and ad copy to reflect the relative performance of different aspects of the campaign, added up to steady forward progress and an increasingly efficient lead-generation machine.

Finally, when his slow season arrived (he sells deck furniture, so buying begins to slow in early August) Paul could always shut the campaign down or lower the daily budget to take a wait-and-see approach, and focus on other aspects of his business, such as traveling to visit international suppliers. And when he was ready to go full bore again, the same well-tweaked AdWords campaign—that same lead-generation machine we had perfected—could simply be reenabled for the next busy season and monitored as before.

Imperfect World Case #2: Corporate Furniture Retailer

Let's look at another example of a client I worked with on post-click tracking. The tracking methodology we used seemed simple at first, but more complex problems revealed themselves in the process of trying to measure the profitability of the pay-per-click campaigns. In the end, we were forced to accept a degree of uncertainty in data while gaining a solid picture of which parts of the campaign were performing. (The industry segment has been changed slightly to protect the client's anonymity. I'll use the fictional name Cubicles Etc. for the purposes of this narrative.)

Cubicles Etc. sells a range of corporate furniture products to businesses from a large online catalog. When I took on the account, they told me they were confused about tracking. They felt unsure about "where the money was going," even though their previous consultant's in-house tracking tool seemed to offer plenty of data to someone willing to take the time to analyze it. The problem may not have been with the tracking tool so much as with the junior staffer charged with interpreting campaign results. Had the same staffer been working on a campaign to sell discount neckties to consumers from a large catalog, she might have been able to give adequate interpretations of what was going on, since there is typically a short sales cycle in that type of sub-$100 item. For large corporate furniture orders of $3,000 and up, by contrast, there is an initial "dance" that may involve seeing a sample, getting a budget approved, and comparison shopping. No wonder the client had difficulty knowing "what was going on"! No simple ROI calculation was possible here. Only an experienced analyst with some appreciation for the client's sales cycle would be able to properly advise on the best approach to measuring success.

As I learned from many subsequent conversations, Cubicles Etc. was taking an inappropriate approach to interpreting their data, but it wasn't all their fault. Their previous consultant had given them simplistic advice and had encouraged a form of tracking that shut off keywords if they didn't perform well on a cost-per-order basis over a period of just a few hours. If cash outlays in a single day did not result in immediate sales (in spite of the automated bidding technology being tuned to maximize ROI), the client began to get agitated, wondering why things were "falling apart" and "losing money that day"—a concern that would indeed have been appropriate had they been blowing out hundreds of designer neckties on a daily basis. Yet this approach bore no resemblance at all to their corporate customers' complex buying patterns as they had described them meticulously to me.

I learned a valuable lesson here—a couple, actually. First, you can always find useful ways to track even complicated campaigns such as this one. But second and more important, you can get yourself into a lot of trouble if you assume that you should be feeling a kind of "perfect clarity" to whether your AdWords account is "performing." If your business is complicated, you'll never feel like it just "hits you." Someone with a well-rounded business background, liberal arts education, or scientific training (maybe even a mix of all three)—not a junior staffer who only knows the designer neckties business, nor some automated ROI-maximization software—will have to put in some extra brain work to help you figure out whether the investment is paying off.

The story gets worse. After a period of campaign improvement and reconstruction, we coaxed what we thought were better performance numbers out of this campaign, a hunch that was proven right many months later with return on ad spend (ROAS) numbers coming in over 200%. However, my group came under fire for not being able to produce as solid a daily or weekly statistical summary as the previous consultant had done. Our interpretations were not even as good as the previous firm's "confusing" reports, thought the client. I went back and looked at a few of the incumbent agency's daily reports that looked much better from a performance standpoint than anything we had been able to accomplish. The campaign had been extremely profitable on certain days. We could boast of nothing like this. A closer look at the numbers, though, suggested something else. The numbers they showed could not possibly have been true. Where did they come from? We had, by this time, learned that the client closed most of their orders by phone and that many orders resulted from contacts initiated weeks or months earlier. In this context, a good "daily" ROI report was virtually meaningless. At best, the client was looking at reports for a few days of misleadingly high ROI based on sales that resulted from clickthroughs from weeks or months ago. At worst, the previous consultant had sent opaque reports that counted lead requests as orders, lowering the apparent cost-per-order number to something that would have been impossible to reconcile with the client's so-so financial results that month.

Although we, too, had access to daily conversion data, these were often inconclusive. Over half the orders were entered manually in batches based on data from phone reps. Thus, we looked primarily at *monthly* time periods, and for these, the results were unremarkable—about as good as we might have expected. The ROI was hovering around the break-even mark on paper, but the client's business was thriving and growing. Certainly there was no collapse in business. Based on overzealous assumptions about how conclusive daily data ought to look, the client believed that business on any given day was terrible, when in fact it was not.

So I took a harder look at the previous consultant's data and at old emails that had Cubicles Etc. wailing that they needed to hire us because their campaigns were losing money. (Back then, it was real money being lost while the reports the previous consultant had sent were rosy looking.) I could only conclude that the reports they had received from their previous consultant had been doctored in some way. Possibly a junior staffer or intern had taken this step to mask poor campaign performance, without the knowledge of the principals of the firm.

After listening to that long anecdote, I owe you at least an overview of how we took a more balanced approach to tracking. First, we insisted that the client wait three to four weeks after any heavy spending period before jumping to any conclusions about campaign ROI. As things progressed we found that like clockwork, sales did come in consistently, particularly in the days immediately following a heavy spend on expensive core keywords. We soon learned that those keywords were expensive for good reason: they not only converted to sales, they seemed to generate the most serious, high-volume customers.

Our benchmark ROI measure remained ROAS, which we wanted to be about 100%. Although that did not take into account profit margins, the client agreed that this was a good target because repeat business is strong in their industry, and second orders tend to be significantly larger than first orders. The ROAS in the first month turned out to be right around the 100% target—this in spite of ongoing (and in the end exaggerated) subjective commentary about the "terrible" campaign performance, deteriorating lead quality, and so forth.

We grilled the client on typical patterns of sales so we could measure significant user actions on the site that happened more frequently than a sale. It turned out that about 5% of site visitors would fill out a request form requesting a price quote or free sample. The client's own data, furthermore, showed that roughly 20% of those making such a request later returned to make a purchase. As a result, "cost per form" (or cost per lead) became an additional metric that helped us track the relative performance of various keywords, even where actual sales were sporadic. Instead of waiting for the full verdict of monthly sales reports and conversion data, we could look at day-to-day patterns with leads to give us a rough cue as to whether to raise or lower bids in the interim. Automated systems that adjust keyword bids to correspond to an "allowable cost per order" do not have this flexibility. Even if they did, they'd need to be supervised by an operator with faculties of judgment.

Because we were tracking on a keyword-by-keyword basis, many keywords would go days without leading to a single sale. Then, a single keyword would result in a large sale ($5,000 or $12,000). None of these keyword-specific data points are particularly reliable benchmarks of campaign performance. We would have been ill advised to become too depressed if a particular keyword achieved a 0% ROI over a several-day period. Nor would it have made any sense (at least not until a pattern became established) to become too excited by a particular keyword having a 12,000% ROI over a one-week period. Campaignwide performance is a more reliable guide, since this smoothes out the bumps and gives general guidance as to overall performance. A campaign aimed at attracting infrequent, large purchases must be managed differently than one that aims to sell hundreds of neckties every day, one at a time.

As we watched the campaign, keywords that returned an ROAS of 0%–50% might need to have their bids lowered or even be deleted, but depending on click volume, those determinations needed to be made over a period of a month or two.

Getting sales data for this campaign was not automatic, since most sales were handled over the phone. Asking the customer to read a code to phone reps, triggered by a cookie that was made visible on the buyer's computer, allowed us to map these sales to specific keywords (with the help of some custom programming by ConversionRuler staff). But there were frequent delays in receiving the data. Sometimes revenue amounts got lost in translation. Sometimes the codes were improperly recorded by phone staff or not recorded at all, leading us to routinely underestimate the AdWords-generated revenues. By how much? Hard to say, but probably 15% just owing to human error, and another 10%–15% due to miscellaneous technical problems.

Key Discoveries Even in an Imperfect Experiment   After several months, we were able to adjust the campaign to respond to the varying performance of different keywords, and we did reach the conclusion that the AdWords campaign was performing consistently. Indeed, in retrospect, it performed better than any of us realized at the time. Orders kept coming in months down the road, directly traceable to the campaign initiated in summer and fall 2004. Looking at the big picture of a four-month period from July 1 through October 31, I can now see from ConversionRuler data that total revenues directly traceable to the AdWords campaign for that period are $77,753.54 on an ad spend of $36,401.34 for the period. (See Figures 10-2 and 10-3.) Calculating by hand, the ROAS as far as we know was 213.6%. It was probably significantly higher than that, though, as the detail in our conversion tracking shows quite a number of additional sales with no revenues assigned due to technical glitches in the integration of the conversion tracking with the shopping cart. So although we had a limited sense of how things

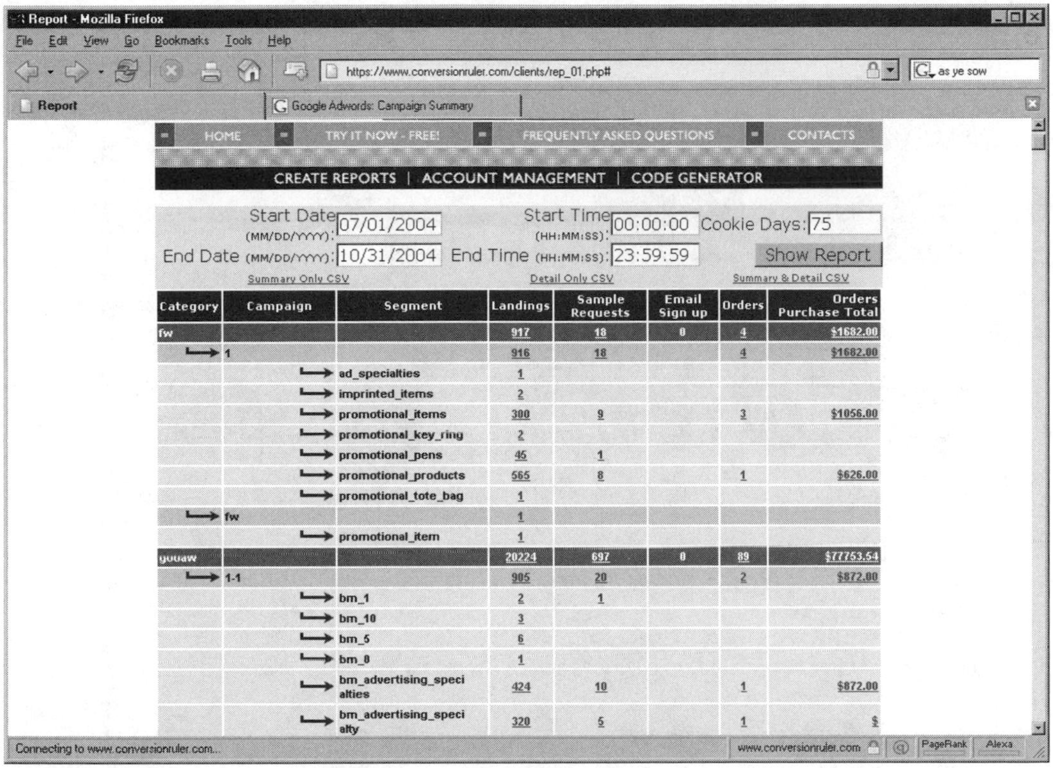

	Category	Campaign	Segment	Landings	Sample Requests	Email Sign up	Orders	Orders Purchase Total
fw				917	18	0	4	$1682.00
		1		916	18		4	$1682.00
			ad_specialties	1				
			imprinted_items	2				
			promotional_items	380	9		3	$1056.00
			promotional_key_ring	2				
			promotional_pens	45	1			
			promotional_products	565	8		1	$626.00
			promotional_tote_bag	1				
		fw		1				
			promotional_item	1				
gouaw				20224	697	0	89	$77753.54
		1-1		905	20		2	$872.00
			bm_1	2	1			
			bm_10	3				
			bm_5	6				
			bm_0	1				
			bm_advertising_speci alties	424	10		1	$872.00
			bm_advertising_speci alty	320	5		1	$

FIGURE 10-2   ROI tracking service ConversionRuler shows $77,753 in revenues over three months.

were performing when we were in the middle of that period, as it turns out the maxim "as ye sow, so shall ye reap" certainly applied to this campaign. We just wish we (and Cubicles Etc.) had had the confidence to sow more.

Just the months of July and August now show an ROAS of (as far as we know for sure) at least 270.3%. That after being led to believe all summer that the campaign was in crisis! The ROI actually got worse in the fall during the busy season in part because competitors began to bid heavily on core keywords. For all the wrong reasons, we began raising our bids over a small number of hours during the working day rather than bidding lower for the full day.

We also learned that the Overture campaign performed about the same on an ROI basis as the AdWords campaign, so we continued to run both. Over the course of this client relationship, we learned a number of interesting things about user behavior. One was that leads generated through

| **FIGURE 10-3** | AdWords interface shows total spend of $36,401 over three months. |

content targeting and AOL Search were, on average, of a lower quality than those generated through Google Search. Looking strictly at cost per lead, these traffic sources were comparable, but qualitative analysis of the content of the request forms filled in by users identified a clear pattern of poorly targeted clicks from content and AOL. Recall that about 5% of all site visitors requested some kind of quote or sample. By looking at the content of the requests, it became apparent which prospects had actually just stumbled on the site looking for an inexpensive one-off purchase, or worse, a freebie of some sort, and which were prospective volume buyers of the type this retailer was targeting. We ultimately gave up on content targeting, and sometimes also turned off search network partners (we unchecked these in the campaign settings) because they were generating too many bogus and low-quality leads, which led to wasted staff time. For this client, too many nuisance leads would be a distraction even if we could bid very low on the content-targeted inventory.

All was not perfect, but the campaign was contributing to steady growth in the business. The growth would have been faster but the client did not want growth to be too rapid, especially given that repeat business and word of mouth also led to rapid order influxes at certain times. Many days, we turned the campaign off at 1:00 P.M. because too many leads were coming in, making it even more difficult to get a true handle on its potential. We never kept it running past 5:00 P.M. Eastern.

Ultimately I found it difficult to escape the conclusion that a high-maintenance, complex-to-interpret campaign such as this one—especially in a high-priced keyword neighborhood—is difficult for the small company to handle, on at least three fronts. First, we (or their previous consultants) could have done a better job for Cubicles Etc. (or they, for themselves) had we been able to spend even more time interpreting data and paying attention to the characteristics of those customers who did make large purchases. Small companies can lose to large companies if they can't find the time or the resources to analyze data. (In this case, the client was quite exacting, but they expected perfection on a tight budget; the work they had in mind could have been nearly a full-time position, a position they didn't have the budget to fill.) Second, it seems inevitable that bid management software of some sort needs to be used in concert with human analysis, especially when the client insists on competing for very high priced keywords and turning the campaign off for the day if a certain spend is exceeded. These tools can be costly; moreover, some tools simply don't work properly. Third, midsized to larger companies may be growth oriented, or already well funded, wanting as much growth as they can handle. In my opinion, managing and tracking a campaign is a little easier when the model is always "growth." In a highly competitive environment (a high-CPC industry), you can still thrive if you maximize the return on a few keyword ideas or some niche that you've figured out better than the competition. Many small businesses have not yet graduated from the "small small business" to the level of a "large small business" that has the capacity and an action plan to handle rapid growth. If you're in a tough AdWords auction in the first place, and have the additional constraint of not being able to handle spurts of growth, you're likely to be at a disadvantage compared to larger companies that leave their campaigns on all the time.

Managing this particular campaign felt a bit like driving a sports car that had been retrofitted with the capabilities of a golf cart. We'd feel like accelerating because we thought we were on a roll, but the darn thing wouldn't get above 20 mph due to the system of rules and cautions we needed to follow. Much later, we kicked ourselves thinking how much money the client could have made had there been more confidence in the limited data we did have. You'll probably notice that the industry leaders in some fields are almost always in customer acquisition mode on AdWords because the ROI here is still low by their standards (compared to offline sources, say). Unless you're realistic, it can be more exhausting to manage a lower-budget campaign because of the unevenness of the methodology used and the tightness of the budget.

Either Keep It Simple and Careful, or Take a Risk and Spend More

Small firms do have advantages, of course. They can reach niche markets and adjust their campaigns more quickly if they have the commitment. But they need to be parsimonious in how they plan and track their campaigns. You can't always just press a button and get perfect responses to complex ROI questions. Someone has to do this stuff (sometimes with the help of software). If you can't handle rapid growth, or you're on a small budget, don't let your reach exceed your grasp when it comes to campaign management and analytics. You're either aggressive or cautious—you can't be both. Aggressive costs more.

If you're being cautious, and thus have fewer human resources to tap into, you may be forced to track fewer keyword groups rather than more. Use proxies for interest (like request forms) and monthly financials to judge performance rather than being in hair-trigger mode, which expects to know the daily ROI for every keyword. If you can't be watching carefully, you can always bid less or lower your daily budget.

The alternative is to have enough confidence in how well your business is doing to keep consistently advertising for three or four months. It takes courage to believe that an ad campaign will pay for itself over time. But as the previous case showed, it can take weeks or months for some campaigns to begin paying off, and no pretty reporting format can (or should) make that reality more palatable or less risky for you.

Cases like this one illustrate vividly how difficult it is to fully capture the behavioral world of users. In such a context, growing a small company relies not on some perfect "shooting fish in a barrel" methodology, but rather on an approach to data that combines inference with instinct. You're not a marksman aiming at a known target so much as you are a detective sifting through forensic evidence. Although you have a clear advantage over a forensic scientist in that you have daily access to new data, there are also some limitations you'll have to live with.

Indeed, recent developments show that users are taking more steps to protect their online privacy, which might make marketers' tracking efforts increasingly inexact. For example, comScore, an agency mentioned throughout this book that tracks online user behavior through a panel-based methodology similar to Nielsen ratings, reports that some of their panelists aren't transmitting behavioral data properly because their anti-spyware software is blocking comScore's tracking module even though it is a legitimate research tool installed voluntarily by the user.[8] In other words, comScore is actually *paying* people to send them behavioral data, yet they aren't receiving reliable data from some of those users because it's being blocked by privacy-protection software the users forgot they had installed. As such privacy-protection software begins to be built into operating systems, companies like Microsoft could conceivably play havoc with the tracking services they don't like, while setting up protocols that protect direct data transmission for themselves in the future.[9] Such developments could influence your choice of tracking methodologies down the road.

Beyond that, though, recent research has shown far more latency to online purchase decisions than once thought. At Search Engine Strategies New York 2005, in a panel on "The Search Landscape," James Lamberti of comScore Networks and Ken Cassar of NetRatings agreed that advertisers must take a much closer look at buying cycles, arguing that 90-day delays are not uncommon from the first click to the decision to buy. Panel moderator Danny Sullivan agreed, saying that he is seeing more and more data showing that "purchases caused by online listings are often neither immediate nor online." In light of emerging research by leading Internet measurement firms, then, it appears that clients like Cubicles Etc. have a lot of company in their uncertain ROI measurements.

The only way to achieve perfect measurement would be with full-scale surveillance of every thought and action of your prospects and customers. Complete Panopticon-like trackability might seem like the direct marketing ideal, but I'm personally willing to exchange a bit of efficiency in my marketing campaigns for the privilege of living in a society where my privacy is respected to a reasonable degree. As a small business owner, I think I'd be willing to allow that sometimes, phone orders might not be tracked perfectly, in exchange for closing a sale with an impatient customer.

First Things First: Landing URL Depends on Tracking Method

When you're getting set to launch a campaign, you need to be clear on the type of tracking you'll be using. For many of my clients, I've used a simple tracking service called ConversionRuler. ConversionRuler, like many of the tracking services available today, works by placing a small snippet of custom Javascript code in the HTML of your landing page and on other key pages on your website. In this case, custom "landing page" code is slightly different from custom code that counts sales, leads, and other desired actions. The fact that you customize the code snippets actually leads to more reliable performance and easier-to-read reports down the road. Fortunately, most of these kinds of companies offer some installation support for the technically challenged.

Tracking services come in a variety of flavors. Some track using advanced logfile analysis, needing no code to be installed on your website, and others use "landing page code" written in Javascript to follow users on your site through to a desired action. Some are installed directly on your server and allow you to download reports, whereas others are hosted applications that are available at all times to anyone with the login information. Some site owners get their tracking from their existing shopping cart, e-commerce package, or affiliate software. This kaleidoscope of different tracking methods, and the fact that the technical underbelly of web analytics can be complicated, will require some shorthand if we're to get through a basic intro here. For the most part, I assume a hosted application that provides at least a report on which parts of a paid search campaign are generating sales or leads. I may use terms like *software, service, package, toolset,* or *analytics solution* interchangeably.[10] Companies like WebTrends and ClickTracks offer their analytics in both "flavors," as it were. For those who wish on-demand service, a hosted application is available. For those who prefer the autonomy of installing a package on their own server, the ability to run unlimited reports, and so on, software is available.

Web analytics won't work without some input from you. First, you'll want to decide whether you'll be tracking by ad group and ad, or by keyword. Tracking by ad group and ad is the simplest method. (In industry vernacular, this is sometimes referred to as "tracking in buckets.") To do this, you'll need to ensure you're matching the correct landing pages to the appropriate ads within your campaign.

Next, no matter which method you use, you'll have to tell it what to track by attaching parameters to the landing URLs you use in the ads in your Google AdWords campaign. Typically, this will be in some arbitrary format based on a nomenclature you choose yourself. For Ad Group 3 within Campaign 2, for example, you might want to use "23" as the code. You might then tag different ads with a letter, so the third ad you test might be "23c." Your landing URL would look something like this:

http://www.pewterz1.biz?source=goog&kw=23c

Or, if you were tracking by individual keyword:

http://www.pewterz1.biz?source=goog&kw=pewter_duck

The words *source* and *kw* or *group* are connected to (dictated by) the analytics package you're using. Parameter names vary depending on the tool you use, but the principles are the same. The labels you use (such as "23c," "pewter_duck") will show up in your campaign analytics reports, so you need to settle on a format you and colleagues will find easy to interpret later.

Increasingly, advertisers are tracking right down to individual keywords. In campaigns with a lot of keywords, it's helpful to use a tracking tool that will generate all the tracking URLs for you and insert them into your campaign to save you the work. But not every campaign requires this level of detail.

One practical solution I've used to good effect is to begin tracking by ad group and ad within a Google campaign to get a sense of how different "buckets" of keywords are performing. I'll then *selectively* track the conversion rate of 10 or 20 specific keywords; typically those that are the most expensive or popular. You can do this in an existing ad group by simply using the powerposting feature of AdWords. Done on a single line within the keyword editing box, with a specific bid corresponding to that keyword alone, the keyword-specific bid and tracking URL would look like this:

"pewter duck" ** 1.14 ** http://www.pewterz1.biz?source=goog&kw=PMpewter_duck

"PM" denotes "phrase match." The label is arbitrary; I devised this system myself and continue to use it for some clients. Exact match is EM, and broad match is BM, in this system. Sometimes I use abbreviated or disguised versions of the keywords in case competitors are spying or lest some users be distracted by overt words appearing in the URL. Figure 10-4 shows the Google interface with a couple of keywords being tracked.

There are many ways to skin a cat (or track pewter duck sales, in this instance). These are only examples. You may settle on a slightly different method.

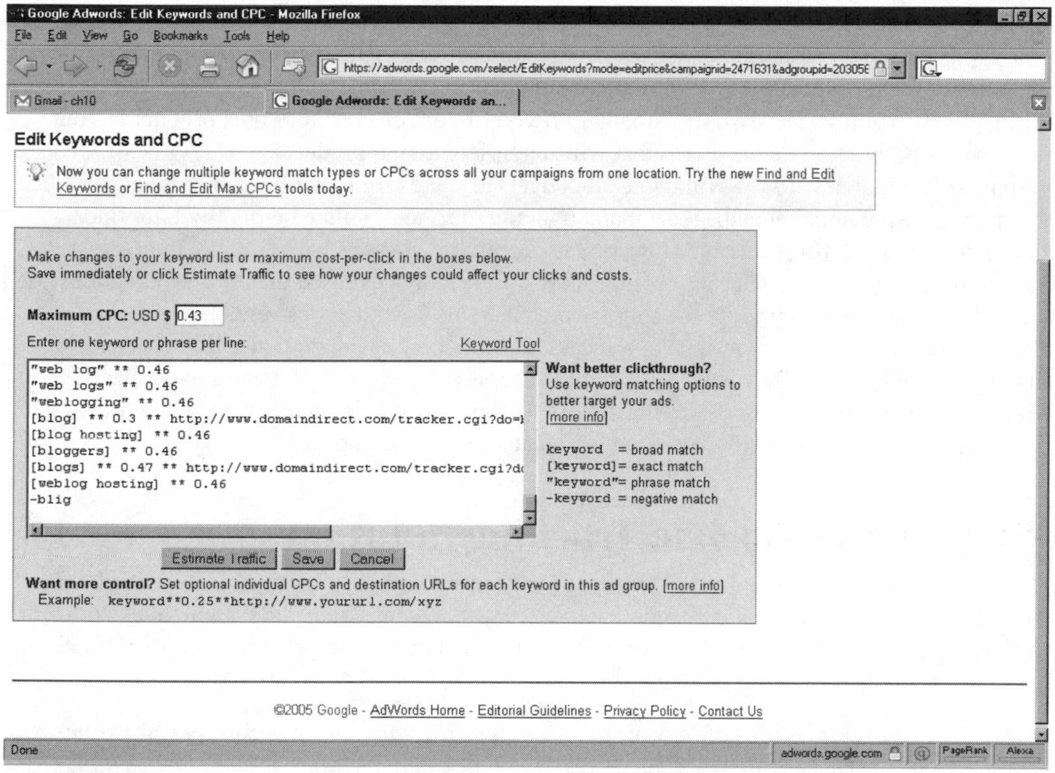

©2005 Google - AdWords Home - Editorial Guidelines - Privacy Policy - Contact Us

FIGURE 10-4   In this keyword list, only a couple of keywords are being tracked separately by designating a special tracking URL following double asterisks.

Google's Relationship with Third-Party Analytics Vendors

Until recently, sellers of basic conversion tracking software have been limited by uncertain relationships with Google. Some vendors, for example, have developed bid management functions or functions that make it easy to generate appropriate "by keyword" tracking URLs and to insert them into an AdWords account from the third-party interface. Other vendors have made less progress because of what appears to be limited cooperation from Google.

This is all about to change. On January 27, 2005, Google released an Application Programming Interface (API) for AdWords that allows authorized access to the AdWords interface by third-party application developers. This basically will provide advertisers using this next generation of applications more direct authorized access to the AdWords interface without necessarily having to log into their AdWords account. Because Google is actually now encouraging developers to think of "creative" ways of accessing AdWords campaign data, I'd expect new services to emerge. One example would be a custom integration between your inventory system and your AdWords campaign: if you run out of inventory on a product in your catalog, you stop bidding on the words that will send users to that product.

Some individual advertisers with large ad budgets at stake will now find it attractive to develop their own campaign management and tracking tools and, unlike before, will not find their access to the AdWords interface thwarted by uncertain relations with Google. In practice, a handful of third parties had been accessing AdWords accounts using semiauthorized methods, and for at least six months prior to the announcement, some key analytics vendors were beta-testing the API. For those beta testers, this access allowed them to create richer ROI reports and manage client bids more effectively. Now that the access procedures have been standardized, we'll likely see an explosion of clever third-party AdWords campaign management and tracking services. As a result, prices will come down and feature sets will improve.

Choosing an Appropriate Tracking Solution

As a consultant, I've tried a number of tracking tools, and I have my favorites. Insofar as clients have installed some of them (in particular, ConversionRuler) quite frequently, sometimes with my company as a reseller, I have direct or indirect financial relationships with some vendors. So take all advice for what it is—a guideline.

CAUTION   *Some consulting firms always recommend their own tool, which makes them far from impartial. This can lock you into consulting that you don't want or an analytics tool that isn't appropriate (or priced right).*

The real trick to choosing a tracking solution is no trick at all, it's common sense. You first determine what your tracking needs are, and then you find the tracking solution that fits those needs. The hard part is figuring out exactly what your tracking needs are. Most of us can boil it down to definitively answering this question: is my AdWords campaign generating sales or other desired actions on my website? Second, which parts of the campaign are performing best? If your tracking solution offers only basic logfile analysis, it may not be able to tell you whether your AdWords campaign is "converting" to sales, or which parts of the campaign are converting better. Look for terms like "conversion tracking" and "ROI reports" in the sales literature of any analytics solution before you decide to test one. Most, especially in the low-price area, offer free 14-day or 30-day trials.

Investing in any of the lower-end conversion tracking services, such as ConversionRuler, Keyword Max, and IndexTools, is fairly safe. Even WebTrends now offers an affordable small-business version ($35/month for the hosted version). If your needs grow, it isn't a big deal to hunt for a more sophisticated analytics package, since your investment in the lower-end services is minimal. Once you make a decision on a lower-end tool, you aren't generally locked into anything.

One thing to watch for is that pricing for almost any hosted service will ramp up for heavy users. WebTrends Small Business gives you a limit of 50,000 page views (the total number of pages viewed by users coming to your website) in a month. If you're going to go significantly over the limits, consider whether using the low-end service is still cost effective or stepping up to the next level makes sense.

What is perhaps a greater concern is the amount of time you might wind up spending with a tool you don't like. Most of the interfaces of today's low-end analytics solutions are not particularly user friendly. Moreover, many still have limited reporting. Fully 35% of my survey respondents noted that the biggest problem with their analytics solution was "not getting all the information I need." Traditional analytics companies like WebTrends have taken care to ensure that their lower-priced packages are not so full featured as to encourage enterprise customers to switch to the most basic version. Healthy competition in the marketplace today should ensure that we receive better value from all players in the near future.

Given the limitations of the available solutions, juxtaposed alongside the great value of having at least basic conversion data at hand, the bottom line is, do something about your tracking, even if it's not perfect.

In the interests of staying relatively vendor neutral, I don't provide an exhaustive review of analytics vendors, but rather, a brief overview of offerings at the inexpensive, middle, and high ends of the price range. In embarking on this exercise, though, I actually learned something odd: the "middle" category seems somewhat artificial in the offerings of many of the name-brand analytics vendors. In some cases the middle category is not in the middle at all—it's expensive. WebTrends 7, for example, comes in small business, professional, and enterprise versions. The small-business version is quite affordable at $35/month for the hosted version or $495 for the software version. It's a big step up to the professional edition. It costs six times as much, but the few additional features you get for that price seem rather arbitrarily chosen.

ClickTracks' new middle-priced Optimizer product is intended to be a middle ground between its high-end Professional (a rich set of web analytics reporting capabilities, priced at $3,000 and up for the software version, $179/month and up for the hosted version, depending on usage) and its inexpensive Analyzer (simple logfile analysis, $495 for the software version, $49/month and up for the hosted version). Optimizer typically runs $1,195 for the software version and $99/month and up for the hosted version. It provides a rich feature set similar to the Professional edition, including the innovative "What's Changed Report"—an intelligent time-saver if there ever was one. An important note, though: ClickTracks Optimizer does *not* provide ROI analysis or conversion tracking! So in essence it presents as a legacy logfile analysis product with added bells and whistles, and it is unsuitable for most readers of this book, since you'll need to get a handle on conversions. This latter task can be accomplished by low-priced solutions or even Google's free conversion tracker. The money you save on superfluous analytics could be invested in custom programming and site development work, both of which you're going to need from time to time.

Any step "up" to the midpriced analytics software or services, then, should be taken with caution. In the case of ClickTracks, your only logical step up would be to the full-priced Professional product. The same could probably be said for WebTrends 7 and numerous others. If you're going to be paying serious money for a full analytics package, the midpriced packages seem bound to frustrate you by withholding features. It's plain that midpriced products are often thrown together as thinly veiled means of inducing you to upgrade to the top-end product.

> **TIP** *Since pricing can be misleading, be sure to ask the right questions and review the fine print. Two key points to remember: technical support may cost extra unless otherwise stated, and hosted services get more expensive with heavy use.*

If you're a small business on a budget, the benefits of an "integrated" web analytics package can be overrated. WebTrends 7's sales literature makes much of the fact that its hosted Small Business edition won't give you information about "search engine spiders." But this same information can be accessed for free or nearly free with a basic log analyzer (perhaps even WebTrends). Most web hosting packages offer entry-level log analyzer capability if you're really curious about search engine spider activity. You don't need to shell out six times more for WebTrends Professional just to get this info, which in any case has no direct impact on your paid search campaign strategy.

I guess if I had to boil down my advice to those just getting their feet wet in web analytics, especially giving the emerging competition in the marketplace that seems bound to offer us more choice and better pricing soon, it would be (1) don't be lazy; but (2) it's OK to be thrifty.

> **TIP** *For a comparison of web analytics software, take a look at the* MarketingSherpa *Buyer's Guide to Web Analytics, available at MarketingSherpa.com. It is useful, but primarily covers big-iron packages more suitable for large companies with several full-time marketers on staff. Basic conversion trackers—which I recommend for small businesses—are largely ignored in Sherpa's report.*

Inexpensive Hosted Tracking

I met Eric Winter, the founder of a small conversion tracking service called ConversionRuler, at a Search Engine Strategies show a couple of years ago. We had a few productive conversations about trends in paid search, and really hit it off. That, and the fact that the product worked simply and immediately for a number of my clients, was enough for me to begin using the tool. Though it was far from perfect, ConversionRuler got the job done. At that time, as amazing as it may sound, tracking ROI was virtually unheard of among many small-business owners. At $19 per month (and up, depending on usage), ConversionRuler was more powerful than some much more expensive products. My criteria for using this product, then, included a healthy dose of trust in the people behind the company.

Currently a couple of dozen viable products in a similar price range are available, and more will be forthcoming. I can't review them all, but two others worth checking out are IndexTools and Keyword Max.

What such tools can do for you is usually fairly similar, since the snippets of Javascript code that they require you to install on your landing pages and "completed action" pages (typically a "thank you for your purchase" or "thank you for your request" page) are fairly standard in the industry. What may differentiate them is under-the-hood management and interpretation of the data that is subsequently collected, on one hand, and how they allow you to view reports on that data, on the other.

Colleagues and I have found IndexTools to offer some nice reporting options, but the downside for me is that it encourages the keyword-by-keyword tracking method, and the reports can be hard to navigate.

By contrast, my team has had great success with ConversionRuler, as simple as its interface may seem for now. (My friend at Iguana Corp. laughed that "it's nothing more than a calculator." It's a bit more than that!) Tracking by ad group and ad, we can essentially view conversions by ad group.

One feature I really like is the "drilldown," where you can access the full raw referring URLs for any class of click. (Later on in this chapter I refer to this as a *micro source analysis* and point out its usefulness in looking for fraud.) For all clicks, all clicks on a given ad, or all clicks that converted, you can click on the numerical result within the ConversionRuler report. Up pops a fuller list of detailed information about each click: the time of the click, the full referring URL (which will tell you the exact way the user typed the search query), the time of the conversion, and the visitor's IP address. This is not something you want to look at all the time, but it can be invaluable in getting a qualitative sense of what is happening with a campaign. It's easier to look for click fraud, for example, by examining traffic as it has clicked on a given ad and knowing whether it converted, rather than examining a long list of "traffic in general" from a log analyzer that doesn't know what converted. In addition, looking at the time and date of the click versus the time and date that the click converted, you can see how long it took between the initial click and the sale. Sometimes it will be five minutes, sometimes 45 days. Like many of its competitors, ConversionRuler is a deceptively powerful little tool.

In any case, most of the inexpensive ROI tracking services offer a big step up for any advertiser who is failing to "close the loop" in terms of measuring the link between a particular keyword or ad and whether these convert to desired actions. Which service you choose may be a matter of taste or simply personal relationships. I've seen mock-ups of a future generation of ConversionRuler that will offer a wider range of reporting options and stats, so I'm sticking with the service for now.

I gave the Small Business version of WebTrends 7 ($39/month) a test drive, but I found that the hosted (on-demand) version did not offer any of the commerce measurements (ROI tracking) that are available in the more expensive versions. Even the software version of WebTrends 7 Small Business comes with these features, so it's a bit frustrating not to be able to use them with the hosted version.

Several providers of low-priced shopping cart technology, such as 1shoppingcart.com, include conversion tracking, and these are better than nothing. Personally I am not comfortable using many of them. It is usually better to go with a dedicated analytics solution.

Midpriced Solutions

As I concluded earlier, the idea of a midpriced analytics package is a bit of a fiction. ClickTracks Optimizer doesn't offer the ROI tracking most of us need, so it's not clear to me who would use it, although I've certainly enjoyed testing its powerful capabilities as a reviewer. Most would be better off just going for the full-featured ClickTracks Pro or, if the budget is tight, using a low-priced conversion tracker coupled with a free or inexpensive log analyzer for occasional perspective on traffic patterns.

Most advertisers who have the budget for midpriced analytics are best off using entry-level products heavily so that they wind up paying more as usage increases. I tend to think that the quality of the lower-priced products will soon increase to the point where they make the middle-market products redundant. If you go into it thinking you can afford the midmarket products, it's quite likely that additional hidden costs will put you well over budget.

WebTrends 7 also tries to offer a middle ground, but it's still out of range for many users. Their midrange Professional version boasts many features, but for its hefty price tag, buyers are probably going to feel deprived of valuable features that are only available with the Enterprise version.

Urchin is one well-respected analytics solution that actually does seem to fit into the middle price range. Better yet, you can sometimes get it thrown in for free with a higher-end web hosting package. If you're in the market for dedicated hosting, find a deal that offers something like Urchin 6.1.1 included (a $900 value). Like many others, Urchin now comes in a hosted on-demand version. This latter is a lot more expensive, at $495/month and up. Urchin boasts that it is the world's most-installed analytics solution. It appears that Urchin has entered a mass-market, savvy-webmaster, and midmarket realm that WebTrends came to neglect. The company's relationship (similar to WebTrends') with web hosting companies has clearly fueled this growth and has established a good reputation. Note that Google has very recently acquired Urchin (as this book went to press). This indicates that Google could begin to offer much fuller featured analytics for its advertising clients. I tend to think this development will drive down the cost of all web analytics packages, especially those in the middle to high price ranges.

If you require a shopping cart or e-commerce package, you may find yourself in the middle range. Companies like Manticore offer e-commerce at a variety of price points. In some cases the included analytics functionality may be more than enough to satisfy your needs. I personally found one client's Manticore e-commerce solution quite helpful with basic conversion data as well as some interesting behavioral data in areas such as repeat purchases. On the other hand, there seemed to be inexplicable holes in the data.

Indeed, I'm often suspicious enough of the data I'm getting from one tracking service that I'd be tempted to use two. MarketingExperiments.com (much of the content is for subscribers only, but see the site for more information) recently performed a systematic study that indeed showed significant disparities in click counts and conversion data across different tracking services. It's enough to make you pull your hair out.

Full-Featured Analytics Suites

ClickTracks Professional is probably the most economical of the full-featured analytics products out there. That said, at least one client tells me that there is a reason for the higher pricing of Omniture SiteCatalyst, WebTrends 7, Hitbox Enterprise, and Manticore Virtual TrafficMaster: these will scale to handle the heaviest users. (ClickTracks couldn't handle my client's volume, much to his chagrin, since the price would have been relatively low at $10,000.) Scalability does, of course, come at a heavy price. A "report card" by CMP Media (for their own network of content sites) included custom quotes from all of these firms (not including ClickTracks), and they all came in around $100,000. Omniture SiteCatalyst received the highest score.

If you use a service like Omniture SiteCatalyst (Figure 10-5), I guarantee you'll be impressed with how customizable it is and with the range of interesting reports you can access from a single interface. If you've also seen quick-and-useful conversion data from a $19/month or free service, however, you're definitely not going to be impressed to the tune of $100,000.

It's the old story about no one ever being fired for buying from IBM. Large enterprises choose vendors with stable, scalable products, who have service departments that can solve problems. Others have their IT department build elaborate custom web reporting. These considerations do not necessarily have a direct relationship with the impact, quality, or usefulness of the reports. As Jim Sterne has rightly pointed out, you need to "measure the ROI on measuring ROI." Divisions of large companies that already deal with a certain analytics vendor can tap into the existing setup without vastly increasing the cost to the parent company. For a small to midsized company of a comparable size, there is a relative disincentive to going with an enterprise-class analytics solution because the cost is higher relative to the size of the business.

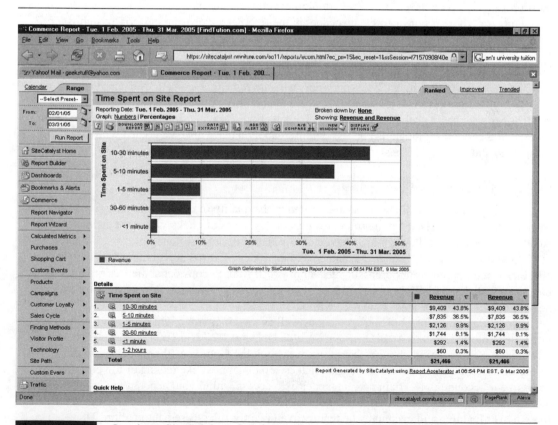

FIGURE 10-5   Omniture SiteCatalyst: full-featured enough for the most exacting users

If you're in the market for full-scale enterprise analytics, you'll need to do plenty of due diligence and request custom quotes from the leading vendors. Service and usage fees increase as your needs do.

Google's Free Conversion Tracker

Google does offer a free conversion tracker, and its performance can be more reliable than third-party services. However, there are downsides. You need to install not only code, but a text notation that states "stats by Google" on your site. Recently, Google upgraded the functionality so that you aren't restricted to tracking only Google campaigns. For example, it now allows you to track Overture campaigns as well.

In spite of the attractive (free) price and the convenience of using a Google-designed service, I recommend against using it. Some advertisers are uncomfortable sharing private business data with a big media company like Google, no matter how robust their privacy policy. After all, Google is selling ads to your competitors. It's to their advantage to learn what industries are most profitable, which they can assess by looking at conversion rates and cost-per-order data in the aggregate. There is considerable precedent in the Internet advertising industry of publishers collecting such data and using it as justification for raising prices. As a partner in a leading paid search management agency told me recently, using Google's tracking tool is like handing over your sales receipts to your office building landlord. This is information they don't need to know.

I'm uncomfortable with analytics providers who are too eager to share even aggregate data as self-promotion tools. As a journalist, I love the availability of aggregate user behavior stats (such as browser share or the ROI on different ad positions). As a customer paying good money for analytics products, though, I'd be less enthused about having my data pooled with other companies' data to help the analytics vendor gain PR.

Other Things to Consider

Today, nearly all of the available tools are limited in the quality of the reporting they can offer because there are details about the sources, times of day, costs of clicks, and other elements, that AdWords does not pass through in a convenient format (API notwithstanding).

While the feature set, ease of use, and cost of analytics products are all important items to consider when making your purchasing decision, you'll want to consider some less obvious factors as well. These boil down to a couple of concerns: will your analytics provider be around next year, and will its product keep pace with your needs?

If you think you'd like bid management as well as tracking, you might want to go with an integrated solution such as Atlas OnePoint, Decide DNA, or PPC Bid Tracker. More of these are on the way. Keep in mind, though, that in the ever-evolving Google AdWords platform, there is a very new bid management capability that makes some features, like raising or lowering bids across your account by a certain percentage, easy to access within your account under the Tools tab. Because anything in the AdWords interface can be accessed by third parties using the API, these newer features will eventually be readily available for rules-based automation. They can be complicated, though. If you're not comfortable with them, don't use them!

The leading firms such as WebTrends, WebSideStory, and Omniture have more infrastructure in place to offer more sophisticated and customizable reports. Their main drawbacks are cost and the potential need for custom programming and ongoing service, which adds yet more cost. You also need to consider the "Microsoft syndrome." When a vendor gains heavy market share, there is a tendency to build a patchwork of new features on an outdated paradigm, or to slow the pace of innovation.

I'm hopeful that these leading firms will be putting more emphasis on their small-business packages because they can count on upselling a percentage of these customers to a much more full-featured solution. Several such firms have been in acquisition mode, further strengthening their offerings (but potentially offering more data to you than you can really handle or act upon). WebSideStory acquired Atomz, a site search technology. WebTrends acquired WebPosition Gold, a tool for analyzing organic search rankings. Recently, WebTrends was acquired by a private equity firm, Francisco Partners, thus detaching it from its publicly traded parent, NetIQ. This could accelerate the pace of innovation at WebTrends, since it was never very well integrated into the diversified firm that owned it. As the industry consolidates, the question is whether the improved feature sets of top-end analytics packages will really help you improve your bottom line, or whether dealing with one of these elephants will cause you to bite off more than you can chew.

Management Strength/Momentum/Integrity

Some of the leading analytics applications are owned by traditional (publicly traded) online ad serving firms. Two of them are 24/7 Real Media (owner of Decide DNA) and Aquantive (owner of Atlas OnePoint), both of which seem relatively healthy. Doubleclick is in trouble financially and is seeking acquisition, and is now directing its clients to Omniture SiteCatalyst if they wish full-scale web analytics. As mentioned earlier, WebTrends has just changed ownership, and some speculate that the new owners are just in it for a "quick flip."

Midsized players like ClickTracks are often led by respected industry veterans with visible track records. ClickTracks is developed in part by veterans of Analog, a log analysis software company of long standing.

As for inexpensive tools offered by smaller companies, check on management's integrity, at least, through word of mouth. You can't guarantee that any company will be around forever, but it helps to feel comfortable that the operator of a hosted application won't misuse or attempt to profit from your private business data, for example. When in doubt, go with a more established firm.

If choosing a third-party service seems like too much of a minefield, consider building basic conversion tracking functionality in-house.

Custom Work

Regardless of which service you choose, everything you need may not come with the default software package. Before you sign up, find out to what extent the provider will work with you on integrating the tracker with an unusual shopping cart. Another question to answer is, do they have experience in custom programming to facilitate tracking of phone orders?

Upper-tier services rely on service fees as a significant part of their business (just as all enterprise software companies do, from IBM down). As a result, most of them offer custom solutions. Midmarket players like ClickTracks have been known to help customers with complicated custom work, but can become overwhelmed. Low-end services like ConversionRuler have done amazing things for my clients, but again, if their market grows too fast, they are going to be unable to provide adequate customer service.

Metrics to Consider

When in doubt, simplify. Many of my clients do very well with a simple measuring stick such as cost per new customer acquired (CPA) or cost per order (CPO). Even though these may not take into account the dollar amounts spent by the customer, they can be reliable measures with a history in any given line of business. Comparing these metrics among various ad sources, keywords, and ads will give you a sense of relative performance.

"Rough" ROI, or ROAS

No one is ever going to be able to prove exactly how well an advertisement paid off. When it comes to retail, of course, profit margins must be taken into account, further complicating matters. With a big product line, profit margins vary wildly, so it can be quite a chore to truly calculate ROI. Indeed, that would be such an inexact science that I know of no business that does so. (Allowable costs per order or costs per new customer acquisition are much more common benchmarks.) What many do instead is accept the "dollars in divided by dollars out" as the working measure of ROI, on the understanding that customer acquisition is the goal and that all of these measures are relative and used to adjust campaign performance. Profit and loss statements are your only real guide to profit or loss. That's why I often refer to "rough" ROI when calculating ROI. Some call this return on ad spend (ROAS). Use the term that works for you.

As with all such measures, it can be more useful as a relative yardstick (comparing performance within or across campaigns, or even across different media) than it is as an absolute measurement of whether your campaign has succeeded. Your company financials will be the ultimate judge of financial success.

Cost per Acquisition

Cost per acquisition (CPA) is a generic term that could cover a newsletter subscriber, or a new customer, or any number of other goals defined by you. Depending on its power, your metrics tool may or may not be able to pull your click costs associated with a given ad group, ad, or keyword into the calculation. Fortunately, you can do a hand calculation of CPA quite easily. Go into the AdWords interface for the appropriate date range, take the total cost associated with the ad group in question, and then divide by the number of actions registered as associated with a given Google AdWords campaign ad group (successful newsletter subscriptions booked, for example). This gives you the average cost per new customer acquired, as associated with that particular ad group (or keyword, or ad). If you spent $420 to attract ten paying subscribers, your CPA is $42.

Cost per Order

Retailers will probably want to look at average cost per order (CPO) related to any given referral source, keyword, ad, or ad group, as this benchmark provides useful comparisons. One of my clients (Iguana Corp., discussed in previous chapters) has an approximate allowable CPO of $30. But obviously they're happier as that gets lower. The key to analyzing CPA and CPO data is not simply to look at the bottom line, but to view it in relation to pushing that number up in "additional" ad groups to increase order volume as well. Hitting an allowable CPO on a narrow band of keywords is no challenge; the trick is to achieve such targets on higher volume.

If order size varies wildly, you'll also want to look at a rough ROI measure (or ROAS measure). An ad group that has a high CPO might tend to generate the occasional volume buyer or high-margin purchase. In such cases, looking at both CPO and rough ROI (revenues divided by ad cost) for a given ad group, ad, or keyword would be the best policy.

Ideally, for Iguana Corp.'s campaign as a whole, I like to see that the campaign is bringing in more cash than it's spending (this would be an ROAS of at least 100%) *and* that the CPO number is below $30. Compared to many of Iguana Corp.'s competitors, these are conservative goals, as many of these competitors are willing to lose money to acquire a customer. Working on this campaign feels comfortable because the client takes no revenue loss as a result of the campaign in any given week, while over time, a significant amount of repeat annual subscription business kicks in at virtually no cost, meaning that profit margins rise gradually over time.

Revenue per Click

Another way of measuring ROI, revenue per click, is again a relative measure that can be compared easily to determine whether a bid is too high or too low on a given keyword, or whether a source like Google is outperforming Overture or other ad server. Some statistics packages report this one.

Propensity for Repeat Business

Jim Novo, owner of Drilling Down (drillingdown.com), is an accomplished web marketer and former executive with QVC, the TV shopping channel. In his presentations he has argued that seemingly money-losing keywords frequently turn out to be the ones that bring in customers with the highest propensity to buy later.

Imagine you run an online wine store or contact lens outlet. Because popular broad-match keywords might attract a lot of nonproductive clicks as well as a few interested buyers, you might find you're losing money on those keywords. According to Jim Novo's studies, the buyers in that stream might be core customers—perhaps better than customers acquired through the use of unusual keywords. Therefore, you may be cutting off a source of future revenue by eliminating those keywords. On the other hand, you won't be able to tell whether certain classes of customer are likely to repurchase unless you perform a long-term study of your own.

Most retailers will find it difficult to track their customers this well, but hiring a consultant like Novo to hook you up with the appropriate tools could be well worth it. Failing that, you can sometimes make your own interesting discoveries. For one retail client, KlinQ.com (a housewares retailer), I found the "repeat buying" reports given by their Manticore Technologies shopping cart e-metrics package very helpful (and reassuring). The most striking pattern seemed to be a method that users employ to see if a retailer is trustworthy. They place a small trial order. Once satisfied that the company is reputable, that shipping and other details are well handled, they may return to place a large gift order or purchase higher-ticket items. I'm increasingly convinced that buying cycles are both longer and more varied than we often assume.

Putting Your Tracking Data to Work

OK, you've got your tracking system in place, and you're compiling all this data. What do you do now? Unfortunately, it's not always clear how you should interpret your metrics. Fortunately, there are some simple rules to follow that will enable you to make the most of your tracking data.

Above all, your tracking efforts should keep you from overhauling your whole campaign unnecessarily. More likely, you'll be making adjustments rather than deciding to scrap everything.

Nonperforming Ads

If you're tracking by ad group and ad, you will usually find that most ads perform about the same from an ROI standpoint, assuming their CTR and associated CPCs are about the same. But sometimes, split-testing ads does show you that one ad attracts better customers, or attracts far too many nonprospects. The proof is always in the numbers, and the measure of a good ad is not just in your AdWords CTR report, but in the ROI-related numbers you're tracking in your conversion analytics tool. The upshot is, in rare instances, your tracking will show a significantly worse ROI on a particular ad, as tagged by you with a tracking URL, against a competing ad for the same ad group. Obviously, in such rare instances, you'll want to shut off the poor-performing ad.

One odd example of this was with Iguana Corp.'s campaign. I thought that ad text with a plural word in it (get your *iguanas*) might plant a seed for prospects to make higher-volume, multiple purchases. Instead, the ad had the opposite effect. Perhaps because they felt pressure, the prospects clicking on this ad were less likely to make any kind of purchase at all. On the singular version of the same ad text (get your *iguana*), prospects not only made low-volume purchases more regularly, but also sometimes made volume purchases in keeping with normal patterns in the industry. Suggesting to prospects that they might want to buy a batch of "iguanas" actually made them less likely to buy even one! You'd never find out something like this if you didn't test and track ads.

Nonperforming Keywords

In a very simple campaign, you may only be tracking "by ad group and ad." That's OK. All this means is that you're tracking the ROI performance of *groups of keywords* as represented by a tracking URL(s) attached to the ad or ads for that group. If ROI for the group is low, you'll need to adjust your bids lower. If you can't make a group work at all, pause it and try it again in a few months.

To put this in perspective, some of my clients find that 80%–90% of their ad groups return an acceptable ROI at some point, so they keep those groups running. But at the opposite extreme, I've seen accounts that have dozens of ad groups that never pan out, while two or three perform quite well. That's a lot of experimenting to find the two or three buckets of keywords in a hundred that really work, but it can be worth it.

In rare cases, you may want to adjust your bids higher because you'll find that consumers buy from you only when they see you in a "trusted" position on the page (in the top one or two spots). If it works, go with it.

In general, finding the fulcrum point, where you're bidding appropriately to each group of keywords (neither too high nor too low based on the revenues or user actions that result from those groups), is an ongoing challenge. Advanced advertisers will attempt to use technology to adjust bids on the fly to maintain acceptable campaign ROI. Decide DNA and Efficient Frontier are two of the various technologies that allow you to set bids to go up or down (or off) in response to "allowable CPO" numbers. Since ROI may be different at different times and on different days, large retailers with big ad spends may find such tools increasingly indispensable. These technologies and the technique may not be ready for prime time, however. Addressing the situation with your own eyes with weekly or monthly analysis is probably a better approach to take for most small businesses.

Incidentally, I have it on good authority that there is some internal skepticism at Google about tools that check and adjust bids too often. One problem with this is that such activity used to be done in an unauthorized fashion. With the API now in place, acceptable third-party access to the AdWords interface will be facilitated, but excessive usage will come with a cost. Google won't go into dollars-and-cents details, but the principle is that access to the API is based on a "token system" that allows a certain number of free accesses per day based on your ad spend. Unless your spend is high, you'll exceed your allotted tokens if your bid management application checks and adjusts bids too often. And yes, if you have 5,000 phrases in your account and you use a third-party tool to adjust them all down by 5%, that counts as 5,000 accesses. A common-sense approach, then, would have you frequently adjusting only the bids that take up the lion's share of your spend, making other adjustments less frequently, or going into the AdWords interface and doing occasional touch-ups manually using Google's new "campaignwide bid manager" tool. Excessive bid tweaking through a third-party interface is going to get costly under Google's API terms. Just how costly is not yet clear. As before, you can do as much tweaking as you wish for free if you actually log into the AdWords interface and use it directly.

If you're using separate tracking URLs for individual keywords, the principle is the same as if you're adjusting bids to the appropriate levels for the ROI on the group of keywords in a whole ad group. You'll simply find that the ROI or CPA for some keywords (often, popular ones that attract bidding wars) do not justify a high bid. But by dropping your bid to the point where you're in ad position 5, 8, or 9, you may find that your ROI comes into an acceptable range. For example, you might be tracking the phrase match for **paint chips** and find that you can bid no higher than 45 cents without losing money. (You'd like to bid higher to be in ad position 3 or higher, because you're often in ad position 6, but moving to a more visible ad position is prohibitively expensive, so you accept the lower volume of sales to ensure you remain profitable.) For the phrase **paint colors**, you might find that the price for the same ad position is a bit lower at 33 cents, but your tracking shows that nearly no one clicking on your ad triggered by this search phrase turns out to make a purchase. This means you are losing money on this keyword. Consequently, you decide to lower your bid to 8 cents. If this phrase continues to be a money loser, you might even eliminate it entirely.

Tracking and bid strategy go hand in hand. The latter flows from the numbers you receive from your tracking. Because this is a marketplace, conditions will change over time as participants come and go. So you're never quite done. You'll always have to monitor your account—even to the point of monitoring ROI on particular keywords—at least to a degree that keeps you from running into serious trouble.

Nonperforming Sources

Most paid search marketers are aware of the numerous second-tier services that will sell you pay-per-click listings: LookSmart, Enhance Interactive, Kanoodle, FindWhat, and so on. In my opinion, FindWhat is the best of this lot. By tagging your landing URLs with "source=" and "goog," "fhwt," "kanoo," and so on, in the proper way to get the conversion stats to display correctly in your software, you will be able to calculate metrics like cost per order quite handily and compare them across sources.

All too often, new clients don't have ROI numbers on the LookSmart or ePilot or 7Search (or other second-tier PPC) campaigns they're running. Frequently, once they start tracking their results, it's only a matter of days before they hurriedly shut those campaigns down permanently, upon discovering very few, or no, conversions. The reason is plain to see when you do a micro source analysis. Essentially, second-tier pay-per-click services are forced to partner with lower-quality sites that may be sending you traffic that was really never intended to convert. It is in some sense "fake" traffic that is deliberately created by the publishers of various search services, low-quality content sites, and others. The only purpose of some of the traffic you receive from some second-tier PPC services is to line the pockets of the publishers at your expense.

A micro source analysis (Figure 10-6) is a fancy name for simply looking at the raw referral data (full URLs, including sometimes lengthy strings of code representing various attributes) and assessing where your traffic is coming from. ConversionRuler is one tracking tool that makes it easy to list that raw data not just in general, but with specific conversion information. This way, you're not just complaining about traffic that seems "fishy" in general, but you have added confirmation that none of that traffic actually converted. There's no sense in rejecting a traffic source out of hand. Sometimes, unorthodox traffic sources, such as parked domain name pages, really convert.

Depending on whether those selling you the traffic are masking the referral information, you may see a lot of referrals from websites you wouldn't choose to display your ad on if you had that choice. A lot of notations of "no referrer" on traffic you've associated with a particular traffic source (by using, say, "?source=looksmt" in your tracking URL) are a red flag, since you now have no idea where that visitor came from. (You know you probably paid LookSmart for the click, but you don't know what partner it came from.)

Landed	Category	Campaign	Segment	Referer	User IP
1/21/04 7:22 PM	Undefined	look2		http://search.mysearchnow.com/search.cgi?src=dtsb&s=www.google.com	64.32.92.39
1/21/04 7:42 PM	Undefined	look2		No Referrer	200.76.240.11
1/21/04 7:42 PM	Undefined	look2		No Referrer	80.54.229.152
1/21/04 7:45 PM	Undefined	look2		http://www.flashlightsearch.com/search.aspx?q=http://search google.com /	63.201.24.6
1/21/04 7:46 PM	Undefined	look2		http://www.looking4links.com/search/?keywords=google	4.63.147.61
1/21/04 7:49 PM	Undefined	look2		http://www.searchingbooth.com/partner/darcjd/searchresults.php?terms=google.com	152.8.76.96
1/21/04 7:52 PM	Undefined	look2		http://is1.websearch.com/_1_26JHT7H03S934Z1__websrch.iepan.main/dog/results?otmpl=dog/webresults.htm&qkw=google&qcat=web&top=1&start=&ver=28141	66.130.11.199
1/21/04 8:26 PM	Undefined	look2		http://www.searchingbooth.com/partner/xcess/searchresults.php?terms=google search	150.208.38.76
1/21/04 8:28 PM	Undefined	look2		http://srch.lop.com/search/search.cgi?affid=66&src=searchbar2&s=google	24.150.144.33
1/21/04 8:33 PM	Undefined	look2		http://www.ugosearch.com/selink.php?terms=google. com	24.13.64.11
1/21/04 8:38 PM	Undefined	look2		http://www.searchingbooth.com/partner/xcess/searchresults.php?terms=google	24.121.55.203
1/21/04 8:39 PM	Undefined	look2		http://yessearch.net/aaa/ppcws/index.php	206.81.129.21
1/21/04 8:41 PM	Undefined	look2		No Referrer	24.11.109.131
1/21/04 8:45 PM	Undefined	look2		http://www.searchingbooth.com/partner/rubyred/searchresults.php?terms=google. com	12.220.116.23
1/21/04 8:50 PM	Undefined	look2		No Referrer	159.226.24.22
1/21/04 8:56 PM	Undefined	look2		http://www.nicheseek.com/seek2/search.cgi?keywords=google&xsearch=google	65.33.215.199
1/21/04 9:25 PM	Undefined	look2		http://www.letsgofind.com/selink.php?terms=google. com	67.123.164.15
1/21/04 9:35 PM	Undefined	look2		http://www.nicheseek.com/seek2/search.cgi?keywords=google.com&xsearch=	66.67.41.15

FIGURE 10-6	Raw data shows that LookSmart sends a high volume of traffic from some highly questionable partners.

Most importantly, if you purchase thousands of clicks from a second-tier PPC service and not a single one translates into desired actions on your site, you need to shut down that click source immediately. Your parting shot to the provider might be to request a refund, but only if you feel that they've significantly misled you as to the sources of the traffic you'd be receiving. For more on this, check out the upcoming section, "Looking for Click Fraud."

Search vs. Content Targeting

ClickTracks Pro is one of the few existing metrics packages that can easily compare ROI numbers on your search campaign within an AdWords campaign against the "content-targeting" listings within the same account.

For packages that don't support this, you can track content separately by setting it up in a separate, parallel campaign with identical keywords and separate tracking codes on ads, as I did for Iguana Corp. This also allows you to react to the ROI data you get, by bidding less on the content-targeted traffic. How much less depends on your results.

Looking for Click Fraud

A full primer on auditing click fraud is beyond the scope of this chapter. Some consultants and metrics companies now bill themselves as click fraud "experts." Again, I like to eyeball "raw" referral strings to look for unusual patterns. But keep in mind: when it comes to duplicate clicks and certain repeated clicks from malicious clickers, Google's fraud detection might have already chosen not to charge you.

The major PPC providers, Google included, have departments devoted to analyzing click patterns to assess potential fraud. Obvious duplicate clicks are not charged. But in addition, a variety of suspicious patterns may be identified and you may receive refunds on those clicks. Google doesn't disclose details to avoid tipping off the perpetrators of fraud to their fraud detection methods.

Key culprits in fraudulent activity are typically common, expensive keywords; and dishonest publisher partners in Google's AdSense program. As a last resort, fraud in the first instance can always be dealt with through reduced bids based on your ROI numbers, emphasizing other areas of your campaign. In the second area, until recently, you had less control than you'd like. Google has made big strides towards improving publisher accountability. A "publisher exclude" feature is now built into the AdWords interface to help you screen out content publishers you don't feel you can trust. Google must continue to police its content partners. Recently, Google launched a lawsuit against one AdSense publisher who conspired to generate fake clicks to bilk AdWords advertisers. It's a start, but more will have to be done to keep fraud to a minimum.

By doing your part and tracking diligently, you won't be one of those advertisers who is unwittingly buying low-quality traffic and enriching bad publishers and Google as a result.

Advanced Tracking

In addition to basic tracking strategies described throughout this chapter, several more advanced techniques may come in handy depending on your business and the time you have available to invest in tracking.

Tracking Phone Orders

It's not easy to track phone orders in the same way that you track online orders. It will typically require some hand calculation and custom work. Setting up a different phone number for an AdWords campaign isn't particularly difficult; you might even reference different "extension" numbers on different landing pages, corresponding to different ad groups within a campaign.

One advertiser I talked to told me he had 50 different 800 numbers at his disposal; so tracking up to 50 online sources—even 50 different AdWords keyword groups and/or high-volume individual keywords—would be possible by simply sending searchers to different landing pages from the AdWords campaign, with each landing page containing a dedicated 800 number. I was not aware that some providers of bundled phone services are making more numbers available to customers at a very reasonable cost. To me, this method is one of the simplest solutions to an often thorny tracking problem. Some businesses believe that their brand identity or business continuity depends on using the same phone number all the time. This solution won't work for them.

Another approach is to have a programmer place a visible unique alphanumeric identifier on the page for every new user who comes to your site and who is uniquely cookied. If that user makes a purchase, the phone sales staff could be instructed to ask that user for the code that appears on the page. The associated sale data must then be manually entered into your tracking tool, and if all goes well, these will be mapped to the appropriate ad group or keyword that generated the initial site visit. Such custom work isn't uncommon, but it's not exactly a cakewalk for do-it-yourselfers. If you or your webmaster can't figure it out, seek expert help.

Be suspicious of anyone who claims total automation or "ease of use" in this realm. Extra legwork is usually involved in tracking offline orders.

Data Loss, Sales Cycles, and Proxy Expressions of Interest

The earlier discussion of phone order tracking highlights the fact that you won't always be able to track everything perfectly. In the case of phone orders, it's easy to understand why. But when advertisers who are diligently tracking still get poor visibility with their online campaigns it's a little more complex.

Those who work for analytics firms can enumerate dozens of reasons for why every user is not tracked perfectly from click to final purchase. Some users might have privacy settings enabled on their computers. Some might do their shopping and research from home, making the purchase at work (or vice versa). These, plus a number of other glitches can occur.

For some campaigns, tracking might be 90% accurate. For others, you might only "give due credit" to 50%, 30%, or 10% of all the sales that ultimately do trace back directly or indirectly to your AdWords campaign.

While cookies may stay active on a user's computer for a long time, clearly the longer the time lag, the less likely a purchase will be accurately tracked. There is always data loss over time. Tracking becomes less certain the longer the sales cycle.

This, incidentally, is why intermediate expressions of interest (such as visiting an About Us page, downloading a free white paper, or requesting a catalog) are great alternative metrics that can help you measure campaign success in industries where purchases are typically researched thoroughly beforehand. Figure out how to incorporate such intermediate expressions of interest (or *proxies* for interest) into your tracking. This will give you more to go on when comparing the relative performances of campaigns, even if you have trouble capturing the actual dollars in and dollars out on campaigns for high-ticket, offline-centric, or long-sales-cycle products or services.

In long or unpredictable sales cycles, many advertisers go with the old-fashioned method of tracking: the anecdotal or superstitious method. "When I advertised, they came to the store," many used to say. "When I stopped advertising, they stopped coming in." In some cases that's actually true. But by designing a sales process that captures proxies for interest, you can at least tell if your traffic is relatively targeted.

To delve deeper into user on-site behavior, experienced marketers will sit back with data on "click paths," time spent on different pages, and so forth. That's when the power of the upper-tier analytics packages really comes in handy. Advanced marketers will want to learn how much time is spent on certain pages, or what types of users navigate to certain informational or category pages. But be sure you're attacking the basic conversion ratios and adjusting your campaign before you get into the heavy-duty, big-iron, analytics.

Time of Day

Today's high-volume, low-margin online retailers often go on instinct or retail lore when it comes to shutting off campaigns during periods perceived to be "poor converters," such as nights or weekends. If everyone did this, though, prices would fall, the market would take care of the problem, and you wouldn't have to bother dayparting. Most advertisers lack the capacity to study their own data to correlate sales with time of day. The ability to run sophisticated reports of this nature is sorely lacking from the average analytics package. It will soon become a must-have feature. As things stand, many marketing managers are circumventing inadequate analytics packages and doing their own hand calculations to learn as much as they can.

Geographic Breakdowns

If you run an international campaign, the Google AdWords interface won't even give you a breakdown of how much you're spending in each country. That's a huge drawback that I can't imagine continuing much longer. Understanding which geographic areas (even regions or cities) are converting to sales should be relatively easy to do in a fairly accurate way. It will add another dimension that advertisers will analyze to rapidly improve their campaign efficiency.

As a workaround, you might want to set up a separate AdWords campaign using the regional targeting feature. By using different tracking codes from your regionally focused campaign(s), you'll get a great sense of the differential performance of clicks emanating from IP addresses in different regions.

Deeper Behavioral Analysis

Pressure will increase on search engines and portals to gather more data on registered users and to use this to assist advertisers in targeting more deeply to demographic groups based on age, sex, ethnicity, sexual preference, past buying habits, and anything else you can imagine. The flip side of this potential is the concern about user privacy. Google has done well as an Internet company that doesn't ask users a lot of questions. However, it's dabbling in various services such as Gmail, the social networking site Orkut, Google Groups 2 (a discussion service), and other places where users are asked to become registered Google accountholders just as they are on Yahoo or AOL.

There's no question that advertisers will be doing more behavioral analysis and demographic targeting as more data is made available about users. All the same, the smartest advertisers won't push too hard on this one. The Internet must remain a "pull" medium to maintain the confidence of users. Some take a different perspective and argue that most users will exchange privacy for convenience or cash. But will Google be the one to spearhead a change in the way they treat their current user base? Time will tell. If competitors like Microsoft can maintain a much cleaner data pipeline between themselves and Internet users, Google's advertisers may demand that they follow suit.

Still a Burgeoning Field

There is no shortage of technology, so the real cost lurks quietly behind the scenes: the cost of hiring competent human analysts and problem solvers. While you're thinking about this: what about the analytical capabilities of those who do web development or marketing work for your company? It may be time to ask them to upgrade their skills, perhaps by attending the E-Metrics Summit, led twice a year by Jim Sterne.

As Bryan Eisenberg recently pointed out in a statement at the founding of a new Web Analytics Association, 1,598 jobs for "web analytics" come up when you search a popular job board. But, laments Eisenberg, "The fact is there is not enough talent or knowledge out there at the moment to fill all those positions."[11] Few of us have all the tools we currently need, or the proper training, to do this job as well as it could be done. But we're getting there.

Endnotes

1. Jim Sterne, "I'm a Marketing Guy," October 2000, archived at Targeting.com.

2. See Jim Sterne, *Web Metrics: Proven Methods for Measuring Website Success* (Wiley, 2002), Chapter 3, "Raising the Flag and Convincing the Boss." In particular, see the sections on IT centralization, pp. 40–41.

3. For an opposite view that would praise the freedom to build such "skunk works exercises" as a means of connecting with customers and as a tool to retain innovative employees, see Christopher Locke, et al., *The Cluetrain Manifesto: The End of Business as Usual* (Perseus, 2001); Christopher Locke, *Gonzo Marketing: Winning Through Worst Practices* (Perseus, 2002); David Weinberger, *Small Pieces Loosely Joined: A Unified Theory of the Web* (Perseus, 2003).

4. For exhaustive examinations of such measurements, consult Eric Peterson, *Web Analytics Demystified* (Celilo Group Media, 2004).

5. An October 2004 study by Jupiter Research characterized 75% of search marketers as "unsophisticated," meaning they failed to use advanced bidding and measurement techniques. See Pamela Parker, "Study: Most Search Marketers Unsophisticated," ClickZ.com, October 27, 2004.

6. Nowhere is the need for actionable data and fast feedback cycles better explained than in Seth Godin's *Survival Is Not Enough: Zooming, Evolution, and the Future of Your Company* (Free Press, 2002).

7. Jim Sterne, "Hold Onto That Turf," *Webmaster Magazine*, September 1995, archived at Targeting.com. See also "Customer Interface: Building Bridges," June, 1998, archived at Targeting.com.

8. Rob McGann, "'Spyware' Label Slapped on Legit Research Software," ClickZ.com, February 18, 2005.

9. Simon Avery, "Microsoft's IT Security Plans Spark Controversy," *The Globe and Mail*, February 21, 2005, B5.

10. For an intelligent discussion of web "services" today, as against "objects" and "components," see Roger Sessions, "Fuzzy Boundaries: Objects, Components, and Web Services," *ACM Queue* 2:9 (Dec.–Jan. 2004–2005); archived at acmqueue.com. I'm no programmer, but as a user, I love the convenience of hosted web services that clients, my staff, and I can log into anytime, from anywhere.

11. Rob McGann, "Web Analytics Trade Group Formed," ClickZ.com, February 18, 2005.

Chapter 11

Increasing Conversion Rates

Conversion science, which attempts to define those factors most critical to turning a casual click into a profitable action, is one of the hottest trends in Internet marketing today. But it hasn't been an overnight success. Earlier generations of web marketers often threw together websites hastily, optimistic that they'd get rich as long as they could find visitors. Such a strategy might have worked then, but certainly not in today's competitive marketplace.

NOTE · *Conversion science is an emerging field, so some terminology used in this chapter will be new. I am coining the terms conversion science and conversion scientist in an attempt to describe a particular group of Internet marketers—those who specialize in increasing clients' online conversion rates. I consider online conversion science as a subset of the broader field of web analytics. Conversion scientists are not only interested in measurement issues* per se; *they are engaged in "doing something about it."*

There are few famous *conversion scientists* yet. Many have toiled behind the scenes in marketing positions, improving the ROI on online marketing campaigns for their employers by testing various online buying processes. Much of the work has been experimental and based on trial and error.

A typical unsung hero in this field is Marc Stockman, an email marketing consultant who was formerly a marketing VP with TheStreet.com. As a publicly traded online content company in the financial field, TheStreet.com was suffering from regular quarterly losses. In 2001, TheStreet.com only generated $15.2 million in revenues for the entire year, posting an operating loss of $31 million. To come closer to breakeven, the company wanted to dramatically increase the conversion rate of its free email newsletter subscribers to paying subscribers. Under Stockman's tutelage, the layout and sales copy in emails, as well as the layout, copy, and checkout process on the website, were all tested and improved. This resulted in a surge in paid subscriptions and a material improvement in TheStreet.com's profit picture. TheStreet.com's market valuation today is about $93 million, and it runs at or slightly above breakeven. The company generated $9.5 million in revenues, and a slight profit, in the final quarter of 2004. These are not stellar results, but impressive for a company that barely had any revenues and was written off for dead by analysts years ago.

Stories like TheStreet.com's are common. Many online content companies needed to replace lost ad revenues that had put a serious hole in their business model. Many promised investors that they'd make a transition to paying subscribers, but many did a poor job of converting free readerships into paying subscribers. The rate at which prospects convert into paying customers can make or break companies of all sizes.

Today, Stockman has a few high-end clients but is so busy that he may be inaccessible to the average business. The knowledge a conversion scientist can bring to the table is so valuable in terms of increased revenues that the better ones can pick and choose from high-paying jobs, and they don't share all their secrets.

Experience has taught us that conversion science has a number of elements, each of which plays an important part in moving an online visitor from curiosity to action. These elements include, in addition to your actual offering, the aesthetics of the user interface, ease of use, content, and credibility of your website.

User Interface

While many small, independent online entrepreneurs were working haphazardly at converting visitors, large companies and organizations were studying user interface issues as part of their mandate to do a better job for their customers. What they found was that the more enticing and easier to use they made the website, the higher the conversion rate became.

A website, after all, is a user interface. So much is known about user interface design, yet only a small percentage of those putting together websites have the proper training to understand how people interact with such technologies. You can bet that large companies like Google and Amazon plow considerable resources into making sure people don't have any trouble using their sites.

NOTE   *According to legend, Google, known as one of the world's easiest-to-use sites, got its user-friendly design by accident. As the story goes, the plain layout of the site came about as a result of the cofounders of the company being more interested in math and search algorithms than web programming, design, and HTML. By not caring about design, Google.com started out as a search box and little else.*

The lesson to be learned is that it's impossible to overestimate the importance of the user interface design. In this chapter I'll try to guide you with some key principles drawn from a variety of experts and from my own experiences. If you talk to just about anyone in web development or web marketing, at some level, they all have concrete experiences in "making over" a website or landing page in order to improve its salesworthiness. Using my own considerable experiences I will marshal as much of the available knowledge as possible and provide you with practical steps to perform your own makeover.

At the same time, I'll try to present a clear picture of why certain methodologies tend to create better user response online. While much of this advice is contingent on the specific users and on the different industries, there are many common threads to all discussions of online user behavior. Once you digest this chapter along with a few of the books suggested in my footnotes, you'll begin to develop your own conversion science.

General Conversion Science Principles

Before we delve into the meat of conversion science, I want to cover a couple of general principles. To begin with, conversion science isn't about turning water into wine, or putting "lipstick on a pig." Trying to sell a blah product or a poorly conceived service on a great website is generally a prescription for failure. Therefore, make sure your offering is solid before assuming that problems converting sales are the fault of the usability specialists, data analysts, or web developers who are advising you.

The truth is, you stand a better chance of success with a great product and a poor website. An example that springs to mind is Silicon Investor, a stock discussion site that was acquired by a publicly traded company, Go2Net, in the late 1990s. In spite of their rather cheesy website, they became quite successful. The reason was simple. They offered something compelling that wasn't available elsewhere.

The second point I want to make is that poor conversion rates matter far more when you're paying for traffic than when you aren't. The argument is sometimes made that if prospects are interested enough, they'll find what they need on your site, and if they don't go looking for it, maybe they weren't interested anyway. There is some truth to this. Certain pages may have a history of performing adequately for a business owner. When a certain layout or page has been the foundation upon which an entire business has been built over the years, the business owner may become pretty attached to the status quo. But the status quo may no longer cut it when traffic becomes more and more costly.

You can't take a passive approach to site design and persuasive sales copy once you start paying heavily per click. Too many business owners start by blaming Google AdWords (or other sources of paid traffic) for "not converting" when, with a few simple changes to the website, their campaign economics would improve significantly.

Common Errors That Kill Conversions

These may become obvious as we study the subject in more detail, but at this point it may be useful to catalog some of the key errors made in online navigation and design that make it difficult to achieve a positive ROI on a paid search campaign.

Error #1: Not Understanding What a Landing Page Is

A landing page, of course, is the destination URL that users "land on" after they've clicked on your paid search listing. Landing pages are a fundamental variable that can make or break your numbers, but so many businesses neglect them.

Here are some things to keep in mind concerning landing pages:

■ Virtually the entire goal of the landing page must be to induce users to take a particular action, such as making a purchase or requesting information.

■ Some landing pages are better than others at achieving that goal.

■ Designing your landing page with an understanding of what is likely to work will get you reasonably close to optimal performance from the start.

■ Testing in real time is ultimately the only way to determine what kind of landing page converts best.

While it is true that both your site navigation and design as a whole, and the layout and message of a particular landing page, influence user behavior, it pays to focus primarily on the landing page. Yes, your "site" is important. But excessive focus on "the site" does not necessarily help you understand how to create results. Isolating the user's experience with the page he is actually on is always helpful to understanding your task at hand.

Error #2: Overloading the Landing Page with Information

One of the most common mistakes site designers make is trying to cram too much information on the landing page. The impulse to get everything in front of the potential customer while you've got his or her attention can be irresistible.

However, when you're paying for traffic, you need to be very clear on what you'd like the user to do and avoid wavering from that goal. A good approach is to limit your landing page to one primary goal, plus a secondary, fallback goal. The possibility of the user finding another part of your site through an easy-to-understand navigation interface might be the third priority. Keep your options open without overwhelming the user.

Landing pages that present the user with too many options rarely perform well. For example, if you're thinking that flag animation or a "site counter" somehow enhances your credibility, think again. Eliminate what isn't necessary. If users are particularly interested in researching your company, they can and will navigate to your About Us page.

Often, all that is accomplished in asking users to pay attention to "something else" is that you squander or divide the attention you've paid 10 cents, 50 cents, or $3 to purchase. Why ask them to pay attention to something else (see Figures 11-1 and 11-2), especially if they barely know who you are or what your main offer is?

In the case of Urban Challenge Online, you can see that all of the ideas competing for attention on the page shown in Figure 11-2 are good ideas. It's certainly not a bad idea to indicate who your charitable and corporate partners are, for example. As a page whose sole goal should be to convert visitors to registered players of a game, however, it's cluttered both in a visual sense and in the sense of priorities facing the user. Most users have no idea what this is all about, and most have no intention yet of registering as players, but the page seems intent on changing the subject by referring to distracting issues such as an entirely different contest they could enter. At the very bottom of the page, the user is asked to "send this page to a friend." How about converting that user to a registered contestant first?

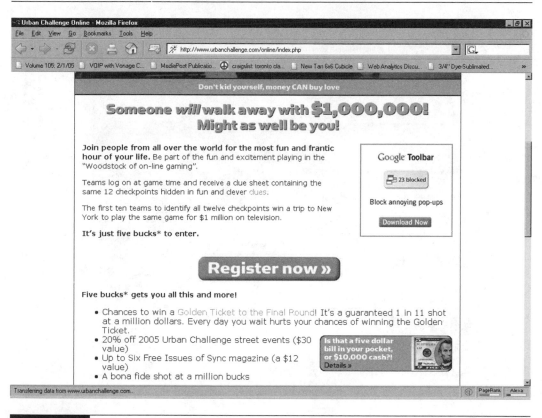

FIGURE 11-1   The user's precious attention is divided three ways.

If your landing page isn't tightly focused on inducing users to take a particular action, they're likely to take no action, and your paid search campaign will be bleeding cash. Can you imagine my walking up to a person I've never met, and instead of shaking his hand and saying, "Hi, Andrew Goodman, pleased to meet you," I abruptly bark, "My wife likes daffodils!" I'm guessing they'd be very eager to talk with someone else.

Error #3: Assuming That the Best Landing Page Is the Home Page

Many site owners have the attitude that "the site has all kinds of stuff on it, so we'd better let them come to our home page and discover what we have to offer." This rarely works. It typically leads to users browsing around indecisively, or worse, to their simply not caring that they are on "your company page" and promptly leaving. If you got them there to look at an offer, especially if

FIGURE 11-2   A fourth contest detail competes with six corporate logos.

that offer is related to a niche keyword, give them an offer. Depending on the type of business you're in, you'll be better off bringing the searcher to a tailored lead-generation-oriented landing page, a product description page, or a product category page. Don't be coy. You got them there to buy something, or at least to express an interest in you as a vendor. Lead them into that process.

According to Misty Locke of Range Online Media, a Texas-based online marketing agency, requiring just one additional click at the beginning of your sales process could result in a 30% higher abandonment rate. Don't lose that first 30% by taking them to an introductory page that makes them decide, for example, which part of your company they want to deal with. If you have a carefully targeted AdWords campaign, you should already know who you're targeting, so you should be able to lead users to exactly the page that contains the information you want to show them. Don't risk even a single extra click if you don't have to. Urban Challenge's main corporate page wouldn't be a good page to bring a paid click to, for example (Figure 11-3).

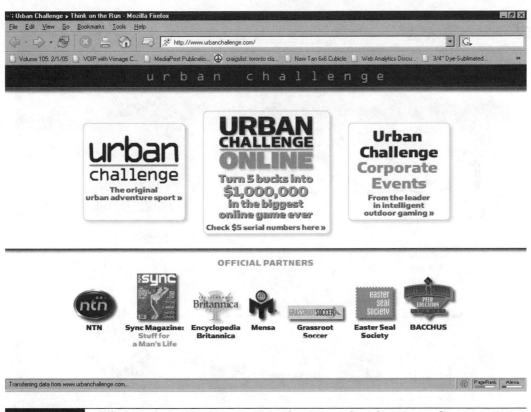

FIGURE 11-3   Why start here when you can start the user on the relevant page?

Error #4: Assuming That the Best Landing Page Is a Contact Form

If you're in the lead generation business, don't expect users to be so excited by your offer that they immediately give you their contact info. For example, I clicked on a banner ad on Yahoo for a specialized service by Gomez Advisors, a consulting firm. The ad took me to a raw contact page with no accompanying copy. I had absolutely no incentive to fill out the form. A better approach would be to offer a few paragraphs of information, followed by the contact form.

Another example I ran across is in the competitive credit counseling industry. Although the landing page (see Figure 11-4) has some info in the form, a few bullets, and looks like it's been optimized for visual appeal and credibility, it still doesn't offer enough to encourage the casual visitor to take action. In a highly competitive industry, your visitor has plenty of alternatives

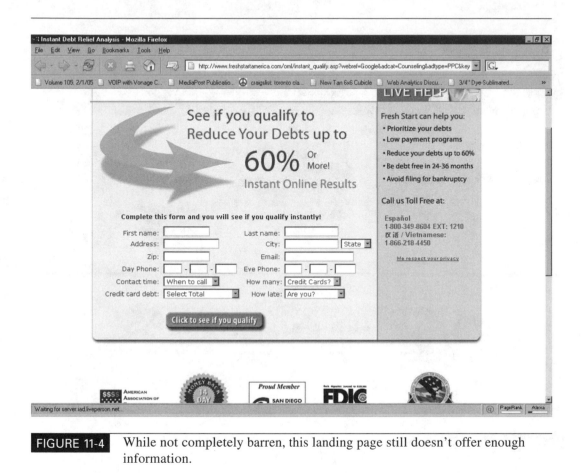

FIGURE 11-4   While not completely barren, this landing page still doesn't offer enough information.

if your landing page doesn't do the job. Your goal is to grab each prospect when you have the chance—you may not get another.

Error #5: Assuming That the Best Copy Is Brief Copy

If clutter is bad, some may reason that six paragraphs should be chopped to three. But that is not always the case. The more abbreviated some companies seem to get with their copy, the more they appear to be talking in industry gibberish that only makes sense at internal company meetings. If you're Apple and there have been 40,000 news stories written about the iPod, you can get away with any length of sales copy. But if you're a relative unknown, it often helps to tell a story.

Check out the big car companies' sites. While sometimes difficult to navigate, they generally contain a lot of material describing every facet of their vehicles, right down to the characteristics of their new All-Wheel-Drive system, braking, airbags, and so on. Imagine that you made or sold the airbags, or the brakes, since you probably don't make cars. It would probably help to have more than a couple of words on your site to describe the features and benefits of the product, or the reason other customers like to buy it from you.

As you can see in Figure 11-5 this telecommunications equipment vendor has proper descriptions on some of his product pages, but not on others (Figure 11-6). An early version of the site had many such omissions. Conversion rates were low. Costly clicks were not translating into buyer interest because the site seemed inhospitable and uninformative.

TIP   *Having proper, full-length product descriptions on your website will help you attract more "stumble-in" search engine traffic as well (often at no cost to you). Without words, search engines have nothing to index.*

FIGURE 11-5   This product page provides rich detail for shoppers to sink their teeth into.

FIGURE 11-6   Inconsistency in adding product copy to each page has a tangible result: poor conversion rates and wasted ad dollars.

Two Schools of Thought: Economists and Ideologues

A lot of conversion experts are clamoring for attention these days. I think this field somewhat parallels broad schools of thought in economic policy and public administration, and I like to break down approaches to increasing conversions into two schools of thought:

- **Economists**   These are the conversion experts who promote removal of undue barriers to commerce as the way to increase conversion rates.

- **Ideologues**   Conversion gurus in this camp are convinced that you need to convince or persuade users to buy your product through sales copy, pricing, psychological triggers, limited-time offers, comparisons, and other emotional elements.

Seth Godin, in *The Big Red Fez: How to Make Any Website Better*, falls into the "economist" camp. At one point in this short beginner's guide to usability, he compares a website to a Japanese game of chance, Pachinko. In Pachinko, disks are dropped into the top of a wooden box that contains pegs and "scoring holes" at the bottom. Whether or not you win depends on whether the disks bounce crazily off the pegs in such a way that they land in the right scoring area. It's an interesting analogy and, along with other examples given in the book, falls into the economist camp. Godin rightly reminds readers that the business owner needs to be working with a clear endpoint in mind when designing a site and particularly when designing a landing page. Any site may require users (disks) to "bounce off a few pegs" (navigate around a bit), but the amount of bouncing around should be minimized to heighten the probability that the user winds up in the scoring area (buys your stuff or signs up for something).

The most extreme ideologues are the ones who want you to believe that if you just adopt the right design elements and, in particular, choose the right words to "hypnotize" prospects, you'll create an audience of automatons willing to lap up your wisdom and buy your stuff. Some even delve into neurolinguistic programming to add scientific cachet to their advice and training. But if you can achieve your goals without consulting experts at that extreme, I'm not sure these theories are much more than interesting curiosities. At the very least, they're not appropriate for everyone.

Bryan Eisenberg (along with his brother, Jeffrey, and his team at Future Now, Inc.) is one of the best-known conversion scientists in the world today, and he seems to marry elements from both camps. On balance, though, I'd place him in the ideologue camp for his frequent use of terms like "persuasive architecture" and "persuasion scenarios." Eisenberg often relates conversion stories anecdotally, tossing in elements of barrier-removal and usability as well as mentions of the persuasiveness of the sales copy on a given landing page. This case study method can be effective for those who already have a strong grounding in web marketing.

In one brilliant section of his new book, *Call to Action*, Eisenberg asserts that shopping cart abandonment may not be the real problem facing online retailers, although many of them seem to focus excessively on the problem. E-tailers tend to focus on such matters as why shoppers leave the checkout process at such a high rate, assuming that their own abandonment rate is somehow an anomaly and that something in the checkout process may be wrong. That appears to be related to tunnel vision on the part of business owners: they can't believe that people don't buy, so something must be wrong with the cart. According to Eisenberg, it ain't necessarily so. E-tailers, in his view, are often better off improving their home pages and landing pages, and working on "persuasion scenarios."[1] That sounds complicated, but some of it can be boiled down to serving up more appropriate content. You see, Eisenberg's data show that once a user has stayed on your site for a while (more than a minute), drop-off rates are relatively low. If you "focus on providing relevant and persuasive content based on understanding visitor intent, easily inferred from keywords (or ad copy, or the e-mail they arrived from), you'll have a much higher overall conversion rate."[2] Eisenberg wants us to understand who's coming to our site and to create content tailored for them. That's persuasion. It's logical to work harder on providing this relevant content to visitors, considering that it's often you, with your carefully written ad triggered by carefully chosen keywords, who induced the user to visit the site in the first place!

Advanced marketers will study their data and hold regular internal meetings to discuss the characteristics of their target markets. In that respect, soon more online advertisers will move to the more sophisticated side of the continuum, making better use of some of the more advanced analytics packages mentioned in Chapter 10, such as ClickTracks Optimizer, ClickTracks Professional, or Omniture SiteCatalyst. Something as simple as understanding how long certain types of users spend on the site can be a real help in developing persuasion scenarios. Recently, by looking at data generated by ClickTracks Optimizer, I learned something significant about the users on one of my sites. Those who bought something or filled out a quote request form stayed on the site for an average of seven minutes. Many of them not only read the long copy on one landing page, but also looked at the About Us and other background pages to ensure that they felt comfortable with me and my business. By contrast, those who didn't take action—those who stumbled in from search engines, for example, but quickly found they weren't interested—lasted only an average of 15 seconds on the site. Those users who spent seven precious minutes of their time reading through my material are the most interesting to me. Experiences like these bear out Eisenberg's theories about persuasion. Probably only a small percentage of new site visitors are interested in what you or I have to offer. But for those who are interested, it's simply a myth that they're in a big hurry. Many businesses would do better if they did more to inform and persuade that small subset of hot prospects.

Well-known online copywriters like Nick Usborne should also be considered ideologues. Usborne likes sites to have persuasive copy, and lots of it, but his style is more muted than some, perhaps because he often works for large firms that don't want to be too "salesy." Usborne often focuses on articulate, direct writing that is appropriate for the particular audience being spoken to. Sounds simple, but copywriting professionals who can actually achieve this are rare.

Remove Barriers to Conversion (Economists)

Think of all the reasons you didn't buy something online this year because it was difficult to do so:

- The site was too slow to load.
- The page was broken somehow.
- The site wasn't optimized to properly display in your browser.
- The site wanted you to install a plug-in.
- The checkout process was lengthy.
- You had to become a member before you could buy (or read) anything.
- There were so many options, you got confused and left.
- There was a form that you needed to fill out that didn't include "District of Columbia" as one of the available states, or Canadian provinces, or in some other way made it impossible for you to "exist."
- The credit card security system didn't like the fact that you were traveling, so your purchase was declined, but there was no alternative means of purchasing.

These and countless more issues are the worst kinds of problems because they deter even eager prospects from completing a transaction or forming a relationship with you. If there are serious barriers to people doing business with you, they usually won't. As Godin has been known to say with respect to the online sales process: "Make it smooth." As Amazon.com chief Jeff Bezos frequently stated on his way to becoming a billionaire: "We're trying to make it easy for people to buy." They both know what they're talking about.

I offer the analogy with economics because I believe that while there is a certain logic to the idea of removing barriers to trade as a way of promoting more of it, it might not be enough. Indeed, those who pursue a consistent marketing campaign or lobby effort promoting the value of an economic region (to pump up tourism or investment) will probably mitigate some of their need to remove every possible barrier. If people want to do business in your region and feel that it's highly appropriate to do so, they'll put up with slight inconveniences, even extra costs. Usually that happy scenario is reached by providing as much relevant information to prospects as possible.

Extending the analogy to your business, since you're not Amazon.com, you can't create "1-click ordering." You probably don't have the user's credit card already on file. You may be constrained in how much free shipping you can offer. You might not be able to create a site that is quite as smooth as Amazon's. But by making people really want to buy from you (by persuading them), you reduce the need to be absolutely perfect in your site architecture, shopping cart, or other elements of the sales process.

Given the sorry state of so many websites, though, the economists still have a persuasive argument. People will be far less likely to buy from you if your site is hard to use or literally broken. There are probably already people who want to do business with you. If you do nothing else, at least don't put roadblocks in their way. That means taking users to appropriate landing pages (instead of the wrong ones). It means ensuring that your web hosting is adequate, that your shopping cart works, that your pages load into all major browsers, and so on. If you do nothing else, get started by removing the most obvious barriers to trade.

Persuade, Convince, Use Psychology (Ideologues)

Getting rid of barriers to commerce may not be enough. In a sea of conflicting commercial messages, the one that inspires may be the one that gets the sale. To use a dating analogy, sure, removing major barriers is the first step, since getting a date is nearly impossible if, say, you never get out of the house to meet anyone. Removing the obvious impediment of hermit-hood (with online dating, even that barrier is reduced) might be a first and necessary step to getting a date, but it doesn't change the fact that at some point, somebody has to like or be inspired by you. You have to convince! You need to make an attractive offer, even if that's only making sure you have fresh breath when you say, "I know a great coffee shop near here."

The same goes for your business. The fact that you sell jewelry, and that your shopping cart isn't broken, is definitely not going to be enough to convince a high percentage of prospects to buy jewelry from you. There are a lot of jewelers. Why should prospective buyers buy a particular product? Why should they buy from you? If your landing page or site as a whole doesn't provide the answer to that question, then only a small percentage of prospects—those in an enormous hurry, for example—are going to take the plunge and buy.

There are two primary elements to persuasion online: copywriting and design. Writing good copy is the most obvious of these. Beyond that, web credibility and "brand cues" are indirect persuaders. We'll discuss these later in the chapter.

Copywriting

Great sales copy doesn't grow on trees. Like anyone else in this business, I've tried to mix and match a variety of areas of expertise, grabbing insights wherever possible. If you don't have the budget to hire an experienced sales copywriter for your site, you're going to have to develop a little bit of expertise yourself.

The most basic requirement (don't laugh) is that you have copy. I've seen far too many sites with basic three-word product names and pictures of products and little else. Some amateur sellers appear to believe the Web is just an order-taking system, a big catalog that will attract plenty of eager buyers no matter what.

I've come across some mind-bogglers: for example, a successful offline sports apparel business from near Kalamazoo, Michigan, that set up shop online under an entirely different name. They chose a domain name that evoked nothing more than that they were some kind of generic online seller of sports apparel. The site, too, was generic. They had terse product descriptions and little else. No mention was made of their successful bricks-and-mortar presence. What if they had chosen a catchy name like Kalamazoo Sportswear and populated the site with not only full-fledged product descriptions, but an engaging story about the business, including the positive local PR they'd received in newspaper articles?

So don't be shocked when I tell you that the worst kind of copywriting is no copywriting. There are tens of thousands of online businesses out there with virtually no copy on their sites. As a result, they have virtually no online presence.

Believe it or not, some of the advice that is useful for writing small AdWords ads also comes in handy for pages of sales copy that might go on for many paragraphs. It seems to be something of a universal law that in spite of wide variation in industry-specific terminologies, most readers—even prospects of a complicated niche business—get turned off by jargon. Sure, you do have to pay some attention to your prospects' reading level and degree of expertise to avoid talking down to them. But even for the niche reader, wading through jargon-laden presentations can be tedious. Moreover, copy that is too dry can actually suck the enthusiasm out of a prospect. Not every line of business can be "fun," but your potential customer shouldn't approach her relationship with you as if it will be pure drudgery, either.

Don't hesitate to tell a bit of a story, provided the story quickly turns to focus on the benefits of your product or service to the customer and, above all, to the offer you're making and the action you hope the prospect will take.

Be clear and direct in your language. Inject emotional appeal and even sex appeal into your copy wherever that's appropriate. For a software product, you'll want to talk about ROI (money is emotional) and problem solving (alleviating headaches is very emotional). For a motorcycle jacket, referring to a celebrity that once bought one from you would add sex appeal. Certain adjectives like *racy*, *heavy-duty*, or *vintage* would also add sex appeal, for those who wanted to infer it, or at the very least a sense of status or authenticity.

Let me give you an example from my own portfolio. An enterprise software company was experiencing poor conversion rates on their AdWords campaign, even though they were an industry leader in their human-resources-related field. What was needed was a rescue operation on the landing page copy.

The rescue required two steps. First we eliminated the landing page list of cold, unemotional bulleted points. Next we tackled the industry jargon. In the end we turned a sterile, confusing landing page into an appealing and informative tool to motivate visitors to take action.

Here are a few brief "clips," if you will, of before-and-after copywriting from that landing page:

Before: "performing regular talent inventory gap analysis of your human capital assets"
After: "identifying talent gaps in your current workforce"

Before: "unparalleled level of domain expertise"
After: We eliminated this, along with a variety of other empty boasts, replacing them with concrete information.

Before: "largest group of customer references in the industry"
After: Here, we asked either that they provide a list of testimonials or delete this boast. At first, the only testimonial that appeared on the site was jargon-laden and lukewarm, which was inconsistent with this claim of customer satisfaction.

Before: "...facilitates the end-to-end process of identifying..."
After: "facilitates the process of identifying..." (eliminated redundant buzzword)

Over time, the longer, more detailed sales presentation is likely to hold more interest than bulleted points would for serious buyers. Moreover, the clearer version should convert better than the initial pass with the jargon-laden long copy.

I'd say probably over half of the people doing sales copy out there are self-taught, and many people do their job very well. A book like *Net Words* by Nick Usborne can help you to understand what works well online. Pick up a copy and begin practicing. If you feel you need something with a little more "sizzle" or "hype," look off the beaten track, at the work of direct-response copywriting gurus such as Marlon Sanders or Joe Vitale. They should be considered extreme ideologues, but Sanders is known for his advocacy of sites involving a simple one-page sales letter. So he also advocates focus and ease of navigation to the purchase point.

Writing product descriptions that appeal to a target audience in retail is often driven by demographic research. It might be difficult to prove that one adjective beats another in writing descriptions for Chanel purses, but it's probably safe to say that experienced fashion writers would do a better job at injecting flair into copy for such products than the average person off the street. In a small business, the owner or owners must absolutely become directly involved in communicating with customers and writing sales copy. If you sell designer purses or complicated home renovations, is it realistic to expect your 21-year-old webmaster (for example) to feel the necessary intimate connection with the audience? Yet I've seen businesspeople delegating the task of writing website copy to just such an uninformed person.

One overlooked area in marketing copywriting is the tendency to exclude potential clients by using language that is actually too obsessed with a particular target market. Car manufacturers are notorious for writing copy targeted at affluent males in the 22–34 demographic, because they assume that's their target audience. So why do I see 50-year-old women driving around in those same cars? Could it be that they, too, are a valuable market? I often wonder whether many companies (online or off) wouldn't be more profitable if they understood how to avoid alienating audience members with unconscious biases based on gender, ethnicity, nationality, age, sexual orientation, language, and lifestyle. It's one thing to have a certain style, and quite another to take that style to such extremes that enthusiastic customers feel like you don't care about them. Do you have testimonials on your site? Consider the power of diversity there. Might you make more sales in the UK if one of your happy customers is from there?[3]

Design Cues

In large part, persuasive design comes back to the improved focus, reduced clutter, standards-based design, brand cues, and other elements discussed elsewhere in this chapter.

But some conversion enthusiasts also like to experiment to discover emotional responses to certain layouts, colors, shapes, images, and much more. The complex and allegedly subliminal psychology of design has long been studied by a few experts. Especially in an offline environment, for larger companies with a lot of capital investment at stake, like mall owners and store designers, such studies are indispensable.[4]

Be wary of overestimating the hidden benefits of details such as punctuation, font color, button shape, and imagery. Some of these matters, indeed, could be summed up in a key credo offered by researchers on web credibility: get a site that "looks professionally designed." Now a photo of the business owner may well improve conversion rates, and a high-quality photo might do this better than a low-quality one. But is this really a hidden benefit, or an obvious application of a principle of web credibility and the need to offer cues to brand quality? There are benefits to certain layouts and designs, no question about it. But I don't think they are as mysterious as some would have us believe.

Multivariate tests and extensive overhauls of sites and page layouts are typically more effective and measurable than tests intended to measure the impact of, say, two different colors of font in a heading. To illustrate: Iguana Corp. tested their main landing page by completely overhauling it, stripping out clutter, changing many visual elements, adding a person's face, and more. The new page converted better (most of the time), but Iguana didn't come up with that page by studying every variable over a three-year period. The design team put together a new page that would best be described as "completely different" from the old page.

Many elements of the new design probably count as professional competence in the field of landing page design. Professional competence and emerging standards that are shared among professionals can frequently offer useful shortcuts that allow us to achieve the results we need without starting from Square One in the lab. If I were given the choice between hiring a well-trained design professional for $5,000 (who worked in tandem with my marketing team) and hiring a testing group that offered to run a battery of complicated experiments for $50,000, guess who I'd be inclined to hire! (Hint: I'm cheap. I don't want free advice, but I'm not going to overpay wildly for it either.)

For reasons explained later in this chapter ("On Statistical Validity"), many companies lack the traffic levels to conduct effective tests on small variations in page layout. Amazon.com is like a giant laboratory for such testing. But most of us have to be realistic and test far fewer elements, far less often.

Those who focus on navigability, focus, clear communication, image/brand, and basic salesmanship (such as making sure there is an offer or that a lead is collected) have the right focus, in my opinion. Most of us should start with those basics before getting bogged down in the treatment of every tiny detail.

The cartoonish image of advertising and marketing as somehow being able to force or hypnotize intelligent consumers into doing things they wouldn't normally do has persisted since the original advertising critiques came down the pike in the 1950s. I side with Bob Garfield, a critic of many modern ad campaigns. Garfield insists that many campaigns are so poorly executed that advertising is often not persuasive at all![5] If you can't get your overt message out there, what value could there possibly be in contemplating subliminal techniques?

So stop thinking you're Dr. Evil. As Garfield argues, rather than being some kind of magic act that will hoodwink consumers into doing your bidding, advertising and marketing—and I presume this includes the sales copy and design of landing pages on your website—can be a positive force for clear communications with consumers. Economic growth depends on advertising and marketing. Communicating the differences among products and services, telling prospective customers about your innovations or track record of reliability, and so on, are not as one sided an exchange as critics would have us believe. This is precisely why some now argue that it's companies with authentic stories to tell (not carefully crafted "hypnosis") that quickly grab market share as their competitors overemphasize aspects of manipulation.

Careful experimentation intended to measure the psychological impacts of design and layout, however valuable to some larger e-commerce retailers and direct marketing pros, also needs to be weighed against consistency in look and feel. Better designers maintain libraries of styles, and they design the overall look and feel of a site to be appropriate for the job at hand. If a certain color scheme or general layout is deployed throughout a corporate website, the fact that a different color or bold layout might convert better in a vacuum needs to be weighed against the consistency of your design. Longer term, your audience may hold you in higher regard if you integrate your attempts at increased conversions comfortably within your existing design scheme. If a big red "buy now" button converts slightly better over the short term, but the closest color to red that is really consistent with your site's style is reddish-brown, you may prefer to maintain a certain dignity by making the button reddish-brown. This is especially important for upscale brands, which are always willing to sacrifice a few short-term sales for the sake of consistent positioning in the marketplace.

The Quality of Your Offer

Of course you do need to spend time testing the actual content of your offer. What is your customer getting, for what price? You can always test to see if highlighting the following elements improves your conversion rates:

- Free shipping
- Free gift or add-on
- Time-limited discount
- Bulk discount
- Price increase or decrease

The last element is one that many sellers overlook. Sellers of software and information often underprice their material. Unless you test the total revenue potential of different price points, you may be leaving money on the table. You might also be projecting a discount image that could hurt you long term. On the other hand, your goal might actually be to increase your customer base quickly, if you calculate that lifetime value is potentially high. In that case, you might consider lowering prices if you can see a significant volume increase at that lower price point. There are any number of ways to try these things, but multiple landing pages and multiple product codes are one way of going at it.

If They Don't Buy, Get Them to Do Something

Many businesses sell products and services with a price point that is just so high, the conversion rate is too low to gain any measurable feedback for many months. If your business is like this, you need to create *proxy* metrics. If a potential customer of Cubicles, Etc., requests a fabric sample, for example, this generates zero revenue at first. But if fabric sample requests tend to convert into sales at a consistent rate, then the conversion rate from clicks to fabric sample requests becomes a valuable metric, one that occurs with more frequency than sales.

When you're measuring conversion rates, then, keep in mind that in looking at final sales, you might not be measuring the most *appropriate* or *helpful* conversion rate. By helpful, I mean the conversion rate that will help you analyze data and quickly adjust your campaign to respond to it. In numerous places in this book I've provided examples. Brookbend Outdoor Furniture considered distribution of a color catalog to be an important metric even in the absence of an immediate sale. Similarly, Bruce Baird's California Golf Schools considers a brochure request as an important metric, along with an online information request (a lead, if you will). Many service businesses capture leads or other "weak" expressions of interest given the infrequency of, and delay in, completing, sales. The goal is that you organize your sales process so you're measuring *something*, so you can take the feedback on that conversion rate and improve from there, for example by adjusting bids, deleting ad groups, or turning off content targeting.

What Are Typical Conversion Rates?

Just a few of the examples in this chapter indicate the wide variety in conversion rates. As I'll discuss later in this chapter, two Anonymizer.com landing pages tested by Lee Mills were widely disparate at 3.2% and 9.6%, respectively.

My advice is, don't try to guess what others in your industry are "converting at." These numbers can be artificial anyway. If your AdWords account is restricted to only very highly targeted words, you might convert at a very high rate. But that might mean your volume is too low. The more words you add in an attempt to increase volume, the greater the chances that your average conversion rate will fall. But if these new words were quite inexpensive, they'd perform well from an ROI standpoint regardless of the actual conversion rate number.

If you read reports on typical industry conversion rates, take them with a grain of salt. Conversions are highly dependent on what type of listing users clicked on, what type of search they did, and so on. Conversions also might vary from product to product.

For those generating certain types of leads, conversion rates could be higher or lower depending on how much effort is required of users filling out a contact form or survey. On its core (most targeted) keywords, an insurance-related campaign I worked on saw 20% of the visitors who clicked on an ad beginning to fill out a survey that would ultimately generate a lead for the sales force to follow up. Only about half that number—10%—completed the survey, thus counting as a "lead." That might have indicated problems with the usability and smoothness of the survey process, but some of the drop-off could be attributed to a normal filtering process, where inappropriate prospects dropped off as they discovered they did not qualify. There is always something to improve in any online sales process, but by and large, this result was satisfactory. What wasn't so easy to take was the escalating prices on clicks for those core keywords! Once generated, only about 10% of the leads turned into sales. Because 10% of clicks had turned into leads, only about 1% (10% of 10%) of the clicks on these core words ultimately turned into sales, meaning that 100 clicks were required for each sale. So in this case, at a hypothetical cost of $5 per click, the cost per sale was $500.

Depending on how you look at it, this could indicate a problem with the sales force, but it also could have been attributed to the quality of the leads. Or, it might simply have been normal for the industry. Of course, large competitors are very unlikely to share their data on various stages of their sales processes, so it's tough to know what's typical. What you do know is that you need to continue to test ways of improving that result. In a large company, that may mean overcoming considerable inertia. Usability testing may not have a clear champion in every organization, but it ought to in any large company, no matter how long that road may seem at first.[6]

The horrible secret (though it should come as no surprise to anyone with empathy for consumers) is that products and services that aren't in demand generate conversion rates close to zero. Confused visitors clicking on misleading ads convert at rates near zero. And inappropriate, poorly thought-out landing pages convert at rates near zero. No matter whether your industry benchmark is 0.5%, 1%, or 10%, you're clearly getting nowhere and likely losing money quickly when your conversion rate is zero. I wish I could say that never happened. In reality it does, because in a competitive marketplace there are often too many sellers of goods and services, and not enough buyers.

One area to be careful of is clicks on content targeting as opposed to clicks on search results within your AdWords campaign. In many cases, content may convert at a different rate than search. If it converts much worse, you may need to disable content targeting.

The conversion rates on different ads and keywords in your account will affect the viability of your campaign, your decision to keep or reject certain ads, and how high you should bid (as discussed in Chapter 10). But the rate per se is really trivial considering that you are likely bidding differently on different keywords. Measures of ROI should be the ultimate arbiter of how you manage your account.

Use Models and Follow Conventions

If you're stumped for what's likely to convert best, do what most experienced marketers do: take a shortcut. If you know of pages or site layouts that have been effective for others, there's nothing wrong with emulating their general principles, at least as a starting point. That does not, of course, mean you should rip off copyrighted material! A number of the successes cited in this chapter—the Anonymizer.com and PierOne.com landing pages, for example—are worth looking at.

Ideally, you'd marry your personal or corporate style with sound principles learned from others. The public doesn't necessarily want to see cookie-cutter material, but in almost all cases, they are hoping for a conventional approach to communicating features, benefits, and an offer, as well as supporting material such as company background. Perhaps most importantly they're looking for a simple, conventional navigation scheme.

In some circles there seems to be a misperception that the Internet is the preserve of wigged-out visionaries. Last time I checked, though, web users were a lot like motorists. They would rather drive on asphalt. If you pave their route to the convenience store with tapioca, they're going to get ticked off.

Landing Page Design

As discussed earlier, the landing page is the most important page of your site when it comes to converting a click to a profitable action. Let's take a closer look at the elements of a good landing page.

Category Page vs. Single-Product Page

If you run a site with a catalog involving a lot of individual products, what converts better, a category page listing a variety of products under a given heading, or a product-specific page? For starters, that depends on the ad. For example, a specific brand name attached to a wristwatch wouldn't take potential customers to a huge selection of all watches. At the same time, they probably wouldn't take them to the page for a single watch unless their selection was small or that watch was a particularly hot item. They usually wouldn't get more specific than a category page for, say, a variety of Timex watches, simply because most watch makers have hundreds of individual models and it would usually be impractical to build a campaign with several thousand ads all going to separate landing pages.

Most of the experts I've talked to lean towards category pages, but none of them rely exclusively on them. A category page, as long as it looks inviting (such as the nicely designed "coffee, tea, & espresso" page at KlinQ.com, shown a bit farther along, in Figure 11-14), offers an interesting happy medium between the home page and a single product page.

Keep in mind that if everyone already knew that they wanted a "Beacon Hill Sugar Bowl with Spoon," there would be no need for search! Consumers, at least those who are shopping for gifts or housewares to upgrade their current lifestyle, want to browse various designs, brands, and sizes. A category page is often a great place to start. This can be enhanced with "featured suggestions" to give the user a sense of the breadth of the site's selection.

The thing about rules, such as "minimize clicks at all costs" or "reduce the number of items on the page," is you need to have enough flexibility to violate them for a good reason. By all accounts, there is absolutely nothing wrong with showing the shopper images of several related products in a category. If a brand is strong enough, or if the site makes a lasting enough impression on users, they may return later to buy one or more products, or they may decide to buy something they weren't considering when they first performed a search.

Your site may not have an obvious category that relates to every popular keyword that you're bidding on, but you can still take the user to a dynamically generated "site search results URL." The Pier 1 Imports site has no category page for "director's chairs," for example, but users are still taken to a page full of director's chairs by way of the URL for a site search. (Depending on your situation you may want to work with your site developer to hard-code such results pages and make them into shorter URLs, or indeed turn them into category pages.) Misty Locke of Range Online Media, who works on Pier 1's campaign, has stated that pages like this selection of director's chairs in Figure 11-7 do quite well in terms of conversions from click to sale.

Locke has also found that successful results came as a result of testing the search advertising copy. She found that an ad with flair, including the phrase "lights, camera, action," produced higher conversion rates on director's chairs. She believes this may be partly as a result of Pier 1's strong brand and middle-class target audience, who already know basically what type of product they want.

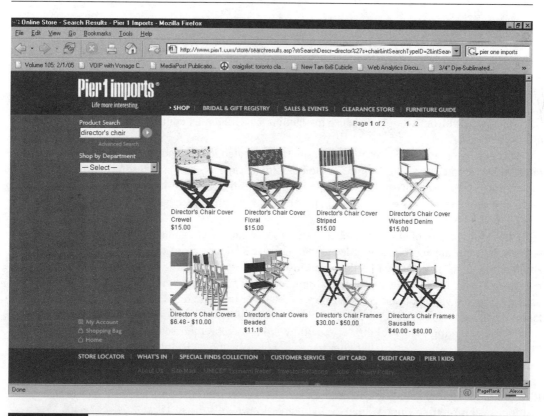

 FIGURE 11-7   While singular in focus, this page offers the shopper an easily navigated selection of director's chairs.

Advanced shopping cart functionality (or even more advanced personalization technology at leading destination e-commerce sites like Amazon) will do a good job of suggesting related items that the searcher might also want to look at. While that may appear to violate my rule of thumb "don't suggest other things until they've become a customer," some retail environments are more amenable to users browsing among various items. Indeed, some sales of lower-priced items may have virtually zero profit margins, so it's incumbent on retailers to make potentially well-heeled customers aware of a couple of related higher-priced items as well.

Ensure Ads and Tracking Codes Refer to Correct Page

One of the biggest errors you can make is to advertise grass seed in your ad and send users to a completely wrong page on the site, such as a page advertising dog food.

If you do nothing else, go inside your AdWords campaign and click on every ad (if you do it from inside the campaign, you won't be charged). Double- and triple-check that all landing pages are working and that you haven't crossed any wires.

Ensure Keywords Are on the Landing Page

In search, consistency is key. You already know that ads often receive a higher CTR when you include the searched-for keywords in your ad title and/or ad copy. This applies to landing pages as well. Presenting case studies on his clients Anonymizer.com and St. Bernard Software, Lee Mills has stressed on several occasions that taking care to add core keywords to the landing page will almost always raise conversion rates. In some cases, it also ensures that your ads will get editorial approval from Google, because the landing page contains content consistent with what users are seeking.

This is why many companies will write several dedicated landing pages to improve conversion rates. For example, if you're running ads on **car insurance** as well as **personal watercraft insurance**, you'd probably get better response if you had a separate landing page for each including those keywords on the page, rather than taking all searchers to the same generic **vehicle insurance** page.

One of my former clients, a financial institution, wanted to focus heavily on home mortgage refinancing; but during the AdWords campaign, their IT department was slow in creating a tailored landing page for that product line. Instead, those who clicked on the ad for mortgage refinancing were taken to an application form tailored to new homeowners! Needless to say, conversion rates were poor, as many visitors to this page immediately left. When a more targeted landing page was finally developed, conversion rates doubled.

People are going to be looking for specific words based on their search query and the content of your ad. Make sure that's what your page is explicitly about. Ralph Wilson offers a funny example of a home gym company that has two kinds of ad: one that focuses on the fact that "guys with muscles get the girl" and one that talks about muscular definition ("getting ripped"). If the ad the user sees is focused on the "get the girl" theme, and the user lands on a page that just focuses on "getting ripped," they're likely to ask "where's the girl?"

Information Galore: Becoming the "Only" Solution

Dr. Harold Katz is a world-renowned "breath doctor" and founder of the California Breath Clinics. The remarkable thing about his website is the wealth of free, hard-to-find information there—the sort of specialized clinical information that could only be offered by someone who has spent a lifetime in the same business. Dr. Katz sells a range of bad-breath-abatement products targeted at the significant segment of the population who suffer from problem halitosis. But he knows he can't count on the lucrative repeat business that comes with this territory until he has formed that first relationship resulting in a first sale.

As one of my colleagues discovered when working on the California Breath Clinics paid search campaign, the site converts nicely in general. But one of the specific conversion mechanisms is worth noting. For people who want to save time, Dr. Katz has produced an e-book that condenses decades worth of medical research into a single handy guide. Such guides tend to be good sales tools. In fact, 20% of those who download the free e-book become buyers of his products. And since problem bad breath is rarely cured, repeat business is strong.

Sometimes, what converts best for your business might conflict with what usability experts (or Google) advise. You may need to use your own judgment and get creative. The reality, to which marketing experts like MarketingSherpa's Anne Holland bear witness, is that many working online marketers today find that certain aggressive tactics—like pop-ups—have become necessary components of an aggressive marketer's conversion strategy. Dr. Katz promotes his free e-book, collecting email addresses in exchange for the download, with a pop-up that shows up to any user visiting his site who clicks on three or more links. This is an interesting compromise, ensuring that users are moderately interested before asking politely (but still quite assertively) if they want to deepen their relationship and find out more about his research. All they need to enter is their first name and email address (Figure 11-8), and they can go back to browsing the site. This seems to get around Google's editorial policy against bringing AdWords clicks directly to pages that show pop-ups.

Elsewhere on his site, Dr. Katz sells a line of tooth-whitening products. This is a logical extension of his breath line, since the same people who are concerned about the image impact of oral hygiene are likely to be interested in both. At one point early in his article "A Few Secrets About Teeth Whitening That Your Dentist Hopes I'll Never Tell You," he cleverly evokes his Los Angeles location, noting that in that area, people are particularly image conscious no matter what their social class or occupation. (Referring to the fact that "factory workers" are getting their teeth whitened, he's well on his way to removing the initial objection that "I'm not the type of flashy person who goes for that sort of thing.") He also points out that he started practicing dentistry in that area in 1975, back when tooth whitening meant "using Pearl Drops toothpaste." In essence, he is saying "tooth whitening is for everyone," and "I care about patients and understand the evolution of the field, since I have 30 years' experience." The article itself is an excellent sales tool. It does the following things:

- It establishes his objectivity. Dr. Katz talks about the inflated expense of current tooth whitening, saying that "dentists love it," and that "most dentists would 'shoot' him for revealing some of the secrets he discusses in the article."

- It establishes his scientific expertise and experience.

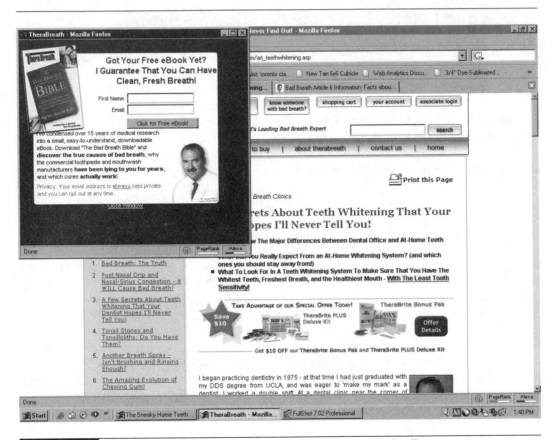

FIGURE 11-8   Dr. Katz's site informs, collects email addresses, and sells.

- It examines the pros and cons of various methods, leading the reader through the purchase research process towards the most effective and cost-effective solution.

- Although critical of some dentists and some methods, overall, it's respectful. He doesn't lower the level by engaging in muckraking.

- It refers to the kit he sells and offers a guarantee.

- It offers before-and-after photos, but doesn't rely solely on these. They are realistic; the patients look healthy rather than glamorous.

- It contains his photo and signature, for added directness. The printed name under the signature is "Harold Katz, DDS." He's a doctor, not a salesman. But does he ever know how to sell!

The sales page, for the user that clicks there, is also effective. It contains, among other things, a testimonial from a user who relies on her image because of "frequent entertaining at corporate parties." That's a nice touch. Even if you're not a movie star, this reinforces the fact that the product could help your career.

There is one more sales tool built into the "A Few Secrets About Teeth Whitening" article. If a reader lingers more than five seconds on the part of the article "above the fold," a *pop-in* (like a pop-up, but built into the HTML page) is inserted (see Figure 11-9) that asks if you'd like to download a brief, free e-book that contains a description of how Dr. Katz whitens his own teeth. Unlike a pop-up, a pop-in leaves your screen (is stuck in place) as you scroll down. Google Editorial does not typically consider these as pop-ups, so will not generally disapprove your AdWords ad if you use them.

Dr. Katz and his marketing team deserve credit for a fine effort. The Therabreath.com site proves that assertive online marketing doesn't have to be annoying. After all, the people coming to the site are already interested in his line of business. Many are eager to find out more. In search marketing, relevancy rules.

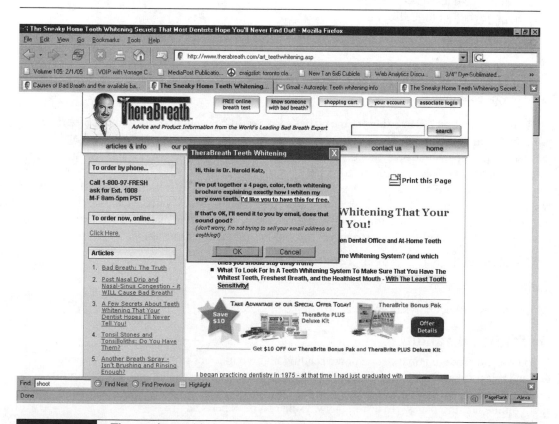

FIGURE 11-9 The pop-in graphic inserted in this article assertively asks if you want to download a related free e-book.

A/B Landing Page Split-Testing

If you're going to improve on landing pages, you need a scientific way to test them. Fortunately, you should already understand the basics of split-testing from the discussion in Chapter 7 about split-testing ads.

If you have two landing page designs and want to find which one converts best, AdWords offers a better, faster, and easier way to gather the requisite data than most any other method available.

A Simple AdWords-Powered Split-Testing Methodology

Since AdWords is supposed to rotate ads evenly if two or more ads are run in the same ad group, you don't need fancy methods to split-test ads. (Sometimes, the ad rotator doesn't seem to function properly. If you find you have problems in this area, you may need to contact your Google Support rep.) One element of your AdWords ad creative, remember, is the destination URL. Nothing is stopping you from running the same ad head to head, altering only the destination URL, so the only variable being tested is the landing page. This would offer a true head-to-head test at the same time of day during the same days of the week; so it's as close to a lab experiment as you're going to get—better than a sequential test, for example.

Let's say your ad looks like this:

Bulk Bridge Mix

Party hearty with the tastiest
Confections. Bulk savings!
www.chocoholyx.biz

In the destination URL setting for the ad, let's say you'd be sending users to the appropriate page for **bridge mix**, at http://www.chocoholyx.biz/bmix1.asp. Run a second ad, with exactly the same title, copy, and display URL, but point the destination URL to the second landing page you want to test. Let's say that destination URL is http://www.chocoholyx.biz/bmix2.asp. As soon as AdWords begins placing both ads into even rotation, you'll be testing the impact of these two landing pages on conversion rates, provided you're properly tracking conversions. If your tracking solution requires tracking codes, you'd need to add a question mark and some unique parameters at the end of the URL string, so it would look something like this:

http://www.chocoholyx.biz/bmix1.asp?source=goog&kw=24a_lp01

and

http://www.chocoholyx.biz/bmix2.asp?source=goog&kw=24a_lp02

On Statistical Validity

If you run a major e-commerce site or are sending high volumes of traffic to a page, you can test and retest frequently. However, I believe that it's possible to oversell the notion of rapid experimentation. Many companies generate too little traffic—especially if they have multiple low-volume landing pages—to test in the ways that some experts advise.

Several other factors make split-testing more complicated than some would let on. To be sure, understanding basic principles of statistical reliability is helpful, and simple tools like the Vertster "Clickthrough Rate Validity Checker" (see www.vertster.com/adwords-tool/default.asp) can help you get a feel for this (see Figure 11-10). Using the tool, I told it I had received 28 clicks from ad A and a CTR of 3.0% (which means that I must have had, according to the tool, 933 impressions). For ad B, I told it I got 39 clicks for a CTR of 4.3%, which means that I must have had 906 impressions of that ad. One of the things these tools are good at demonstrating is how you reach a high level of reliability in a split-test sooner when there is a wider gap in CTR performance. In this case, the gap is fairly wide—4.3% to 3.0%. Vertster's statistical analysis tells me that 80% of the time, the current winner will continue to be the winner in the future.

It wouldn't be too difficult to use a similar tool to assess the reliability rate of landing pages, either, but it can take a surprisingly long time to arrive at an 80% reliable test, which in statistical terms, isn't all that reliable. If you were using that tool to assess the conversion rate of clicks to sales, for example, the numbers for the example just given would be "28 sales" and "39 sales," not clicks.

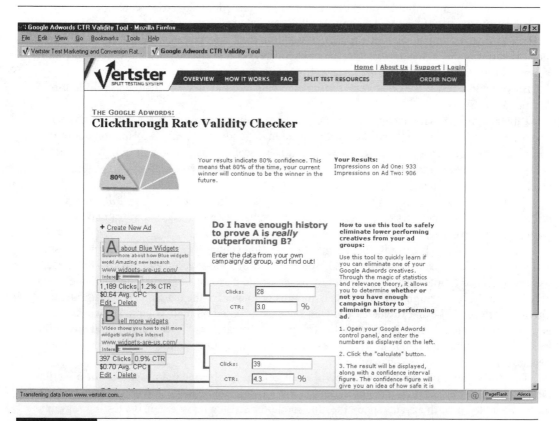

FIGURE 11-10   Vertster's Clickthrough Rate Validity Checker

Unfortunately, the reality here is complicated. What if your CTRs or conversion rates don't diverge as much as this example? Given the wide variety of user motivations and mind-sets as they arrive on your site, how can you know that a conversion rate of 0.70% is really significantly better than 0.63%? It might take you quite a while to find out. This suggests to me that you are often better off gaining a deeper understanding of your marketplace and of web persuasion theories that will ultimately allow you to create new landing pages with *vastly* improved performance. If you go from 3% to 9%, you won't have a tough decision as to which page performs better. So I think it's a myth that testing landing pages is about making dozens of minute tweaks. It's about rethinking your communications strategy so that you're making big leaps forward in performance. Those leaps are the ones that make you feel confident about making permanent changes.

There are several reasons why you don't get as much reliability as Vertster says on your CTR test, let alone on a landing page split-test. Of course it can be done, just not as easily or as quickly as many think. At the Google AdWords account level, there is actually built-in uncertainty in terms of CTRs on search partners (AOL, and others) as opposed to Google proper. For the purposes of ad rank, AdWords uses the CTR on Google only, but shows you data in the aggregate. To a certain extent, you're always flying blind (Google's fault)!

There are a number of other quirks to take into account. Many advertisers aren't aware of the quiet editorial review process on new ads that can delay proper rotation for four to six days. When a four-to-six-day delay needs to be factored into the time you allow your tests to run, the idea of churning through a new test every couple of days is fantasy, and even a week is too short. You need two weeks at least.

As you add a few more of these distorting elements into the mix, the math gets a little more complicated still.

Take a company with a long sales cycle. On high-volume core keywords, at least, the large financial institution I recently worked with was able to generate reliable information about the conversion rate of clicks to leads on the various ads we were testing, although in light of editorial delays and internal bureaucracy, it took us a while to realize that we needed to wait at least two weeks for every new test, rather than one week.

However, those leads converted to actual sales at vastly different rates. So while we used the initial click-to-quote conversion rate as a decent benchmark, we also needed to wait six to eight weeks for the revenue information to come in.

On higher-volume keywords, that information would eventually be valuable to us within six to eight weeks, at least. Not so, though, in ad groups built around low-volume keywords. On these, we either needed to infer that ads and landing pages would perform similarly to those related to the core keywords, or we might need to wait six months or longer for the data to become significant. Obviously this may be an extreme case if your business is based on high-volume keywords that generate high-volume sales, but the point is you need to be careful of how you interpret any split-test. There is no major harm in tacking an extra week or month onto your testing schedule, just to be sure that what you're seeing is reliable.

Typically, there are politics involved in even getting a cohesive plan together for a single landing page test. Marketing managers, developers, outside consultants, and company execs may all be afraid to show their ignorance of testing methods; so they resist extensive testing regimens that may pull any of them away from more familiar (and possibly more productive, given where their expertise may lie) tasks.

My friends at Iguana Corp.—and they do generate high volumes of traffic—eventually did organize a single split-test of their main landing page. The new page was different in several areas, so the multivariate approach to testing was in keeping with the advanced thinking of scientists (like Genichi Taguchi, a leader in the Total Quality Management Movement).

We found that the new page did outperform the old one on most (but not all) of our keyword groups. (The two main features that seemed to contribute to the improvement were a reduction in clutter and the addition of an image of a friendly female face.) But for Iguana Corp., like so many other companies, this kind of testing has no champion in the company, outside of perhaps the CEO, who is busy with a great many priorities. A fresh test might be undertaken once every 6–12 months; no more often than that.

Yes, you can and should strive to improve. But some of the testing and iterative improvement methods that may be applied to factory management or other capital-intensive businesses do not translate well to many online marketing campaigns. Unless the budget permits a team of specialists to work full time on improving the sales process, you can't expect to improve your AdWords campaign and landing pages like some division of General Electric might try to perfect a manufacturing process at an overseas factory. For most small to midsized businesses, it's practical to compromise in terms of how many stages of landing page improvement you go through; you'll no doubt wind up a bit farther from perfection than some larger company might. The reality is, at a certain point you'll need to devote your time to other aspects of the business: answering the phone, getting out and meeting customers, interacting with coworkers, attending seminars, or whatever you fill your day with. By all means make major improvements where possible, and reap the benefits of improved conversion rates. But you cannot afford to sweat the small stuff.

All the more important that you adopt best practices and get reasonably close to an optimal landing page design from the beginning. And more than that, you should pursue a broad strategy of making your prospective customers comfortable with you and your site on their first visit, and on subsequent visits.

Split-Testing Services

If frequent split-testing or advanced multivariate testing of landing pages does seem appropriate to your company's goals and traffic volumes, you'll find an increasing number of services that will help you do this. Some leading ones are Optimost, Offermatica, and Sitespect.

Anonymizer.com: A/B Testing That Defied Expectations

Lee Mills, a marketing consultant who has alternated between independent consulting through his firm Beyond Clicks and in-house marketing roles, has conducted a number of landing page tests for clients seeking improved conversion rates. One such test, for Anonymizer.com, showed surprising results. The first landing page (Figure 11-11) had fairly brief sales copy, a clear offer, and was attractively laid out. Mills and the client didn't believe that the conversion rate of 3.2% could be improved upon very much.

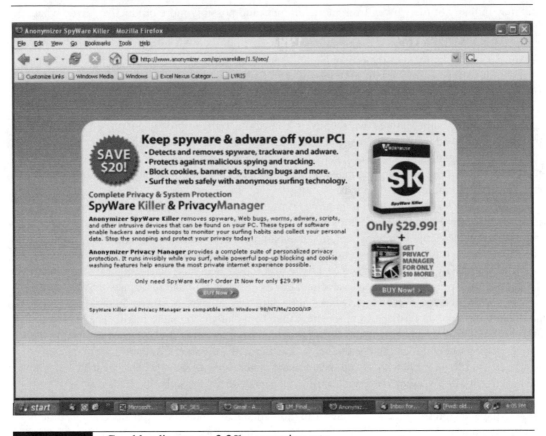

FIGURE 11-11   Good landing page: 3.2% conversion rate

Indeed, this does seem to be a nice page, and 3.2% was a fine result. Nonetheless, a much longer page was also tried (Figure 11-12). It included more sales copy, more education about the dangers of spyware and threats to Internet privacy, and more information about the benefits of the product. It even included screen shots. This page did far better than the first attempt—it converted at a rate of 9.6%!

In his presentation at a conference in August 2004, Mills said he and his team were surprised by the result because they'd always assumed it was important to minimize scrolling—to keep all the vital information "above the fold." The result doesn't surprise me. We often hear nonsense about the fact that people don't like to read a lot of information—"Keep it simple, stupid"—that sort of thing. Obviously, with a result more than three times better than the short page, this longer page had something going for it. Having extensive sales copy does not necessarily conflict with the need to maintain a singular focus on converting the prospect into a buyer.

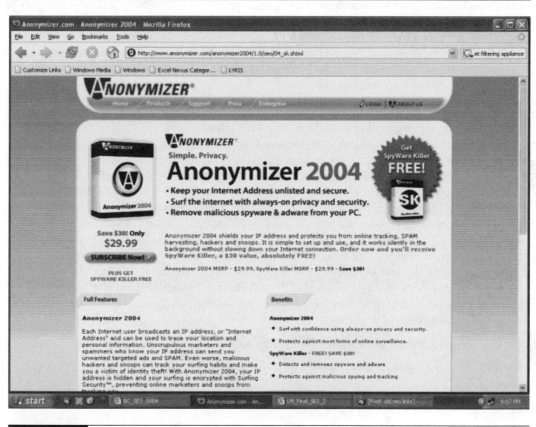

FIGURE 11-12   Great landing page: 9.6% conversion rate

Web Credibility

The state of mind of many new visitors to your site can probably be summed up in one word: incredulous. Who are you? Why should they believe you? Will you deliver on your promises? Will you rip them off?

When I go through the swift process of buying a book on Amazon.com, I'm 99.9% certain that the information I see is reliable and that my order will be fulfilled to my satisfaction. That degree of certainty drops significantly if a site is less familiar to me.

Unless you are a major brand or are dealing with a repeat customer, you have a fair bit of work to do to ensure that the visitor is "in your camp," taking your word for what you claim on the site.

I'm convinced that if everyone took the various principles of web credibility seriously, starting with a deep understanding of the fact that online interaction can still feel distant and unfeeling to many, most of the other pieces of the puzzle of creating better conversion rates would fall into place relatively easily. Do yourself a favor and pick up a copy of B. J. Fogg's book, *Persuasive Technology*, and focus on Chapter 7, "Credibility and the World Wide Web."

B. J. Fogg and Stanford Research on Web Credibility

Web surfers face an ongoing challenge: to "determine what information is credible." Web designers, to connect businesses and organizations with potential clients, must "create highly credible sites."[7]

Do we actually know what increases or decreases web users' perception that the information they find on a site is credible? Thanks to studies carried out by the Stanford Persuasive Technology Lab, we actually have a very good idea. Between 1999 and 2002, Fogg's team conducted large-scale studies as well as some smaller pilot studies involving over 6,000 participants in total. The 1999 study involved 1,409 participants, and the 2002 study involved 1,649. The average age in the first study was 32.6 years; in the second, 35.5. More than half the participants were Finnish; most of the rest were American. Gender was about 45% female and 55% male in both studies. Participants were typically middle-income college graduates with extensive Internet experience.[8]

By and large, the findings do not contradict the investigators' hunches about what factors increase and decrease credibility scores. According to the Stanford studies, the following are some key factors that increase credibility:

- The site gives the organization's physical address.
- The site gives a contact phone number.
- The site looks professionally designed.
- The site lets you search for past content.
- The site is linked to by a site you think is believable.
- The site has articles containing citations and references.
- The site lists authors' credentials for each article.
- The site provides a quick response to customer service questions.
- The site was recommended by a friend.
- The site represents an organization you respect or a news organization.

Want to blow your credibility? The following seem to be no-no's:

- The site is sometimes unexpectedly unavailable.
- The site makes it hard to distinguish ads from content.
- The site is rarely updated with new content.
- The site is difficult to navigate.

- The site has a typographical error.

- The site's domain name does not match the company name.

- The site links to a site you think is not credible.

- The site has a link that doesn't work.

- The site automatically pops up new windows with ads.

- The site takes a long time to download.

The people—at least those in this study—have spoken, and the preceding are the factors they say most influence their perceptions. In the real world, some of these mistakes can be even more damaging than the study might indicate. And some of the "must-haves," like providing contact information, are becoming more important all the time.

Bear in mind that Fogg and his researchers believe that credibility is made up of two dimensions: perceived trustworthiness (unbiased, fair, honest) and perceived expertise (knowledgeable, experienced, intelligent).[9] So in the case of Dr. Katz's Therabreath.com site, discussed earlier, credibility derives from two sources. Most of what I emphasize is related to Dr. Katz's perceived expertise, and his 30 years in business is testament to his expertise. His perceived trustworthiness (lack of bias) also goes up because he seems to be providing articles that don't merely talk about his own products, but rather the evolution of products in his field. That in itself wouldn't be enough; he would have to provide good customer service to maintain that trustworthiness.

TIP   *For a handy summary of web credibility guidelines, visit http://credibility.stanford.edu/ guidelines/index.html.*

Should You Blog?

Dr. Katz makes effective use of articles on his site as a means of establishing his expertise. In a previous chapter I mentioned Ray Allen's "This Week in Wildflowers" weblog as a great way of putting a human face on his online store. A weblog is simply the latest means of simple content management for website owners who want to post date-stamped entries on their website. (Google owns one of the leading blog software providers, Blogger. There are dozens of others, including Blogspot, Blogware, Movable Type, and the list goes on.) Weblogs, or *blogs*, have become full featured and include easy means of posting photos, allowing feedback, and so on. Bloggers have many different styles. Some companies just allow execs to quietly blog their thoughts about trends in business. Some execs may blog "off to the side," attracting a wide following. This can help or hurt careers. There is evidence of both happening. But this isn't about your career, it's about whether a new form of communication might help you convert more sales or create a better conversion environment for your business over the long haul.

Blogging per se is relatively new, but posting thoughts on a website is of course not all that new. Nonetheless, the principle blogging represents—standing up and being counted on a regular basis—fits in well with the general idea of developing a persuasive online voice and offering something fresh so visitors are aware you're alive and doing business.

Whether you consider blogging or just make a point of communicating with your audience through articles, books, conference presentations, press interviews, and other means, your credibility will improve if you are "out there," building your brand. But the process is subtle.

Blogging is not a magic bullet in itself. I tend to think the heavy focus that some of today's "blogging for business" consultants place on the activity is a bit faddish. The number of blogs in existence today is staggering, but there is little evidence to show that many of them contribute directly to a company's bottom line. At a certain point, content is content. Columnists in the newspaper have visibility, even brand appeal. But no one is going to tell you that the best way to triple sales at a chemical company is to get one of your people a column at the *Miami Herald*.

Broadly speaking, visible business owners tend to gain brand recognition ahead of less visible peers. After all, aren't all wildflower seeds pretty much the same in the customer's eyes? Self-promotion in general can be an important skill. But for now I am not inclined to carry the torch for blogging as a self-promotion tool that applies well across the board. Self-promoters whom I've seen create rapid growth in competitive industries are often like Christine Magee, president of Sleep Country Canada. They buy huge blocks of late-night television advertising time, and appear personally in the ads, until you can't think of anywhere else to buy a mattress. Sleep Country Canada went from zero to 81 stores in eight years, all without a blog.

If blogging is part of a happy scenario for you, keep it up. (I blog, but long before that, I wrote articles and posted them online. I actually created a bloglike format on that site to facilitate posting short entries when I got tired of writing long articles. This was before anyone called this "blogging.") Even though my (now blog-centric) site, Traffick.com, has had a fairly loyal readership, I don't think of blogging in terms of its direct impact. Indirectly, it could help improve your position as an industry authority, but you'd better do it for a long time and do it well. I can't even prove to you that one of the better examples—Ray Allen with his blog entries about spring flowers, complete with photos—is helping his business by doing this. I believe that Ray and I both do this, in the end, because we are born to communicate. (As Aristotle said, we are political animals.) But Ray has also found himself quoted in the *New York Times* and appeared on a recent *Biography* episode on TV (no, not about Ray). In other words, he's always trying to get his message across. Ray would probably tell you that he blogs because (1) his customers like it; (2) it's fun!

I've run across some innovative uses of blogs that are more commercial in nature than most. That's the interesting thing. People can adopt different styles for blogs and use them for different purposes. Blogging can be a time-saving way to post new offerings, products, and specials. One example I ran across recently was during a search for commercial office space. Most small companies searching for serious office space in a metropolitan area will have a certain area in mind, and they may already know the dozen or so main suitable spaces that have vacancies at any given time. As I did some research, I came across a Toronto office real estate blog that had a sole purpose: to post new vacancies. The entries only came every week or so and simply mentioned the address of the building, the square footage of the space, and linked to the detailed particulars at a site called Space4Lease.com. In essence, the blog was an easy way for the owner of Space4Lease.com to keep prospects aware of fresh information. This would not have been as easy to do with the complex site layout of Space4Lease.com. Visitors to the site might not have had a good sense of what vacancies were truly fresh; or perhaps people just like blogs these days and find them easier to digest. In essence, the blog seemed like a bit of a workaround to help the site owners communicate fresh info to searchers in a way that the main site was ill suited to accomplish. I found it a rather addictive little blog; even though I eventually found an office space, I can't help stealing back onto it to see the latest available offerings in the market. I'm sure a lot of residential realtors could make good use of this blogging tactic, too.

One practical element of blogging that any businessperson should be aware of is that savvy Internet users will know how to "subscribe" to the blog as long as it's compatible with RSS (Really Simple Syndication). That is a great way of keeping contact with customers who may not want email. The headlines of your blog entries might appear, for example, on someone's personalized My Yahoo home page. The problem is, your subscribers are anonymous. There is generally no subscriber list.

If blogging isn't your bag, then focus on more practical aspects of communicating your online offerings (better copy on the home page, including a regularly updated brief of what's new, for example), and don't bother with blogging.

Don't Neglect "Site Search"

Recall that an element of web credibility is the ability to search for archived material. On an e-commerce site, people are looking for products, not articles. It's vital that there be a search box to help consumers who are having trouble navigating through your categories to find the item they're looking for. Site search has become increasingly sophisticated. Successful e-commerce site developers know which options are available and whether they are built into the shopping cart package you're using, or whether a customized version of a third-party solution might be required. Be wary if your developer seeks to reinvent the wheel by throwing together his own "homemade" search engine. Product search and the ability of a site search tool to suggest related items can be a complex matter.

NOTE   *Amazon.com is one of the world's top search technology companies. The ability for users to browse their huge catalog without getting lost is an important driver of Amazon's current profitability, since this increases the average order size.*

If you want to maximize your conversion rates and you have more than a few pages on your site, you need quality site search. Some low-cost and free site search options are offered by companies like Atomz and Google, but make sure that you investigate fully. The lowest-end products might not be sufficient for your needs. A useful resource on site search products is Avi Rapoport's SearchTools.com.

Factors Outside Your Control

Don't confuse luck with brains. Sometimes, you don't have total control of how users will behave from day to day. However, while you may not be able to control these factors, you can plan for them.

Seasonality

Every market has up and down seasons. Housing, taxation, and retail gifts are three of the most obvious examples. Unless you have at least two years' worth of conversion data at your disposal, it can be difficult to know whether your site is converting well or not, adjusted for season. What appears to be a drop-off or an increase might simply be normal activity. How well do you understand your own business?

Hot Sectors

If you've begun working on a campaign for a product that is just hitting the market and is hard to find, you could wind up reaping windfall profits because that's what search is really good for: connecting users with niche areas quickly. GPS phones were hard to find not long ago. One site owner in this area reaped windfall profits as a result. The design of the site had very little to do with the high conversion rates, and the drop-off in ROI that will inevitably occur as more competitors move in can't be blamed on AdWords campaign techniques or site design.

Hot sectors will eventually cool off. Users in more mature industries know that they can comparison shop. You need to allow for that. The reason people don't comparison shop when something is brand new is likely because early adopters come to the table with a status-driven "must have" mentality. If the iPod cost $1,500 and sold out very quickly from retail stores, you can bet that there would be a few bleeding-edgers who would buy from the site that could promise them fast delivery regardless of price.

360-Degree View: Create a Good Conversion Environment

The popularity of the TV show *What Not to Wear* has convinced a certain segment of the population that no matter how comfortable you may be in ripped jeans and a 30-year-old hairstyle, your career could suffer if you wear these to work. I wish more site owners—especially smaller businesses—understood that principle as it relates to the conversion rate on their paid traffic.

Online, more than anywhere else, you suffer from a need to prove yourself to skeptical prospects in an environment that feels very "cold" to those prospects. They haven't met you face-to-face. They may not have heard the positive word of mouth that you've generated. They haven't sampled the quality of your products. They can't see the line of customers outside your store. In short, unless you take particular steps to position yourself as a business with some kind of status, prospects may assume you're third rate.

A large part of how status is conveyed online is visual. Recall that in the studies by Fogg's Stanford Persuasive Technology Lab, a "site that looks professionally designed" scores as one of the strongest means to increase "surface web credibility" for an online business or organization.[10]

That's obviously a very general goal. "Professionally designed" means different things to different people. In *Selling the Invisible*, Harry Beckwith argues, "Prospects look for visual clues about a service. If they find none, they often look to services that do have them. So provide clues."[11]

Beckwith's examples include visible company "front men," which can be real men such as Joel Hyatt (Hyatt Legal Services) and Dave Thomas (late founder of Wendy's Restaurants), or the pillars at law offices, an accountant's conservative attire, or a financial adviser's prosperous-looking leather portfolio. Online, though, what people see is not just images, but how those images are presented. They see your design. If your site resembles a dead skunk lying in the middle of the road, chances are your prospect will assume your company stinks, too. Good design isn't cheap, but you should buy as much as you can afford, rather than as little as you can get away with.

A client I recently worked with, the Rotman School of Business at the University of Toronto, certainly grasped this concept. With the high cost of MBA programs, special attention needed to be paid to the look and feel of the website for their Omnium Global Executive MBA. They hired an agency, Sonic Boom Creative Media, to design a site (Figure 11-13) that "looks expensive"—as expensive as the pricey degree. Obviously, a solid image is only the first step—the site must also be effective in converting to desired outcomes—but in an organization like the Rotman School, fostering an image of solidity and quality contributes to building a globally recognized

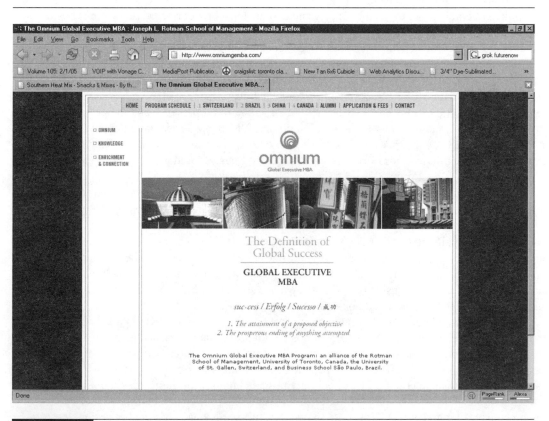

FIGURE 11-13   The Omnium Global EMBA home page: classy from head to toe

brand for the long haul. An even better site that combines the proper feel with improved usability and better landing pages is planned for the future. The classy feel isn't enough to generate improved conversion rates by itself, but it does provide a solid foundation and enhances the organization's brand.

Leveraging Feel and Brand in Small Retail Operations

Let's look at a couple of examples of how small companies can create a brand with a quality feel, in spite of not having a nationwide chain of retail stores or the budget to hire a top ad agency.

KlinQ.com

KlinQ.com is an online housewares business owned by Michael and Frieda Lichter. I'd worked briefly with them on their previous site, CrystalPorcelain.com. CrystalPorcelain.com had done very well on search engines. The AdWords campaign generated high clickthrough rates and was quite profitable. But overall, their feeling was that the niche was too narrow and their audience was limited to an older demographic. They wanted to launch a broader-based housewares business that appealed to a youthful, more adventuresome audience. They also felt there was a market for higher-end designer kitchenware and drinkware products that wasn't adequately being tapped into.

To create the new brand concept and to develop the visual look and feel of the new site, the Lichters turned to Joel Miller, head of a Montreal-based interactive agency, Nekouda Creative. In conversations with Miller I learned that Nekouda believed strongly in the relationship between appropriate visual elements and "quality cues" in an online retail presence and the propensity of buyers to purchase and repurchase high-margin products. Miller was adamant that the investment in the right kind of retail experience creates higher conversion rates. After all, offline retailers have been studying these kinds of relationships for many years. Should it be any different online? Expertise pays.

To make a long story short, Miller's theory proved exactly correct, and his previous experience as a creative director for TV campaigns was put to solid use in planning the appropriate visual feel for the site. KlinQ.com's paid search campaigns did very well for a brand-new site. We launched an AdWords campaign in October 2003, and it was profitable from the outset. Remarkably, repeat buying started to make up a significant portion of sales as early as late November, something we were able to confirm using the Manticore Virtual Traffic Master analytics package. It was obvious that users were a bit apprehensive at first, so they made small trial orders to see whether they'd be fulfilled. Then they came back and bought multiple gifts for friends.

December went about as well as could be expected, to the point where KlinQ was backlogged with orders and needed to slow down their campaign. I noticed that an unusual number of shoppers did not buy the first item they searched for, but rather, browsed and purchased some other item—in most cases, I supposed, this would have been a gift for someone else. This confirmed for me that users found the site (Figure 11-14) not only upscale enough for their tastes, but easy and fun to navigate. The Lichters showed foresight in taking the plunge and betting on Nekouda's comprehensive "brand concept." It goes to show that a full-service agency's quality design doesn't

FIGURE 11-14 A beautifully laid out category page with custom photography and a youthful, cosmopolitan flair

have to cost hundreds of thousands of dollars. To be sure, it's not necessarily easy to find agency-quality work at a fraction of the usual price, but to those who scoff at the value of such initiatives, case studies like "CrystalPorcelain.com becomes KlinQ.com" might help change minds.

NutsOnline.com

Jeff Braverman, another client of mine, is a savvy businessperson. His site does very well, though for competitive reasons I can't share exact numbers. There are two primary reasons. First, Braverman has humanized his site and injected web credibility into it. NutsOnline is "real." The site contains not only contact information, but a whole history of the family business, a roasted nut stand in New Jersey (Figure 11-15). "In 1929, on the brink of the Depression," begins Braverman's heartfelt sales copy, "my grandfather Sol took a bold step." There's even a picture of Sol in front of the shop in the 1930s. It would be hard to say that the Braverman family doesn't care about nuts.

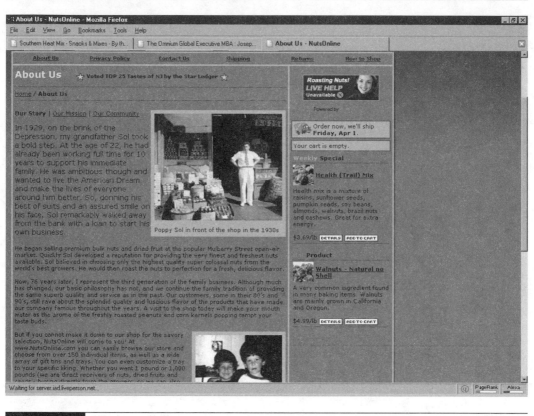

FIGURE 11-15   Web credibility and personal accountability create a good backdrop for customer loyalty.

Braverman also obsesses about the quality of his site. The checkout process and other details are important to him. If you're lost and use the site search box to look for **almonds**, you'll be served a page with a couple dozen product options. Everything on this website seems to work the way it's supposed to.

Perhaps the most impressive detail Braverman has obsessed over is the look and feel. It looks simple and straightforward, but that doesn't mean it was easy to put together. Rather than posting stock photos of nuts, he hired a food photographer to take proper photos of the products the Bravermans actually deliver to their customers (an example is in Figure 11-16). Nothing keeps it more real than accurate photographic images. But more than that, a professional food photographer knows how to make food look appealing.

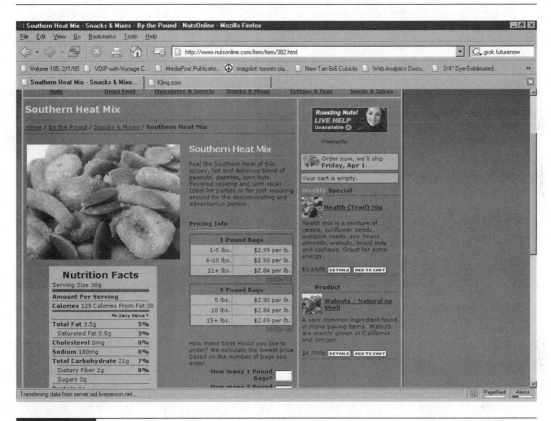

FIGURE 11-16 Jeff Braverman employed a food photographer to convey the quality of his products.

Summing Up

To improve conversion rates, think in terms of four broad priorities. First, make it smooth. Remove the most obvious barriers getting in the way of the user performing a desired action. Clutter and lack of focus are the subtlest, most insidious barriers. Broken links and nonworking checkout processes will literally kill any chance of a sale.

Second, test copy and layout elements that may serve to persuade a skeptical prospect that you deserve her business. That includes matters as basic as improving product descriptions on a retail site, testing different sizes of "purchase now" or "add to cart" buttons, or expanding on and clarifying too-brief, jargon-laden sales copy on a business-to-business site.

Third, make sure that you don't blow your web credibility when a hot prospect starts to scrutinize you more closely. Have contact information available; spell everything correctly; don't look desperate by hitting him with pop-ups; keep the material fresh; and so on.

Fourth, be image conscious in the broadest sense: heed Harry Beckwith's advice in *Selling the Invisible*. In business, companies have always been judged on superficial matters such as the shine on a salesman's shoes, your area code, your BlackBerry, whether or not you use giant orange letters in emails, and so forth. Beyond mere web credibility, the visual impact and basic architecture of your site can make the difference between becoming a real player with brand appeal, or just another peddler with a story to tell and stuff to unload. Ask yourself: are you so afraid of offending your current "web person" that you've allowed yourself to turn off potential customers? Not all web developers and designers are created equal.

I hope that by now, when you assess whether your site—or any site, for that matter—converts well, you'll be able to look into the matter with these four broad elements of conversion science in mind. Not every company can afford a full-scale usability testing regimen. But by implementing best practices and testing alternate landing pages, you can more often than not turn a money-losing campaign into a profitable one. Remember, one step at a time. Perfection is not possible.

Conversion science can't fix it if your product or service stinks, either. At a certain point, your marketing will fail if you don't deliver the goods. As Harry Beckwith argues, if people don't seem to embrace your sales pitch or your page layout, it may be time to stop worrying so much about pitching and formatting, and "get better reality."[12]

Additional Resources

Reading material by the authors footnoted in this chapter should help you get a bit deeper into conversion science. You'll also find GrokDotCom (www.grokdotcom.com), a newsletter published by conversion rate specialists Future Now, Inc., useful. For a capsule overview and straightforward how-to guide (though not necessarily tailored to AdWords advertisers), check out two e-books by Dr. Ralph Wilson, "How to Develop a Landing Page that Closes the Sale," and "How to Optimize Your Landing Pages Scientifically," available at www.wilsonweb.com.

Endnotes

1. Bryan Eisenberg and Jeffrey Eisenberg, *Call to Action: Secret Formulas to Improve Online Results* (Wizard Academy Press, 2005), 175.

2. Eisenberg and Eisenberg, *Call to Action*, 175.

3. Needless to say, you can take this line of thinking too far. Not excluding important members of your target audience is not the same as contriving "phony inclusions," such as transparently naming your rock band "Asia" because you hope to sell more records in Asia. But I digress (and regress, to the 1980s).

4. Paco Underhill, *Why We Buy: The Science of Shopping* (Simon & Schuster, 1999).

5. In *And Now a Few Words From Me* (McGraw-Hill, 2003), Garfield writes: "In the ordinary course of events, the effect of advertising falls smack between Vance Packard's *The Hidden Persuaders* and Randy Rothenberg's scenario of extraneousness; it influences our buying decisions but by no means dictates them. For every 'Where's the beef?' deployment of poison gas there is a benign bicarbonate like Alka-Seltzer, which provided campaign after delightful, memorable, hilarious campaign and lost market share the entire way" (p. 191). Although the discussion in this chapter considers your landing pages and website as a whole, rather than just your ad, the argument seems fair to apply to your entire sales process. The original and current (lazy) critics of advertising, from Vance Packard to *Adbusters* magazine, probably should have been considering the entire sales process, too. When I see an ad for Harry Rosen's menswear in the newspaper or on TV, no matter how bamboozled I am by the promotion, I still need to go into the shop and interact with a suit salesman, find a garment that fits, and budget enough money to make a purchase. By rights, then, the "hidden persuaders" critics ought to be going far beyond looking at the ads. They should be following me into the store and watching as I take a follow-up sales call on my home phone six months later. By that time, though, they might have to conclude that I actually like the suit I bought and appreciate the service provided to me by this retailer, including the time the sales rep offered to drive to the airport to deliver my recently altered overcoat.

6. Jakob Nielsen, "Evangelizing Usability: Change Your Strategy at the Halfway Point," *Alertbox*, March 28, 2005, archived at useit.com.

7. B. J. Fogg, *Persuasive Technology: Using Computers to Change What We Think and Do* (Morgan Kaufmann, 2003), 149.

8. *Persuasive Technology*, 152. Fogg notes that the 2002 study was a "snapshot," conducted in collaboration with a private research lab. He is not as clear as he could be about the methodologies or sample sizes of various studies. This area cries out for more funding and more definitive, up-to-date research.

9. *Persuasive Technology*, 156.

10. *Persuasive Technology*, 168.

11. Harry Beckwith, *Selling the Invisible: A Field Guide to Modern Marketing* (Warner Books, 1997), 187.

12. Harry Beckwith, *Selling the Invisible*, 3. "Get better reality" is attributed to Guy Kawasaki. For a deep exploration of this theme, see Seth Godin, *Free Prize Inside: The Next Big Marketing Idea* (Portfolio, 2004); Seth Godin, *All Marketers Are Liars: The Power of Telling Authentic Stories in a Low-Trust World* (Portfolio, 2005).

Chapter 12

Online Targeting: Past and Present (and Maybe the Future)

In recent years, the practice of "futurism" has inspired oft-deserved derision. An IBM commercial, wherein the consultant has supplied the cantankerous CEO with "business goggles" that require the user to "put in another quarter" if he wants to see the future, comes to mind. My personal favorite is *The Simpsons'* portrayal of the Epcot Center as how "people in 1965 thought things would look in 1987."

The only phenomenon that regularly attracts as much scorn as futurism is futurism coupled with bullishness about the contributions the Internet will make to the economy. It is indeed possible to oversell the contributions made by the Internet as compared with progress in other fields. Because I don't work in those industries, I find the ability of Daimler Chrysler to use more and more robots to build cars with fewer and fewer design flaws more mind-boggling than I find a client's ability to find a customer. I'm more impressed by the huge increases in the survival rates for some types of cancer than I am in an e-commerce site's ability to sell a tooth whitening system.

But let's not underestimate the contribution of online functionality to the global economy, either. Internet models can either add layers to the economy or remove them, making it possible for a buyer to work through an intermediary or an aggregated form of information if they choose, or to gain more direct access to information related to a transaction than they might have had 20 years ago. The Internet offers a postmodern form of choice, which means we needn't feel trapped by a particular unidirectional macrotrend in any given industry (getting rid of intermediaries versus the rise of new intermediaries, for example). Increasingly, we can actually choose more or less of a given attribute (such as how "raw" or "packaged" we want information to be).

No, online innovation isn't always rocket science, but it can create cracks in old armor that eventually transform whole industries. Online stock trading precipitated huge changes in the retail securities brokerages, for example, driving commissions way down on routine transactions.

AutoInsights.ca is the online front end of a business that helps users go through a process of requesting several new-car quotes from local dealerships—real-life offers to sell specific vehicles for set prices. For those of us who know exactly what we want already, it saves us the pain of having to haggle with a salesperson to find the actual lowest amount over invoice that the dealer is willing to go. You can look at such developments any way you like. You can completely minimize their impact, or add them all up and realize that online functionality and online search are acting as catalysts for sweeping changes in many industries.

Indeed, online search has shown so much promise in terms of getting what we need more easily, more quickly, at a better price, that it's driving us to demand more of traditional businesses. Once we're empowered by the combination of online search and easy online transactions, it's tough to go back to the old ways. Recently, my wife and I drove fifteen minutes west of the city to Structube, a furniture store, to look at coffee tables and such. Having settled on a couple of bulky items, we naturally inquired about delivery. Turns out that delivery to our home would cross the border between Mississauga and Toronto, so would cost $129 instead of $49. Kind of steep for a $300 coffee table! We then entered into a lengthy discussion as to whether we should cram the items into our small car, just pay the extra money, or visit the downtown location of the store, which was in the same delivery area even though technically farther away from our home than the Mississauga location. Not pleased with the bad service, we walked away empty-handed, but we still like the coffee table and will probably wind up either visiting the downtown store (to save $80 on delivery) or borrowing a bigger vehicle to transport the item. No wonder people shop online! I already know what I want, so why can't I just click a couple of times, be informed of the delivery terms and costs, process my transaction, and be done with it? Structube's website is quite attractive, but at present you can't order from it. That's a big opportunity missed. The ability to order online would be especially welcome among repeat customers who really don't feel like going through the rigmarole of dealing with unhelpful salespeople who appear to have less product knowledge than the customers, and who have never even been to the company's website. At Structube, I had to inform the salesman that the shelving unit I was looking at was made of poplar, and that the white color wasn't accurately depicted on the company website. All news to him.

Businesses that don't get the Web—and even those that don't understand how consumers' hunger for information, transparency, and context is being driven by their ability to search online—are going to face a lot more dissatisfied customers in the coming years. Inertia can be costly.

As entrepreneurs create new ways of putting buyers and sellers together online, thousands of new business practices are emerging today that will need to be studied by economists decades hence. Revolutions in fields like high finance, where pioneers invented ways of packaging and pooling almost any financial asset or risk category to be bought and sold, have unleashed massive efficiencies on the global economy, and are duly studied. Many of the changes wrought by Internet entrepreneurs are humbler than that. But when you add them all up, some powerful math is lurking behind what seem to be modest changes in how consumers behave and how businesses interact. The improvements in our ability to communicate, target, and transact business are far reaching. Reductions in "economic friction" predicted by writers in then-avant-garde publications like *Wired* and *Business 2.0* in the mid-to-late 1990s are now coming to pass. The real challenge becomes how to manage these surges in economic productivity so that they don't consume us. Many have already arrived at the point where "always on" is more of a curse than a badge of honor.

More than the economy, these changes are about widespread access to specialized communities and freedom of information. Citizens and consumers have unprecedented access to information and sources of enlightenment that were once the province of a few. Many will not have the initiative or the educational background to take advantage of those opportunities. Someday, proponents of Internet community, Internet research, and Internet business will need to take a breath and go back over the knowledge utilization literature to remind themselves that the availability of information affects change in less-than-obvious ways, and sometimes not at all. Experts argue that rather than directly informing decisions, a growing body of evidence is often brought to bear on a specialized field over a period of years or decades and informs decisions in the background by replacing what was once thought of as common sense with a new kind of common sense.[1]

The Internet has become synonymous with sweeping economic change. And so should it be.

As you read in Chapter 2, search-centric companies like Google and Yahoo—and the pay-per-click model—have surged ahead of traditional online advertising brokers. Things may look quite different in a couple of years, but for now, the proportion of Google's revenues derived from advertising is closer to 100% than it is to, well, 95%. The world's leading search company is the world's leading online advertising vendor.

While the successes of these new leaders aren't likely to be ephemeral, it is likely that the dominance of a relatively narrow form of online advertising—Google AdWords and Overture paid search results charged "by the click"—will give way once again to a wider variety of targeting methods.

Just as email, banners, and other forms of online targeting lost ground and suffered bumps and bruises, paid search faces key challenges such as click fraud, bidding wars, and low volume. As a result, the leaders will be forced to innovate.

The exciting thing for companies like Google is that they've made a name for themselves by providing a highly efficient platform within which advertisers can manage targeted, measurable campaigns. As the search metaphor insinuates itself into various aspects of people's lives—online and off—advertisers will be able to reach more customers in more ways using an AdWords-like bidding platform. Thus your efforts to learn the ins and outs of AdWords will be applicable to future developments in marketing and advertising generally.

Google AdWords: Emerging Trends

While it's interesting to speculate on longer-term transformations in the marketing landscape, from a practical standpoint, most of us need to keep an eye on near-term developments that may affect our campaign strategy. What lies directly ahead for Google AdWords advertisers are advances in campaign management and ROI tracking.

Bid Management and Other Campaign Aids

There have been subtle shifts in Google's philosophy on providing advertisers with additional tools to manage their campaigns. In the early days of AdWords, I was told that Google believed strongly that in certain areas, especially reporting and tracking ROI, third parties were better suited to help their advertisers. Over time, this shifted to "we'll try to offer our advertisers more tools that will help them manage their campaigns in less time."

The campaign management functions that Google has already rolled out indicate that the company now has a regular process of soliciting advertiser needs and rolling out significant upgrades to the AdWords interface. For example, a recent upgrade allows advertisers to change maximum CPCs across an entire account by a certain percentage. That feature is rules based, allowing advertisers, for example, to raise all bids by 10% on any keywords whose current bids exceed (say) $1.20 (see Figure 12-1). Even this first "take" on bid management appears to be quite sophisticated, so we can probably expect Google to continue down this path, offering simple scheduling or dayparting, for example, for advertisers who want their ads to be bid lower on weekends. This may reduce your potential reliance on third-party bid management vendors, but the case can be made that third parties will always come out with interesting custom features and reports that Google doesn't care to offer.

Other recent initiatives are open to interpretation. Google has recently released a "campaign budget optimizer" (Figure 12-2) whose goal could be interpreted as helping media buyers spend their money quickly (by raising bids throughout the day if necessary) to attempt to exhaust the set daily budget. Google may be trying to increase their revenues by giving some media buyers

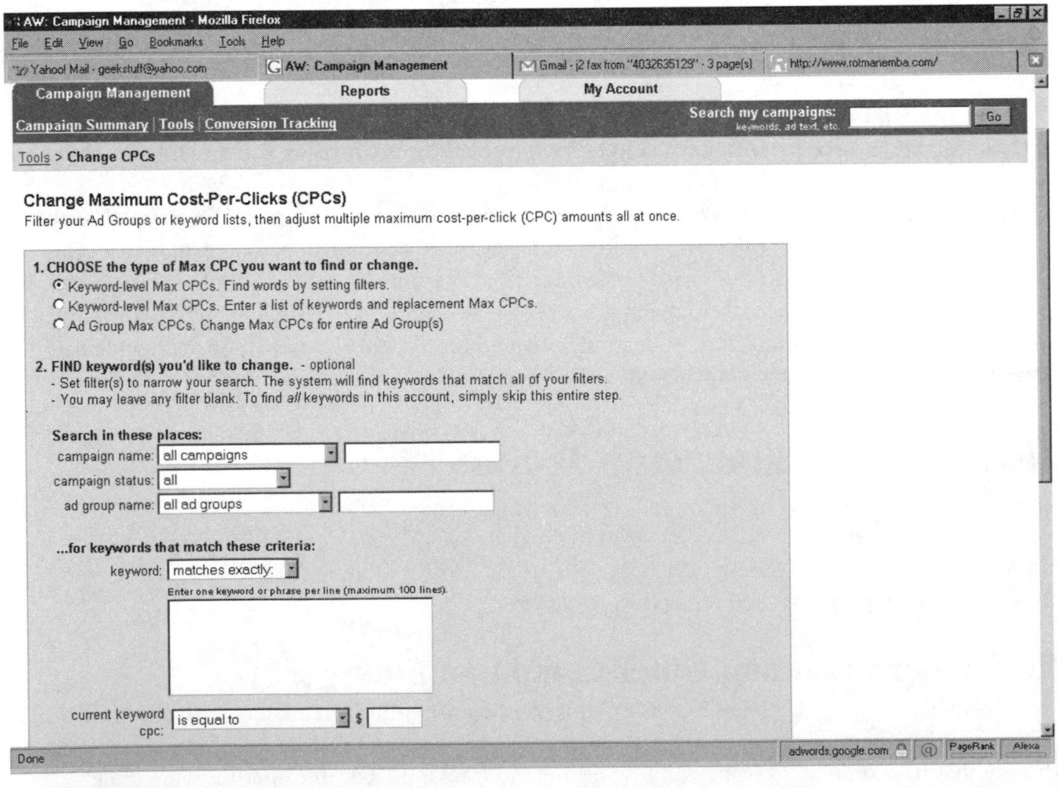

FIGURE 12-1   Google is beginning to offer basic bid management tools within the AdWords interface.

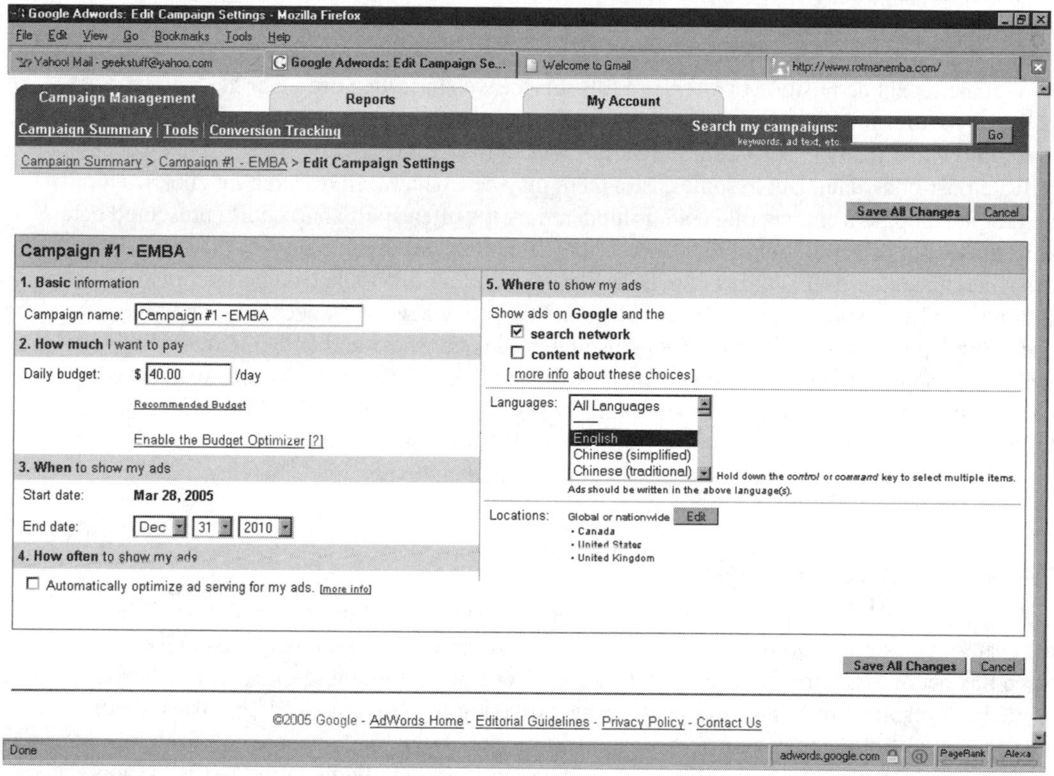

FIGURE 12-2 The Budget Optimizer (under How Much I Want to Pay) may help eager spenders "spend the budget."

the opportunity to spend quickly and perhaps foolishly. No observer of online advertising should be surprised that a company like Google is taking steps to allow "dumb big money" to spend more heavily when it has ad money to burn. What is still important to recognize is that "smart big money" and even "smart little money" still get rewarded for careful campaign management. "Dumb little money" has no chance of survival. In that regard, given the different budgets advertisers and agencies bring to the table, the system isn't purely Darwinian. Big dumb dinosaurs may roam freely for a long time. But it will still pay to be smart. Indeed, the majority of advertisers will need to be more careful than ever to avoid getting caught up in bidding wars for top positions on certain keywords at certain times of the year.

ROI Tracking

Google already offers a free conversion tracker. I'm impressed with the full level of support they provide for the product, including tutorials. The customized reporting options, for those so inclined, are also improving. You might not be aware that Google's conversion tracking will now also track your Overture campaigns! You can even use it for cross-channel tracking, including email. So if you can overlook the drawbacks to allowing Google to see into your private business data, this is a powerful and useful service.

With the recent acquisition of Urchin, a full-service web analytics firm, Google may be gearing up to offer more full-service analytics solutions to its advertisers. Time will tell. You already know that many experts believe that the cons outweigh the pros of Google having access to private post-click data. But in some cases, there may be a benefit. In researching click fraud, for example, Google's engineering team is hindered by the often spotty and poorly presented data that its advertisers can pull out of their server logs. If Google has direct access to that data (in cases where the advertiser is also using the hypothetical future full-scale Google/Urchin analytics solution), they'll be able to assess click quality, and they may have a stronger case when it comes to prosecuting, reprimanding, or otherwise punishing rogue publishers within their content network. Recall that Google's Smart Pricing on content-targeted clicks is influenced by data that Google can access from the campaigns of advertisers who have Google's free conversion tracker installed.

On the whole, Google's entry into the analytics space through the acquisition of Urchin seems likely to put downward pressure on prices for full-featured and midmarket analytics packages.

Google Projects to Watch

Since they're a primary supplier of traffic to your business, it probably wouldn't hurt to be curious about Google's future direction. For search advertisers and searchers alike, Google Search has become a primary obsession. In the parlance of advertising guru Kevin Roberts, Google both inspires love and commands respect, making it a "lovemark."[2] That isn't about to change soon. But we may gain some insight from speculating on how some of Google's various projects could affect advertisers down the road, and on how they might affect Google's competitive position in the race for online user loyalty (what were quaintly referred to as "the portal wars" back in the 1998–2001 era).

Froogle

Despite a slow start, Google's shopping engine, Froogle, appears to be an integral part of its offerings to searchers and advertisers. As with other shopping engines, retailers must upload product information through a special "feed." For now, advertisers don't pay a dime to list in Froogle. Google's competitors typically charge on a per-click basis.

Shoppers may access Froogle directly, but in addition, they're reminded of Froogle's existence when they perform a commercially oriented search, and Google suggests Froogle results by placing them at the top of a page of search results.

Froogle's availability will likely be expanded internationally. Froogle UK is already up and running. According to my sources, Google plans to launch Froogle Canada shortly. The launch has been delayed due to the time involved in convincing smaller Canadian retailers to participate in "feed management" to properly upload their product offerings to the shopping engine.

To make sure you're on shopping engines like Froogle, you may want to contact an agency that offers feed management, or investigate software that can help you automate the process. Froogle feeds can also be used to augment your AdWords keyword list. Experts who understand the ins and outs of tactics like this can be found lurking on forums like WebmasterWorld. See www.webmasterworld.com/forum96/.

Orkut

Named after Orkut Buyukkokten, the Google engineer who spearheaded its development, Orkut is a social networking site that allows friends and "friends of friends" to communicate, form groups of interest, and much more (Figure 12-3). In principle, Orkut is separate from other Google initiatives. But observers believe that the extensive personal information Orkut collects could be a big step towards Google developing a large "user base" like the one Yahoo has built. MSN Search has already begun offering its advertisers demographic targeting options based on user data available from Hotmail. Google might follow suit.

It seems likely that Google will someday offer advertisers access to deeper demographic targeting options. Projects like Orkut not only create a potential revenue stream for Google, they give Google "users," along with all that entails. Google is stealthily increasing its global footprint.

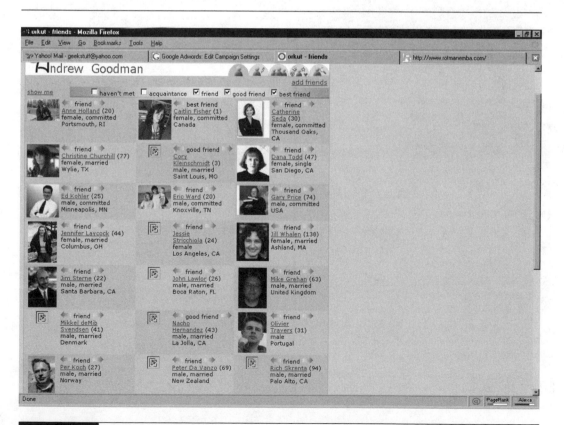

FIGURE 12-3   Whether they're using it for business or dating, Orkut users provide extensive demographic information.

Google Labs

An interesting repository of half-baked Google experiments is Google Labs (labs.google.com).
They certainly don't share everything they're working on, but it's refreshing that they do sometimes
show off "not yet ready for prime time" features.

Some of Google's most important features, such as Google Maps and Google Scholar, are
listed under Google Labs. Google continues to play the game of downplaying major initiatives
by calling them "beta" or "experimental," but no one is fooled. A lot of the "experiments" listed
under Google Labs will play a big part in the future of search.

If you're not using Google Maps yet, you should be. It works better than any of the available
mapping services. Unfortunately, the best features are restricted to North American users. Recently,
Google added a satellite mapping feature at no extra charge (Figure 12-4). Cool!

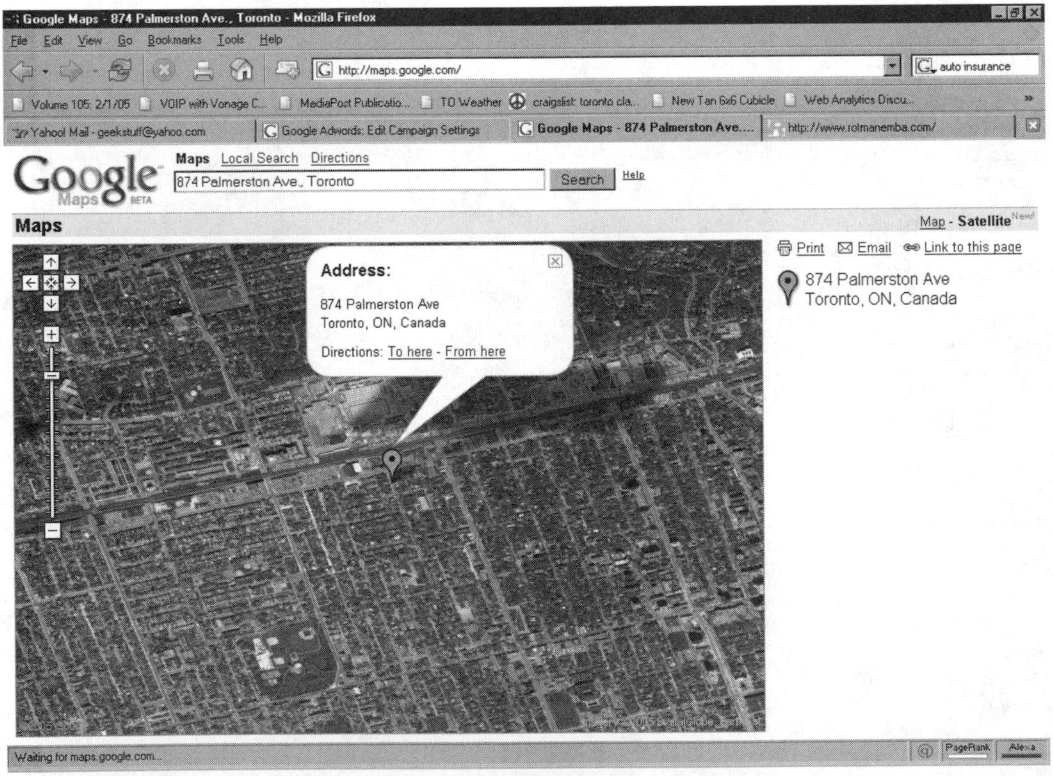

FIGURE 12-4   Want a satellite image of your neighborhood? With Google Maps powered by
recently acquired Keyhole, it's no problem.

Google Video is another avant-garde lab experiment. Based on closed-captioning transcripts, it allows users to find episodes of favorite TV shows (Figure 12-5). Down the road, Google seems likely to move quickly into the field of search and retrieval of video clips. Can you say "voice recognition"? Ample opportunities for targeted advertising exist in this realm, though it's pointless to speculate at this stage how it might work.

More concretely, though, Google Video is now testing an upload feature available to anyone who has produced video content (preferably in MPEG and MP3 formats). Publishers must be approved by the program. Videos can be labeled with keywords (metadata) to help searchers find them better. You can even set a price for users to download your video; Google will take a revenue share for connecting you with buyers. Here's a marvelous new targeting opportunity. Who knows how far Google can take this little venture. The first company to try something like this was a company called SingingFish, recently acquired by AOL. They were a bit ahead of their time. Unlike Google, which prohibits "obscene material," at first SingingFish seemed to be focusing rather heavily on the "adult" area. By and large, SingingFish suffered

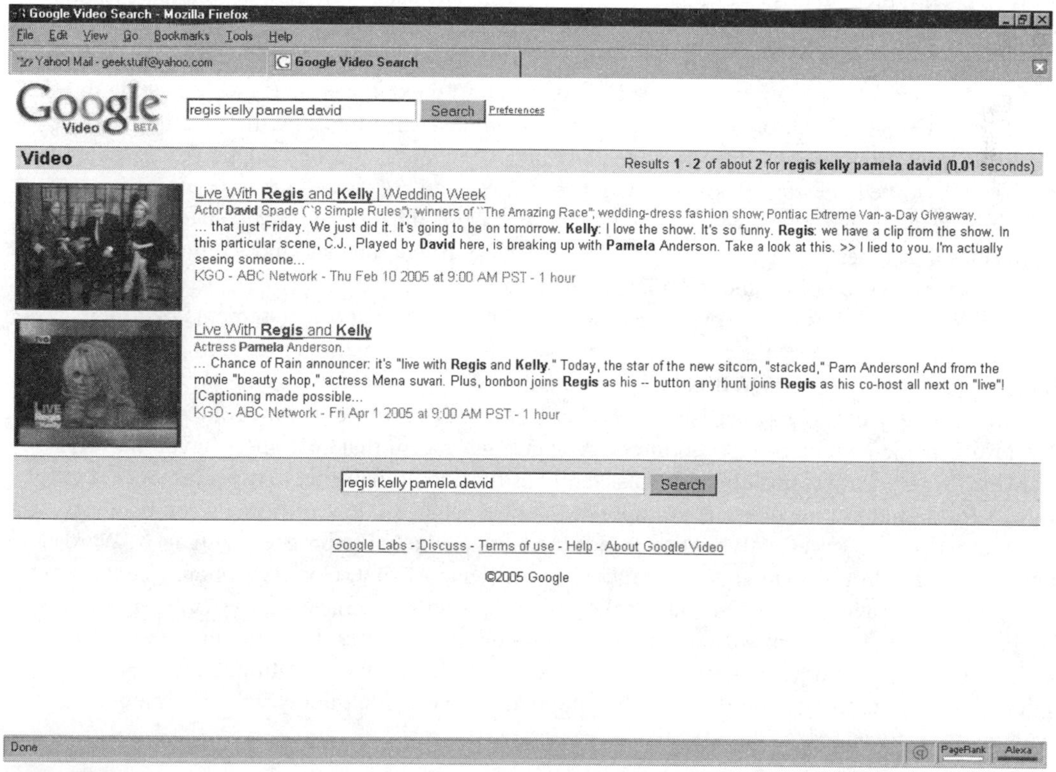

FIGURE 12-5   Google Video: what are they up to?

from a shortage of quality publishers of multimedia content, and an even more serious shortage of viewers and buyers. With Google acting as a second mover, a lack of publishers and viewers shouldn't be a problem.

I suggest that you check back into Google Labs from time to time, just to see what they're up to.

The Ecosystem: Google's Competitors and Partners

Advertisers go where the customers are. Today, Google and a couple of other companies are leading options for your online ad campaigns. To be honest, relative stability in Google's immediate ecosystem makes it easier on most of us. But that stability can't be counted on. Google's ability to compete as well as cooperate will affect your relationship with them in the coming years.

Google vs. Everybody Else

If you read the papers, you hear a lot of negative stories about any new, brash company. Google is no exception. I have often been critical of Google, but I also try to give praise when it is due, which is also often. No matter what any analyst says, the decisions taken at companies like this may often be based on careful thought processes that aren't shared with outsiders. We might misinterpret certain messages. If Google seems too cold, aloof, and "maddeningly too geeky to care about money" in some cases, it's probably because top management cares passionately about developing the next great product. Developing new mobile search applications, for example, carries with it a high degree of difficulty. Google people are laser focused on difficult tasks like this, and they seem to assume that profitability flows foremost from succeeding in developing the best product possible (even if they haven't worked out exactly how that will happen). So I do understand why the company seems downright apathetic when it comes to certain worldly matters. It isn't, but it may have a different set of priorities than other "advertising" companies, which can be confusing to those unfamiliar with how the biggest successes in Silicon Valley got that way.

Google's mantra has been "serve the user." They've made powerful statements that their focus is on the user experience even if it means not always maximizing revenue. In that regard, Google has had the foresight to build a beloved online destination with staying power.

Their relationship with advertisers and other partners has been less cozy. Like competitor Overture, Google's youth and (sometimes) arrogance has meant that customers haven't always been dealt with as professionally and consistently as they could have been, especially in the early days. A recent but not uncommon example of this was when a client of mine, a top business school at one of the largest universities in North America, wanted to proceed with an AdWords campaign, but didn't want to go the usual credit card route. At first, Google's finance department shrugged and turned them down flat for the invoicing option, suggesting the cumbersome "prepay" option. The client was so unhappy about this, we simply decided "no" wasn't an acceptable answer, and tried again. After six weeks of delay and an additional seven days of paperwork, the campaign could finally be enabled. A seven-week delay was detrimental to a campaign that was seasonal in nature.

What's supposed to be exciting about AdWords is that the system treats you with respect even if you run a niche business that only receives a handful of clicks for a high-ticket item. In the case of the business school, Google's sales, service, and finance team for a time decided they were unimpressed by this blue-chip client's "spend" and even their potential spend. Fair enough, but not every client is selling discount travel and churning through $10,000 a day. You would think that somewhere a light would go on that giving credit terms to a major business school is just, well, good business.

(To be fair, it all worked out eventually, thanks to some very helpful people who talked to other helpful people. I merely offer it as a not-uncommon example.)

I've been fortunate to deal with a wide variety of caring, conscientious individuals at Google, but they quite simply need more of those individuals. Yet the most desperate pleas for new blood (most recently, out in the open at the bottom of the Google Labs home page) seem to be for new engineering talent.

From such indications, it's hard not to conclude that Google is a search engine company in the same vein as those that came before it. The revenue stream is seen as just that: a tap that flows and keeps the lab running. Advertisers are a necessary evil. Isn't that a strange way to feel about a client base that makes up 98% of your annual revenues?

At its heart, Google remains a traditional Silicon Valley powerhouse with an engineering culture. Many of the eye-opening tales that have leaked out into the press appear to have been reported reasonably faithfully.[3] Empathy for paying advertisers can be cultivated over time, but there are questions to be asked as to whether Larry Page and Sergey Brin can foster this kind of deep empathy with consumers and partners. We know little of their management style or personal interactions with employees, but it seems erratic, introverted, and aloof by contrast with visionary leaders like Apple's Steve Jobs, or even Microsoft's Bill Gates. Yahoo's Jerry Yang long ago developed the sort of rounded edges and steadiness that has kept that company pointing in the right direction. None of these billionaires needs to go into work every day, so their motivations must come from somewhere—either the internal drive to dominate a market or external feedback from customers and partners.

Google is arguably just far less seasoned than its key competitors, so it hasn't developed a good feel for the complexity of its environment. At this stage the company still seems slightly bemused by external forces other than end users, which it understands well. The willingness to take the suggestions of random anonymous message board posters as seriously as long-standing clients, for example, was endearing at first. But lately, the act has been getting old. The traditional advertising business always recognized that clients are people with names and faces that you remember and keep tabs on. Google isn't somehow immune from that reality.

Can the paradox persist? Google as one of the world's leading brands, yet their leaders remaining so enigmatic? Whatever might happen, we know that Larry Page, Sergey Brin, and Eric Schmidt are likely to remain firmly in control. In spite of the appearance of a democratic culture, power at Google is concentrated in the upper ranks, a state of affairs sealed by a dual share structure that gives ordinary shareholders little control over the company's direction.

Top management and investors in more traditional firms likely would have blanched at some of Google's experiments. Aspects of the initial public offering and other aspects of Google's relationships with economic power structures have been treated as more opportunities for innovation. Some, me included, feel that a company like Google can make important contributions by challenging conventions in areas like investment banking. But when every area of the company's operations, including billing and clickthrough reporting, seem to be treated as "cool hacks" rather than mission-critical bedrocks of client relations, it's not hard to imagine future crises of confidence if and when tales of the most gravity-defying inventions leak out.

The sky probably isn't falling, though. In the few minutes it took to write this section, I instinctively searched for background material using, you guessed it, Google Search. Carolyn came into the room and reported, per her search on Google News, that a Toronto transit strike was averted at the 11th hour.[4] A prospective client's request for a quote came through to my Gmail account. Google is entrenched in people's daily lives, and that's probably what counts most.

Amazon and eBay

Amazon and eBay are the two largest e-commerce companies in the world. Unsurprisingly, their fortunes are deeply intertwined with Google's.

eBay advertises heavily on Google, both directly and indirectly through affiliates. But it also competes with Google, and future product development by both companies threatens to create even hotter competition. Take online classifieds. eBay has bought a 25% stake in popular classifieds site Craigslist and has also created Kijiji, its own international local classifieds service that it plans to roll out in a variety of markets. Google has high hopes to become the world leader in local search listings. In that regard, any company hoping to move into the local classifieds arena is bound to find themselves on a collision course with Google. In studying the success of such competitors in addition to keeping close tabs on the user response to Google's rapidly evolving local platform, Google may be well equipped to design new listings services and features that take a bite out of traditional media companies' revenues, as well as those of its direct online competitors like eBay. Google has thus far only taken baby steps into the "look directly for ad listings" arena, with a link that sometimes appears at the bottom of AdWords results that says "see all sponsored listings." If they take this concept and run with it, look out. In June 2005, Google acknowledged that it was working toward two new offerings: a payment processing service, and a new classified listings service. The latter certainly competes with eBay's core business. Eric Schmidt denied that the payment processing service would compete directly with eBay's PayPal division, but that depends on how you define "directly."

eBay versus Google seems to be a moderately competitive relationship. But for now, both sides have more reasons to work for one another than they do to work against one another.

One interesting potential catalyst may be television. Who makes the strongest leap to TV to cement their brand? Thinking of the popularity of shopping channels and infomercials, if eBay develops a popular channel (or several) that caters to the home shopping crowd, for example, or some kind of modified TV pitch concept that offers a certain degree of interactivity, they could head off potential threats by becoming increasingly ubiquitous. Google, MSN, and Yahoo will, of course, be considering how to do something similar. It is quite possible that all can coexist.

Amazon and Google appear to have a strong relationship. Even here, though, both have launched initiatives that could threaten one another.

Google Print (Figure 12-6) is a fascinating new repository for digital documents. Anyone may submit their copyright material to be archived in Google Print. Combine this with a new payment processing technology, and it's not a huge stretch to imagine a world in which Google goes into the "book business."

Amazon has some of the most sophisticated search technology in the world. It uses this to help users navigate its site and to find related products. But with the recent release of the A9 search engine, Amazon is also showcasing its search expertise for a general audience. Users have not embraced A9, however. Its market share is insignificant.

Reading these particular tea leaves, I don't sense much animosity between these two companies. It seems most likely that both will keep a hands-off attitude towards any initiative that would seriously threaten the other. They currently have many interests in common. Google AdWords derives revenues from Amazon Associates affiliate advertisers who run ads promoting products and books on Amazon. Since affiliates take the risk of running the ads, Amazon gets free referrals for nothing. Google Search also ranks many Amazon.com pages well for free. Both companies derive ad revenue by showing AdWords ads on many pages throughout the Amazon site and

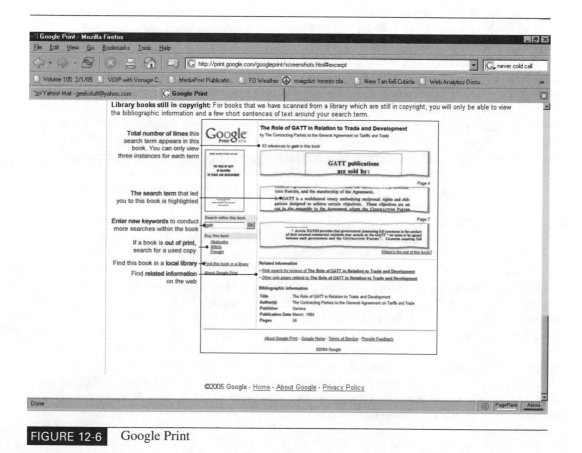

FIGURE 12-6   Google Print

on Amazon-owned Alexa.com. Finally, A9 doesn't really compete with Google Search, so informally it could become a way for Google to run lab tests of new search features without arousing the same degree of interest from competitors or the press as they would if they ran the same tests themselves. Google versus Amazon seems to be more a story of cooperation than competition, then.

Portal Wars: AOL, Yahoo, MSN, IAC

Google's closest competitor is Yahoo. They compete as the top two players in paid search, of course. They also hold down the top two spots in terms of search market share, which isn't unrelated to their positions as leaders in revenue derived from search. Increasingly, though, as Google attempts to "take over the world," they compete with Yahoo on many fronts, as portals that want to attract as many users as possible to their brand and their network of online services. Predicting where things will wind up or where the new hot product category or feature will take us is difficult, but it seems clear that due to the presence of the other, neither company can get too comfortable.

In a category like online email, Google entered the space boldly and continues to give Yahoo fits by offering more features and more storage. Advantage? Slight advantage to Yahoo, as the incumbent that still has a product that integrates well with calendars, address books, and personalized home pages. But Gmail has the cool factor and is coming hard.

In desktop search, Google seems to have grabbed user attention. The product is best in category and installs easily, making slow, inefficient Windows desktop searches a thing of the past. Yahoo and several other companies have released similar products, but none are getting the same attention as Google's.

Google Groups 2 is a direct competitor to Yahoo Groups, a flexible discussion platform that allows users to interact online or through email. The pace of Google Groups 2's development has been slow, however. Yahoo Groups seems to be well ahead of Google's offering, and Google seems to be making little effort to close the gap. That could be because both companies are thinking more along the lines of next-generation services that supersede these groups' offerings.

Because both companies now own related "sharing and communicating" services—Google with Blogger and Picasa, Yahoo with Flickr, 360, and more—it seems likely that they'll continue to release new versions of their various disparate services, possibly knitting some of them together to make them more useful. Keeping up with all the developments is tough.

In industry shorthand—and if you asked them it would be confirmed by the CEOs of the two companies—Google is a technology company and Yahoo is a lifestyle company. Google CEO Eric Schmidt led two major technology companies before taking the Google post; Terry Semel reportedly didn't even use email before taking the digital helm at Yahoo. The latter company has done a great job of seizing market opportunities in everyday areas like personals. Google has made its mark by releasing products that work better, faster, cooler. Both make money, both are loaded with technical talent and growing sales forces. There is no reason why these two can't coexist.

Ultimately, despite all the background noise of new features, hacks, and promotions, observers of the search scene will want to know which company is leading in terms of paid search revenue and in terms of search usage. And that's where Google, for now, seems likely to hang onto its lead.

Recently, Yahoo introduced a special new feature that offers free template websites for small businesses, linked to its Yahoo Local product. That should be a great way for small business to gain local customers. It might even be said that Yahoo is working harder to understand the needs of small business than Google is. But ultimately, the significance of providing better service and options for listings and placements is overridden by the importance of search market share. Both Yahoo and Google are on the cutting edge of local search, and both are viable new promotional options for smaller businesses seeking customers. For advertisers, though, what matters most in the end is which local search service users wind up choosing. Both companies are in a position to hook local search users in two ways: through continued product development, and through acquisitions of growth companies in the local search area.

News search is a hot category,[5] though I'm not sure anyone understands precisely how to make money from it. You can show advertising on "content," but figuring out the exact dollars and cents is anyone's guess in a world where so much is changing. Google's highly popular Google News service seems to be another way of extending Google's brand as a search leader, but they don't directly draw ad revenues from it, and users are quickly sent away to the sites of news publishers. Insofar as many of those sites are AdSense publishers, Google does indirectly earn revenue from "sending users away" in this manner. Neat trick.

Most of what can be said about the rivalry between Google and Yahoo applies to Google versus MSN as well. MSN has strong search products, marketing muscle, an entrenched email brand, and of course the support of the leading browser and operating system. The acute threat that Microsoft's continued dominance of the user's computing platform poses to competitors like Google suggests that Google may indeed feel the need to continue working on a competing browser to Internet Explorer. Or perhaps Google will simply continue to be merely "supportive" of the increasingly popular Mozilla Firefox browser. Who knows, maybe Google is actually working on a new computer system or operating system. It's fun to speculate on what a Google-Apple merger might bring.

The logic of Google-powered rivalries "in search and all things" applies less so to slowly fading, but still steady, AOL, and even less so to Interactive Corp. (IAC), which has recently acquired Ask Jeeves and seems worthy of consideration for the ominous crown of "fifth-place portal." (Fifth portals have never fared too well, as increasingly irrelevant Lycos, and now-defunct Excite, can attest.) IAC has mostly made itself an annoyance by acquiring Ask Jeeves, a property which, along with IAC-owned CitySearch, might have been a useful acquisition for one of the leaders. Pieces of IAC may well be parceled up and sold to one of these rivals if the price is right.

Think Small to Get Big: What Search Marketing Will Look Like in 2010

Throughout this book, I've emphasized the features of search marketing that give businesses of all sizes unprecedented access to niche markets. Large businesses will need to adapt to think more about micromarkets. This is a trend they've been following anyway. The number of products and choices has exploded in most industries over the past 30 years. In that respect, search marketing has blossomed in tandem with the postmodern global economy. Increasingly, consumers and businesses want products, services, and information to be available on demand. Conducting a search is the quintessential form of expression of such increasingly impatient demands.

As large businesses adapt—sometimes too slowly—to emerging demands, small growth businesses can get big fast. Many will grow faster than their ability to manage that growth.

Today, most of us think of a search in terms of a fairly consistent practice: typing keywords into a box, using a search engine site like Google.com, within an operating system like Windows or Macintosh, on a browser like Internet Explorer or Mozilla Firefox.

Of course the present-day reality isn't that narrow. Many consumers are becoming adept at shopping search, news search, local search, and other forms of specialized searching. Some install toolbars in their browsers. A few are searching on mobile devices, or even reading commands into their cell phones, getting information from voice-recognition services provided by companies like Google. Luxury cars now come with navigation systems. Within ten years, nearly all new vehicles are likely to come with sophisticated local search capabilities.

The availability of new forms of targeting will give advertisers new access to a variety of new forms of "searcher" behavior. Don't be too restrictive in your definition of a searcher. It's unlikely that the next generation of searchers will restrict themselves to the forms of information retrieval that are most recognizable to us today.

The Revolution in Media Buying

I've argued in this book that the automated advertising auction systems developed by Overture and Google put significant pressure on online media buying. Yet traditional media buying has yet to be revolutionized. As AdWords-like methods spill over into offline advertising buys, advertisers will likely be able to bid on a variety of targeting options in late-night cable TV, product placements, billboards, newspaper ads, and more. This will change some of the skill sets required of those in the advertising business, but it will likely benefit both publishers and advertisers. Just as Google Search can monetize less desirable ad inventory by making it available at sell-off prices, offline advertisers might benefit from an automated system that created more bidding wars on (let's say) desirable billboard locations, while allowing them to command at least some minimum amount for less desirable properties. Advertisers could simply log on and bid for the inventory they desired, provided of course that they had already fed in their graphics and were a trusted paid-up member of some sort of ad buying program.

As I write this, Google is launching some new targeting options that make it clear they're bent on expanding their role in the world of online advertising. The pricing on content targeting ads has been changed effective May 2005 to a CPM (cost-per-thousand-impressions) model. Google has also decided to allow animated graphical ads in the content program. Finally, the flexibility of the targeting is improving. Advertisers will have the option to target their ad to specific websites (such as www.nytimes.com) subject to a maximum CPM bid, rather than being purely at the mercy of Google's matching technology that up until now has decided which pages (not sites) make the best match for your ads. And the AdWords interface will offer suggested lists of related websites so advertisers can decide whether to include those in their campaign as well. This development doesn't affect the search side of AdWords at all, and not all advertisers will make heavy use of the advanced content targeting features. But it is an example of how Google's approach to targeting is constantly evolving to meet the needs of different types of advertisers. Traditional media buyers at interactive agencies may be particularly impressed with this new offering.

Tying into the growth of targeting and bidding in all types of advertising is the need for advertisers to measure response more effectively. As more is known about the ROI on various pieces of campaigns, we'll see shifts in ad pricing.

High Mobility, Personal Devices

We now move into an era of Internet access that is both converged and mobile. Much of the talk of not-yet-realized "media convergence" over the past ten years has revolved around the future convergence of television and the Internet.

In the meantime, the explosion of new mobile phone technologies, email-enabled devices such as the BlackBerry and other advanced PDAs, and new ways of wirelessly accessing the Internet, such as Wi-Fi, has put a new spin on what convergence might do for us on a practical level. VOIP telephony has reduced costs for basic phone service and may continue to create disruptions for formerly comfortable telecommunications devices. Another mobile phenomenon, the increasing power of music storage devices like Apple's iPod, opens our eyes to the implications of advances in ergonomic design, massive increases in computing power, and unprecedented mobile access to digital content.

Brands like Apple, Google, Microsoft, and Yahoo will compete for status as indispensable information providers and platform owners not just in your living room, but wherever you may be. Some of what they develop will not be as partners of traditional phone or cable monopolies, but as owners of entirely new systems. Sooner than you think, Google or Apple could literally become your new phone company. Yahoo recently acquired VOIP telephony company DialPad, and speculation is rampant that a fast-growing player in free Internet-based telephony, Skype, could be snapped up by Google or Microsoft.

This potential to control future communications channels may explain why the stocks of companies like Google trade at what seem to be unrealistically high multiples.

A Transparent World

As the search metaphor bleeds into other realms, particularly into the commercial realm, consumers will grow increasingly impatient with artificial impediments to enlightenment.

I used to think it was normal not to know where to find a particular item in a supermarket. Now, it makes me impatient. I think a supermarket should act like a search engine. Before too long, many of them will.

Before the last round of the 2005 Masters golf tournament, commentators on the Golf Channel sat around the table responding to a deluge of emails on the subject of why no televised coverage was available of "leftover" Sunday morning play from the rain-delayed third round. These defenders of the status quo sided with the powers that be at CBS, making it clear that "full 18-hole coverage" means coverage of the leaders only, and plenty of gaps in coverage of players a bit farther behind in the pack. Since the leaders had not completed their Saturday round due to poor weather earlier in the tournament, they played as many as nine holes of their third round on Sunday morning before the fourth and final round began. CBS golf analyst Peter Oosterhuis—who, according to his bio, led the 1984 PGA tour in sand saves—told the Golf Channel team that "it's simply not possible to show every hole of every tournament." Yet viewers were obviously dismayed by the fact that they didn't have the chance to view live coverage of Tiger Woods overtaking Chris DiMarco for the Masters lead on Sunday morning. That morning, Woods turned a five-shot deficit into a three-shot lead on the strength of a record-tying charge of seven consecutive birdies. This was hardly "every hole of every tournament." It was the sort of drama golf fans spend all year waiting for, and years reminiscing about—if they get to watch it live, that is.[6]

In the short term, it's no doubt true that neither the Augusta National club, nor a network like CBS, nor cable networks, will bend over backwards to address logistical problems that result in disappointed viewers. In that sense, it will continue to be "impossible" to watch what they find inconvenient to show us. But to hear that making such adjustments is impossible rings hollow in this day and age. Just a few days before, after all, I'd been able to access a satellite photo of my street using Google Maps, absolutely free of charge. In a context where information and images of all types seem readily available on demand, expectations go up accordingly.

Augusta National is a private club, and the networks remain powerful organizations that have every intention of playing by Augusta's rules. That rules out, say, placing low-cost cameras in various spots around the course, or placing small cameras around the necks of caddies and various patrons so that enthusiasts could access coverage of any shot of any player in the final round of the tournament. But the principle here is that it's less and less credible to claim that information and digital content are impossible to access. For better or for worse, in a full-disclosure world, you really cannot hide. And you come off looking silly and defensive when you try to.[7]

The New Geography

My maternal grandparents, and their parents before them, lived and worked on a farm near Seaforth, Ontario. In such tight-knit communities, especially for those who were lucky enough to live off the land in a fertile region, life was comfortable. A restricted set of choices were part and parcel of this relative prosperity, though. Banks, suppliers, and distributors could dictate the terms of doing business. Searching for different options meant nothing less than packing up lock, stock, and barrel and moving somewhere else. Business was transacted in places like Wingham, Blyth, Monkton, Goderich, and Mitchell, no more than 20 miles from home. It was an hour's drive to the largest city in the region, London. They'd get there about once a year.

Life in farm country has changed fairly dramatically in spite of outward appearances. With the advent of e-commerce and online search, farmers do have the ability to compare banks, insurance companies, and other financial services. There is growing use of computer technology to monitor crops and animals. Families can investigate options for their children's postsecondary education years in advance. The small, cash-based craft businesses or bed-and-breakfast operations that many rural residents run on the side, or as retirement projects, can be widely publicized online at low cost. Some will dabble in eBay transactions, making a few dollars here or there. Others will hit a rich vein of market demand and find themselves facing the challenge of running a growing business.

My parents and I have lived in a variety of urban and suburban settings, much different from life on the farm. Even though we're only 24 years apart in age, my work habits—and, perhaps, whole concept of professional geographic reach—are already considerably different from my dad's. For a significant proportion of his life, he was fortunate enough to walk to his office only a few blocks away. His bailiwick, Burlington, Ontario, was local by definition. (Since my father is an urban planner by profession, though, it would be bad news if I were to write here that he didn't have an advanced grasp of shifting concepts of work and geography!) He had the opportunity to travel to professional conferences in various North American cities, but it was nothing like the frequent airline travel of today's business road warriors.

Until recently, after a long stint in graduate school got me used to the habit, I worked solely from home, while reaching a global audience of clients and professional contacts. (This flowed nicely from the precedent set in universities, where professors and graduate students were some of the first people to use email to communicate systematically and cheaply, and sometimes eloquently, with global colleagues. The main reason for this is that until the early 1990s, few outside of government, military, and university circles had free access to email.) Now, I divide time between home and a downtown office, and even that temporary reality feels like it could change as technology and tastes evolve. The office itself is different from traditional offices insofar as wireless technology (and the probability that many of us will do work from home or while traveling) has made it less necessary to set up desktop computers for every employee. This office, like many others in Toronto's downtown west area, is dominated by knowledge work that carries a light physical footprint. We chose the 1920's art deco building as much for its ceremony as for its functionality. We liked the psychological effects of natural light, a vibrant business and arts community, and proximity to public transit, among other things. (The photo of the place posted on our website will also boost our web credibility. A sense of place is doubly important to prospects who are looking for assurances that someone solid will be handling their account.) Unlike my grandparents' farm (or my other grandfather's machine shop), the business we do could theoretically be transacted anywhere. It feels like we had a choice.

The choices people have mean that talent does seem to gravitate towards certain kinds of cities today. In the old days, factories and buildings seemed to hire people. Today, a lot more workers choose a lifestyle, then find a job. That has translated into growth for wired fresh-air locales such as Bend, Oregon, and Victoria, British Columbia. It's also meant a concentration of high-tech talent in places that have the best restaurants, neighborhoods, and culture.[8]

Granted, it's probably an advantage for a high-tech business to locate in a high-tech hub such as Silicon Valley or Waterloo, Ontario, which can seem limiting. But at any given moment, new work styles are being tried all over the place. Geographically dispersed project teams are experimenting with new ways of getting more done using collaboration tools. Employees of utility companies are handling billing using wireless remote devices that give them on-the-go access to customer data. One corporate executive I recently read about decided to take a job at a high-tech firm in New Brunswick without relocating his family from Tennessee. He drives to the head office, works two or three long days in New Brunswick as needed, and spends the rest of his time with family. The new economy makes such choices possible. My grandparents wouldn't know what to make of it. They only left the farm for more than a day three or four times in their entire lives. Once, to Ottawa, to visit my family, and two or three times to Toronto, for business and pleasure. They probably wouldn't have gone far if given the choice to go anywhere or do anything they wanted, because choice can be paralyzing. Today's knowledge worker needs to be comfortable with this bewildering freedom to choose.

Another habit I've picked up is that I work late. Not as bad as some hackers and scribblers who still can't kick the 4 A.M. habit, but pretty different from my ancestors who had to get up to milk the cows. How rampant odd hours are is anyone's guess, but gauging from the habits of clients and colleagues, it's not easy to pin down when someone is available. And more often than not, it's important to get to know someone well enough to understand when they'll be groggy and out-of-sorts on the phone, and when they'll be primed for a productive meeting. For those uncomfortable with 9–5, the flexibility of working life today offers a variety of devices and excuses for behavior that might have been written off as bizarre 20 years ago. But by adjusting to different work styles, progressive companies might well be fostering a significant increase in productivity.

All in all, businesspeople today need to take a flexible approach to their concept of geography. When one's geographic focus broadens, one also becomes accustomed to a shifting concept of time, yet another development that presents both an opportunity and a burden to knowledge workers. I'm not here to argue that no one relies on local communities anymore or that no one punches a clock; in many cases, the ability to dominate a local market is a great advantage, and work schedules are more flexible for skilled freelancers and those in senior positions. But growth companies today will do well to re-evaluate preconceived notions of where or how employees should work, or where their best customers and best suppliers are likely to be located.

Business Is Global

Google is a great example of a company that operates globally and that facilitates the efforts of customers who want to operate globally. It's perhaps trite to say it, but your company is going to find it imperative to explore international opportunities in the coming years. From the standpoint of AdWords, targeting searchers anywhere in the world is relatively easy. The flip side of that growth potential is that many businesses are not ready for it. A sales presentation for an Asian audience might require more than just verbal translation, for example. It might require credible imagery of local customers and other relevant cultural references.

Business Is Local

Meanwhile, millions of businesses just want to operate in a single locale, or in a few cities. If you were to travel ahead five years, I think you'd be amazed at how many new ways you'd have to access information about local businesses. People's habits will change, gradually at first, but eventually radically. The supposed decline of flesh-and-blood interaction is the supposed drawback of online culture. That myth will be turned upside down. Store clerks who mumble and condescend will be treated with increasing degrees of contempt from device-wielding information junkies. The visitor to Ikea will be able to access all sorts of comparative information while right in the store, including user reviews of the products.

On the way to some of this advanced functionality, niche players who find a middle ground, providing relatively uncomplicated means of connecting customers with vendors, will thrive.

Craigslist today is a simple, friendly online classifieds site that has enough following in several cities that users feel a sense of community and see enough listings that they keep coming back. Want a funky office space to sublet? Need a ride? That's the type of thing you can get on Craigslist. This should probably be called Local Commerce 1.0. By the time we hit 3.0, we'll wonder what we did without it.

Niche directory providers will increasingly beat traditional offline listings services, classifieds, and general online directories at their game by being relentlessly focused and sales oriented. Professionals and small businesses will get so many quality, detailed referrals from such sites that they will continue to advertise on them. Breeders.net is one example among thousands of interesting ones out there today. The site connects Canadians with reputable dog breeders in their area.

Considerable wealth has been amassed by the publishers of modest offline classified publications such as Auto Trader and The Buy and Sell Newspaper. When similar principles are applied more widely by more online entrepreneurs, the increase in economic productivity will be significant, and that next generation of "classifieds entrepreneurs" stand to become an order of magnitude or two wealthier than the previous generation.

Work Is Decentralized

Shortly after I began my personal strange journey towards an Internet marketing career, friends and relatives began asking in an accusatory-sounding way: "Do you actually *know* any of these people? Have you met them face-to-face, I mean?" By now, I've met a lot of "these people"—from my Traffick.com cofounder Cory Kleinschmidt, to various competitors, to clients and readers, to famous web superstars like Danny Sullivan, Larry Chase, and Jakob Nielsen—face-to-face. It makes a difference, of course. But it's always been a funny question to me. Subscribers and clients are not clustered politely in an easy-to-tour set of road stops like Toronto, the Bay Area, New York, and Chicago. My U.S.-based clients and readers have come from every state and every area code. To "know" them all by flying out to meet them would be one heck of a bad economic proposition for all of us, though the airlines would love it. Fortunately, as more online marketers have begun taking this field seriously enough to get out and mingle at various trade shows, we get the opportunity to speak, listen, and have a coffee with just about anyone who counts, including folks we work with remotely.

Online relationships are odd things, but they're real, as real as any nontraditional work pattern. In other words, they're real, but different.

The *wheres* and *hows* of people's work are influenced by a range of factors. Urban geographers and armchair planners debate theories about the rejuvenation of downtown areas, the overlooked diversity of the suburbs, the decline of "inner suburbs," the rise of "edge cities" and "exurbs" as upscale business hubs, and more.[8] Many professionals are able to arrange their work to suit their lifestyles or to satisfy family obligations. Globalization aside, many companies shift the distribution of work to new locations based on new economic calculations and convenience. This has always happened to some extent, but what seems new is the blurring of lines between urban, suburban, and rural locales. Old metaphors like "fly-over states" need to die soon. They're meaningful only to certain elites—mostly, it seems, broadcast journalists in two or three major cities.

For our purposes, the overarching theme, and one that tends to embolden those who have shed traditional work patterns (be it a 9–5 schedule, a time-consuming commute, or a traditional mecca for any given industry), is that you can make a fortune (or simply hold down a steady, rewarding gig) from just about anywhere. No one will ever dispute the fact that face-to-face contact is vital in many fields. Indeed, increased prosperity for many free agents and entrepreneurs translates into a heavy travel schedule. But today's enterprise, and today's worker, often demands more flexibility than ever before.

The ability to work on projects with decentralized work teams or to buy an antique milk pitcher from a vendor in Albuquerque are apparent upsides to the new economy, but the downside may be the difficulty of "reading" people from afar. The forces that drive us to the comfort of our own lifestyles and our own work patterns, and that allow us to transact business with total strangers, may have unintended consequences. True trust-building in the form of face time becomes a relative rarity. Indeed, as long as such trends bewilder those uncomfortable with change, we'll hear endless stories in the mainstream press about online dating scams, credit card fraud, spam gangs from Korea, and of course personality disorders caused by spending too much time staring at a screen. (All caused by the evil Internet, of course!) I don't mind such tales. I'd rather my efforts to forge into uncharted territory be relatively uncluttered by weak-kneed types.

In any case, there are some real drawbacks to the impersonality and accelerated pace of work that may be fostered by a decentralized, always-on economy. Companies, workers, free agents, buyers, and sellers (with the possible exception of Michael Dell and Bill Gates) will need to take extra steps to cement their credibility, preserve their sanity, and to forge alliances in the offline world. Perhaps the rise of online business networking is a response to feelings of disintegration brought on by the fast pace of economic change and the decline of traditional organizations, public or private. Whatever you do, stay as connected as possible, online and off. And it goes without saying, never be dismissive of any businessperson, no matter what their area code.

Discussion Groups for AdWords Addicts

You may find the following communities useful for discussion and networking on the topic of Google AdWords and related areas:

- SEM 2.0, a not-for-profit discussion group for search engine marketers that I created and currently administer on the Google Groups 2 platform:

  http://groups-beta.google.com/group/SEM2

- Webmaster World, a Google AdWords forum, privately owned by Brett Tabke:

  http://www.webmasterworld.com/forum81/

- Search Engine Watch forum, a Google AdWords forum, privately owned by Jupitermedia, led by Danny Sullivan, and administered by Elisabeth Osmeloski.

  http://forums.searchenginewatch.com/forumdisplay.php?f=31

Communications + Mobility = Productivity

Investment in information technology over the past 30 years has reduced the costs of doing business, sometimes dramatically. As forms of information retrieval and communication (like search and email) get cheaper and cheaper to operate, the cost to start up a new business falls. The cost to find and retain customers, the cost of searching for employees, the cost of running a wireless LAN, all of these can potentially drop to the point of near insignificance as compared with outmoded methods. As this occurs, the balance of power shifts. Many traditional monopolists lose their hold over entrepreneurs. But new power brokers will emerge.

Google is one of those power brokers. You don't really get to choose how history unfolds. Which types of companies become powerful (new media companies, say) and which lose their power (downtown office tower developers and local phone service providers, for example) is completely out of your hands and mine. But it can be fun to watch some traditional monopolies topple. Even more fun can be attempting to benefit from the new environment by exploiting new niches quickly and avoiding the same old ruts that used to force businesses to devote outsized amounts of their capital to basic infrastructure.

Conclusion: What about Peanut Butter?

At age four, I began a love affair with peanut butter that carries on to this day. Fairly early on, I discovered that I liked crunchy better than smooth. I also found that adding process cheese slices to my peanut butter on toast horrified adults and tasted pretty good to boot. I credit the constant flow of protein with helping me get decent grades in high school while coming at least third in several regional cross-country ski races. (Unfortunately, I also liked potato chips, which, along with too much joke telling and book reading, got me bounced from the team.) I later upped the ante by adding dill pickles to the peanut-butter-and-cheese recipe. But there's more to the story, much more.

What kind of relationship do you have with peanut butter? If you're young or relatively affluent, chances are you know a bit about what's "good" for you and what's "bad."

Growing up, we didn't know anything. Peanut butter came with hydrogenated vegetable oil and plenty of salt and sugar, and that was that. Weird professors' children ate that natural stuff and drank skim milk from powder. We just assumed it was because they were poor. I consumed brands like Kraft and Squirrel, and some store brands.

In the 1980s, I was introduced to Skippy. "Super Chunk" was surely sublime. It was also loaded with the same old hydrogenated vegetable oil. And icing sugar. Icing sugar!

For the past ten years or so, I've been on relatively high moral and nutritional ground... or so I thought. I've been eating nothing but store-label "natural" peanut butter. Because I thought this was healthy (no hydrogenated oil, no sugar), I ate a lot of it... until I began to hear rumors that peanuts are loaded with pesticides. I began paying far too much for tiny jars of organic peanut butter, until further Internet research convinced me that regular natural peanut butter is perfectly fine and subject to regular government testing.

You see a lot of rumors flying around and little in the way of solid facts. Sites like peanutbutterlovers.com are actually run by peanut farmers' marketing boards. The state of information on peanut butter does seem to be relatively undeveloped. It has been a long time since anyone as great as George Washington Carver has turned his attention to the peanut.

What we have here, I believe, is merely one example of an emerging market demand: a demand for better, healthier, more interesting peanut butter, and preferably not in a tiny overpriced jar.[9] It's a relative micromarket for now, but it could be a lucrative one. (Think pinot noir, zinfandel, syrah, or some other once-obscure wine variety.) It's a demand, moreover, that some large companies have had an interest in resisting. But the tide is turning.

At this stage of his online research, the peanut butter connoisseur feels himself hitting a wall. Sure, he's a bit more educated about the gooey brown paste than he was a year ago. But he doesn't have access to a wide product selection. He doesn't have access to discussions and debates about peanut butter. There are no clubs. No tastings to attend. Few if any awards to be won. No Hollywood blockbusters about yuppies making their way through "peanut country." But we'll have our day sooner than you think.

> *Fact: Even natural peanut butter will keep for two to three months without being refrigerated. But it does need to be kept in a relatively cool, dry place. If you put your peanut butter in a wine fridge to ensure that you get the temperature just right, you're well on your way to yuppie peanut butter connoisseur status.*

While the big brands do market studies and busy themselves trying to control shelf space and spend millions on solidifying their brands, someone will begin shipping a new variety of organic, crunchy peanut butter directly to the consumer. (Of course, it's already happened, but it hasn't reached the tipping point required for full-on peanutbuttermania.) Someone else, be it a small local organic food retailer or the Whole Foods Market, will begin to see the light on how they could promote their peanut butter selection through local search, driving floor traffic from that single item and perhaps gaining an educated, long-term customer for their whole selection of organic foods.

> *Fact: Several large brands now offer natural peanut butter. One has even attempted product differentiation with a product straight out of the R&D lab: natural peanut butter that does not undergo oil separation, thus doesn't need to be stirred.*

Soon, as the availability of both alternative products and alternative information grows, communities will form. The first serious peanut butter blog will be launched. FAQs and other resources will support the further development of peanut butter culture. Do-it-yourselfers will begin clamoring for newer, better peanut-butter-making paraphernalia. PB&J sandwiches, popular in an ironic sort of way at college refectories, will make their way into certain food outlets, even at airports. Much like Starbucks or Seattle's Best, some retailer will develop its own unusual way of over-roasting the peanuts and a new way of serving the PB&J sandwich, perhaps on a huge piece of toasted pumpernickel based on a family recipe. The "combo" would come with a glass of milk.

Peanut butter on fries, sometimes served with cheese curds, will become a popular dish in Quebec.

Emerging market demands are always interesting to watch unfold. Big companies and small companies alike are becoming increasingly adept at responding to them, aided by new forms of market research and a culture in which customer demands are always being communicated, sometimes loudly. Even as entrenched interests vainly try to control and restrict the flow of information, the peanut butter enthusiast community will force them to adapt, or will take their business elsewhere.

The coming peanut butter craze won't require fundamental shifts in human nature. No one will need to deviate from their basic love of peanut butter. Things will just get a bit more specific. Yuppies will waste time considering the sublime qualities of different varieties. Kids will continue to love the stuff and scarf it down at every opportunity, eating dozens of jars a year. The difference this time around will be that their parents pay more attention to the available research to ensure that the product is less likely to kill them. Who bought bicycle helmets 30 years ago?

Even if eating jars and jars of the old kind of peanut butter was relatively harmless, it's all about perception. How many more pleasure points do I get out of a $20 bottle of wine than I do out of a $10 bottle? Does it matter, if I'm bound and determined to spend the $20 today because I have to know how something tastes? How many people now run perfectly good tap water through a Brita filter? When the market wants something, give it to them. And if you can, create some kind of online resource or hub that actually fosters and supports that demand.

Emerging market demands aren't the same as needs, but they can be even more powerful. To best serve them, think bottom-up, not top-down. Whatever size of company you work for, the tests you can run on a platform like Google AdWords give you the ability to tap into such demands before anyone else knows what's going on.

Some large companies are true innovators, and others are pretty savvy second movers. But it's probably most exciting that the small entrepreneur can nudge his or her way into a niche with little risk and decent prospects for success. If a bunch of folks are selling peanut butter ahead of you, you can specialize in peanut butter–making equipment. You can launch a peanut butter festival. You can create a recipe book or a line of funny hats or special engraved knives. You could upload a video to Google Video of you smearing peanut butter on your bald head, and charge for it. There is always an opening somewhere. As long as you have a couple thousand dollars in a savings account, some supportive friends and family standing by, and, of course, eager and interested prospects, then you should feel free to do as the spirit moves you.

Go forth and target.

Endnotes

1. Carol H. Weiss, "Knowledge Creep and Decision Accretion," *Knowledge: Creation, Diffusion, Utilization*, 1(3): 381–404.

2. In the words of one copywriter from Turkey: "Google is my best friend! Google is my best friend! Google is my best friend! Google is my best friend! Google is my best friend!" From Kevin Roberts and A. G. Lafley, *Lovemarks: The Future Beyond Brands* (Powerhouse Books, 2004), 182.

3. John Heilemann, "Journey to the (Revolutionary, Evil-Hating, Cash Crazy, and Possibly Self-Destructive) Center of Google," *GQ*, March 2005.

4. And Walter, our cat, made it clear that he didn't care if Google's founders suddenly developed the lovable candor of Warren Buffett or ran away to join the circus.

5. Including CNN.com and other news leaders, Yahoo News has drawn more unique visitors than any other rival in 6 of 14 months leading up to April 2005, according to Nielsen/ NetRatings. See Kevin J. Delaney, "What's Clicking at Yahoo Is News," *The Wall Street Journal*, April 14, 2005, seen in syndication at *The Globe and Mail*, April 14, 2005, p. B13.

6. Anti-CBS opinion from competing news organizations was easy enough to find with a couple of mouse clicks over to Google News; viz., Kevin Scarbinsky, "CBS Needs More Journalism, Less Genuflecting," *The Birmingham News*, April 11, 2005; Bob Harig, "Ratings Soar, Not Coverage," *St. Petersburg Times*, April 12, 2005.

7. For a deeper exploration of this theme, see Don Tapscott and David Ticoll, *The Naked Corporation: How the Age of Transparency Will Revolutionize Business* (Free Press, 2003).

8. So-called "gay-index" research has discovered that high-tech talent is attracted to cities which, for similar reasons, are home to large gay populations. Richard Florida, a regional economic development professor at Carnegie Mellon University in Pittsburgh, wondered if economic development was driven as much by where workers chose to live as it was by where companies decided to locate. He further discovered that indices of high-tech economic development generated a list of cities that looked very similar to the list of cities with large gay populations: San Francisco, Boston, Seattle, and Washington, DC. Bill Catlin, "Gay Index Measures High-Tech Success," Minnesota Public Radio, June 5, 2001, archived at news.minnesota.publicradio.org.

9. For an excellent recent account from the standpoint of the new economy entrepreneur, see Om Malik, "Escape from Silicon Valley," *Business 2.0*, November 10, 2004. Even the purported advantage that certain far-flung "alternative business hubs" have— broadband access—will soon seem trite as this access spreads everywhere.

10. Micromarkets based around a single fruit, vegetable, or legume seem to be one example of an "enthusiast area" that is currently underserved and perfectly tailored to online marketing. On the weekend of Saturday, August 27, 2005, 25,000 visitors will once again descend on Zurich, Ontario, population 860, for the annual bean festival. It should be noted that Zurich is not The White Bean Capital of Canada. That distinction goes to Hensall, a few miles down the road. One of the experts cited in this book (who shall remain nameless) is a regular attendee of the Stockton Asparagus Festival in California. The festival's website estimates that the festival has a $19 million economic impact on Stockton.

Index

INTERNATIONAL CONTACT INFORMATION

AUSTRALIA
McGraw-Hill Book Company
Australia Pty. Ltd.
TEL +61-2-9900-1800
FAX +61-2-9878-8881
http://www.mcgraw-hill.com.au
books-it_sydney@mcgraw-hill.com

CANADA
McGraw-Hill Ryerson Ltd.
TEL +905-430-5000
FAX +905-430-5020
http://www.mcgraw-hill.ca

GREECE, MIDDLE EAST, & AFRICA
(Excluding South Africa)
McGraw-Hill Hellas
TEL +30-210-6560-990
TEL +30-210-6560-993
TEL +30-210-6560-994
FAX +30-210-6545-525

MEXICO (Also serving Latin America)
McGraw-Hill Interamericana Editores
S.A. de C.V.
TEL +525-1500-5108
FAX +525-117-1589
http://www.mcgraw-hill.com.mx
carlos_ruiz@mcgraw-hill.com

SINGAPORE (Serving Asia)
McGraw-Hill Book Company
TEL +65-6863-1580
FAX +65-6862-3354
http://www.mcgraw-hill.com.sg
mghasia@mcgraw-hill.com

SOUTH AFRICA
McGraw-Hill South Africa
TEL +27-11-622-7512
FAX +27-11-622-9045
robyn_swanepoel@mcgraw-hill.com

SPAIN
McGraw-Hill/
Interamericana de España, S.A.U.
TEL +34-91-180-3000
FAX +34-91-372-8513
http://www.mcgraw-hill.es
professional@mcgraw-hill.es

UNITED KINGDOM, NORTHERN,
EASTERN, & CENTRAL EUROPE
McGraw-Hill Education Europe
TEL +44-1-628-502500
FAX +44-1-628-770224
http://www.mcgraw-hill.co.uk
emea_queries@mcgraw-hill.com

ALL OTHER INQUIRIES Contact:
McGraw-Hill/Osborne
TEL +1-510-420-7700
FAX +1-510-420-7703
http://www.osborne.com
omg_international@mcgraw-hill.com

Know How

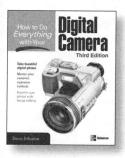

How to Do Everything with Your Digital Camera
Third Edition
ISBN: 0-07-223081-9

How to Do Everything with Adobe Acrobat 7.0
ISBN: 0-07-225788-1

How to Do Everything with Photoshop CS
ISBN: 0-07-223143-2
4-color

How to Do Everything with Windows XP
Third Edition
ISBN: 0-07-225953-1

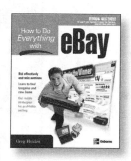

How to Do Everything with eBay
ISBN: 0-07-225426-2

How to Do Everything with Your eBay Business
Second Edition
0-07-226164-1

How to Do Everything with Your Palm Handheld
Fifth Edition
ISBN: 0-07-225870-5

How to Do Everything with Your iPod & iPod mini
Second Edition
ISBN: 0-07-225452-1

How to Do Everything with Your iMac
4th Edition
ISBN: 0-07-223188-2

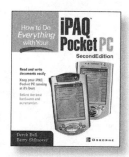

How to Do Everything with Your iPAQ Pocket PC
Second Edition
ISBN: 0-07-222950-0

OSBORNE DELIVERS RESULTS!

www.osborne.com

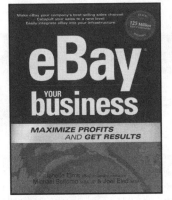
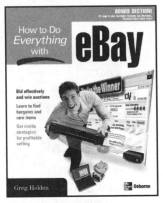

First, maintaining your relationship to God is essential. If you are caring for your soul, spending time in prayer, nurturing your soul on scripture, fellowshipping with other Christians in church, and making yourself accountable to a Christian friend or your pastor, you are far less likely to be easily tempted to wander. The urge may come but you will be better equipped to reject acting on the urge. The closer you are to God, the less likely you are to allow yourself to become compromised emotionally or sexually.

Second, be realistic about consequences and outcomes. Don't allow fantasy to overwhelm reality and reason. Think through the fantasy to what would actually happen if you were to live it out. Think about the people who would be hurt, including your children. Think about what kind of witness your life will be if you act on your marriage-breaking fantasies. If another man or woman is willing to destroy their marriage to be with you, how far can you trust them to not repeat the behavior and leave you later? How will your relationship with your children be affected? What will your colleagues at work think? Get REAL!

Also be realistic about the nature of human beings. All people are sinful. All are imperfect. Leaving your spouse for another is merely trading a relationship with one imperfect, fallible person for a relationship with another imperfect, fallible person. Plus, just as there were a myriad of things you didn't discover about your spouse until after you were married, the same will be true with any new person you become involved with. Any new relationship will be just as challenge-filled as any old relationship. A relationship born from infidelity will even be more complicated. Get REAL!

Third, maintain an attitude of forbearance, forgiveness, and thankfulness in your marriage. Act toward your spouse as you want them to act toward you. Extend to your spouse the love, kindness, forgiveness, and tolerance that you desire for yourself. Deal with issues quickly and fully. Pray together every day. Forgive each other every day. Renew your commitment to each other every day.

Fourth, if issues and tensions begin to mount, get help immediately. Go see your pastor. Go to a Christian marriage counselor. Do all that you can to deal with the issues and soothe the tensions with the help of a counselor and the help of the Holy Spirit. Look for solutions, not an escape. Work at staying together, not tearing your marriage apart. Refocus your attention on the positives that brought you together in the first place. Count the blessings you have enjoyed since you were first married. Invite Jesus into your situation and ask him for strength, guidance, and help. Choose to turn toward each other and not away. Couples who hang tough during rough times will find contentment down the road.

For Her

Just as you don't want your husband to eye other women, you should not encourage other men to eye you! How much flesh do you expose? Just because it's the style doesn't make it appropriate. What's more important, being stylish or being modest in your dress? Be sexy and seductive at home, not when you're strolling through the mall or sitting in church. Allowing yourself to be a slave to fashion could lead you to contribute to another woman's husband stumbling sexually. Your sexiness and sexuality belong to your husband, and no one else.

If you realize that you are starting to think about someone else, and involvement with someone else, ask yourself this question: How is my marriage? Inevitably you and your spouse are going through some stress and strains. The very fact that you are thinking of someone else is a red flag that should cause you to "take every thought captive" and "make" yourself think of how you and your spouse are going to deal with your troubles. Perhaps you should seek professional help. Don't give the enemy a foothold.

If you start thinking of somebody else chances are you know that person personally. Choose to protect your marriage even if you think in your head that the possibility of actually crossing the line is slim. Do not meet with that person alone under any circumstances. Not even for lunch in a restaurant. Do not keep any secrets from your spouse about who you are meeting with, ever. Make a confession of your temptation to a trusted Christian friend of the same sex. When light is brought into darkness the enemy flees and can't gain a foothold.

Part of preserving our marriages and avoiding adultery is the simple recognition of those times when we are emotionally vulnerable. The enemy knows our weaknesses and if sexual temptation is our weakness the enemy will try to entice us in that direction when we are vulnerable. It is when we are vulnerable that we must be the most vigilant. Our vulnerability is a season; it will pass, but the consequences of marital infidelity can last a lifetime.

Marital fidelity is a matter of covenant. Exodus 34:14-15 reads:

> "You must worship no other gods, but only the LORD, for he is a God who is passionate about his relationship with you. Do not make treaties of any kind with the people living in the land. They are spiritual prostitutes, committing adultery against me by sacrificing to their gods." (Exodus 34:14-15)

God's covenant with us is often explained by illustrating the marriage covenant and relationship between husband and wife. The Lord wants us to know that he is passionate about his relationship with us. He has committed himself to us. Likewise, a spouse who is committed to their marriage feels passionate about their relationship with their spouse. Following after other gods causes one to commit adultery against God. Such is the result when men and women look to others. It is the breech of a covenant. Whether in the mind or in actuality, we commit adultery against our spouse when our mind and/or our body wanders.

How to Love the One and Only One

Practical application of how to love your mate is something only you can determine. But there are a few general guidelines that can help you.

- *Listen to them.* Take time to really hear the heart of your mate and understand what makes them tick. Learn their desires, dreams, and goals.

- *Support them.* Be positive toward your spouse about the effort they expend on behalf of the family. Whenever possible, be on their side in issues, and be verbal about it. Encourage each other in the faith and to be active in a church.

- *Love them.* Love is a choice. Once you've made that choice and committed it to marriage, live it out.

- *Care for them.* Help out around the house. Share in chores. Cuddle on the couch while watching a movie together. Prepare great meals for each other.

- *Pray for them.* Every day, whether you pray with them or when you're alone, pray for your spouse. It doesn't have to be a long or complicated prayer. Whether it's a single sentence or ten minutes long, thank God for your spouse and ask God to bless your spouse.

Dr. Truth

The knowledge that our spouse is faithful to us alone, the assurance that no matter what they would never stray from us, gives us a deep surety inside our being. Knowing that our spouse will keep all their sexual energy inside our marriage gives us respect and admiration for them even if we're really angry. Faithfulness is fulfilling. It pours into our souls and provides a protective covering for our marriage.

Chapter 22

Faith Is Sexy

Everything is "sexy" these days, even things having nothing to do with sex. Ideas are "sexy," buildings are "sexy," trends are "sexy," and on it goes. In this sense, sexy means exciting or interesting. But when we say faith is sexy, we mean that within marriage, faith can heat up a couple's sex life.

It's Okay to Pray for Good Sex

Yes, indeed it is. God created us as two who would become one. It is within God's glory for his creation to come together in unity, sexually, for the complete joining of hearts, souls, bodies, and spirits. Ecstasy.

God created us as sexual beings for our pleasure and enjoyment of each other. It is sad that because sin entered the world, Satan has used sex against people in so many ways, enticed them into all sorts of misuse of their bodies that it takes some a serious effort to recognize the beauty of God's creation and accept it as "good."

It is married Christians who ought to have the most complete satisfaction in marital sex. This is the only circumstance where Father God blessed sexual union and sexual expression. Knowing the wonders of God and the wonders of his created world, married couples who worship and follow God Almighty should be having the best sex ever.

Non-Christians have seen Christian people be so uptight about sex that they think Christians are supposed to repress themselves sexually. How untrue! The Lord makes it clear what the parameters are within which we are to express ourselves sexually. Within those parameters it should be greater than great, the best.

If married sex is a beautiful gift from God, why wouldn't we want to praise him for it and thank him for it like we praise him and thank him for every other blessing in our lives?

"The Lord knows what we need before we ask him, but he tells us to ask anyway." (Matthew 6:6) Take the Holy Spirit, for example. The Holy Spirit is given to us when we ask, when we believe and accept Jesus Christ, when we are baptized. "Yet, the Lord Jesus himself tells people they need to 'ask' for the 'good gifts' of the Holy Spirit." (Matthew 7:7-11, Luke 11:9-13) We are told to "make our requests known." (Philippians 4:6)

Word from the Wise

"Don't worry about anything; instead, pray about everything. Tell God what you need, and thank him for all he has done." (Philippians 4:6)

Pray about everything. Everything means *everything*. Sex is not excluded. The Lord knows we need sex in our marriages—he created us with sexual desires and responses. Sex is one of God's gifts to us. We are told clearly to "ask," so let's ask!

Sex is just one of the things we can pray for. Nobody wants bad sex. If we're going to have sex we want it to be good, as good as possible, as good as it gets. This is not contrary to God's will or plan for us as married people. It is a gift like any other and we can ask for the gifts God offers us and bring them into reality.

Bringing God into the Bedroom

Oooooh, this may feel weird for a lot of people. Like Adam, many people think they need to cover themselves before God. It's because of sin and shame that we feel like this. It need not be this way.

"Don't you think the Lord has seen your nakedness? Yes, from your mother's womb no less." (Psalm 139) What can we hide from him? Nothing.

We think nothing of inviting the Lord Jesus to our dinner table as we give thanks to him for his bountiful gifts. What is stopping us from inviting the Lord Jesus to our bedroom to bless our sexual union and give thanks for that?

Remember the two sentence prayer you learned earlier? After a great night of sex we ought to give thanks to God for it in the morning.

1. Give thanks to God for something good about your spouse.
2. Ask the Lord for something good for your spouse for that day.

Being one who loves the Lord, how can you not have a thought to praise him during or right after great sex with your spouse?

There are couples where one spouse (or both) has been sexually abused. Sex can be difficult. The bedroom can be filled with much more than just the couple. There can be many spiritual anomalies that can interfere with the God-given pleasures of sex and intimacy. In this situation you want to specifically pray for protection and ask the Lord Jesus to stand guard over your marriage bed so that you can enjoy the sex God has given to you.

Some of the symptoms of an evil presence in your bedroom include: a facial change in your spouse, a cold shiver going through your body, seeing shadows, hearing voices (cackling, laughing, or talking), a rancid odor, hair standing up on the back of your neck, feeling there is a wall between you and your spouse, and fear. Refer to Appendix D for prayers you can pray to protect your bedroom and your bed from the effects of evil.

 For Him

You need to take the initiative to be the spiritual head of your household. To be effective, you need to keep your spiritual life fired up through spiritual disciplines that include prayer, Bible study, and fellowship. Personal holiness will exhibit itself in loving and kind behavior toward your spouse and children. If there's ongoing friction in the marriage, take a close look at where you are spiritually and make any needed adjustments.

Sex and the Bible

It's amazing when you come across the "Song of Songs" (a.k.a. Song of Solomon) in the Old Testament. It's like, "Where in the world did that come from?" Have you ever heard anyone preach anything from this book? It's doubtful that you've ever heard anybody mention it.

When Sybil was in seminary years ago she wrote a research paper titled "The Song of Lovemaking." As she researched the Song of Songs she came across one particular passage that led her to believe that sexual intercourse was indeed a part of the writings in the Song of Songs, specifically chapter 7 verse 12:

> Let us get up early and go out to the vineyards. Let us see whether the vines have budded, whether the blossoms have opened, and whether the pomegranates are in flower. And there I will give you my *love*. (Song of Songs 7:12)

There are 20 Hebrew words for "love" in the Old Testament. Only one makes reference to sexual intercourse. The Hebrew word *dod* is an unused root word and found in only 60 different passages in the Old Testament. It is translated three ways, as either beloved, love, or uncle. Only eight times in the Bible is it translated "love" as in Song of Songs 7:12.

Proverbs 7:18, Ezekiel 16:9, and Ezekiel 23:17 also contain this rare word. In each of these passages it is clear that the meaning of the word "dod" is sexual intercourse.

What about the other places in the Song of Songs where we find the word "dod"? Let's take a look at the references to sexual intercourse:

> "Kiss me again and again, for your *love* is sweeter than wine." (Song of Songs 1:2)

> "We praise his *love* even more than wine." (Song of Songs 1:4)

> "How sweet is your *love*, my sister, my bride! How much better is your *love* than wine, and the fragrance of your oils than any spice!" (Song of Songs 4:10)

Read the passages again from the Song of Songs. Beautiful, aren't they? How sweet is the taste of *love*, sweeter than wine! Those who compiled the books of the Bible did so under the guidance and direction of the Holy Spirit. The Lord made sure that this book was in our Bibles. Take a read. Can anyone say this book does not endorse passion? Marriage? Intimacy? Sexual expressions of love?

For Her

Remember how special you are in God's creation. He gave you a clitoris for no other purpose than for your sexual pleasure. No matter what you've been told, God is pleased with his creation and desires for his creation to be pleased with what he gave us. Your sexual responses are for your own pleasure and for you to share with your husband. Don't let your past history stop you from enjoying the gift God gave you in your sexuality.

Sex and the Church

The church, out of necessity, has had to preach on sexual sin and repentance from sexual sin because Christ came for those who are sick. "Sexual sin is a spiritual sickness and it must be addressed to save the sinful." (Matthew 9:12, Mark 2:17) There is sexual sin outside of the church and inside the church. Christians struggle with sexual sin in a big way. Temptation is everywhere.

The church has spent so much time trying to preach people out of sexual sin that it hasn't invested the time into teaching healthy sexuality.

There has been fear that if we teach people about sex they will become preoccupied with it and will fall into sexual sin. But we all need information about sex and we're going to get it one way or another. If godly healthy information isn't available, people will get whatever information *is* available.

Children want to hear their parents' values and the reasons why parents hold on to those values. Give your children a reason to keep their sexuality for themselves and for sharing with their spouse when they get married. Talk with them about how Father God knew of the pain that comes when people share their sexuality outside of marriage and he doesn't want them to feel that pain. Father's prescription of keeping sex within marriage is for our health and well-being, not to keep us from something good, but to give us the best he has for us.

Dr. Truth

It is not only our children who need to know what healthy sexual boundaries are—so do single adults, even people who have been previously married. We are a community of faith. We look out not only for ourselves but for our weaker brothers and sisters, whoever they may be. Be prepared to have "sexual boundary" talks with anyone in the church, at any time. Someone needs to be addressing these issues and it might as well start with you.

When we leave our children in the dark about sexual issues we leave them vulnerable, like lambs before wolves. It is our responsibility to give our children something to hold on to. We need to talk with our children about healthy sexual boundaries when dating: kissing, hand-holding, hugging, "keeping your pants on and zipper zipped," and "keeping your hands off the boobs." Oral sex and anal sex is a sin outside of marriage. Father God was not only referring to vaginal intercourse in the Bible, he was referring to the union of flesh! Save your nakedness for your wedding night. Learn about sexual touching and intimacy with the person who has already committed themselves, before God and man, to love you, guard you and uphold you, all the days of your lives.

It is such a delight to hear some of the young Christian singles talk these days, isn't it? To hear these young adults talk about the conversations they are having with people they are starting to date. They are speaking right up right away, telling the other person what their sexual boundaries are. If their date can handle it, fine. If not, they can take a hike.

It's good for us to teach our children when they are 8 to 12 years old how to handle those first few dates (when they are older) and making sure things don't happen in secret, in the dark, or unexpectedly. Let them know the things they should be up-front about with someone they are interested in or who is interested in them so that they don't have to deal with those sexually uncomfortable, unpredictable, "I wish I'd never done that" moments. Lack of knowledge of how to handle dating situations is what makes our children vulnerable.

It's just great that in the last 20 years Christian publishers have been willing to start printing books like this to teach Christians about healthy sexuality. Professional Christian counselors get training in human sexuality as part of their university/seminary programs. Christian marriage counselors can now provide sex therapy for couples. Churches are sponsoring marriage retreats and Marriage Encounter continues to flourish. Pastors have begun to preach on healthy marital relations and God's place for sex in his creation.

Word from the Wise

"But if you are unwilling to serve the Lord, then choose today whom you will serve. Would you prefer the gods your ancestors served beyond the Euphrates? … But as for me and my family, we will serve the Lord." (Joshua 24:15)

Choosing together, as husband and wife, to serve the Lord will bring blessing to you individually and to every member of your family.

Chapter 23

Talking Can Be a Turn-On

The myth is that women never shut up and men never speak up. In reality, studies have shown that men actually talk more than women. Some women would say that while that may be true, men still don't say much!

Talking. This is where problems often begin, and it is in talking that they are resolved. Conversation of any kind between the sexes can be a minefield. Men and women differ in the way they talk and what they mean when they talk. Problems often arise when these differences are overlooked.

Talking can be a turn-on and lead to sex. It can also be a real turn-off. Which one is often determined by timing.

What to Say

What you say before, during, and after you have sex can have an impact on your sexual life. We've pretty much covered the generalities of being kind, respectful, loving, and so forth. These qualities need to be expressed in the words you use and in the topics you choose.

How you talk to each other about sex will need to be negotiated carefully between the two of you. There may be certain sexual slang words that one finds offensive but the other sees as a turn-on.

Ordinary words may have emotionally painful memories attached to them. You may push a button without realizing what you said. Talking will help you realize what is offensive to your spouse and why. There may be tears associated with this for one of you. Sensitivity is important. You don't want to offend your spouse.

There are a lot of words that mean the same thing, particularly when it comes to sexual things. There may be words that your spouse uses for sexual things that you've never heard and you may need some definitions. Talk through gently what you can both agree is acceptable language for the two of you.

Not only are you dealing with the differences between male and female, you're also dealing with the differences in backgrounds and personalities.

> **Word from the Wise**
>
> "Let me see you; let me hear your voice. For your voice is pleasant, and you are lovely." (Song of Songs 2:14)
>
> We love to hear the sound of our lover's voice over the phone when we are apart. Even more pleasant is the sound of their voice when they are nearby.

A person from a conservative background or who is shy may be hesitant to talk openly about sex. They may also not know how to put their thoughts about sex into language because they have never talked about it before. It could be best to bring up only one item at a time and chop up your conversations about sex into short segments.

Sexual verbal teasing outside of the bedroom may or may not be acceptable to your spouse. Sexual teasing can be a part of "getting thrilled" for intimacy but it can also just be a way of connecting with your spouse during the day. Again, see what your spouse has to say about this. Perhaps they would find it cute and loving for you to tell them how sexy they are, how voluptuous they are, how horny you are for them, how much it excites you just to look at them, or to tell them what a great lover they are.

When to Say It

Timing is critical. If you are concerned about the way your husband puts on a condom, waiting until the heat of passion is upon you both before bringing it up probably will bring a chill into the room. And we all know what happens when male genitals get cold! Just as you need to think before you speak, a little planning is good, too.

Talking about sexually transmitted diseases (STDs) needs to happen before you are married. You have the right to request your fiancé get a full battery of testing for STDs and to insist that you are in the room when the doctor delivers the results. If you didn't do this, then you must bring it up before you have sex on your honeymoon or as soon as possible thereafter. If there is any reason to have any suspicion about STDs (if your spouse is not a virgin) you have a right to make an issue out of it and to insist on the use of a condom until the testing is completed.

You should also have a general discussion about sex with your spouse-to-be after you are engaged and before you say your vows. If you have fears or concerns, share them with each other. If there are certain sexual practices or positions you are loath to try, say so. Find out what you both think you'll be comfortable with on your wedding night. Later, you are both free to reintroduce ideas for reconsideration.

While you are making love, if it's a turn-on for both of you to have a little sex talk, go ahead. But, if it's a turn-off for one of you, make love in quietness. Perhaps play some soft music. Talking isn't a necessary ingredient in sexual intimacy once foreplay begins. You may not want to talk since you will be busy doing and enjoying other things!

If your spouse does something you are uncomfortable with or that is painful, you'll have to gently let them know in the moment.

After making love, if you are both open to it, gently and lovingly talk about the experience and what you enjoyed or did not enjoy or would like to try next time. Be careful! It may be better to wait and just bask in the afterglow for the time being.

For many people conversations about sex can't happen in the bedroom. For others, it must happen in the bedroom. In any event, it must be in private. Nobody else should be privy to your conversations about improving the details of your sex life. Protect your children from this talk—this is nothing that involves them.

For Him

Many women are under the mistaken idea that the focus of sex is the husband getting what he wants and the wife being submissive and undemanding. Please, validate her right to sexual satisfaction in her marriage and never force your demands upon her. Encourage her to help teach you what you can do to make her feel as loved, cared for and pleased sexually as possible. As you focus on her you will find that she becomes more mentally and physically involved in lovemaking. You both win!

How to Say It

Proverbs 4:24 states, "Avoid all perverse talk; stay far from corrupt speech." And Psalm 19:14 declares, "May the words of my mouth and the thoughts of my heart be pleasing to you, O LORD, my rock and my redeemer."

These two verses, and several others you are probably familiar with, provide clear guidelines on how you should speak to one another on any topic. Anything you discuss with your spouse needs to be spoken with kindness and love. At least that should be the goal.

Given our sinful natures, it won't always happen that way. In anger, you will speak harshly to your spouse. If hurt, you will retaliate and lash out. If you're not feeling well or are tired, you cut your spouse off, speak out of turn, ignore them, or engage in any number of actions that will yield offense and possibly spark an argument.

> ### Word from the Wise
>
> "And the tongue is a flame of fire. It is full of wickedness that can ruin your whole life. It can turn the entire course of your life into a blazing flame of destruction, for it is set on fire by hell itself." (James 3:6)
>
> This verse can sound harsh but we know how words that are out of control, coming from our sinful nature, can destroy relationships for good.

When discussing issues of sexuality, it is especially important to be tender, compassionate, and patient. Sex is a delicate subject that touches the core of your being. It is a topic to be handled with care.

Talking about sex can be delicate. Whatever you wish to comment on, do your best to be positive and not accusatory. It's better to make positive statements about what you would like to see happen, what you would like to try, or what you find especially stimulating rather than to make statements about what your spouse did wrong. You don't want your spouse to feel that they can't please you—you want to equip them so that they can please you. Everybody responds better to encouragement than to criticism. Think before you speak!

For the person who really struggles to talk about sexual things the couple may, out of necessity, have to write letters to each other, e-mail, or talk on the phone. Some couples are most comfortable when one of them is out of town and they talk about sex over the phone .

If your spouse is struggling to talk with you about sex, write them a letter and ask them what would be the best possible way for the two of you to communicate on this topic.

For Her

Many women have the mistaken idea that men have no limits sexually or could not be totally satisfied. They fear that if they let their husbands open up about what they want sexually they will be aghast with what his expectations or desires are. All men are not insatiable sexual carnivores. Don't presume your husband is. It's unfair to him, to you, and your marriage. Take the risk of knowing his heart about sexual desires. If you end up with any concerns, you and your husband can deal with them together. Meanwhile, he's probably easier to satisfy than you think.

When to Shut Up

Knowing when to keep quiet is a real talent. In an argument, you always want to get in the last word or respond to and negate each point raised by your spouse. Even in a calm discussion, both may want to appear more knowledgeable than the other and, as a result, actually talk past what they know. We see and experience examples of talking when one should be quiet almost every day.

When it comes to sex, the same problem exists. During sex, even if you both enjoy a little banter, there will usually come a time to shut up and focus on the pleasure you are giving and receiving. Some people cannot attain orgasm when distracted by their spouse's talking. Pay attention and if your spouse sweetly indicates that the time for talking is passed, just relax and enjoy your lovemaking.

At other times when talking about sex, avoid haranguing your spouse about an issue or pressuring them to talk beyond what they are comfortable with at that moment. Sometimes, just bringing up the topic is enough for one session. With your spouse aware, he or she can begin to mentally prepare for a more detailed discussion. Breaking a topic up into smaller chunks can allow time in between for both of you to become comfortable with the issue being raised.

Dr. Truth

In her book *That's Not What I Meant!*, Deborah Tannen states, "Male-female conversation is cross-cultural communication." What does she mean? Essentially that men and women are wired differently and that boys and girls are raised differently. How women talk with other women is usually radically different than how men talk to other men.

If, however, you have a pressing issue that really needs to be talked about and every time you've raised it your spouse becomes defensive or refuses to even consider a discussion, it may be time to see a therapist or your pastor. If your spouse won't go with you, go alone. Your therapist may be able to help you resolve the issue on your own or provide you with strategies for encouraging your spouse to open up.

The extroverted spouse talking to the introverted spouse may have to make a number of adjustments to talk about sex. They may need to decrease intensity, restrain themselves from over-talking, and create intermissions so their spouse can respond. The intermissions may have to be minutes or days long. The extroverted spouse will likely have to work to invite their introverted spouse into conversation and be prepared to be quiet and listen.

If a conversation about sex becomes heated and anger erupts, you may both need to zip it. That goes for any conversation that degrades to a sand box brawl. Get a grip on yourself! See a therapist to find out why your buttons got pushed. There may be individual, personal issues that need to be dealt with.

 ### Word from the Wise

"Please be quiet! That's the smartest thing you could do. Listen to my charge; pay attention to my arguments." (Job 13:5)

Like Job, we need to be heard by those who love us. To really hear the heart of our love, we have to stop talking and pay attention to what they are telling us. There are moments when love is just listening.

24

Housecleaning for Three Houses

Marriage joins two people who bring into the relationship two sets of preferences, opinions, tastes, likes, and dislikes. Prior to marriage, despite the hours and hours you spent together, there were far more hours you were apart. You will discover that some assumptions you made about your new spouse based on that limited interaction were wrong. After you say "I do," that's when the negotiations begin regarding issues of chore sharing, décor, and more. The good news is, it can all be fun, and even sexy.

When the Unexpected Creates a Problem

In marriage, the unexpected will pretty much be par for the course. It makes no difference who you are married to. Even Prince Charming or Cinderella will have their surprising little quirks, issues, emotional baggage, odd relatives, and more that they'll bring with them into the marriage.

Add to this list the general uncertainties of life and many of your marital expectations are certain to become casualties. But this doesn't mean that your marriage has to become a casualty as well.

Many unexpected issues are minor if you can maintain any sense of objectivity. For example, you may expect your spouse to use the same toothpaste and squeeze the tube just as you do. Yet, what you discover is they use a type of toothpaste you can't stand and squeeze the tube from the middle. These kinds of issues crop up everywhere—how towels are folded and shelved, what laundry detergent is best, what brand of foods to buy and what grocery store to buy them from, where to take the car for servicing, and so on.

None of these little differences are issues until they are perceived as a problem by one or both. Perhaps your spouse couldn't care less whether the toilet paper unrolls from the top or bottom and is happy to comply with your preference. However, while you can accept that she uses a different brand of toothpaste, you can't stand that he or she squeezes the tube in the middle. Since you each have your own tubes, he or she figures there's no problem, but that improperly squeezed tube stares you in the face every time you're at the sink! So you resqueeze it neatly from the bottom. He or she takes offense at your "help" and the argument begins.

Believe it or not, such nitpicky things can be what triggers issues of control, issues from the past, and issues of our basic humanity, knowledge or instinct. Anytime we overreact to what someone else does we need to ask ourselves what's going on with ourselves. What kind of needs for control do we have? What thought or memory does this behavior trigger from my past? Now that you're married, it can't be "his way" or "her way"—we need to find "our way."

 Word from the Wise

"These are the instructions for dealing with infectious mildew in woolen or linen clothing or fabric, or in anything made of leather." (Leviticus 13:59)
Leviticus and other books of the Old Testament include very specific instructions related to cleanliness. Keeping your home, body, and mind clean keeps you healthy and shows reverence and respect for the life and possessions God has blessed you with.

Part of the work of marriage is the normal day-to-day chores that somebody has to do. Clothes need to be laundered, carpets need to be vacuumed, bathrooms need to be scrubbed, dishes need to be washed, trash needs to be taken out, and stuff needs to be organized.

What does all of this have to do with sex? If one spouse feels the other is not doing their fair share of the work or creating more work by being messy, there's a good chance sex won't be happening for either.

It's usually, but not always, the case that the woman is the neater and cleaner of the two. There are situations where the man is the neatnik. Regardless, trouble arises when there are strong differences of opinion as to what constitutes a clean or dirty house, whether or not it's ever appropriate to toss clothes or coats on the floor or furniture, and how often dusting is required.

If your spouse tends to be a little bit of a neat freak, a messy bedroom (or any other part of the house) may actually be a distraction. Some people were raised to equate respect for one's property with how neat you kept your house. A house that was in any way unkempt equated to laziness and a lack of pride or self-respect. To have guests over and not thoroughly clean and straighten the house can be seen as rudeness.

Looking at "Irrelevant" Issues

The key to success when confronted by these types of issues is to put them into context as well as be considerate of one another. Marital unity and oneness can be built through dealing with all these seemingly mundane, nitpicky things. Dealing with these issues shows our spouse whether or not we respect them, trust them, value them, consider them, and listen to them.

For some, using a specific brand of laundry detergent is really important. It could be that they've tried other brands and have determined which one works best for them. Or perhaps they've talked with other people in the area who have recommended a specific brand that works best with the type of water in your area. Or your spouse may have very real memories and emotions attached to a specific brand of detergent.

These kinds of scenarios could be true for any product or service you bring into your home. If your spouse had a strong preference on brands and you don't, let them buy what they want. If you both have strong preferences, then you need to talk and negotiate.

In some instances, one may have better information about the quality and performance of one brand over the other and you can both agree to use the better one. In others, one may have a stronger emotional attachment to a brand. You both may have to concede on items in order to keep things equitable.

Does this whole discussion seem silly to you? Great! Hopefully you and your spouse will never let such minor things come between you. Yet, many couples split up over relatively silly issues such as these. It can be which brand to buy, where to buy it, how much money to spend, how to use an item, or any number of other things, such as what time of day to mow the lawn to how many times to take out the trash during the week. When these sorts of issues are the prime focus of tension where no agreements or concessions are made or kept, there are underlying issues that each person needs to deal with.

The point is you both bring into your marriage hundreds of expectations of all shapes, sizes, and intensity. Sorting out the few really important ones and laying aside the bushels of insignificant issues is important.

In most instances, love, patience, and compromise will eventually find a resolution. A simple way to knock one small thing down to size is simply to hold it up against serious possibilities such as what if one of you is downsized from a job, seriously hurt in an accident, diagnosed with a terminal illness, or loses a parent? Suddenly, toothpaste is nothing more than toothpaste.

For Him

As a kid, your bedroom was generally a mess and decorated in a race car motif. In college the mess continued and your walls were covered with popular posters of the day. As a bachelor, you furnished your apartment in Old West chic. Now you're married to the most wonderful woman in the world, but she wants to put frills and floral prints on everything. Yuck! Get used to it and learn to appreciate her more refined tastes. If you have strong opinions about décor, share those with your wife and be willing to seek compromise.

The Three Houses of Marriage

Some women joke with each other about how it is that God brought men and women together, because men just don't understand women. It's a miracle we can live together at all!

That's sort of how it feels when you're in disharmony with your spouse. You wonder how you'll ever work it out. Sometimes you get so mad and frustrated you want to just bonk them on the head with a rubber mallet, don't you? (Be honest, now.)

In a way, you're like a landlord. Do you realize that you are the caretaker of three houses all at the same time? You have your physical house that you live in. You have to keep it clean. You have to do the chores. You have to clean up messes, sometimes yours, sometimes somebody else's. Every once in a while you need to steam clean the carpets, paint the walls, and put on a new roof. The walls of our house are there to protect us from heat and cold and to keep other threatening forces from harming us. It provides us safety.

Next we have our house of God inside us. We know that our bodies are the temple of the Holy Spirit. This is where God comes to visit with us. It is our internal house. We are told to keep it clean. We need to abstain from sin and when we sin we need to clean out our house. We need to wipe up all the messes we created that keep our houseguest out. We want the Spirit of God to visit upon us so we work to keep our soul and spirit clean before God. Our righteousness is the greatest defense we have against the enemy's schemes.

Next we have the invisible house that surrounds our spouse and us; it is called the relationship of marriage. Marriage is a house that contains a man and a woman. The relationship between the man and the woman requires them to both take responsibility for keeping their marriage clean. To keep their marital house clean they have to clean up messes. They need to do things to take care of their invisible house. They have to do regular maintenance. They have to repair things that are broken. They have to care for it. When they care for "it" they care for each other. When they keep their marriage clean it becomes a protected place for the man and woman to dwell in peace together.

In the same way that we can't expect our physical house to take care of itself, in the same way that our spiritual house requires us to participate in taking care of it, our marital house also requires us to participate in its upkeep. We know what to do to clean our physical house. "Mr. Clean, here we come!" We know what to do to clean up our spiritual house. "Oh Lord, forgive me for being so dumb!" And to clean up our marital house? "Sweetheart, we need to figure this out."

Cleaning Up Our Marital House

How do we clean up the messes in our marital house? Here are some guidelines.

We need to get a grip on our anger and not allow it to control us.

We need to speak the truth in love.

We need to give our spouse an opportunity to respond to our complaint or concern. They may need time to ponder it before getting back to us.

We need to raise only one issue at a time, state the issue and let it go for a while. Never bring up multiple issues in one sitting.

We need to truly hear our spouse, stop all we're doing and just listen. Not listen for the purpose of forming an immediate rebuttal or defense but listen to understand what has caused our loved one such grief.

If our distress is out of proportion to the behavior of the other person, we have to commit ourselves to getting professional help for our problems. We have to protect our spouse from our anger at our past.

We need to remember that our spouse is human, they will mess up, you will mess up, and in the end it will probably even out. In the meanwhile we need to just deal with it.

In any power struggle we need to stop and husbands need to call out to the Lord for his help and protection. We need to wait until we are calmer before we try to talk together. We need to find another way. Not his way. Not her way. We need to find a different way.

Don't sweat the small stuff. Before taking issue with something I will ask myself how important it is that I make an issue of this particular thing.

Try to remember to tell your spouse, without accusation, what it was that they did that bothered you.

We need to apologize when we're hurt or have offended the one we love.

We need to forgive our spouse in love.

We need to remember that we're in this thing for the long haul. We will have trials and tribulations. We must make a commitment to "the marriage" that we will do everything we can to work things out with our spouse. We must be willing to seek the help of a third party while it's still "marriage enrichment" and never let our disharmony get to the point of having to talk with the counselor for "marriage dissolution."

We need to kiss and make up. We have to commit our hearts to each other once again. We need to remember the ways that we have conquered our problems in the past and how we will conquer them in the future.

Perseverance

Sometimes marriage feels like a sheer act of perseverance. At times it is. What did the Apostle Paul say about this? In 1 Timothy 4:11-12 Paul writes, "Pursue a godly life, along with faith, love, perseverance, and gentleness. Fight the good fight for what we believe." A godly life isn't just about faith, love, and gentleness. Hey, we aren't in heaven yet!

Meanwhile we have to deal with some of these seemingly ridiculous, mundane, time-wasting issues. We also have to deal with the very hard issues of abuse and trauma.

Perseverance is part of faith. The Lord never told us it would be easy, only that he'd be there with us as we persevered through it.

It is because we persevere that our faith is shown to our spouse, that our love is shown to our spouse, and that our gentleness is shown to our spouse. It's toughing it out through the hurt, the pain, the arguments, that really tells us that we have a committed spouse who is not just there for the long haul but wants to work things out with us so that our marriage can be healed.

One couple I counseled had worked through a lot of issues. The husband had serious anger problems and the wife was very controlling and had been through severe depressions. They worked hard together over an extended period of time. The wife would sometimes call in desperation at one more "stupid" thing her husband had done. She always had a complaint about him, even though he was working hard on his issues and making significant progress. No matter what he did she was never happy. Finally I confronted her, "You're never happy, no matter what he does. Perhaps you've just had it with this marriage?" She paused for a minute and said, "No way—I've put too much into this guy to get rid of him!" She began to appreciate his growth and started cutting him some slack.

We feel the freedom to truly love when we know that with perseverance we will continue on together through life. It is getting through the tough times that we gain confidence in our mate and in our marriage.

Hey, sometimes it a real relief to think that our spouse is the one person in the world who sees the worst of us and still loves us anyway.

Are you committed to working through your marital issues? Great sex doesn't come in a relationship rife with conflict. Great sex doesn't come in a relationship where you're being a jerk! Great sex doesn't come in a relationship where you're doing all the work and your spouse is a millstone around your neck. Nope. Intimacy comes from equitable involvement and commitment to the marriage.

If you're reading this book solely to try to find out how to get good sex, forget it. Nothing can help you. First you need to focus on taking care of each other in every way. You need to take care of all three of your houses.

Get your physical house in order. Help clean the house, wash the clothes, do the dishes, care for the kids, paint the fence, mow the grass, take out the trash, clean the toilet, and vacuum, vacuum, vacuum.

Next, get your spiritual house in order. Get on your face before God and clean up your act and keep it clean. You are solely and completely responsible for taking care of this house. (And you husbands have added responsibility to care spiritually for your entire household.)

Now, clean up your marital house. Work through your issues with your spouse. If you can't resolve them between you go to a trained marriage counselor. If you have brought personal issues from the past into the marriage, take responsibility to seek healing for yourself. Work at maintaining your marital house on a daily and weekly basis.

Only when all of your houses are clean will you be able to enjoy the best sex ever. Sex is so much more than physical bodies. You can learn sexual techniques many places but married Christians who have their houses in order have the corner on the market when it comes to complete and total fulfillment and satisfaction at every level of one's mind, body, soul, and spirit. Oh Lord, thank you that you have made Christian marriage this way!

For Her

Be considerate of your husband's taste when it comes to decorating and furnishing your home. Consult with him on the choices you make. Avoid forcing him to endure a totally feminine environment. That's not fair since you both share your home. It may be rare, but there are men who actually have better taste and decorating sense than their wives.

Chores Can Be Sexy

When all of our houses are clean, keeping a clean house can take on new meaning and adventure!

There are couples who get so turned on by the natural smells of their mate when they start to sweat that sex is the likely outcome. There are those who get more turned on as their spouse starts sweating during lovemaking. There are others who will do something to sweat so that they do get turned on. And hey, there's nothing like a little bit of vacuuming or floor washing to make you sweat.

Sweating, incidentally, produces pheromones. Remember those? Pheromones are believed to be our body's natural aphrodisiac. Pheromones are produced in our sweat glands under our arms. Go ahead and laugh, it's true. (It's those underarm pheromones that get women who live together menstruating together.)

Some like sex when their bodies are clean and dry. That's okay. But, have you ever tried it when you've both been sweating buckets? Of course, here's hoping that the activity that made you sweat hasn't depleted you of so much energy that you have none left for intimacy.

There are couples who "do it" in every room in their house. It's sort of a house-warming thing. It's like they want their love to flow through the whole house.

Who doesn't like the element of surprise? You could surprise your spouse by whispering sweet nothings in their ear while they are performing a chore. You could let your spouse know what you've got in mind if they're interested. Or you could take over their chore and tell them that if they like, you'll do the chore so that they can relax and start thinking about what a wonderful evening you'd like to have with them and how much you'd like to pleasure them later on.

Dr. Truth

What you don't see in your house can be a health hazard. Is there mold growing in your bath-rooms? That neglected dust under the sofa, the unchanged furnace filter, moldiness around the plumbing under the sink, or the rarely vacuumed carpet can all be sources of illness. There were good reasons your mother and grandmother conducted annual spring cleanings that were very thorough.

At least once a year, preferably two or more times clean every nook and cranny of your home. Change the furnace filter at least four times a year (check the instructions on the filter). You may find that a careful housecleaning makes you feel better in more ways than one.

Word from the Wise

"Let everyone see that you are considerate in all you do." (Philippians 4:4)

Whether it's how you care for your home or how you conduct your sex life, be considerate of your mate and of others at all times.

Does your spouse enjoy a little sex play? If they do, and they are open to some spontaneous sexual advances, surprise them once in a while. If your husband likes to have his buttocks squeezed now and then, do it. If your wife likes to have her breasts massaged now and then, do it. If your husband likes you to gently squeeze his crotch now and then, do it. If your wife likes for you to slip your hands down her pants and give her a little tease now and then, do it.

If this type of thing is offensive to your spouse, don't do it. But if your spouse likes to play, then play! Hey, you're only in this body once, you may as well enjoy it!

The only caution here: *never do this sort of thing in front of anybody*, especially not your kids. That is a serious crossing of parental sexual boundaries. Kids should never be party to seeing or hearing about any of this. Ever! This is something just for the two of you. These are sweet little nuggets to share with each other.

Demands and Expectations

This is an immutable fact: You will fight and argue with your spouse. Period. You enter a marriage with certain expectations of your spouse that will feel like demands to them, and vice versa. There will be disagreements, misunderstandings, unrealized expectations, unmet demands, and more. All are survivable. What follows are guidelines as to how.

Fighting the Good Fight

We're human, right? Right. Do we all get along perfectly? Nope. It's a fact.

Who do we fight with the most? The ones who are in our face the most—our immediate family. Why? Because they are there, because each is fully aware of the others' shortcomings, and because home is where we let our hair down (so to speak). It's the old adage "we hurt the ones we love." If we lived with other people it would be the same.

Home is where we live with people who love us for the long haul. Home is where we find people who will forgive us because they have committed themselves to loving us through thick and thin. Home is where we can experience the greatest joy (love, caring, and respect) and the greatest pain (family abuse, violence, and betrayal).

Let's remember that Jesus Christ experienced every emotion and temptation known to humans. Remember how ticked off he was in the temple. He got so angry he twisted rope together and then ran around upsetting all the tables of the money changers and chasing all the animals out of the temple. (John 2:13-15) Jeepers, if you expressed your anger like that someone would be dialing 911!

One thing Jesus didn't do in his anger? He didn't hurt people. He didn't hurt the animals, either. He didn't break the tables. He didn't yell and scream at anybody. He made his point succinctly but strongly, "Get these things out of here. Don't turn my Father's house into a marketplace!" (John 2:14) Jesus exhibited a lot of emotion in his anger but he didn't do any damage and we know that he was sinless in everything. What he did was not sinful.

The Apostle Paul also gives us some guidance on anger. The New Living Translation puts it "And don't sin by letting anger gain control over you. Don't let the sun go down while you are still angry, for anger gives a mighty foothold to the Devil." (Ephesians 4:26-27) The King James Version says "Be ye angry, and sin not." Jesus, we know, was sinless, yet he exhibited anger. Paul tells us that anger is not a sin in and of itself. However, how we deal with it may become sin if we let the devil tempt us to do something sinful with it.

Word from the Wise

"We should be decent and true in everything we do, so that everyone can approve of our behavior. Don't participate in … fighting and jealousy. But let the Lord Jesus Christ take control of you, and don't think of ways to indulge your evil desires." (Romans 13:13-14) Fighting can be indulging an evil desire. Who deserves our decency and our truth more than the one who has made a commitment to love us 'til death do us part?

Just because we are angry doesn't mean we'll fight. But, if we're fighting, it's because we're angry. What have we learned from Jesus? Don't hurt people, don't hurt animals, don't destroy property, stay in the moment, don't bring up the past, express yourself clearly and succinctly, and identify clearly what it is that has ticked you off.

Good fighting is fighting fairly. This means putting into practice all of the above. We need to keep in control of ourselves. If we let ourselves get out of control we have given the devil a foothold.

Jesus also didn't name call, swear, degrade the people, or lecture. He made his point. That was it.

Sometimes we should stop ourselves and ask, "Would I be saying and doing this if Jesus Christ was standing right here watching me?" Well, funny thing, he is. Make him proud of you, whether contented or angry.

Clearing the Air

Once the air is full of negative energy (a.k.a. anger) we need to clean it up. Where is that air purifier when we need it?

If you're upset about something your spouse has done, make a statement about what they did and why it has offended you. Keep to the current issue. Don't pull out all the old laundry. It's not wash day.

If your spouse brings something to your attention that you've done that has really hurt or offended them, own up to what you did. Whether or not you intended to hurt your spouse is important but does not change the fact that your behavior or words have hurt them. The importance of telling your spouse what your intention was is to help them understand that you were not trying to cause them pain. Often when we do something inadvertent that gets a really strong reaction from our spouse it is because it is merely a reminder of other hurts and pains we've had over the course of our lives. We are not just reacting to our spouse but to all of the emotion we have stored up from all past pain that was similar to what our spouse did. If this is happening over and over, chances are you have some inner healing to do. Consulting a professional counselor may be necessary.

 For Him

Husbands, there is no more critical time that your wife needs you to be the spiritual head of the house than when there is conflict in the home. Whether it's you or her or both of you who are angry, *you* must pray. Invite your wife to join you but whether or not she is willing *you* must call out to God on behalf of both of you and ask for his Holy Spirit to come into your house right now. And you must command all evil spirits to leave your house now. Keep praying until the two of you can speak the truth in love with each other.

Part of learning to love each other is finding out the things we do that push our spouse's buttons and choosing not to push those buttons, even when we're really angry. We learn quickly in marriage exactly what to do to really hurt our spouse and make them angry. We hold a lot of power to hurt them. We must choose not to. It's easy to make this choice when we're not angry but it's a sheer act of love to make this choice when it really counts.

Remember the old saying, "Love is a feeling." Wrong! Love is a choice. We make choices every day that tell our spouse either "I love you" or "You don't matter much."

Be Kind When Angry

So much of what we get angry over is cleared up when we "clarify." Lots of times people get upset because they don't have all of the information. When we get angry we have to get a grip on ourselves until we've heard the whole story.

This is why we need to be kind first.

Word from the Wise

"But speaking the truth in love, may grow up into him in all things, which is the head, even Christ." (Ephesians 4:15)

We grow up into Christ when we learn to harness our tongue and speak the truth in love. The truth can hurt but it hurts worse and adds insult to injury if it isn't spoken in love.

Giving Your Spouse a Chance

One day a mother found a folded-up letter in her daughter's pocket when she was doing the laundry. She opened it because she saw some nasty stuff written on it by her daughter. As she read through the letter she saw that her daughter had written a very vicious and horrid note to another girl at school. The mom was upset that her daughter would write such a thing to anybody. What were the mom's options? How many people would lay into the child as soon as they got home from school? This mother, after getting a grip on her emotions, knew she had to give her daughter the chance to tell her story.

The mom took the daughter for a drive after school away from the family. The mom patiently inquired of her daughter how things were going at school, how things were going with the girls in her class, and so on. The daughter wasn't forthcoming about any problem. The mom then mentioned the note she found. The daughter was mortified. Her response was one of shame and embarrassment but not for the reason you might think. The daughter told her mom that that was how she dealt with her feelings. She said that she had been really angry at that girl at school but that writing it all out on paper got all the yucky feelings out of her without being nasty to the girl at school. When the mom asked "So, you had no intention to give this to that girl?" the daughter was stunned that the mother would even think such a thought. "Of course not, I'd never do that." It made the mother proud.

Do we give our spouses this same kind of respect, patience, and care? We ought to. We need to. We need to be kind to each other.

> ### Word from the Wise
>
> "See that no one pays back evil for evil, but always try to do good to each other and everyone else." (1 Thessalonians 5:15)
>
> If you've been offended by your spouse, you have a choice how you respond. You can react in a way that is just as offensive or you can choose to respond kindly.

It's best if there is a bit of a time lag between our being angry and when we bring it to our spouse's attention. We should allow time for our "bomb" to defuse before we open our mouths. Imagine if the mother in the story had laid into her daughter and accused her of doing something terrible. The mother's overreaction would have wounded the heart of her daughter.

This is what is meant by "Be angry yet do not sin." Anger is an emotion we have in reaction to hurt or offense. Our behavior is what we *choose* to do. It is control of our behavior that stops us from sinning and giving the devil a foothold. The devil is just waiting to fuel your anger. You need to let him know who the boss is. You! Be in control of your anger so that you stop him from turning a difficult situation into a catastrophic situation.

Grabbing hold of your anger, containing your reactions, is part and parcel of becoming a safe and trustworthy person in marriage.

Great and Not-So-Great Expectations

Part of what gets people angry are the expectations they have of their spouse that don't get met. These expectations can be apparent or not apparent. Expectations of our spouse can range from "I thought you were going to do the dishes" to "Why did you only give me a card for Valentine's day?" to "If you loved me you'd do more around the house" to "The car has needed fixing for two weeks and you haven't taken it in yet." Expectations of our spouse can arise at any time and can involve both mundane things in life or critical issues.

Our expectations perhaps have been clearly articulated to our spouse or they may be unspoken (and our spouse may be unaware that we have the expectations that we have). Even though we have expressed our expectations to our spouse it is unfair to expect that they'll just do what we want. How do they actually feel about our expectations of them?

Is your marriage plagued by expectations and demands? If so, someone has a control issue. In fact, you probably both have control issues. If you're fighting over who expects what from whom on a regular basis, you're probably having a power battle to see who will control who. Take the covert guerilla warfare to a marriage therapist before WWIII begins.

For Her

Women are generally known to be more verbal than men. If you're angry about something and you want to be truly heard by your husband, pay attention to three things: intensity of emotion, number of words, and intermissions. Keep your emotion low-key, use the least number of words required to get your point across, and provide an intermission so your husband can speak too. (Hey guys, if you're the one with the gift of gab, you need this advice also.)

In a good fight one person confronts the other about some kind of injustice or offense. It can take a lot of guts to confront your spouse. It can take a lot of energy to constrain your anger and get in control of it so that you can talk with your spouse in a loving way. All confrontation puts the relationship in a tenuous place for a time.

Just because you've done a beautiful job at bringing up an issue doesn't mean you'll be well received. It's stressful to wait out your spouse's reaction to what you've told them.

Then there is the one who was confronted. It's not always easy to hear the truth of how much you've hurt your spouse. To think that they are in pain because of something you did that you may have been unaware of at the time can leave one feeling pretty bad.

Fighting is hard on the soul. Sheesh, after a battle you can feel wounded and miserable. Confrontation is hard. Confession is hard too, as is repentance.

It can take a lot of time, energy and tears to deal with this stuff. Most of the time a lot of hurt has to come out of someone before the tears end.

But, finally, reconciliation comes. Forgiveness is sought and given. Your hearts can finally come together again. You have found some peace in your storm.

On a first date, Jerry and Sally were on their way to dinner and a movie. Jerry was a confident, but not an aggressive or dangerous, driver. However, Sally was a very cautious driver, and the perspective from sitting in the passenger seat of a car always made her nervous. Unsure of where they were going and new to Jerry, Sally felt he was driving too fast and changing lanes erratically. On the other hand, Jerry felt they were moving smoothly and comfortably with traffic.

Adding to Sally's tension were bad experiences with her previous husband, Bob, who *was* a dangerous driver. Frequently Bob had cut other cars off, driven faster than the speed limit, and even scared their kids with his driving. More than once Sally and her kids refused to ride in the car unless she drove. Those experiences had made Sally somewhat hypersensitive to how others drove and she was seldom a passenger. She was becoming frightened as she and Jerry drove to the restaurant.

She endured the drive quietly. However, her initial emotions of fear and anger made her want to lash out. She knew, though, that that would have been unfair to Jerry.

At the restaurant, as they were enjoying dessert, Sally cautiously brought up her concerns about Jerry's driving. She explained her general nervousness, the fears from her prior relationship, and how fearful she'd felt as they were driving to the restaurant. Because Sally had allowed her emotions to settle before bringing the issue up, she was able to speak calmly and reasonably.

Jerry listened, a little defensively at first, but quickly understood the basis of Sally's fear. They talked through the situation a bit more and Jerry said he would take care to drive a little more conservatively so that Sally would feel comfortable. As they drove to the movie and later, as Jerry drove Sally home, he did as promised. Sally felt respected and Jerry was appreciative of the calm manner with which she had raised the issue.

Making Up Naked in the Closet

Reconciliation with your spouse is unlike any reconciliation you'll ever have with anybody else. Why? Because marriage is a covenant. There are no other covenanted relationships between human beings.

What is a covenant? J. I. Packer, in his book *Concise Theology: A Guide To Historic Christian Beliefs* (Tyndale) writes that covenants are "solemn agreements, negotiated or unilaterally imposed, that bind the parties to each other in permanent defined relationships, with specific promises, claims, and obligations on both sides (e.g., the marriage covenant, Mal. 2:14)."

Marriage is about oneness and unity of mind, body, soul, and spirit. After the agony of confrontation comes the sweetness of reconciliation. Coming together after emotional pain can take some time. Sometimes we have to let our wounds heal for a few hours or a few days. Just because the air has been cleared doesn't mean that the person who has felt wounded is ready for intimacy. As the wounds are healed and forgiveness is released we begin to draw together again. It's as if the Spirit of God points us toward our spouse.

The desire for complete unity will draw us to sexual unity. We have already united our minds and our souls and we may have united our bodies through cuddles and hugs. But it is sexual unity that is the final evidence of our repentance and forgiveness toward each other. Our choice to again expose ourselves to our spouse tells our spouse, "I've worked it out," "I still love you," "I will trust you again," "I need you," "I love you." Sexual unity seals the deal.

It's time to make up and remember your love for each other. This is a time when many couples can actually find themselves crying during sexual intimacy. The tears are tears of joy and gratefulness that you have found the love of your spouse all over again. The tears are about the joy and gratefulness that you have been forgiven by the one who loves you. The tears are about the joy and gratefulness of the commitment that you have made to each other.

Dr. Truth

Why did God give us a sex drive? To draw men and women into a covenanted relationship. If we didn't have a sex drive Adam and Eve might have been the only two people to have ever lived on the earth. Our sex drive operates both to get us into covenant with each other and to keep us in covenant with each other. Many couples notice that after conflict with their spouse, their sex drive becomes activated and can be highly intense. Restoring sexual unity with our spouses is essential.

Sexual unity after conflict can be some of the most intense sexual experiences a couple has. Sexual unity after conflict is about more than just the sex, it is about apologizing and forgiving, it is about understanding and acceptance. After conflict, because each spouse has just been experiencing intense emotions, emotional intensity follows the couple to bed.

This is a time when a spouse who was reluctant to please their mate sexually in a particular way is suddenly willing to do that special thing. After conflict there is a window of opportunity opened that you could both use to the long-term advantage of your marital sexual satisfaction. This is a time when both of you may be more willing to try new things sexually. You could try things that you find you like and will enhance your sexual repertoire in the months and years to come.

Staying Young Together

Growing old together is inevitable and can be a pleasurable experience. But you'll also want to inject a sense of youthfulness into your relationship even in the golden years. The joints may ache and the sexual response may dim, but being young at heart is possible at any age.

It's All in Your Mind

Once again, it all starts in your mind. When Paul said "take every thought captive" he understood how important it was for each person to be in control of their thoughts (2 Corinthians 10:5) in order to be obedient to Christ.

Every good thing begins in our mind although it does not begin on its own. We make choices to deliberately think and ponder those things that are good and lovely.

How do you, then, stay young together? You decide you are going to do it and then you set your mind on how you will do it.

There are old people who get really, really old. Their minds retire long before their bodies die. In a way, they are the living dead. They checked out long ago. So sad. It need not be this way. After their mind decides to give up life, their bodies begin to whither and atrophy. Their aches and pains are far more than anybody else's. They are hard for others to be around.

Word from the Wise

"Fix your thoughts on what is true and honorable and right ... pure and lovely and admirable ... excellent and worthy of praise." (Philippians 4:8)

Fixing one's thoughts is an intentional act. Paul says to "think about things." This is a decision. The enemy is always trying to tempt us to think about things we shouldn't and draw us into his snare. What begins in your mind, you live out in your life.

What joy there is to find an older person who wants to stimulate their mind, learn new things, try new activities, and go on adventures. They have joy and satisfaction with life. They like to hear new jokes and tell new jokes. Their bodies may be wrinkled and creased but their eyes see what everybody else's see, their heart feels what everybody else's feels, their mind is alive and active even when their body isn't any more. They enjoy life and want to live it to its fullest. It is a joy to be around these folks.

When only one spouse makes the mental decision to stay young it's a real drag for the couple. To sit and watch their mate resign to atrophy is very disheartening. The mate who chooses mental death becomes a millstone around their spouse's neck.

But for those who choose to stay young together? Boy oh boy, what a fun time they can have. How much more they will get out of life!

You and your spouse need to ask yourselves how you want to age together. No matter how old a person is they can feel young if they choose. Once our minds decide, our feelings will follow and flow out of what we choose to do.

When we decide to stay young, we take on a youthful mental attitude toward ourselves, our mate, our children, our grandchildren, the church, and the Lord's kingdom.

And the Rest Is in Your Body

If we decide to stay young together we need to begin to make decisions to get us there and keep us there.

Take a look at what is carrying us through life: our physical body. Our body is a gift to us from God. We are only using it temporarily to hold our spirit and our soul as we pass through this life. Our body is also where the Holy Spirit meets with us. It behooves us to take care of it.

"Our body is not our enemy. Our body is not a burden. Our bodies were created by God, formed by him in our mother's womb. He knew us even then." (Psalm 139) If our

Word from the Wise

"Dear friend, I am praying that all is well with you and that your body is as healthy as I know your soul is." (3 John 1:2)

It is important for both our bodies and our souls to be healthy in order to maximize our love lives.

For Him

Maintain a sense of humor throughout your married life. Appreciate the fact that, despite your body's new, lumpier shape, your wife still finds you handsome. Make an effort to do something out of the ordinary from time to time to break the routine and surprise your wife. Stay playful!

heavenly Father was so intimately concerned about every part of the development of our being, we ought to take what he values and value it too. We need to love what God loves.

Stop being angry with your body and whatever size and shape it is. Be of a mind to love your body, be good to your body, treat it kindly, tell it you are sorry for the injuries it has sustained, and give it good food and exercise it.

Your body can't survive without you. It's a partnership. Be good to it and it will be good to you. You have to treat your body like you would a good friend who is totally helpless to get along in life without you. How well would you feed your friend? If your friend needed exercise, wouldn't you help them to get the exercise they needed?

Your body was built with specific needs. Muscles need to be exercised. Your body needs good clean fuel (a.k.a. food). It's pretty simple. A healthy body will give you the opportunity to live life to its fullest.

As mentioned earlier, couples with healthy bodies also enjoy a better sex life. Sex is a drag if you hurt everywhere. In fact, if you hurt everywhere you won't be too interested in sex, will you?

Taking care of our bodies is only the beginning of staying young together. There are more decisions to make.

Enjoy It While You Have It

Our bodies won't always have fantastic physical capabilities. Our capabilities will decline over the years even when we keep in top physical condition. We may suffer from conditions that could never have been prevented by eating better or keeping fit.

If we're lucky we'll live to a ripe old age. We need to enjoy everything we can while we can. There was an old grandpa whose wife lost a lot of her mental capabilities when they were in their 70's. He kept busy loving her, conversing with her, and doing all that

For Her

You and your husband will both undergo physical changes as you age. Body parts sag and weight gain happens. Keep yourself healthy and attractive yet accept the changes aging brings. Avoid spending too much time complaining about the inevitable changes. Grow old gracefully with your husband.

he could to be humorous, have fun with his children, grandchildren and great-grandchildren. His heart was so full of love. He kept up with the current news as he shared his stories from the old country. His face held a smile that was genuine and sincere. He treated his wife like the sweet little bride he'd married decades before. He looked out for her and wouldn't put her in a retirement home without him right by her side. At 93, she died. He died three days later. It was as if he knew how much she needed him and when she was gone, his purpose was complete. They were only apart three days before he joined her in heaven. That couple unarguably spent a lifetime together.

Continue to do the most you can with what you have—all the time. We never know when our capabilities will be diminished.

Tips for Keeping It

How do you stay young together after you've made up your mind to do it and you've decided to take care of your body?

To keep the mind young read, listen to the news, read to each other, drive a different route to a familiar place, or take a drive somewhere you've never been before. Be a tourist in your own hometown. Keep stimulating those neurons.

Learn new games together: board games, mental games, and physical games. Take up a hobby with your spouse.

Explore a new place. Visit museums, art galleries. Go to a NASCAR race. (Take ear plugs!) Take a bus ride or train ride together. Go to the North West Territories to see the Aurora Borealis. Go to Montreal to the Ice Hotel in the winter. Go to the Butchart Gardens on Vancouver Island. Go to New Orleans and take in a Jazz performance. Go to Disneyland. Go to a football game. Take up rock climbing. Go on a parachute jump. Try some of those things together that you've never done before. Create fun memories together.

Volunteer together in the nursery at church. If nothing else it'll remind you how glad you were when your kids could finally take care of themselves! Volunteer at a local food bank together. Meet new people.

Spend time with your grandchildren. They will help keep you young. Read them stories, toss the ball, take them to a ball game, hockey game, and so on. Teach them a game you played when you were younger.

Laugh. Keep a sense of humor. Go to comedy plays!

We will never be too old to laugh together, play together, and love together. There is so much we can do to stimulate our oneness and our attraction to each other.

Dr. Truth

Keep young mentally but be realistic about the changes happening to your body. You do not have the same reflexes, stamina, and resilience at ages 40, 50, and 60 that you did at 20 and 30. You can injure yourself much more easily and much more seriously.

If you're thinking of taking up skiing, rollerblading, or some other physical activity, take all the precautions you can, wear all the safety items available, and go slow to begin. Check with your doctor and develop a reasonably paced training regimen that will prepare you to participate in the activity. Hundreds of aging baby boomers are injuring themselves annually because they just jump into an activity their bodies aren't ready to handle.

Growing Old Together

You know you're in a satisfying marriage when you ponder getting old together and it brings a smile to your face. After decades or just a few years together, growing old puts the finishing touches on your life together. It seals the commitment you made many years ago. As we look to the final stages of our lives we ought to ponder how we want those last years to look. As our bodies age, as we deal with illness, the companionship we've found in each other ought to bring deep and satisfying contentment. There is nothing sweeter than seeing an elderly couple holding hands together, walking together, and chuckling together with a glow of contentment that goes beyond words.

Aging Happens

We all know that unless we die prematurely through accident or disease, we will grow old. Our bodies will age whether we like it or not. We will sag, bag, and hag. As one middle age man once said, "When I hit 50 my chest fell into my drawers." Well, when we hit 70 or 80 or 90 we will see many more evidences that we are the age we are.

Your Aging Body

For some, our metabolism slowing at middle age leaves us with a belly or a butt that we didn't have before. Some gain weight, others can't keep it on. We can add a chin or two. Our ears get bigger and so do our noses. And we shrink! Once we were five foot seven; now we are five feet even. Our hands start to look bony and the blood vessels protrude. We develop our mother's hands. Our boobs drop down to our waists. Our moles seem to increase in size. And wrinkles? Where do they end?

As our bodies slow down we need more sleep and we don't have the energy we once had. We have to choose what activities are really important and which ones we need to just let go.

All of the injuries our bodies sustained over our lifetimes come back to haunt us.

We can't walk as fast. We can't think as fast. Our memory starts to go to mush. We need "progressive lenses" and hearing aids.

Our taste buds start to die off and nothing we cook tastes good to our kids anymore (because we can't really taste what our cooking tastes like anymore). Hey, when this happens it's time to turn the holiday cooking over to the kids!

We have to decide if we're going to keep dying our hair or finally just let it be as old as we are. What about that hairpiece? Will we finally let ourselves be as bald as we really are?

Menopause finally finishes, much to our husbands' relief, but that leaves us with dry vaginas that now need much more lubrication. "Time to go to the drugstore again, honey."

The ole penis can't keep an erection like it used to, and so much more effort is required to keep it up. "Hey Doc, how about that Viagra?"

We can't stop it. Aging happens. Baby product manufacturers make a bib that says "Spit Happens." Next thing you know the AARP will have a bib for us: "Aging Happens"! (Well, maybe they'll just put it on a T-shirt.) Oh yes, do you remember when you received your first mailing from the AARP? Weren't you angry! "Sheesh! Surely I can't be that old yet?" is probably what you said to yourself. By now you've been a member for decades. You're getting all the seniors discounts, aren't you? See, a few benefits of aging. "My gosh, I've become a senior citizen!"

Grandparenthood becomes great-grandparenthood. Our friends and relatives are all dying. We go to one funeral after another. Life is coming to a close.

You may have gotten too old to do some things, but you'll never be too old for sexual intimacy with your spouse.

Word from the Wise

And Sarah declared, "God has brought me laughter! All who hear about this will laugh with me. For who would have dreamed that I would ever have a baby? Yet I have given Abraham a son in his old age!" (Genesis 21: 6,7)

The incredibly great news here is that Abraham and Sarah were still having sex when Abraham was 100 years old. Wow! Sex at one hundred? Yes, Lord, may it be. Aging has nothing to do with our ability to continue to have marital sexual relations.

Sex and Age

When asked whether she and her husband still had sex, one older woman replied, "Do you ever stop?"

Sags, bags, and all, aging never needs to stand in the way of sexual intimacy. There are couples who have sex less frequently and those who have sex more frequently in their senior years. With an empty house and time on their hands, seniors find the opportunities for sexual intimacy are many. Sex might go from twice a month to twice a day.

For women, as we age, we become more and more able to have orgasm during vaginal intercourse. For us, after we've learned how to get an orgasm, we don't have any trouble getting them whenever we want them, even when we get really old. It seems that a woman's body just keeps improving its sexual capabilities.

If you are currently in your senior years and this is the first book you're reading on marital sexuality, we hope that you have learned a fair amount. When you were young, talking about sex was taboo and there was little healthy information available. The church didn't want to speak about sex back then. We hope and pray that you and your spouse might try some of the suggestions in Chapter 9 and go to bed more often with big fat smiles on your faces.

From the time we are born until the time we die, Father God created us as sexual beings with sexual responses. No, you're never too old to enjoy sex.

For those who married very late in life, or have remarried in your 40s, 50s, 60s, or older, you can still enjoy a very fulfilling sex life together. But keep in mind the reality of your situation. You may be newlyweds but you will not be able to recreate the intensity of your initial sexual experiences when you were both young and newlyweds. All-night sessions or frequent spontaneous sex may not be possible anymore. That's okay! Focus on what is available to you and on the beauty of your new relationship and your new spouse. What you are able to enjoy sexually will still be very fulfilling. You may just want to avoid erotic acrobatics and torso-twisting positions.

Illness

Age alone cannot cause a couple to cease sexual intimacy, but illness can cause problems. It is no surprise that those enjoying sex in their senior years are those who have maintained fit and healthy bodies. Good physical health is positively correlated to satisfying sex.

Old and Healthy, or Old and Sickly?

One thing that we have to decide in our 30's and 40's is how we want our lives to finish. We can recognize that we are going to age and get old, but, when we are young we can decide if we are going to get old and sick or old and healthy. It's one thing to be old. It's another thing to be old and sickly!

There is so much that we can do to keep ourselves healthy or get ourselves healthy. We need to start young.

You've seen the commercial on TV where the woman asks if you want to know what the warning signs are for osteoporosis. Then comes her answer: "There aren't any." Osteoporosis is a terrible condition that affects primarily white, slight, females. What is the only thing that women can do to prevent osteoporosis? To do regular weight-bearing exercise. That's it. You need to start lifting weights at least when perimenopausal symptoms start.

We are what we eat. Gluttony is one of the seven deadly sins and it doesn't start in old age, it starts when we're young. Once we're morbidly obese we're in trouble. America is one of the most obese nations on the face of the earth. We eat way too much fast food, chips, pop, and deep-fried everything. We're literally killing ourselves with food. What God created for our pleasure and nourishment has become the very thing that ends our lives. It need not be this way.

So many conditions are preventable with regular exercise and a good healthy diet. Any time you begin to put these two things into your daily life it is a good thing and the younger the better. If you wait to decide to take care of your body, by the time you make the decision it could be too late.

Of course, many of us have biological predispositions to high blood pressure, cholesterol problems, heart conditions, cancer, and so on. We may end up having lung cancer even if we've never been a smoker, and simply if we've inhaled enough second-hand smoke. We can catch viruses and bacterial infections that can make us very sick or kill us. Sometimes the conditions in our senior years are those that we could never have prevented through all of the dieting and exercising in the world.

Sex and Illness

What does illness have to do with sex? We earlier talked about "sex and nausea being a volatile combination." In our senior years we often deal with conditions that will be with us for the rest of our lives or conditions that are killing us.

What about prescription and nonprescription drugs? Many drugs inhibit one's sexual life. If you have any concern or suspicion that your medications could be inhibiting your sexual response, talk with your doctor. Make sure your doctor knows that you want to be able to have great sex with your spouse and don't want to take medications that would interfere with that. It won't be the first thing on your doctor's mind to ask if your medications are leaving you with sexual side effects. However, you should initiate this conversation with your doctor.

The fact is ill health can cause a person to lose interest in sex completely but not necessarily. It is important even in our aged years to talk with our spouse when we become sick or when they become sick. Our sexual needs and desires don't end because our spouse is sick. Also, just because we have some kind of illness doesn't mean we don't want sexual pleasure.

Couples need to talk. If you can't find a way to talk with your spouse on your own, even at your age, try to get to a marriage counselor.

Believe it or not, some people, even sick in the hospital, want to have sexual contact with their spouse just for the emotional and spiritual connection and for the extra feeling of love that comes with sexual intimacy. Are you willing to stimulate your spouse in their hospital bed if they want you to do that for them? These kinds of things are acts of love. Sexual contact with our spouse helps us not to feel so alone in our pain or illness. Keep in mind, if your spouse is on a lot of pain medication they won't be feeling anything anywhere in their bodies and it's unlikely that they would ask you, but the possibility remains.

When we're sick, medical professionals see our medical need and care for us medically; our close friends and family see our emotional and social need and they keep us company and visit us; our pastor and church family see our spiritual need and they pray for us and share encouraging scriptures with us. We are all that and more. Our sexuality still is part of who we are. The only person we have to care for our sexual needs, even in sickness, is our spouse.

> **For Him**
>
> A woman never gets too old to hear how pretty she is, how desirable she is, or how sexy she is. It's not a matter of what her body looks like, it's about her soul, her spirit, your unity together, and how beautiful it is to you. She knows perfectly well what she looks like. Tell her the things that warm her heart and make her feel special.

Companionship

As young men and women bursting with hormones it seems as if sex has always been and always will be on our minds. It's easy to forget that, before puberty, sex was a vague curiosity and those of the opposite sex were "yucky." Sex takes and holds a preeminent position in your life through many years of your life. It can seem as if you will always be desiring and enjoying sex.

Aging can, and should, shift your focus. Sex is great and sexual intimacy can be enjoyed as long as you live. Yet, it will not happen with the same frequency or level of release you once experienced, and it will take a lot more energy. However, when the sex drive wanes, your happiness as a married couple does not wane as well. In fact, it can increase!

One of the central joys of marriage is the companionship it entails. Being married means you will always have a date for New Year's Eve, a shoulder to cry on, and someone to hold your hand.

In some instances, the effects of aging can seriously impair your ability to have or enjoy sexual intimacy. Yet it does not impair your ability to enjoy your spouse's company. After spending years together, the friction that marked your first few years has left behind a smoother, more easy going relationship. You are very used to and accustomed to one another.

The quality of the companionship you will enjoy is being built every day of your marriage. As you work together to sustain a healthy and loving marriage, as you enjoy sexual intimacy together, you are investing in your future companionship.

For Her

In younger years your husband may have wanted much more sexual activity and you may have felt that his sex drive ran faster than yours (for many women it's just the opposite!). His sex drive has now shifted from 5th gear down to first. He's sauntering along now. Our husbands have become cuddle bunnies. They are looking for emotional connectedness with you in their senior years. Just being together, just holding each other, just sitting or lying side by side brings deep emotional and spiritual pleasure.

Contentment

Song of Songs 8:10 states, "… my lover is content with me." A lot of people are "happy" but not very contented. Happiness is fleeting and too often tied to temporary conditions. Contentment on the other hand is rooted in your soul. Contentment is not necessarily about happiness, but rather is related to a sense of well-being, peace, and being at ease or comfortable. It is possible to be unhappy over a temporary event while still being content with life in general.

As you grow old together, working through issues, overcoming life challenges, growing in the grace of God, you will also grow to become more and more content with your spouse and your marriage.

How you live out your marriage is one indication of how you live out your faith. Timothy 6:6 states, "Yet true religion with contentment is great wealth." True religion for the Christian embodies everything related to one's walk of faith, including your family and your marriage. This is a place of peace, hope, and deep trust in God. There is no more strife in striving, but rather your walk and your marriage are both about attaining and gaining. Instead of getting caught up in working to become a better husband or wife, you are more focused on being in your marriage with your spouse as you both enjoy each other.

Final Mission

What is the final mission of your life together? What is your legacy in the Lord's kingdom?

One of the ways we leave this life in peace is knowing that we have tied up loose ends, that we have mended fences, that we have made amends, that we have apologized to those we have hurt, that we have asked people to forgive us for the stupid things we did, that we have made attempts to reconcile broken relationships, and that we have loved the unlovely.

They say that our children are our future. Maybe not. Children know nothing and they are immature. What grows children into productive members of our society and productive workers in the Lord's kingdom is the investment of mature Christians. It is not the young who have wisdom, but the old. It is not the young who have learned from their mistakes, but the old. Wisdom comes from our elders.

Loving Christian couples have so much to give to the Lord's work and to his kingdom. Is there really any retirement from our calling from God?

Dr. Truth

People enter the final stage of their life and find either contentment or despair. Those who have lived a good life, made the right choices, found forgiveness, found love, shared love, and are at peace with themselves find contentment. Those who have lived a miserable life, treated people miserably, are unforgiving and hard-hearted, find despair and bitterness. One only has to visit a nursing home to see that the residents are a very polarized bunch. There is no middle ground because there is little chance to "fix" a life at this stage.

As your life comes to a close, as your married life finds its end, you will be at peace if you have sought to cultivate the fruit of the Spirit throughout your life. Always remember and practice love, joy, peace, patience, kindness, goodness, faithfulness, gentleness, and self-control. (Galatians 5:22-23)

As we grow old we need to think of how we are investing in the Lord's work. We can invest ourselves with our time and our energy. We can spend time with our grandchildren sharing with them the love of the Lord. We can mentor younger couples who are having troubles. We can visit the homeless.

If we can give thought to our older years we can begin to plan what we will do together for the Lord's kingdom. One mature Christian couple, after retiring from pastoral and counseling ministries, left their homeland and decided to be missionaries in Turkey. They decided to do the Lord's work together, as a team. Retirement was not a concept they believed relevant to those called of the Lord.

An 82-year-old woman once said that she'd thought she'd done enough for the Lord and she just wanted to go home. He made it clear to her that he had plenty left for her to do and he wasn't about to take her home yet. It was her job to inquire of him to see what he still wanted her to do.

The Lord seeks to use us in his kingdom throughout our lives. When the kids are gone and our careers have moved to retirement, it may just be the beginning of your lives of ministry.

 Word from the Wise

"In everything you do, stay away from complaining and arguing, so that no one can speak a word of blame against you. You are to live clean, innocent lives as children of God in a dark world full of crooked and perverse people. Let your lives shine brightly before them." (Philippians 2:14,15)

What greater witness is it to the world than to see a Christian couple whose love and devotion together shines a light into the darkness of the world. As you share your love with each other, share him with the world!

May the peace and love of the Lord Jesus Christ be with you both now and forever! May his mighty angels shield you from the evil one. May you be strong together. May you keep the faith together. May you live, love, and rejoice together. May your love shine as a light in the darkness.

May you go with peace and contentment into his eternity saying to your spouse, "Thank you for all of the love you shared with me. Thank you for all of life's difficulties that you walked through with me. Thank you for forgiving me for all of my faults and shortcomings. Thank you for tolerating me when I was stupid. Thank you for the wounds that you helped me heal. Thank you for the love of God that you brought into my life. Thank you for all of the prayers you prayed for me. Thank you for the intimacy we shared."

Appendix
A

A Brief Glossary

alveoli   The sacs inside the breasts responsible for producing milk.

androgens   Hormones that trigger male sexual development produced in the testicles. Testosterone is the most common.

anorgasmia   Unable to achieve orgasm.

anus   The opening of the rectum.

anal sex   Insertion of the penis into another's anus.

aphrodisiac   Some substance that enhances sexual desire.

areola   The darker skin area around nipples.

autoerotic   Self stimulation of the sex organs (masturbation).

balantis   Often caused by infection due to poor hygiene or an STD, this is an inflammation of the head (glans) and foreskin of the penis.

Bartholin glands   Lubricating glands that are located in the labia minora on each side of the vaginal opening.

bestiality   Sex with animals. Expressly sinful according to the Bible.

bladder   The organ where urine is collected and stored until emptied.

bv (baterial vaginosis)   Vaginitis or inflamed vagina created by a bacterial imbalance.

butterfly kisses   When the eyelashes are blinked open and shut against another person's skin.

candida   The most common type of yeast causing vaginal infections.

castration The surgical removal of the testicles. Removal before puberty prevents development of secondary sex characteristics in men (facial hair, pubic hair, voice change, muscle mass). Castration prevents a man from achieving erection. Castration results in the cessation of male sex drive.

celibacy Abstinence from sexual intercourse (oral, anal, or vaginal).

cervix The lower part of the uterus that opens into the vagina.

cervical cap A contraceptive device for women. A small rubber cap that fits over the cervix.

chlamydia A sexually transmitted disease (STD).

cholesterol High cholesterol causes blockage of blood flow in the veins. Problems with blood flow can affect men and women's sexual responses during foreplay. Their sex organs are not able to fully fill with blood. This can result in a man not being able to get or sustain an erection.

circumcision The removal of the foreskin from the penis.

climax Orgasm.

clitoral hood Skin that covers and protects the clitoris.

clitoris The female sex organ most sensitive to stimulation.

clitoral shaft The part of the female genitalia that is connected, beneath the skin, to the clitoris.

condom Female. A sheath made from rubber and other materials made with a ring at each end, one positions it over the outer vulva and the other over the cervix. It is worn inside the vagina during intercourse to prevent pregnancy and protect against sexually transmitted diseases.

condom Male. A sheath made from rubber and other materials worn over the penis during intercourse to prevent pregnancy and protect against sexually transmitted diseases.

corpus cavernosa Strips of spongy tissue that are located on either side of the urethra in the penis. These fill with blood to cause an erection.

corpus spongiosum Additional tissue inside the penis that also fill with blood during an erection. Similar tissue makes up parts of the glans and clitoris.

cryptorchidism The condition when one or both testicles fails to descend.

cystitis Bladder infection.

ejaculation   Female. The ejecting of fluid from the clitoris at orgasm. Some, but not all women have clitoral ejaculations.

ejaculation   Male. The ejecting of sperm from the penis at orgasm.

embryo   The beginning of created life after the sperm penetrates the egg and cell division begins.

endometrium   The lining of the uterus.

erection   When the penis and clitoris fill with blood they become erect.

erectile disorder   When a man is unable to get or sustain an erection until orgasm. If the problem exists for more than two months, a doctor should be consulted.

Eskimo kisses   The gentle nuzzling of noses.

estrogen   A female hormone produced by the ovaries.

estrus   The period when a woman is fertile.

fallopian tubes   Narrow tubes through which the egg travels to the uterus from the ovaries.

fetus   A fertilized egg (embryo) after about seven weeks.

foreplay   A variety of sexually pleasurable activities that lead up to orgasm.

foreskin   A piece of skin that covers the glans when it is not erect.

G-spot   Woman. Formally known as the Grafenberg Spot. The G-spot is found directly behind the pubic bone about two inches inside the vaginal opening.

G-spot   Man. Formally known as the Grafenberg Spot. The G-spot is found directly behind the pubic bone about two to three inches inside the anal opening.

glans   The sensitive tip of the penis and clitoris.

gonads   In men, they are the testicles; in women, they are the ovaries.

gonorrhea   A sexually transmitted disease (STD).

hymen   A fleshy tissue that covers the opening of the vagina.

Kegel exercises   Those exercises that strengthen the pubococcygeus muscles a.k.a. sphincter muscles. Tightening and loosening of these muscles can help prevent urinary and fecal incontinence and strengthen the muscles around the vagina that can lead to greater sexual pleasure.

introitus   The inner skin of the vulva.

labia majora   The larger outer lips of the vulva.

labia minora   The inner smaller lips of the vulva.

lubricants   Any assortment of gels used on the penis, vagina, and nipples to enhance sexual pleasure.

manarche   A girl's first menstruation (period).

masturbation   Any assortment of techniques that stimulate the penis or clitoris for the purposes of sexual arousal.

menopause   The time when a woman ceases to menstruate, usually around her mid 40s or 50s. Menopause is indicated when she has passed 12 months without menses.

menstruation   The evacuation of the contents (blood, fluid, tissue) of the uterus when there has been no pregnancy.

oral sex   Using the mouth to stimulate your spouse's sexual organs, specifically the penis or clitoris/vagina.

nocturnal emissions   Ejaculation while sleeping.

orgasm   The peak of sexual feeling during intercourse.

ovaries   The organs producing hormones and where the eggs are stored.

ovulation   When the ovary releases an egg.

pelvic girdle   The muscular and bony structure that supports the woman's sexual organs inside her body.

penile pressure and angina   When penile pressure readings are low it is an indication of arterial blood blockage throughout the body. This can cause erectile problems but may also be indicative of impending heart problems.

penis   The male sex organ.

perimenopause   Menopausal like symptoms that can occur six to nine years before formal menopause begins. Symptoms can include short-term memory loss, incontinence, hypersensitivity to touch, need for less than five hours of sleep/night, vaginal dryness, irregular periods, abnormal bleeding, painful contraction of the uterus during orgasm, dizziness, night sweats, and hot flashes.

Peyronie's disease   When a penis is crooked when erect. Peyronie's disease is caused by scar tissue or fibrous plaque in the shaft of the penis.

pheromones   It is believed that our sweat glands produce special odors called pheromones which are said to be involved in the attraction of the sexes. People pick up on the pheromones unconsciously. Commercial pheromones are available and have been shown to increase the attraction of the opposite sex.

premature ejaculation   Lack of ejaculatory control.

prophylactic   Condom.

progesterone   A hormone produced in the ovaries.

prostate   A small walnut-sized organ below the man's bladder that produces ejaculate fluid.

prostatitis   An inflammation of the prostate.

puberty   The point at which a boy or girl begin their transition into adult men and women. Girls bodies begin to produce estrogen and boys bodies begin to produce testosterone. Boys and girls begin to develop their secondary sex characteristics: pubic hair, underarm hair, ejaculation/nocturnal emissions [boys], facial hair [boys], breast development [girls], physical development of the bones and muscles, body fat changes [girls], voice change [boys], menstruation [girls], penis, testicles and scrotum grow larger [boys], oil production on the face and back increase causing acne for some, sweat glands become more active.

scabies   Tiny mites that can be sexually transmitted.

scrotum   The fleshy sac that holds the testicles.

semen   The ejaculatory milky fluid containing sperm.

seminal vesicles   Two small organs producing seminal fluid that are located near the bladder.

seminiferous tubules   Tiny tubes that wind inside the testicles and produce semen and androgens.

sleeping orgasm   An orgasm that occurs at night in men or women when they are asleep, also known as a wet dream.

smegma   A smelly, white discharge produced under the foreskin of an uncircumcised penis.

sperm   Reproductive cells produced in the male.

spermarche   The time when a boy's body starts producing sperm.

spermatogenesis   The producing of sperm.

STD   Sexually transmitted disease.

sterilization   Using surgical means to remove the ability to impregnate or become pregnant.

syphilis   A sexually transmitted disease (STD).

testicles   The testes, which are two round glands that hang inside a man's scrotum and produce sperm and hormones.

testosterone   Androgen that is produced in the testes.

thelarche   The initiation of a girl's breast development.

ureters   Tubes leading from the kidneys to the bladder.

urethra   The tube through which urine is excreted from the body and through which, in men, semen is ejaculated.

uterus   A pear-shaped organ where the baby develops.

vagina   The term referring to the inner canal of the female genitalia beginning at the labia minora and ending at the cervix.

vulva   Refers to the labia majora and labia minora tissues, part of the female external sex organs.

yeast infection   Refers to a bacterial infection in the vagina whose root cause is usually candida bacteria, but not always.

Appendix B

Resources

Books on Sexuality from Christian Publishers

In the previous 20 years, Christians have been blessed with several excellent books on sexuality written by Christians. Here are a few you may want to seek out.

Dillow, Linda and Lorraine Pintus. *Intimate Issues Conversations Woman to Woman: 21 Questions Christian Women Ask About Sex*. Waterbrook Press, 1999.

Dobson, James C. *Marriage and Sexuality: Dr. Dobson Answers Your Questions*. Wheaton, IL: Tyndale House Publishers, 1982.

Kippley, John and Sheila Kippley. *The Art of Natural Family Planning*. Couple to Couple League, 1997.

LaHaye, Tim and Beverly. *The Act of Marriage: The Beauty of Sexual Love*. Grand Rapids, MI: Zondervan, 1976.

Linamen, Karen Scalf. *Pillow Talk*. Baker Book House, 1998.

Penner, Clifford L. and Joyce J. *52 Ways to Have Fun, Fantastic Sex: A Guidebook for Married Couples*. Nashville, TN: Thomas Nelson, 1993.

Penner, Clifford L. and Joyce J. *The Gift of Sex: A Guide to Sexual Fulfillment*. New York: Doubleday Direct, 1997.

Rosenau, Dr. Douglas E. *A Celebration of Sex: Revised and Updated*. Nashville, TN: Thomas Nelson Publishers, 2002.

Shannon, Marilyn. *Fertility, Cycles and Nutrition*. Couple to Couple League, 2001.

Smedes, Lewis B. *Sex for Christians*. Grand Rapids, MI: Eerdmans, 1984.

Wheat, Ed and Gaye. *Intended for Pleasure: Sex Technique and Fulfillment in Christian Marriage* (Third Edition). Grand Rapids, MI: Fleming H. Revell, 1997.

Books on Sexuality from Other Publishers

There are hundreds of books on the topic of sexuality available from secular publishers. Many contain useful and valid information. However, most if not all are written from a nonbiblical perspective and include information that can be objectionable to some people. An inclusion of a book here is in no way an endorsement of its entire contents. Use discernment when reading or pursuing these books.

Bechtel, Stefan. *The Practical Encyclopedia of Sex and Health*. Emmaus: Rodale Press, 1993.

Birch, Robert W., Ph.D. *A Short Book About Lasting Longer: Step by Step Basics for the Management of Premature Ejaculation*. PEC Publishing, 2001.

Buckley, Peter F., ed. *Sexuality and Serious Mental Illness (Chronic Mental Illness Series)*. Dunitz Martin Ltd., 1999.

Kaplan, Helen Singer. *How To Overcome Premature Ejaculation*. Brunner-Routledge, 1989.

Lieberman, Laurence. *The Sexual Pharmacy: The Complete Guide to Drugs With Sexual Side Effects*. New American Library Trade, 1988.

Masters, William H. *Human Sexual Inadequacy*. Little, Brown Medical Division, 1970.

Masters, William H., M.D., and Virginia E. Johnson. *Human Sexual Response*. Lippincott Williams & Wilkins Publishers, 1966.

Masters, William H., M.D., Virginia E. Johnson and Robert C. Kolodny, M.D. *Human Sexuality* (5th Edition). Addison-Wesley Publishing Co., 1995.

Masters, William H., M.D., Virginia E. Johnson and Robert C. Kolodny, M.D. *Masters and Johnson on Sex and Human Loving*. Little Brown & Company, 1986.

Northrup, Christiane. *The Wisdom of Menopause*. Bantam Doubleday Dell Publications, 2003.

Schover, Leslie R. and Soren Buus Jensen. *Sexuality and Chronic Illness*. Guilford Press, 1988.

Articles on Sexuality

Christian Sex Rules: A guide to what's allowed in the bedroom, Louis and Melissa McBurney, Marriage Partnership, Spring 2001, (www.christianitytoday.com/mp/2001/001/4.34.html).

The Basics of Sex, Tim and Amy Gardner, Marriage Partnership, Fall 1999, (www.christianitytoday.com/mp/9m3/9m3056.html).

The Terror of Sex, Ben Patterson, Marriage Partnership, Spring 2002, (www.christianitytoday.com/le/2002/002/20.12.html).

Online Resources

Better Sex (www.christianitytoday.com/marriage/features/bettersex.html)

A collection of articles from *Christianity Today International* publications.

WebMD (www.webmd.com)

Excellent medical information on every topic including sexuality issues. Many other web-based health sites use WebMD articles and information.

Suite 101 (www.suite101.com)

Many articles and links pertaining to a large range of topics include physical and mental health.

Postpartum Support International (www.postpartum.net/)

Provides information and support for women suffering postpartum disorders.

Appendix C

Guidelines for Opposite Sex Friends in Marriage

Is it wrong for a spouse to have an opposite sex friend? No, not necessarily. However, care must always be taken to preserve the marriage. Some guidelines need to be in place that you both need to agree to.

No Secrets

You must never have secrets with your friend. They should never have any information that your spouse doesn't have. Don't discuss anything with your friend that you haven't discussed with your wife.

Never When Vulnerable

When you and your spouse are experiencing difficulties you should not meet with your friend. In addition, if you find yourself fantasizing about your friend you should not meet with them during that time. You need to ask yourself: What's going on in my marriage that is pressing me to look outside for comfort? Fix what's happening at home first.

Couple Activities and Socializing

Your friend must be known to your spouse and vice versa. Your friend ought to be invited to the family home to socialize now and then, eat a meal with your family, or go on a family outing with you.

Your spouse needs to feel free to call and talk with your friend any time. Your spouse should feel free to have lunch with your friend and get to know them on a personal basis.

Your spouse needs to feel comfortable about your friend and the nature of your relationship. If your spouse is not comfortable about it the two of you need to take that seriously. Your spouse may be uncomfortable because he or she can see that this person may be a threat to the marriage when you don't see it.

On the other hand, your spouse may be very uptight about any friend you might have because there is a history of infidelity in their family or in a previous marriage. If this is the case you need to strengthen your marriage first. Your marriage is your first priority. All other relationships come after your marriage. Your spouse must first feel your marriage is secure before they can trust you to be with someone else and not stray from them. These guidelines will be very important to them. However, it may be that you have to suspend your friendship for a time until your marriage strengthens.

This does not mean that your spouse has the right to step in and expect that you terminate all of your friendships. If there is an issue, please consult a professional.

Never in Private

Never meet in private or secret with your friend. Don't have them over to your house when your spouse isn't there. Don't go to their home if their spouse isn't there. Don't meet in an isolated place. Never meet in a hotel room. Keep your meetings in public, open places where there are always other people around.

Never Discuss Sexual Issues

Don't talk about your married sex life with your friend. This is none of their business. You need to protect your spouse and their sexuality. Do not talk to your friend about any of your sexual frustrations with your spouse.

Do not let your friend talk about their sex life either. If they bring it up tell them that's off limits for your friendship.

If you are having sexual problems with your spouse you need to talk with your spouse first. If they won't pay attention to your issues, talk to a professional. This will protect your marriage's need for privacy and ensure that sexual sparks don't start to fly with your friend.

Never Initiate or Allow Any Sexual Contact

Don't be deceived by the enemy. No sexual contact with your friend is ever appropriate or sanctioned by God. It can never be safe.

Never hug your friend unless their spouse or your spouse is present. This protects both of you from sexual sparks flying.

Never kiss your friend except on the cheek, possibly, and only if one of your spouses is present.

Adults don't hold hands with their opposite sex friends.

If your friend initiates any such contact, tell them that it is out of bounds for your friendship.

E-mails and Correspondence

Your spouse should be willing to give you access to his or her e-mail accounts and allow you to read any e-mails that go between you and your friend. You should never have anything to hide.

This protects your marriage from the dangers of secrecy. Any time you start feeling you need to hide something about your friendship from your spouse it's a sign that the enemy has begun to deceive you. Keep yourself accountable to your spouse with all correspondence that flows to and from your friend.

Ensure That Your Friend Will Help Keep You Accountable

You should be able to openly discuss with your friend that you don't want your marriage or theirs to ever be in jeopardy because of your friendship. Discuss these guidelines with your friend and ask him or her to help keep you accountable, especially when you are feeling vulnerable.

A good friend will help reinforce your righteousness when you are feeling vulnerable, not put you in a position where you might compromise your marriage. Tell your friend that if you are sounding vulnerable on the phone or they have any reason to believe that you are vulnerable that they should refuse to meet with you alone. Instead they should encourage you to seek out your male friends, your pastor, or a counselor.

Ensure That Your Friend Is Accountable to Someone Else

Does your friend recognize his or her own humanity? Does your friend value your desire for righteousness and their own? Ask your friend to make himself or herself accountable to someone else about your friendship. Ask them if they begin to feel attracted to you sexually or start fantasizing about you that they will deal with this with someone else and never bring it into the friendship. Ask them to not agree to meet with you if they are struggling with these issues. Ask them to protect you in case they are in jeopardy of crossing the line.

Same Sex Friends Can Be a Threat, Also

Reality is, many people are vulnerable to homosexual encounters with same sex friends. There are those who find out after years that their husband or wife was carrying on sexually with their best friend (the maid of honor or best man at the wedding). If you have any concerns about the nature of your spouse's relationship with their same sex best friend, bring it into the open. If you can't bring it up alone, raise the issue with a counselor.

Warning Signs of Major Depression and Postpartum Depression

Symptoms of Clinical Depression

According to the Diagnostic and Statistical Manual of Mental Disorders IV–TR (American Psychiatric Association, 4th edition, June 2000), a person is suffering with major depression if they meet the following criteria:

A. Five (or more) of the following symptoms have been present during the same two week period and represent a change from previous functioning; at least one of the symptoms is either (1) depressed mood or (2) loss of interest or pleasure.

(1) Depressed mood most of the day, nearly every day, as indicated by either subjective report (e.g., feels sad or empty) or observation made by others (e.g., appears tearful).

(2) Markedly diminished interest or pleasure in all, or almost all, activities most of the day, nearly every day (as indicated by either subjective account or observation made by others)

(3) Significant weight loss when not dieting or weight gain (e.g., a change of more than five percent of body weight in a month), or decrease or increase in appetite nearly every day.

(4) Insomnia (up all night can't sleep) or hypersomnia (can't stop sleeping) nearly every day

(5) Psychomotor agitation (e.g. jittery hands or legs) or retardation (very slow motions, the body can hardly get going) nearly every day (observable by others, not merely subjective feelings of restlessness or being slowed down).

(6) Fatigue or loss of energy nearly every day.

(7) Feelings of worthlessness or excessive or inappropriate guilt nearly every day (not merely self-reproach or guilt about being sick).

(8) Diminished ability to think or concentrate, or indecisiveness, nearly every day (either by subjective account or as observed by others).

(9) Recurrent thoughts of death (not just fear of dying), recurrent suicidal ideation without a specific plan, or a suicide attempt or a specific plan for committing suicide.

Clinical depression is diagnosed only if the above symptoms are not the result of other complications (e.g. neurologic or hormonal problems) or illnesses (e.g. cancer or heart attack), and are not the unexpected side effects of medications or substance abuse.

Maternal Signs

Shortly after birth a woman's body is attempting to get back to its pre-pregnancy state. A woman's hormones are working overtime. The hormonal shifts can cause a woman various degrees of depressive feelings as her body tries to return to normal. Please consider the following symptoms and pay attention to yourself. Husbands, keep an eye out for any problems your wife may have.

Postpartum Blues

Most mothers will experience some Postpartum blues. It may be as short as a few days or last for a few weeks. These hormonal surges can produce the blues.

A woman may feel tearful and cry at the least little thing (even just looking at a plant can do it). Some women find it impossible to pray during this time because they just start to cry. They can feel irritable, experience nervousness, or hyperactivity.

They can feel very vulnerable and overwhelmed. Their confidence may plunge and they may have trouble sleeping.

As her hormones regain their balance, the Postpartum blues will decrease and then completely fade away.

Postpartum Depression

One or two women of every ten will develop Postpartum depression. Depression is when Postpartum blues start but don't stop, and the situation worsens for the new mom. She may experience many of the blues symptoms but will also develop symptoms of major depression (see list above). Her ability to cope with her baby's needs becomes impaired. She will feel like she's not a good enough mother. Her memory may become severely impaired. She may become despondent and stare off into space. She may feel like she's going crazy and her thoughts may begin to scare her. She may start thinking of hurting her baby.

If you notice that these symptoms persist more than two weeks, you must get immediate medical and psychological help. Both the woman and the baby (and other children) can be at great risk of danger.

Postpartum Psychosis

Less than one in a thousand women will experience Postpartum psychosis. It begins about the same time as the blues, just days after delivery.

The mother's symptoms will be disconcerting for those close to her. She will be very confused, incoherent at times, and her thoughts can become totally irrational. She may express suspiciousness, paranoia, and fear. She may talk rapidly, not be able to stop what she is doing and be manic (ridiculous spending, speeding, sexual indiscretions, not sleeping). She may refuse to eat. She may have hallucinations—see or hear things nobody else sees or hears.

A woman with these symptoms after childbirth needs immediate and emergency medical attention. Take her straight to the emergency room. She is a definite risk to herself, her children, and possibly to her spouse. Women in this state have killed their children and committed suicide.

The mother must be admitted to the hospital immediately and started on medications. She should not leave the hospital until the medications begin to take effect.

Once she leaves the hospital she must make regular weekly appointments with a mental health specialist until she is completely clear of this condition. It may take her a year.

Make sure she is properly diagnosed and treated. If you don't have confidence in her care, take her to another facility.

Index

Introducing a new series from Alpha Books with a clear Christian family focus

christian family
guide to

Christian Family Guides are warm, conversational books jam-packed with expert content, Scripture quotes, meditations, family perspectives, and helpful resources.

Well-known Christian book author and former editorial director for Moody Press, Jim Bell Jr., serves as the *Christian Family Guide* series editor.

christian family
guide to
Buying and Selling a Home

Series Editor: James S. Bell Jr.

ISBN: 0-02-864436-0

christian family
guide to
Pregnancy and Childbirth

Series Editor: James S. Bell Jr.

ISBN: 0-02-864442-5

christian family
guide to
Total Health

Series Editor: James S. Bell Jr.

ISBN: 0-02-864443-3

Christian Family Guide to Managing People	ISBN: 0-02-864454-9
Christian Family Guide to Starting Your Own Business	ISBN: 0-02-864476-X
Christian Family Guide to Organizing Your Life	ISBN: 0-02-864493-X
Christian Family Guide to Family Activities	ISBN: 1-59257-077-1
Christian Family Guide to Family Devotions	ISBN: 1-59257-076-3
Christian Family Guide to Married Love	ISBN: 1-59257-078-X
Christian Family Guide to Surviving Divorce	ISBN: 1-59257-096-8